895.11   Sunflower splendor.
Sun

DATE DUE

DEMCO 128-8155

90039420

Sunflower Splendor

Three Thousand Years
of Chinese Poetry

❀ ❀ ❀

CO-EDITED BY

Wu-chi Liu

and

Irving Yucheng Lo

Indiana University Press
Bloomington and Indianapolis

Selected lines by Conrad Aiken from *Collected Poems* by Conrad Aiken. Copyright © 1953, 1970 by Conrad Aiken. Reprinted by permission of Oxford University Press, Inc.

Selected poems by Lu Yu from Burton Watson (tr.): *The Old Man Who Does as He Pleases, Selections from the Poetry and Prose of Lu Yu*, New York: Columbia University Press, 1973, by permission of the publisher.

The following poems: "Let Me Gallop, Let Me Go," "South Mount Soaring High," "I've Had the Wagon Hauled Out," and "The Fourth Month" are reprinted by permission of the University of California Press from C. H. Wang, *The Bell and the Drum: Shih Ching as Formulaic Poetry in an Oral Tradition*. Copyright © 1974 by The Regents of the University of California.

The following poems: "Mulberry by the Path," "Telling of Innermost Feelings," "Pleasure of Returning to the Fields: A Prelude," "Song of River Goddess," and "The Charm of Nien-nu" are reprinted by permission of the University of California Press from Cyril Birch (ed.), *Studies in Chinese Literary Genres*. Copyright © 1974 by The Regents of the University of California.

Selected poems by Yen Shu, Liu Yung, Ch'in Kuan, Su Shih, and Chou Pang-yen from James J. Y. Liu, *Major Lyricists of the Northern Sung, A.D. 960–1126*. Copyright © 1974 by permission of Princeton University Press, pp. 27, 69–70, 81, 116, 62–63, 102, 148, and 177. Reprinted by permission of Princeton University Press.

Hellmut Wilhelm's translation of two poems by Chang Chih-ho and two poems by Ch'en Liang are reprinted by permission of the Swiss Society of Asian Studies and appeared in the Society's journal *Asiatische Studien/Etudes Asiatiques* resp. Vol. XVIII/XIX (1965), pp. 100–101 and Vol. XXV (1971), pp. 81–83.

Hans Frankel's translation of "Ballad of the Orioles in the Fields" and "A Song of Lament" by Ts'ao Chih are reprinted by permission of the American Oriental Society, Inc. and appeared in *The Journal of the American Oriental Society*, Vol. 84 (1964), pp. 3 and 10–11.

Hans Frankel's translation of "They Fought South of the Walls" reprinted from *VENTURES, Magazine of the Yale Graduate School*, Vol. V, Number 1, Winter 1965.

Selected poems of the "Tzu-yeh Songs of the Four Seasons" translated by Michael E. Workman from *K'uei Hsing: A Repository of Asian Literature in Translation*, edited by Wu-chi Liu, F. A. Bischoff, Jerome P. Seaton, and Kenneth Yasuda. Copyright © 1974 by Indiana University Press, Bloomington. Reprinted by permission of the publisher.

First Midland Book Edition 1990

© 1975 by Wu-chi Liu and Irving Lo
Originally published in 1975 by Doubleday, Anchor Books.

A Chinese character text edition, under the title *K'uei Yeh Chi*, is available in cloth from Indiana University Press.

The paper used in this publication meets the minimum requirements of American National Standard for Information Sciences—Permanence of Paper for Printed Library Materials, ANSI Z39.48-1984. ∞ ™

Manufactured in the United States of America

Library of Congress Cataloging in Publication Data

Main entry under title:

Sunflower splendor.

Bibliography: p. 523.
Includes index.
1. Chinese poetry—Translations into English. 2. English poetry—Translations from Chinese. I. Liu, Wu-chi, 1907– II. Lo, Irving Yucheng, 1922–
PL2658.E3S84   895.1'1'008   90-39420
ISBN 0-253-35580-X   0-253-20607-3 (pbk.)

2   3   4   5   94

"Exiled are we. Were exiles born. The 'far away,'
language of desert, language of ocean, language of sky,
as of the unfathomable worlds that lie
between the apple and the eye,
these are the only words we learn to say.
Each morning we devour the unknown. Each day
we find, and take, and spill, or spend, or lose,
a sunflower splendor of which none knows the source."

—Conrad Aiken, "A Letter from Li Po"

Acknowledgments

This is one of the volumes sponsored by the Asian Literature Program of The Asia Society, New York, under a grant from the National Endowment for the Humanities.

Acknowledgments are also made to the following translators and publishers to reprint materials from copyrighted publications:

To *Asiatische Studien* for Hellmut Wilhelm's translation of two lyrics by Chang Chih-ho and two lyrics by Ch'en Liang.

To Columbia University Press for Burton Watson's translation of six poems by Lu Yu reprinted from *The Old Man Who Does As He Pleases,* 1973.

To *Journal of American Oriental Society* for Hans H. Frankel's translation of two poems by Ts'ao Chih.

To Princeton University Press for James J. Y. Liu's translation of one lyric by Yen Shu, three lyrics by Liu Yung, one lyric by Su Shih, two lyrics by Ch'in Kuan, and one lyric by Chou Pang-yen, all reprinted from *Major Lyricists of the Northern Sung,* 1974.

To University of California Press for Hans H. Frankel's translation of "Mulberry by the Path" reprinted from his article *"Yüeh-fu* Poetry" to appear in *Studies in Chinese Literary Genres,* ed. Cyril Birch [in press]; also from the same volume, for James J. Y. Liu's translation of one lyric by Ku Hsiung and one lyric by Chiang K'uei reprinted from his article "Some Literary Qualities of the Lyric." Also for C. H. Wang's four translations of the *Shih Ching* poems reprinted from *The Bell and the Drum,* 1974.

To *Ventures,* Magazine for the Yale Graduate School, for Hans H. Frankel's translation of "They Fought South of the Walls."

To Indiana University Press for Michael Workman's translation of nine lyrics included in *K'uei Hsing.*

Preface

This volume, which involves the effort of many individuals, aims to present new translations of Chinese poetry written in classical meters from the earliest time down to the mid-twentieth century. In execution and design, the book represents an unprecedented dimension of collaboration among scholars, a new venture in solving old problems.

First, this anthology is comprised of translations done by over fifty contributors. With rare exceptions (which are noted in the text) in the case of translations that have appeared originally in scholarly journals, all the translations have been specially prepared for this volume. A few of them, subsequent to the submission of the manuscripts to us, have appeared in books published within the last few months. In some instances, a popular poem has elicited several different translations, and it became the hard task of the co-editors to use what is considered the most successful version. Our contributors are mostly East Asian specialists on the faculty of American or Canadian colleges and universities, or younger scholars who have received many years of graduate training in the language. Each contributor, of course, has his or her own style. This variety of approach, in itself desirable and fitting, is also intentional: it helps to enliven a very long tradition which has produced many styles too often stifled in a book of translation done by one person.

Secondly, in the matter of selection, we have aimed, within the limitation of space, at inclusiveness by giving balanced representation to all major genres and periods and, within each, the chief exponents of major schools of Chinese poetry. It is our contention that the richness and variety of the poetic tradition in China cannot adequately be conveyed by a period anthology or by the work of one individual poet. This seemingly trite observation calls attention to a fact, lamented by many students of Chinese literature, that the general public has been ill-served for too long by having access only to a fragment of Chinese poetry, such as the *Three Hundred Poems of T'ang* (618–907), which alone has more than one English translation and which, in reality, is an eighteenth-century Chinese compilation culled from the extant works of close to 49,000 poems by 2,300 poets!

Finally, with respect to the process of translation, we recognize the inherent difficulties, especially in view of the fact that Chinese is an allusive and non-inflectional language. But we do not subscribe entirely to the theory that poetry is untranslatable from one language to another. We have paid, therefore, the most scrupulous attention to the original texts and insisted upon accuracy as well as readability. The translation aims at preserving, in idiomatic English, the identity of the original, including most of its grammatical and stylistic features (parts of speech, word order, line length and enjambment, the use of parallelism, and sometimes even auditory devices); however, no attempt has been made, except in the rarest instances, to reproduce the rhyme scheme.

Each translation in this volume has been checked against the Chinese source by at least three different readers; and, in most cases, the translation has been tested before a larger select audience. As a mode of accommodation between two languages, translation is an art that is bound to improve with each generation as more and more problems are grasped and understood. For such a task, it is not enough that a person must be fluent in both the target and the host languages; fidelity in translating poetry presupposes a thorough understanding of the original as a poem: its meaning, its structure, and its nuances. This is the process observed by all our contributors. We do not recognize as legitimate the use of informants, which was so often resorted to by missionaries and amateurs even in the not so distant past.

In compiling this anthology, we have constantly kept in mind these three principles of operation which, we hope, will save us from committing errors knowingly. In general, we prefer to include in it poems that have not been translated before, and we accept new renderings of previously translated poems only when we are convinced of either the significance of the original as great poetry or the merit of the present version. But a man's reach is one thing, his grasp another. Someone's favorite poet, or poem, will be found missing from our volume; others may question our "taste" in preferring one poet, or one poem, to another. For all our errors of omission or commission, we ask for the understanding of our readers.

We are grateful to all our contributors for making this anthology possible, for giving us unstintingly of their time and sharing with us the benefits of their research. Special thanks are due to three of our respected colleagues for reading certain portions of our manuscript, after they have been completely assembled, and offering us invaluable suggestions for improvement: Professors William Hung, now retired from Harvard University (on Tu Fu); James J. Y. Liu of Stanford University (on Li Po and Li Shang-yin); and F. W. Mote of Princeton University (on Kao Ch'i). And to our younger colleague at Indiana University, Professor Eugene Eoyang, whose contribution to our anthology goes far beyond his own translations in this volume.

We wish to express our regret to our contributors for the failure to print all the translations which we originally intended to use. During the final stage of editing we made the disconcerting discovery that the material being assembled had exceeded by a third the generous space allotted by our publisher. Consequently, we felt compelled to reduce the number of poems selected for this volume from over 1,300 to about a thousand—a process made rather difficult by the abundance of good translations. To all our contributors, we offer our apologies for having to effect this change.

For generous financial assistance to our project, we are grateful to The Asia Society, New York, especially to our friend Ms. Bonnie Crown, Director of the Asian Literature Program of The Asia Society. We are also indebted to the Office of Research and Advanced Studies and to the East Asian Studies Program at Indiana University for grants-in-aid in the preparation of the manuscript, and to the Department of East Asian Languages and Literatures which has brought the two of us together, as exiles to this new land, and made possible our pleasurable association. We derive equal pleasure from our contact with our present and former students in the department, many of whom have contributed to this volume. One final word of appreciation is due to our wives for their patience and understanding, in particular to Lena Dunn Lo for her help in reading through the typescript and improving the quality of the manuscript with her experience and insight as an editor.

Wu-chi Liu and Irving Y. Lo

Bloomington, Indiana
June 1, 1974

Introduction

I

In what ways does Chinese poetry differ from Western poetry? First, it enjoys an unbroken three-thousand-year-old tradition out of which have evolved many forms, meters, and styles. The word *shih,* for example, is used by the Chinese as a generic label for poetry in a rather broad sense, excluding only the *tz'u* ("poems in the lyric meter") and the *ch'ü* ("song-poems"), or to refer specifically to the earliest anthology of Chinese poetry known as the *Shih Ching.* Chinese verse compositions of the *shih* form are often called by their subgeneric names such as *ssu-yen shih* ("four-word poems"), *lü-shih* ("regulated verse poems"), etc.[1] Even when one form is no longer in vogue, it is never completely supplanted, and often continues to appeal to contemporary poets for its archaic flavor.

Secondly, from the very beginning, Chinese poetry has been intimately related to music. The *Shih Ching* is made up of (1) folk songs and ballads; (2) festive songs sung at court banquets; and (3) temple hymns performed to the accompaniment of music and dance. With only a few exceptions, these songs were compiled by unknown poets in the Yellow River region in North China. The *sao* tradition, which developed quite independently in the South, and which crystallized in the works of the poetic genius Ch'ü Yüan (343?–278 B.C.), may have originated from shamanistic chants performed as part of folk religion practiced by the people of the Yangtze region in what is now Hunan and Hupeh. Ancient music, not having been transcribed on bamboo tablets or stone monuments, proved more ephemeral than ancient verse, and has been, for the most part, lost. But new musical in-

---

[1] For other forms see Explanations, No. 7: "Subgeneric Names of Poetry: *Shih, Tz'u,* and *Ch'ü.*" While *tz'u* and *ch'ü* are composed according to the prescribed prosody of the tune pattern used, every one of the *shih* forms can be in the four-syllabic meter, the five-syllabic meter, or the seven-syllabic meter and are called the "four-word," "five-word," or "seven-word" poems. The four-syllabic line, the most common meter in the *Shih Ching,* was not popular in later times; but T'ao Ch'ien's (365–427) "The Seasons Come and Go" and Kung Tzu-chen's (1792–1841) "The Lute Song" were composed in this meter.

struments and tunes were introduced into the Middle Kingdom from the border peoples of the West and the Northwest and helped to revitalize folk poetry at different times.[2] Even when the musical context for lyrics had been forgotten, poems were still written to be chanted, not just read aloud.

Thirdly, underlining the affinity of poetry with music is the nature of the Chinese language itself, which dictates that each written graph, or character, has a monosyllabic pronunciation. Hence, the rhythmic quality of Chinese verse is based not on a system of stressed and unstressed syllables, but (except for ancient poetry) on a patterned alternation of words of different tone, or pitch.[3] The use of tonal meter has been the most distinctive character of Chinese verse since the seventh century; other auditory devices used by Chinese poets include those familiar to students of Western poetry—such as end rhyme, internal rhyme, alliteration, assonance, and onomatopoeia.

A fourth difference, and another characteristic of the language that has imparted a special flavor to Chinese poetry, is the frequent omission of the subject of a sentence in classical Chinese. In Chinese grammar, there are also no explicit distinctions made in tense for verbs, number for nouns, or case and gender for pronouns. Thus, a line of Chinese poetry tends to be more compact, almost telegraphic. Sometimes this grammatical sparseness contributes to deliberate ambiguity as, for instance, in a line by Li Shang-yin (813?–858):

> *tso   ying   tang   chiu   chung*
> sit   oriole   like   wine   heavy

---

[2] This took place at least twice in Chinese history: once during the early Han, when the Music Bureau (*Yüeh-fu*) was reactivated around 120 B.C. to supervise the collecting of court music and folk tunes, as well as of songs and music of nomadic Tartar tribes, thus contributing to the birth of a genre of balladry known as the *yüeh-fu*. Another instance was during the eighth and ninth centuries, when new music was brought to the T'ang capital by traders and soldiers from Persia and other parts of Central Asia, exerting decisive influence on the tunes and melodies of the *tz'u*.

[3] The two contrasting groups of tones used for poetry are called "level" or "even" (*p'ing*, meaning the "high-level" or "high-rising" pitch) and "deflected" (*tse*) tones, the latter referring to the three "low-rising" (*shang*), "high-falling-to-low" (*ch'ü*), and "entering" (*ju*) tones. The "entering" tone, though no longer present in modern Chinese (except in some dialects), is still used in the writing of classical poetry; in ancient Chinese it had a consonantal ending of *p*, *t*, or *k*. For paradigms of major verse forms of the "modern-style poetry" (*chin-t'i shih*) of T'ang and some of the tune patterns of *tz'u*, readers may consult James J. Y. Liu's *The Art of Chinese Poetry* (University of Chicago Press, 1962), pp. 26–27, 32–33 and Liu's *Major Lyricists of the Northern Sung* (Princeton University Press, 1974).

A perch for orioles, as if weighed down with wine
("Little Peach Blossoms in the Garden")

But, more often, the context of a poem indicates very precisely both the implied subject and tense of verbs, as in the following line by Shen Yüeh (441–512):

yi	*lai*	*shih*	*cho-*	*cho*	*shang*
(I) remember	(she) come	time	bright	bright	(she) climb-up

chieh-   *ch'ih*
steps-in-courtyard

> I recall the time she came,
> Radiantly treading up the steps.
> ("Four Recollections")

The non-inflectional nature of Chinese and the terseness it permits are matters of linguistic convention rather than poetics: readers should not assume that poetry lies in brevity alone.[4]

Fifthly, on the social provenance of Chinese poetry, one must conclude that, despite the exalted status enjoyed by poetry as a literary form, there is no special class of people, or profession, in traditional Chinese society designated as poets. Chinese poetry has, from the earliest days, drawn its inspiration from two distinct groups; namely, the common people, with their colloquial idiom and plain style of speech, and the literati, with their vast erudition and sophisticated sensibilities. From time to time, there are interactions between the two groups (cf. "Bamboo Branch Song" or other village ditties, which attracted many a literary poet and were imitated by them). The patronage of literature before the seventh century, however, was generally confined to the nobility and the courtiers (cf. the Chien-an poets). When poetry emerged, under the T'ang, as an important, if not the chief, criterion in the selection of officials, many scholars—by means of imperial exami-

---

[4] It is this quality that endeared Chinese poetry to many imagist poets in America during the twenties, and may have fostered a style of translation which dispenses with prepositions and articles, akin to pidgin English. Conceivably, when carried to an extreme, the translation of Li Shang-yin's line quoted above might read as "Sit oriole like wine-heavy." We believe in preserving the structure of the original, but within the control of the target language, and not at the expense of intelligibility. Chinese grammar must be understood in terms of English grammar. For example, stative verbs in Chinese may occur as adjectives. Hence, to supply a verb in the translation in this instance, or a subject when it is implied, need not necessarily detract from a line of poetry as poetry.

nations (or, in special cases, private audience)—achieved the coveted *chin-shih* (a term meaning "presented scholar") degree and appointment to official posts. Therefore, a number of poets, especially during the T'ang and early Sung eras, were primarily high officials; and the writing of poetry was considered among the literati as an avocation, a personal accomplishment, or a means of self-expression. The broad class of people trained in the writing of poetry included many women, either from good families or from the courtesan profession; some Taoist and Buddhist monks were also noted for their poetic talent. This tradition has continued to the present time.

There were, to be sure, disaffected intellectuals such as the T'ang poet Meng Chiao (751–814), or banished officials like Ch'ü Yüan. But they were not *poètes maudits:* the training they had received in the Confucian classics had imbued them with a sense of duty and service. When literary excellence was no longer valued by the rulers, as under the Yüan (Mongol) dynasty, artistic talents of the time were channeled into other art forms such as drama and painting. Or, when the road to officialdom was beset with insurmountable obstacles and dangers, as under the autocratic rule of the Ming emperors, poets earned their living by selling calligraphy and painting in which they excelled. Even in the modern era, a fighter for social and political reform, Lu Hsün (1881–1936), who was also a giant of modern (*pai-hua,* or colloquial) literature, chose to express his innermost thoughts in traditional verse. Chinese poets see as their primary mission in life not the writing of poetry, but the fulfillment of their ambition and aspirations for a successful career. And this includes the business of governing the empire, as in the case of the founder of the Han dynasty, Liu Pang, and the leader of the Chinese Communist Party, Mao Tse-tung.

Finally, with respect to themes in Chinese poetry, perhaps a few explanations are needed to account for the high incidence of certain topics. Chinese poetry has traditionally been closely related to the life and activities of the people. For the last three thousand years, China has been an agricultural country; hence, the importance attached to the change of seasons, the observance of rituals, or the concern for the lot of the farmers is readily apparent in the poetry of any period. The use of poetry as a form of social intercourse has also been a pronounced feature. As early as during the Spring and Autumn period (770–466 B.C.), verses were recited from memory at state functions by officials in the course of diplomatic receptions; as recently as February 26, 1974, Premier Chou En-lai of the People's Republic of China, in welcoming President Boumediene of Algeria at a banquet in Peking, quoted a line, "Flowers fall off, do what one may,"[5] from Yen Shu's (991–1055) lyric, to prove a point. Another popular practice is the exchange of poems between friends, written by using either the same rhyme-words as the original poem or words from the same rhyme-category.[6]

The particular fondness of the Chinese poets for the theme of parting should be understood in the real-life context of the difficulties of travel in pre-modern China. In addition, a monarch with absolute power could decree the banishment of any of his subjects to a remote, often uninhabitable part of the empire, and such separation usually meant lifetime exile, or even death. By the traditional way of thinking, to live far away from one's native district (except in the capital or while serving as officials in the provinces) was considered undesirable since it would mean that one could not care properly for one's ancestral tombs, nor fulfill one's duties to the family. In conformity with the Confucian teaching, the concept of friendship is also viewed with special reverence: regarded as one of the five basic "human relationships," it closely follows in importance the relationship between the emperor and subject, father and son, husband and wife, elder brother and younger brother.

Compared to friendship, sex seems to be a theme of minor importance in Chinese poetry. When women's position was generally cast in a subservient role, and the institution of the pleasure houses existed, women were rarely the objects of adoration. Hence, Chinese love poems are seldom endowed with the same spiritual intensity as one finds in the love poems of the West. Still, there are disarmingly charming love songs of folk origin, subtle and ironic "impersonations" of boudoir feelings, and touching apostrophes between lovers. There are also love poems addressed to one's wife (during a period of forced separation and travel); elegies written for one's wife (a Chinese scholar is reticent to show in public his feeling for his wife while she is living) or concubines; and passionate poems and lyrics inspired by unrequited love. A jaundiced view that Chinese poetry does not treat

---

5 *Peking Review* 17:10 (March 8, 1974), 6 and *Renmin Ribao* (February 28, 1974). For a translation of this lyric, see James J. Y. Liu, *Major Lyricists of the Northern Sung*, pp. 18–20.

6 The terms used for this kind of poetry are either *tz'u-yün*, or *ho* (sometimes translated as "harmonizing"); they are rendered as "Following the Rhyme of" or "Replying to" in this volume.

romantic love is very much mistaken: rather, the manners of express-
ing love are different and reflect different social conventions.

II

How is this assortment of themes treated and accommodated in
Chinese poetry during the different periods of its long history? It must
be said that Chinese poems will be found to show different levels of
technical accomplishment: from the simplest and the least adorned to
the most allusive and sophisticated. Compare these two poems, one a
love song written before the sixth century B.C., and the second a lyric
by the highly stylized poet of the ninth century A.D., Wen T'ing-yün:

> Lovely is the modest girl,
> She awaits me at the corner of the wall—
> I love her, but do not see her;
> I scratch my head, not knowing what to do.
>   ("Lovely Is the Modest Girl")

> Frozen in flight, two butterflies adorn
> A blue pin, gold-stemmed, in her hair.
> Who knows the inmost secrets of her heart?
> Only the bright moon and the flowering branches.
>   (Tune: "Deva-like Barbarian")

The differences in verbal texture and emotional intensity are unmis-
takable. Or, take the following statement of the familiar *sic transit
gloria mundi* theme made by T'ao Ch'ien (365–427), a poet noted
for the spontaneity of his style:

> Bright blossoms seldom last long:
> Life's ups-and-downs can't be charted.
> What was a lotus flower in spring,
> Is now the seed-husk of autumn.
>   ("Miscellaneous Poems, No. 3")

And compare these lines with those of Han Yü (768–824), a difficult
and allusive poet:

> The cosmos turns in endless periods
> And the essence given every thing differs

> yet each, attuned to time, attains its place—
> no need to treasure the evergreen
> ("Sentiments at Autumn, No. 2")

It becomes immediately clear, as Thomas De Quincey once said, in comparing "things of immortal beauty" with "works of nature," that "they never absolutely repeat each other, never approach so near as not to differ; and they differ not as better or worse, or simply by more and less; they differ by undecipherable and incommunicable differences . . ." ("The Poetry of Pope," 1848).

The complexity of a Chinese poem, both technical and intellectual, results from a confluence of several intellectual sources—chiefly Confucianism, Taoism, and Buddhism. While Confucianism inculcates the ideals of order and stability and of human brotherhood, the teachings of Lao Tzu and Chuang Tzu expound the theory that the world is governed by impermanence and flux, maintaining also that to live in harmony with nature is the only way to assure man's survival. Philosophical Taoism is reinforced by the teachings of Buddha introduced in China during the Han dynasty. The breakup of the first stable, universal empire ushered in an age of great creativity in many areas: in philosophical debate, in studies of phonology (influenced by the study of Sanskrit), in literary criticism, in landscape appreciation, in calligraphy and painting. Poetry, heir to all these intellectual pursuits, spoke for the first time with a multiple voice.

The poets of the T'ang cra[7] devoted their exclusive energy and talent to the refinement of the various forms of *shih*, culminating in the artistry seen in the works of Li Po (701–62) and Tu Fu (712–70). The break from the elegant tradition of the Six Dynasties' verse occurred at the beginning of the dynasty in the poetry of Lu Chao-lin (c. 641–80), among others, and especially Ch'en Tzu-ang (661–702); while even more individualistic voices began to be heard in the works of Wang Wei (701–61) and the Buddhist monk Han Shan, who probably lived during the eighth century.

Following the great chaos of the An Lu-shan rebellion in the middle of the eighth century, there emerged more loudly the voices of satire and realism, such as exemplified in the works of Po Chü-yi

---

[7] The T'ang dynasty produced so many poets and poetic styles that Chinese literary historians, since the Ming, often speak of them in terms of four periods: the Early T'ang (618–712), the Flourishing, or High, T'ang (713–65), the Mid-T'ang (766–846), and the Late T'ang (847–907).

(772–846) and Yüan Chen (779–831). In the works of the best T'ang poets, a concern for craftsmanship goes hand in hand with the attempt to broaden the scope of poetry. The two strains of realism and lyricism are combined in the frontier poems, the earlier exponents of which style were Kao Shih (702?–65) and Ts'en Shen (715–70), and in the narrative poems which are found in such great numbers. (Attempts have been made in this anthology to include those titles less well known to English readers, like Yüan Chen's "On Lien-ch'ang Palace" and Wei Chuang's [836–910] "The Lament of the Lady of Ch'in" rather than the more familiar poems.)

With the decline of the material culture, extraordinary geniuses who were poetic rebels—like Han Yü, Meng Chiao, or P'i Jih-hsiu (c. 833–83)—manipulated the traditional themes even more boldly; and some turned more and more inwardly to the abyss of their soul. (Except for Han Yü, their poetry was often neglected by scholars of later times and by anthologists, accounting for their relative obscurity among Western readers; hence, they are given substantial representation in this volume). While philosophical poetry had its champions in Han Yü and, to a lesser extent, in Liu Tsung-yüan (773–819)—becoming more and more Buddhistic toward the end of the era (cf. Ssu-k'ung T'u, 837–908)—there also occurred the exuberant, aesthetic poetry of Tu Mu (803–52), Li Shang-yin, and Wen T'ing-yün (813?–70) toward the end of the dynasty.

During the second period of division (the Five Dynasties era, 907–60), the new vogue of the "lyric meter," which started in Ch'ang-an and spread as far as the remote frontier town of Tun-huang, miraculously flourished in two centers of civilization far apart from each other: in the kingdoms of Shu (Szechwan) and Southern T'ang (with its capital in what is now Nanking). The sophisticated artistry of the *tz'u* reached a new level in the works of Li Yü, the Last Ruler of Southern T'ang (937–78), and of the many poets represented in the *Hua-chien chi* (the earliest *tz'u* anthology, compiled in Shu, preface dated 960).

With the unification of the empire under the Sung, the early Sung poets continued for a time to imitate the technical aspects of late T'ang poetry, resulting in the so-called Hsi-k'un style of verse. But the genius of such poets as Mei Yao-ch'en (1002–60), Ou-yang Hsiu (1007–72), and Su Shih (1037–1101) succeeded in arresting this trend and brought poetry into closer contact with the life of the prosperous Northern Sung society in all its aspects—secular, intellectual, and artistic. The realistic poetry grew more and more popular, and the exponents of this style included most of the major *shih* poets of the Southern Sung such as Yang Wan-li (1124–1206) and Lu Yu (1125–1210).

The greatest achievement of the lyric poets of the Sung eras appears to be their ability to assimilate not only the new music and new vocabulary of the market place, but also the intellectual discourses of all persuasions. This ferment, sustained by the heroic and patriotic temper of the times, reached the highest level of intensity in the works of Lu Yu and Hsin Ch'i-chi (1140–1207). Living in a vibrant yet precarious time, they were eager to accommodate all the forces of their *milieu* and to blend words and ideas and music into one integrated art form. (It is probably not accidental that many of these poets were also famous for their calligraphy, the visual appeal being but another dimension of Chinese poetry.) Toward the end of the Southern Sung period, when lyric poetry became more and more concerned with technical details of embellishment, it soon lost its vitality.

During the one century of Mongol rule in the Yüan period, new musical melodies and a new poetic genre emerged in China. Like the *tz'u*, the *ch'ü* poems in which the Yüan writers excelled have multiple tune patterns and a set of complicated prosodic requirements. But this new form admits even more freely the use of everyday colloquial speech, the idiom and slang of the common people, and extra or "padded" words in addition to what is required by the melody; it also bears the mark of the vocabulary and music of the Mongol conqueror. Poems were again written to be sung, especially by girls in pleasure houses and by actors and actresses. The non-dramatic songs, known as *san-ch'ü* (to be distinguished from the dramatic songs, *hsi-ch'ü*), were compiled by poet-dramatists, usually commoners or minor officials, and by poets who were high officials though they still disdained the acting profession during the most flourishing period of Chinese drama. Of the poet-dramatists, Kuan Han-chi'ing (c. 1220–c. 1300) and Ma Chih-yüan (1260?–1334?) contributed significantly to the development of the *ch'ü*, while poets like Chang Yang-hao (1269–1329) and Chang K'o-chiu (1265?–1345?) consolidated this verse form by working exclusively in it.

The themes and contents of the *ch'ü* are as varied as any other form of Chinese poetry. As a whole, the *ch'ü*, again like the *tz'u*, is basically lyrical in nature. In spite of its dramatic potentialities, the poets made little attempt in using the *ch'ü* as a medium of narrative poetry, except in some of the "song-sequences" (*t'ao-ch'ü*), several examples of which are also included in this volume. On the other hand, the writers of the non-dramatic songs were skilled in their descriptions of sceneries and situations, persons and objects (sometimes trivial and humorous), and thoughts and sentiments. These are sometimes compressed into a single short song (*hsiao-ling*) or elaborated into the "song-sequences" which usually lend themselves to political or social satire. While fresh and innovative in the early phase of its development, this new subgenre became formalized and conventional in later periods (from late Yüan through the Ming and Ch'ing dynasties), during which the *ch'ü* continued to be written but steadily lost its popularity as a form of poetry.

The last six hundred years in China produced many talented poets, but, compared to those of T'ang and Sung, no major figures. Under the Ming, there were the tragic genius Kao Ch'i (1336–74) and poet-painters like Shen Chou (1427–1509), T'ang Yin (1470–1523), and Hsü Wei (1521–93). In the Ch'ing dynasty founded by the Manchus, Chinese people labored in great restraint under a long tradition and foreign rule; they compiled a large number of outstanding anthologies and established schools of poetry, as if in search of a magic formula with which to produce great poetry upon prescription. But this conformist age also produced some unconventional geniuses: poets like the Sinicized Manchu noble Na-lan Hsing-te (1655–85), the painter-calligrapher Cheng Hsieh (1693–1765), and the frustrated Kung Tzu-chen (1792–1841). Toward the end of the dynasty, providing continuity with our own age, were men like the reformist-poet Huang Tsun-hsien (1848–1905), a diplomat who had visited four continents; the revolutionary poet Liu Ya-tzu (1887–1958), founder of the Southern Society (Nan-she), active during the early twentieth century; and the pessimistic scholar-poet Wang Kuo-wei (1877–1927), whose suicide by drowning seemed to echo the legend of the death of China's first poet, Ch'ü Yüan. The works of these men all reveal a painful awareness of the modern temper, a deep consciousness of China's weakness as a political entity, and a sense of estrangement from modern society.

III

If one scans the long tradition of Chinese poetry, two salient features stand out clearly: (1) its utilitarian or didactic aspect, and (2) its function as a means of self-expression or self-cultivation. To illustrate the first strain, we need only to point to the use of poetry as conventions in polite society or as attempts of the poets to allegorize their situations in life. Indeed, from Ch'ü Yüan to Lu Hsün, the satiric thrust of Chinese poetry has never been blunted: poetry is a tool for social reform to both banished officials and modern revolutionaries. The second tendency, to consider poetry as no more than a skill in self-cultivation, may also be exemplified by both practice and precept. As early as the sixth century, the scholar Yen Chih-t'ui (531–91) wrote in a book of family instruction that the function of all types of literature was "to develop one's native sensibility,"[8] adding as an afterthought: "or to give others unembarrassed advice." Remembering this dual nature of poetry, Yen's dictum seems consonant with an earlier critical view, by Liu Hsieh (?–473), that literature can be dichotomized into "refinements" (*wen;* literally, "the characteristic markings on animal skin" and hence "ornamentation") and "utility" (*pi;* literally, "the brush," or "pen"). And one is tempted to say that a majority of Chinese poems, though written in their multifarious forms and styles, belong to either of two traditions—those written by poets to please or console themselves and those written to move others (both gods and men).

In the sense of affording self-cultivation, or self-expression, on the one hand and purposefulness on the other, poetry is generally regarded by the Chinese more as "a literature of power" than as "a literature of knowledge." While Chinese poetry is deeply rooted in the daily lives of the people, the Chinese never lose sight of its loftier goal, shared by all imaginative literature (which, typically, in the West reaches the highest level of development in epic and drama). As described by the critic De Quincey, in discussing Homer, Sophocles, and Shakespeare, this goal is to "restore to man's mind the ideals of justice, of hope, of truth, of mercy, of retribution, which else (left to the support of daily life in its realities) would languish *for want of sufficient illustration.*" (Italics mine.) And the English critic goes on boldly to predict that such literature will triumph forever "as long as the languages exist in which they speak or can be taught to speak." In the modest idiom of Conrad Aiken, such a language exists in the faraway "language of desert, language of ocean, language of sky"—all of which communicate a "sunflower splendor" of which no one really knows the source.

Irving Yucheng Lo

---

[8] A more literal translation of this phrase: *t'ao-yeh hsing-ling* is "to mold and shape [one's] own nature and spirit"; cf. *Family Instructions for the Yen Clan,* translated and annotated by Teng Ssu-yü (Leiden: E. J. Brill, 1968), p. 85. We follow James J. Y. Liu in his translation of *hsing-ling* as "native sensibility" (*The Art of Chinese Poetry,* p. 74).

Explanations

1. Romanization: Chinese words and names are given in the Wade-Giles system according to Mathews' Chinese-English Dictionary, with the following modifications: the circumflex above the *e, en, eng* or the breve above *u* (in *ssu, tzu,* and *ts'u*) is omitted; *i* is spelled (with the exception of published titles) as *yi* for easier pronunciation. Also, the name of the Chin dynasty (265–420) is spelled as "Tsin," to avoid confusion with the name of the Jurched "Chin" (the word for "gold") dynasty, 1115–1234.

2. Geographical names: Well-known place names are given in the form most commonly used (Soochow instead of Su-chou); others are spelled out with a hyphen (thus Chia-hsing instead of Kashing.

3. Personal names: Except with pen names, the "formal names" (*ming*) of the poets are used instead of their sometimes more familiar "courtesy names" (*tzu*) or "style names" (*hao*). Thus Su Shih instead of Su Tung-p'o, but Lu Hsün (a pen name) rather than Chou Shu-jen. The biographical information provided in the Background section includes, inside the parentheses, both a poet's courtesy name (given in italics) and, if he has one, his style name (given in small capital letters). If a poet has more than one such name, only the most widely used will be given.

4. Bibliography: The bibliography lists only important works and translations in English (and a few major European studies).

5. Citation of Chinese Sources: For Chinese works cited, abbreviations are used (see key for identification). To avoid cluttering the notes, citations, wherever possible, are made to the larger anthologies such as the *Ch'üan T'ang shih* (CTS), "Complete T'ang Poems," or the *Ch'üan Sung tz'u* (CST), "Complete Sung Lyrics," rather than to individual works, although the latter are always consulted in the most authoritative editions.

Except for modern texts, the page reference is indicated with the use of a virgule when there is more than one *chüan* (Chinese volume): the numeral to its left indicates the *chüan* number (Roman numerals I or

II following this number indicate *shang* or *hsia*); and the numeral to the right gives the page number, followed by "a" or "b" to refer to recto or verso page.

6. Footnotes: In the translations, footnotes are kept to a minimum; only those which are deemed necessary to the comprehension of the text are provided. Most of these are explanations of historical or literary allusions, but efforts have been made in a few special cases to keep the more extensive notes submitted by our contributors on some major poems.

7. Subgeneric Names of Poetry: *Shih, Tz'u,* and *Ch'ü.*

(a) Referring to the line lengths of *shih* poetry, the following terms are used: "five-syllabic" poem, for *wu-yen-shih,* and "seven-syllabic poem," for *ch'i-yen-shih,* referring to the number of words or syllables per line. ("Character," "syllable," and "word" are used interchangeably.)

(b) Designating the forms of *shih* poetry, the terms for the more basic types are as follows:

ancient-style poems:	*ku-shih*
Music Bureau poems (or ballads):	*yüeh-fu*
modern-style poems:	*chin-t'i-shih*
"regulated verse" poems:	*lü-shih*
"truncated verse" (or quatrain):	*chüeh-chü*

(c) *Tz'u* is translated as "poems in lyric meter" or simply as "lyric." *Ch'ü,* or *san-ch'ü,* often translated as "non-dramatic verse," is called a "song-poem" in this volume.

8. Titles: A title given inside parentheses indicates the tune-title. The tune-title (*tiao-ming*) of a *tz'u* or *ch'ü* composition is given only in English translation, but at its first occurrence in the anthology it will be followed by the romanized Chinese name appearing in parentheses. (An index of all the *tz'u* and *ch'ü* tune-titles in their romanized version is provided.) When a *tz'u* or *ch'ü* composition has a subject-title, it will be given immediately following the tune-title. What appears inside square brackets preceding a *ch'ü* title indicates the *kung-tiao,* or mode of music, of that particular tune; and no translation is provided.

9. Chronology: The poems of Li Po and Tu Fu are presented roughly in the chronological order of compositions as far as can be ascertained; for other poets, no similar attempt is made in the arrangement of the

selections. Dates of composition for the works of modern authors, while they are available, have not been included.

10. Key to Abbreviations:

CCSC	*Chien-chai shih-chi,* by Ch'en Yü-yi. SPPY.
CFYCC	*Ch'in-fu yin chiao-ch'ien,* by Wei Chuang. Ed. Ch'en Yin-k'o. Kunming, 1940.
ChCSC	*Ch'ing-ch'iu shih-chi,* by Kao Ch'i. SPPY.
CKLTSH	*Chung-kuo li-tai shih-hsüan.* Ed. Ting Yin. Hong Kong, 1960.
CKLTTH	*Chung-kuo li-tai tz'u-hsüan.* Ed. Lo Ch'i. Hong Kong, 1962.
CNSK	*Chien-nan shih-kao,* by Lu Yu. SPPY.
CPCC	*Cheng Pan-ch'iao chi,* by Cheng Hsieh. Shanghai, 1962.
CSPCTP	*Ch'ing-shih p'ing-chu tu-pen.* Hong Kong, 1939.
CSH	*Ch'ing-shih hsüan.* Ed. Wu Tun-sheng. Shanghai, 1936.
CST	*Ch'üan Sung tz'u.* Ed. T'ang Kuei-chang. 5 vols. Peking, 1965.
CTPC	*Ch'u-tz'u pu-chu,* by Ch'ü Yüan *et al.* Ed. Hung Hsing-tsu. SPPY.
CTS	*Ch'üan T'ang shih* (reprint of 1781 edition). 16 vols. Taipei, 1961.
CYSC	*Ch'üan Yüan san-ch'ü.* Ed. Sui Shu-shen. 2 vols. Peking, 1964.
FSHC	*Fan Shih-hu chi,* by Fan Ch'eng-ta. 2 vols. Shanghai, 1962.
HCC	*Hsiao-ch'u chi,* by Wang Yü-ch'eng. SPTK.
HCSC	*Ho-ching shih-chi,* by Lin Pu. SPPY.
HHSC	*Huai-hai shih-chi,* by Ch'in Kuan. SPTK.
HKCCC	*Hsi-k'un ch'ou-ch'ang chi,* by Yang Yi *et al.* SPTK.
HWCSC	*Hsü Wen-ch'ang sun-chi,* by Hsü Wei. Taipei reprint, N.D.
HYC	*Hsiao-yao chi,* by P'an Lang. *Chih-pu-chu chai ts'ung-shu.*
JCLST	*Jen-ching-lu shih-ts'ao (ch'ien-chu),* by Huang Tsun-hsien. Shanghai, 1957.
Jen	*Tun-huang ch'ü chiao-lu.* Ed. Jen Erh-pei. Shanghai, 1954.

KTCCC   *Kung Tzu-chen ch'üan-chi.* 2 vols. Shanghai, 1959.

LCC   *Lin-ch'uan chi,* by Wang An-shih. SPPY.

LCCC   *Li Ch'ing-chao chi,* by Li Ch'ing-chao. Shanghai, 1962.

Legge   *The She King, The Chinese Classics,* Vol. IV. Tr. James Legge, Hong Kong, 1871; N.Y., 1961.

LHCC   *Lu Hsün ch'üan-chi,* by Chou Shu-jen. 10 vols. Peking, 1958.

LJC   *Liu-ju chi,* by T'ang Yin.

LYTSTH   *Liu-Ya-tzu shih-tz'u hsüan.* Ed. Liu Wu-fei *et al.* Peking, 1959.

LYWSH   *Lin Yüan-wai shih-hsüan,* by Lin Hung. *Sheng Ming pai-chia shih.* 1566 Edition.

MCCHC   *Mu-chai ch'u-hsüeh chi,* by Ch'ien Ch'ien-yi. SPTK.

MCHST   *Mao chu-hsi shih-tz'u (ch'ien-chu),* by Mao Tse-tung. Ed. Chang Hsiang-t'ien. 4 vols. to date. Hong Kong, 1969–71.

MCSH   *Ming Ch'ing shih-hsüan.* Hong Kong, 1939.

MSCC   *Man-shu ch'üan-chi,* by Su Man-shu. Ed. Liu Ya-tzu. Shanghai, 1928.

NLT   *Na-lan tz'u,* by Na-lan Hsing-te. SPPY.

NTECTHC   *Nan-T'ang Erh-chu tz'u hui-ch'ien* Ed. T'ang Kuei-chang. Shanghai, 1936.

OYWCC   *Ou-yang Wen-chung chi,* by Ou-yang Hsiu. SPPY.

PHSSCCC   *Pai Hsiang-shan shih Ch'ang-ch'ing chi,* by Po Chü-yi. SPPY.

PHSSHC   *Pai Hsiang-shan shih Hou-chi,* by Po Chü-yi. SPPY.

PSTC   *Pu-shu-t'ing chi,* by Chu Yi-tun. SPPY.

PSTJSC   *Pai-shih tao-jen shih-chi,* by Chiang K'uei. SPPY.

SKNC   *Shan-ku nei-chi,* by Huang T'ing-chien. SPPY.

SKPC   *Shan-ku pieh-chi,* by Huang T'ing-chien. SPPY.

SKWC   *Shan-ku wai-chi,* by Huang T'ing-chien. SPPY.

SPPY   *Ssu-pu pei-yao* edition. Shanghai, 1927–35.

SPTK   *Ssu-pu ts'ung-k'an* edition. Shanghai, 1920–35.

SSCC   *Su Shun-ch'in chi.* Ed. Shen Wen-cho. Shanghai, 1961.

STC   *Shih-t'ien (hsien-sheng) chi,* by Shen Chou. Taipei reprint, N.D.

SY   *Shuo-yüan,* by Liu Hsiang. SPTK.

THCK   *Tz'u-hsüeh chi-k'an.* Ed. Lung Mu-hsiung. 3 vols. 1933–36.

Ting	*Ch'üan Han san-kuo nan-pei-ch'ao shih.* Ed. Ting Fu-pao. 6 vols. Taipei, 1961.
TLYC	*Ts'ang-lang (Yen hsien-sheng) yin-chüan,* by Yen Yü. *Shih Yüan Ts'ung-shu.*
TPC	*Tung-p'o chi,* by Su Shih. SPPY.
TPHC	*Tung-p'o hsü-chi,* by Su Shih. SPPY.
TYHHC	*T'an Yu-hsia ho-chi,* by T'an Yüan-ch'un. *Chung-kuo wen-hsüeh chen-pen tsung-shu.* Series I. No. 8. Shanghai, 1935 reprint.
Wang	*Ming san-shih-chia shih-hsüan.* Ed. Wang Tuan. 1822; 1873.
WKTCC	*Wang Kuan-t'ang (hsien-sheng) ch'üan-chi,* by Wang Kuo-wei. 16 vols. Taipei, 1968.
WLC	*Wan-ling chi,* by Mei Yao-ch'eng. SPTK.
WSCL	*Wu-shih chi-lan,* by Wu Wei-yeh. SPPY.
WYHC	*Wu-yi hsin-chi,* by Yang Yi. *P'u-ch'eng Sung-Yüan-Ming ju yi-shu.*
YCCSC	*(Yang) Ch'eng-chai shih-chi,* by Yang Wan-li. SPTK.
YJHLC	*Yüan-jen hsiao-ling chi.* Ed. Ch'en Nai-chien. Shanghai, 1958.
YSW	*Yi shih-wen.*
YYCHL	*Yü-yang (shan-jen) ching-hua-lu,* by Wang Shih-chen. SPPY.
YYSSC	*Yüan Yi-shan shih-chi,* by Yüan Hao-wen. SPPY.

Contents

PART II

A World Fragmented: Multiple Voices in a Period of Intellectual Foment
(3rd Century B.C.–A.D. 6th Century)

PART III
Expanding Horizons and the Full Flowering of the Shih
(During the T'ang Dynasty, 618–907)

Wang Fan-chih (590?–660?)

Wang Chi (590?–644)

Lu Chao-lin (c. 641–680)

Ch'en Tzu-ang (661–702)

Han Shan (date uncertain)

Ts'en Shen (715–770)

Ssu-k'ung T'u (837–908)

Yü Hsüan-chi (c. 843–868)

Tu Hsün-ho (846–904)

Li Shan-fu (fl. 874)

T'ang Yen-ch'ien (fl. 880)

Li Hsün (fl. 896)

Han Wo (fl. 902)

Anonymous

PART IV

Cross-pollination: The Predominance of the Tz'u,
or Lyric Meters
(In the Five Dynasties and the Sung Eras,
10th–13th Century)

Huang T'ing-chien (1045–1105)

Ch'in Kuan (1049–1100)

Lu Yu (1125–1210)

PART V
The Rise of the San-ch'ü, *or Song-poems*
(In the Mongol-ruled Society, 1234–1368)

PART VI

In the Long Tradition: Accommodation and Challenge
(Ming, 1368–1644; Ch'ing, 1644–1911;
The Republic, 1912–   )

Kung Tzu-chen (1792–1841)

Ku-t'ai-ch'ing (1799–?)

Chiang Ch'un-lin (1818–1868)

Huang Tsun-hsien (1848–1905)

PART I

In the Beginning: The Legacy of Shih *and* Sao

(12th Century B.C.–3rd Century B.C.)

Shih Ching

Lovely Is the Modest Girl

Lovely is the modest girl.
She awaits me at the corner of the wall—
I love her, but do not see her;
I scratch my head, not knowing what to do.

Pretty is the modest girl.
She gave me a red reed;
The red reed is bright,
But I delight in the beauty of the girl.

From the pasture she brought me a tender blade,
Truly beautiful and rare.   10
No, it is not that you are beautiful,
You are the gift of a beautiful girl.
(LEGGE, PP. 68–69)   (TR. WU-CHI LIU)

Near the East Gate

Near the East Gate
Young women go
Like so many clouds all day:
Like drifting clouds
A thought of them
Soon blows away.

> There. White robe
> and a blue scarf—
> she makes my day.

Near the Great Tower and Wall   10
Go slender girls
Like reeds by river's edge:
Like bending reeds
A thought of them
Soon passes by.

There. White robe
and a purple scarf—
she makes me rejoice.
(LEGGE, P. 146)   (TR. HENG KUAN)

A Simple Rustic You Seemed

A simple rustic you seemed,
Carrying cloth to barter for silk.
But you did not come to buy silk;
You came with a design on me.
I saw you off, wading the river Ch'i[1]
As far as Tun-ch'iu.
"It is not that I'd put off the date,
But no good go-between you have.
Please, do not be angry;
Autumn is the time we meet again."   10

I climbed that ruined wall
To look towards Fu-kuan.
I did not see Fu-kuan;
My tears flowed in streams.
After I had seen Fu-kuan,
How I laughed and talked!
You'd consulted the shell and the stalks,[2]
And there was nothing inauspicious.
You came with your carriage
And carried me away and my goods.   20

Before shedding from the mulberry tree,
How glossy green the leaves are!
Alas, you turtledove,
Eat not the mulberries!
Alas, you women,
Do not dally with men!
When a man dallies,
He will still be pardoned;

---

[1] The Ch'i River, along with Tun-ch'iu (Tun Hill) and Fu-kuan (Fu Pass),
   was located in the state of Wei, in northern Honan.
[2] Oracle bones and milfoil stalks used in divination.

But when a woman dallies,
No pardon will she have. 30

The mulberry leaves have fallen,
All yellow and sere.
Since I came to you,
Three years I have tasted poverty.
The waters of the Ch'i are full;
They wet the curtains of my carriage.
The woman remains constant,
But the man has altered his ways:
He is lacking in faith
And changeable in his conduct. 40

Three years I was your wife,
I never tired of household chores.
Early I rose and late I went to bed;
Not a morning was I without work.
First you found fault with me,
Then treated me with violence.
My brothers, not knowing this,
Jeered and laughed at me.
Quietly I brood over it
And myself I pity. 50

Together with you I was to grow old;
Old, it has made me wretched!
The Ch'i, at least, has its banks,
And the swamp, its shores.
At the feast of the "tufted hair,"
We talked and laughed gaily.
You pledged solemnly your troth,
Little recking that it would be broken.
No, I never thought that it could be broken,
And that this should be the end. 60
(LEGGE, PP. 97–101)   (TR. WU-CHI LIU)

In the Wilds There Is a Dead Doe

In the wilds there is a dead doe;
In white rushes it is wrapped.

There was a girl longing for spring;
A fine gentleman seduced her.

In the woods there are tree stumps;
In the wilds lies a dead deer,
Wrapped and bound with white rushes.
There was a girl fair as jade.

"Ah, not so hasty, not so rough!
Do not move my girdle kerchief;   10
Do not make the dog bark."
(LEGGE, P. 34)   (TR. WU-CHI LIU)

Let Me Gallop, Let Me Go

Let me gallop, let me go
To share with the Lord of Wei, my brother, his woe!
I'd urge my horse on the long long road
Till I should halt at Ts'ao![1]
A deputy has journeyed over the grassland and streams.
My heart is stricken with grief.

You have denied my wish to travel;
I cannot go back like that.
You think my plan baleful;
I have no way of relieving my sorrow.   10

You have denied my wish to travel;
I cannot be crossing the river.
You think my plan baleful;
I have no way of stopping the thoughts.

I climb the sloping hill,
To pick the toad-lilies.
Thoughts abound in a woman like me,
Sure can find her way right to follow.

---

[1] On the border of Wei state. The poem was said to be a lament of the wife
of the Baron of Hsü, a smaller state also in Honan, who wished to go home
to console her brother, the Marquis of Wei, on the desolation of his state.

The people of Hsü blame my intent;
These people are childish, presumptuous! 20

I walk into the fields,
The grains are thick and rich.
To a great land I would plead for aid,
But where shall I go, on whom can I rely?
O you great officers, nobles,
Don't lay blame on me:
The thoughts of all the hundred of you,
None can really match my single proposal!
(LEGGE, PP. 87–89) (TR. C. H. WANG)

South Mount Soaring High

South Mount soaring high
A sly male fox treads;
Broad is the road to Lu, open,
The daughter of Ch'i[1] traveled to wed.
Yet once she made the way to wed,
How can you think of her anymore?

Fiber shoes five by pairs
Ribbons on the cap are two, matched.
Broad is the road to Lu, open,
For the daughter of Ch'i to use. 10
Yet once she took the road to use,
How can you be after her anymore?

What does one do when he plants hemp?
Across and along he dresses the rows.
What does one do when he takes a wife?
He makes it known to her parents.
And once it was known to her parents,
How can you indulge in her anymore?

What does one do when he splits firewood?
Without an ax he cannot succeed. 20

---

1 Wen Chiang, a daughter of the house of Ch'i, married to the Marquis of Lu
 (in modern Shantung), also known as Duke Huan.

What does one do when he takes a wife?
Without a matchmaker he cannot get her.
But once he has succeeded and had her,
How can you touch her anymore?
(LEGGE, PP. 155–57)   (TR. C. H. WANG)

Heavily Flapping Are the Bustards' Plumes

Heavily flapping are the bustards' plumes:
They have perched on the oak.
The king's business never ends:
I cannot plant my millet;
What will my father and mother rely on?
O you blue Heaven far away,
Is there a day when all this will settle?

Heavily flapping are the bustards' wings:
They have perched on the thornbushes.
The king's business never ends: 10
I cannot plant my millet;
What will my father and mother eat?
O you blue Heaven far away,
Is there a day when all this will end?

Heavily flapping are the bustards in row:
They have perched on the mulberry.
The king's business never ends:
I cannot plant my millet;
How can my parents have a taste?
O you blue Heaven far away,   20
When will everything go back to its good, old way?
(LEGGE, PP. 183–84)   (TR. C. H. WANG)

In the Seventh Month

In the seventh month the Fire-star declines,[1]

---

[1] *Liu-huo* ("cascading fire"), occurring in the formulaic first line of the first
three stanzas of this poem, refers to Antares, the first-magnitude star in the
Scorpius constellation, which appears bright red in the southern sky at dusk
in summer nights. When this star passes the meridian, the days get shorter.

In the ninth month winter garments are handed out.
The eleventh month[2] comes with the blustering wind;
The twelfth month, with the shivering cold.
> Without cloak or serge
> How are we to see the year out?
The first month comes with the tending of the plough,
The second month, with the measuring of field.
> Together with our wives and children
> We carry food to the southern acres;   10
> How the overseers of the field rejoice!

In the seventh month the Fire-star declines,
In the ninth month winter garments are handed out.
> Spring days bring us the sun's warmth,
> And the orioles sing.
> Girls carrying deep baskets
> Go along narrow pathways,
> Look for young mulberry leaves.
> As spring days lengthen,
> In crowds they gather the southernwood.   20
A young girl's heart is sad and troubled,
Fearing that she may have to go home with her lord.

In the seventh month the Fire-star declines,
In the eighth month we gather sedges and reeds.
In the silkworm month[3] we trim the mulberry trees.

See Joseph Needham, *Science and Civilization in China,* Vol. III (Cambridge University Press, 1959), pp. 242, 244, and 245.

[2] Reference to dates in this poem are made in two different ways—either to the more traditional Hsia calendar (also known as the "farmers' calendar"), when simply the month is given, as in lines 1–2, or to the newer, Chou calendar. The Hsia calendar is known as the *Hsia Hsiao Cheng* ("the lesser annuary of the Hsia dynasty," cf. Joseph Needham, *Science and Civilization in China,* Vol. III, pp. 194–95), although it has nothing to do with the Hsia dynasty. In making reference to the Chou calendar, the original reads as "On the day of the First [Month]," "On the day of the Second [Month]," *etc.* (translated as "when the -th month came . . ."). To avoid confusion for Western readers, I have converted this type of reckoning to correspond to the traditional Hsia calendar references. The traditional Hsia calendar begins the year in the spring according to the Julian calendar, while the Chou calendar begins the year two months earlier. For "eleventh month" in this line, the original reads "on the day of the First [Month]."

[3] The only deviation in this poem from the two ways of reference to dates occurs in this line when "silkworm month" is used, referring most probably to the third month in the traditional calendar.

Taking those axes and hatchets,
We lop off the higher' boughs,
And strip the young ones of their leaves.
In the seventh month the shrikes cry,
In the eighth month we tend to spinning   30
Of both dark and yellow silk.
Most becoming is the silk I dye bright red,
Which I shall make into a cloak for my lord.

In the fourth month the small grass sprouts,
In the fifth month the cicadas sing.
In the eighth month we harvest the field,
In the tenth month the leaves begin to fall.
The eleventh month comes with the hunting of badgers;
    Taking those foxes and wildcats,
    We make into fur coats for our lord.   40
The twelfth month comes with the public exercise,
With hunting and training for martial deeds.
    One-year-old boars we keep for ourselves,
    The three-year-olds we offer to our lord.

In the fifth month the locust stirs its legs,
In the sixth month the grasshopper vibrates its wings.
    In the seventh month, out in the fields;
    In the eighth month, under the eaves;
    In the ninth month, about the doors.
    In the tenth month the crickets   50
    Get under our beds.
We fill up chinks to smoke out the rats,
We block the northern windows, plaster the doors.
    Come, my wife and children,
    Another year is ending;
    Enter and live in the house.

In the sixth month we eat wild plums and grapes,
In the seventh month we cook sunflower and lentils.
In the eighth month we strip trees of their dates,
In the tenth month we bring home the harvested rice,   60
    We make it into spring wine
    For the nourishment of the old.

In the seventh month we eat the melons,
In the eighth month we cut the bottle-gourds.
In the ninth month we collect the hemp seeds,
Sow thistle and rotting plants for fagots,
For the use of our farmhands.

In the ninth month we prepare the threshing ground,
In the tenth month we bring out the harvested grains,
Millets of both kinds, early and late;   70
Rice in husk, hemp, beans, and wheat.
    Come, my farmhands,
    Our harvest is done.
    Let's go to attend to our houses.
Mornings we gather rushes for thatching,
Evenings we braid them into ropes.
    Be quick to roof our houses,
    Before we start again to sow the grains.

The twelfth month comes with the chopping of ice—clanging stroke
    after stroke;
The first month comes—we bring ice to the cold-house for storage; 80
The second month comes—we rise early
And make offering of garlic and lamb.
In the ninth month comes the severe frost,
In the tenth month we clean the threshing ground.
With a pair of goblets we hold a village feast.
    Let's slaughter sheep and lamb,
    And ascend to the public hall.
    Raising our cup of rhinoceros-horn, we toast
    Our lord, "Long life without end."
(LEGGE, PP. 226–33)   (TR. IRVING Y. LO)

I've Had the Wagon Hauled Out

I've had the wagon hauled out
To stand on the pasture-ground.
From where the Son of Heaven is
Have come the orders that I be here.
I've commandeered the groom,
And told him to load it up.

The king's business is to bring me many hardships;
It is a very tense affair, always urgent.

I've had my wagon hauled out
To stand beyond the walls.   10
Here they set up the snake-turtle banners,
There you raise the oxtail pennons;
The falcon standards and the snake-turtle banners
Flutter flapping all around.
Worry in my heart, I am very anxious,
And the groom is already tired out.

The king has ordered Nan-chung[1]:
Go and build the forts on the frontier at Fang!
Wagons rumble out in array, many and powerful,
Bright are the flags with twisted dragons and snakes in twin.   20
"The Son of Heaven has given me the order,
That I must build some forts on the Northern frontier!"
Awesome, awesome is Nan-chung,
Sent to have the Hsien-yün expelled.

Long ago when I was taking leave,
The millet was in flower.
Now as I am returning,
Fallen snow covers the road.
The king's business brings us so many hardships.
I had no time to rest, or to bide.   30
Did I not long to go home?
I feared the inscriptions on the tablets.

Dolefully chirp the cicadas;
Jump and skip the grasshoppers.
"When I could not see my lord,
My heart was sad, never at rest.
But now that I have seen my lord,
My heart is still, finally at ease."
Awesome, awesome is Nan-chung;
He has stricken the Western barbarians!   40

---

[1] The leader of a military expedition against the Hsien-yün, a non-Chinese
northern tribe.

The spring days are long, drawing out,
Plants and trees exuberant in leaf;
Orioles sing tunefully in harmony,
And asters are being gathered, in abundance.
We have captured and tried the culprits,
And now I am on the way home.
Awesome, awesome is Nan-chung:
He has leveled down the Hsien-yün.
(LEGGE, PP. 261–65) (TR. C. H. WANG)

The Fourth Month

The fourth month: summer already;
In the sixth month I drag in the heat.
My ancestors: were they not men?
How can they continue to see me suffer?

The autumn days are chilly, cold:
All plants and grasses decay.
Tumults and wandering have made me very sick;
What shall I do, how can I go home?

The winter days are fierce and bitter.
Whirlwinds: a gust blasts against another. 10
Nobody gets less than how much he desires—
Why do I alone have to undergo such troubles?

On the mountains there are fine trees:
This is chestnut and that is plum;
And now, that is torn up and this is cut—
I wonder what crime they have committed.

Look at the streamwater from a spring:
Now clear, now polluted!
Yet I have to meet calamities every single day.
How can I wait to become better off? 20

Immense waters flow, the Chiang and the Han,[1]

---

[1] I.e., the Han River, which flows into the Yangtze (the Chiang) near modern Hankow, Hupeh.

Main-threads of the Southern Land.
I have drained my vigor to serve,
But why don't I have some support?

Neither am I an eagle, a falcon,
That can flap and soar up to heaven;
Nor am I a sturgeon, a snout-fish,
That can plunge to hide in the deep.

On the mountains there are brackens,
In the swampgrounds, red thorns.   30
I, a gentleman, have made the song,
In order to release my sorrows.
(LEGGE, PP. 357–59)   (TR. C. H. WANG)

He Measured Out His Spirit Tower

He measured out his spirit tower
Measured it and planned it;
All the people rushed to work
And they built it in a day.
Measured it out, saying "No hurry,"
All the people flocked like children.

The King[1] rests in his spirit park
Where doe and stag lie about,
Doe and stag so sleek
And the white birds glisten.   10
The King stands by his spirit pond
Where fishes leap all around.

On solid cedar H-frames, spiked,
Hang the dented ornaments:
Grand drums and bells all perfectly tuned
To the ceremony of his crescent moat.

Grand drums and bells all perfectly tuned
To the ceremony of his crescent moat:

---

[1] King Wen, father of King Wu, the founder of the Chou dynasty. He built near his capital of Hao (close to modern Sian, Shensi) an observation tower, called Lin-t'ai ("Spirit Tower"), complete with a park and animals.

B'ung, b'ung, lizard-skin drums—
Blind musicians make report of public event.   20
(LEGGE, PP. 456–57)   (TR. HENG KUAN)

O Magnificent and Many

O magnificent and many:
The tambourines and drums we set up!
A thud and again a thud on them we make,
To delight our glorious ancestors.
It is for the descendant of T'ang[1] that we play,
To assure that our ceremony is properly done.
The drumbeats reach far and deep;
Shrill, shrill is the music of the flutes:
Harmonious—ah yes—concordant
Together with our sonorous chimes of jade.   10
O grand great is T'ang's descendant;
Lovely and fine the symphony of his!
The bells and the drums are splendid;
The *wan* dance goes on gracefully.
We have a number of welcome guests:
None of them is less delighted than we.
Long since very old in the past,
With ancient people did all this rightly begin:
Be meek and mindful by day and night,
Everything we do let it be according to the rule.   20
May they turn to us and enjoy the offerings,
Which the descendant of T'ang has prepared!
(LEGGE, PP. 631–33)   (TR. C. H. WANG)

Ch'ü Yüan (343?–278 B.C.)

Hymn to the Orange

Fairest of trees under heaven and on earth,
The orange came to be acclimated here.

---

1 King T'ang, the founder of the Shang dynasty. The *wan* dance was an elaborate
  ritual dance of pre-Chou origin. Cf. Arthur Waley, *The Book of Songs* (Grove
  Press, 1960), pp. 338–40.

Thus destined, it will not live elsewhere,
But grows in our southern land.
Deep-rooted, it cannot be transplanted,
And has, moreover, a singleness of purpose.
Green foliage—white blooms—
How lovely and exuberant it looks!
With its dense twigs and prickly thorns,
The rotund fruit hanging in clusters: 10
A riot of blending green and yellow,
Gleaming in a gay composition!
Elegant in color, pure inside,
Like a person loaded with virtue,
It is luxuriant, and fit for trimming.
Here is beauty without blemish.

I admire your youthful aspiration,
So different from the rest of us.
Standing alone, you will not easily budge—
Truly, how praiseworthy it is!   20
Deep and firm, you can hardly be moved;
Broad-minded, nothing else you seek.
Wide awake in this world, you stand alone,
Unyielding, not shifting with the tide.
Your heart secluded, you act with care,
Without committing any error in the end.
Endowed with virtue, not selfishness,
You rank with heaven and earth.
I wish, despite the passing of time,
To be forever your friend.   30
Genial and graceful, free from excess,
Resolutely you follow the principles.
Though young in years,
You are a teacher to us.
Your conduct is like Po-yi's[1];
A pattern you set for mankind.
(CTPC, 4/29a–30b)   (TR. WU-CHI LIU)

---

[1] The eldest son of the ruler of a small principality, Po-yi lived toward the end of
the Shang dynasty. When his younger brother refused his offer to succeed their
father as the new ruler, they both fled the state to live in the wilds. Later, when
King Wu of Chou was about to attack Shang, the two brothers remonstrated
with him against the expedition. When their advice went unheeded, they starved
themselves to death rather than becoming subjects of the new dynasty.

Lord of the River Hsiang[1]

You, my Lord, have tarried long in your journey.
Ah, who has kept you in the middle of the islet?
Beautifully dressed and finely adorned,
I cross the stream in a cassia raft.
I bid the Yüan and Hsiang still the waves,
And the waters of the river flow placidly.
I look for my Lord, but he stays behind;
Playing the panpipes, of whom do I think?

Driving the winged dragon, he travels northward,
As I wend my way to Lake Tung-t'ing.   10
With ivy and orchids for a curtain,
Oars made of iris, banners of magnolia,
I'll sail toward Ch'en-yang on the distant shore.
As I cross the Great River, my spirit form I reveal.

Revealing my spirit form avails naught;
Tenderly, my maid heaves for me a long sigh.
My tears coursing down in a stream;
In my seclusion, I think of you without end.

With cassia oars and magnolia planks,
I chop ice on piles of snow;   20
Pluck woodland vines in the water,
Or gather lotus flowers on the treetop.

When hearts are alien, matchmaking is labor lost;
Affection lightly given is lightly severed.
Over rocky shoals the waters flow sluggishly,
While the winged dragon soars into the sky.
Faithless friendship leads to long complaints.
Failing to come as promised, he tells me he's not free.

---

[1] The spirit of the River Hsiang has been variously interpreted as either a male (as in this translation) or a female deity. The disappointed lover in the song is supposed to be a shaman (in this case, a female one), who failed to meet the lord of Hsiang in a rendezvous. The rivers, lake, and other places mentioned here are found in the Hunan-Hupeh region, which at that time formed a part of the state of Ch'u.

At dawn I gallop along the riverbank;
At dusk I halt my steps in a northern islet.   30
The birds alight on the roof top;
Waters gird my house below the hall.

I cast my jade ring into the river,
Drop my girdle gems on the shore of the Li.
Plucking sweet herbs in this fair island,
I'll send them as a token to my handmaid.
Time once gone by will never come back;
I will just loiter around to ease my mind.
(CTPC, 2/5a–8b)   (TR. WU-CHI LIU)

The Great Arbiter of Fate

Wide open are the gates of Heaven.
On clusters of dark clouds I ride,
Bidding the whirlwind herald my way,
And icy rain sprinkle the dust.

You, my Lord, are circling the sky and descending;
I'll cross the Mulberry Hollow to follow you there.
Teeming with people are the Nine Continents,
Yet in me rests the power of life and death.

The Lord soars aloft, roams serenely in the sky;
Borne on pure air, he drives the light and shade.   10
I and my Lord advance together with speed
To greet the Sovereign on the Nine Ridges.[1]

With my spirit robe long and flowing,
My jade pendants in variegated hues,
A male and a female I blend[2]—
What I've been doing is unknown to men.

I pluck the holy hemp and jasper blooms
To bestow on those who live far from home.

[1] The Nine Ridges are the nine mountain peaks, one in each of the Nine Continents, which constituted the Chinese world of antiquity.
[2] The shaman spirit, who attends upon the Great Arbiter of Fate, apparently has, like her Lord, the power of creation as well as that of life and death over men.

As creeping old age draws nigh to an end,
Not to be close together is to drift apart.   20

Riding a dragon carriage, the wheels rumbling,
High he gallops as he mounts the sky.
Here I tarry, twining the cassia sprigs into a knot.
The more I think of him, greater becomes my sorrow.

My sorrow is great, but nothing avails.
I only hope the present will last and get no worse.
Of man's life there is indeed an arbiter.
Who could do anything about parting and reunion?
(CTPC, 2/12a–14a)   (TR. WU-CHI LIU)

Li Sao: Selections

I

A descendant I am of Emperor Kao-yang;
My august father, now deceased, is Po-yung.
When the year-star reached *shê-ti,*[1] in the first month,
On the day of *keng-yin,* I was born to the world.[2]

The august one, surveying the state of my birth,
First bestowed upon me an auspicious name:
He called me "Pattern of Righteousness,"
Then styled me "Spiritual Balance."

With a profusion of innate virtues I was endowed;
Augmented them with many cultivated talents.   10
Clad myself in selinea and shady angelica,
I wove together autumn orchids for girdle pendants.

It seemed I could hardly keep up my race with fleeting time.
Dreading that the years wouldn't wait for me,

---

[1] *Shê-ti* is a poetic name for *yin,* the third of the twelve terrestrial branches, when the zodiac sign points to Gemini. The *yin* year is the year of the tiger.

[2] From this and the previous lines, scholars have deduced that Ch'ü Yüan was born on the *keng-yin* day of the first month of the *yin* year, which could be the year 343 B.C. But, as the *yin* year occurs every twelve years, it could also be 355 B.C., 331 B.C., etc.

Mornings, I plucked magnolia blossoms on a mound,
Evenings, I gathered winter sedges in the islet.

The sun and moon sped away and never lingered;
Spring and autumn followed each other in succession.
As grass and trees will wither and fall,
I also feared the Lovely One would decline in old age. 20

"You won't cherish your youth or abandon the filthy;
But, why can't you mend your ways and manners?
Come, gallop forth on your spirited steed,
And I'll guide you on the road ahead!"

In former times, the three kings[3] were true and pure;
It was with them that the fragrant plants abided:
Mountain peppers mixed with cassia,
Also, garlands of melilotus and valeriana.

Those rulers, Yao and Shun,[4] were great and glorious;
Following the right principles, they found the way. 30
But how wild and licentious were Chieh and Chou![5]
They took the narrow path and they stumbled.

For partisans who indulged themselves in lust,
The road was dark, narrow, and dangerous.
I was not afraid of falling into disaster myself,
But I feared the wreck of the royal carriage.

Hastily I rushed back and forth,
To follow the footsteps of former kings.
The Fragrant One[6] failed to discern my inner feelings;
Instead, he believed in slanders and raged against me. 40

I knew, for sure, my obdurate loyalty would cause me trouble;
I would rather be patient but could hardly constrain myself.

---

3 These kings are Yü, T'ang, and Wen, respectively founders of the Hsia, Shang, and Chou dynasties.
4 Two sage kings of antiquity greatly admired and extolled by Confucian scholars as model sovereigns.
5 Respectively, the last rulers of the Hsia and Shang dynasties, considered by Confucian scholars as tyrants.
6 Literally, a kind of fragrant herb. See also note 7.

I pointed to the Nine Heavens as my witness—
All that I did was for the sake of the Holy One![7]

At first, he gave me his plighted words,
Soon he pretended to have other thoughts.
It wouldn't be difficult for me to leave him,
Yet I grieved for the Holy One's constant fickleness.

I had once cultivated nine fields of orchids;
Also I planted a hundred acres of melilotus,   50
A plot of lichens and rumex,
Together with asarums and sweet-scented angelica.

Expecting their branches and leaves to grow and flourish,
I longed for the time I could harvest them.
Even if they should wilt and die, there was no cause for grief,
I lamented only that fragrant plants were overgrown with weeds.

The crowd vied with each other for sordid gain;
Insatiable they were in craving and extortion.
While measuring others according to their own standard,
They each set their mind on envy and malice.   60

To rush about in mad pursuit
Was not my most pressing concern.
As old age slowly came upon me,
I worried that my good name had not been established.

Mornings, I drank dewdrops on magnolia flowers;
Evenings, I ate the fallen petals of autumn chrysanthemums.
If only my feelings were genuine and refined,
What harm, though I were long famished and sallow!

I gathered tree roots to tie valeriana into a knot,
Strung together the wistaria's fallen stamens;   70
I straightened up cassia twigs on which to hang melilotus,
And bound ivy vines neatly into a sheaf.

---

[7] It seems that the Holy One as well as the Lovely One (l. 20) and Fragrant One (l. 39) are used interchangeably in the poem to symbolize the king.

That I followed the examples of former sages
Is not what the vulgar world would approve.
Though they did not please the men of modern times,
I'd carry out the instructions bequeathed by P'eng Hsien.[8]

Long I sighed and my tears I wiped away—
I grieved that people could suffer so much.
Though I have loved virtue and curbed my emotions,
I was reviled in the morning and rejected at night.   80

I was rejected for wearing melilotus as pendants;
I was reproached for plucking fragrant valeriana.
These were the things my heart desired,
And I wouldn't regret even if I died a thousand deaths.

I lamented that the Holy One was remote and licentious;
He never understood the people's true desires.
Those women envied me for my beautiful looks,
And spread rumor that I was given to lewdness.

Truly, the trend of the times was to practice artifice,
To mend errors without compass and square.   90
Disregarding the straight ruler, they pursued crooked ways,
Vying with each other to vaunt appearance as truth.

Listless and distressed, I stood irresolute.
Alas, that alone I should be in trouble at this time!
I'd rather die a quick death than to wander in exile,
But I could never allow myself to assume such manners.

That hawks would not flock with common birds
Has been true since ancient times.

---

[8] Chinese scholars, beginning with Wang I, the Han dynasty commentator and
editor of the *Ch'u Tz'u,* believed that P'eng Hsien was a wise minister of Shang,
who, having been alienated from the king, committed suicide by drowning.
There is, however, no historical evidence to prove the existence of such a per-
son, and modern critics have variously considered him as a recluse and even a
shaman. (There are references to a Shaman P'eng and a Shaman Hsien, but not
to a Shaman P'eng Hsien.) The name also appears several times in other
poems attributed to Ch'ü Yüan. When taken together, these references seem to
point to P'eng Hsien as a man of great moral integrity whom Ch'ü Yüan ad-
mires and extols as his model.

How could a square fit into a circle,
And people of diverse views live peacefully together?   100

I'd humble my heart and curb my ambition;
I'd endure reproaches but drive away disgrace and shame.
To suffer for purity and die for righteousness
Is what the sages esteemed in bygone days. . . .

II

Oftentimes, I grew dejected and sobbed,   180
Bewailing that I had fallen foul of the times.
With tender melilotus petals I wiped away the tears
That streamed down and soaked the lapel of my robe.

Kneeling down, I adjusted my clothes and stated my case—
How splendid that I had kept my integrity!
I rode the phoenix carriage, drawn by a team of jade dragons,
And before long, on a gust of wind, I ascended the Heavens.

At daybreak I started my journey from the Ancient Mound,
And arrived in the evening at the Hanging Garden.
I wished to linger awhile at Heaven's carved gate.   190
When the sun sank suddenly and darkness descended.

I asked the Sun-charioteer to slacken his pace,
Not to hasten as we neared the Sunset Cave.
The road was unending, the journey long and tedious.
I'd like to explore the regions high and low.

I watered my horse at the sun's bathing pool;
I fastened my reins on a sacred mulberry tree.
Plucking a golden bough to brush the sun,
I roamed around, leisurely and carefree.

I ordered the Moon-charioteer to lead the way,   200
The Wind-God to rush along and follow behind.
The King-phoenix acted as my herald,
But Master Thunder told me that he was not ready.

I bade the phoenix to soar aloft,
To press on by day and by night.
The whirlwinds gathered and then scattered,
Marshaling the clouds and rainbows to greet me.

In confused masses they merged and dispersed;
In variegated hues they drifted above and below.
I enjoined Heaven's gatekeeper to open the portal,   210
But he leaned on the door and stared at me.

As the day grew dark, I felt exhausted;
I tarried there, tying lonely orchids into a knot.
The world was foul, forgetting all distinctions,
Seeking to cloak man's beauty, in spite and malice.
(CTPC, 1/3a–13a, 1/19b–23b)   (TR. WU-CHI LIU)

A Lament for Ying[1]

August Heaven has failed in its divine ministration.
How it has thrown the hundred families into dire confusion!
The people are dispersed, one lost from the other,
When in mid-spring we begin our exodus eastward,
Leaving our native village for the distant shores,
Along the Great River and the Hsia in aimless wandering.
I set forth from the city gate with sorrows in my bosom.
In the morning of the first, we start our journey
From Ying, the capital, and bid farewell to our old home—
In what godforsaken country will all this end!   10

The oars are lifted in unison, the mind is set at ease,
But I lament that never again shall I see our sovereign.
Watching the giant catalpas along the bank, I sigh long,
My tears rain like sleet in an endless stream.
As we pass the mouth of the Hsia and waft westward,
I look back toward the Dragon Gate but can see it no more.
With anxieties in heart, in deep pain and distress,
I gaze afar, but know not whence I could rest my feet.

---

1 Ying, capital of the state of Ch'u, fell to the invading army of Ch'in in 278 B.C.
The Great River (Yangtze), the River Hsia, and the Lake Tung-t'ing are all in
Ch'u along the route of exodus of the fleeing inhabitants. The Dragon Gate here
is one of the city gates of Ying.

Borne by winds and waves, the boat floats on—
On the water's vast expanse, a wanderer I drift. 20

We ride on the Lord of the Waves' surging crest;
Suddenly we soar, not knowing where it will take us.
My heart is tied in a knot that cannot be loosened,
And anxious thoughts, zigzagging, are not to be straightened.
We are about to turn the boat downstream,
To sail up Lake Tung-t'ing and thence down the river,
As we take leave of our ancestral abode,
To follow at ease an eastward course.
Alas! How my spirit longs to return home!
There is not a moment when I could forget it. 30

The banks of the Hsia now behind us, my thoughts travel westward:
I mourn that the old capital is every day farther away.
I mount the big mound in the water to gaze into the distance,
Hoping in this way to comfort my saddened heart.
I sigh for the peace and joy that was once in this land,
And bewail now the lingering wind over the stream.
Blocked by the Lord of the Waves, where could we go?
Water everywhere—where would this southern journey take us?
I wonder, have the lordly mansions been reduced to mounds,
And the two eastern gates overgrown with weeds? 40
My heart has not known happiness for a long time,
While sorrow and grief are interlinked.
Ah, the road to Ying is far and beyond,
The Great River and the Hsia can no longer be crossed!

Promptly I was sent away when I failed to gain *his* trust;
Since then nine years had elapsed without my being recalled.
I was overcome by a pent-up sadness that suffocates;
Thus dispirited and distressed, I had been filled with grief.
Outwardly they put on pleasing manners to curry favor,
And *he* was too meek and softhearted to hold his own. 50
Imbued with loyalty, I would fain present myself,
But their jealousy ran rampant and barred my path.

The lofty conduct of the sage-kings Yao and Shun,
So wise and farsighted, could extend to the heavens;
Yet, the host of slanderers, filled with envy,

Accused them of unkindness and gave them a bad name.
He dislikes the sedate and studious, those who cultivate beauty,
But loves others who brag loudly about their worth.
The crowd, ever pressing forward, advance themselves each day,
While beauty is left behind and kept at a distance.   60

Envoi

I stretch my gaze to look hither and thither;
I hope one day to return, but when would it be?
The birds fly back to their old roost,
And dying foxes lay their heads on the mound.
Truly, it wasn't my fault that I was discarded and exiled.
Day and night, how could I ever forget my plaint?
(CTPC, 4/11a–14b)   (TR. WU-CHI LIU)

Anonymous

Song of the Boatswain of Yüeh[1]

What a fine evening is this,
    that I've come to this islet midstream!
What a fine day is this,
    that I share a boat with you, my prince!
Unworthy that I'd be so desired,
    when have I ever felt such shame?
My heart's perplexed to no end,
    that I've come to know you, my prince!
There are trees in the mountain, and branches on trees.
I yearn to please you, and you do not know!
(SY, 11/10b–12a)   (TR. IRVING Y. LO)

---

1 This poem has the unique distinction of being the earliest composition translated
from one Chinese dialect into another. First sung by a boatswain in the dialect
of Yüeh (modern Chekiang and Kiangsu), it was heard by a prince from the
state of Ngo (in the Warring States period), who had it transcribed in the Ch'u
dialect. The earliest mention of this poem, along with the story, was in Liu
Hsiang's (77–6 B.C.) *Shuo-yüan*, or *Forest of Anecdotes* (11/10b–12a). The
poem preserves the stylistic features of the *Ch'u Tz'u* anthology, as in the use
of the sound-carrier particle *hsi* which marks the division between the half
lines in each line.

PART II

A World Fragmented: Multiple Voices in a Period of Intellectual Foment

(3rd Century B.C.–A.D. 6th Century)

Hsiang Chi (232–202 B.C.)

Song of Kai-hsia[1]

Strength I had to uproot hills,
    my spirit dominated the age;
Now in this hour of misfortune,
    my dappled steed cannot flee.
Dappled steed, unable to break away,
    what hope is left?
Ah, Lady Yü, my Yü!
    what will become of you?
(TING, P. 67)   (TR. RONALD C. MIAO)

Liu Pang (256–195 B.C.)

Song of the Great Wind

A great wind rises,
    clouds fly and scatter;
With power over the four seas,
    I return to my homeland;
Where shall I get brave warriors
    to safeguard the four quarters?
(TING, P. 45)   (TR. RONALD C. MIAO)

Liu Ch'e (156–87 B.C.)

The Autumn Wind

Autumn winds rise,
    white clouds fly,

---

1 Kai-hsia (in modern Anhwei) was the site of Liu Pang's decisive defeat of
Hsiang Chi, better known as Hsiang Yü. As a result, Hsiang Yü committed
suicide; with him at the time of his death were his famous charger, the "dappled
steed," and the Lady Yü, his favorite consort.

Grass, trees are yellow and sere,
    geese return south.
The orchids are resplendent,
    the chrysanthemums, fragrant;
Tenderly I think of the lovely one,
    I cannot forget her.
Sailing in a pavilion boat,   5
    we cross the Fen River,[1]
Cutting across the current,
    white ripples scatter.
Fife and drums play,
    the oarsman's song begins;
As joys reach their end,
    sorrows multiply
Brief is the vigor of youth—
    helpless before old age!
(TING, P. 47)   (TR. RONALD C. MIAO)

Anonymous

Nineteen Poems in Ancient Style: Eight Selections

[1]

Going on always on and on
alive, but parted from you
gone ten thousand miles and more
each to a far edge of the sky

the road is hard and long
with nothing sure about meeting again
Tartar horses lean to the northern wind
Viet birds nest on southern boughs

days advance, the parting grows long
days advance, the sash grows loose   10
floating clouds hide the bright sun
the wanderer can think of no return

---

1 A major river in Shansi which flows southwest into the Yellow River.

loving you I became old
suddenly the time is late—
enough   I speak no more
try hard to stay well
(TING, P. 71)   (TR. CHARLES HARTMAN)

[2]

Green is the grass on riverbanks,
Dense are the willows in the garden.
Fair is the woman upstairs,
Bright as the moon at her window.
Lovely is her rouge-powdered face,
Slender are her white hands.
At one time she was a singing-girl,
Now she is a wanderer's wife.
He went away and has not returned,
An empty bed, hard to keep alone.   10
(TING, P. 71)   (TR. DELL R. HALES)

[3]

I cross the river to pluck hibiscus,
In the orchid marsh, many scented plants.
I pluck, but whom should I give them to?
For my love resides in a distant land.
Turning my head, I look toward home,
Along that vast and endless road.
Our hearts are one, yet we dwell apart,
Worrying and grieving till we grow old.
(TING, P. 71)   (TR. DELL R. HALES)

[4]

In the courtyard is a marvelous tree
its green leaves spreading a profusion of flowers
I bend a branch and gather blossoms
to send to the one I love

sweet smells fill my lapels and sleeves
but the road is long and nothing can reach you

these things have no value as precious gifts
they only remind me how long you've been away
(TING, P. 71)   (TR. CHARLES HARTMAN)

[5]

Distant and faint the Herd-Boy Star,[1]
Bright and lustrous the Heavenly River[2] Maid;
Gently plying her slender white hands,
Cha-cha hum her shuttle and loom.
Day after day, her pattern unfinished,
Her tears fall in droplets like rain.
The Heavenly River, shallow and clear,
Divides them now by only a space;
Lovely and tender, with the river between,
Longingly, they look but cannot speak.   10
(TING, PP. 71–72)   (TR. DELL R. HALES)

[6]

a speeding carriage climbs through eastern gate
to view far off the tombs past northern wall
white poplar's leaves all a rustle
evergreens line the broad ways

below these are men long dead
come through dark to endless dusk
sunken in sleep under Yellow Spring[3]
never waking for a thousand years or forever

yin and *yang*[4] turn round in ceaseless flow
spans of years like morning dew   10
men's lives go fast like stops overnight
old age lacks the fixity of iron or stone

---

1 The Herd Boy and the Weaving Maid are the two stars positioned, respectively, to the south and north of the "River of Silver," the Milky Way. Popular belief holds that the two constellations are lovers, destined to meet only once a year on the seventh day of the seventh lunar month. On that day magpies build a bridge for the stellar lovers to cross.

2 *Ho-han,* the Milky Way.

3 I.e., the nether world, also referred to as the Nine Springs.

4 *Yin* ("dark") and *yang* ("light") represent respectively the female and the male principles of the universe.

eons on end we saw them off
no saint nor sage that found escape
some took drugs to find the potions were wrong

better to drink good wine
and clothe yourself in satins and silks
(TING, P. 112)   (TR. CHARLES HARTMAN)

[7]

The chilling breath of midwinter arrives,
Bitter cold is the north wind.
Full of grief I know the night is long,
I look up at the clusters of stars.
On the fifteenth day, the bright moon is full;
By the twentieth, a quarter is gone.
A traveler came from a distant land,
And handed a letter that was meant for me:
First you speak of your lasting love,
Then you say how long we've been apart.   10
I put the letter in my sleeve,
For three years the words remain clear;
With all my heart I clutch these trifles,
But I fear you will never know.
(TING, P. 113)   (TR. DELL R. HALES)

[8]

The bright moon white and silver
lights my silken bed screens
worries and grief allow no sleep
with gathered robes I rise and walk
(though traveling may have its joys
none equals an early return)
out the door alone to pace, anxious
no one to tell sad thoughts
neck craning I enter the room again
tears drop and dampen my clothes   10
(TING, P. 72)
                                                  (TR. CHARLES HARTMAN)

"Mulberry by the Path"

The sun rises at the southeastern corner
And shines upon our Ch'in family's house.
The Ch'in clan has a fair daughter,
She is called Lo-fu.
Lo-fu likes to work with silkworms and mulberry leaves;
She picks mulberry leaves at the wall's south corner.
Green silk strands form the basket cord,
A cassia twig forms the basket handle;
On her head, a "falling" chignon,
On her ears, "bright moon" pearls;   10
Of yellow silk her skirt below,
Of purple silk her jacket above.
The passers-by who see Lo-fu
Put down their loads and stroke their beards.
The young fellows who see Lo-fu
Take off their caps and adjust their headcloths.
The tillers forget their ploughs,
The hoers forget their hoes.
When they go home they find fault and are wroth
Just because they've looked at Lo-fu.   20

The Prefect comes from the South,
His five steeds stop and hesitate.
The Prefect sends his men to ask,
"Who is this pretty woman?"
"The Ch'in clan has a fair daughter,
She is called Lo-fu."
What is Lo-fu's age?
Not quite twenty yet,
A little more than fifteen.
The Prefect asks Lo-fu,   30
Would she ride with him?
Lo-fu steps forward and replies:
"How stupid is the Prefect!
The Prefect has his own wife,
Lo-fu has her own husband.

"In the East, among more than a thousand horsemen,
My husband holds the top position.
How can you recognize my husband?
A white horse walks behind a black colt.
With green silk strands is tied the horse's tail,   40
With yellow gold is harnessed the horse's head.
At his hip a sword with 'pulley' hilt,
Worth more than a million.

"At fifteen he was county clerk,
At twenty, provincial court councilor,
At thirty, palace attendant,
At forty, lord governor.
His personal appearance: a pure white complexion,
Fine hair and a slight beard.
Slow is his pace, as becomes a dignitary;   50
With stately, graceful steps he moves around the office.
The thousands of men assembled there
All say my husband looks superior."
(TING, PP. 123–24)   (TR. HANS H. FRANKEL)

"They Fought South of the Walls"

They fought south of the walls,
They died north of the ramparts.
Lying dead in the open, they won't be buried,
     the crows may eat them.

Tell the crows for me:
Please enjoy a sumptuous meal!
Lying dead in the open, they surely
     won't be buried.
How can their rotting flesh get away from you!

The water runs deep and clear,
The rushes and reeds are dark.
The brave war steeds have died in battle,   10
The worthless nags neigh, running hither
     and thither.

The bridges have been made into buildings,
How can one go south?
How can one go north?
The grain is not harvested, how shall our lord eat?
And we who want to be loyal vassals, how
          can we succeed?

I think of you, fine vassals.
Fine vassals, indeed one should think of you.
In the morning you went out to attack,
In the evening you didn't come back for the night.   20
(TING, P. 62)   (TR. HANS H. FRANKEL)

Ts'ai Yen (*c.* A.D. *200*)

The Lamentation

When the power of Han decayed,
Tung Cho[1] betrayed Heaven's way:
Bent on regicide and usurpation,
He slew the ministers loyal and good;
He forced the court to move to the old capital,
He held the Emperor hostage to exalt his own sway.

A righteous army was raised by the nation
To punish this wicked and evil man.
Tung Cho's troops moved eastward,
Their golden armors glittering in the sun.   10
Feeble and weak were the Chinese
When the Tartars and the Ch'iangs[2] came to invade.

---

1 During the troublesome times of the Later Han dynasty, Tung Cho, a frontier
general, led his army to the capital (Lo-yang) and after having killed the court
eunuchs, seized power himself. He later moved the capital to Ch'ang-an in the
west and then dethroned the reigning monarch, putting a child emperor in the
latter's place. In A.D. 192, Tung was overthrown by a coalition of civilian
officials, and was stabbed to death by his adopted son.

2 One of the five most powerful non-Chinese tribes, the Ch'iangs came from the
Tibet-Kokonor area. See Yi-tung Wang, "Wu-hu t'ung-k'ao" ("Notes on the
Five Barbarians"), *Bulletin of Chinese Cultural Studies* (Ch'engtu, 1943), 57–
79.

Like hunters they swooped on city and town,
Destroying all as they pressed forward.
Few were spared slaughter and death;
Corpses of the slain lay entwined.
Men's heads dangled from the sides of horses
As they carried away the captive women.

Westward, beyond the T'ung Pass[3] they rode;   20
The road behind lay tortuous and forbidding.
As we gazed back toward distant homes,
Our livers and spleens seemed to tear and rot.
Ten thousand captives all told,
Forbidden to encamp together.

Even among brothers and sisters,
None dared to converse with the other.
Trifles often infuriated our masters,
They shouted, "Death to the captured slaves!
You deserve the blades of our knives—
We have no need to keep you alive."   30

No reason had we to care for life
As we swallowed insults and curses.
They whipped and scourged us as they pleased;
Brutally, mercilessly were we beaten.
All day we marched on, sobbing,
We sat wailing all night long.

We wished to die, but found no way.
We wished to live, but knew not how.
Oh, what sins have we committed
To deserve such bitterness and misery?   40

Border people are nothing like us Chinese,
They pay no heed to righteousness or reason.
They live in a land of frost and snow;

---

[3] The T'ung Pass was a strategic point in Shensi dividing China into east and west. In the last years of the Han period, the regions east of the pass were virtually controlled by non-Chinese tribes.

When Tartar winds rise in spring and summer—
Fluttering, they blow open my garment;
Biting cold, they nip at my ears.
Moved by the seasons, I thought of my parents,
Causing me ceaseless sighs and laments.

Sometimes when visitors came from afar,
We rejoiced as we greeted them.   50
But never was there the news I sought:
No word for me of my village and home.

Unexpectedly, fortune fulfilled my wishes:
My close relative came with ransom for me.
Sweet release ended my long bondage,
But purchased by abandoning my sons.
A mother's love knits heart to heart.
Once I left, there could be no reunion,
Separated forever, in life and death—
How could I bear to turn away from them?   60

Clinging to my neck, the children cried out,
And asked where Mother was going:
"We hear you'll be leaving us soon,
But when will you come back again?
Our mother has always been kind,
Why should she be cruel to us now?
We are so young, so little.
How can you bear to leave us behind?"

Seeing this, I felt my body collapsed,
My spirit shattered, my mind crazed.   70
Caressing my children, I wept, I wailed.
Again and again I turned to gaze at them.

Many others had been captured with me
And some came to bid me goodby,
Envious that I alone could go home.
Their wails and laments wrung my heart.
For the moment the horses stood still;

The chariot wheels would not turn around:
The spectators sobbed as they watched,
Even passers-by wept at our departure. 80

Gone, gone! cut off from loved ones,
I hurried homeward on my long journey.
Three thousand leagues separating us,
Could we hope to see each other again?
I thought of the children I had borne,
My heart felt as if stabbed.

Home, I found my family all gone;
Not even cousins had survived.
City walls turned to woody mounds,
Courtyards overgrown with thorns and brambles. 90
Bleak bones knew not to whom they belonged:
Unburied, uncovered, scattered far and wide.

Outside the door, I heard no human voice,
Only howling and barking wolves.
All alone, I gazed at my shadow.
Fear seized me and robbed me of all my senses.

Climbing a mound, I looked into the distance.
My soul seemed to have left my body;
I felt as if my life had ended.
But bystanders revived and comforted me, 100
Only then did I force myself to live on.

Though I live, what hope can be mine?
I entrust my life to my new husband,
Sustaining myself the best way I can.
Rootless, despised and miserable,
I constantly fear to be abandoned again.
Human life lasts but a moment,
But grief is my lot till my days end.
(TING, PP. 104–5)   (TR. YI-T'UNG WANG)

Hsü Kan (171–214)

Boudoir Thoughts, Four Selections

[1]

The deepening shadows bring on sorrow,
Oh for whom is this sorrow felt?
I'm thinking of our separation:
Each in opposite corners of the world.
There's no hope yet of joyful reunion,
Within me there's only grief and pain.
It's not that I suffer from want of food,
True sorrow comes from feelings starved.
I sit down in tense abstraction,
And imagine your radiant face.   10

[2]

Steep, steep the lofty mountain peak,
Distant, distant the thousand-*li* road.
You left, sir, so long ago,
Affliction has made me old.
Man lives but for a time—
Briefly—like the grass at spring's end.
Time cannot be recaptured,
Why fill the mind with pensive thoughts?
Yet when I praise your past great love,
I despair of ever repaying you!   10

[3]

The drifting clouds, distant and vast,
I wish they could convey my message.
Yet floating above, they are beyond reach,
Vainly we trust our loving thoughts to them.
When people separate they always reunite,
You alone, sir, have not returned.
Since you went away,

My bright mirror lies dim, untended.
My love for you is as the flowing waters,
How can there ever be an end?   10

[4]

Sadly, sadly the season draws to an end,
Once again the orchid petals wither, fall.
I vent long sighs of grief,
Only the hope of your return comforts me.
Tossing and turning I'm unable to sleep,
How endless the long night!
I put on slippers, rise, and go outside,
Gaze up at the constellation Orion;
I regret that desires cannot be fulfilled,
Tears stream down as from a pulsing spring.   10
(TING, P. 260)   (TR. RONALD C. MIAO)

Wang Ts'an (177–217)

"Seven Poems of Lament," Three Selections

[1]

The Western Capital[1] is in turmoil,
Wolves and tigers[2] create chaos.
Once again I leave the Central Realm,[3]
Cast myself to the Ching barbarians.[4]
Family and relatives face me in grief,
Friends pursue and cling to me.
As I leave the gate, all is desolation:
White bones cover the plain.

---

[1] The Western Capital refers to Ch'ang-an, one of the two capitals of the Han dynasty; the Eastern Capital was Lo-yang.
[2] Wolves and tigers refer to the rapacious generals of Tung Cho (d. 192), a military dictator of the time who had kidnapped the last Han emperor.
[3] Central Realm is equivalent to "China."
[4] The Ching barbarians inhabited the humid and pestilential territory of Ching-chou (in modern Hupeh) in south central China. This was to be the poet's place of refuge. There is pathos in the notion that he, a true Chinese, was on the point of seeking sanctuary among the uncivilized Ching tribes.

On the road there are starving women,
Hugging their children, they leave them in the grass,   10
Turning back, they hear howling and crying.
They wipe their tears and go on;
"I don't know yet where I will die,
How can I care for us both?"
Driving on my carriage, I leave them behind,
Unable to stand such pitiful cries.
In the south I climb the Pa-ling ridge,[5]
Turning my head, I gaze at Ch'ang-an.
Understanding now the poet of the "Lower Springs,"[6]
I sigh in heartfelt agony!   20

[2]

The land of the Ching tribes is not my home,
Why have I stayed here so long?
Side by side, boats sail upstream on the Yangtze,
The sun sets, twilight touches my thoughts.
On the mountain ridge there is an afterglow,
On the rocky slopes the deep shadows lengthen.
Foxes scamper into their dens,
Soaring birds hover above their wooded nests;
Rippling waters stir fresh echoes,
Monkeys whimper above the shore.   10
A brisk wind blows against my sleeves,
Silvery dew moistens my lapel.
In the lonely night I cannot sleep,
Gathering my robe, I rise to pluck the zither.
Silk strings on *t'ung*-wood answer my mood,
A sad melody echoes in response.
A stranded traveler has no hope to break away,
And melancholy thoughts are strong and hard to bear!

[3]

This frontier post brings me sorrow,
Once before I came through here.

---

[5] The Pa-ling tumulus was the burial site of Emperor Wen of the Former Han
dynasty. It is located to the east of the Western Capital.
[6] "Lower Springs," an ode from the *Book of Songs,* sings of longing for the
worthy rulers of the past and their peaceful reigns.

Ice and snow slash muscles and skin,
The wind howls without end;
For a hundred *li* there are no people,
Grass and trees lie untended.
Climbing the ramparts I view the outpost and beacons,
Fluttering, fluttering fly the garrison banners.
A man on campaign does not count on returning,
Once he leaves the gate, he leaves home forever.   10
Many sons and brothers are now captives,
Weeping and wailing go on without end.
The world is filled with happy places,
Why linger here, on and on?
The smartweed insects[7] are used to bitter hardship,
Coming and going they question no more.
(TING, PP. 257–58)   (TR. RONALD C. MIAO)

"Joining the Army: A Song"

I follow the army to campaign on distant roads,
To punish our southeastern barbarians.
Side by side, boats glide on the broad river,
Evening comes, yet we have not moored.
The white sun is half over the western mountains,
There's an afterglow in the mulberry and catalpa.
Crickets sing along the banks,
A lone bird flies fluttering by.
A warrior's heart is full of longing—
Bitterness and sorrow bring him pain.   10
I get off the boat, climb a high ridge,
Dew-wet grass moistens my robe,
Turning back, I go to bed and sleep.
To whom shall I confide my sorrows?
My body serves the mission of shield and spear,
How can I even think of personal wishes?
One goes to war when the lord commands:
Such decrees cannot be disobeyed.
(NO. 3 FROM A SERIES OF 5; TING, P. 255)   (TR. RONALD C. MIAO)

---

7 In *Ch'u Tz'u,* there is mention of the smartweed insect who has become so used to the acrid taste of the plant that it no longer thinks of moving on "to the sweet mallow plant."

Occasional Verse

Rows of carriages, grooms at rest—
A festive scene by the green water-margin:
The dark orchids release glorious fragrance,
The lotus radiates a red glow.
A hundred birds, how they flap and flutter,
With winged tumult the flocks chase each other.
"Cast the nets, pull in the deep-hiding fish;
Draw back the crossbow, down the high-flying ones"—
The sun is already hidden in the west,
With such happiness, who thinks of going home?   10
(NO. 2 FROM A SERIES OF 4; TING, P. 256)   (TR. RONALD C. MIAO)

Ts'ao P'i (187–226)

Untitled Verse, Two Poems

[1]

Deep and boundless, the long autumn night,
Fierce and cutting, the chill northern wind.
I toss and turn, unable to sleep;
Putting on a robe, I rise and pace
Back and forth; suddenly it is late;
White dew moistens my gown.
I gaze down at the clear rippling water,
Glance up at the brilliant moonlight.
The "Heavenly River" streams back westward,
Countless stars glitter in every direction.   10
How melancholy the cry of the insects!
A solitary goose wings southward;
Heavy are the thoughts inside me,
Endlessly I think of home.
I long to fly away, yet have no wings—
I long to cross the river, yet there's no bridge.
Facing the wind, my sighs pour forth,
A broken spirit knows only torment!

[2]

In the northwest there is a drifting cloud,[1]
High and isolated like a chariot canopy.
Sad that it should meet an untimely fate,
Encountering gusty winds!
"Away I am blown to the southeast,
On and on, to Wu and Kuei[2]—
Wu and Kuei are not my home,
How can I linger there for long?"
Come, let it go and speak no further—
A wanderer is often a frightened man.   10
(TING, PP. 197–98)   (TR. RONALD C. MIAO)

The Lotus Pond

I take the royal carriage for an evening outing,
Leisurely to stroll about the western gardens.
Twin canals irrigate the park,
Splendid trees surround the open streams.
Low branches brush against the feathered canopy;
Tall, slender twigs stroke the azure sky.
A sudden gust blows against the chariot wheels,
While flying birds glide before me.
Roscate mists encase the bright moon,
Stars like blossoms peer between the clouds.   10
Heaven sheds its brilliant radiance,
Different shades of pristine light.
Not able to live as long as Sung or Ch'iao,[1]
Who can acquire divine immortality?
Let me roam at will to free the spirit—
To preserve myself and live long life.
(TING, PP. 196–97)   (TR. RONALD C. MIAO)

---

1 According to one interpretation, Ts'ao P'i uses the cloud metaphor to express his
  fear that he has lost his father's favor.
2 Wu and Kuei refer to the commanderies of Wu and Kuei-chi located in the
  Kiangsu-Chekiang region.
1 I.e., Ch'ih-sung-tzu and Wang Tzu-ch'iao, famous Taoist immortals who attained
  the status of *hsien jen* or "transcendent persons." (These mythical beings
  possessed immortality and the power of flight.)

"Song of Yen"

Autumn winds whistle sadly, the air grows chill,
Plants wither, leaves fall, dew turns to frost.
Swallows fly homeward, geese wing south;
I think of your distant wandering and am filled with love.
Longingly you think of returning to your old home,
Why linger on in remote places?
Forlorn, your wife keeps to the deserted room;
Misery cannot make me forget my love.
Unaware of the tears that moisten my gown,
I play zither tunes in the *ch'ing shang*[1] mode,   10
The songs are brief, the breath, weak—nothing lasts.
The brilliant moon shines upon my bed,
Stars, the Milky Way, stream westward; the night not even half over.
Herd Boy and Weaving Maid, you gaze at each other from afar,
Why are you confined alone to the "river" bridge?
(NO. 1 FROM A SERIES OF 2; TING, PP. 191–92)   (TR. RONALD C. MIAO)

Ts'ao Chih (192–232)

"Ballad of the Orioles in the Fields"

The tall trees are full of sad wind;
The sea water rises in billows.
Without a keen sword in hand,
What's the use of plentiful ties of friendship?
Don't you see the oriole in the hedge?
Seeing a hawk, he tumbles into the net.
The fowler is glad to get the oriole.
A young man is sad to see the bird caught.
He grasps his sword and cuts the net away.
The oriole gets free, he flies and flies.   10
He flies and flies, upward, touching the blue sky,
And down again, to thank the young man.
(TING, P. 218)   (TR. HANS H. FRANKEL)

---

1 The name of an ancient *yüeh-fu* tune.

"Seven Poems of Lament"

A bright moon shines upon the pavilion,
The streaming moonlight moves and lingers;
In an upstairs chamber, a melancholy wife,
Her long sighs express much sadness.
If you ask, "Who is sighing?"
She would say, "A wanderer's wife.
My lord's been away for more than ten years,
His lonely wife now sleeps by herself.
He is like the light dust of the road,
And I, the mud of turbid waters: 10
Floating or submerged, we're each in different places,
When shall we be together again?
Let me become the southwest wind,
To be swept away to his breast.
Yet if he won't receive me,
I'll have no one to turn to."
(TING, PP. 230–31)   (TR. RONALD C. MIAO)

"Song of Heavenly Ascent"

Where the Fu-sang tree[1] grows,
There is the natal gorge of the morning sun.
Its central trunk rises up to the Heavens,
Its outspread branches canopy the horizons.
As the sun rises, it ascends the eastern trunk,
At dusk, it sinks into the western branches.
Oh, to have the reins that entwine the sun,
To bring the sun galloping eastward again!
(TING, P. 208)   (TR. RONALD C. MIAO)

---

[1] The sun-myth theme is treated in this poem; "ascent" here is not concerned with the levitation of Taoist immortals, but with the mythical Fu-sang tree, mandala of the organic universe, and a widely adopted symbol in Indian mythology.

"Roaming Immortal"

Human life does not reach a hundred,
Year after year there is little joy!
I long to soar with six-feathered wings,[1]
To cleave the mists and transcend the vermilion void.
A cicada sheds its skin[2]: I shall be as Sung and Ch'iao.[3]
With a flutter I ascend from Tripod Lake,
Glide and drift above the Ninth Heaven.[4]
I spur myself on to distant spaces:
Eastward to view the glittering Fu-sang tree,
Westward to overlook the Limpid Water current,   10
Northward stopping at the Dark Heaven Isle,
Southward in winged ascent up Cinnabar Hill!
(TING, P. 212)   (TR. RONALD C. MIAO)

"A Song of Lament"

Woe, this tumbleweed,
How lonely his life in the world!
Far away from his native roots he travels,
Day and night without rest or leisure,
East and west along the seven paths,
South and north beyond the nine roads.
Suddenly I meet a twisting storm arising,
He blows me right into the clouds.
Expecting to stay forever on Heaven's road,
All of a sudden I drop to the deepest abyss.   10
A startling whirlwind pulls me out,
Thus I'm back in the midst of those fields.

---

1 A synecdoche for wings; in particular the wings of large waterfowl, which in
Chinese lore "could lift with 'six feathers' a thousand miles."

2 A metaphor for the mystical process whereby one sheds the onus of the mun-
dane world.

3 I.e., Ch'ih-sung-tzu and Wang Tzu-ch'iao, Taoist immortals.

4 The place names have their symbolic significance in Taoist mythology. They are
closely identified with particular cardinal directions according to the cosmology
of the Han period. The persona in his mystical flight makes a characteristic
tour of the compass; in so doing he symbolically embraces all of creation.
The flight itself is a realization of escape from worldly cares and confinement,
a return to spiritual freedom and unity with the universe.

Now the direction is south, then it changes to north.
Now I expect to go east, then it's back to the west.
Swept about, where can I find a hold?
Now on the point of sudden death, then alive again.
Drifting, shifting, around the Eight Marshes,
Gliding, sliding, past the Five Mountains,
Floating, rambling, without a fixed abode,
Who is aware of my bitter distress?   20
I wish I were a grass in the midst of the grove,
To be burned by the forest fire in autumn.
'T would hurt, of course, to be destroyed,
But at least I could stay with my roots.
(TING, PP. 215–16)   (TR. HANS H. FRANKEL)

Juan Chi (210–263)

Poems Expressing My Feelings, Three Selections

[1]

Deep in the night and unable to sleep
I rise and sit to play my singing lute,
thin curtains mirror the bright moon
clear breezes tug my lapels

a single swan shrieks past the fields
hovering birds cry in the north woods,
pacing round, what is it that awaits me?
anxious thoughts alone that hurt the heart.

[2]

Autumn's onset means cooling breezes
and crickets that sing in bedroom curtains,
to feel a thing is to sense the many cares
the sorrows that cause a heart to grieve

Many words all saying nothing
and endless phrases addressed to no one

Gentle winds flap my silken sleeves
the bright moon beams out pure splendor,
at dawn a rooster sings from high trees
I order a carriage to come and take me home.   10

[3]

Long ago there was an immortal man
who lived on the slope of Shooting Mountain[1]
riding clouds and commanding flying dragons
he did his breathing and supped on precious flowers

He could be heard, but not seen,
sighing sorrows and full emotion
self-tortured he had no companion
grief and heartbreak piled upon him
"Study the familiar to penetrate the sublime"[2]
But time is short and what's to be done?   10
(NOS. 1, 14, 78 FROM A SERIES OF 82; TING, PP. 300, 302, 315)

                      (TR. CHARLES HARTMAN)

T'ao Ch'ien (365–427)

The Seasons Come and Go, Four Poems

The seasons come and go: late spring is upon us. The spring garments are ready and, as the scenery is inviting, I stroll out by myself, with feelings of joy mixed with sadness.

[1]

By and by, the seasons come and go,
My, my! What a fine morning!
I put on my spring cloak
And set out east for the outskirts.
Mountains are cleansed by lingering clouds;

---

1 Ku-she Shan, the abode of the immortals, from the chapter "Roaming the Universe" (*Hsiao-yao yu*) from *Chuang-tzu.*
2 A quotation from *Lun-yü* (*The Analects*), XIV:24.

Sky is veiled by fine mist.
A wind comes up from the south,
Winging over the new sprouts.

[2]

Bank to bank, the stream is wide;
I rinse, then douse myself.
Scene by scene, the distant landscape;
I am happy as I look out.
People have a saying:
"A heart at peace is easy to please."
So I brandish this cup,
Happy to be by myself.

[3]

Peering into the depths of the stream,
I remember the pure waters of the Yi,[1]
There students and scholars worked together,
And, carefree, went home singing.
I love their inner peace,
Awake or asleep, I'd change places,
But, alas, those times are gone—
We can no longer bring them back.

[4]

In the morning and at night
I rest in my house.
Flowers and herbs are all in place;
Trees and bamboos cast their shadows.
A clear-sounding lute lies on my bed,
And there's half a jug of coarse wine.
Huang and T'ang[2] are gone forever:
Sad and alone, here I am.
(TING, PP. 597–98)   (TR. EUGENE EOYANG)

---

1 Alluding to the ancient lustration rites held in the spring, on the bank of the Yi
  River, as described in *Lun-yü*, XI:25.
2 I.e., the legendary emperors Huang-ti and Yao.

On Returning to My Garden and Field, Two Selections

[1]

When I was young, I did not fit into the common mold,
By instinct, I love mountains and hills.
By error, I fell into this dusty net
And was gone from home for thirteen years.
A caged bird yearns for its native woods;
The fish in a pond recalls old mountain pool.
Now I shall clear the land at the edge of the southern wild,
And, clinging to simplicity, return to garden and field.
My house and land on a two-acre lot,
My thatched hut of eight or nine rooms—   10
Elms and willows shade the eaves back of the house,
Peach and plum trees stand in a row before the hall.
Lost in a haze is the distant village,
Where smoke hovers above the homes.
Dogs bark somewhere in deep lanes,
Cocks crow atop the mulberry trees.
My home is free from dust and care,
In a bare room there is leisure to spare.
Long a prisoner in a cage,
I am now able to come back to nature.   20

[2]

I plant beans at the foot of the southern hill;
The grass is thick and bean sprouts are sparse.
At dawn, I rise and go out to weed the field;
Shouldering the hoe, I walk home with the moon.
The path is narrow, grass and shrubs are tall,
And evening dew dampens my clothes.
Wet clothes are no cause for regret
So long as nothing goes contrary to my desire.

(NOS. 1, 3 FROM A SERIES OF 5; TING, P. 605)   (TR. WU-CHI LIU)

Begging for Food

Driven by hunger I leave my home
With no idea where I'm heading,
But walk on until I come to this village;
I knock at the gate—too embarrassed for words.
The master of the house knows what I want,
Gives me food so my coming isn't in vain.
We talk and joke the whole day till dusk;
Wine is brought in, cups are constantly emptied.

I rejoice that I have found a new friend,
I compile and chant this poem: 10
I'm grateful that your favor is like the washing woman's—
But I'm sorry that I lack Han Hsin's talents.[1]
I don't know how to express my thanks,
So I'll repay your kindness in the hereafter.
(TING, P. 607)   (TR. WU-CHI LIU)

Passing Ch'ien-hsi as Military Adviser
in the Third Month of the Year Yi-ssu [405]

I don't travel much in these parts:
The months and years—how they've piled up.
Dawn to dusk, I see mountains and streams,
Everything just as they were before.
Fine rain awash on tall groves,
Fresh wind riffling through cloud-feathers.
That's what I see: things as they are;
A fair wind doesn't cut everyone off,
And so, what about me?
Plodding along, tied down to this post: 10
A body, it seems, with no will of its own,

---

[1] In his youth, Han Hsin, who later helped the First Emperor of Han to establish his dynasty, was in great poverty. Hungry and without food, he went to fish under the city wall. There he met an old washwoman who took pity on him and fed him for several days. After Han Hsin became a great general, he repaid her kindness with a thousand ounces of gold.

A simple soul that no one can change.
Fields and gardens daily haunt my dreams—
How long must one remain abroad?
My hope is forever in a boat bound for home,
And my happiness among the frost-nipped juniper.
(TING, PP. 617–18)   (TR. EUGENE EOYANG)

Drinking Wine, Four Selections

[1]

Unsettled, a bird lost from the flock—
Keeps flying by itself in the dusk.
Back and forth, it has no resting place,
Night after night, more anguished its cries.
Its shrill sound yearns for the pure and distant—
Coming from afar, how anxiously it flutters!

It chances to find a pine tree growing all apart;
Folding its wings, it has come home at last.
In the gusty wind there is no dense growth;
This canopy alone does not decay.   10
Having found a perch to roost on,
In a thousand years it will not depart.
(NO. 4 FROM A SERIES OF 20; TING, P. 621)   (TR. WU-CHI LIU)

[2]

Old friends know what I like:
They bring wine whenever they come by.
We spread out and sit under the pines;
After several rounds, we're drunk again.
Old men chatting away—all at once;
Passing the jug around—out of turn.
Unaware that there is a "self,"
How do we learn to value "things"?
We are lost in these deep thoughts;
In wine, there is a heady taste.   10
(NO. 14; TING, P. 623)   (TR. EUGENE EOYANG)

[3]

A green pine grows in eastern garden,
Dense underbrush obscures its beauty.
When a nipping frost ruins all other plants,
Its lofty branches emerge majestically.
Unnoticed among trees,
Standing alone, it becomes a wonder.
I take a pot of wine to hang on the wintry bough,
Then look afar, over and over again.
Life alternates between dreams and illusions,
Why should I tie myself to this worldly bondage?   10
(NO. 8; TING, P. 621)   (TR. WU-CHI LIU)

[4]

Autumn chrysanthemums have beautiful color,
With dew in my clothes I pluck their flowers.
I float this thing in wine to forget my sorrow,
To leave far behind my thoughts of the world.
Alone, I pour myself a goblet of wine;
When the cup is empty, the pot pours for itself.
As the sun sets, all activities cease;
Homing birds, they hurry to the woods singing.
Haughtily, I whistle below the eastern balcony—
I've found again the meaning of life.   10
(NO. 7; TING, P. 621)   (TR. WU-CHI LIU)

Miscellaneous Poems, Six Selections

[1]

A man has no roots.
Blown about—like dust on the road,
In all directions, he tumbles with the wind:
Our lives are brief enough.
We come into this world as brothers and sisters:
But why must we be tied to flesh and blood?
Let's enjoy our happiness:

Here's a jug of wine, call in the neighbors.
The best times don't come often:
Each day dawns only once.   10
The seasons urge us on—
Time waits for no man.

[2]

Bright sun lights out over the western bank,
Pale moon comes out from behind the eastern ridge.
Far-reaching, this million-mile brilliance;
Transcendent, this scene in space.
A breeze comes through the window in my room.
At night the mat and pillow are cold.
The weather shifts: I sense the seasons change;
Unable to sleep, I know how long the night is.
I'd like to say something, but no one's around,
So I raise my cup, and toast my own shadow.   10
Days and months pass by—
One cannot keep pace with ambition.
Thinking these thoughts, I am depressed;
Right through till dawn, I find rest impossible.

[3]

Bright blossoms seldom last long;
Life's ups-and-downs can't be charted.
What was a lotus flower in spring,
Is now the seed-husk of autumn.
Severe frost freezes the wild grass:
Decay has yet to finish it off.
Sun and moon come back once more,
But where I go, no sun will shine.
I look back longingly on times gone by—
Remembering the past wounds my soul.   10

[4]

A noble ambition spans the four seas;
Mine is simpler: not to grow old.
I'd like my family all in one place,

My sons and grandsons all caring for each other.
I want a goblet and a lute to greet each day,
And my wine casks never to run dry.
Belt loosened, I drink pleasure to the dregs:
I rise late, and retire early.
How can today be compared to yesterday?
My heart harbored both ice and coal.   10
In time, ashes return to ashes, dust to dust—
And vain is the way of fame and glory.

[5]

When I was young and in my prime,
If times were sad, I was happy on my own.
With brave plans that went beyond the sea,
I spread my wings, and dreamt of great flights.
But the course of time has run me down,
And my zest for life has begun to wane.
Enjoyment no longer makes me happy,
Each and every thing means more worry.
My strength is beginning to peter out,
I sense the change: one day's not like the last.   10
The hurrying barge can't wait for a moment:
It pulls me along and gives no rest.
The road ahead: how much farther?
I don't know where I will come to rest.
The ancients begrudged a shadow's inch-of-time:
When I think of this, it makes me shudder.

[6]

Years ago, when I heard the words of my elders,
I'd cover my ears, not liking what they said.
Now that I am fifty years old,
These things suddenly matter.
To recapture the joys of my youth—
Does not appeal to me in the slightest.
Going, going, it's very quickly gone.
Who ever lives this life twice?
Let's use the household money for entertainment,

Before the years catch up with us.   10
I have children, but no money left:
No use leaving post-mortem trusts.
(NOS. 1–6 FROM A SERIES OF 12; TING, PP. 628–30)

(TR. EUGENE EOYANG)

In Praise of Poor Scholars

All creatures, each has a home:
The solitary cloud alone has none.
Here and there, into thin air, it vanishes:
When do you ever see its traces?
Morning glow breaks through night's mist;
Flocks of birds fly off together—
One by one, winging out of the woods,
Not to return again until nightfall.
Know your strengths, keep to trodden ways.
Who hasn't known cold and hunger?   10
Those who know me: if they are no longer here—
That's it then. Why complain?
(NO. 1 FROM A SERIES OF 7; TING, P. 631)   (TR. EUGENE EOYANG)

Hsieh Ling-yün (385–433)

Passing Through My Shih-ning Estate[1]

While a child I longed to be staunch in virtue,
But then I tarried in pursuit of worldly goals.
It seems only yesterday I turned against my will,
Yet a good two dozen years have passed.

Blackened and ground, I've renounced the clear wilderness[2];
Tired and spent, I'm shamed by the upright and firm.

---

[1] Hsieh's family estate was in Shih-ning District on the Kuei-chi peninsula (Chekiang). On his way to assume office as magistrate in Yung-chia in 422, he paid a brief visit to this estate. Hsieh had just been the victim of a political intrigue in the capital, and his new office was a demotion tantamount to exile.

[2] *Lun-yü* XVII:7: "But is it not also said that there are things 'So hard that no grinding will ever wear them down,' that there are things 'So white that no steeping will ever make them black?'" (Arthur Waley's translation.)

But stupidity and illness together sustain me—
I return to gain the boon of quietness.[3]
With my magistrate's tally I'll rule the blue sea,
But first I set sail for my native hills.   10

Trekking these hills, I comb their heights and depths,
Crossing rivers, I exhaust their courses upstream and down—
Cliffs sheer down from the closely layered ranges,
Islets weave round the endless line of shoals;
White clouds enfold dark boulders,
Green bamboos bewitch clear ripples.

I'll rethatch the roof overlooking the winding river,
And raise a belvedere among the storied peaks.
Waving my hand, I'll say to the villagers:
"Three years in office, and then I'll return.   20
See that the elms and coffin-trees are planted—
Don't neglect this wish of mine."
(TING, PP. 809–10)   (TR. FRANCIS WESTBROOK)

Leaving West Archery Hall at Dusk[1]

Stepping out through the west-wall gate,
I gaze afar at peaks west of the city wall—
An unbroken barrier piling cliffs upon crags,
Where the deep blues darken, and sink away.

Under morning frosts the maple leaves turn scarlet,
In the evening dusk mists grow shadowy.
As the season passes one's grief is not slight;
Sorrows come and memories weigh down.

The stray hen yearns for her former mate,
A lost bird longs for its old forest: 10

---

[3] *Tao Te Ching* 16: "This return to the root is called Quietness; Quietness is called submission to fate." (Waley.) "Stupidity" (*cho*) may refer to failure in government service in the capital, but has a predominantly favorable Taoist connotation.

[1] West Archery Hall was located near Yung-chia: the imagery of the poem emphasizes Hsieh's separation from his home and friends.

Choked by feeling, they still ache with love—
Then what of myself, deprived of my closest friends.

I rub the mirror where my black temples show flecks,
And pull at my belt, where once snug folds are slack.
"At peace with the order of things"—mere empty words.[2]
Obscure and alone, I turn to my singing lute.
(TING, P. 811)   (TR. FRANCIS WESTBROOK)

Climbing a Solitary Islet in the River

I'm tired of seeing sights south of the river,
But I've neglected to roam north of the river.
With my love of the new, the road runs ever farther,
As I seek the unusual, the scenery never tarries.[1]

The turbulent flow hurtles upon a sheer barrier,[2]
The solitary islet is bewitching in mid-river.
Sun and clouds reflect each other's brilliance,
The water and air are equally fresh and clear.

These revealed marvels are things no one enjoys;
The hidden immortals—who has told of them?[3]   10
When I imagine the beauty of the K'un-lun Mountains,
Far removed from the world of causality,
I begin to believe in the arts of An-ch'i,[4]
That I might fulfill the years of a nourished life.
(TING, P. 812)   (TR. FRANCIS WESTBROOK)

---

2 Quoted from *Chuang-tzu* 6.
1 The word *ching* (here translated "scenery") is ambiguous, and the couplet
  might also be translated: "I desire the new, but the way is tortuous and far;/I
  seek the unusual, but the light does not last."
2 Following a variant reading, this line might also be translated: "I cross the
  turbulent current, hurrying to the solitary islet."
3 Hsieh seems to speak of his perception of the islet's magical manifestations,
  but the word *chen* for "immortals" also means "truth" and the couplet suggests
  the poet has found an esoteric spiritual edification.
4 An-ch'i was a well-known Taoist immortal (biog. *Lieh-hsien chuan* 30). The
  K'un-lun Mountains, a famous haunt of immortals, were the home of the
  Queen Mother of the West.

Climbing Stone Drum Mountain Above the Shores of Shang-shu

A traveler's thoughts stretch on forever,
Sorrow follows grief and grief follows sorrow.
The road home is interminably far,
The rivers and highlands are impassable.
Wandering on, with no one to share a happy moment,
Now at the start of spring I devote myself to climbing.

Since I cannot share my joys and hopes,[1]
Perhaps my melancholy is most in place.
Extending my gaze leftward, I see the broad plains,
Around to the right, I behold a narrow gorge.   10
As the sun sinks the waters grow choppy,
And clouds form midst the multiplying ranges.[2]

White flag vies with new trumpet-creepers;
Green duckweed sets forth its first leaves.
Picking fragrant plants, their fragrance brings no forgetting;
I would delight in music, but the music is discordant.[3]
The prospect of a tryst is remote and vague;
I gaze out wildly—who would call me content?[4]
(TING, P. 814)   (TR. FRANCIS WESTBROOK)

---

1 Possibly this line should be understood to mean: "Since my joy [of the moment, inspired by the beauty of the mountains in the spring] and my aspirations [to end the "traveler's" existence and reunite with old friends] are not compatible . . ."

2 The couplet seems to refer to the flickering of light and shadow in the water at sunset, and the layers of mist rising between the ranges of mountains.

3 An alternate translation seems equally possible for this couplet: "Picking fragrant plants, their fragrance is unforgettable:/Happy and delighted, my delight is discordant."

4 In the first, third, and last couplets Hsieh paraphrases the *Ch'u Tz'u* anthology. Frequently, in his poetry Hsieh equates his separation from understanding friends with the convention of the shaman's frustrated search for a goddess (Fair One) in the Ch'u poems.

Climbing the Tower by the Pond

Hidden dragons entice with their mysterious forms,[1]
Flying geese echo their distant cries,
Resting in the sky, I am shamed by the clouds' floating,
And lodged by the river, humbled by its fathomless depths.

Too stupid to advance in virtue,[2]
Too weak to retire to the plow,
I followed my salary to the remote seaside,
And lie sick facing the empty woods.

With quilt and pillow I blotted out the season;
Then opening up, I briefly look out.[3]   10
Inclining my ear I listen to the surging billows
And raising my eyes behold the craggy peaks.

Early spring has replaced the drawn-out winds,
The new sun changes the old shadows.
The pond is growing springtime plants,
Garden willows have turned to singing birds.

"Droves"—I am pierced by the song of Pin,[4]
"Lush and green"—moved by the tune of Ch'u.[5]
Living apart can easily last forever;

---

1 "Hidden dragons" is the first of several allusions in this poem to *I Ching*, Hexagram 1. Submerged in the river's depths, it represents creative energy held in potential readiness to act, a man of character who is unrecognized but remains true to himself (see R. Wilhelm, *The I Ching*, translated by Cary F. Baynes [Princeton University Press, 1967], p. 7). The geese and clouds in this quatrain suggest unrestrained freedom.

2 "Advance in virtue" is another reference to Hexagram 1. The phrase characterizes a superior man who exerts himself and keeps in harmony with the time. For "stupid" see note 3 to "Passing Through My Shih-ning Estate." Here Hsieh seems deliberately to deprive the word of any favorable connotation. "Retiring to the plow" is a cliché for Taoist reclusion.

3 This couplet was lacking in Li Shan's *Wen-hsüan* text.

4 An allusion to *Shih Ching* 154/2; on a spring day young girls are out in crowds picking white flowers and one of them grieves that her man is far away.

5 An allusion to *Ch'u Tz'u*, "Chao Yin-shih," lines 7–8: "A prince went wandering/And did not return./In spring the grass grows/Lush and green." (Translation by David Hawkes.)

It's hard to quit the flock with a tranquil mind. 20
Holding to principle is not only a thing of old;
That I am without regret is proven today.[6]
(TING, P. 811)   (TR. FRANCIS WESTBROOK)

Passing White Banks Pavilion

Brushing my clothes,[1] I followed the sandy dikes,
Till, slackening my pace, I entered this thatched pavilion.
A nearby brook trickles over closely packed stones,
Far-off hills gleam through scattered trees.

Their empty blue cannot be forced into a name,[2]
But when fishing, one easily becomes bent.
Grasping the ivy, listening by the green cliffs,
Spring and my heart are conjoined.[3]

"Chiao-chiao," cry the yellow birds on oak trees,[4]
"Yu-yu," bleat the deer feeding on artemisia.[5]   10

---

6 Again an allusion to *I Ching*, Hexagram 1: a person with the character of a dragon withdraws from the world without regret (Nine at the beginning: commentary on the lines).

1 It was customary to brush off one's clothing before starting a journey. The occasion of this poem probably is Hsieh's return home to Shih-ning after retiring from office in 423.

2 An illusion to *Tao Te Ching* 25, which states that the Way (*Tao*) can only have a name forced on it. The fisherman in the next line represents the Taoist who lives spontaneously, without forcing distinctions. The word *ch'ü*, here translated as "bent," may allude to *Tao Te Ching* 22: "If you are bent, then you are whole." But *ch'ü* also might mean "song": the fisherman, in contrast to forcing names, easily makes his song. This seems to be an instance of deliberate ambiguity.

3 This line suggests that Hsieh has eliminated all distinction between his conscious self and the season, or the natural world. But there probably also is an allusion to the end of the *Ch'u Tz'u* piece, *Chao Hun:* "One's gaze extends a thousand *li*, and the *spring heart* is grieved." Hence the line is ambiguous and foreshadows the unpleasant allusions which follow.

4 An allusion to *Shih Ching* 131/1: the song concerns three outstanding servitors who were sacrificed and went to the grave with Duke Mu of Ch'in in 621 B.C. It laments that each of these servitors is worth a ransom of a hundred other men. Hsieh evidently is alluding to the "sacrifice" of himself and several friends who failed in a power play to promote the Prince of Lu-ling for the throne in 422.

5 An allusion to *Shih Ching* 161/1: at a banquet a host lavishes hospitality upon his virtuous guests. Hsieh seems to be rejoicing, no doubt with considerable irony, in the good fortune of his friends who have not yet been sacrificed and remain in the government's good graces.

I grieve for the hundred sorrows of those men,
And rejoice at your happiness on receiving baskets of favor.

Prosperity and decline alternately come and go,
Failure and success turn to joy and sorrow.
Better to live forever a life of retirement,
Of all possible courses, to be constant in Simplicity.[6]
(TING, PP. 818–19)   (TR. FRANCIS WESTBROOK)

Spending the Night on Stone Gate Mountain

At dawn I plucked orchids in the park;
I feared they would wither in the frost.
At night I return to dwell at the clouds' edge,
Enjoying here the moonlight on the rocks.[1]

Birds cry, revealing their nocturnal roost;
Leaves fall and I know the wind has risen.
Separate sounds can be heard perfectly together,
Variant echoes carry with equal clarity.

If no one appreciates these marvelous things,
With whom can I enjoy this fragrant wine?   10
The Fair One never comes;
I dry my hair in vain on Sunny Bank.[2]
(TING, P. 819)   (TR. FRANCIS WESTBROOK)

Journeying by Stream: Following Chin-chu Torrent I Cross the Mountains

When the gibbons howl one is sure it's dawn,
Though in the valley gloom no light can be seen.
Beneath the cliffs clouds are just forming,

---

6 "Simplicity," that is, "embrace the Uncarved Block," live in unity with the Way. See *Tao Te Ching* 19.
1 This quatrain may allude to Hsieh's past political career and present retirement at Shih-ning.
2 The third line of this poem, as well as the final couplet, allude to one of the Nine Songs of the *Ch'u Tz'u* anthology: in vain a shamaness seeks a tryst with a male deity (Fair One), and imagines bathing with him in the Pool of Heaven. Hsieh again laments his isolation from close friends.

While on the flowers dewdrops still glisten.
Winding about through nook and crook,
I tortuously ascend to the notches and peaks.
Crossing streams I drench my clothes in the rapids,
Scaling cliff-ladders I traverse far spans.
The river's bank often doubles back;
I enjoy going with the meandering stream.   10
Duckweed floats on the murky depths,
Darnel and rushes cover the limpid shallows.

On tiptoe atop a stone I cup a waterfall,
And climbing a tree pull down leafy branches.
I fancy seeing someone in the mountain's fold:
The fig-leaf coat and rabbit-floss girdle are before my eyes.
Taking a handful of orchids, I try in vain to entwine them;
I break off hemp—to whom can I open my heart?[1]
To my mind appreciation is beauty;
This thing is obscure—who can ever discern it?   20
Viewing this scenery I discard worldly cares;
Awakened once and for all, I'll gain total abandonment.[2]
(TING, P. 818)   (TR. FRANCIS WESTBROOK)

Entering the Mouth of P'eng-li Lake

A traveler tires of nights on the water.
The wind and tides are unpredictable:
Around islets they suddenly swerve and rejoin,
And the banks often come crashing down.

By moonlight I hear the mournful gibbons,
And dampened by dew, I smell fragrant iris.
At spring's end, the green wilds flourish;
Where the cliffs rise highest, white clouds amass.

---

1 These four lines allude to the Nine Songs: Hsieh puts himself in the place of
the shaman-suitor who cannot succeed in presenting gifts to the fickle deity. The
twining of orchids also suggests forming bonds of friendship.
2 To help explain this paradoxical line (the original literally says "gain what is
abandoned") commentators cite a passage from the Hsiang/Kuo commentary to
Chuang-tzu 2, which suggests that Hsieh is so far beyond the distinction of
discarding and gaining that he even abandons abandonment.

A thousand memories gather day and night,
A myriad sorrows brim dawn and dusk.   10
Scaling cliffs, I find my reflection in Stone Mirror,
Parting the leaves, I enter Pine Gate.[1]

The stories of the Three Rivers are mostly lost,
The Nine Tributaries exist only in name.
The marvels here begrudge their curious treasures;
The Immortals withhold their ethereal souls.[2]

The Essence of Gold has doused its bright light,
The Liquid Jade has stopped its radiant flow.[3]
In vain I play the "Thousand-Mile Song";
The strings snap and memories multiply.   20
(TING, P. 823)   (TR. FRANCIS WESTBROOK)

Pao Chao (?–466)

"Going Out Through the North Gate of Chi": Imitation of a Ballad

Winged bulletins issued from frontier outposts;
Beacon fires extend into the city of Hsien-yang.[1]
Cavalry are sent to garrison Kuang-wu[2];
Infantry dispatched to the aid of Shuo-fang.[3]
Rigorous autumn stiffens bows and shafts;
The Hunnish formations are spirited and strong.
The Son of Heaven lays a hand on his sword in anger;
Couriers catch sight of one another in the distance.
Climbing stony roads in echelon formation,
Crossing over flying bridges in single file.   10
Flutes and drums flow with memories of the Han;
Banners and armor are covered with the frost of the steppes.

---

[1] Stone Mirror was on the summit of Pine Gate Mountain in Kiangsi east of P'eng-li Lake.
[2] This quatrain refers to the lore and magical manifestations of the region. Compare the last six lines of "Climbing a Solitary Islet in the River," p. 60, with which this poem, written almost ten years later, markedly contrasts.
[3] Hsieh refers to ingredients for mixing elixirs of immortality.
[1] The ancient capital of Ch'in.
[2] Located in Shantung, a frontier town in Han times.
[3] Another frontier town, located in the southern part of Sui-yüan.

A howling wind arises and assails the frontier;
Sand and grit soar aloft and float.
The horses' coats are as stiff as hedgehog spines;
Horn-trimmed bows cannot be drawn.
When times are hard, we see steadfast officials;
When the world is in chaos, we know the loyal and the good.
They cast away their lives in the service of a great ruler,
Their own deaths offered as a sacrifice to the nation.   20
(TING, PP. 847–48)   (TR. DANIEL BRYANT)

"In Imitation of Ancient-style Poetry"

The grass has not yellowed on the paths by the river;
Nomad geese are already stretching their wings.
Autumn crickets sing all around the door;
A shivering wife completes her weaving for the night.
"Last year some men returned from the war,
Bringing word that they had known you long ago.
They told me that when you were climbing up Mount Lung
You gazed long toward the east and heaved a sigh.
Your clothes and belt are different from former times;
In the morning you show a face greatly changed.   10
What can I do, worrying over these troubles?
As nights grow long, my sorrow is all the more.
My bright mirror lies closed in its dusty case;
Cobwebs spread over my jade-trimmed lute."
(NO. 7 FROM A SERIES OF 8; TING, P. 881)   (TR. DANIEL BRYANT)

Presented as a Farewell to Secretary Fu

The nimble swan plays in the river pool;
The lonely goose comes to roost on the island sand bar.
For a while by chance the two of us were close,
In thought and feeling together without a break.
Wind and rain blew us apart, east and west;
Once parted we drifted for ten thousand leagues.
I pursue my memories of the times we stayed together,
Your voice and appearance fill my mind and ears.
As the sun falls, the river isles grow cold;
Mournful clouds rise and enfold the heavens.   10

These short wings cannot soar aloft;
And hesitate here amid the mist and fog.
(TING, PP. 873–74)   (TR. DANIEL BRYANT)

"The Weary Road," Two Selections

[1]

Water spilled on level ground
Runs east, west, south or north, and whichever way it pleases.
　　A man's life is also governed by fate,
Then why must we always sigh as we journey and grieve as we sit?
　　Drink your wine to please yourself;
Raise your cup and forswear singing "The Weary Road."
But since a man's heart isn't wood or stone,
　　How could it be without feeling?
Thus I weep, I hesitate, I dare not speak.

[2]

Have you not seen the grasses on the riverbank?
　　They wither and die in winter, overspread the road in spring.
Have you not seen the sun above the city wall?
　　It grows dim, sinks, and disappears;
　　The next day it will come out again.
Now, at what time in my life can I be like this?
Once gone, I'll forever perish in the Yellow Spring!
Life is full of bitterness but scant in joy;
To be high-spirited belongs to the prime of life.
So I wish, ever so often, when I enjoy success,   10
There'll always be money at my bedside to buy wine.
To be immortalized in bamboo or silk is not what I want:
Life or death, honor or debasement, I leave to Heaven.
(NOS. 4–5 FROM A SERIES OF 18; TING, P. 860)   (TR. IRVING Y. LO)

Liu Chün (*430–464*)

In Imitation of Hsü Kan ("Since You Went Away")[1]

Since you went away
Gold and green hairpins have lost their glint.
My longing thoughts of you, like sun and moon,
Circling round and round, rise day and night.
(TING, P. 740)   (TR. JAN W. WALLS)

Shen Yüeh (*441–512*)

"Song of Woe"

The wanderer was in love with the spring of the year
And the spring in love with the wanderer.
Languid sunbeams in the morning draped their splendor,
Gentle dew at dawn lay frozen by the ford.
Seasonal bird songs lilted through the new-grown leaves
While scented airs were stirring in the early duckweed.

Then one morning found me far from my old home,
Ten thousand *li* had come between me and that dawn.
(TING, P. 1214)   (TR. RICHARD B. MATHER)

"Hand in Hand: A Song"

Dropping the reins, we dismount from the ornate carriage
And change our clothes to celebrate the couch of jade.
Drooping hairpins reflected in autumn waters,
Open mirror rivaling spring's beauty.

What I dread is red-cheeked youth's swift fading,
When your love may not be made to last.

---

1 This poem is also attributed to Hsü Yao-chih.

With pheasant cap,[1] when once you have an heir,
Will you then miss the cassia bough when it is gone?
(TING, P. 1215)   (TR. RICHARD B. MATHER)

"Four Recollections"[1]

I recall the times she came,
Radiantly treading up the steps,
Tenderly telling what it was to be parted,
Gravely protesting how she missed me,
How our visits were all too short,
How seeing me made her forget her hunger.

I recall the times she sat,
A tiny thing before the silk-gauze screen:
Now singing four or five refrains,
Or playing twice or thrice upon the strings.   10
When laughing she was quite beyond compare,
When vexed, more lovable than ever.

I recall the times she ate,
Above the dishes changing her expression,
Starting to sit and then too shy to sit,
Starting to eat and then too shy to eat,
Holding small morsels in her mouth as if not hungry,
Raising her cup like one who'd lost her strength.

And I recall the times she slept,
With others sleeping, forcing herself to stay awake: 20
Untying her gauze dress, not waiting to be coaxed,
But on the pillow once more needing to be led,
Distrustful lest the one beside her see,
Sweetly ashamed before the candlelight!
(TING, PP. 1249–50)   (TR. RICHARD B. MATHER)

---

1 I.e., the cap of a court attendant, decorated with pheasant feathers.
1 The original title is "Six Recollections" (*Liu-yi-shih*), but with only four
stanzas extant.

The Fishing Rod

My cassia boat, adrift and free,
Past verdant banks winds in and out.
Light silken line stirs tender water plants,
While muffled oars arouse a lone wild duck.
Tapping the gunwales heedless of the sunset
To my last years I will make this my pleasure!
(TING, P. 1215)   (TR. RICHARD B. MATHER)

Wild Geese on the Lake

When the white waters fill the spring embankments
Migrating geese each year come winging back.
Gabbling in the swift flow they tug the tender cress,
Their folded wings still crusted with residual frost.
In flocks they swim along, stirring light ripples,
Or singly drift, chasing a lonely sunbeam.
Hovering above in flight some never come to rest,
While others rise confusedly, ranks yet unformed.
And then with flapping pinions, undulating in the air,
In one grand sweep they all return to their old home.   10
(TING, P. 1236)   (TR. RICHARD B. MATHER)

A Response to Wang Ssu-yüan's Poem on the Moon

Splendor of the moon shines down on quiet night,
And night is quiet, quenching fumes and dust.
Square moonbeams flood in at the door
While rounded flecks come filtered through the cracks.
On her high tower they wound the yearning wife;
In western garden sport with men of talent;
Through curtained casement gleam from pearl-sewn threads;
Before the gate shine on the verdant moss;
But in the inmost chamber where the dawn has not yet come—
The limpid radiance—ah, how far away!   10
(TING, P. 1235)   (TR. RICHARD B. MATHER)

The Fragrant Tree (In Memory of Hsieh T'iao)

It put forth buds at the end of the Nine Splendors,[1]
Opening its blossoms by the edge of the Chilly Dew.[2]
Its pervading perfume was no single scent,
A wild profusion, its many and varied hues.
Then suddenly one night a wintry wind arose;
Blasted and sere, the tree no longer can be known.
While sleet and snow swirl by in gusty bouts,
Standing before it here, I heave long sighs.
(TING, P. 1213)   (TR. RICHARD B. MATHER)

Spending the Night in the Eastern Park

The road where Ts'ao Chih watched the fighting cocks,
The path where P'an Yüeh gathered firewood—
The Eastern Suburb—has it changed from yesteryear?
Let me at leisure wander there again.
Roads through the wilds not only twist and turn,
Paths between weed-grown paddies, too, cross back and forth.
Hibiscus hedgerows sparse and dense;
Thornwood gates, both old and new.
In treetops howl the gusty gales,
At grass roots gathers the frosty dew.   10
The startled deer move on and do not rest,
Migrating fowl from time to time look back.
From a thatched ridgepole shrills the mournful owl,
On level moor runs by the shivering hare.
The evening dark enfolds the layered hills,
Long mists draw out light silken skeins.
The fleeting daylight suddenly oppresses me—
Is it the year alone that's ending now?
If only I could get the West Hill herbs,
My failing years might still be made to last.   20
(TING, P. 1232)   (TR. RICHARD B. MATHER)

---

1 Summer.
2 Autumn.

I Say Goodby to Fan An-ch'eng

In the usual way of the young
                we made appointments
and goodby was easy.
Now in our decay and fragility,
separation is difficult.

Don't say "One cup of wine."
Tomorrow will we hold this cup?
And if in dreams I can't find this road,
how, thinking of you,
              will I be comforted?
(TING, P. 1238)   (TR. LENORE MAYHEW AND WILLIAM MCNAUGHTON)

Lament for Hsieh T'iao

This young mandarin had undoubted genius.
His startling lines vibrated with rare sound.
His poems were like bronze bells and musical stones.
His thoughts climbed the wind to the high clouds.
Who can explain such excess of talent?
Now, suddenly, he's gone.
How unjust that this young man of rank
already has his place in the grave mound.
(TING, P. 1242)   (TR. LENORE MAYHEW AND WILLIAM MCNAUGHTON)

Hsieh T'iao (464–499)

"Jade Steps Plaint"

Palace at dusk, the pearl blind is lowered,
Drifting fireflies glide and come to rest;
Through the long night I sew a fine silk jacket—
My thoughts of you, when will they end?
(TING, P. 1001)   (TR. RONALD C. MIAO)

"The Wandering Gentleman"

Green grass tendrils like silk,
Trees burgeoning with pink blossoms;
You needn't say "I'm not returning,"
When you return, the fragrance will be gone.
(TING, P. 1001)   (TR. RONALD C. MIAO)

Hsiao Yen (464–549)

"A Spring Song of Tzu-yeh"

On the stairway fragrance assails the bosom;
In the garden flowers light the eye.
Once the spring heart is like this,
Love comes without bounds.
(NO. 1 FROM A SERIES OF 4; TING, P. 1060)   (TR. JAN W. WALLS)

Anonymous

"Song of Tzu-yeh"

The night is long, she cannot sleep,
A bright moon glitters, glitters;
She imagines hearing a vague voice calling,
"Yes," distractedly she replies to the air.
(NO. 32 FROM A SERIES OF 42; TING, P. 688)   (TR. RONALD C. MIAO)

"Tzu-yeh Songs of the Four Seasons," Twelve Selections

Spring

[1]

Spring breeze stirs a springtime heart,
Wandering eyes gaze upon mountain and grove;

Mountain and grove are full of wondrous color,
Spring birds trill limpid sounds.
(NO. 1 FROM A SERIES OF 20; TING, P. 688)   (TR. RONALD C. MIAO)

[2]

Luminous winds flicker in the moonrise.
In the woodland spreads a brocade of flowers.
Lovers frolic under the spring moon,
And bashful maidens trail robes of gauze.
(NO. 3; TING, P. 689)   (TR. MICHAEL E. WORKMAN)

[3]

Before jade pavilions the new moon dims.
Silk dresses cling to the light breeze.
The lure of spring holds back a song,
The cassia wine makes my cheeks shine.
(NO. 5; TING, P. 689)   (TR. MICHAEL E. WORKMAN)

[4]

Bewitching the blossoms of the spring grove,
Poignant the meaning of spring birds;
Spring breeze brings love thoughts—
Gently parts my skirt of gauze.
(NO. 10; TING, P. 689)   (TR. RONALD C. MIAO)

[5]

Young swallows trill their new tune.
Cuckoos vie in the morning racket.
The thrush won't stop chattering—
I stroll to ease this spring heart.
(NO. 11; TING, P. 689)   (TR. MICHAEL E. WORKMAN)

[6]

Plum flowers all fallen and gone,
Willow catkins disperse with the wind.
How I lament that in the spring of life
No young man has beckoned me!
(NO. 12; TING, P. 689)   (TR. MICHAEL E. WORKMAN)

Summer

[1]

Toss and turn on bamboo mat;
No need for gauze curtains.
Young man, don't rush in now,
Before I've made myself ready.

[2]

At dawn I stand on cool roof garden.
At eve I sleep by the orchid pond.
In moonlight I gather lotus flowers[1];
Each night I husband lotus seeds.[2]

[3]

All winds died this hot day
As summer clouds lift in the dusk.
Hand in hand beneath dense foliage
We float melons and sink ripe plums.

[4]

Green lotus leaves, a canopy on the pond.
Each lotus flower conceals a ruby crown.
The gentleman longs to pluck me off.
But my heart yearns for the lotus seed.

[5]

These scanty clothes too drab.
Even a whirlwind brings no relief.
When will these stifling summer days pass,
So I can put on rouge and powder?

---

[1] A pun on *fu-yung*, the lotus, which is homonymic with "a husband's face."
[2] "Lotus seed" (*lien-tzu*) suggests "children."

[6]

Though humid summer's unfit for excursions,
As muliple cares snarl about me,
I long to sail in the lotus lake
To scatter my thoughts among lotus seeds.
(NOS. 2, 8, 9, 14, 19, 20 FROM A SERIES OF 20; TING, P. 690–91)

(TR. MICHAEL E. WORKMAN)

"A Song of Parable"

A young man is a pitiful wretch,
Leaving home in constant fear of death;
Corpses decay down in narrow gulleys,
And bleached bones lie unclaimed.
(NO. 1 FROM A SERIES OF 4; TING, P. 1587)   (TR. JAN W. WALLS)

The Ballad of Mulan[1]

A sigh sounds and a sough replies,[2]
Mulan must be at the window weaving.
You can't tell the sounds of the loom
From the sighs of the girl.
Ask her whom she's longing for!
Ask her whom she's thinking of![3]
She's longing for no one at all,
She's thinking of no one special:

---

1 For further references concerning the historical background of this poem cf.
Margret Barthel, "Kritische Betractungen zu dem Lied-Gedicht Mulan," *Mitteilungen des Institutes für Orientforschung*, 8 (1961), 435–65. Suffice it to say
that Mulan was of northern, I.e., non-Chinese, stock and lived during the Six
Dynasties period (A.D. 220–588).
2 The first line reminds one of the oral origins of this poem. Several versions of it
exist. The present translation is based on the reading (in modern Mandarin
transliteration): *"Chi chi fu chi chi,"* where the syllable *"chi"* is both an
onomatopoeic representation of a sigh and the sound made by a loom.
3 This line and the preceding two are formulaic. They also occur in *"Che yang-liu chih ko"* ("Song on Breaking the Willow Branch"), *Yüeh-fu shih-chi* (SPTK
ed.), Ch. 25, fol. 6a and 6b. On formulaic language in the popular poetry of this
period cf. Hans H. Frankel, "The Formulaic Language of the Chinese Ballad
'Southeast Fly the Peacocks,'" *Bulletin of the Institute of History and Philology, Academia Sinica*, 39 (1969), pt. 2, 219–44.

"Last night I saw the draft list—
The Khan's mustering a great army;   10
The armies' rosters ran many rolls,
Roll after roll held my father's name!
And Father has no grown-up son,
And I've no elder brother!
So I offered to buy a saddle and horse
And campaign from now on for Father."

In the eastern market she bought a steed,
At the western a saddle and cloth;
In the southern market she bought a bridle,
At the northern a long whip;   20
At sunrise she bade her parents farewell,
At sunset she camped by the Yellow River;
She couldn't hear her parents calling her,
She heard only the Yellow River's flow surge and splash.

Dawn she took leave of the Yellow River,
Evening she was atop the Black Mountains;
She couldn't hear her parents calling her,
She heard only the Tartar horse on Swallow Mountain
   whinny and blow.

Hastening thousands of miles to decisive battles,
Crossing mountains and passes as if flying!   30
The northern air carries the sentry's drum,
A wintry sun glints off her coat of mail.

After a hundred battles the generals are dead,
Ten years now, and the brave soldiers are returning!

Returning to audience with the Son of Heaven,
The Son of Heaven, sitting in his Luminous Hall.[4]
Their merits quickly moved them up the ranks,
And rewards, more than a hundred thousand cash!
Then the Khan asked what Mulan desired:

---

[4] The Luminous Hall was the most important temple of the ancient Chinese
rulers. There ancestors and Heaven were worshiped, the provincial lords pre-
sented themselves annually, and various rites which ensured the natural pro-
gression of the universe were performed.

"I have no use for a minister's post,[5] 40
Just lend me a famous fleet-footed camel[6]
To send me back to my village."

"When my parents heard I was coming,
They helped each other to the edge of town.
When my big sister heard I was coming,
She stood at the door, putting on her face.
When my little brother heard I was coming,
He ground his knife in a flash and went for a pig and a sheep.

"I opened myself the east chamber door,
And sat myself down on the west chamber bed; 50
Took off my wartime cloaks,
And draped myself in my robes of old.
At the window I put up my cloudy black tresses,
Before the mirror I powdered my face,[7]
Came out the door to see my camp mates,
My camp mates so shocked at first!
They'd traveled together for many a year
Without knowing Mulan was a girl!"

The hare[8] draws in his feet to sit,
His mate has eyes that gleam,[9] 60

---

5 Literally "I have no use for [the position of] *Shang-shu lang.*" This was a powerful position during and after the Tsin dynasty, but here it probably indicates generally any high position.

6 This is a variant line based upon the text given in the *Yu-yang tsa-tsu.* On the meaning of the term *ming-t'o,* here translated as "famous . . . camel," cf. Edward H. Schafer, "The Camel in China Down to the Mongol Dynasty," *Sinologica,* 2 (1950), 270–72.

7 Literally "Before the mirror I put on flowery yellow." "Flowery yellow" refers to the yellow makeup commonly used, especially by the nomadic women of the north, to powder their foreheads; cf. also Edward H. Schafer, "The Early History of Lead Pigments and Cosmetics in China," *T'oung Pao,* 44 (1956), 419.

8 The selection of the hare for this image may have aural overtones: "hare," *t'uo* in archaic Chinese, is very similar to the archaic word for "soldier" or "companion," *d'uo.*

9 Although the epithet *mi-li* describing the female rabbit's eyes is usually interpreted to mean "dull" or "dim," we have followed Hoshikawa Kiyotaka's note which glosses it as "the glittering gleam of the eyes" (*Kan shi taikei,* vol. 5, p. 357); this better approximates the bright, natural appearance of the rabbit's eyes.

But when the two run side by side,
How much alike they seem![10]
(TING, PP. 1594–96)   (TR. WILLIAM H. NIENHAUSER)

---

[10] The difficulty in distinguishing a male rider from a female rider is also men-
tioned in another folk poem of this period; cf. Barthel, op. cit., 439.

PART III

Expanding Horizons and the Full Flowering of the Shih

(During the T'ang Dynasty, 618–907)

Wang Fan-chih (590?–660?)

Eight Untitled Poems

[1]

Grass hovel filled with wind and dust,
Not even a tattered blanket to sleep on.
A guest comes, I ask him in:
On the ground, a straw mat to sit on.
In the house, there are no coals,
Only willow hemp to start a fire.
Bland wine is stored in an earthen jug;
The wine kettle has two broken legs.
There're three or four strips of dried deer meat
And five or six chunks of rock salt.   10
I see! This isn't good enough for you,
It hurts; the laugh's on me.

[2]

I saw another man die:
My stomach burned like fire.
Not that I felt sorry for him:
I was afraid I'd be next.

[3]

That fellow rides a big horse,
While I straddle a donkey.
Turn around: someone's toting wood—
So easy to take on airs.

[4]

On the outskirts, dumplings of mud;
Stuffed with what's still in town,
One for each of us to eat:
Don't say it has no taste.

[5]

No one lives past a hundred:
Why not write immortal rhymes.
Forge iron to fence off evil—
Demons just watch: clap hands and laugh.

[6]

I, Fan-chih, wear my socks inside out:
Everyone says it's wrong.
But I'd rather be an eyesore
Than hide my feet under a bushel.

[7]

Having power is nothing to be concerned about
But cheating others is risky business;
Just look at the fire in the wood—
It goes out when the wood burns through.

[8]

Yellow gold's not precious:
Learning's better than pearls;
A man who has no abilities
Leaves not a trace on his times.
(TUN-HUANG MSS.: P2914, S3391 *et al.*)   (TR. EUGENE EOYANG)

Wang Chi (590?–644)

Sent to Recluse Ch'eng

A man's life is a hundred years' constant vexation;
Ten thousand affairs all bring anxious thoughts.
The sun sets when it wants to set,
The river flows following its inclinations.
Ritual and music imprisoned Tan of the Chi clan,[1]
And K'ung Ch'iu[2] was hamstrung by *Songs* and *Documents*.

---

1 The well-known Duke of Chou.
2 Confucius.

It would be better to rest on a high pillow
And occasionally take to drunkenness to let sorrow dissipate.
(CTS, P. 304)   (TR. HELLMUT WILHELM)

In Praise of Carnations

Lush grow the leaves on green stems,
Resplendent red flowers bend low.
I am only afraid that a frost will fall
And deny them their life's fulfillment.
Sighing, I get to thinking about myself:
Does this life really conform to my wishes?
In the time before I was born `
Who was it who made me sprout?
Things once discarded won't be displayed again,
Why should such natural change give me fright?   10
(CTS, P. 302)   (TR. HELLMUT WILHELM)

Lu Chao-lin (c. 641–680)

Lotuses on the Crooked Pond

A floating scent encircles the curved shore,
Round shadows cover the flowery pond.
How I fear when autumn wind rises early,
To be blown adrift—you'll not know.
(CTS, P. 328)   (TR. PAUL KROLL)

"Mount Wu Is High"[1]

endlessly gaze at Mount Wu
gaze and gaze as morning fog descends

---

[1] The title of a *yüeh-fu* tune originating in the Han dynasty. Mount Wu is situated southeast of Wu-shan prefecture in Szechwan province. It was on this mountain that King Huai of Ch'u (329–299 B.C.) had a dream in which a beautiful woman appeared to him and slept with him all night. At dawn she vanished, telling the king that she was the goddess of Mount Wu who manifested herself as clouds in the morning and as rain in the evening.

indistinct trees where gibbons cry
while I fix my gaze on the clouds of the goddess

surging waves convulse the vein of water
lashing rain darkens the patterns on the peaks

soaked clothes even up here:
how much more when I think of you far away
(CTS, P. 325)   (TR. ROBIN D. S. YATES)

"The Weary Road"

Don't you see, north of Ch'ang-an, by the bridge over Wei River,
Withered trees fallen flat in the ancient fields?
In times past, they were flushed red and flushed with purple,
Always retaining the dew and retaining the mist.
In spring light, in spring wind, their flowers were like snow;
Perfumed carriages and jade chairs rumbled endlessly past.
There were no travelers who did not rival in gathering their flowers;
There were no courtesans who did not come to pluck their twigs.
Singing girls with precious kerchiefs and dragon skirts;
Young lords on silver saddles, thousands and ten thousands galloped
     by.   10
Yellow orioles, one by one, glided gracefully towards the flowers;
Blue birds,[1] in pairs, led their chicks in play.
Their branches a thousand feet long, twigs a hundred—
Moon-laurels and star-elms[2] overspread and eclipsed each other.
On their coral leaves paired love birds[3];
In the phoenix's nest, fledglings.[4]
Now, the nest tipped, twigs broken, and the phoenix gone:
Branches withered, leaves dropped, carried away by the wind.
One day stripped bare and no one asks why;
For ten thousand generations destroyed and how are you to know?   20

---

1 According to Taoist legends, blue birds were the messengers of Hsi Wang Mu,
   the queen of the Western Paradise, in the K'un-lun Mountains. She had peach
   trees whose fruit matured once in three thousand years and gave immortality to
   those who tasted them.
2 The laurel tree grew in the moon, stars were thought to be celestial elm trees.
3 Love bird, or mandarin duck, was a symbol of marital fidelity.
4 The *chu-yüan* was a species of fabulous bird, here the phoenix.

In a man's life, fortune knows no beginning or end:
Suddenly, in a moment, gone: hard to rely on it for long.
Who can stop the sun over the western hills?
Who can dam the waters flowing east?
By the grave mounds of Han, trees crowd the Ch'in River,[5]
Coming and going, all is mourning and sorrow.
From of old, lords and nobles of highest rank
All intended their glory and brilliance to last ten thousand years:
I do not see their red lips and fair complexions;
I've only heard about green brambles and the yellow stream.   30

Gold headgears and sable coats[6] were sometimes exchanged for good wine;
Jade-handled stag tails[7] were often brandished: the cost went uncounted.
I wish to say to my seated guests in the rank of immortals:
Life and death are where friendships meet.
You need not tarry beneath the Green Dragon Turret[8];
I must leave for the White Crane Mountain.[9]
Among the clouds, on the sea far away, so difficult to meet:
When is the time for all sincere hearts to understand one another?
Would that the reign of Yao had lasted a million years!
Then to be a Ch'ao-fu or a Hsü-yu,[10] I would forever
    resign myself.   40

(CTS, P. 323)   (TR. ROBIN D. S. YATES)

---

5 The Ch'in stream flows in the northwest province of Kansu.
6 Gold headgears and sable fur were sewn on the hats of officials of the Ministry of War. Wang Fu of the Tsin dynasty (265–420) bartered this hat for wine, an act that resulted in his impeachment.
7 Wang Yen of the Tsin, an immensely wealthy man, had these brushes specially made for him.
8 Green Dragon Turret was situated in the eastern part of the Wei-yang Palace.
9 White Crane Mountain in Szechwan province was the home of the Han Taoist Wu-an. The poet means he will fly off from there to become an immortal.
10 The legendary emperor Yao was considered to have been the perfect monarch of the perfect society. Ch'ao-fu and Hsü-yu were hermits who refused the throne when Yao wished to abdicate.

Ch'en Tzu-ang (661–702)

A Song on Climbing the Gate Tower at Yu-chou

I fail to see the ancients before my time,
Or after me the generations to come.
Thinking of the eternity of Heaven and Earth,
All alone, sadly I shed tears.
(CTS, P. 512)   (TR. WU-CHI LIU)

Inscription on a Tree atop Mount Sacrifice (Ssu Shan) and Sent to Censor Ch'iao [Chih-chih]¹

The Han court honors clever eunuchs;
The Cloud Pavilion² disdains frontier deeds.
How sad is the envoy on a piebald horse—
His hair white, whose hero now?
(CTS, P. 519)   (TR. GEOFFREY R. WATERS)

Impressions of Things Encountered, Three Selections

[1]

As the crescent moon is born from the Western Sea,¹
A dimmed sun begins to rise and take its place.
When this gleaming sphere floods the east,
The shadowy soul will already be frozen in the dawn.
From the Great Ultimate heaven and earth were born,²
The three great ones³ will rise and fall in turn.

---

1 Ch'iao Chih-chih (d. 697), poet and official, was killed by Wu Ch'eng-ssu, one of Empress Wu's favorites.
2 Yün-t'ai, where portraits of Han generals were painted on walls in recognition of their meritorious service.
1 It is conventional to speak of the crescent moon as rising or appearing in the west, as it is there that it first becomes visible (when it rises in the east it is still day) in the early evening during the first week of the lunar month.
2 The usual allegorical interpretation of this poem identifies the usurper, Empress Wu (reigned 684–705), with the moon, and her son, the legitimate ruler, with the sun, whose light will soon be so strong as to make his mother's invisible.
3 This line refers to the full moons of the first, seventh, and tenth lunar months.

The quintessence, I suspect, resides there,
But who could ensure the fullness of the moon?[4]
(NO. 1 FROM A SERIES OF 38; CTS, P. 505)

(TR. WILLIAM H. NIENHAUSER)

[2]

Orchids grow through spring and summer,
Their luxuriance so green and lush.
Secluded and alone, they color the groves in vain,
Their red petals rising from purple stems.
Ever so slowly, daylight turns to dusk;
Ever so finely, autumn winds are born.
The season's flowers have withered and fallen,
How could one fulfill their sweet intent?
(NO. 2; CTS, P. 505)   (TR. WILLIAM H. NIENHAUSER)

[3]

Kingfishers nest on South Sea islands,
Male and female in vermilion-colored groves.
How would they know the minds of fair ladies
Who cherish them far more than gold?
Their bodies slain in the land of burning sun;
Their feathers cast in a dark corner in a jade hall.
Resplendent, they glitter as hair ornaments;
Lush, they decorate the embroidered quilt.
It isn't that you can't keep your distance:
A forest official's net will suddenly seek you out.   10
To be born with talents is to invite disaster:
I heave a sigh at this fabulous bird.
(NO. 23; CTS, P. 506)   (TR. IRVING Y. LO)

---

4 Literally, "three and five," i.e., the fifteenth of the lunar month, the time of the full moon.

Han Shan (*date uncertain*)

Four Untitled Poems

[1]

Parrots dwell in the west country.
Foresters catch them with nets, to bring them to us.
Lovely women toy with them, morning and evening,
As they go to and from their courtyard pavilions.

They are given lordly gifts of golden cages—for their own storage!
Bolted in—their feathered coats are spoiled.
How unlike both swan and crane:
Wind-swirled and -tossed, they fly off into the clouds!

[2]

Swine gobble dead men's flesh.
Men gobble dead pigs' guts.
Swine do not disdain the smell of men.
Men even talk about the scent of pork.

But—
Should a pig die—it is cast into the water.
Should a man die—the soil is dug to hide him.
Then—
Neither finds the one or the other to his taste.
Yet—
Lotus flowers will live in boiling water!
(CTS, PP. 4675, 4678)   (TR. EDWARD H. SCHAFER)

[3]

Man lives his life in a dust bowl,
Just like vermin in the middle of a pot:
All day going round and round,
Never getting out from the inside.
Blessedness is not our lot:

Only nettlesomeness without end.
Time is like a flowing river—
One day, we wake up old men.

[4]

There is a poetaster named Wang
Who laughs at much-flawed verse.
He says: "This line sounds waspish"[1]
And: "That line runs on knobby knees."[2]
"You have no command of versification,
But put words willy-nilly on the page."
I laugh and say: "The poetry *you* write
Is like a blind man faintly praising the sun!"
(CTS, PP. 4686, 4690)　　　　　　　(TR. EUGENE EOYANG)

Shih Te (*date uncertain*)

Four Untitled Poems

[1]

You can see the moon's brightness,
Illuminating all under heaven.
Its round radiance, suspended in the Great Void,
Is lustrous, pure, and ethereal.
Others say it waxes and wanes;
That which I see is eternal, never declining.
With an aura like the Mani pearl,[1]
Its brilliance knows no day or night.

[2]

Since apes are still able to learn,
Shouldn't men study with renewed zeal?

---

1 Literally, "wasps' waists," referring to one of the "eight blemishes" in the composition of poetry, in which the second and fourth words in the line have the same tone, according to Shen Yüeh's principles of prosody.
2 Literally, "stork's knees," referring to another of the "eight blemishes," in which the fifth and fifteenth words have the same tone.
1 The Mani pearl is a bright, luminous pearl, symbol of the Buddha and his doctrine.

When the lead carriage falls into a pit,
The rear carriage must alter its course.
If you are not aware of this,
You'll meet, I fear, with evil and destruction.
Even if you were born a Yaksa,[2]
Change your ways and you'll become a Bodhisattva!

[3]

I laugh at my failing strength in old age,
Yet still dote on pines and crags, to wander there in solitude.
How I regret that in all these past years until today,
I've let things run their course like an unanchored boat.

[4]

Far, faraway, steep mountain paths,
Treacherous and narrow, ten thousand feet up;
Over boulders and bridges, lichens of green,
White clouds are often seen soaring.
A cascade suspends in mid-air like a bolt of silk;
The moon's reflection falls on a deep pool, glittering.
I shall climb up the magnificent mountain peak,
To await the arrival of a solitary crane.
(CTS, PP. 4693, 4692, 4694)   (TR. JAMES M. HARGETT)

Meng Hao-jan (689–740)

Passing the Night on a River in Chien-te

I guide my boat to mooring by a misty islet,
With the setting sun, a traveler's sorrows revive.
Wilds so vast, the sky stoops to the trees;
The river so clear, moon close to man.
(CTS, P. 913)   (TR. PAUL KROLL)

---

2 Yaksa are demons who are malignant, violent, and devourers of human flesh.

The First of Autumn

Unnoticed the first of autumn as nights grow longer,
A pure breeze wafts and drifts, redoubling the chill of loneliness.
The blazing flame of summer wanes; the thatched studio is still:
Beneath the steps, clustered sedge keeps the glitter of dew.
(CTS, P. 914)   (TR. PAUL KROLL)

On the Street of Lo-yang[1]

Pearl pellets, resplendent young dandies;
Golden bridles, roaming gallants;
Drunk with wine, as the white sun sets,
Ambling on horseback, enter the red dust.
(CTS, P. 913)   (TR. PAUL KROLL)

Paying a Visit to Monk Yung's Cloister

A monk's robe hangs in a cloister in the hills.
Outside the window I find no one but passing birds.
Dusk has come up halfway down the mountain road;
Then I hear the sound of the spring cling to the green-tinted slope.
(CTS, P. 914)   (TR. JOSEPH J. LEE)

Starting Early from Yü-p'u Deep[1]

Eastward, the faint glimmer of the early dawn,
And the birds on the islet already awakened and clamoring.
Lying down, I listen at the mouth of Yü-p'u Deep,
To the sound of paddles splashing dimly by.
As the sun rises and the mist clears,
I begin to make out the breadth of the river's way—
A beautiful woman who always rises late

---

[1] The original title of this poem reads: "Written on the Street of Lo-yang in the Company of Ch'u the Twelfth." "Pellets" in line 1 refer to those used with a small crossbow.
[1] Located on the upper reaches of the Che River estuary, southwest of the city of Hangchow.

Casts her reflection, dabbling with the rushing stream.
  I am fearful of alarming the monkeys who drink at the river,
  Sometimes I see an otter "sacrificing" fish.[2]   10
My boat moves along at ease and without concern,
The more so with the unfolding of this clear view.
(CTS, P. 896)   (TR. DANIEL BRYANT)

Crossing the Hsiang River at Night

A wandering traveler anxious to make the crossing
Takes the ferry over the River Hsiang by night.
In the dew-laden air I scent the fragrant pollinia
And by their songs know the gatherers of lotus blossoms.
The boatmen steer for the fires upon the shore;
Fishermen anchor for the night deep in the mist.
From time to time this wayfarer inquires of them,
"Which way to get to Ts'en-yang?"
(CTS, P. 907)   (TR. DANIEL BRYANT)

Parting from Wang Wei

Forlorn and lonely, my time will never come;
Day after day, I return by myself in vain.
I wish to go away, to seek fragrant herbs,
But regret that I must leave an old friend behind.
On whom among those in power might I depend?
Few in this world hear the same music[1] as I.
All I can do is keep to my lonely solitude,
And just close the gate of my old garden.
(CTS, P. 901)   (TR. DANIEL BRYANT)

---

2 Otters were believed to sacrifice fish, an action probably related to the food-washing of raccoons.

1 Referring to the lutenist Po Ya, who smashed his instrument on the death of his friend Chung Tzu-ch'i, saying that there was no one left who could understand his music. The phrase "know music" has thus come to mean one who understands and appreciates the highest ideals and capabilities of a friend.

Stopping at a Friend's Farm

My old friend prepares chicken and millet
And invites me to visit his home in the fields.
Green trees enclose the country village,
Blue hills slope upward from the outskirts.
Opening the window, we face fields and garden,
Lifting our cups, talk of mulberry and hemp.
Wait till the Autumn Festival comes again,
I will return in time for the blooming of chrysanthemums.
(CTS, P. 906)   (TR. DANIEL BRYANT)

Spending the Night at the Hillside Lodge of Master Yeh and Waiting for My Friend Ting, Who Does Not Arrive

The evening sun sets beyond the western ranges,
And in a moment, all of the valleys grow dark.
The moonlit pines bring forth the cool of night,
Wind and running water fill my clean hearing.
    Soon the woodsmen will be back in their homes;
    Birds find their roosts now in the misty trees.
It is you that has not come by the time agreed;
And I wait alone with my lute in the vine-grown lane.
(CTS, P. 894)   (TR. DANIEL BRYANT)

Seeking Hsin E in the Western Hills

In a swaying boat drifting along with the stream
I am on my way to visit my old friend's lodge.
The setting sun lies in the clear,
Who says I am here only to "admire the catch"?[1]
    Peering deep into stony depths through the clear water,
    Passing slowly through the bends between the sandbanks,
    I see a hook dangling from a bamboo-grown islet,
    And hear a book chanted in a thatched studio.

---

1 Alluding to an aphorism from the *Huai-nan Tzu*, "Admiring the catch is not so good as going home and making a net."

Deep in our words we forget the fall of night;
This pure pleasure belongs to the first cool of autumn.   10
Ah, Hui! with his simple drinking gourd[2];
Such a sage, constantly in a state of peace.
(CTS, P. 912)   (TR. DANIEL BRYANT)

Wang Wei (701–761)

Seeing Someone Off

Dismounting, I offer you wine
And ask, "Where are you bound?"
You say, "I've found no fame or favors;
"I must return to rest in the South Mountain."
You leave, and I ask no more—
White clouds drift on and on.
(CTS, P. 685)   (TR. IRVING Y. LO)

To Subprefect Chang

In late years, I love only the stillness,
The world's affairs no longer trouble my heart.
Looking at myself: no far-reaching plans;
All I know: to return to familiar woods—
The pine winds blow and loosen my sash;
The mountain moon shines upon me playing the lute.
You ask for reasons for failure or success—
Fisherman's song enters the riverbanks deep.
(CTS, P. 698)   (TR. IRVING Y. LO)

Birdsong Brook

Mind at peace, cassia flowers fall,
Night still, spring mountain empty.
Moon rising startles mountain birds
Now and again sing from spring brook.
(CTS, P. 714)   (TR. IRVING Y. LO)

---

2 Alluding to Confucius' praise of his favorite disciple Yen Hui as a man un-
discouraged by poverty so extreme that he had only a gourd to drink from.

Red Peonies

Such radiance of green,
    so casual and composed;
The tint of her dress
    blends crimson with pink.
The heart of a flower
    is nearly torn with grief:
Will spring's brilliance
    ever know her heart?
(CTS, P. 715)   (TR. IRVING Y. LO)

The Farms at Wei River

Slanting rays shine on the hamlet,
Through narrow lanes oxen and sheep return.
An aged rustic thinks of herdboys,
Leaning on his staff, waits by the bramble door.
Pheasants cry, barley sprouts flourish;
Silkworms sleep, the mulberry leaves are sparse.
Farmers with shouldered hoes approach,
Meet each other and chat—linger.
This I admire: leisure and peace;
And wistfully hum "O to go back!"   10
(CTS, P. 688)   (TR. PAUL KROLL)

On Returning to Sung Mountain

The clear stream girdles the long copse,
Carriage horses amble with ease, with ease.
Flowing water seems to be purposeful.
Evening birds in pairs return.
Barren city walls overlook the old ford,
Fading sunlight fills the autumn mountains.
Far and distant—below Sung's height;
I've come home, and close the gate.
(CTS, P. 702)   (TR. PAUL KROLL)

Suffering from Heat

The red sun fills the sky and the earth,
And fiery clouds are packed into hills and mountains.
Grasses and trees are all parched and shriveled;
Rivers and swamps, all utterly dried.
In light white silks I feel that my clothes are heavy;
Under dense trees I grieve that the shade is thin.
My mat of rushes cannot be approached;
My clothes of linen are washed again and again.

I long to escape beyond space and time;
In vast emptiness, dwell alone and apart.   10
Then long winds from a myriad miles would come;
Rivers and seas would cleanse me of trouble and dirt.
Then would I find that my body causes suffering;
Then would I know that my mind is still unawake.
I would suddenly enter the Gate of Pleasant Dew[1]
And be at ease in the clear, cool joy.
(CTS, P. 689)   (TR. HUGH M. STIMSON)

Enjoying Coolness

Lofty trees, ten thousand or more trunks:
A clear stream threads through their midst.
In front, I look out on the mouth of a great river,
While broad and spacious comes the wind from afar.
Gentle ripples moisten white sand;
A pale carp seems to swim in air.
I lie down upon a broad stone,
And rolling waves flow over my trivial body.
I rinse my mouth in the water and wash my feet.
In front, I face an old man angling for fish: 10

---

[1] The term "Gate of Pleasant Dew" is found in the Buddhist classic the *Fa Hua Ching,* and refers to the entrance into nirvana.

How many in all are those who lusted for bait
And now vainly long to be "east of the lotus leaves"?[1]
(CTS, PP. 689–90)   (TR. HUGH M. STIMSON)

Ch'u Kuang-hsi (fl. 742)

The Cowherd: A Song

It matters not if the pasture is far;
It matters not if the slope is steep.
Whether or not the cattle are tame or wild,
The cowherd's mind is always calm.
A round bamboo hat over my head,
And a long palm-leaf coat to cover my body.
They're good against summer showers
And good for days cloudy and cold.
The big cows are hidden behind the slopes;
The little ones dart in and out of nearby woods.   10
All things seem to please each other;
And they move me to sing and chant.
Joy is found in a moment;
Who would ask for a finer tune?
(CTS, P. 765)   (TR. JOSEPH J. LEE)

Farm Routine

The rushes daily grow taller;
Apricot blossoms daily more lush.
As an old farmer, I enjoy the view;
Everything I do according to the seasons.
I rise early to feed the cows;
Then yoke a pair to farm in eastern acres.
Earthworms crawl in and out of the ground;
Field crows follow me around—

---

[1] The quotation is from an old song, the *Chiang-nan Ch'ü*, which has a line that goes: "Fish play east of the lotus leaves," a happy place, apparently, which the fish in Wang Wei's poem had to give up, because of their fatal passion for worldly food.

In flocks they peck and cry,
As if to tell me of their hunger.   10
My heart is full of compassion;
Looking at this, I pity both them and myself.
I give my food to the crows;
At dusk I return with an empty basket.
My family greet me with mocking smiles;
But never would I have changed my mind.
(CTS, P. 770)   (TR. JOSEPH J. LEE)

Wang Ch'ang-ling (?–756)

Listening to a Wanderer's "Water Melody"

A lone boat, a sliver of moon facing the maple woods—
A wanderer's heart is entrusted to his flute.
Mountain views merge with thousand sheets of rain,
And the last chord fades as our ears fall.
(CTS, P. 802)   (TR. JOSEPH J. LEE)

"Following the Army on Campaign," Three Selections

[1]

The *p'i-p'a* begins the dance, midst changing new sounds,
Always the mountain pass, old feelings of leave-taking.
Disturbing is the frontier sadness, heard without end,
High, high the autumn moon shines upon the Great Wall.

[2]

In the citadel of Jade Gate Pass, elm leaves early scatter yellow,
At the sunset of the day, clouds, sand, an ancient battlefield.
A memorial begs the troops return to cover dusty bones,
Let not men, officers weep over White Dragon Wilderness!

[3]

At Jad Gate Pass mountain ridges several thousand-fold,
North, south of the mountains, always the beacons.

Men on distant garrisons must watch for fire,
Horses tread the deep mountains, unseen their traces.
(NOS. 2, 3 7 FROM A SERIES OF 7; CTS, P. 800)   (TR. RONALD C. MIAO)

Ch'ang Chien (fl. 749)

A Visit to the Broken Hill Temple

At the break of day I come to an old temple,
As the first rays of the sun glow on the treetops.
A path in the bamboo grove leads to a quiet retreat—
A meditation hall hidden behind flowering boughs.
Here, mountain scenery delights the birds,
And the reflections in the pond empty a man's mind.
All murmurings are stilled in this presence,
But for the echoes of chimes and bells.
(CTS, P. 809)   (TR. JOSEPH J. LEE)

Li Po (701–762)

Calling on a Taoist Priest in Tai-t'ien Mountain but Failing to See Him

A dog barks amid the sound of water;
Peach blossoms tinged by dew take on a deeper tone.
In the dense woods at times I see deer;
By the brook I hear no bells at noon.
Wild bamboos divide the blue haze;
Tumbling waterfalls hang from the green cliff.
No one can tell me where you are,
Saddened, I lean against the pines.
(CTS, P. 1021)   (TR. JOSEPH J. LEE)

Seeing Meng Hao-jan Off to Kuang-ling

My old friend, going west, bids farewell at Yellow Crane Terrace,
Among misty blossoms of the third month, goes down to Yang-chou.

His lone sail's far shadow vanishes into the azure void.
Now, only the Long River flowing to the sky's end.
(CTS, P. 981)   (TR. PAUL KROLL)

"Song of Hsiang-yang"

The setting sun about to vanish west of the Hsien Hill,
Lost among the flowers, I wear a hat upside down.
The children of Hsiang-yang clasp their hands,
Blocking the streets and singing "A White Horseshoe."
The spectators ask what they are laughing at,
They laugh at Master Shan, who is as drunk as mud.[1]
A cormorant-ladle!
A parrot-cup!
There are thirty-six thousand days to a hundred years,
And each day one must drain three hundred cups.   10
From afar, the mallard-green of the Han River
Resembles grapes about to ferment.
This river could be turned into spring brew,
The grains piled up would have been a tower of dregs.
I offer my thousand-gold steed for a sing-song girl,
Seated in my carved saddle, I laugh and sing a tune of "Falling
    Plums."
Beside my carriage I hang aslant a jug of wine,
Escorted by the music of phoenix-pipes and dragon-flutes.
Why mention the yellow hounds when one is about to die in Hsien-
    yang?[2]
It's better to empty gold goblets in the moonlight.   20
Do you not see the stone tablet of Lord Yang[3] in Tsin times,
Its carved turtle head falling off, overgrown with moss?
I cannot shed tears;
I cannot feel sad.
Pure breeze and bright moon cost not a single coin,

---

[1] Shan Chien (A.D. 253–312) was once a governor of the region and well-known
for his drinking bouts.
[2] Refers to Li Ssu (?–208 B.C.), the prime minister under the First Emperor of
Ch'in. Upon being taken out for execution, Li Ssu turned around and told his
son how much he missed hunting with his yellow hounds.
[3] Yang Hu (A.D. 221–78) served as a governor in Hsiang-yang. After his death,
the people from the district erected a stone memorial.

The jade mountain crumbles[4] by itself, with no one pushing.
A Shu-chou-ladle!
A figurine-cup!
Li Po vows to live and die with you.
The clouds and rain of Prince Hsiang have left not a trace,[5]   30
The river flows east and the gibbons cry at night.
(CTS, P. 941)   (TR. JOSEPH J. LEE)

"Moon over Mountain Pass"

A bright moon rising above T'ien Shan[1];
Lost in a vast ocean of clouds.
The long wind, across thousands upon thousands of miles,
Blows past the Jade-gate Pass.
The army of Han has gone down the Pai-teng Road,[2]
As the barbarian hordes probe at Ch'ing-hai Bay.[3]
It is known that from the battlefield
Few ever live to return.
Men at garrison look on the border scene,
Home thoughts deepen sorrow on their faces.   10
In the towered chambers tonight,
Ceaseless are the women's sighs.
(CTS, P. 928)   (TR. JOSEPH J. LEE)

In Imitation of Ancient Songs

I ford a river to play with autumn water;
I love the freshness of lotus flowers.
I pluck the lotus and play with the pearls

---

4 "The jade mountain crumbles" alludes to the poet Hsi K'ang (A.D. 223–62),
who was described as "tall as a solitary pine . . . When he gets drunk, he is a
staggering giant, a mountain of jade about to come crushing down" (*Shih-shuo
hsin-yü*, Ch. 14).
5 From Sung Yü's "Shen-nü Fu." In this *fu* a story is told of King Hsiang's
encounter with the Goddess of Mount Wu who appears as clouds in the morn-
ing and rain in the evening.
1 Literally, the Celestial Mountains, between Russia and Chinese Turkestan.
2 Pai-teng Mountain, east of Ta-t'ung in modern Shansi, where the first emperor
of Han, Han Kao-tsu, was besieged by the Hsiung-nu for seven days.
3 Literally, Blue Sea (Ch'ing Hai), i.e., KoKo Nor, a district in the extreme west-
ern part of China, named after a large lake in the area. Later, in T'ang time,
it was occupied by the Tu-fan (Tibetans).

That tumble on its leaves and are round no more.
Our meeting is beyond the colored clouds,
The sky is vast and I have no way to send a gift.
I think of her but I can't see her,
Dejected, I stand before the cool breeze.
(NO. 11 FROM A SERIES OF 12; CTS, P. 1023)   (TR. JOSEPH J. LEE)

Thoughts While Studying at Hanlin Academy
Sent to My Colleagues at the Chi-hsien Academy

At dawn I hasten toward the Purple Hall,
At dusk I await edicts from the Golden Gate.
I read book after book, scattering rare manuscripts all around.
I study antiquity to search for the ultimate essence.
Whenever I feel I understand a word,
I close my book and suddenly smile.
Black flies too easily defile the pure,
A lofty tune like "White Snow" finds few echoes.
By nature carefree and unrestrained,
I've often been rebuked for eccentricity.   10
When the cloudy sky becomes clear and bright,
I long for visits to woods and hills.
Sometimes when the cool breezes rise,
I'll lean on the railings and whistle aloud.
Yen Kuang[1] angled in his T'ung-lu Creek,
And Hsieh K'e[2] climbed his Ling-hai Peak.
When I finish my task in this world,
I shall follow them and try my fishhook.
(CTS, P. 1024)   (TR. JOSEPH J. LEE)

"The Road to Shu Is Hard"

Alas! behold! how steep! how high!
The road to Shu is hard, harder than climbing to the heavens.
The two kings Ts'an-ts'ung and Yü-fu[1]

---

[1] Yen Kuang (37 B.C.–A.D. 43), friend and adviser to Liu Hsiu, who later became Emperor Kuang-wu of Eastern Han (reigned A.D. 25–58).
[2] I.e., the poet Hsieh Ling-yün (A.D. 385–433).
[1] Shu, the ancient name for Szechwan, was said to be ruled at one time by five brothers, the eldest being Ts'an-ts'ung and the third being Yü-fu. Having no

Opened up this land in the dim past;
Forty-eight thousand years since that time,
Sealed off from the frontier region of Ch'in!
The Great White Peak blocks the west approach, a bird track,
Just wide enough to be laid across the top of Mount Omei.
Earth tottered, mountain crumbled, brave men perished,[2]
And then came stone hanging-bridges, sky-ascending ladder inter-
    locked.   10
Above, on the highest point, the Six-Dragon Peak curls around the sun;
Below, the gushing, churning torrents turn rivers around.
White geese[3] cannot fly across,
And gibbons in despair give up climbing.
How the Mud Mountain twists and turns!
Nine bends within a hundred steps, zigzagging up the cliffside
To where one can touch the stars, breathless!
Beating my breast, I heave a long sigh and sit down.

May I ask if you expect to return, traveling so far west?
Terrifying road, inaccessible mountain peaks lie ahead,   20
Where one sees only dismal birds howling in ancient woods
Where the female and the male fly around and around.
One also hears cuckoos crying beneath the moon at night,
Grief overfills the empty mountain.
The road to Shu is hard, harder than climbing to the heavens;
Just hearing these words turns one's cheeks pale.

Peak upon peak less than a foot from the sky,
Where withered pines hang inverted from sheer cliffs,
Where cataracts and roaring torrents make noisy clamor,
Dashing upon rocks, a thunderclap from ten thousand glens.   30
An impregnable place like this
I sigh and ask why should anyone come here from far away?

---

    language, the people lived in peace and had no contact with Ch'in until 311
    B.C.
2 According to legend, a king of Ch'in promised five young women in marriage to
    the ruler of Shu, who sent five brave men to meet and escort the young
    women. On the way, they encountered a huge snake; and while they were fight-
    ing off the snake, mountains crumbled and all the party met death. The five
    women were transformed into five mountain peaks.
3 Reading *ku* ("snow-white goose") for *ho* ("crane").

There the Dagger Peak stands erect and sharp:
With one man guarding the pass,
Ten thousand people can't advance.
Should those on guard prove untrustworthy,
They could have turned into leopards and wolves.
Mornings, one runs away from fierce tigers;
Evenings, one runs away from long snakes—
They gnash their fangs, suck human blood,   40
And maul people down like hemp.
The Brocade City might be a place for pleasure,
But it's far better to hurry home.
The road to Shu is hard, harder than climbing to the heavens.
Sideways I look westward and heave a long sigh.
(CTS, PP. 922–23)   (TR. IRVING Y. LO)

To Secretary Lu Ch'ien of Jen City

A sea bird knows the coming of storm,
He seeks refuge east of Lu city-gate.
A cup before him, he would not drink;
Flapping his wings, he desires to fly high.
He finds no delight in bells and drums,[1]
And no one would share with him mist and frost.
Ready for return home, he could not bear to leave;
Tears flow as he bids farewell to herons and ducks.
(CTS, PP. 949–50)   (TR. JOSEPH J. LEE)

T'ien-mu Mountain[1] Ascended in a Dream:
A Farewell Song

Sea voyagers talk about fairy islands,
Lost in mists and waves, and hard to reach.
The men of Yüeh speak of the T'ien-mu Mountain,
Sometimes it can be seen when clouds gather or disperse.
T'ien-mu Mountain links to the horizon and extends heavenward—
Its majesty surpassing the five sacred peaks and overshadowing Mount
    Ch'ih-ch'eng.

---

1 Symbols of wealth and power.
1 A mountain in Chekiang regarded as sacred by Taoists.

Nearby, the T'ien-t'ai Mountain, five hundred thousand feet high,
Appears to sink low, leaning to the southeast.

How I would like to dream of Wu and Yüeh,
And fly one night with the moon over Mirror Lake!   10
The lake-moon shines on my shadow
And takes me to Shimmering Stream.
The place Lord Hsieh[2] lodged is still here,
Where blue waters ripple and gibbons cry.
Wearing Lord Hsieh's clogs,
I scale the mountain among azure clouds.

Halfway up appears the sun in the sea;
In midair is heard the Cock of Heaven.
Among thousands of crags and ravines, the road meanders.
Lured by flowers, I lean on a rock and suddenly it becomes dark.   20
Bears roar, dragons chant—the thundering cascade;
Deep woods quake with fear and towering ridges tremble.
Clouds turn dark with a hint of rain;
On the placid waters mists rise.
Lightning flashes and thunder rumbles;
Crags and peaks crash and crumble.
The stone gate in the fairy cave
Splits asunder with a shattering sound;
Its blue depth is vast, the bottom is invisible.
The sun and moon shine on the Towers of Gold and Silver;   30
Clad in rainbow raiments and riding on the wind,
The Lords of Clouds descend in long processions,
Tigers playing the zither and phoenixes drawing the carriages;
The fairies stand in rows like a field of hemp.
Suddenly startled, my soul shivers;
Dazed, I awake in fright and I heave a long sigh.

At this moment, I am conscious only of my pillow and mat;
Gone are the mists and clouds of a while ago—
Likewise are the pleasures of this world;
Since ancient times, myriad affairs vanish like waters flowing east.
Taking leave of you, I have no date for return.   40

---

2 The poet Hsieh Ling-yün was the Duke of K'ang-lo.

I would tend a white deer on the green cliff
And ride it whenever I go to visit famous mountains.
How could I lower my eyebrows, bend my waist to serve those with
    power and wealth,
And deny myself the joys of a smiling face and a buoyant heart?
(CTS, P. 978)   (TR. WU-CHI LIU)

"They Fought South of the Walls"

Last year we fought
At the source of the Sang-kan River[1];
This year we campaign
On the road to Ts'ung-ho.[2]
We wash our weapons in the waters of the T'iao-chih Sea[3];
And graze our horses on the grass in T'ien Shan's[4] snow.
Fighting and more fighting for ten thousand miles,
Until the soldiers all grow weak and old.
The Tartars live on killing and slaughter;
Since of old there have been white bones in the yellow sands.   10
Where the Ch'in built a wall[5] to keep out the Tartars,
The Han still light a beacon fire.
Beacon fires are lit without cease,
And fighting goes on without end;
Men die in the wilds,
And horses of the vanquished wail mournfully towards the sky.
Vultures feed on human guts,
Carry them flying, then leave them hanging on withered mulberry
    branches.
Soldiers fall, their blood smearing grass and bushes;
The generals have striven in vain.   20
How well we know the curse of war;
May the wise rulers follow it only as the last recourse!
(CTS, P. 923)   (TR. JOSEPH J. LEE)

---

[1] A major battle was fought in 742 on the Sang-kan River south of Ta-t'ung, Shansi.
[2] Ts'ung-ho, or Ts'ung-ling-ho, is a river in Sinkiang which a T'ang expedition crossed in 746.
[3] T'iao-chih refers broadly to the region in modern Iran.
[4] See Li Po's "Moon over Mountain Pass."
[5] I.e., The Great Wall of China.

Drinking Alone Beneath the Moon, Two Selections

[1]

A pot of wine among the flowers:
I drink alone, no kith or kin near.
I raise my cup to invite the moon to join me;
It and my shadow make a party of three.
Alas, the moon is unconcerned about drinking,
And my shadow merely follows me around.
Briefly I cavort with the moon and my shadow:
Pleasure must be sought while it is spring.
I sing and the moon goes back and forth,
I dance and my shadow falls at random.   10
While sober we seek pleasure in fellowship;
When drunk we go each our own way.
Then let us pledge a friendship without human ties
And meet again at the far end of the Milky Way.

[2]

If Heaven weren't fond of wine
Wine Star would not be found in Heaven.[1]
If Earth weren't fond of wine
There could be no Wine Spring[2] on earth.
Since Heaven and Earth are fond of wine,
In Heaven being fond of wine can't be judged wrong.
Clear wine, I've heard, is compared to sages,

---

1 According to the chapter on astronomy in *Tsin Shu* (*History of Tsin Dynasty*), written by the T'ang mathematician Li Shun-feng (seventh century), the "Wine Pennant Star" (*chiu-ch'i hsing*) was the name of three stars situated south and at the right corner of Hsüan-yüan, or Leo; it was also the pennant of wine officials.

By repeating the same words in pivotal positions in the lines, Li Po was imitating T'ao Ch'ien, who, in his poem "On Stopping Wine," used the word *chih* ("to stop") in every line. See James R. Hightower's translation of that poem in *The Poetry of T'ao Ch'ien* (pp. 157–58).

2 Name of a town in Kansu since Han times, known for its underground spring with the taste of wine.

Also the unstrained wine spoken of as worthies.[3]
Since I've drunk both sages and worthies
Why must I seek out the immortals?   10
Three cups penetrate the Great Truth;
One gallon accords with Nature's laws.
Simply find pleasure in wine:
Speak not of it to the sober ones.
(NOS. 1–2 FROM A SERIES OF 4; CTS, P. 1018)   (TR. IRVING Y. LO)

Sitting Alone in Ching-t'ing Mountain

Flocks of birds fly high and vanish;
A single cloud, alone, calmly drifts on.
Never tired of looking at each other—
Only the Ching-t'ing Mountain and me.
(CTS, PP. 1020–21)   (TR. IRVING Y. LO)

To Amuse Myself

Drinking alone without knowing the coming of dusk,
I discover my robe covered with fallen petals.
Drunk, I rise to walk along the moonlit creek—
The birds have gone and few are the people around.
(CTS, P. 1021)   (TR. JOSEPH J. LEE)

Listening to a Monk from Shu Playing the Lute

A monk from Shu, carrying a precious lute,
Comes down from the western peak of Omei Mountain.
As he lifts his hands to play for me,
I seem to hear the sound of pines from a thousand glens.
The flowing stream[1] cleanses a traveler's heart,
Its dying strains fade into the first bells of frost.[2]

---

3 "Sages" and "worthies" were slang expressions referring respectively to strained
and unstrained wine used in a time of prohibition in T'ang times. (Note sup-
plied by James J. Y. Liu.)

1 This possibly alludes to the story of Po Ya and his friend Chung Tzu-ch'i. For
the story, see note to Meng Hao-jan's poem "Parting from Wang Wei."

2 Literally, *shuang-chung* ("frost bell"), alluding to the legend from the *Classic
of Mountain and Sea,* "At the time when frosts fall, the nine-ear bells at Mount
Feng resounded." It is believed that metal corresponds to the season of frost.

Dusk comes unnoticed over the green hills,
And autumn clouds begin to darken layer after layer.
(CTS, P. 1026)   (TR. JOSEPH J. LEE)

Songs of Ch'iu-p'u,¹ Four Selections

[1]

Ch'iu-p'u teems with white gibbons;
They leap and bounce like flying snow.
They tug and pull their young hanging from the branches,
Come down to drink and play with moon in the water.

[2]

How like a bolt of white silk is this water,
Turning the earth into a flattened sky!
But I would rather seize this moonlit night,
To board a wine-boat and view the flowers.

[3]

The furnace fire lights up earth and sky,
Red sparks fly pellmell into purple smoke.
Young men's faces are flushed in the moonlit night,
And a song reverberates in the cold river.

[4]

My white hair of thirty thousand feet
Has grown so long because of grief,
But I don't know how in that mirror
Has gathered so much autumn frost.
(NOS. 5, 12, 14–15 FROM A SERIES OF 17; CTS, PP. 945–46)
                                              (TR. IRVING Y. LO)

---

1 Ch'iu-p'u is located in Ch'ih-chou, lying southwest of modern Kuei-ch'ih in
Anhwei province. The Ch'iu-p'u Water, said to be thirty *li* wide and over eighty
li long, was one of Li Po's favorite places. The district produced silver and
copper, and poem [3] could be referring to the metal smelting industry of
the time. A less plausible explanation, suggested by some commentators, is that
the furnace, or stove (*lu*), refers to the Taoist practice of turning cinnabar
into elixir.

Written in Behalf of My Wife

To cleave a running stream with a sword,
The water will never be severed.
My thoughts that follow you in your wanderings
Are as interminable as the stream.
Since we parted, the grass before our gate
In the autumn lane has turned green in spring.
I sweep it away but it grows back,
Densely it covers your footprints.
The singing phoenixes were happy together;
Startled, the male and the female each flies away.　　　　10
On which mountaintop have the drifting clouds stayed?
Once gone, they never are seen to return.
From a merchant traveling to Ta-lou,
I learn you are there at Autumn Cove.
In the Liang Garden[1] I sleep in an empty embroidered bed;
On the Yang Terrace you dream of the drifting rain.[2]
Three times my family has produced a prime minister;
Then moved to west Ch'in since our decline.
We still have our old flutes and songs,
Their sad notes heard everywhere by neighbors.　　　　20
When the music rises to the purple clouds,
I cry for the absence of my beloved.
I am like a peach tree at the bottom of a well,
For whom will the blossoms smile?
You are like the moon high in the sky,
Unwilling to cast your light on me.
I cannot recognize myself when I look in the mirror,
I must have grown thin since you left home.
If only I could own the fabled parrot
To tell you of the feelings in my heart!　　　　30

(CTS, PP. 1033–34)　　　　　　　　　(TR. JOSEPH J. LEE)

---

1 A region in southeastern Honan.
2 Yang Terrace refers to the general area on the Yangtze. The line alludes not only to Li Po's whereabouts, but also to Sung Yü's "Shen-nü Fu." See note 5 to Li Po's "Song of Hsiang-yang."

Climbing Phoenix Terrace at Chin-ling

The phoenix birds once frolicked on Phoenix Terrace,
The birds are gone, the terrace empty, and the river flows on.
Flourishing flowers of Wu Palace are buried beneath dark trails;
Caps and gowns of Tsin times all lie in ancient mounds.
The Three-peaked Mountain half visible under the blue sky,
The two-forked stream separated by White-egret Isle.
It's always the clouds that block the sun,
I do not see Ch'ang-an and I grieve.
(CTS, P. 1010)   (TR. JOSEPH J. LEE)

Ancient Airs

The great odes[1] have had no revival,
Who will continue the effort after I am gone?
The ways of ancient kings were overgrown with weeds,
Brambles thrived everywhere in the Warring States.
Dragons and tigers tore at one another,
Long battles did not end with the power-crazed Ch'in.
How the true voice grew weak and dim,
Then sorrow and lament inspired the *sao* poets.
Yang and Ma aroused the ebbing tide,[2]
And new currents began to flow everywhere.   10
Though their rise and fall alternate time and again,
Still, the great tradition suffered a great decline.
Ever since the time of the Chien-an masters,[3]
Fine phrases and ornate style have been overpraised.
Our great age has restored the ancient tradition,
As His Majesty values only what is pure and true.
A host of talents flock to the enlightened court;
Availing themselves of the happy trend, they all leap to recognition.
Style and substance lend each other brilliance,
Like myriad stars blinking in an autumn sky.   20

---

1 *Shih Ching* (*The Book of Songs*).
2 Yang Hsiung (53–18 B.C.); Ssu-ma Hsiang-ju (179–117 B.C.).
3 Referring to the Seven Literary Masters (including Wang Ts'an and Hsü Kan)
   of the Chien-an period (196–220).

I desire to select and transmit the old,
So that its splendor will last a thousand ages.
If I could keep to the tradition of the sage,
I'd stop writing at the capture of the unicorn.[4]
(NO. 1 FROM A SERIES OF 59; CTS, P. 917)   (TR. JOSEPH J. LEE)

Kao Shih (702?–765)

"The Youth of Han-tan: A Song"

He is a young knight from the south of Han-tan.
Proudly he tells of his adventures in the town.
A thousand gambling throws depleted not his wealth;
And he survived many bloody feuds.
His mansion is filled with songs and laughter day after day.
Outside his gate horses and carriages gather, thick as clouds.
There's none to match his ideal of friendship:
He looks back to the time of Lord P'ing-yüan.[1]
Do you not see,
Fellowship holds little value of late,   10
And companions disappear when gold is gone?
That's why I bid farewell to my old friends
And stop minding the affairs of the world.
I might as well enjoy good wine with young gallants,
And now and then go hunting in western hills.
(CTS, P. 1201)   (TR. JOSEPH J. LEE)

"Song of Yen"

In the twenty-sixth year of the K'ai-yüan reign,[1] a man came back from
Censor Chang's[2] mission to the frontier, and showed me his "Song of
the Yen Country." Moved by his depiction of the life of war and garri-
son duty, I write the following poem in response to his.

---

4 According to tradition, Confucius terminated his compilation of the *Spring and
Autumn Annals* upon the capturing of a unicorn.
1 A feudal prince of the Warring States period known for his generosity toward
men of talent.
1 A.D. 738.
2 Chang Shou-kuei, see *T'ang Shu,* 133:6a–7b.

Border clashes flare northeast of the Empire;
Our general marches out to destroy the enemy.
Young men are by nature eager for brave deeds,
The Son of Heaven deigns to bestow them many favors.
Amid the sound of drums and gongs we head for Yü Pass[3];
Our flags snake round the Pinnacle Hill.[4]
Military dispatches speed across the desert;
Tartar chieftain's hunting fire lights up Wolf Mountain,[5]
The land is desolate to the farthest frontier;
Tartar riders storm past like wind and rain.   10
Half of our warriors fall on the battlefield;
Back in the camp beautiful girls still dance and sing.
In the vast desert, frontier grasses wither in late autumn;
In the lone city at sunset few fighting men remain.
We brave the enemy's attack because of His Majesty's favors;
But the city is still under siege despite our efforts.
Clad in armor, we labor long and hard at garrison;
In streams of tears our loved ones should lament this separation.
South of town, young wives are about to break their heart;
To the north of Chi[6] our soldiers vainly turn their head.   20
How could one pass the day in wind-blown frontiers?
In the vast expanse of the borderland all is desolate.
The air of death hangs for hours[7] like masses of clouds;
All night long in the cold watch, alarms continue to sound.
The dripping blood on our naked swords is all we see:
It is not for glory that we risk our lives.
Do you not see
The hardships of war on the battlefield?
Even now we still remember the exploits of General Li.[8]
(CTS, P. 1201)   (TR. JOSEPH J. LEE)

---

[3] Shan-hai Kuan, the eastern terminus of the Great Wall.
[4] In Hopeh on Po-hai Bay.
[5] Lang-chü-hsü Shan, a mountain in Mongolia.
[6] Hopeh.
[7] *San-shih*, literally, three Chinese hours. The term can also be interpreted as the three seasons (spring, summer, and autumn).
[8] Li Kuang (?–25 B.C.), a famous general of the Han, did much to secure the frontiers of the empire and further Han expansion into Central Asia.

Liu Ch'ang-ch'ing (709–780?)

Replying to a Poem by the Monk Ling-yi at the New Spring

To the eastern grove where a spring rises
I've come from afar to meet my host;
Where rocks form shallows in the cold river,
And the moon sets on the empty mountains.
Between dreams I listen to the crisp currents,
My cares washed away by the clear ripples;
To be active or passive is never by design—
Only a transcendent mind can understand.
(CTS, P. 825)   (TR. WILLIAM H. NIENHAUSER)

At an Inn in Yü-kan[1]

Toppling down as the sunset sky grows distant,
The frosted leaves are thinned from the maples;
A deserted city wall closed to the river,
A solitary crow flies away from men;
By the ford the moon's just risen,
But the fishermen next door aren't back.
A homesick heart about to break:
Where comes that sound of pounding clothes?[2]
(CTS, P. 824)   (TR. WILLIAM H. NIENHAUSER)

Sent to the Taoist of Dragon Mountain,
Hsü Fa-leng

On and on in the white clouds
he lives alone, guest of the verdant mountains;
Midday in the grove he lights the incense,
and with the cassia blossoms shares the stillness.
(CTS, P. 820)   (TR. WILLIAM H. NIENHAUSER)

---

1 Presently the seat of a county in Kiangsi, located on an estuary at the south-
eastern shore of Lake Po-yang; it was a mere village during the T'ang dynasty.
2 The sound of a woman washing clothes suggests home.

Encountering a Snowstorm, I Stay with the Recluse of Mount Hibiscus

Dark hills distant in the setting sun,
Thatched hut stark under wintry skies.
A dog barks at the brushwood gate,
As someone heads home this windy, snowy night.
(CTS, P. 819)   (TR. DELL R. HALES)

Saying Goodby to the Monk Ling-ch'e

Dark and dim, the Bamboo Grove Monastery,
Faint and faraway, the sound of bells at dusk.
Your bamboo hat carrying home the evening sun,
Alone you return to the distant green hills.
(CTS, P. 820)   (TR. DELL R. HALES)

Listening to the Washblock in the Moonlight

Evening calm envelops the cold city—
Whence come these sharp claps from a washblock?
Unceasing echoes thump the autumn moon,
Tormenting my thoughts for the garrison at Lu-lung.

I have been unable to contact my soldier,
And I grieve at the frost and the dew.
(CTS, P. 836)   (TR. DELL R. HALES)

Tu Fu (712–770)

For Li Po

Two years I've been in the Eastern Capital,[1]
And had my fill of cunning and conniving.

---

[1] *Tung-tu,* i.e., Lo-yang.

I'm a simple man when it comes to meat and fish:
Vegetables will not satisfy my hunger.
Is there no real meat[2] to be had
To bring color back to my cheeks?
I am poor, and cannot afford herbs:
In the hills and forests, the paths are unfrequented.
Mr. Li, late a scholar of the Golden Court,[3]
Retired in search of occult mysteries,   10
You're also traveling in Liang and Sung[4]:
I hope you find the precious herbs you're after.
(CTS, P. 1220)   (TR. EUGENE EOYANG)

To Li Po

Autumn, and we're still like the will-o'-the wisp,
Not having found the elixir, like Ko Hung.[1]
Drinking to excess, singing with abandon, idly passing the day;
Flitting here and there, flailing about,[2] to impress whom?
(CTS, P. 1299)   (TR. EUGENE EOYANG)

Frontier Songs, First Series, Three Selections

[1]

Sad, sad they leave their old village,
Far, far they go to the Chiao River.
Officials have an appointed time of arrival,
To flee from orders is to run afoul of capture.
The ruler is already rich in lands,
Expanding the frontier brings no gain!

---

2 *Ch'ing-ching,* a concentrate in popular medicines, composed of southern flame-grass (*nan chu-ts'ao*) leaves mixed with bark, cooked in a broth, then steamed to give it a greenish color, and dried in the sun. It was said to stimulate the blood, fill the stomach, strengthen the marrow, and subdue the "three worms" (*san ch'ung*).

3 The Hanlin Academy, i.e., the Academy of Letters.

4 Liang and Sung: in the present-day area of K'ai-feng and Kuei-te in Honan.

1 Early fourth-century Taoist herbalist and alchemist, famed for his treatise *Pao P'u Tzu.*

2 *The T'ang History (T'ang Shu)* relates the story that Li Po, perhaps recalling his youthful adventures as a would-be knight-errant, was known to affect chivalrous exploits by displays of swordsmanship.

Abandoned forever is the love of father, mother,
Sobbing, they march away with spears on their backs.
(NO. 1 FROM A SERIES OF 9; CTS, P. 1241)　　　(TR. RONALD C. MIAO)

[2]

Sharpen the sword in the Sobbing Waters,[1]
The water reddens, the blade wounds my hand.
How much I want to hush the sound of anguish;
Too long entangled are the strands of my heart!
When a man of courage promises life to his country,
Then what is there to regret and lament?
Deeds of fame live on in the Unicorn Pavilion,
Bones of soldiers will quickly decay.
(NO. 3; CTS, P. 1241)　　　(TR. IRVING Y. LO)

[3]

If you draw a bow, draw the strongest,
If you use an arrow, use the longest:
To shoot a man, first shoot his horse,
To capture rebels, first capture their chief.
In killing men, also, there are limits,
And each state has its own borders.
So long as invasion can be curbed,
What's the use of much killing?
(NO. 6; CTS, P. 1241)　　　(TR. RONALD C. MIAO)

The Elegant Women

On the third day of the third month, in fresh weather,
The elegant women of the capital stroll on the riverbank—
Their manner regal and remote, their faces delicate,
Their figures shapely and pleasing.
Wrapped in filmy silks bright with peacocks and silver unicorns,
They illumine the spring evening.

---

1 Wu-yen Shui is also the name of a river in Sui-te, Shensi, where, according to
legend, the eldest son of the First Emperor of Ch'in, Fu-su, was sent and
murdered under instructions of Chao Kao, who forged the emperor's edict;
hence the sobbing sounds of the river keep on lamenting the heir apparent's
fate.

What do they wear in their hair?
The kingfisher headdress with jade leaves dangling
Past their lips.
What do you see upon their shoulders?
Capes with crushed pearls at their waists that cling
To their bodies.   10
One even glimpses from time to time,
Glittering beneath the canopies of the empresses' pavilion,
Those great ladies of the empire, Kuo and Ch'in.

Purple steak from the camel's hump broiled in a glistening pan
And the white flesh of fish are set out in rows of crystal dishes.
But the satiated ones stay their rhinoceros chopsticks,
And morsels minced by belled knives lie untouched.
Yet still the palace eunuchs arrive.
They rein in their horses without so much as stirring dust,
And set before the guests food rare as jewels
Brought from the eight corners of the earth.
The music of pipes and drums, strange enough to move the dead,
Accompanies the feast. A vast retinue blocks the main road.   20
Then in measured paces a saddled horse arrives;
The rider dismounts and enters on embroidered carpets.
Willow-down drifts like snow, masking white duckweek flowers;
And a bluebird flies off with a scarlet kerchief in his beak.
Be careful! So great is his power, his lightest touch can burn.
Do not approach the prime minister too close.
He may be angry.
(CTS, P. 1224)   (TR. MARK PERLBERG)

Ch'iang Village, Two Selections

[1]

From the jagged edges of purple clouds to the west,
The sun sets its foot on level plain.
Above wicket gate sparrows start chattering,
As I return home from a thousand-*li* journey.
My wife and children, amazed at my being alive,
Wipe their tears when they get over their surprise.

In these troubled times I have drifted thither and yond;
Returning home alive is but an accident.
Neighbors are all over the garden wall;
They sigh and sob uncontrollably.   10
As night draws on, I call for candles;
Then we look at each other as if in a dream.

[2]

Flocks of chicken clucking from every corner,
They fight each other as visitors arrive.
After I have chased the chickens up the tree,
I could hear the knocks at the wicket gate.
Elders of the village, four or five,
Come to ask me about my long journey.
Each carrying something in his hand,
They pour out jugs of good and poor wine.
"Hope you won't mind if the wine tastes too weak:
No one has been able to attend to farming.   10
And since we're still in the midst of battles,
All our children have gone to the eastern front."
Then I ask to sing for the elders a song;
In these hard times, I'm deeply moved by their affection.
Singing done, I look up to the heavens and sigh,
And tears stream down the cheeks of all who sit around.
(NOS. 1, 3, FROM A SERIES OF 3; CTS, P. 1233)   (TR. IRVING Y. LO)

Journey North

I

The second year of the emperor's reign, in autumn,
in the Extra Eighth Month, in Beginning Luck,[1]
I, Master Tu   about to journey north
vast, vague   wonder about my home.

---

[1] The extra or intercalary eighth month in the second year of the T'ang emperor Su-tsung's reign begins on the day corresponding to September 18, 757, of the Western calendar. "Beginning Luck" is a term used in ancient times for the first week of a month, but here Tu Fu might be using it for the first day.

These times have brought us hardship, sorrow;
in or out of court, there are few free days;
yet (I feel shame for favors specially granted)
a decree permits a return to my vines and brambles.

I bow farewell,   pay respects in the palace,
fearful, alarmed   a long time before I come out.   10
Although I lack the temperament to admonish,
I fear the Ruler may still have some errors left:
the Ruler truly is lord of our rising again,
about state affairs certainly diligent;
but the Eastern Hu² rebellion is not yet over,
so his servant Fu is anxious about what is pressing.

I wipe my tears   long for the Travel Locale³
on roads and trails   still muddled
the universe   endures its gaping wounds
sadness, sorrow   when will it ever end?   20

II

Slow, slow   we cross paddy paths
men, smoke   sparse in the desolation
those we meet   most of them wounded
groaning, sobbing   and even bleeding

I turn my head back toward Feng-hsiang⁴ town:
its pennons and banners at dusk grow bright, go out.
On and up   into folds of wintry hills
often we come across   grottoes where horses are watered

The land around Pin⁵   goes deep into the earth

---

2 Throughout the poem, Tu Fu refers to the rebels as Hu, a derogatory term
  for non-Chinese people to the north, because An Lu-shan's native land is north-
  east of China proper. (For the An Lu-shan rebellion, see background materials
  on Tu Fu.)
3 The emperor's provisional court during exile is euphemistically called the
  "Travel Locale," or *hsing tsai.*
4 Feng-hsiang, the site of the emperor's court in exile, is about a hundred miles
  to the west of Ch'ang-an, the Western Capital.
5 At about a third of the total distance from Feng-hsiang to his wife's place in
  Fu-chou in the north, Tu Fu passes through the town of Pin, through which
  flows the Ching.

waters of the Ching   crash in its midst   30
a fierce tiger   stands in front of us
gray cliffs   at his roar, split

Chrysanthemums háng   blossoms of this autumn
rocks carry   ruts of ancient chariots
blue clouds   move me to elation
secluded things   are, after all, a joy

Mountain berries   most of them tiny, delicate
spread and grow   mixed with acorns and chestnuts
some red   like dust of cinnabar
some black   like dots of lacquer   40
wherever rain or dew moisten,
whether sweet or bitter, all bear fruit
My longing thoughts   are by Peach Spring[6]
more sighing   for the clumsiness of my life's course

Hilly land   and I gaze at Fu Altar[7]
cliffs and valleys   emerge and disappear
my own path   has reached to the bank of the stream
my servant   is still in the tips of the trees

An owl   calls from a brown mulberry
field mice   fold their paws in a mess of nests   50

The night is deep   and we pass through a battlefield
the wintry moon   shines on white bones
at T'ung Pass[8]   a million warriors
at that time   why did they scatter so fast?
thus it happened   and half the people of Ch'in
were broken, wounded   or turned into other beings

But what about me?   I fall into Hu dust
and now go home   my hair all flecked with white.

---

6 Referring to T'ao Ch'ien's essay on the Peach Blossom Spring.
7 A landmark near where Tu Fu's family had moved.
8 The poet-historian cannot help thinking of the disastrous battle fought earlier
  during An Lu-shan's rebellion at T'ung Pass, in an area also known by its
  anciet name, Ch'in, where nearly 200,000 loyal troops were killed—euphemis-
  tically, "turned into other beings."

III

It's been over a year   I arrive at my thatched house
wife and children   clothes with a hundred patches   60
our bawling   returns with sounds of pines
a sad brook   shares our stifled sobs
Our son, spoiled all his life,
face whiter than snow,
sees his dad   turns his back and weeps
dirty, grimy   feet unsocked

In front of the bed   our two little girls
patched tatters   barely passing their knees
a seascape   broken ripples and waves
from an old embroidery   out-of-line crooks and snaps   70
Sky Wu   and Purple Phoenix[9]
upside down   on the coarse cloth of their jackets

An old man   sick in mind and chest
vomiting, diarrhetic   I lie down several days

"How could I not have   in my satchel, silks
to save you   from the cold, the shivering?"
powder and eye-black   also unwrapped from their parcels
quilts and curtains   gradually displayed
and my thin wife   has her face aglow again
our silly daughters   their hair they comb themselves   80
they copy their mother   there's nothing they don't do
morning makeup   free-handed smeared
at another time   I give them rouge and powder
and they messily paint   their eyebrows wide.

Come back alive   I face the children
it's as though I'm about   to forget the hunger and thirst

---

[9] One of the things that catches Tu Fu's attention upon returning home is the condition of his children's clothes of coarse fabric, torn and patched with fine embroidery cut and resewn in such manner that the lines of waves and background patterns are disturbed and some of the images, such as those of the mythological animals Purple Phoenix and Sky Wu, the water spirit, are inverted.

they ask questions   and fight to pull my beard
who could bring himself   to shout at them?

I turn back my thoughts   to the sadness of being among rebels
and sweetly submit   to a disorderly din   90
newly come home   ready to be comforted
—how can I bring up our making a living?

IV

The Most Revered is still covered with dust[10];
how many days before he stops training the troops?

I look up and see   the sky's colors have changed
I sit and sense   weird vapors dispersed
A dark wind comes out of the northwest,
sad, dull, following the Uighurs.
Their king wants to help, as an ally;
their folk are good at the "galloping ambush."[11]   100
He sends soldiers, five thousand men,
and fast horses, ten thousand mounts.

Of such people,   just a few would be best
everyone agreed to this brave decision.
Using them, always as "eagle steeds,"
will smash the enemy faster than an arrow.
The Holy Heart waits with great composure;
but at current discussions, spirits begin to flag.

At the Yi and the Lo   a finger-palm recovery
the Western Capital   not needing to be stormed[12]   110

---

10 The emperor—the "Most Revered"—is still covered with the dust of exile.
11 The year before (756), the king of the Uighur allies in the northwest sent
   troops to help the loyal forces in a campaign that was so successful that the
   T'ang emperor, who was then Su-tsung, made the Uighur prince ceremonial
   brother to Su-tsung's son, an honor not lost on the foreign noble. The Uighurs
   were expert horsemen, one of whose most successful maneuvers was the "gal-
   loping ambush."
12 Lo-yang, the Eastern Capital, located between the Yi and the Lo rivers, will be
   recaptured by loyal forces in an operation that is as easy as pointing a finger
   toward a palm: Ch'ang-an, the Western Capital, will be recovered in an opera-
   tion taking less effort than it takes a hand to pluck a weed.

The government armies ask to penetrate deeply:
their latent valor can be released all at once!
Then will you rise and open up Ch'ing and Hsü,
whirl your gaze, capture the Heng and the Chieh.[13]

A vast sky piles up frost and dew
a corrective spirit includes stern destruction
misfortune reversed it's the year to destroy the Hu
the force is gathered it's the month to take the Hu
Hu destiny can it last for long?
The imperial strand was never meant to be broken!   120

V

Recall how before, when things got out of control,
matters were different from those of ancient times;
the vicious minister has been chopped to bits;
his companions in evil have since then been dispersed.
We do not hear that the Hsia and the Yin declined
because they themselves put Pao and Ta to death.[14]
Chou and Han achieved their reconstruction;
Hsüan and Kuang were indeed clear-sighted and wise.[15]
Martial, martial is General Ch'en,[16]
grasping his battle-ax, roused in his loyal zeal: 130
had it not been for you, all men would have ceased to be;
today, the nation still lives!

---

13 Ch'ing-chou occupies what is now Shantung; Hsü-chou, the adjacent state to the south. Heng Mountain and Chieh-shih Mountain recall another ancient state, northwest of Ch'ing-chou, near the homeland of the Hu, the heart of the rebel nation.

14 The Hsia and Yin (or Shang) dynasties fell because of the moral failings of their last rulers, reflected in their preoccupation with their beautiful consorts. Ta Chi, a concubine of the last ruler of Yin, was an accomplice in his unkingly revels and helped bring about the downfall of that dynasty. Pao Szu was a favored concubine and later queen of King Yu of the Chou dynasty, who was assassinated because of an instance when he catered to her whims.

15 The T'ang dynasty, like the dynasties of Chou and Han benefiting respectively from the efforts of reconstruction of King Hsüan and Emperor Kuang-wu, is destined to continue in civil peace.

16 During Emperor Hsüan-tsung's journey into exile at the time of An Lushan's rebellion, it was General Ch'en Hsüan-li who engineered the death of the minister Yang Kuo-chung and who persuaded the emperor to have Yang Kuei-fei executed.

Desolate   is Great Unity Hall
quiet, quiet   White Beast Gate
men of the capital   look for kingfisher splendor
as the auspicious spirit   moves toward the Golden Tower[17]
the parks and tombs   truly have their gods
are swept, sprinkled   often and without fail
bright, bright   the Great Founder's deed
his establishing   most broad and pervasive!   140
(CTS, PP. 1232–33)   (TR. HUGH M. STIMSON)

Meandering River, Two Poems

[1]

A single petal swirling diminishes the spring.
Ten thousand dots adrift in the wind, they sadden me.
Shouldn't I then gaze at flowers about to fall before my eyes?
Never disdain the hurtful wine that passes through my lips.
In a small pavilion by the river nest the kingfisher birds;
Close by a high tomb in the royal park lie stone unicorns.
This, a simple law of nature: seek pleasure while there's time.
Who needs drifting fame to entangle this body?

[2]

Returning from court day after day, I pawn my spring clothes;
Every time I come home drunk from the riverbank.
A debt of wine is a paltry, everyday affair;
To live till seventy is rare since Time began.
Deep among the flowers, butterflies press their way;
The slow-winged dragonflies dot the water.
I'd whisper to the wind and light[1]: "Together let's tarry;
We shall enjoy the moment, and never contrary be."
(CTS, P. 1309)   (TR. IRVING Y. LO)

---

[17] The emperor, Su-tsung, on his return to the capital (Great Unity Hall and White Beast Gate) and his residence in the Golden Tower will, so Tu Fu hopes, bring good luck to the nation so that the imperial tombs can then renew their ritual lustrations, and the great work of the founder of the T'ang dynasty can be continued.

[1] Following William Hung's reading of *feng-kuang* (*Tu Fu*, I, 129). This compound also means "scenery."

Dreaming of Li Po, Two Poems

[1]

Parted by death, we swallow remorse;
Apart in life, we always suffer.
South of the river, miasmal place,
From the banished exile, not a word!
Old friend, you appeared in a dream,
It shows you have long been in my thoughts.
Perhaps it wasn't your living soul[1]:
The way's too far, it couldn't be done.
Your spirit came: and the maples were green:
Your spirit left: the mountain pass darkened.   10
Friend, now that you're ensnared down there,[2]
How did you manage to wing away?
Moonlight shines full on the rafters,
Yet I wonder if it isn't your reflection.
The waters are deep, the waves expansive:
Don't let the water-dragon get you!

[2]

Drifting clouds pass by all day long;
The wanderer is long in getting here.
Three nights now you've entered my dreams—
Which shows how good a friend you are.
But your leave-takings are hurried,
Bitterly you say, it's not easy to come;
The river's waters are wind-blown and choppy,
And you're afraid to lose your oars.

---

[1] The popular conception distinguished between the soul of a living being and the soul of a dead being. The soul of a living being was more circumscribed in its movements, but the soul of the deceased could roam at will across great distances.

[2] The image of the net plays an important role in both this and the next poem. Here reference is made to the net of the law. The injustice of this net moves Tu Fu to write in "Twenty Rhymes to Li Po": "When they applied the old laws to your case,/Was there no one to point this out?" It is against this net of the law, which has kept Li Po in exile away from the capital, that Tu Fu rails.

Outside the door, you scratch your white head,
As if a lifetime's ambition were forfeit.   10
Officials teem in the capital city,[3]
Yet you alone are wretched.
Who says the net is wide,[4]
When it tangles such a man in his old age?
An imperishable fame of a thousand years
Is but a paltry, after-life affair.
(CTS, P. 1240)   (TR. EUGENE EOYANG)

Farewell of an Old Man

"No peace or quiet in the countryside,
Even in old age I find no rest.
My sons and grandsons lost in war,
What's the use of staying home to save my skin?"
He throws away his cane and strides out the gate;
Tears come to his old comrades-in-arms.

"I'm lucky. I still have my own teeth
Though I regret the marrow dried in my bones.
Now that I'm a soldier properly clad in armor,
I'll make a long bow to bid farewell to the magistrate.   10

"My dear old woman lies crying by the road,
It's late winter; her clothes are thin.
Who can be sure this won't be our final farewell—
I cannot stop worrying over her suffering in the fierce cold.
I do not expect to return from this march,
Yet her gentle urging to eat well stays with me.

---

3 Cf. "For Li Po," "Two years I've been in the Eastern Capital,/And had my fill
of cunning and conniving."

4 Here, the net is the net of Heaven (cf. Ch. 78 of the *Tao Te Ching:* "Heaven's
net is wide; Coarse are the meshes, yet nothing slips through"—Waley transla-
tion). Hawkes (*A Little Primer of Tu Fu*, Oxford University Press, 1967, p. 97)
contrasts the net here with that in the first poem: "The net here is not the net
of the law . . . but the net with which the Emperor, as a fisher of men, gathers
up men of talent to put in positions of responsibility. Li Po, one of the biggest
fish of all, has managed to elude the imperial fisherman." This contrast, between
the "net of the law" and "the net of Heaven," is critical to an understanding of
both poems.

"The walls at T'u-men have been fortified;
The ferry at Hsing-yüan will thwart the foe.
Conditions are different from our defeat at Yeh;
Even if I must die, there is still some time left.   20
Life has its partings and reunions,
Why fuss about your age; everyone must die.
But when I think back on the days of my youth
I can't help pausing—and sighing.

"The whole empire is a military camp;
Beacon fires have spread to each ridge and peak.
Corpses in piles foul fields and woods,
Blood reddens streams and plains.
If I knew where Heaven was
I wouldn't linger on this earth longer.   30
To leave for good this humble cottage and home
Will crush a man."
(CTS, P. 1237)   (TR. MICHAEL E. WORKMAN)

Recruiting Officer of Shih-hao

At dusk I sought lodging at Shih-hao village,
When a recruiting officer came to seize men at night.
An old man scaled the wall and fled,
His old wife came out to answer the door.

How furious was the officer's shout!
How pitiable was the woman's cry!
I listened as she stepped forward to speak:
"All my three sons have left for garrison duty at Yeh;
From one of them a letter just arrived,
Saying my two sons had newly died in battle.   10
Survivors can manage to live on,
But the dead are gone forever.
Now there's no other man in the house,
Only a grandchild at his mother's breast.
The child's mother has not gone away;
She has only a tattered skirt for wear.
An old woman, I am feeble and weak,
But I will gladly leave with you tonight

To answer the urgent call at Ho-yang—
I can still cook morning gruel for your men." 20

The night drew on, but talking stopped;
It seemed I heard only half-concealed sobs.
As I got back on the road at daybreak,
Only the old man was there to see me off.
(CTS, P. 1237) (TR. IRVING Y. LO)

At Horizon's End, Thinking of Li Po

Chill wind stirs at horizon's end:
My friend, what news?
When will the geese arrive?[1]
Autumn swells river and stream.
Writers abhor worldly success[2];
Mountain demons like to entrap us.
Perhaps we should talk with the abused soul,
By sending a poem to the River Mi-lo.[3]
(CTS, P. 1315) (TR. EUGENE EOYANG)

Seven Songs Written While Living at T'ung-ku in 759

[1]

There's a wanderer, there's a wanderer, his name is Tzu-mei.[1]
His head is white, his tangled hair tumbles past his ears.
He lives all year on acorns he gathers like Master Tsu the monkey trainer,[2]
Under the cold sky at dusk in mountain valleys.

---

1 Traditionally, migrating geese were associated with messages or air-borne letters (the conceit was reinforced, no doubt, by the formation of the geese which indeed did form "air-borne letters").
2 Cf. Tu Fu's "Dreaming of Li Po, #2": "An imperishable fame of a thousand years/Is but a paltry, after-life affair."
3 The famous river where Ch'ü Yüan was said to have drowned himself. In 759, Li Po was in the Lake Tung-t'ing region, in the vicinity of the Mi-lo.
1 The courtesy name of the poet.
2 Alluding to the story from *Chuang-tzu* about Master Tsu, the keeper of monkeys, who outwits his herd into obedience by promising them four chestnuts in the morning and three in the afternoon, when they demand three chestnuts in the morning and four in the afternoon.

There is no news from the Central Plain; he cannot return.
His hands and feet are frostbitten, his skin and flesh numb.

Alas! This is my first song, oh! a song already sad;
A pitying wind comes to me from the sky.

[2]

Long hoe, long hoe, with your raw wooden handle,
I entrust my life to you, you are my only provider.
The yams have no shoots, the mountain snow is deep.
I pull down my short coat many times; it won't cover my shins.
Today we return empty-handed, you and I;
My son groans, my daughter moans, the four walls are quiet.

Alas! This is my second song, oh! I begin to sing it loud.
My neighbors' faces are distressed on my behalf.

[3]

I have younger brothers, I have younger brothers, all far away.
All three were sickly; have any gotten stronger?
We live apart, drifting farther; we never see each other.
Tartar dust obscures the sky, the road back is long.
Wild geese fly east, then the cranes follow.
Can they carry me to your side?

Alas! This is my third song, oh! I sing it three times.
Will you know where to come to find your elder brother's bones?

[4]

I have a younger sister, I have a younger sister, she lives in Chung-li.[3]
Her husband died young, her children all are giddy.
The waves are high on the long Huai, and the dragon rages.
Ten years without a meeting: when will it ever come?
I long to go in my little boat, but arrows are all I see.
The South is dark and far away, filled with soldiers' flags.

---

3 In modern Anhwei province.

Alas! this is my fourth song, oh! I sing it four times,
And the apes in the forest cry for me in broad daylight.

[5]

The wind blows in the mountains around, the creeks run fast.
Cold rain falls in sheets, withered trees are sodden.
Yellow weeds grow on the old city wall below unbroken clouds.
White foxes jump around, yellow foxes stand.
Why must I pass my life in this lonely valley?
At midnight I rise, beset by countless cares.

Alas! This is my fifth song, oh! I draw the notes out long,
But I cannot call back my soul that it might return home.

[6]

There is a dragon in the South, oh! in a mountain pool.
The old tall trees round about, their branches intertwined.
Their leaves turn yellow and fall; then the dragon sleeps.[4]
A poisonous snake comes from the east, roaming the waters.
I walk in fear, how dare I go out?
I draw my sword to strike, but it may be better to wait.

Alas! This is my sixth song, oh! a singer's thought lingers.
May the creeks and valleys show their spring colors again for my sake.

[7]

I am a man who's made no name, already I've grown old,
Wandering hungry three years on barren mountain roads.
In Ch'ang-an the ministers are all young men;
Wealth and fame must be earned before a man grows old.
In the mountains here are scholars who knew me long ago.
We only think of the good old days, our hearts full of pain.

Alas! This is my seventh song, oh! with sorrow I end the refrain,
Looking up to the wide sky where the white sun rushes on.
(CTS, PP. 1244–45)   (TR. GEOFFREY WATERS)

---

4 I.e., so the dragon will come out of hibernation and eat the snake. Some critics
believe that the dragon refers to the emperor, and the snake, Shih Ssu-ming.

A Spring Night—Rejoicing in Rain

A good rain knows its season
Comes forth in spring
Follows the wind, steals into the night;
Glossing nature, delicate without a sound.
Clouds on country road, all black,
Sparks of a lantern from a river boat, the only light.
Morning will see red-steeped spots:
Flowers heavy on the City of Brocade.
(CTS, P. 1322)   (TR. WILLIAM H. NIENHAUSER)

Strolling Along the Riverbank, Looking for Flowers: Seven Quatrains, Two Selections

[1]

Masses of flowers and plants envelop the riverbanks;
Walking there, unsteady in my steps, I'm really afraid of spring.
My verses and my wine I can still manage:
There's no need yet to look after this white-haired one.

[2]

'Tis not I pity the flowers are about to die:
I only fear when flowers are gone age will hurry me on.
Lush branches too easily may be despoiled;
To these tender buds I say: you open a petal at a time.
(NOS. 2, 7, FROM A SERIES OF 7; CTS, P. 1328)   (TR. IRVING Y. LO)

Random Pleasures: Nine Quatrains

[1]

See a traveler in sorrow: deeper is his grief
As wanton spring steals into the river pavilion—
True, the flowers will rush to open,
Yet how the orioles will keep up their songs.

[2]

Those peach and plum trees planted by hand are not without
    a master:
The rude wall is low; still it's my home.
But 'tis just like the spring wind, that master bully:
Last night it blew so many blossomed branches down.

[3]

How well they know my study's low and small—
The swallows from the riverside find reason to visit me often:
Carrying mud to spot and spoil my lute and books,
And trailing a flight of gnats that strike my face.

[4]

March is gone, and April's come:
Old fellow, how many more chances to welcome the spring?
Don't think of the endless affairs beyond the hereafter;
Just drain your lifetime's few allotted cups.

[5]

Heartbroken—there springtime river trickles to its end:
Cane in hand, I slowly pace and stand on fragrant bank.
How impertinent the willow catkins to run off with the wind;
So fickle, the peach blossoms to drift with the stream!

[6]

I've grown so indolent I never leave the village;
At dusk I shout to the boy to shut the rustic gate.
Green moss, raw wine, calm in the grove;
Blue water, spring breeze, dusk on the land.

[7]

Path-strewn catkins spread out a white carpet;
Stream-dotting lotus leaves mound up green coins.
By the bamboo roots, a young pheasant unseen;
On the sandbank, ducklings by their mother, asleep.

[8]

West of my house, young mulberry leaves are ready for picking;
Along the river, new wheat, so tender and soft.
How much more is left of life when spring has turned to summer?
Don't pass up good wine, sweeter than honey.

[9]

The willows by the gate are slender and graceful
Like the waist of a girl at fifteen.
Morning came, and who could fail to see
Mad wind had snapped the longest branch.
(CTS, P. 1328)   (TR. IRVING Y. LO)

Two Quatrains

[1]

I lounge on the jetty in the fragrance of catalpa
The fresh young buds all seem too young to fly
I'll stay drunk until the wind's through blowing
Could I bear, if I were sober, the rains come smash, and scatter?

[2]

Beyond the gate the cormorant had gone and not returned
Now on the sandbank, suddenly, he greets my waiting eye
From this moment he must know my mind
And every day return a hundred times.
(NOS. 1–2 FROM A SERIES OF 3; CTS, P. 1328) (TR. JEROME P. SEATON)

A Tired Night

Bamboo's chill creeps into the chamber,
A wilderness moon floods the garden nook,
Heavy dew trickles in little drops,
Scattered stars appear and disappear.
In dark flight, a glowworm lights itself
As river-dwelling birds call back and forth.

Everything involved with war,
Vainly I sigh as the clear night moves on.
(CTS, P. 1334) (TR. JAN W. WALLS)

No Word

Haven't seen my friend Li Po for some time:
It's really too bad, his feigning madness.
The whole world would want him executed,
Save I, who cherish his abilities.

A thousand fine and spirited poems he's written,
With a cup of wine, and wandering in solitude.
Here I am in K'uang Shan,[1] where he used to study:
He'd do worse than come back—now that his hair's turned white.
(CTS, P. 1331) (TR. EUGENE EOYANG)

Rain, Four Poems: Two Selections

[1]

Light rain doesn't slick the road;
Broken clouds slack, then move again.
The foot of racing purple cliffs—black,
At the horizon the white birds—bright.
The autumn sun casts damp new shadows,
On the cold river, old familiar sounds of rain.
A brushwood cottage overlooks a rustic mill;
Half wet, the fresh-hulled fragrant rice.

[2]

This southern rain nourishes the mossy stones,
As it slows news from the capital.
In mountain's cold, a black bull lows;
By evening's river, a white gull cries his hunger.

---

1 In the region of Shu, north of Mien-chou. Tu Fu had moved to Ch'eng-tu in
Szechwan at the very end of 759. William Hung conjectures that this poem may
have been written during the farewell parties given in honor of his friend Yen
Wu, who was being summoned to the capital by the new emperor, Tai-tsung.

Patterned hairpins of the Goddess drop;
The mermaid, sitting by her loom, mourns.
Cares will not come untangled,
Streaming down all day
In silken threads.
(NOS. 1, 4 FROM A SERIES OF 4; CTS, P. 1367)

(TR. WILLIAM H. NIENHAUSER)

The City of White Emperor

Above the city of White Emperor the clouds leave by the city gate;
Below the city wall, rain pours down as if from an overturned bucket.
In the swelling river and gulping gorges, thunders battle,
Ancient forests and hoary vines darken the sun and moon.
A war horse tenses, unlike an idle horse returning home.
Of the thousand families, only a hundred have survived.
Sadly, sadly, the bereaved women, ruined by the heavy toll—
Which villages on the autumn plain have raised these mournful cries?
(CTS, P. 1354)   (TR. WU-CHI LIU)

Night

Over sheer banks a menacing wind moves,
In a cold room the candle shadow dims,
The mountain ape sleeps out in the frost,
And the river bird flies deep into night.
Sitting alone I befriend a manly sword,
With a mournful song, sigh at my short gown.
Smoke and dust encircle the palace gate;
White head pays no heed to a stout heart.
(CTS, P. 1367)   (TR. JAN W. WALLS)

Two Poems on Night

[1]

White night, the moon an unstrung bow,
The charred lampwick has half dozed off.
Mountain winds howl; deer unsettled;

Tree leaves drop: cicada alarmed.
For a while I remember delicacies east of the river,
And recall a boat under falling snow.
Barbarian songs arise, invading the very stars;
I'm empty, here at the edge of the sky.

[2]

By the city wall a flute mourns the dusk,
Over the village market a few wings pass.
Wars and weapons for so many long years;
Taxes collected, I return in the depth of night.
Leaves fall from darkened trees along the cliff,
And the Galaxy grows dim skirting the frontier.
The Dipper aslant, I crane my neck to see;
The moon thins, and magpies cease to fly.
(CTS, P. 1368)   (TR. JAN W. WALLS)

Written on the Thirtieth Day, Ninth Month, Second Year of the Ta-li Reign [767]

No end in sight to the days of my wandering,
My autumn grief draws to a close toward dusk.
Miasmic vapors hover above the old kingdom of K'uei[1];
A light frost falls on Ch'u's imperial palace.
Grasses rival the kingfisher sheen of mountain mist,
The flowers stay on as chill leaves turn crimson.
Year after year there's just a little shedding:
It's so unlike the garden back home.
(CTS, P. 1369)   (TR. IRVING Y. LO)

I Spend the Night in a Room by the River

Darkness still shadows the mountain road
As I gaze from my study above the water gate.
Streamers of cloud seem to rest upon the brow of a cliff,

---

1 K'uei-chou, where Tu Fu wrote this poem. Nearby is the Witch Mountain (Wu-shan), with a temple built in memory of King Hsiang of Ch'u. For the legend about Mount Wu, or Witch Mountain, also see note 5 of Li Po's "Song of Hsiang-yang."

While the lonely moon tumbles among the waves.
A line of cranes winds overhead in silent flight.
Below, a pack of wolves quarrels over food.
I am grieved by the war and have not slept.
Who has the strength to right heaven and earth?
(CTS, P. 1350)   (TR. MARK PERLBERG)

Thoughts on Historical Sites: Wang Chao-chün[1]

Massive hills, numberless valleys, all point to Ching-men,[2]
Where the Radiant Lady was born and reared; there's her village.
Once gone from the purple palace, she was lost to northern desert,
Only her green mound remained, looking toward yellowing dusk.
A painter might well have recognized a face lovely as the spring
    breeze;
Now, pendants jangling, her soul returns in vain on moonlit nights.
For a thousand years the lute[3] speaks in an alien tongue,
Clearly her resentment and grief are told in these tunes.
(NO. 3 FROM A SERIES OF 5; CTS, P. 1357)   (TR. IRVING Y. LO)

Climbing the Heights

When winds rage and the sky is high, gibbons cry mournfully;
Over white sands on a clear riverbank, birds fly and whirl.
Leaves fall from deep woods—rustling and soughing;
The Long River rolls on, forever, wave after wave.

---

1 Wang Chao-chün, or Wang Ch'iang, of the first century B.C., was known in
    court as Ming-fei ("Radiant Lady"). Conscious of her unsurpassed beauty, she
    refused to bribe the court painter, Mao Yen-shou, who did the portraits of the
    ladies of the imperial harem. As a result, she was painted as homely-looking,
    and she was picked by the emperor to be married off to a Hsiung-nu chieftain.
    When the emperor discovered the fraud, he regretted his selection and had the
    painter executed. Later, because Ming-fei refused to marry her husband's son
    at the death of the khan, she committed suicide. It was said that her grave,
    located in modern Sui-yüan, had green grass growing on it all year round.
2 Ching-men Mountain is located in Ching-chou (modern Hupeh), where there
    is a village known as Chao-chün Village, although Wang Ch'iang was said to
    be a native of K'uei-chou in Szechwan, where Tu Fu wrote this poem.
3 *P'i-p'a,* "balloon-guitar," a foreign instrument brought to China in Han
    times, is generally associated with Wang Chao-chün; many paintings depict
    her carrying this musical instrument.

Ten thousand miles away in sad autumn, I often find myself a
        stranger;
My whole life afflicted by sickness, I mount alone the high terrace.
Beset by hardships, I resent the heavy frost on my temples;
Dispirited, I have by now abandoned my cup of unstrained wine.
(CTS, P. 1335)   (TR. WU-CHI LIU)

Autumn Thoughts, Three Selections

[1]

Jade dews deeply wilt and wound the maple woods;
On Witch Mountain, in Witch Gorge,[1] the air is somber, desolate.
Billowy waves from the river roar and rush towards the sky;
Over the frontier pass, wind and clouds sink to the darkening
        earth.
These clustered chrysanthemums, twice blooming, evoke the tears
        of yesteryear;
A lonely boat, as ever, is moored to the heart that yearns for home.
To cut winter clothes, women everywhere ply their scissors and
        foot-rulers—
Below the White Emperor's tall city wall is heard the urgent
        pounding of the evening wash.

[2]

I have heard the affairs in Ch'ang-an are like a game of chess;
For a hundred years, the business of the state has caused sorrows un-
    bearable.
Over there, the mansions of great nobles and princes all have new
    owners,
And the court dresses of officials and generals have changed from
        former times.
Straight north, on the mountain pass, gongs and drums shake the earth;

---

1 The ancient city of the White Emperor was situated on the top of the White
Emperor Mountain east of K'uei-chou, where Tu Fu lived for two years (766–
68). The city faces the Yangtze River as it enters the Witch Gorge below the
Witch Mountain. A rebel general who seized Szechwan and claimed himself
emperor built the city in the first century A.D.

To horses and chariots in the westward expedition, war dispatches race.[2]
Here, the fish-dragon is solitary and the autumn stream cold—
To live peacefully in the old country is all I cherish.

[3]

The waters of K'un-ming Pool recalled the achievements of Han times,
As the banners and standards of Emperor Wu[3] unfurled in my mind's eye.
The Weaving Maid, with silk on her loom, wasted away a moonlit night;
On the stone whale, scales and crusts moved in the autumn wind.[4]
Like lowering clouds, wave-tossed rice grains blackened;
From dew-cooled lotus pods, flower pollens dropped red.
The frontier pass reaching to the skies reveals only a bird track;
On the rivers and lakes wanders far and wide an old fisherman.
(NOS. 1, 4, 7 FROM A SERIES OF 8; CTS, PP. 1356–57) (TR. WU-CHI LIU)

Two Quatrains

[1]

Late sun, the stream and the hills; the beauty
Spring breeze, flowers and grasses; the fragrance
Steaming mudflat, swallows flying.
Warm sand, and mated ducks, asleep.

[2]

Birds the more white, against green stream
Blooms burst to flame, against blue hills
I glance, the spring is gone again.
What day, what day, can I go home?
(CTS, P. 1339)   (TR. JEROME P. SEATON)

---

2 While the An Lu-shan rebellion had been over almost ten years ago, the T'ang borders were threatened at that time by the Uighurs in the north and the Turfans (Tibetans) in the west.
3 Emperor Wu of Han built, in 120 B.C., a large artificial lake forty *li* in circumference to the southwest of Ch'ang-an as a replica of the K'un-ming Lake in Yunnan, to be used for the training of his navy.
4 On the K'un-ming Pool stood the statues of the legendary Weaving Maid and Cowherd; also a carved jade whale.

Upon Seeing the Fireflies

On Witch Mountain the fireflies flit in the autumn night:
Cleverly they enter the open lattice to alight on my clothes.
Suddenly I am startled at the coldness of my lute and books in the
    room;
Then I confuse the fireflies' light with the sparse stars over the eaves.
Rounding the well's railings, they come in an endless file;
Passing by chance the flower petals, they gambol and glow.
On this cold riverbank, my hair white, I feel sad when I look at
            them—
By this time next year, shall I have returned home?
(CTS, P. 1375)   (TR. WU-CHI LIU)

Night Thoughts Aboard a Boat

A bank of fine grass and light breeze,
A tall-masted solitary night boat.
Stars descend over the vast wild plain;
The moon bobs in the Great River's flow.
Fame: is it ever to be won in literature?
Office: I should give up, old and sick.
Floating, floating, what am I like?
Between earth and sky, a gull alone.
(CTS, P. 1347)   (TR. JAMES J. Y. LIU AND IRVING Y. LO)

Ts'en Shen (715–770)

Autumn Thought

Suddenly aware that the good year is almost over,
Sitting down, I look at the chilling leaves fall.
I cannot even be like the decayed grasses
That whirl up and transform into fireflies.
(CTS, P. 1142)   (TR. C. H. WANG)

Fisherman

The boatman of Ts'ang-lang is quite old,
But his heart is as clean as flowing water.
He never talks about where he lives,
And nobody knows exactly what his name is.
At dawn he cooks on the riverbank;
Nightfalls, he glides into the rushes and sleeps.
He sings too, one song after another,
And he holds in hand a bamboo pole:
The line at the end of the fishing pole
Is more than ten feet long.   10
He rows and rows, following where the river goes,
And he doesn't have a permanent abode.
How can anyone in the world imagine
What the old man really thinks?
The old man looks for what he himself thinks fit,
And he never cares about the fish.
(CTS, P. 1125–26)   (TR. C. H. WANG)

Song of the White Snow: Saying Farewell to Supervisor Wu Returning to the Capital

North wind whirls low
Breaking up white grasses.
Tartar's sky in the eighth month
Is filled with snow (as though
A spring breeze,
Overnight, had returned,
Thousands of pear trees
Have come to blossom):
It sprays through the pearl curtains,
Wets the blinds.   10
The fox-fur coat is cold,
And the silk cover feels thin.
The general's horn-tipped bow
Can hardly be drawn,
But the freezing mail of iron

Remains on the commander.
Over the cracked desert, ice
Piles up a thousand feet;
Under the overhanging clouds, bleak darkness
Stretches for ten thousand miles.   20

The army commissioner drinks
To a homebound traveler,
Amid the barbarian tunes
Of the lutes and pipes.
Evening snow falls and
Falls on the camp's gate;
Strong wind assails the red flags—
They are frozen, and do not flap.
As I bid farewell to you
At the East Gate of Lun-t'ai,   30
Snow has blocked
The T'ien-shan trails.
The road turns in the mountain's fold,
And I lose sight of you;
But the hoofprints remain,
Telling of your journey in the snow.
(CTS, P. 1119)   (TR. C. H. WANG)

Composed at Sunset at the Dunes of Ho-yen

On the sands is seen the sun rising,
On the sands is seen the sun setting.
Regret for having come ten thousand *li:*
Achievement, fame, what things are these?
(CTS, P. 1142)   (TR. RONALD C. MIAO)

Replying to "On the Occasion of Morning Audience After Snow" Poem by Assistant Secretary Wang of the Board of Sacrifices

Ch'ang-an after snow resembles spring returning;
White drifts, crystal blossoms merge in the morning light—
Jade bridles are made brighter to dazzle horsemen at dawn;
Silver candles shining on court robes take on greater brilliance.

Over Western Hills the setting moon looks down on the Celestial
  Stavesmen;
Above the Northern Gate the clouds, clearing, rise above the inner pal-
  ace.
One hears that an Immortal Gentleman has sung a Song of White
  Snow;
Who can hope to reply to such exquisite songs?
(CTS, P. 1139)   (TR. DANIEL BRYANT)

On Climbing the Pagoda[1] of the Temple of Gracious Benevolence with Kao Shih and Hsüeh Chü

The might of this pagoda seems to erupt upwards,
Rising alone until it brushes the halls of Heaven.
To climb it and look down is to leave the world behind;
Its stone stairway winds around in the void.
Majestic and imposing, towering over this sacred land,
So immense and lofty as to seem the work of gods.
Four corners block the bright sun;
Seven stories rub against the blue sky.
We gaze down to point at the soaring birds,
We bend to hear the fearsome wind rumble below.   10
Ranges upon ranges are like ocean's waves
Surging onward as though courtiers hastening eastward to attendance.
Dark green locusts line the broad post roads;
How lovely and bright the palaces and mansions there!
The beauty of autumn comes in from the west,
A wan aura filling the basin within the pass.[2]
The five royal tombs of Han stand on the plain to the north[3];
Dim and misty green for a thousand ages.

---

1 This pagoda, built in 652 by Hsüan Tsang (i.e., Tripitaka, Buddhist monk,
  pilgrim to India), was in the southeastern part of the T'ang capital, Ch'ang-an,
  near the "Serpentine" Park. Kao Shih is often paired with Ts'en as a frontier
  poet. His reputation thus stands much higher than that of Hsüeh Chü, of whose
  work only a dozen poems survive. All three men were friends of Tu Fu.
2 *Kuan-chung* ("within the passes") was the usual name for the region around
  the capital, roughly equivalent to southern Shensi.
3 The five tombs were those of five emperors of the Han dynasty (206 B.C.–A.D.
  220). They were located across the Wei River to the north and northwest of the
  capital. They would have been from 10 to 25 miles distant from the pagoda and
  over eight hundred years old when this poem was written.

At last I feel enlightened to the pure doctrine,
Though I have long revered the superior truth.   20
I am resolved to resign my official post,
Knowing this Way of enlightenment to be of eternal worth.
(CTS, P. 1113)   (TR. DANIEL BRYANT)

A Song of the Running Horse River: Presented on Seeing General Feng[1] Off on a Campaign to the West

Do you not see the Running Horse River flowing along the Sea of
  Snow,
Where the sandy plain stretches vast and brown into the sky?

In November the night wind howls over Lun-t'ai,
And a river full of broken rocks big as bushel baskets
Covers the earth with careening stones blowing with the wind.

The horses of the Hsiung-nu[2] fatten when autumn yellows the grass;
And west of the Altai[3] we see the black dust of rebellion fly;
A great general of Han leads his army to the west.

The commander's iron armor is never taken off through the night;
Halberds clank in a midnight march;   10
The wind like a knifeblade, soldiers' faces hurt as if slashed.

Snow clings to the horses' coats, their sweat steaming,
Only to turn to ice again on their dappled backs;
As dispatches are drafted in tents, ink freezes on the slab.

---

1 General Feng Ch'ang-ch'ing, who appears in the titles of several of Ts'en's
  poems, was at this time the military governor of the western frontier with the
  title Protector of Pei-t'ing. Ts'en Shen joined Feng's staff in 754 at the age of
  forty. He hoped by doing so to satisfy his ambition to rise to a high place in
  the government, an ambition which remained frustrated while he was in metro-
  politan China in spite of his literary talents and distinguished family back-
  ground. General Feng's career came to an unhappy end within a few years. He
  was defeated by the rebel An Lu-shan and subsequently put to death.
2 The Hsiung-nu had been the most important nomad enemies of the Chinese
  during the Han dynasty. Although they were ancient history by the time of
  Ts'en Shen, he uses the name to refer to the barbarians of his own day.
3 "Altai" translates the term "Metal Mountains."

Shouldn't the Hunnish horsemen tremble when they hear?
They dare not cross their short swords with ours.
Let victory greet our return at the west gate of Chü-shih.[4]
(CTS, P. 1121)   (TR. DANIEL BRYANT)

A Song of the Bay Steed of Governor Wei

The bay steed of your stable could not be caught in a portrait,
The color of peach blossoms circling about in a whirlwind.
    Crimson reins, scarlet bridle, crop of coral,
    Jade saddle, embroidered blanket, and bit of gold.

Harness and bring him out, please, that I may see you ride,
His long tail brushing the earth like a scarlet thread.
You yourself boast that there is no horse his equal,
Even as you think back to when you bought him for a hundred coins.

On the scented streets and purple paths of our Phoenix City,[1]
The wonder and envy of all who see him!   10
With your crop held high, at a sudden gallop, how white his perspirations!
Admiring his own shadow, in his haughty gait, such shattering sounds
    of his jade shoes.

A brown-whiskered nomad youth with a pair of golden scissors
Trims tall the three mane plumes in the early morning light.
    Seen standing in his stall, his spirit shines forth;
    Led from the herd, his mettle and valor are without peer.

You ride him out to hunt along the base of the southern hills;
Foxes and hares are found south of the walls no more.
A speck on the grass sends it galloping as though in flight,
Leaving even the green falcons fluttering behind.   20

---

4 A Han dynasty term, referring to the area around the eastern part of the T'ien-shan, modern Dzungaria and Turfan.
1 I.e., the capital. "Scented streets" (*hsiang chieh*) and "purple paths" (*tzu-mo*) are epithets for boulevards and walks in the imperial compound, alluding no doubt to the elegant fashions of court ladies and the colors of the robes of high officials.

How I remember seeing you come to court at Wei-yang Palace[2]—
Bridle-jades jingling, canopy held aloft, fragrance filling the streets,
The riches and glory of frontier generals I knew for the first time,
Entrancing sight of man and mount setting one another aglow!

Such can be the joy that a man's heart may feel;
A fleet horse with a long neigh as north wind blows.
He awaits your going east to sweep away the nomad dust,
To cover for you a thousand miles in a single day!
(CTS, P. 1123)   (TR. DANIEL BRYANT)

Yüan Chieh (719–772)

The Palace of Rocks,
Four Verses

[1]

At the palace of rocks, spring clouds white—
white clouds are best for the green moss;
brush apart the clouds, tread the rocky path:
what ordinary man could come along?

[2]

At the palace of rocks, summer waters cold—
cold waters are best for the tall grove;
a distant wind rustles ivy and vine:
the rustic delights in the cool shade.

[3]

At the palace of rocks, autumn air clear—
clear air is best for the mountain vale;
falling leaves chase the frosty wind:
the hermit loves bamboo and pine.

---

2 Built during the Han dynasty, but the name often appears later with the meaning "imperial palace."

[4]

At the palace of rocks, winter sun warm—
warm sun is best for the hot springs;
morning rays settle a watery fog:
the recluse can sleep soundly.
(CTS, P. 1459)   (TR. WILLIAM H. NIENHAUSER)

Ku K'uang (725?–c. 814)

Written upon Returning to the Mountains

My worries: several strands of white hair;
My livelihood: a stretch of green hills.
A deserted grove, snow-covered, is waiting;
On an ancient road there's no one, I return alone.
(CTS, P. 1584)   (TR. IRVING Y. LO)

On the River

Across a limpid stream white birds aslant,
    An idle oar tangles among duckweed flowers.
As I listen to the songs of lotus-gatherers till dusk,
Moonlight, eddying on the pond, settles upon the sand.
(CTS, PP. 1583–84)   (TR. IRVING Y. LO)

Upon a Brook

A girl gathering lotus upon a brook,
Timid in a tiny boat that shifts in the wind,
Startles a pair of mallards from their sleep;
Water and clouds are splattered red.
(CTS, P. 1584)   (TR. IRVING Y. LO)

"Sonny"[1]

Sonny grows up in Fukien;
The officers of Fukien seize him,
Then they castrate him,
Hold him as fugitive and slave,
And receive gold that fills up the house.
They shave him and brand him,
Treat him like grass and plants.

"Unknown are the ways of Heaven,
So I fall into their venomous hands;
Unknown are the ways of gods,   10
And they receive their blessing."
Daddy bids farewell to Sonny[2]:
"How I regret giving you birth!
At the time of your birth,
People warned me never to rear you;
I didn't heed that advice,
And now I come to this misery."
This is Sonny's farewell to Daddy:
"My heart's crushed, and I can only weep blood,
As I'm parted from heaven and earth   20
Till I come to Yellow Spring,
I shan't be able to stand in front of Daddy."
(CTS, P. 1568)   (TR. IRVING Y. LO)

---

1 *Author's note:* "Sonny is to lament the fate of Fukien. [This refers to selling
slaves as eunuchs, a practice probably rampant at the time in the coastal
province of Fukien.]" This is the ninth from a series of thirteen verses en-
titled "Supplemental Didactic Poetry of Remote Antiquity."
2 The words translated as "Sonny" and "Daddy" are both dialectal words found
only in the Min dialect spoken in northern Fukien. The poet appends a note as
follows: "This word is pronounced the same as *kịän:* [Karlgren 143f; *ch'ien*
in modern Chinese]; it was the usage in Fukienese to call *tzu* ("son") as
kịän: and *fu* ("father") as *lâng* [Karlgren 753r]—*b'jịẹ* [Karlgren 26a; *lang-pa*
in modern Chinese]." The reconstructed Ancient Chinese pronunciation, the
language of Ch'ang-an around A.D. 600, follows Bernhard Karlgren, *Gram-
mata Serica Recensa* (Stockholm: Museum of Far Eastern Antiquities, 1957;
1964), pp. 58, 195, 27.

Tai Shu-lun (*732–789*)

Living in the Mountains

Deer gather in flocks by nature;
What man comes up to these white clouds?
In the mountains there are no worldly concerns:
To the end of my days mellowed in wine.
(CTS, P. 1649)   (TR. WILLIAM H. NIENHAUSER)

Wang Chao-chün[1]

To the palaces of the Han

                 she can only return in dreams,

How often in the yurt

                 have tears dampened her robes?

More dejected than

                 these shadows of the border geese,

For on the autumn winds

                 they can still fly south.
(CTS, P. 1651)   (TR. WILLIAM H. NIENHAUSER)

An Accidental Meeting with an Old Friend
While Traveling at Night[1]

The season is fall and the moon's full too,
The gate tower looms a thousand stories in the night;
Unexpectedly we meet south of the river—
Bewildered—like a dream encounter;
Wind in the branches startles a hidden magpie.
Frost on the grass covers a cold cricket;

---

1 For the story of Wang Chao-chün, see note 1 to Tu Fu's poem of that title.
1 Since city gates were usually closed at dusk, night travel was uncommon in
T'ang China. The poet here has arrived at a city during the night and could
not gain admission. By chance he met an old friend in similar circumstances.
The morning bell in the last line of the poem signaled the reopening of the
city gates and thus the hour of parting.

We wayfarers must keep in drink and
Stay one another dreading the morning bell.
(CTS, P. 1639)   (TR. WILLIAM H. NIENHAUSER)

Wei Ying-wu (737–?)

"Longing in My Heart"

Shall I ask the willow trees on the dike
For whom do they wear their green spring dress?
In vain I saunter to the places of yesterday,
And I do not see yesterday's people.
Weaving through myriad courtyards and village squares,
Coming and going, the dust of carriages and horses—
Do not say I have met with no acquaintances:
Only they are not those close to my heart.
(CTS, P. 1070)   (TR. IRVING Y. LO)

In Imitation of T'ao P'eng-tse [T'ao Ch'ien]

When frost and dew have caused a hundred plants to wither,
The season's chrysanthemums alone look comely.
The nature of things being what it is,
Can heat or cold do anything to them?
I pluck a bloom to float in unstrained wine;
When the sun goes down, I meet farmers in their home.
To lie drunk under the thatched eaves:
Should the meaning of life be found only in abundance?
(CTS, P. 1042)   (TR. IRVING Y. LO)

On Dewdrop

A drop of dew on an autumn lotus leaf,
In a clear night it falls from the dark heavens.
On this jade plate it comes to rest;
Only because it's unsettled, we know it to be round.
(CTS, P. 1083)   (TR. IRVING Y. LO)

On Sound

Ten thousand things are heard when born,
But the highest heaven's always still.
Yet everything must begin in silence,
And into silence it vanishes.
(CTS, P. 1083)   (TR. IRVING Y. LO)

Crossing the Lang-yeh Mountain with a Friend
(Chao P'i-ch'iang, a Young Student)

Snow on Stone Gate,[1]
    but there's no trace of footprints.
In the pine ravine, mist congeals;
    the air filled with many fragrances.
Upon the leftover food discarded in the courtyard,
    wintry birds swoop down;
A tattered robe hangs on a tree,
    the old monk is gone.
(CTS, P. 1081)   (TR. WU-CHI LIU)

Tune: "Song of Flirtatious Laughter" (*T'iao-hsiao ling*)

Hunnish horse,
Hunnish horse,
Left grazing afar under the slope of the Yen-chih Mountain.
    Trots through sand,
        trots through snow,
            neighing alone.
Looks east, looks west, has lost its path.
    The path is lost,
    The path is lost,
And frontier grass has no end when the sun sets.
(CTS, P. 5120)   (TR. HELLMUT WILHELM)

---

[1] *Shih-men,* the Stone Gate Mountain, located near Yung-chia, Chekiang, once visited by the poet Hsieh Ling-yün. Cf. Hsieh's poem "Spending the Night on Stone Gate Mountain."

Wang Chi-yu (fl. 766)

Viewing Mr. Yü's Landscape Painting on the Wall

A rustic person like me seldom spends a night in a mountain home.
I wake and watch the dawn come to these hills:
On the wall the clouds still hover above the peaks;
And I open the window to set free the birds in the lake.
Who is this man sitting alone under the tall pine?—
To my repeated greetings he is slow in response.
Mr. Yü lets loose a hearty laugh and says,
"It is my painting that deceives you so."
(CTS, P. 1546)   (TR. JOSEPH J. LEE)

Chang Chih-ho (c. 742–c. 782)

Fisherman's Songs, Three Selections

[1]

Near the rim of Hsi-sai Mountain,[1] white egrets fly;
Peach blossoms, flowing stream, and perches full grown.
Oh, for a broad-brimmed bamboo hat, and a cloak of straw!
Slanting wind, fine rain, one need not go home.
(NO. 1 FROM A SERIES OF 5; CTS, P. 5119)   (TR. IRVING Y. LO)

[2]

Oh, about the joy of owning a crab hut at Sung-chiang!
A dish of wild rice and watercress soup make a repast taken in company.
The maple leaves drop,
The flowers of the wild chrysanthemums are dry.
Drunk on a fishing boat one does not feel the cold.
(NO. 4; CTS, P. 5119)   (TR. HELLMUT WILHELM)

---

1 Hsi-sai Shan, located 250 *li* southwest of Wu-hsing, Chekiang.

[3]

Before dusk on the lake, the moon just full,
The fisherman from Pa-ling chants incessantly his boatman's songs.
Fishing gear,
A boat with an up-turned bow,
To be happy in wind and waves one need not be a saint.
(NO. 5; CTS, P. 5119)   (TR. HELLMUT WILHELM)

Lu Lun (*fl. 770*)

"Frontier Songs": Replying to
Assistant Executive Secretary Chang, Three Selections

[1]

Woods darken, grasses startled by wind,
The general at night draws his bow;
In daylight he looks for the white plume,
Buried within the rock's fissure.

[2]

Moon blackens, geese fly high,
The kaghan[1] at night takes flight;
We lead light horsemen in pursuit,
A great snow covers bows and swords.

[3]

Select fine arrows and call for falcons,
All have heard of our uncommon skill;
Rout the fox and close in upon pheasants,
Flush out the ancient hills and mounds!
(NOS. 2, 3, 5 FROM A SERIES OF 6; CTS, P. 1678)   (TR. RONALD C. MIAO)

---

1 *Ch'an-yü,* or "chieftain," in the original text.

Li Yi (c. 749–c. 829)

At Night atop Shou-hsiang Citadel, Hearing
Tartar Flutes

Before Hui-le Peak, sands like snow.
Beyond Shou-hsiang Citadel, the moon like frost.
From somewhere the reed pipes are blowing,
And all night through the soldiers long for home.
(CTS, P. 1716)   (TR. PAUL KROLL)

Looking in a Mirror the Day Before
the Advent of Autumn

Everything fades away beyond oneself.
Life is all here in this mirror:
Just that my temples are covered with snow,
With which to front the autumn winds tomorrow.
(CTS, P. 1713)   (TR. WILLIAM H. NIENHAUSER)

Meng Chiao (751–814)

Ballad of Ching Mountain

Swarms of flies crowd my sick horse,
Its blood flows, can't get going.
On the road behind, night's color rises.
In the mountains ahead, I hear the cries of tigers.
At this time the wanderer's heart
Is a pennon in the wind, a hundred feet high.
(CTS, P. 2234)   (TR. STEPHEN OWEN)

Expressing My Feelings

Pull up the stems, grass doesn't die,[1]
Take out the roots, the willow still flourishes.
Only the man who's a failure
As in a trance walks, strengthless.
Before, he was a branch entwined with others,[2]
Now is the sound of a breaking lute-string.[3]
As a twined branch—then he was honored,
Now as a broken string he is made light of.
I will go forward in my lonely boat
To the great gorges where the water isn't smooth;   10
I will ride my carriage and horse
Over the T'ai-hang Mountains where the roads are rocky.
A single spirit lies at the root of all things—
How can they then destroy one another?
(CTS, PP. 2217)   (TR. STEPHEN OWEN)

Failing the Examination

For a dawn moon, hard to hold its light,
For a sorrowful man, a heart troubled.
Who says that all things flower in spring?—
Can't they see the frost on the leaves?
An eagle, losing its powers, sick;
Wrens that soar on borrowed wings.
Cast off once, cast off again—
My feelings like a knifeblade's wound.
(CTS, P. 2221)   (TR. STEPHEN OWEN)

Seeing Off Master T'an

A poet suffers making poems—
Better to waste your efforts trying to fly!

---

1 Punning on *hsin* as both "stem" of a plant and "heart."
2 *Lien-li chih* refers to two trees with branches entwined; in this case it refers to the poet's companions in Ch'ang-an before taking examination.
3 The breaking of lute-strings indicates the loss of intimate friends.

My whole life, a spirit of useless squawking,
Not of remonstrating and not of mocking—
Bare, leafless twigs hang from cold branches,
Cast off as though a tiny ball of spittle.
Step after step you beg
For scrap after scrap of clothing.
Those who have relied on poetry for a living
Since ancient times have never gotten fat.   10
This old man, hungry from poetry, is not bitter,
But your suffering tears fall like rain.
(NO. 12 FROM A SERIES OF 12; CTS, P. 2248)   (TR. STEPHEN OWEN)

Laments of the Gorges, Two Selections

[1]

The edges of the gorges hack up sun and moon,
Sun and moon always ruined in their shining.
All things grow warp and slanted,
Bird's wings fly warped and slanting.
Teeth on sunken stones locked;
Spirits of the drowned summoned but don't return.
A blur—armor-shells in a clear spring,
Splotched, the emerald robes on stone.
Hungrily lapping up the howl of rushing waters;
Slavering, seems like whirling, swirling oils.   10
Don't go strolling through the gorges in springtime—
Stinking grasses grow tiny, tiny.

[2]

Owls mimic human speech,
Dragons suck in mountainous waves.
They can, during broad daylight,
Coax you with pleasant clear breezes,
Shake judgment, make all living things stumble,
Gather reeking smells to spread from deep vines.
Toothed streams, bleak and bottomless,
Hacksaw froth, found everywhere.
Slanted trees where birds won't nest,

Dangling gibbons swing past them.   10
You can't listen to the laments of the gorges,
For nothing can be done about the bitterness there.
(NOS. 7, 10 FROM A SERIES OF 10; CTS, PP. 2257–58)

(TR. STEPHEN OWEN)

Apricots Die Young, Six Selections

Apricots die young: their flowers are nipples which the frost cuts and
they fall. They lead me to grieve over my late child and to write these
poems.

[1]

Don't let freezing hands play with these pearls—
If they play with these pearls, the pearls will surely fly loose.
Don't let the sudden frost cut off springtime—
If it cuts off spring, no bright flowering.
Scattering, falling, small nipple buds
In colorful patterns like my dead baby's robes.
I gather them—not a full hand's grasp,
At sunset I return home in hopeless sorrow.

[2]

In vain I gather up these stars from the ground,
Yet on the branches I see no flowers.
Sad—a solitary old man,
Desolate—a home without children.
Better the duck that sinks in the water,
Better the crow that gathers twigs for nesting.
Duckling in the waves, breaks through them, still flies,
Fledglings in the wind, ruffled, boasting to one another.
But blossoms and baby will live no more,
I sigh in vain, facing these creatures.   10

[3]

It must have been a single thread of tears
That entered the heart, the trunk, of this spring tree.

On branch after branch, they never became flowers,
Petal after petal fell to the cutting metal.
We cannot lengthen the life of spring,
But my lament of the frost has gotten even deeper.
Usually in this season I bathe in streams of blossoms,
But on this day my robes are bathed in tears.

[4]

When my son was born, the moon was not bright;
When my son died, the moon first gave light.
My son and the moon took each other away,
So my son's life was not long at all.
Why is it that these blossoms too
Become lament to the blue skies?
Heaven willingly let them fall into dust
And make no blossoms in later ages.

[5]

When I tread the earth, I fear to hurt the ground
And harm the roots of these flowering trees.
Yet Heaven did not know this sincerity,
When it cut and cast off my descendants.
Thousands have fallen from drooping branches—
Of the blossoms' lives, not one survived.
Who says of a family of the living
That spring's beauty does not enter their gate?

[6]

Nipping chill, the frost killed spring,
From branch to branch it seemed a tiny knife.
Since the flowers have fallen from the tree's trunk,
Like mountain caves the hollows cry out in vain.
Spot after spot—the blossoms that fell to earth,
Dot after dot—like oily drops of light.
Now I know that between heaven and earth,
The millions of things are all fragile.
(NOS. 1–6 FROM A SERIES OF 12; CTS, P. 2258)   (TR. STEPHEN OWEN)

Autumn Meditations, Four Selections

[1]

Bones of the lonely-wretched spend no quiet nights:
The cicadas keep them company with endless chirps.
Old men weep no drivels or snivels;
For them, the pitter-patter of autumn dew.
The prime of life has passed, brief as an arrow's flight;
Withering age approaches, tangled like a web from the loom.
The senses touched, no fresh feeling;
Clustered grief, the lingering memory.
How could I bear chasing after southern sails,
To tread my past over mountains and rivers?   10
(NO. 1 FROM A SERIES OF 15; CTS, P. 2223)   (TR. IRVING Y. LO)

[2]

In autumn moonlight the face turns icy;
Old wanderer, the force of his spirit spent.
Chill dew drips a dream to pieces,
A rugged wind combs the bones cold.
On the mat, prints pressed by sickness,
In the heart, writhing coils of grief.
These feelings of doubt are based on nothing,
Listen in vain to things—mostly without cause.
A paulownia tree, bare and towering,
Its echo like plucking a lament.   10
(NO. 2; CTS, P. 2223)   (TR. STEPHEN OWEN)

[3]

Autumn finds me old and poorer;
My home in ruins lacks a door.
A slivered moon drops onto my bed,
The wind from four walls enters my garment.
Broken dreams no longer travel far;
A faint heart easily turns to home.
Autumn vines about to shed their green leaves
Twist all around to catch the sun's last rays.

To step out into the wilds—such occasions often missed;
In sickness—all my plans go wrong.   10
For the insects hidden by grass clumps,
Life's strivings, as with me, are feeble.
(NO. 4; CTS, P. 2223)   (TR. IRVING Y. LO)

[4]

Old and sick, many strange broodings,
Dawn and evening, the heart's not the same.
Autumn insects weep for the declining cycle.
I cannot unravel their tangled echoes.
Autumn grass frail as hair,
A pure fragrance adorning sparse cassia blooms.
Yet how can this late fragrance last long?—
The speeding sunlight also darkens easily.
In vain I'm ashamed of my studies as a youth,
To what can I apply my wisdom in these twilight years?   10
I displayed my talent and it was slandered,
Then, early the wisdom within me deepened.
Fending off that depth, not fending off eminence,
Was the attitude the ancients warned against.
(NO. 7; CTS, P. 2224)   (TR. STEPHEN OWEN)

Lament for Lu Yin

Poets are usually pure, rugged,
Die from hunger, cling to desolate mountains.
Since this white cloud had no master,
When it flew off, its mind was free from care.
After long sickness, a corpse on a bed,
The servant boy too weak to manage the funeral.
Your old books, all gnawed by famished rats,
Lie strewn and scattered in your single room.
As you go off to the land of new ghosts,
I look on your features white as old jade.   10
I am ashamed that, when you enter the earth,
No one calls after you, to hold you back.
All the springs lament for you in vain,
As the day lengthens, murmuring waters mourn.
(NO. 1 FROM A SERIES OF 10; CTS, P. 2258)   (TR. STEPHEN OWEN)

After Passing the Examination

The wretchedness of my former years I have no need to brag:
Today's gaiety has freed my mind to wander without bounds.
Lighthearted in the spring breeze, my horse's hoofs run fast;
In a single day I have seen all the flowers[1] of Ch'ang-an.
(CTS, P. 2222)   (TR. IRVING Y. LO)

Wang Ya (c. 764–835)

"Song of Spring Journeying"

Ten thousand almond trees by the riverbank
Burst freshly into bloom after one night's wind.
All over the park, colors dark and light
Are reflected there in the green waves.
(NO. 1 FROM A SERIES OF 2; CTS, P. 2045)   (TR. IRVING Y. LO)

"Song of Autumn Night"

A new moon has come up and the autumn dew is light,
Her dress of soft gauze is too thin before she has time to change.
All night long she plays tenderly on the silver flute;
With a timid heart, she can't bear returning to an empty room.
(CTS, P. 2046)   (TR. IRVING Y. LO)

"Palace Poem"

A snow-white terrier brushes the ground as it walks;
Used to sleeping on red carpet, it has no sense of fright.
Who could have come to the palace's innermost quarter?
It barks only at evening fireflies by the gold-inlaid steps.
(NO. 13 FROM A SERIES OF 27; CTS, P. 2047)   (TR. IRVING Y. LO)

---

1 "Flower" in Chinese poetry is often used as a metonymy for beautiful women
and, more specifically, sing-song girls.

Han Yü (*768–824*)

Sentiments at Autumn: Eleven Poems

[1]

Out past the window two trees in splendor,
all their leaves alight with lushness
as autumn wind excites a gentle breeze
soughing, make sound unceasing

The dim lamp lights a futile bed
where depths of night, reckless, invade the ear
Anxious sorrows arise, uncaused
with mournful sighs
        I struggle up

in morning's light
        and look at my face
(not the same as it was before)   10
Hsi-ho drives the sun and moon
against his speed there's no defense

The floating life has many paths
the rush to death a single trail
Why then, heedless, in self-torment?
Take wine
      Enjoy

[2]

White dews drop on the hundred grasses
brushwood and orchid fade together
but vibrant green under the hedgerows
will bloom again
        and cover the ground

Cold cicadas for an instant
          still
crickets sing out
        to self-content

The cosmos turns in endless periods
and the essence given every thing differs
yet each, attuned to time, attains its place—
no need to treasure the evergreen   10

[3]

How fast
        speed these times
How far
        my goal is
The War Chief, out of work,
        drank wine in leisure
Lien P'o, the old general,
        kept strength to eat

With nothing days on end in the school to do
I spur my horse who wanders at will,
far-reaching the roads that leave my gate
I want to go, just to reassure myself

Home again I scan through texts
(words ocean-like and limitless)   10
Who searches the ancient traces but me
a humble pleasure that makes no precious gift

Men hold firm to their views
but discontent grows great in women

[4]

Every day now
        autumn air more troubling sad
        autumn skies more trembling cold

Above
        no cicadas on the branches
below
        no flies in the bowls

Who's not stirred by the season's change
that rids the senses of these small pains

In dawn's light I close my books and sit
watching the high ridges of the Southern Mountains
below which, the clear pool's water
where dragons, chilled cold, can be caught   10
Oh but I cannot go there
yet who would say I lack the skill?

[5]

Tearing inside there gnaws a baseless grief
a needless vigilance envelops me fearfully
Dews sparkle the tops of autumn trees
insects mourn the cold night's eternity
Drawing inward I adopt a new timidity
Plotting my life lament the former rage

Return to the simple and know the tranquil road:
to draw up antiquity takes a long rope,
a shallow fame still holds disgrace
but basic joys bring real content   10
If remorse and blame were left behind
then here would be my hidden retreat

[6]

Unable to get up this morning
I sat in bed exhausting the day's light
Now insects serenade the house, deep-hidden,
the window spews out the moon all aglow

My heart went lost like bearings unclear,
shallow thoughts pique (fish bones in the throat)
too lazy to serve in the dust and wait
with writing, fruitless, I run myself round,
but again must prod my intransigence
to the king's business at morning court   10

[7]

Autumn night cannot dawn
Autumn day turns bitter dark

I have no driving desires
so why prevails this discontent?

Cold rooster futile on his perch
the silvered moon I strain to watch

Take my zither
                    tune strings and stops,
play again
                    to hear more limpid notes

Ancient sounds
                    vanished long ago,
now, no way to know   10
                    pure from false

With sinking heart I follow time's speed,
take great pains only to manage the moment—
like a sailboat riding the wind
can't be hawsered, once free

Nothing compares with poring through texts
red brush in hand making notes in the margin
What use is there in craving an excess?
a few bushels of grain are all I need

[8]

Leaves fall in gentle swirls to the ground
wind-borne, speeding past the eaves
they whisper sounds as though self-willed
somersaulting, chasing one another

In the empty hall at ambered evening
I sit serene nothing to say
the boy comes from outside
lights the lamp in front of me
questions me, I do not answer
offers me food, I do not eat   10

retires to sit by the western wall
and read some books of poems aloud

The authors are not our men of today,
a thousand years are gone since then,
their words besiege my emotions
bring to me anguish and pain again

I turn and say to the boy:
"Put away the books and go to sleep."

A man may have his thoughts in a moment
Though fruition knows no final year   20

[9]

Frosting winds invade the *wu-t'ung* tree
where leaves all dangling dry from the branches
drop, each alone to the empty steps
crackling like pendants of jade shook

This speaks the breath of night's decease—
the moon's carter let fall his sphere
(nowhere to rest in the blue expanse,
his flying tracks unsure, hard of hold)

Fearful, I'm up out the door to look,
leaning on the post long tears flow   10

Sorrows and grief consume the gnomon's shadow
(sun and moon like juggler's balls)
return from delusion counts no distance,
for you the dusty saddle shall halt?

[10]

Evening darkness comes, the guests depart,
the common din with each subsides
Resting calm in the night's silence
autumn light untired enwraps me

Suddenly worldly concerns invade my thoughts
outside cares infiltrate the true soul

A strong spirit swells but not to fullness,
memories of weakness lapse then surge again,
I bend, stoop to elude the snares of talk,
in darkness infinite touch the heart's edge   10

Failure recalls a thousand in gold renounced,
Success like the bud of an inch-small herb
To know shame makes moral strength
since who shall enjoin a mind at peace?

[11]

Chrysanthemum fresh in the frost
what use your beauty so late?
Butterfly cheerful in the fragrance,
your life neither comes too early,
at cycle's end you both meet
your youth and grace intact till death

Western wind, snakes and dragons hibernate,
all the trees with days' advance fade and dry
Such are the parts destined by fate,
who could express total extinction?   10
(CTS, PP. 1983–84)   (TR. CHARLES HARTMAN)

Occasional Poem

Ancient annals strewn left and right
Poetry and *History* placed front and back,
How do I differ from a bookworm,
From birth to death encased in words?
The ancient way dulls and stultifies
ancient words cage and fetter.
Modern times differ indeed from antiquity,
Who today can share such pleasures?

Hand in hand alone with Master No Speech
We mount together the K'un-lun peaks.   10

Distant winds flapping lapels and hems
We rise and soar the lofty vault.
Below we sight the nine domains of Yü—
a dust speck held on a brush tip.
We tour in delight just a while—
Eons of years elapse below.

The loud disputants of yesterday—
A myriad grave mounds weight their skulls.
Sad the perverse clutch to opinions,
They could not separate white from black!   20
My indignation cries out in anguish
Tears surge like the Nine Rivers.
With faultfinders mutually accusing, slurring,
Even returned to the present, who would befriend me?
Nimbly gliding we drop to the Great Expanse
Hair flying, galloping on unicorns.
(CTS, P. 2012)   (TR. CHARLES HARTMAN)

To the Wooden Hermit, Two Poems

[1]

Scarred by flame, hollowed out by waves
you've stood here for ages.
Your roots look like somebody's face
and your trunk like a human body.
Just because you were called "The Wooden Hermit"
people came to pay homage and pray for fortune.

[2]

This tree trunk honored as "spirit"
is worth less than an old log
adrift in the gutter.[1]
At least someday someone
might rescue the log from the flame,

---

[1] *Chuang-tzu:* A hundred-year tree was made into a sacrificial goblet, with green
and yellow decors. When it floats adrift in the gutter, it's certainly prettier than
a rotten log in the gutter; however, with respect to losing its nature, the two
are no different from each other.

and make something good of it.[2]
But you—you are rotten, brittle,
would break under knife or saw,
and even the best craftsman
wouldn't know what to make of you.
(CTS, PP. 2025–26)   (TR. KENNETH O. HANSON)

Poem on Losing One's Teeth

Last year I lost an incisor
and this year a molar, and now
half a dozen more teeth fall out
all at once—and that's
not the end of it either.
The rest are all loose, and I know
there's no end till they're all gone.
The first one, I thought
what a shame for that obscene gap!
Two or three, and I thought   10
I was falling apart, almost
at death's door. Before, when one
loosened, I quaked and hoped
wildly it "wouldn't." The
gaps made it hard to chew
and with a loose tooth I'd
rinse my mouth gingerly.
Then when at last it fell out
it felt like a mountain collapsing.
But now I've got used to this   20
Nothing earthshaking. I've
still twenty left, though I know
one by one they'll all go.
But at one tooth per year it will
take me two decades, and gone,
all gone, will it matter

---

[2] *Hou-Han Shu,* the biography of Ts'ai Yung: In the district of Wu someone used *t'ung* as firewood. Ts'ai Yung heard the cracking sound in the fire and knew that it was fine wood. He asked for it and made it into a lute. The lute had beautiful sounds but the end remained burned. His contemporaries named it "Lute with Burnt End."

they went one by one
and not all at the same time?
People say when your teeth go
it's certain the end's near.   30
But seems to me life has
its limits, you die when you die
either with or without teeth.
They also say gaps scare
the people who see you. Well
two views to everything
as Chuang Tzu noted: A blasted
tree need not necessarily
be cut down, though geese
that don't hiss be slaughtered.[1]   40
For the toothless who mumble
silence has its advantage, and
those who can't chew will find
soft food tastes better. This is a poem
I chanted and wrote
to startle my wife and children.
(CTS, P. 2003)   (TR. KENNETH O. HANSON)

The Girl from Flower Mountain

On street corners east and west
    they teach the Buddhist sutras
Banging bells, blowing horns
    rattling the court
Much is made of sins and blessings
    to seduce and awe
the listening crowd shoving
    —floating waterweeds pressed—
A yellow-robed Taoist also
    preaches his texts,

---

[1] Chuang Tzu saw a huge tree which the woodsman would not take because its wood was useless. Chuang Tzu said, "This tree is useless, thus it can live its natural life." Chuang Tzu then visited a friend and stayed at his house. The friend ordered a boy to slaughter a goose for the meal. One of the geese could sing and the other could not. The boy asked which goose to slaughter; the friend said, "Kill the one that cannot sing."

below his pulpit people are scarce
    like morning stars

The girl from Flower Mountain
    (her family follows the *tao*)
wants to dispel the strange teaching
    and return people to the immortal Spirit
She washes makeup away, scrubs her face
    puts cap and mantle on,
white neck, red cheeks   10
    long black eyebrows
come then to climb the pulpit,
    explain the true mysteries

It's not allowed to open the bolt
    on the temple door
yet unknown someone leaked
    the news around,
now crashing, a shaking
    like thundering lightning
sweeping clean the Buddhist temples
    empty of human tracks,
thoroughbred horses block the street,
    strings of covered carriages,
people inside fill the temple
    others sit outside,
latecomers have no space,
    no way to hear
They take out hairpins, pull off bracelets,
    undo jade pendants,
heaped gold piled up jade   20
    gleaming a green light
Worthies from the portals of Heaven
    convey the imperial command—
the Inner Palace desires to learn
    the teacher's face and form

The Jade Emperor nods his head
    allows her return

riding dragons mounting cranes
  she reaches the blue void
Young lords of noble houses
  know little of the *tao*
come circling a hundred turns
  with ceaseless feet
Clouded windows misted belvederes
  these enraptured affairs
double-folded kingfisher curtains
  deep golden screens
The immortal ladder is hard to climb
  worldly ties are heavy,
idly they trust the blue birds   30
  to carry their youthful regards
(CTS, P. 2016)   (TR. CHARLES HARTMAN)

Southern Mountains

I

I heard that south of the capital city[1]
There thrived a menagerie of mountains amassed,

East and west bordering both seas,[2]
I struggled to delve into all, both great and small.

The Mountain Classic[3] and other geographical works
Are confused and vague without oral traditions.

So collecting my phrases I tried writing an abstract,
But knew each point recalled meant a thousand forgotten.

I should have stopped but truthfully was unwilling,
So roughly I recount now only things I saw.   10

---

1 I.e., Ch'ang-an.
2 Probably no two specific bodies of water are meant. "East and west" simply means "everywhere" as in the line of Tu Fu: "From east to west news is rare." (Davis, A. R., *Tu Fu*, New York: Twayne Publishers, 1971, p. 63.)
3 The *Shan-hai Ching*, or *Classic About Mountains and Seas*, an ancient work of cosmography.

II

I climbed a high knoll[4] and viewed—
Fold after fold, vistas massed on themselves.

Clear and bright, angled horns emerged—
Silken veins, fragments of broken brocade.

Alpine hazes swirled together
Suddenly strung inward and outward,

Without wind, alone they winnow and turn,
Dissolve to moisture, warming vegetation.

Flat clouds frozen still,
Point by point cap the many caverns.   20

In heaven's vastness float long eyebrows,
Vibrant green and newly drawn.

A lonesome tor, a steep drop—
A bathing simurgh lifting his beak.

III

Spring's vigor hides in sodden marshes
Then brightly disgorges dense flowers.

Towering crags, impassively steep,
Yet fluent like liqueur swished in the mouth.

In summer's blaze the forests flourish,
Shaded and bushy, multiplying their cover.   30

The daily exhalations of divine spirits
Vie with the clouds in building formations.

---

4 In Ch'ang-an.

When autumn frost crushes like wheels,
Flayed stand the mountains, thin-worn,

All uneven piled on themselves
Ever majestic, spanning the sky.

Winter comes with somber silence,
Ice and snow sculpting in white jade.

A new sun lights the summits
Stretching heights and breadths millions of feet.   40

From morning till night no lingering shape—
A moment changes conditions and forms.

IV

Great Clarity[5] commands the southwest,
Straight up unflanked by seconds.

Defending the capital, matching its element—
Dividing the house, holding south and center.[6]

Roaming in leisure, it passes the southwest
Reproached in censure, sinks in northwestern bogs.[7]

Empty, vacuous, shivering and fearful—
The wind's force bites like an arrow.   50

---

[5] T'ai-po Shan, south of Wu-kung county, 200 *li* from Ch'ang-an, was a permanently snowcapped mountain.
[6] This verse is based upon correspondences drawn from the *I Ching* hexagrams, the five elements, and the ten celestial stems. T'ai-po Shan is located to the southwest of Ch'ang-an. Southwest corresponds to "earth," the element of the T'ang dynasty. Thus T'ai-po is seen as the protector of Ch'ang-an and the T'ang. *Ting* is for *ping-ting* and the direction south; *wu* is for *wu-chi* and center. The entire Ch'in-ling range is seen here as one family or "house" with three peaks: T'ai-po in the west, Chung-nan in the center, and Hua-shan in the east. It is, however, not clear why T'ai-po is said to occupy south and center. Perhaps simply for the rhyme word *wu*.
[7] The meaning of this line is unclear.

On the austral side the sun almost burns
On the boreal hail jumps in confusion.

V

Gone for a look north of the Greak Lake[8]
Of Assembled Brilliance I chanced on clear daylight,

Looking down, everywhere silken floss strings
Inverted, imprisoned in limpid submersion.

Slight ripples stir the surface—
Scrambling monkeys leaping with excitement

Yelping in fear the mountain shattered—
Look up, surprised it hasn't fallen.   60

VI

Once before, I passed the villas of Tu,
Dust-covered and squalid was End Plateau.[9]

Climbing high up steep trails
Suddenly I saw a wealth of views.

On and on almost infinite
Peaks and plateaus running together.

Irate I thought to cleave them apart
Whose covering and concealing I could not forgive.

If the River Spirit or K'ua-o's sons
Came peddling their services, certainly I would buy them![10]   70

---

8 For K'un-ming Lake in Ch'ang-an, see note 3 to Tu Fu's poem "Autumn Thoughts." Lines 55–60 all deal with the reflections of the mountains in the lake.
9 The village of Tu-ling. End Plateau was the burial place of Kings Wen and Wu of the Chou dynasty, and according to the *Shih Chi* was 28 *li* southwest of Ch'ang-an.
10 An allusion to the "Western Capital *fu*" of Chang Heng where the River Spirit splits the mountains at the bend of the Yellow River in two halves—Hua Shan to the southwest and Shou-yang Shan across the river in Shansi. Cf. von Zach, E., *Die Chinesische Anthologie,* Cambridge: Harvard University Press,

Yet still I wonder if the Maker's intent
Was not to preserve his natural creation—

Human power can push and move
But fears the rebuke of thunder and lightning.

Climbing upward, arms and legs give out
Stranded-exhausted, I reach a well-like hollow.[11]

Confused I strain to lift my head,
Hemmed in by earthen clods, my ignorance mounts.[12]

The majestic forms die, lost in isolation—
The near and new block the far and old.   80

Bound to my office, counting the days,
I wanted to go on, but could not return.[13]

VII

So therefore I watched a pool[14]
Whose clear depths concealed water dragons.

Bending I could gather fish and prawns,
But who dares plunder divine beings?

Fearful birds rescue drooping leaves
About to fall from tree branches,

Fighting to take them and circle above,
Then eager to drop them and feed their young.   90

1958, p. 2. For the story about the Old Man Who Wished to Move the
Mountain and about the exploits of K'ua-o's two sons, cf. *Lieh-tzu* (translated
by A. C. Graham, London: Rider & Co., 1960, pp. 99–101).
11 Literally, "amassed well-tiles."
12 The meaning seems to be that he cannot see the distant peaks because of a
depression in the trail where the stones seem stacked up like tiles in a well.
13 The poet, having failed to find a path to the summit, cannot return for another
attempt.
14 The Coal Valley Pool in the mountains 40 *li* south of Ch'ang-an.

Looking backward, off the returning road,
The towering trunks emerged strong again.

Sighing admiration, I think it is strange—
The nature of a mountain peak can change!

VIII

Several years ago meeting with exile,
My sight-seeing chance came unexpected.

I entered the mountains, at Indigo Field,[15]
Craning my head till the neck was stiff.

Then Heaven darkened into a vast snowstorm—   100
Tear-filled eyes blurred to blindness.

The steepening road, straight up
Like a waterfall, was stretched into ice.

With robes tucked up I pushed my horse,
Stumbling falling sliding back again.

Flurried-confused I forgot the distant horizon—
Saw only left and right.

Pines and bamboos seen as halberds
Glittering-gleaming—a collection of armor.

All my heart wanted a tranquil road—
A danger surpassed outweighs a stench avoided.[16]   110

IX

Yesterday I met with clear skies
And an old wish was happily fulfilled.

---

15 *Lan-t'ien*, a strategic town in Shensi, on the route leading to Szechwan. Cf.
poem "Demoted I Arrive at Lan-t'ien Pass . . ."
16 Alluding to a story in the *Lü-shih Ch'ün-ch'iu* of a man who smelled so
strongly that his family could not live together in the same house with him.

Climbing up high I reached the summit,
Quickly bolting squirrels and weasels scattered.

Before and below opening wide,
Scattered and strewn corrugations piled up:

Some joined like marriage
Or constrained like combat

Or relaxed like lying prostrate
Or alert like startled pheasants   120

Or dispersed like broken tiles
Or guided like spokes to the hub

Or floating like boat travel
Or direct like horses running

Or backed off like enemies
Or face to face like partners

Or confused like bamboos germinating
Or swollen like cauterizing moxa

Or disarrayed like lines in a sketch
Or sinuous like Great Seal Script   130

Or meshed like star configurations
Or dense like hovering clouds

Or buoying up like waves
Or breaking apart like plows

Or like the valiants Meng Pen and Hsia Yü[17]
Who gamble victory fighting for the prize—

The victor strong exuding power,
The defeated stunned grumbling his anger.

---

[17] Two men famous in antiquity for their strength. Cf. Giles, L., *Biographical Dictionary*, Taipei Reprint, Nos. 1525 and 684.

Or like the grandeur of a ruler
Who gathers at court the humble and youthful: 140

Intimate, yet never too familiar;
Distant, yet never estranged.

Or like facing a banquet table
With dishes in excess spread for show,

Or like traveling through Nine Plains[18]
Where grave mounds embrace their coffins.

Or stacked up like a double-boiler
Or erect like a sacrificial urn[19]

Or upturned like terrapins sunning themselves.
Or collapsed like sleeping quadrupeds   150

Or undulating like hidden dragons
Or wings flapping like a captured condor

Or equal like friends
Or following like first and second[20]

Or adrift like exile
Or pensive like waiting

Or antagonistic like enmity
Or close like marriage

Or solemn like high miters
Or swirling like dancing sleeves   160

---

18 *Chiu-yüan* was the burial ground for the ministers of the state of Tsin during the Spring and Autumn period. Located in Shansi, it came to be a term for cemeteries in general.
19 Cf. the illustration in Couvreur, S., *Dictionnaire classique*, Taipei Reprint, p. 872.
20 "First" and "second" are used for the wives of an older and a younger brother respectively.

Or immovable like battle formations
Or encircling like the great hunts

Or submissive—flowing east[21]
Or restful—head to the north[22]

Or like the blaze from a roasting fire
Or like vapor rising while steaming rice

Or moving and not pausing
Or left and not gathered

Or aslant and not inclined
Or slack and not taut   170

Or naked like bald temples
Or smoking like a wooden pyre

Or like the cracks on tortoise shells
Or like the lines of the eight trigrams

Or level on top like *po*
Or broken underneath like *kou*[23]

X

Elongated-like: broken then joined again
Unbending-like: deserting then meeting again

Agape-like: fish mouths gasping from duckweed
Sparse-like: constellations traversed by the moon   180

Majestic-like: trees tall in the courtyard
Peaked-like: granaries stacked up high

---

21 Perhaps because most rivers in China flow eastward.
22 Coffins in China were placed in the grave with the head facing northward.
23 The parallelism is more complete than meets the eye. *Po,* hexagram 23, signifies "collapse, splitting apart, the symbol of dispersion" (*I-ching,* Legge-Ch'ai ed., New York: Bantam, 1969, p. xxii). *Kou,* hexagram 44, signifies "meeting, intercourse, the symbol of coming to meet" (Ibid., p. xxiii).

Pointed-like: halberds standing sharp
Glittering-like: holding jade and jasper

Opening-like: flowers unfurling the calyx
Dripping-like: rain falling from broken eaves

Leisure-like: stretched out and calm
Obstinate-like: familiar and pushy

Superior-like: emergent and speeding
Squirming-like: frightened, unwilling to stir.   190

XI

How large! rising between heaven and earth
Their patterns copying the skin's network.

In their beginning, who spread them out?
Who worked, who advised,

Creating them simple and ingenious,
Combining strengths to endure the toil?

Did they use axes to hew,
Or borrow power from magic invocations?

Since nothing is known of the Primal Darkness,
This stately achievement goes unacknowledged.   200

Learning from the shrine attendant that the mountain spirit
Descended in person to inhale the sacrificial fragrance,

With rhetoric I composed this poem,
Hoping by it to offer my gratitude.
(CTS, PP. 1982–83)   (TR. CHARLES HARTMAN)

The Pond in a Bowl, Five Poems

[1]

In old age
I'm back
to childhood pleasures.

A bowl in the ground
Just add water—
it's a pool!

Throughout the night
frogs croaked
till it dawned,

as they did
when I fished
as a child at Feng-k'ou.

[2]

Who says
you can't make a pond
out of a bowl?

The lotus sprig
I planted not long ago
has already grown full size.

Don't forget,
if it rains
stop in for a visit.

Together we'll
listen to raindrops splash
on all the green leaves.

[3]

Come morning,
the water brightens
as if by magic.

One moment alive
with thousands of bugs
too small to have names,

Next moment
they're gone,
leaving no trace,

Only the small fish
this way and that
swim in formations.

[4]

Does the bowl
in the garden
mock nature

when night after night
green frogs gather
to prove it's a pool?

If you choose to come
and keep me company
need you fill

the dark with noise
and endless squabble
like husband and wife?

[5]

Say the bright pond
mirrors the sky
both blue.

If I pour
water, the pond
brims.

Let night
deepen
the moon go

how many stars
shine back
from the water!
(CTS, P. 2029)   (TR. KENNETH O. HANSON)

Short Poems on Various Subjects, Two Selections

[1]

Don't shoo the morning flies away
Nor swat mosquitoes in the evening.
Between the two, they fill the world.
So many, should you fight them all?
And yet, how short a time they live.
While they last, give in and let them bite you.
October, and a cold wind wipes them out.
You don't remember then they ever were.

[2]

Mornings the sparrow twitters seeking food
The dove at evening coos to woo her mate.
Only the crane knows its hours[1]
Cries but not for itself.
And the dumb female cicada never cries
What she feels she does not display.
Only the frogs croak with no good reason
Making up a tumult of noise and nuisance.
(NOS. 1, 4 FROM A SERIES OF 4; CTS, P. 2022)
                    (TR. KENNETH O. HANSON)

---

[1] Proverbially, the cranes cry at midnight.

The Officer at the Rapids

Southward bound over sixty days
Starting down rapids at Ch'ang-lo
Dangers, indescribable hazards
Rocks and boats pound together
I question the officer at the rapids:
"How many leagues yet to Ch'ao-chou?
When may I expect to arrive?
What are the customs like there?"
The officer dropped his hand and laughed,
"Why ask foolish questions, Your Excellency?   10
Suppose you're stationed in the capital,
How'd you know anything about Eastern Wu?
'Cause Eastern Wu's the home of traveling officials—
That's how you'd know.
But Ch'ao-chou—that's a place
For criminals and exiles.
Lucky I never broke the law;
How should I come to know the place?
You'll be there soon enough, Excellency,
So what's the use of stupid questions?"   20

Unexpected, suddenly embarrassed
Sweat came with shame and dismay.
"Just sportin' with Your Excellency a little!
I was there on official business once.
Ling-nan's pretty much the same all over.
The road you'll travel's terribly long:
Three thousand leagues from here,
That's where the prefecture called Ch'ao starts.
Poison vapors gather over the Fetid River,
All the time thunder and lightning crash.   30
There're crocodiles bigger than boats
With teeth and eyes that'll scare you to death.
Twenty or so leagues south of the prefecture
There's ocean—no heaven or earth.
Sometimes, when typhoons come,
It churns and surges to chaos.

When a good emperor's in the land,
His bounty reaches all things:
Lately I heard about fellows imprisoned there
That even returned alive.   40
But don't prejudge the place, Excellency,
Just 'cause it's where criminals are exiled.
No need to press for details about why
You're here in times as good as these:
If you're not careful, Excellency,
You'll end up the same way.
Why mope around for so long here
On the riverbank with your mind in a fog?
A cask is big, a cup is small.
But each one holds what it can.   50
If you don't first measure yourself,
You're begging things to overflow.
Tradesmen and peasants may be common folk,
But each one minds his own affairs.
I don't know if you did any good
For the country or not while at court.
Weren't you maybe just a parasite,
Neither a military nor a civil official,
Covering yourself with 'altruism' and 'righteousness,'
And corrupting others with treachery and deceit?"   60

Head to the ground, I thanked the officer.
My former shame turned now to self-disgust.
Over twenty years I served the state
And never repaid the imperial favor.
Of all the officer's angry rebukes,
Sadly enough, most are true.
Only through death by metal or wood
Could I realize imperial favor.
Although Ch'ao-chou is distant,
Although its dangers cannot be survived;   70
Still to be alive is truly a lot,
So why shouldn't I wish myself well?
(CTS, P. 2017)   (TR. CHARLES HARTMAN)

Demoted I Arrive at Lan-t'ien Pass and Show This Poem to My Brother's Grandson Han Hsiang

A sealed epistle submitted
  at dawn to Nine-fold Heaven—
exiled at dusk to Ch'ao-chou
  eight thousand leagues to travel

Wishing to save His Sagacious Brilliance
  from treacherous evils,
could I have cared for the years that remain
  in my withered limbs?

Clouds straddle the mountains of Ch'in
  where is my house?
snows crowd the pass at Lan
  horse will not move

I know what the reason must be
  that makes you come so far—
the better to gather my bones
  from the shores of miasmic water
(CTS, P. 2035)   (TR. CHARLES HARTMAN)

Hsüeh T'ao (768–831)

The Moon

The crescent, tiny as the curtain hook;
The fan, woven on the Han loom, is round.
The slender image, its nature, to gain fullness—
Where else on earth is this seen?
(CTS, P. 4659)   (TR. ERIC W. JOHNSON)

Farewell to a Friend

The water country's reeds and rushes, night, covered with frost;
The moon's coldness, the mountains' cast share a bleak, pale blue.

Who can say, from this night on, a thousand *li* away,
My dreams of you, dim as the distant frontier?
(CTS, P. 4660)   (TR. ERIC W. JOHNSON)

Willow Catkins

Flowers of the willow, light, fluffy by the second moon,
Sway wildly in spring breezes, tugging sleeves of passers-by.
They are by nature heartless things indeed,
Who just gave them to fly north and fly south.
(CTS, P. 4663)   (TR. ERIC W. JOHNSON)

Autumn Spring

The cold hue newly clears, a belt of haze;
The mysterious sound gurgles afar, the ten-stringed lute.
Endlessly to my pillow they come, to draw thoughts of love,
Not letting this pensive soul half the night to sleep.
(CTS, P. 4663)   (TR. ERIC W. JOHNSON)

Wang Chien (768–833)

"A Boatman's Song"

Oh, it's hard to grow up at the way-station side!
The officials've set me to pullin' station boats;
Painful days are more, happy days are few,
Sleepin' on water, walkin' on sand, like birds of the sea;
Against the wind, upstream, a load of ten thousand bushels—
Ahead, the station's far away; behind, it's waters everywhere!
Midnight on the dikes, there's snow and there's rain,
From up top our orders: you still have to go again!
Our clothes are wet and cold beneath our short rain cloaks,
Our hearts're broke, our feet're split, how can we stand the pain?   10
Till break of dawn we suffer, there's no one we can tell,
With one voice we trudge along, singing as we pull;
A thatch-roofed house, what's it worth,
When we can't get back to the place of our birth!

I would that this river turn to farm plots,
And long may we boatmen stop cursing our lots.
(CTS, P. 1789)   (TR. WILLIAM H. NIENHAUSER)

"Weaving at the Window"[1]

Sighing high and
          again a sigh![2]
In the garden are dates
          which the passers-by crave[3];
A girl of poor family
          for a rich one must weave,
Her parents beyond the wall
          can give her no help;
Cold water, rough hands,
          and fine thread so easily breaks!
Stitch in, stitch out,
          it tears at her heart!
Insects swarm in the grass,
          to cry beneath her loom,
In two days she must do
          one roll and a half;
When each tax is paid
          only odd pieces are left![4]
Her mother-in-law has no new dress,
          how could she wear one?   10

---

1 A T'ang imitation of the *yüeh-fu* ballad.
2 The first line suggests similar formulaic lines of the Six Dynasties period. These lines are often (for example in "The Ballad of Mulan") uttered by a girl who is weaving. Although weaving and silk-raising were the normal day-to-day occupations of women in traditional China, the figure of a woman weaving often suggests her solitude—that she is unmatched or unrequited in love.
3 Alluding to a Six Dynasties *yüeh-fu* poem, "Breaking a Willow Branch." The first couplet reads: "In front of the gates there stands a jujube [date] tree,/That never grows old, though it lives on year after year"; (original text: *Yüeh-fu shih-chi*, 25:6a [SPPY ed.]). Though the tree does not seem to age and still attracts the passers-by, the girl is growing older and has no visitors.
4 Referring to the taxes on silk. Yüan Chen (779–831) has a contemporary poem dealing with the taxes on silk, cf. *Yüeh-fu shih-chi*, 94:1b–2a (SPPY ed.).

From her window she can even envy
those green-bower girls,[5]
Their ten fingers idle,
while clothes fill the hamper.
(CTS, P. 1788)   (TR. WILLIAM H. NIENHAUSER)

"Palace Poems," Nine Selections

[1]

At home I loved to wear old clothes,
Now in vain I set crimson combs and wear makeup;
As I hurry down the stairs my skirt comes loose,
Can it be time for me to see my lord?[1]

[2]

Wanting to welcome the emperor
who has gone flower viewing
I come down the golden stairs,
but turn and stay;
Afraid of seeing that old courtyard
of those who've lost his favor,
I go back and muse to the
sounds of my zither.

[3]

A spring breeze blows the rain,
sprinkles the flagstaff,
Out from the depths of the palace,
I feel no chill;
Boasting that I can straddle
any horse,
I ride straight through the garden
to catch his eye.

---

5 Sing-song girls; they lived in green two-storied buildings, cf. Arthur Waley, "The Green Bower Collection," *Secret History of the Mongols and Other Pieces* (London, 1963), pp. 89–107.
1 According to T'ang belief the accidental loosening of a skirt was portentous of happy conjugal relations.

[4]

Palace girls up early,
                smile as they call one another,
But who's that new fellow
                sweeping the steps?
With strings of cash they struggle
                to inquire of him,
If things outside still resemble
                the life they have within.

[5]

Early autumn, white rabbits
                big as fists,
Red ears and frosted fur,
                sleeping in the grass;
The emperor won't allow
                anyone to shoot them,
His jade-handle whip screens them
                from his horse's hooves.

[6]

Her silken gown rustles,
                heavily embroidered,
With golden phoenixes and silver geese,
                each in a flock;
Every time she dances,
                it opens wide:
"Peace and Long Life!"
                are written there inside.

[7]

A pair of green-painted eyebrows
                locked in the Pondweed Palace[2];

---

[2] The persona of this poem is a palace lady, to date unattended by the emperor,
longing for a visit from him. The Pondweed Palace was located in the Ku-chin
Park north of Ch'ang-an on an island hill in a pond.

All the places the Emperor goes,
             yet he's never been here!
Now the bed of the pool
             has no need for brocade,
Where water chestnuts and lily pads
             have slowly spread.

[8]

A red lantern calls the spring clouds from my sleep,
Clouds gather, it's the third watch—my time of duty[3];
Rain comes to the golden steps, the going is slippery,
So my maid and I lift up our skirts with the hidden flowers.

[9]

Long the flimsy skirts
             of these green-bower girls,[4]
Who've finally signed up
             for the Imperial Music School[5];
At the spring banquet before the hall
             in rows as dancers,
By the door to the tent
             they each plead for a new dress.

(NOS. 51, 38, 33, 69, 23, 17, 18, 27, 84 FROM A SERIES OF 100; CTS,
PP. 1816–20)   (TR. WILLIAM H. NIENHAUSER)

---

[3] I.e., her time to attend the emperor. She is awakened and accompanied to the emperor by her attendant.

[4] Courtesans lodged themselves in green bowers and were often recruited into the Imperial Music School.

[5] This institution, with three branches in the city of Ch'ang-an and one in the palace itself, trained musicians, singers, and dancers for imperial performances. The members of this "school" were virtually slaves, cf Martin Gimm, *Das YUEH-FU TSA-LU Des Tuan An-chieh* (Wiesbaden: Harrasswitz, 1966), pp. 574–75, n. 9. The force of this comes to the reader of this poem in the contrast between the suggested independence of the courtesans' lives in the first couplet, and the depiction of their regimented, collective, and almost pitiable existence in the last two lines.

Liu Yü-hsi

Liu Yü-hsi (772–842)

Sorrowing for the Past at Western Pass Mountain[1]

When the towered galleys of Wang Chün came down from Yi-chou,
The royal air of Chin-ling retreated dull and dim.
A thousand leagues of iron links sank to the river's bed;
Flags of surrender rose in a file over the Wall of Stone.
So many times in human life we grieve for bygone things:
The mountains' form, as long ago, lies pillowed on the cold flow.
Now all within the four seas has come under a single house,
And the old battlements sigh forlornly in an autumn of reeds.
(CTS, P. 2144) (TR. DANIEL BRYANT)

Chin-ling

Mountains surround the ancient kingdom in a massive circle;
The tide that beats on the emptied city, in desolation, recedes.
At Huai River's eastern edge—the moon of old,
As night deepens, still it returns, passing over earthen walls.
(CTS, P. 2174) (TR. PAUL KROLL)

"Looking at My Knife-hilt Ring: A Song"

I have always regretted the shallowness of words
Compared with the depth of human hearts.
Today the two of us look at one another,
Silently, but with feelings a hundredfold.
(CTS, P. 2167) (TR. DANIEL BRYANT)

---

[1] Wang Chün was a general in the service of Ssu-ma Yen, who had usurped the throne from the descendants of Ts'ao Ts'ao in 265. In 280, he proceeded down the Yangtze River from the old capital of Liu Pei, Yi-chou (modern Ch'eng-tu, Szechwan), with a fleet of large warships to attack Wu, the last of the Three Kingdoms. At Western Pass Mountain, downstream from Wu-han, he succeeded in defeating an attempt to destroy his fleet by means of an iron chain stretched across the river. Soon afterward, Chin-ling (modern Nanking), the Wu capital, guarded by the Wall of Stone, was forced to surrender and China was reunified after 60 years of division.

Willow Branches

A thousand strands of willow at spring river's bend,
The same old plank bridge twenty years ago—
I once parted from a beautiful lady on the bridge,
And regret now there's no news of her to this day.
(CTS, P. 2181)　　　　　　　　　(TR. DELL R. HALES)

Song of Miss T'ai

Miss T'ai was formerly the chief singer in the house of Grand Secretary Wei, who came by her while serving in the commandery of Wu. He ordered a music master to instruct her in the *p'i-p'a,* so that she might sing and dance for him. In no time at all she had mastered these arts and after a year or two he brought her back to the capital with him. As there were in the capital many skilled performers in the latest modes, Miss T'ai gave up her old techniques and used the new styles in her performances, with the result that her name was everywhere on the lips of the highest class of people. Early in the *Yüan-ho* period (806–21), Secretary Wei died in the Eastern Capital and Miss T'ai went to live among the common people. After some time had passed, she came into the possession of Chang Sun, the prefect of Ch'i. Sun later ran afoul of the law and was banished to the commandery of Wuling. When he died, Miss T'ai had no home to return to: Wu-ling itself was remote and uncivilized and there was no one there who could appreciate her beauty or her skill. So every day she took up her instrument and cried aloud in an anguished and mournful tone. A visitor from Lo-yang heard her and made a song about her story, so that it might be passed on in ballad form.

Miss T'ai's old home was west of the Ch'ang-men Gate[1];
Before the gate, green water ringed the adamantine dikes.

On days when the weather was fine, she would make herself pretty
And stroll over the Kao Bridge to play at plucking flowers.

---

[1] One of the eight gates of the city of Soochow, the seat of the commandery of Wu, of which Liu was governor from 832 to 834. The Kao Bridge was named after a Han notable named Kao Po-t'ung.

Grand Secretary Wei, the dashing and gallant Commandant,
Saw her by the roadside and halted his troops of falcon banners.
Bright pearls in quart measures, birds to carry his messages;
Indigo carriage screens welcomed her into the presidential residence.

Her long hair like a cloud, her garments like mist;
Brocade cushions and gauze mats bore her light steps.   10
    Her dancing copied swans rising in alarm by a river terrace
        in springtime;
    Her songs teased the honored guests, evenings in the Orchid Hall.

She followed His Excellency westward into the heart of the Imperial
    City;
The hatpins of noble visitors piled up by her fragrant lattice windows.
With hanging tresses and idle glances she embraced the bright moon;
Slim fingers' turbulent strumming gave rise to the desert wind.

Then suddenly this gay life of luxury faded away and died;
The inscribed sword lost its gleam and the sound of his sandals ceased.
In Lo-yang the old grounds are grown over with tangled weeds;
In Tu-ling[2] the pines and cedars grieve in moans and sighs.   20

In her powder case, gather cobwebs thick as silk cocoons;
A hill-shaped Po-shan censer tips and spills out cold ashes.

His honor, young Prefect Chang of Ch'i-chou,
Came on his white horse for the first time to the Bronze Camel
    Quarter,[3]
Announcing he was there to buy smiles, he threw his gold around.
Then it was that the moon first dropped behind the clouds.

Who could have known that a great owl would fly in and perch on a
    corner of his mat[4]
Leaving a lonely wandering soul that could not be summoned back?

---

2 Ch'ang-an's residential district for the aristocracy.
3 The entertainment district of Lo-yang.
4 Alluding to the opening lines of the "Owl *fu*" by Chia Yi (201–169 B.C.), where
  the arrival of the owl is mentioned as an omen that the master will soon de-
  part.

The mirror of Ch'in Chia[5] showed only a bond of former days;
The scent of Han Shou[6] faded with his robes in an old chest.   30

Few people live in the hill town, the river flows jade green;
Geese gone, gibbons grieve, evening wind and rain.
   Crimson strings broken now for one who understood her song[7];
   Cloudy tresses not yet in their autumn, she sorrows for herself
    apart.

Raising her eyes to wind and mist not those of former days,
She follows in a homeward road with many twists and turns.
What can she do but with these thousand streaming tears
Sprinkle once again the stained bamboo of the River Hsiang?[8]
(CTS, PP. 2111–12)   (TR. DANIEL BRYANT)

"Bamboo Branch Song," Two Selections

Songs everywhere use the same notes, even though they have a
different sound. In the first month of this year I came to Chien-p'ing,
where the village lads sing sets of "bamboo branch songs," playing
short flutes and beating drums to keep time. The singers raise their
sleeves and look sidelong as they dance; he who knows the most songs
is considered the most accomplished. To the ear they seem to be in the
submediant of C and their codas reveal hidden feelings like the music
of Wu. Although they are rustic and one can hardly tell one note from
another, they are filled with subtle meanings and as rich in tone as the
"Cove on the Ch'i" Ode. Long ago, when Ch'ü Yüan lived near the
Yüan and Hsiang rivers, the songs with which the common people
summoned the spirits were vulgar and unrefined. Then he wrote the
"Nine Songs" which are still sung and danced today in the regions of
Ching and Ch'u. I have likewise written these nine bamboo branch
pieces, so that good singers can make them known as additions to the

---

5 When Ch'in Chia parted from his wife, he gave her a mirror as a symbol of
  their union.
6 Han Shou's secret affair with the daughter of the high official Chia Ch'ung was
  discovered by the latter when he noticed that Han's clothing smelled of the
  rare scent which his daughter used.
7 Alluding to the story of Po Ya's lute.
8 Alluding to the legend about Emperor Shun and his two consorts. Also see note
  on *pan-chu* in Po Chü-yi's "Painting Bamboo: A Song."

tradition and later men who hear songs of the districts of Pa and Yü
will know from what the styles of these latter-day odes have developed.

[1]

The gorges of Wu are hoary and dim in the season of mist and rain;
Keening gibbons cry out from the highest branches.
Amid all this, the heart of a sorrowing man just breaks
Of its own accord and not, after all, of these mournful sounds.

[2]

Up in the hills are bank on bank of blossoming peach and plum trees;
Amid the clouds the household smoke of families who live there.
Silver armlets and golden hairpins come down to bear water;
Long knives and low bamboo hats go out to burn over the new fields.
(NOS. 8–9 FROM A SERIES OF 9; CTS, P. 2171)   (TR. DANIEL BRYANT)

"Willow Branch Song"

In the days when they were first planted before the Calyx Tower,
They vied for thinness with the lovely waists on the upper floors.
Now, though, they lie abandoned in the long boulevards.
Whom would they mourn, these dew-laden leaves that seem to weep?
(NO. 5 FROM A SERIES OF 9; CTS, PP. 2171–72)   (TR. DANIEL BRYANT)

Coming Again to Heng-yang,
I Mourn for Liu Tsung-yüan

During the *yi-wei* year of the *Yüan-ho* period (815), I parted from
my old friend Liu Tsung-yüan by the Hsiang River. He was sailing to
Liu-chou, while I proceeded overland to Lien-chou. Five years later,
I came back from the Cassia Range by the same road and reached the
place where we said our farewells. But he had died in the south, and
so I wrote this poem to express my grief.

I remember a former day when I and a friend
Said farewell on the bank of the River Hsiang.
In the sunlit woods, my horse neighed;
Into a curve of the hills his sail vanished.

My horse's neigh follows the old road,
The sail vanishes like a flash of lightning.
Spring comes to a thousand leagues of water weeds,
But now my old friend cannot be found.
(CTS, P. 2105)   (TR. DANIEL BRYANT)

A Song of Spring, Replying to a Poem by Po Chü-yi

Down she comes from her vermilion tower, her face freshly adorned.
Deeply immured spring light fills the courtyard with sadness.
She strolls to the center of the garden to count blossoms,
As a dragonfly flies up and alights on her jade hairpin.
(CTS, P. 2177   (TR. DANIEL BRYANT AND RONALD C. MIAO)

Tune: "Ripples Sifting Sand" (*Lang t'ao sha*)

Ripples lap the sand on the beach of Parrot Isle;
I gaze on spring from a green tower as the sun begins to set.
Little swallows race back to their nests with bites of mud;
My headstrong man, the only one who does not think of home.
(NO. 4 FROM A SERIES OF 9; CTS, P. 2172)   (TR. DANIEL BRYANT)

Po Chu-yi (772–846)

Grass on Ancient Plain: A Song of Farewell

Spreading here, spreading there, the grasses on the plain,
A cycle, a year of flourishing and decay—
Wild fires burn but can't kill them off,
When spring wind blows, they grow again.
Faraway fragrance overruns ancient roads,
Bright emerald tint spreads to ruined walls.
Again it's time to bid you farewell,
Lush growth teems with my parting thoughts.
(CTS, P. 2572)   (TR. IRVING Y. LO)

Watching the Wheat-reapers[1]

Farm families have few leisure months,
In the fifth month chores double up.
When south wind rises at night,
Fields and dikes are covered with golden wheat.

Women old and young carry baskets of food,
Children and toddlers bring out porridge in pots,
Following each other with food for the farmhands,
Those stout fellows on the southern knoll.

Their feet steamed by the sultry vapor from the soil,
Their backs scorched by the sun's burning light;   10
Drained of all strength to feel any heat,
Their only regret, summer days are too short.

Then there are those poor womenfolk,
Their children clinging to their side.
With their right hand they pick up leftover grains;
On their left arm dangles a broken basket.

To hear their words of complaint—
All who listen will grieve for them:
Their family land stripped clean to pay tax,
They now glean the field to fill their stomach.   20

What deeds of merit have I done?
I've neither farmed nor raised silkworms;
My official's salary, three hundred piculs of rice,
And at year's end there is surplus grain to eat.

Thinking of this, I feel guilty and ashamed;
All day long I cannot keep it out of my mind.
(CTS, P. 2470)   (TR. IRVING Y. LO)

---

1 Subtitle of the poem: "Written While I Was Magistrate of Chu-chi" [806].

Bitter Cold, Living in the Village

In the twelfth month of this Eighth Year,[1]
On the fifth day, a heavy snow fell.
Bamboos and cypress all perished from the freeze.
How much worse for people without warm clothes!

As I looked around the village,
Of ten families, eight or nine were in need.
The north wind was sharper than the sword,
And homespun cloth could hardly cover one's body.
Only brambles were burnt for firewood,
And sadly people sat at night to wait for dawn.   10

From this I know that when winter is harsh,
The farmers suffer most.
Looking at myself, during these days—
How I'd shut tight the gate of my thatched hall,
Cover myself with fur, wool, and silk,
Sitting or lying down, I had ample warmth.
I was lucky to be spared cold or hunger,
Neither did I have to labor in the field.

Thinking of that, how can I not feel ashamed?
I ask myself what kind of man am I.   20
(CTS, P. 2476)   (TR. IRVING Y. LO)

The Old Man of Hsin-feng with the Broken Arm[1]

An old man from Hsin-feng, eighty-eight years old,
Hair on his temples and his eyebrows white as snow.
Leaning on his great-great-grandson, he walks to the front of the inn,
His left arm on the boy's shoulder, his right arm broken.
I ask the old man how long has his arm been broken,

---

1 I.e., the eighth year of Yüan-ho, or 813.
1 Author's subtitle: To Warn Against Militarism: "New Music Bureau Ballads"
(*Hsin Yüeh-fu*), No. 9. Each poem in Po Chü-yi's "New Music Bureau Ballads"
carries a similar subtitle, which states the moral implied.

And how it came about, how it happened.
The old man said he grew up in the Hsin-feng district.
He was born during blessed times, without war or strife,
And he used to listen to the singing and dancing in the Pear Garden,
Knew nothing of banner and spear, or bow and arrow.   10
Then, during the T'ien-pao period, a big army was recruited:
From each family, one was taken out of every three,
And of those chosen, where were they sent?
Five months, ten thousand miles away, to Yunnan,
Where, it is said, the Lu River runs,
Where, when flowers fall from pepper trees, noxious fumes rise;
Where, when a great army fords the river, with its seething eddies,
Two or three out of ten never reach the other side.

The village, north and south, was full of the sound of wailing,
Sons leaving father and mother, husbands leaving wives.   20
They all said, of those who went out to fight the barbarians,
Not one out of a thousand lived to come back.
At the time, this old man was twenty-four,
And the army had his name on their roster.

"Then, late one night, not daring to let anyone know,
By stealth, I broke my arm, smashed it with a big stone.
Now I was unfit to draw the bow or carry the flag,
And I would be spared the fighting in Yunnan.
Bone shattered, muscles ached, it wasn't unpainful,
But I could count on being rejected and sent home.   30

"This arm has been broken now for over sixty years:
I've lost one limb, but the body's intact.
Even now, in cold nights, when the wind and rain blow,
Right up to daybreak, I hurt so much I cannot sleep,
But I have never had any regrets.
At least, now I alone have survived.
Or else, years ago at the River Lu,
I would have died, my spirit fled, and my bones left to rot:
I would have wandered, a ghost in Yunnan looking for home,
Mourning over the graves of ten thousands."   40

So the old man spoke: I ask you to listen.
Have you not heard of the Prime Minister of the K'ai-yüan period,
  Sung K'ai-fu?
How he wouldn't reward frontier campaigns, not wanting to glorify
  war?
And, have you not heard of Yang Kuo-chung, the Prime Minister of
  the T'ien-pao period,
Wishing to seek favor, achieved military deeds at the frontier,
But, before he could pacify the frontier, the people became
  disgruntled:
Ask the old man of Hsin-feng with the broken arm!
(CTS, P. 2492)   (TR. EUGENE EOYANG)

Red Embroidered Carpet[1]

Red embroidered carpet:
Selected cocoons are first dressed and boiled in clear water;
The choicest silk, thus reeled, is soaked in safflower juice;
Then the fibers, dyed more reddish than blue,[2]
Are woven into a carpet for the Hall of Spreading Fragrance.

Fragrance-spreading hall is over a hundred feet long,
The embroidered carpet barely enough to cover the floor.
Silk of brightest sheen is fine and soft, and the fragrance
    wafts in the breeze.
Delicate threads, embossed flowers, can hardly stand the weight,
As beautiful ladies come treading on it, singing and dancing;   10
Their gauze stockings and embroidered shoes sink with every step.

The carpet from T'ai-yüan is coarse, its fabric hard;
The quilt from Ch'eng-tu is thin, its brocaded flowers cold—
How could they compare with this carpet, warm and soft?

---

1 In the Sung edition, the title reads *Hung-hsiu t'an,* instead of *Hung-hsien t'an*
  ("red-thread carpet," a general term designating carpets made of fine threads of
  many colors). Author's subtitle: To Express Concern for the Wastefulness of
  Sericulture, "New Music Bureau Ballads," No. 29.
2 The Chinese name for safflower is "red and blue flower."

Every year, in the tenth month, when orders come to Hsüan-chou,[3]
The Governor has the carpet woven in a new elegant design,[4]
Stating that, as His Majesty's servant, he knows how to do his best.
When a hundred men together carry it into the palace,
The fabric is so thick, the silk so lavish, that it
    can't even be rolled.

Governor of Hsüan-chou, don't you know: 20
One carpet ten feet long—
A thousand ounces of silk thread?
The floor may not feel cold but people need warmth,
Please be sparing in robbing people of clothes to cover the ground!
(CTS, P. 2498)   (TR. WU-CHI LIU)

An Old Charcoal Seller[1]

An old charcoal seller
Cuts firewood, burns coal by the southern mountain.
His face, all covered with dust and ash, the color of smoke,
The hair at his temples is gray, his ten fingers black.
The money he makes selling coal, what is it for?
To put clothes on his back and food in his mouth.
The rags on his poor body are thin and threadbare;
Distressed at the low price of coal, he hopes for colder weather.
Night comes, an inch of snow has fallen on the city,
In the morning, he rides his cart along the icy ruts,   10
His ox weary, he hungry, and the sun already high.
In the mud by the south gate, outside the market, he stops to rest.
All of a sudden, two dashing riders appear;
An imperial envoy, garbed in yellow (his attendant in white),
Holding an official dispatch, he reads a proclamation.
Then turns the cart around, curses the ox, and leads it north.
One cartload of coal—a thousand or more catties!
No use appealing to the official spiriting the cart away:

---

[3] In modern Anhwei, a scenic area also known for the manufacture of a fine
grade of paper.
[4] *Author's note:* "In the middle of Chen-yüan reign, the Governor of Hsüan-chou
presented a carpet made of extra silk in new patterns (*k'ai-yang chia-ssu*)."
[1] Author's subtitle: To Complain of the Royal Commissionary System, "New
Music Bureau Ballads," No. 32.

Half a length of red lace, a slip of damask
Dropped on the ox—is payment in full!   20
(CTS, P. 2498)   (TR. EUGENE EOYANG)

A Traveler's Moon

I, a traveler, came from south of the river,
When the moon was only a crescent.
In my long, distant journeying,
I've seen thrice its clear light in full.
At dawn I travel with a waning moon;
When night falls, I lodge with the new moon.
Who says that the moon has no feeling?
It has kept me company for hundreds of miles.
In the morning I set out from the bridge of the Wei River,
In the evening I enter the streets of Ch'ang-an.   10
But I wonder about the moon tonight:
In whose home will it be a guest?
(CTS, P. 2559)   (TR. CHIANG YEE)

Painting Bamboo: A Song

Preface: Music Supervisor Hsiao Yüeh is good at painting bamboo and considered without equal by his contemporaries. Hsiao himself prizes his art—so much so that there are those who spend years begging him without avail for but one twig or spear. Knowing that by nature I love those things, he makes me a present of a painting with fifteen spears. Touched by his feeling for me, and valuing his art, I write this song to reciprocate. All together, 186 words [in the Chinese original].

Of all the plants, bamboo is the most difficult to paint.
Among ancient and modern painters, none has caught its likeness.
Master Hsiao's brush alone brings out the similitude—
He's the one supreme artist in the history of painting.

Others paint the bamboo thick and gnarled;
Hsiao paints each spear lean and sturdy.
Others paint the bamboo tufts lifeless, limp, and drooping,
Hsiao paints the branches alive, as if each leaf were seen to move.

Without roots, these bamboos grow from his mind;
Without shoots, these bamboos are shaped by his brush.   10
By a deserted creek, beside a winding bank,
Two clusters, fifteen spears, dense and luxuriant.
Pretty like a girl with a softly powdered face,
Somber, summing up all the aura of wind and mist.

I look up and suddenly forget it is a painting;
Inclined my ears to listen in quiet, I seem to hear their sounds.
In the western corner, seven spears vigorous and strong—
I clearly remember seeing them before a rock at T'ien-chu Monastery[1];
In the eastern corner, eight spears sparse and lean—
I recall having seen them in the rain at the Temple of the Goddess
    Hsiang.[2]   20

Elegant airs, deep thoughts, are appreciated by few;
We look at each other, and I sigh in vain.
What a pity Master Hsiao is getting old,
His hands tremble, his eyes dim, his head the color of snow!
He says that this is his last painting;
From now on such bamboos will be the hardest to find.
(CTS, PP. 2560–61)   (TR. IRVING Y. LO)

On a Moonlit Night, Sent to My Brothers and Sisters[1]

Hard times, bad year, and a family dispossessed—
Brothers all stranded in strange lands, east and west.
Field and garden made desolate by the ravages of war,

---

[1] T'ien-chu ("Heavenly Bamboo") Monastery is located on T'ien-chu Mountain near Hangchow.

[2] This temple is located on Chün-shan, in Lake Tung-t'ing, near Yüeh-yang, Hunan, believed to be inhabited by two sisters, consorts of Emperor Shun. According to legend, the sisters wept so bitterly at his death that the bamboos growing there became streaked with their tears. Henceforth, this variety of bamboos comes to be known as *pan-chu,* or "streaked bamboos."

[1] The original title reads as follows: "Having encountered fighting in Honan and delays and starvation within the pass, with my elder and younger brothers scattered to various places, I was moved, while watching the moon, to write down my thoughts. Sent to Eldest Brother at Fu-liang [in modern Kiangsi], Seventh Brother at Yü-ch'ien [in modern Chekiang], Fifteenth Brother at Wu-chiang [in modern Anhwei], and also given to my younger brothers and sisters at Fu-li [in modern Anhwei] and at Hsia-kuei [in modern Shensi]."

Flesh and blood cast adrift upon the road.
Dispersed—the lonely shadows of far-ranging wild geese;
Uprooted—the scattered tumbleweeds of autumn.
As we all watch the bright moon, there should be tears;
One night the homesick heart at five places feels the same.
(CTS, P. 2574)   (TR. IRVING Y. LO)

Reading the Collected Works of Li Po and Tu Fu: A Colophon

The time the Hanlin scholar was south of the River,[1]
The junior official made his home in Szechwan.[2]
You two never held any high rank or position,
Still you met with turmoil and hardship.
The remorse of a wanderer in the evening of his life;
The laments of a banished Muse in this floating world—
Both your songs and rhymes will last a thousand ages,
Your fame and renown will move the barbarians.
The learned world draws on your elegant lines,
The Music Bureau[3] awaits your new verses.   10
Heaven's wish you certainly have fulfilled:
For all people love great poetry.
(CTS, P. 2593)   (TR. IRVING Y. LO)

Parrot

Talk all day and then keep silent;
Midnight, still restless on its perch.
Body imprisoned for its bright plumage;
Heart embittered by understanding.
Dusk arouses thoughts of return to nest;
Springtime multiplies mating calls.

---

[1] Referring to the time when Li Po was on the staff of Prince Yung (Li Lin), whose rebellion against the throne implicated the poet.
[2] Referring to the time Tu Fu was living in Szechwan after the An Lu-shan rebellion and served on the staff of Governor General Yen Wu.
[3] *Yüeh-fu* ("Music Bureau") poetry, which generally contains social criticism, was always regarded by Po Chü-yi as in the mainstream of Chinese poetic tradition.

Who can break this cage open,
Released, to joy in flight and song?
(CTS, P. 2617)   (TR. IRVING Y. LO)

"Lotus-gatherer's Song"

Caltrop leaves tug on the waves, the lotus quivers in the wind;
Where the lotus flowers grow dense, a small boat passes through.
Wishing to speak to her lover, she nods her head and smiles—
A hairpin of green jade falls into the water.
(CTS, P. 2631)   (TR. IRVING Y. LO)

"Song of the Rear Palace"

Tears wet her gauze kerchief, she cannot sleep,
Night deepens, she taps to the tune from the front palace;
A pink complexion unaged, yet favor already lapsed,
Leaning by the incense burner, she sits till dawn.
(CTS, P. 2623)   (TR. RONALD C. MIAO)

Evening View at River Pavilion, Inviting Guest

Eastward the sea and sky, and a lengthening evening;
The massive looks of the hills, and the serpentine river—
Lamplights in ten thousand homes all around the city,
The River of Stars[1] reflected like a ribbon in the water.
The wind blows on ancient trees—rain on a sunny day;
The moon shines on level sand—frost in a summer night.
Won't you come to my river pavilion to escape the heat?
Your thatched hut can't compare with this for cool breeze.
(CTS, P. 2638)   (TR. IRVING Y. LO)

"The Crow Cries at Night"

Late, when it returns from the city wall;
Perilous, where it perches for the night in a courtyard—
The moon brightens a leafless tree,

---

[1] I.e., the Milky Way.

Frost makes slippery the windy branches.
Crying hoarse, its throat is parched;
Flying low, its frozen wings droop.

The parrots in the painted hall
Do not know cold from warmth.
(CTS, P. 2690)   (TR. IRVING Y. LO)

Tune: "Flower Unlike Flower" (*Hua fei hua*)

A flower, and yet not a flower
Of mist, and yet not of mist
At midnight she comes
And at daybreak, leaves.
She comes like a spring dream, for how long?
She goes like morning dew, without a trace.
(PHSSCCC, 12/11b–12a)   (TR. EUGENE EOYANG)

Tune: "Ripples Sifting Sand," Two Lyrics

[1]

How can the tide of the river be compared to your love?
Or the waters of the sea to a woman's heart?
Missing you, I'd rather have the tide that keeps its promise;
Longing for you, I begin to realize the ocean is not as deep.

[2]

There'll be a day when dust flies at the bottom of the sea.
And the time will come for the mountainside to crumble into stones.
Who'd know that when a young lover casts aside his woman,
Once he has boarded a boat, there is no date of his return?
(NOS. 4–5 FROM A SERIES OF 6; PHSSHC, 12/13b)   (TR. IRVING Y. LO)

Liu Tsung-yüan (773–819)

Viewing Mountains with His Reverence Hao Ch'u
To My Friends and Relatives in the Capital

These coastal mountains are as sharp as swords;
When autumn comes each cleaves my sore heart.
If my body could dissolve into a thousand selves,
I'd have them scattered on the highest peaks to gaze homeward.
(CTS, P. 2074)   (TR. JAN W. WALLS)

Arriving at North Pond by Stupid Brook
on a Morning Walk After the Rain

Hovering clouds scatter over the islet,
early morning sun brightens the village;
in tall trees by the clear pond
a breeze startles last night's raindrops.
My mind is meant for idleness
and by this chance we become guest and host.
(CTS, P. 2083)   (TR. JAN W. WALLS)

Written in Jest on Elder Stonegate's
Eastern Balcony

Elder Stonegate treats the body like a dream;
his hand-planted sandalwood has grown into a grove.
He sits and ponders, ponders, that he is not a man of old:
Lotus Blossoms[1] everywhere, and for whose use?
Now at seventy he has forgotten the contentions of the world,
forgotten love and desire, his sinews weak.
He'd better not gaze from Eastern Balcony over the spring fields:
blossoms are blooming, the sun rising, and pheasants in flight.
(CTS, P. 2083)   (TR. JAN W. WALLS)

---

1 "Lotus Blossoms" refers to the *Saddharma Pundarika* ("Lotus of the Wonderful Law"), one of the important Mahayana sutras in the Chinese Buddhist Tripitaka.

Drinking at Night in the Western Pavilion
of the Fa-hua Temple

In the Jeta Pavilion of the Setting Sun
together we pour the Samadhi wine.
Mist darkens—the stream floods to the stairs;
the moon shines bright—blossoms cover the lattice.
Don't tire of getting drunk from the cup;
see how many heads are not yet white.
(CTS, P. 2083)   (TR. JAN W. WALLS)

Meditation Hall

Clear the land, thatch the rush for roof,
all around cherish the empty, the pure.
Mountain blossoms fall by a secluded door,
within, one who has forgotten the world's schemings.
Concern with existence needs no possession,
comprehending the void does not wait upon reason.
All things are of conditions born,
profound is the silence in the midst of clamor.
A man's mind is very much the same:
a bird in flight, leaving no tracks behind.   10
(CTS, P. 2085)   (TR. JAN W. WALLS)

Feeling Old Age

I've always known that old age would arrive,
and suddenly now I witness its encroach.
This year, luckily, I've not weakened much
but gradually it comes to seek me out.
Teeth scattered, hair grown short,
To run or hurry, I haven't the strength.
So, I cry, what's to be done!
And yet, why should I suffer?
P'eng-tsu and Lao Tzu no more exist;
Chuang Tzu and K'ung Tzu too are gone.   10
Of those whom the ancients called "immortal saints"

not one is left today.
I only wish for fine wine
and friends who will often help me pour.
Now that spring is drawing to a close
and peach and plum produce abundant shade
and the sun lights up the azure sky
and far, far, the homeward goose cries,
I step outside, greeting those I love,
and climb to the western woods with the aid of my staff.   20
Singing out loud is enough to cheer me up;
the ancient hymns have overtones.
(CTS, P. 2080)   (TR. JAN W. WALLS)

Farmers, Two Selections

[1]

Beyond the bamboo fence, cooking fire and smoke,
an evening when neighboring farmers chat.
From courtyard's edge autumn insects chirrup,
scattered hempstalks, now desolate and alone.
Silk from the worms all surrendered as tax,
loom and shuttle lean idly on the wall.
An officer passes through one night,
and is served a feast of fowl and millet.
Everyone says the official is harsh,
his language full of reprimands.   10
East villagers are behind in their rent
and wagon wheels sink in mire and bog.
Officials' residences are short on mercy;
where whips and rods are given fiendish rein.
We must attend cautiously to our work,
for flesh and skin are to be pitied.
We welcome now the new year's arrival,
fearing only to tread on the former tracks.

[2]

By an ancient road, abundant thistle plants
writhe around the curves of the old town wall.

Smartweed blossoms blanket the dike,
water in the dam is cold and clear.
Now, the reaping of the harvest done,
woodsmen and herdsmen return with the setting sun.
Elm and willow are sparse in the strong winds,
pear and date ripen under heavy frost.
The traveler at a loss: to go or to stay,
wild birds struggle for a roosting spot.   10
Old farmers, smiling, bid each other
to be cautious on high grounds when darkness falls.
This year we are thankful for a fair harvest,
with sufficient rice and gruel.
(NOS. 2–3 FROM A SERIES OF 3; CTS, P. 2086)   (TR. JAN W. WALLS)

On Covering the Bones of Chang Chin, the Hired Man

The cycle of life is a worrisome thing,
a single breath that gathers and scatters again.
We come by chance into a hubbub of joy and rage
and suddenly we're taking leave again.
To be an underling is no disgrace,
neither is nobility divine;
all at once when breathing stops,
fair and ugly disappear in decay.
You slaved in my stables all your life,
cutting fodder, you never complained you were tired.   10
When you died we gave you a cheap coffin
and buried you at the foot of the eastern hill.
But then, alas, there came a raging flood
that left you helter-skelter by the roadside.
Dry and brittle, your hundred bones baked in the sun,
scattered about, never to join again.
Luckily an attendant told me of this,
and the vision saddened me to tears,
for even cats and tigers rate a sacrificial offering,
and dogs and horses have their ragged shrouds.   20
Long I stand here mourning for your soul
yet how could you know of this act?
Basket and spade bear you to the grave

which waterways will keep from further harm.
My mind is now at ease
whether you know it or not.
One should wait for spring to cover up bones,
and propitious is the time now.
Benevolence for all things is not mine to confer;
just call it a personal favor for you.   30
(CTS, PP. 2088–89)   (TR. JAN W. WALLS)

Yüan Chen (779–831)

Three Dreams at Chiang-ling[1]

I

When one dreams of another,
Are both aware of it?
We're apart as darkness is from light,
My dream soul exists only for you
True nothing can be gained from dreams,
But without them how would I see you?
Tonight and how many nights
Have they chanced us a meeting!
Shadowy, the clothes you wore before,
Dimmed, but still your former visage;   10
You never mention what keeps us apart,
You only say you have to go.
Your sewing's still strewn about,
The curtains yet are folded;
You often ask after the child,
Countless the tears you've shed.

---

1 This poetic series written c. A.D. 809 describes the dreams of a husband for his
wife who had died, usually understood specifically as referring to the poet and
his wife. It was popularly believed in T'ang dynasty China that there were two
souls: a *hun* or spiritual soul, and a *p'o,* the animal soul. The *hun* not only con-
tinued to exist after death, but could also wander about during dreams. The
first poem of this series presents a dream dialogue between two such souls
(*hun*).
    In the autumn of 809, because of antagonism between Yüan Chen and
prominent eunuchs, he was sent to Chiang-ling (in modern Hupeh), where he
served until 813.

You said: "We have only this daughter,
And sighed to have no son[2];
I remember her then, so naughty and cute,
I can't bear to think of her hungry or cold!   20
You showed no interest in the family,
You took a post, left things behind!
No need to mention the bonds of official duties,
How could you have paid heed to private affairs?
Others have caused us to be alienated;
We were often deceived by our servants—
So long as you're around there'll be someone to trust,
But if you should leave, who's to care for the child?"

Her speech ended, tears choked her throat,
I, too, wept a fountain of tears—   30

Grieved and startled; I am suddenly awake,
Sitting or sleeping it's as if I were mad;
The shadow of the moon has blackened half the bed,
The sounds of insects drift across the gloom of the grass;
My senses come back to me slowly,
Though awakened, I still am distraught;
Alone as I picture your face
Tears come and never seem to end!
Life's final parting is already ours,
How could a single dream bring so many sorrows?   40
Sorrow for our daughter you spoiled,
Whom I've left behind, unable to follow me here[3];
Ch'ang-an is more distant than the sun,
Mountains, rivers, and clouds separate us![4]
Even if I could sprout wings,
The net of worldly affairs binds me hand and foot![5]
Tonight my tears drop down,

---

[2] Yüan Chen married a Miss Wei in 802; their only child was Fan-tzu, a daughter, cf. Yüan Chen's laments on her death, *Yüan Shih Ch'ang-ch'ing chi* (SPTK ed.), Ch. 9, fol. 6a.
[3] Referring to Yüan Fan-tzu, see note 2 above. The girl was evidently left in the capital city when Yüan Chen took up his provincial post in 809.
[4] Yüan Chen's wife was buried at Ch'ang-an, cf. poem II of this series.
[5] The nets of the law, a not uncommon trope to depict the plight of an exile at this time.

Half for the partings I've endured in life!
They stir me toward your soul down there,
They move my thoughts nearer the stream: 50
I can't even cross a single river,
And the Styx, it has no shores![6]
This longing: how can it end?
This dream: how to pursue it?
I sit here watching the sky about to light,
The river wind humming in the trees.

II

In the ancient plain,[7] a thirty-foot tomb,
Buried deeply, a sprig of coral[8];
Slides have shut the mountain's door,
Mist has joined the grave mounds now sprouting grass;   60
Long upon those wild slopes I sat,
But now I have gone away to distant villages;
Startled awake by the moon flooding my bed,
Wind and waves are heard from the river.

III

Your bones have long since turned to dust,
My heart for just as long to ashes!
A hundred-year life has no end!
For three nights you've come to me in a dream.
The flowing waters have passed and are gone,
The floating clouds, where are they now?   70
As I sit watching the morning sun come up,
A flock of birds by twos returns.
(CTS, P. 2384)   (TR. WILLIAM H. NIENHAUSER)

---

6 Literally, the "Yellow Springs," the Chinese Hades.
7 This plain, like the plain in Yüan Chen's poem "The Pitcher" (cf. Arthur
  Waley's translation, *Madly Singing in the Mountains* [New York, 1970] p. 189),
  is that of the graveyard at Ch'ang-an.
8 The sprig of coral refers to Yüan Chen's wife.

To the Waters of the Chia-ling,[1] Two Poems

[1]

Long ago you were perhaps
                    a river flowing down a mountain!
Since then you've been flowing,
                    deepening your bed;
If I could make a river current
                    understand human feeling,
Then you might know my mind
                    on coming from so far.

[2]

You, waters with no feeling,
Have you regrets as you flow east?
In my heart are things I cannot express,
Does that make me different from you?
(CTS, PP. 2429, 2411)   (TR. WILLIAM H. NIENHAUSER)

Drunk Too Soon

Today before a goblet of wine I was shamed,
My third cup unfinished, I couldn't pour another.
Wondering why I am always drunk beneath the flowers,
Perhaps the spring breeze has made me tipsy.
(CTS, P. 2413)   (TR. DELL R. HALES)

Recalling When I Was Drunk

I sigh to myself I am traveling far,
Curse the wine that delays my return;
Today we chance to meet, sober we part;
Wind dries my tears as I recall being drunk.
(CTS, P. 2413)   (TR. DELL R. HALES)

---

1 These two poems were written while the poet was en route to a remote and unimportant post in Szechwan, virtually an exile.

Sobering Up

Drinking until drunk, the day is nearly gone;
I sober up when night is almost over.
Wind fans the flame in the dim lamp at dawn;
By the river window, the spring mat is cold.

My belt still untied around me;
Wobbly, my cap falling on the pillow.
I call my son to ask about all this mess,
Fancying I am still in a happy dream.
(CTS, P. 2408)   (TR. DELL R. HALES)

Late Spring

Evening swallows keep twittering by my curtain,
Pairs of sparrows squabble, stir up dust on the steps;
The wind closes my wicker gate at sundown,
Quietly the flowers fall one by one, but no one comes.
(CTS, P. 2413)   (TR. DELL R. HALES)

Sent to Lo-t'ien [Po Chü-yi] for Thinking of Me After the Rainfall

Treacherous rain and perilous bridge made me fear for my life,
Indeed one faulty step would be the last of me.
In a way T'ung-chou is not different from the nether world:
The deeper I sink into the mud, the closer I approach it.
(CTS, P. 2431)   (TR. ANGELA JUNG PALANDRI)

Apricot Garden

Carriages and horses stir up Ch'ang-an's thick dust—
Brought here by the wild wind each spring.
In front of my door is only a void,
Why plant flowers then to delude others?
(CTS, P. 2412)   (TR. ANGELA JUNG PALANDRI)

Mourning My Son

May you be reborn in the supreme lotus, the realm of truth,
But *Tushita*[1] is far away from the ways of this world.
Our karma differs; you and I will be apart—
I do not know if in a future life we shall meet again.
(NO. 4 FROM A SERIES OF 10; CTS, P. 2386)

(TR. ANGELA JUNG PALANDRI)

Song of the Weaving Woman

Busy is the life of the weaving woman!
Silkworms are about to grow old after their third sleep,
And soon the silkworm goddess will start to make silk;
Early too comes this year's levy of the silk tax.
This early tax is not the evil doing of the officials—
The government has been waging wars since last year:
Soldiers in bitter fighting bandage their sword wounds;
The great general, his merits high, changes his gauze curtain.

She'd continue her effort to reel threads and weave silk,
But the tangled skeins on the loom give her trouble.   10

In the house to the east, a white-haired man has two daughters;
He won't marry them off because they're skilled in embroidery.
Amid the floating gossamers on the eaves,
A spider nimbly plies back and forth.
Admirable are the insects that understand Heaven's way:
They know how to spin a gossamer web in the void.
(CTS, PP. 2439–40)   (TR. WU-CHI LIU)

---

1 The text reads *tou-shuai,* a transliteration for the Sanskrit *tushita,* or "one of
the heavens," and specifically the heaven resided in by Maitreya, the future
Buddha. Actually, Yüan Chen got this mixed up with the heaven of Amitabha
(symbolized by lotus) in the previous line.

On Lien-ch'ang Palace[1]

Lien-ch'ang Palace was overgrown with bamboo,
Long years untended, it turned into a thicket;
The double-flowering peach trees,[2] towering above the walls,
Shed red showers when the wind stirred.

By the palace gate an old man with tears told me:
"Once in my youth I was there to bring food to the palace.
The Grand Emperor was in the Fairy-viewing Hall,
T'ai-chen leaned against the railing by his side.
Above the hall and in front, whirled jade and pearls;
Sparkling, they reflected heaven and earth.   10
I returned as in a dream, and with my senses gone.
How could I relate in full these palace affairs?

"The Feast of Cold Food had just come,
        a hundred and six days after winter solstice,
No chimney smoke rose from rooftops
        and palace trees were turning green.
At midnight when the moon was high
        string music was heard upstairs—
Master Ho's p'i-p'a[3] set the stage for chamber music.

"Then Eunuch Kao passed along the order to search for Nien-nu,[4]
Who was elsewhere entertaining her guests in private.
Soon she was found and urged to hurry;
By special edict, the streets were lit with candles.   20

---

1 Lien-ch'ang Kung, built in 658 by Emperor Kao-tsung, was located near Lo-yang, known as the "Eastern Capital." In his poem Yüan Chen employs as the narrator an old rustic who was supposed to have witnessed the vicissitudes of the country before and after the An Lu-shan Rebellion. T'ai-chen was the name of Hsüan-tsung's Royal Consort, Yang Kuei-fei.

2 The Chinese equivalent is *pi-t'ao*, another name for *ch'ien-yeh t'ao*, literally "thousand-leafed peach," which is used in the original text. I choose to use "double-flowering" because it enhances the imagery of the "red shower" in the following line.

3 Ho Chih-huai, a famous *p'i-p'a* player of the T'ang dynasty.

4 Nien-nu was a favorite courtesan of the T'ien-pao period (742–55), famous for her singing.

Her eyes full of spring coyness as she reclines in red silk,
Tidying her cloud-like hair she hurriedly dressed.

"When she sang her voice soared to the ninth heaven,
Followed by the treble of a young musician's[5] flute.
The twanging music of Liang-chou[6] filled the palace,
The deeper tunes of Kuchah[7] followed along.
Outside the palace wall, holding the flute, Li Mu[8]
Stole several new melodies he overheard.

"At dawn the imperial entourage departed from Lien-ch'ang,
And thousands of people danced in joy along the road;   30
Processions of officials avoided the path of Princes Ch'i and Hsüeh[9];
In their carriages, the Yang sisters[10] raced with the wind.

"In the tenth month next year, the Eastern Capital fell:
The imperial road, still intact, the rebels now trod.
Pressed for provisions, no one dared to hide.
Silently the people shed secret tears.

"Six or seven years after both capitals were restored,
I came back to search for my homesite near this palace—
The village was razed by fire, only dried wells remained;
The palace gate was shut: trees and gardens were still there.   40

---

5 The text reads "Er-shih-wu-lang" (Young Master Twenty-fifth), a famous pipe
  player of Pin-chou.
6 The music from Liang-chou became very popular during the T'ang times and
  was adopted as court music.
7 The Chinese transliteration is "Chiu-tzu," a country in Central Asia.
8 There was a legend that when Emperor Hsüan-tsung went incognito into the
  city of Lo-yang during a lantern festival, he suddenly heard the music of a
  flute coming from a tavern and recognized it to be the melody which he had
  just composed and which the court musicians had tried out the night before.
  The following day he had the flute player arrested and brought to the palace
  for questioning. The young man said that he was Li Mu of Ch'ang-an. While
  enjoying the moon on the Bridge of Tientsin, he overheard the music coming
  out of the palace and recorded it on the railing of the bridge. The Emperor
  was impressed and had the young man dismissed.
9 I.e., Prince Ch'i (Li Fan) and Prince Hsüeh (Li Yeh); both were younger
  brothers of Hsüan-tsung, who erected Hua-o-Lou (mentioned later in the poem)
  for them to occupy.
10 The three Yang sisters were cousins of T'ai-chen.

"Since that time six emperors[11] have ascended the throne,
But Lien-ch'ang Palace remains long unvisited.
Young travelers coming here, talked about Ch'ang-an:
They said the Hsüan-wu Tower[12] was now completed but Hua-o
    abandoned.

"Last year an order came to cut down the palace bamboo,
By chance I found the gate open and stepped in:
Thorns and brambles thickly clogged the imperial pond,
Proud foxes and doltish hares capered around trees;
The dance pavilion had collapsed, its foundation still there;
The ornamented windows were dim, but the screens still green;   50
Dust covered the old filigrees on painted walls;
Crows had pecked the wind chimes, scattering pearls and jade.

"The Grand Emperor specially loved terraced flowers,
His royal couch still lay aslant above the garden steps.
Snakes emerging from swallows' nests coiled and fought on the beams;
Mushrooms grew on the altar in the central hall.
Adjoining the royal bedchamber was the Tuan-cheng Tower,[13]
Where T'ai-chen once washed and combed her hair.
In the early dawn the curtains cast their dark shadows—
Even now, by coral hooks, hung there upside down.   60

"Pointing out these to others, I could not but grieve,
My tears continued to fall long after I left the palace.
Since then the palace gate has been closed once more,
Night after night foxes climb up to the gate and towers."

---

11 Although the poem was undated, internal evidence indicates that it was com-
posed about 816–17, during the last years of Hsien-tsung's reign (806–20).
Consequently, there could be only five emperors that succeeded the throne since
Hsüan-tsung. Since all editions of this poem have "six" instead of "five," it
could not be a typographical error. Some critics tend to think that perhaps the
text was tempered by Eunuch Ts'ui T'an-chün, who changed the "five emperors"
to "six" in order to include the new emperor Mu-tsung (reigned 821–24), to
whom he had presented Yüan Chen's poems. One other explanation is that the
poet purposely created the error to indicate the faulty memory of the old man.
See Ch'en Yin-k'o, Yüan Pai shih chan-cheng k'ao (Taipei, 1963), p. 76.
12 Hsüan-wu Lou, built during Te-Tsung's reign (780–804), used to house palace
guards; Hua-o-Lou was built by Hsüan-tsung for his brothers.
13 Tuan-cheng Lou was actually in the Hua-ch'ing Palace in Ch'ang-an and not
in Lien-ch'ang Palace.

Hearing his words, I ached in my heart and bones:
Who brings peace to the empire? Who brings war?
"What difference is there," said the old man, "to a peasant like me?
I tell only of what my ears have heard and my eyes have seen.

"When Yao Ch'ung and Sung Ching were ministers[14]
Their counsels to the emperor were firm and earnest.　　　　70
The *yin* and *yang* in accord, harvest was full;
Harmony prevailed and peace reigned over the land,
High officials were upright, local magistrates just.
For they were all chosen by the ministers.

"K'ai-yüan[15] period closed with the death of Yao and Sung,
Gradually, the imperial consort had her way at court.
Since she brought An Lu-shan into the palace as an "adopted son,"
In front of Madame Kuo's mansion, 'twas busier than a market place.

"I have forgotten the names of those powerful ministers
But vaguely remember they were Yang and Li,[16]　　　　80
Who caused disorder in government that shook the four seas—
For fifty years the nation has groaned from its wounds.

"Our present Emperor is wise and the ministers have foresight,
No sooner was the imperial edict issued than
　　　Wu and Shu were pacified[17];
Now government troops have captured Huai-hsi from the rebels[18];
When those rebels are quelled, the world will be at peace.
For years we have tilled the waste land before the palace,
Now I won't send my sons and theirs to do the plowing."

---

14 Yao Ch'ung (650–721) was President of the Board of War under Hsüan-tsung;
　Sung Ching (662–737) was Minister of State.
15 I.e., 713–41.
16 I.e., Yang Kuo-chung (d. 756) was a cousin of T'ai-chen; Li Lin-fu (d. 752)
　was of imperial extraction, and became the President of the Board of Rites
　through his friendship with another imperial concubine before Yang came into
　favor at court.
17 The rebel leader of Shu was Liu P'i, and that of Wu was Li Ch'i.
18 The rebel leader of Huai-hsi was Wu Yüan-chi. It took three years of fight-
　ing before he was captured in the twelfth year of the Yüan-ho period (817).

I am deeply moved by the old man's thoughts;
Let's spare no effort to put an end to all wars.   90
(CTS, P. 2443)   (TR. ANGELA JUNG PALANDRI)

Chia Tao (779–849)

Weeping for the Zen Master Po-yen

Moss covers his stone bed fresh—
How many springs did the master occupy it?
They sketched to preserve his form practicing the Way,
But burned away the body that sat in meditation.
The pagoda garden closes in snow on the pines,
While the library locks dust in the chinks.
I hate myself for these lines of tears falling—
I am not a man who understands the Void.
(CTS, P. 3473)   (TR. STEPHEN OWEN)

Evening View as the Snow Clears

I lean on my staff, gaze at the sunlit snow,
Clouds and gullies in countless layers.
The woodcutter returns to his plain hut,
As the winter sun falls behind sheer peaks.
A wildfire burns over the grass of the hills;
Broken patches of mist rise from among the rocks and pines.
Then, turning back on the mountain temple road,
I hear the bells ring in the evening sky.
(CTS, P. 3485)   (TR. STEPHEN OWEN)

Spending the Night at a Mountain Temple

A host of peaks rear up into the color of cold,
At this point the road splits to the meditation hall.
Shooting stars pierce through bare trees,
And a rushing moon retreats from moving clouds.
Visitors come but rarely to the very summit;

Cranes do not flock together in the tall pines.
There is a monk, eighty years old,
Who has never heard of what happens in the world.
(CTS, P. 3488)   (TR. STEPHEN OWEN)

Passing by a Mountain Village: Evening

For several miles I have heard the chill waters,
Homes in the mountain, no one else around—
Strange birds scream over the broad plain;
The setting sun puts fear into the traveler's heart.
A new moon before the twilight's gone,
Beacons of war never come this far—
There in the gloom beyond the mulberries
Are home fires to which I gradually draw closer.
(CTS, P. 3488)   (TR. STEPHEN OWEN)

Sick Cicada

A sick cicada, unable now to fly,
Walks over onto my palm.
Its broken wings can still grow thinner.
And its bitter songs are clear as ever.
Dewdrops stick on its belly,
Dust specks fallen by mischance in its eyes.
The oriole and the kite as well
Both harbor the thought of your ruin.
(CTS, P. 3483)   (TR. STEPHEN OWEN)

Chang Yu[1] (*fl. 810*)

Presented to a Lady Within the Palace

Forbidden gate, palace trees, a moon's flitting trace,
Seductive eyes gaze askance at night-nesting egrets.
Leaning, she plucks her jade hairpin in the lamplight,
Pricks apart the ruddy flame to save a flying moth.
(CTS, P. 3082)   (TR. RONALD C. MIAO)

---

1 Chang's given name is sometimes written Hu.

"Song of Farewell" in the Tartar Mode[1]

The sheen of the willows spreads ten thousand feet,
The fragrance of peach blossoms fills the park.
But when the wind blows it past the curtain,
There's only the scent that clings to the dress.
(CTS, P. 3079)   (TR. IRVING Y. LO)

Yellow Sunflower of Szechwan

Rare flower, leaf-fringed, of tender yellow gold—
Its sheen, reflected on my studio window, penetrates the bamboo grove.
What could prevent a beautiful girl from casually smelling it?
I almost thought it was her lover's mouth[1] imprinted in the center.
(CTS, P. 3085)   (TR. IRVING Y. LO)

Li Ho (791–817)

In Protest

South Mountain![1] So full of sorrows!
Ghost-haunted rains damp its forsaken grass.
On autumn midnights in Ch'ang-an
How many are growing old in that mountain wind!
Dim and uncertain, its footpaths at dusk;
Writhing upward, dark oaks line the road.
When the moon is high, trees rise from their shadows,
And over the whole mountain—a white dawn!

---

1 The original title of this poem reads: *Hu Wei-chou,* a *yüch-fu* title. Wei-chou, or Lung-hsi, in Kansu, was a traditional place of parting.
1 *T'an-k'ou,* literally "sandalwood mouth," referring to the color of the sunflower at the center, but it also puns on *t'an-lang* (*t'an* written with the same character), which means "husband."
1 I.e., Chung-nan Shan, lying southeast of Ch'ang-an. Scattered over its slopes were many graveyards.

Lacquer grave-lamps greet the new arrivals;
Fireflies by shadowy tombs are flickering, flickering[2] . . .   10
(NO. 3 FROM A SERIES OF 5; CTS, P. 2331) (TR. MAUREEN ROBERTSON)

Ravine on a Cold Evening

White foxes[1] howl at mountain wind beneath the moon;
Its autumn cold sweeps up clouds and leaves a sapphire void.
Jade mists shimmering wet are white as curtains;
The Silver Channel's[2] arcing swell flows to the eastern sky.
By the stream a sleeping egret dreams of migrating geese;
Faint ripples, without a murmur, drift slowly by.
Twisting cliffs of layered hills, dragons coil on coil;
Bitter bamboo[3] sound for a stranger their sighing flutes.
(CTS, P. 2341)   (TR. MAUREEN ROBERTSON)

Pleasures of the Night

Red silk lines the chamber curtains, their tassels fringed with gold;
A chased candelabra's nine branches are hung with figures of carp.
Gorgeous girls, shimmering in the moonlight, unfasten the ringed latch;
They serve up spring freshets of wine from a gibbon-shaped jar.
The price is dear—a casket of incense, ten sticks;
Gold nuggets (pink "melon-seeds" and dark "bran-meal");
A green jade duck, with a cover worked in five colors—
But A Hou[1] requires these gifts with a measureless wealth of smiles!
Over her south rooms, when heaven's river recedes, shadows fade from
    blinds;
Crows call from the *t'ung* groves, snug in nests with their young.   10
The fine sword and whip he carries are crusted with green quartz and
    pearls;

---

[2] Fireflies were thought to be metamorphosed from wet, rotting matter and hence
    were known as the embodiments of the *yin* principle of the universe.
[1] White animals, especially foxes, often appear as manifestations of the super-
    natural in Chinese lore.
[2] I.e., the River of Heaven, or Milky Way.
[3] A variety of bamboo used in the manufacture of song-flutes.
[1] The nickname of a beautiful and accomplished fourth-century woman whose
    connection with the statesman Hsieh An became the subject of stories. Li Ho
    calls this latter-day girl A Hou as a tribute to her charm and beauty.

His white steed snorts froth that congeals on the frosty mane.
As the water clock brims, she sends jade pendants off to Ch'eng Ming
    Lodge[2];
The storied pleasure house looms high, lonely in the moonlight.
The next guest dismounts as the old guest goes;
And again she touches up jet brows, combs her shining dark coiffure.
(CTS, P. 2345)   (TR. MAUREEN ROBERTSON)

Young Man with a Yellow Hat[1]

Young man with a yellow hat,
You jump into your boat and leave, not to return.
By the southern bank, shadowing the water,
Red lotus, grieving, droops its head.

Sounds of water recall the girdle-pendants of Lady Hsiang[2];
Bamboos weep in the dew-lit mountains in the moonlight.
A jade zither plays the tune of the "Green Gate"[3]:
Clouds among the rocks moisten the yellow vines.[4]

Above the sand, deer-parsley flowers bloom,
The autumn wind has already come.   10
Will she, broom in hand, sweep the gossamer mat,
And warm the mandarin ducks with incense?[5]
(CTS, P. 2327)   (TR. MICHAEL FISH)

Temple of the Orchid Fragrance Goddess

Ancient spring year after year abides,
Idle greenery sways beneath warm clouds,

---

2 Pendants were insignia of high office; hence, a metonymy for an important
  official ("guest" in l. 15) who was staying at Ch'eng Ming Lodge while waiting
  for an audience with the emperor.
1 The "Yellow Hat" was the customary dress or insignia of boatmen. The color
  yellow symbolizes earth, and in the Five Elements' schema, earth conquers
  water.
2 "Lady Hsiang" could be plural or singular; in either case it refers to the God-
  desses of the Hsiang.
3 "Green Gate" refers to a song no longer extant.
4 The "yellow vines" in the original are the "yellow ko (plants)."
5 "Mandarin ducks" refers to an incense burner in the shape of the ducks, which
  symbolize a happy marriage.

Pine fragrance lingers amid evening flowers;
The setting sun hovers over willow banks.
On sand and stones falls a full red glow.
In the rocky spring grows watercress;
Within the dense grove, the young powdery green bamboos—
And eyebrow hills of bluish tint, aslant facing her gate at dawn.[1]
Orchid too weak to bear the dew,[2]
The prettiest of mountains grieves in the spring sky.   10

Her dancer's girdle-pendants, clipped from a phoenix wing,
Her trailing sashes streaked with light silver.
Orchid and cassia waft rich fragrance,
Caltrop and lotus are the offerings piled high.

Viewing the rain, she meets the Jade Princess,[3]
Sailing her skiff, she chances on the River Goddess.[4]
Playing her flute, drunk with wine,
She knots a girdle about her gold-threaded skirt.
Racing through heaven, she scolds her white deer,
Roaming the waters, she whips the bright-hued scales.   20
From her thick hair the done-up hairdo seems to take flight,
Her cheeks glisten with the tints of flowers smoothly blended.
Two spiraled tresses frame her dimples,
Her dark eyebrows shelter a pair of small lips.
As ethereal as fluttering butterflies,
Wind and sun grow timid at her slender body.

Inside secluded curtains, the golden duck chills,[5]
On the mirror on her cosmetic-box, the imprisoned phoenix gathers
    dust.
Treading the fog and riding the wind she returns,
Her jangling jade pendants heard only on mountaintop.   30
(CTS, P. 2341)   (TR. MICHAEL FISH)

---

[1] I.e., the eyelids.

[2] As in the "Li Sao," where flowers are used to represent people, the "weak orchid" is suggestive of a name of a person.

[3] She is the Goddess of Mount Wu; cf. note 5 on Li Po's "Song of Hsiang-yang." The "rain" here reinforces this identification.

[4] The commentators identify the "River Goddess" with the goddesses of the Hsiang. This is strengthened by the phrase "Sailing her skiff," which is similar to the wording of two songs on the goddesses of the Hsiang found among the Nine Songs in the *Ch'u Tz'u.* See Ch'ü Yüan's "Lord of the River Hsiang."

[5] The "golden duck" refers to an incense burner.

Lamentations of the Bronze Camels[1]

Unsettled, unhappy, near the end of April—
I've gone searching for flowers in the eastern suburb.
Who's there to sing a song of farewell to spring?—
Only the lamentations of the bronze camel on the banks of the Lo!
South of the bridge gather travelers on horseback,
The northern mound teems with men of generations past.
The traveler drinks all there is in a wine-cup,
The camels have grieved for ten thousand springs.
Don't toil in vain while living;
The candle on the plate dies in the wind.   10
Wearied of seeing peach trees all smiles,
The bronze camels weep when night arrives.
(CTS, P. 2337)   (TR. IRVING Y. LO)

Ch'ang-ku[1]

In rice fields of Ch'ang-ku, by the fifth month,
Fragile new green covers the level waters.
Hills in the distance pile layer on layer
Such precarious deeper greens one worries they may fall.
Here is sparkling freshness, without a hint of autumn,
Pervading coolness, breathing airy grace to all things.
Still groves are replete with the scent of bamboo,
The chalky joints streaked with new iridescent emerald.
Long grasses droop hair from sorrowful brows,
Glittering dew on it weeps secret tears.   10
Ascending by levels through winding sunlit glades,
The path is sweet with flushed reds, full-blown.
On ancient willows worms etch out their patterns,
Cicadas are shrilling in high and hidden reaches.
Long sashes, yellow creepers trail the ground,
Purple rushes mesh over narrow streambanks.

---

1 In Lo-yang there was a Bronze Camel Street, where, outside the palace gate,
two nine-foot bronze camels cast in Han times stood.
1 The township in which Li Ho's family home was located, about 50 miles south-
west of Lo-yang.

Moss-coins, strewn, thickly cushion rocks,
Full leaves bunch in heavy clusters.
Smooth and white lie water-rinsed sands,
Where the horse stands, hooves print dark signs.   20
As evening comes, bright scales grow playful here,
A thin crane stands alone, immobile in the dusk.
Droning, droning—voices of mud crickets,
And from the gurgling spring, sudden splashes.
Circuitous and slow, the way to the Pure and True,[2]
To the divine maiden deep among marsh orchids.
Streamers of moss entangle the stream's rocks,
Mountain fruits dangle scarlet and purple.
Fronds of small cypresses are layered fans,
Full-branched pines spurt cinnabar sap.   30
A singing current sends on resonant rhythms
Where catalpas trail their shining seed pods.
Orioles trill, songs of girls from Min,[3]
Waterfalls hang capes of silk from Ch'u.
Dew in the breeze fills laughing eyes
That in clefts and niches everywhere bloom and fade.
A riot of dwarf bamboo juts from the rocky slopes,
Chattering from tiny throats rises from midstream bars.
Now the sun's last rays sweep aside the veil of dusk
And new clouds rise up in a glorious mass.   40
Just as summer's sultry stillness begins to pall,
A breeze from the west speaks in freshening accents.
Above me, luminous, a jade-white presence rises,[4]
As I burn cinnamon and pray at the Pedestal to Heaven.
Her robes of mist billow and stream on the night;
At the altar she sleeps in a dream of perfect purity.[5]
The mythic bird has aged, waiting for a royal carriage;

---

[2] Located in the Ch'ang-ku area, the temple was dedicated to the Goddess of Orchid Fragrance; it contained a shrine to the spirit of a girl said to have ascended to Heaven from a pedestal of rock still standing by the temple.

[3] The Min dialect spoken in northern Fukien was said to sound like birdsong; the ancient state of Ch'u was known for the fine quality of its silk.

[4] Numerous textual variants exist for this line, which begins two couplets referring to the shrine of the Goddess of Orchid Fragrance.

[5] Description of another local site, the Fu-ch'ang Palace, begins abruptly here. Originally built for his royal consort by Emperor Yang (reigned 605–617) of the Sui dynasty, the buildings were restored in 657 by the T'ang emperor; the place was abandoned at the beginning of the ninth century.

Pepper-smeared walls[6] in the ancient palace are moldering.
Small bells on the eaves ring with a remote tinkle,
Bringing a desolate mood to this estranged official.　　　　　50
Darkening vines bind the imperial red door-bolt;
The dragon-screen now hides mountain bogeys.
Flowering tamarisk stretches a green embroidered canopy;
Fragrant coverlets wait upon a vanished nobility.
Dust, unstirred by songs, lies on worm-rotted rafters
Where colored dancing skirts drape like shreds of cloud.

Precious district—a swath cut from figured silk!
Village ways preserve honesty and justice;
When a neighbor is in mourning, sounds of mallets cease,[7]
And in times of plague, no one resorts to sorcery.　　　　　60
Wrinkled old folks are loving and kind;
Children with temple-knots know how to blush.
In the county, no demand for judges;
At our doors, no dunning tax collectors.
In bamboo thickets I repair my ancient books,
On rock jetties, drop in bait and hook.
The curving stream, my encircling satin belt;
Leaves on banana trees, the finest paper of Shu.
Mountain summits for splendid silken mantles,
Setting sun's one disk to erase all my worldly anxieties.　　70
This spring—a beaker of T'ao's own wine,[8]
The moon—Hsieh's lady's lovely brow.[9]
Tolling—a bell hidden by distance,
Far above—a lone bird winging home.
Peaks in the afterglow lift ridges of red and black,
Sheer-falling cataracts sound out their altercations.
A pale moth glides over still, crystalline blue,
Beset by wisps of cloud, she gleams faint and sad.

---

[6] In ancient China, the walls of the inner rooms of the palace were painted with a paste made with the oil of a pepper plant, which emitted a strong fragrance.

[7] According to *Li Chi* (*Book of Rites*), the customary practice of the Chou dynasty was that when a neighboring family was observing mourning, one was not to allow the sounds of thrashing or singing to distract the bereaved family. The poet characterizes the simplicity and purity of the village life in Ch'ang-ku by suggesting that their ways were those which Confucius would have approved.

[8] I.e., the poet T'ao Ch'ien.

[9] Referring to Hsieh An, a fourth-century aristocrat-official known for his love of excursions in the company of beautiful women.

Then in cold light breaking upon the streambank
I know, profoundly, what it means to be in mountains.   80
As the fisherboy casts his midnight net
A frostwhite bird flaps up on misty wings.
Over the fathomless mirror flows slippery dragonspume
And the idling fish exhales his floating pearls.
Wind-filled *t'ung* trees, zithers in jasper cases,
The starlights of fireflies, envoys to Brocade City.[10]
Willow-leaves threaded make long, bright trains,
Bamboo shakes in the wind that plays its flutes.
The base of the cliff emerges from green mosses,
Sprouting reeds plunge roots into reddish marsh-bottom.   90
Ripples and eddies toy with the image of heaven,
Ancient evergreens link arms with the clouds.
Heartsick for the moon, curtains of climbing rose shine red,
Clouds are caught by the thorns of flowering vines.
The level sweep of wheat-tassels runs for a hundred *li*,
In the untilled spaces, a thousand neighborhood shops.
This man of the Ch'eng-chi line, once so ambitious,
Now gives himself to the way of old Master Wineskin.[11]
(CTS, P. 2336–37)   (TR. MAUREEN ROBERTSON)

About Horse, Two Selections

[1]

Last month of the year, grass roots taste sweet;
On the broad avenues, snow resembles salt.
Before you know if your jaw is firm or soft,
Try first to bite on the bitter briars.[1]

---

10 Fireflies were compared to shooting stars, which, according to a Han story,
once appeared as harbingers of envoys from the court to the city of Ch'eng-tu
(nicknamed Brocade City for its scenic beauty). The figure in the Han story
who divined the meaning of the shooting star was named Li Ho (though the
given name is written differently from that of the poet). The poet also likens the
scenic beauty of Ch'ang-ku to that of Ch'eng-tu.
11 The name assumed by Fan Li in his wanderings after he declined the rewards
of his king (king of Yüeh), whom he had helped to victory over the state of
Wu.
1 *Chi-li*, a kind of thorny medicinal plant identified as *Tribulus terrestris*. "On
account of the spiny character of the fruit it is called *Chih-hsing* ('preventing
walking')," from Li Shih-chen's *Peng-ts'ao kang-mu*, published 1578, translated

[2]

The master dragon-tamer[2] has fled the world,
And nobody today raises the dragon-steed.
When night comes and frost presses down on the stable-shed,
The bones of a brave steed crack in the west wind.
(NOS. 2, 9 FROM A SERIES OF 23; CTS, PP. 2327–28) (TR. IRVING Y. LO)

New Bamboo in the North Garden at Ch'ang-ku

I've peeled off the shiny green bark,
    on which to write my songs of sorrow[1];
Lustrous fragrance and spring's chalky powder[2]
    mingle with my black ink.
I'm empty of love and full of regret,
    but who's there to care?
The dew presses down on thousands of bamboo branches
    and the mist sheds tears.
(NO. 2 FROM A SERIES OF 4; CTS, P. 2330)   (TR. IRVING Y. LO)

Young Noble at Night's End: A Song

Swirling, swirling—aloeswood-scented smoke
Crows are crying, scene of a worn-out night
In a curving pond, ripples among the lotus
On his circling sash, a white jade, cold
(CTS, P. 2323)   (TR. MAUREEN ROBERTSON)

Chu Ch'ing-yü (*fl. 826*)

"Palace Poem"

Quiet season of flowering, the courtyard gate is shut,
Lovely ladies, side by side, stand near the ornate rail;

---

by F. Porter Smith and G. A. Stuart, *Chinese Medicinal Herbs,* San Francisco: Georgetown Press, 1973, p. 441.
2 The text reads Liu-shu, or Liu-shu An, a legendary tamer of rare animals in the time of the legendary emperor Shun.
1 The text reads *Ch'u Tz'u.*
2 Referring to the white powder on the surface of bamboo skin.

Feelings held back, they wish to talk of palace matters,
Yet before the parrots they dare not speak.
(CTS, P. 3097)   (TR. IRVING Y. LO)

"Gathering Lotus"

Across the mist flowers and grass appear far and hazy,
How I regret we came here not by the same path.
Just where we stop our oars and chance to meet,
Mandarin ducks fly off into the swift current.
(CTS, P. 3108)   (TR. IRVING Y. LO)

The Great Wall

The Ch'in emperor guarded the land against Tartar foes;
His vigilance, though, proved doubly grievous.
It only a single man were virtuous,
All within the four seas could have been one family.
The universe survives the affairs long past;
The ruined foundation lies hidden by brushwood.
Till now the bones of corvée laborers
Still weep in the wind and sandstorm.
(CTS, P. 3108)   (TR. IRVING Y. LO)

Tu Mu (803–852)

Climbing Up to the Lo-yu Plain

Soaring into the distant sky, a lone bird disappears.
Ten thousand ages dissolve and vanish in this instant.
Look, where are the deeds of the Han empire?
The Five Mounds[1] lie treeless where autumn wind rises.
(CTS, P. 3140)   (TR. IRVING Y. LO)

---

[1] I.e., the five imperial Han tombs—Ch'ang-lin, An-lin, Yang-lin, Mao-lin, and P'ing-lin—outside of Ch'ang-an. Also cf. Ts'en Shen, "On Climbing the Pagoda . . .", note 3.

Pond in a Basin

It breaks up green moss ground
And steals a piece of Heaven;
White clouds grow in the mirror,
A bright moon falls upon the steps.
(CTS, P. 3157)   (TR. EDDIE TSANG)

Sighing over Flowers

How I regret being late to see the flowers blossom,
Those I saw last year before they bloomed!
Now despoiled by the wind, the flowers lie helter-skelter,
Green leaves have become shade and flower pods all over the branches.
(CTS, P. 3162)   (TR. EDDIE TSANG)

Red Embankment[1]

Stalagmites in spring caves rise to more stalactites;
Ponds avoid the turning cliffs' dog-toothed edges.
I smile at myself curling into the womb, horns on my head pulled in,
Returning coiling on the misty steps, just like a snail!
(NO. 3 FROM A SERIES OF 3; CTS, P. 3143)   (TR. JOHN M. ORTINAU)

Returning Home

My children tug at my coat and ask,
"Why have you returned so late?
With whom did you struggle for years and months
To win that head of white hair?"
(CTS, P. 3161)   (TR. JOHN M. ORTINAU)

The Crane

With a pure note he welcomes the evening moon,
With sad thoughts he stands on cold bulrush.

---

[1] I.e., *Chu-p'o,* located at Fan-ch'uan, the poet's childhood home.

Red head and cheeks like Hsi shih's;
Frosty feathers and beard all white like the Four Venerable Old
    Men's.[1]
Beneath jasper clouds, moving and stopping restlessly;
To him the spirit of the white egret is coarse.
All day long without the companionship of a flock,
By the side of the gully he laments his shadow's solitude.
(CTS, P. 3150)   (TR. JOHN M. ORTINAU)

Early Geese

By the Gold River,[1] in mid-autumn, the bows of our enemy are drawn;
Startled, you fly beyond the clouds, then disperse and wail.
A single shadow once flew past the Immortals' Palms[2] under a bright
    moon;
By a dim lamp several notes were heard in the Long-gates Palace.[3]
You should know that hordes of Tartar riders are still here,
So why must you chase after spring wind and return one by one?
Don't disdain the Hsiao and the Hsiang[4] rivers where people are few.
Where the water is full of fragrant rice and banks are overgrown with
    moss.
(CTS, PP. 3149–50)   (TR. IRVING Y. LO)

Egrets

In cloaks of snow, hairs snow-white, and beaks of blue jade,
They gather to hunt for fish, their reflection in the brook;
Startled they fly off, cast their distant shadows on green hills.
And all the blossoms of a pear tree fall in the evening breeze.
(CTS, P. 3150)   (TR. IRVING Y. LO)

---

1 Alluding to *Ssu-hao,* the "Four Venerable Whitebeards," four legendary old
  men known for their integrity.
1 Chin-ho, in Sui-yuan province, Inner Mongolia.
2 Alluding to the bronze plates atop tall pillars erected by Emperor Wu of Han
  in his Chien-chang Palace, to catch the dew of heaven.
3 Alluding to the story of Empress Ch'en; cf. note to Wang An-shih's "Song of
  the Radiant Lady."
4 Two rivers in Hunan often mentioned together in Chinese poetry for their
  scenic beauty.

Li Shang-yin (813?–858)

The Richly Painted Zither

The richly painted zither, for no reason, has fifty strings;
Each string, each bridge, recalls a burgeoning year.
Master Chuang, dreaming at dawn, was confused with a butterfly[1];
Emperor Wang consigned his amorous heart in spring to the cuckoo.[2]
By the vast sea, the moon brightens pearls' tears;
At Indigo Field, the sun warms jade that engenders smoke.[3]
This feeling might have become a memory to be cherished,
But for that, even then, it already seemed an illusion.
(CTS, P. 3235)   (TR. JAMES J. Y. LIU)

Without Title

"Coming" is an empty word, "going" leaves no trace.
The moon slants over the roof, the bells strike dawn.
Dreaming of long separation, who can be summoned to cry?
A letter written in haste, the ink not yet thickened.
The candlelight half encircles the gold and kingfishers' feathers[1];
The musk perfume subtly permeates the embroidered lotus flowers.[2]
Young Liu already regretted that P'eng Mountain was far,[3]
Now a myriad more P'eng Mountains block his way.
(NO. 1 FROM A SERIES OF 4; CTS, P. 3244)   (TR. JAMES J. Y. LIU)

---

[1] The philosopher Chuang Tzu dreamt of being a butterfly, and on waking could not tell whether it was he that dreamt of being a butterfly or vice versa.

[2] According to legend, Emperor Wang had a love affair with his prime minister's wife and died of shame. After his death he was metamorphosed into the cuckoo.

[3] For possible allusions involved in these two lines and a detailed discussion of the whole poem, see James J. Y. Liu, *The Poetry of Li Shang-yin*, Chicago: University of Chicago Press, 1969, pp. 44–57.

[1] Quilts decorated with gold mixed with kingfishers' feathers.

[2] On the bed curtain.

[3] Young Liu alludes to Emperor Wu of Han; P'eng Mountain means Fairyland. For a detailed discussion of this ambiguous poem, see Liu, *The Poetry of Li Shang-yin*, pp. 62–64.

Fallen Flowers

From the tall pavilion the guests have all departed;
In the little garden, flowers fly, pell-mell.
They fall at random on the winding path,
And travel far, sending off the setting sun.
Heartbroken, I cannot bear to sweep them away;
Gazing hard, I watch them till few are left.
Their fragrant heart, following spring, dies;
What they have earned are tears that wet one's clothes.
(CTS, P. 3245)   (TR. JAMES J. Y. LIU)

Wang Chao-chün[1]

Mao Yen-shou, your painter's brush seems to move the gods.
How can you bear to turn your eyes from beauty for gold?
On horseback, the tune of the lute travels ten thousand *li*,
And Han Palace shall enjoy eternal spring[2] in the hereafter.
(CTS, P. 3266)   (TR. IRVING Y. LO)

Night Chill

Trees surround a wide pool, the moon casts many shadows;
Beyond the wind-blown vine, in the village and on the bank,
     the pounding of wash and the sounds of the flute.
In the west pavilion, the kingfisher quilt leaves a fragrance that fades;
All through the night, my sorrow turns toward the wilted lotus.
(CTS, P. 3272)   (TR. EUGENE EOYANG AND IRVING Y. LO)

Hibiscus Flowers

Chill wind and dew repeat the autumn scene:
Pity! Flowers that bloom and fade in a day.

---

[1] For the story of Wang Chao-chün, whose portrait was painted by Mao Yen-shou, see Tu Fu's "Wang Chao-chün."
[2] According to one commentator, this refers to the legend that the grass at the grave of Wang Chao-chün stays green all year long.

In the Emperor's palace,[1] three thousand girls:
Preserve your pretty faces, but not his grace.
(CTS, P. 3263)   (TR. EUGENE EOYANG AND IRVING Y. LO)

Boudoir Feelings

Red dew on floral chamber,[1] white honeycomb—
Yellow bee and purple butterfly, both in disarray,
At spring's casement, awakened from a dream of love:
They share the same bed, and do not know it.
(CTS, P. 3251)   (TR. EUGENE EOYANG AND IRVING Y. LO)

For Lotus Flower[1]

Leaves and flowers are never rated the same:
Flowers put into pots of gold, leaves turn to dust.
Still there are the green foliage and the red blooms.
Folded, stretched out, open or closed: all naturally beautiful.
These flowers, these leaves, long mirror each other's glory:
When their greens pale, their reds fade—it's more than one can bear.
(CTS, P. 3262)   (TR. EUGENE EOYANG AND IRVING Y. LO)

About Geese

Asleep on the sand, dozing on the water, they form a flock.
Jagged shoreline, fading light, clouds over distant bank.
They don't know in their heart the plight of the peacock:
The female fettered, forever apart from the male.
(CTS, P. 3248)   (TR. EUGENE EOYANG AND IRVING Y. LO)

In a Day

A year's flowers in the grove die in a day;
At the pavilion by the river I linger in grief.
Chanting over and again, and fingering them,
        really what's the use?

---

[1] The text reads *Wei-yang kung,* or Wei-yang Palace, built by Emperor Kao-tsu of
Han.
[1] *Hua-fang,* meaning the calyx of a flower.
[1] Possibly intended for a woman.

Already falling but still blooming, like grief not fully let go.
Mountain hue spreads, enveloping the small park;
Springtime shadows long to linger by the high tower.
Golden saddles flash out, silver water clock drips:
In whose house shall I get drunk, and play the hook-of-white-jade?[1]
(CTS, P. 3243)   (TR. EUGENE EOYANG AND IRVING Y. LO)

Little Peach Blossoms in the Garden

All through the day, little peach blossoms in the garden
(A thaw in the cold, yet only a hint of warmth[1])—
A perch for orioles, as if weighed down with wine;
They see guests out, appear profusely over the wall.
Cry a long time, face-powder worn thin.
Dance a lot, fragrant snow fluffed up.
More's the pity, the moon's not yet full,
Coming out too soon to shine on evenglow.
(CTS, P. 3262)   (TR. EUGENE EOYANG AND IRVING Y. LO)

Cicada

To fly high hardly fills the belly.[1]
Wasted effort, distressing, your useless crying
At dawn, intermittent, about to break.
A whole tree stands indifferently green.
A hapless official, flotsam floating about,[2]
My old garden is already level with weeds.
Much obliged I am for your admonition:
I too, with my family, live on thin air.
(CTS, P. 3236)   (TR. EUGENE EOYANG AND IRVING Y. LO)

---

1 *Pai-yü-kou*, referring to the game of "hiding the hook," said to have originated
from the time of Han Wu-ti and once played by the emperor and the ladies in
the palace. Li Shang-yin mentions this game in another love poem; cf. James
J. Y. Liu, *The Poetry of Li Shang-yin*, pp. 86–87.
1 Punning on the expression *han-hsüan* ("cold and warmth"), which has also the
sense of exchanging pleasantries and getting acquainted.
1 It was generally assumed that cicadas subsist on dew, and the air would be
thinner, though purer, on higher branches.
2 Alluding to the fabled dialogue between a clay idol and the fallen branch of a
peach tree, both swept along by a flooding river, as to their relative helplessness
in their respective situation. The story is found in *Chan-kuo ts'e* (*Intrigues of
the Warring States*), SPTK, 4/31b–32a.

Willow

Awakening spring: how many leaves!
Rustling dawn: how many branches!
Does she know the pangs of love?
Never a time she wouldn't dance.

Pussy willows aflutter—hide white butterfly,
Tendrils hanging limp—bare yellow oriole.
All-conquering beauty,[1] perfect through and through:
Who would enjoy just the brows of her eyes?
(CTS, P. 3237)   (TR. EUGENE EOYANG AND IRVING Y. LO)

Wen T'ing-yün (813?–870)

A Song of Chang Ching-yüan Picking Lotus Flowers

Ching-yüan was Yang K'an's singing girl, and her beauty was the wonder of the age. K'an himself composed two lyrics to the tune "Picking Lotus Flowers." Among *yüeh-fu* poems still extant, the original theme of this mode has been lost; consequently, I compile this song for a future collection of poetry. The facts are all contained in the *History of Liang*.

Essence of orchids in her tumbled hair, a goddess of spring,
She takes the swallow hairpin from her nape, loosens coiled tresses.
Under the willows by west gate, near the bridge at dusk,
Moated waters past doorways, dabbled, riffled flow.
A prince of rare talents, visitor to the imperial court,
Shell fittings on his saddle all ajangle, crosses the spring lane.

Dancing effortlessly on an open palm,[1] her sheer skirt,
Tailored shagreen dress, best the colors of spring.

---

[1] *Ch'ing-kuo*, literally "toppling a kingdom," alluding to a song by Li Yen-nien of the Han dynasty describing a beautiful woman as someone whose "one glance topples a city/(and) a second glance (from her) topples a kingdom."

[1] Said of Chao Fei-yen, reputedly so small of stature she could dance on a man's open hand.

Like wafting smoke embracing the moon, waist one measure round,
Scent of musk and dragon marrow, how lovely, graceful is she!   10

Clouds like autumn curtains brush the water—fragments of bright
    movement;
Dew-laden, flowers in profusion, their fragrance unfading.
Mandarin ducks go to and fro on the brimming pond,
'Midst duckweeds green like tassels, and short lotus stems.

One evening the west wind comes bringing showers,
Scaring, stripping bare the flowers, a melancholy pale red.
Boat prows sever lotus stems, but strands unseen hold fast,
For lotus roots, lotus seeds, preserve a mutual bond.
His heart is like the moon, a moon not yet on the wane,
Clear, bright and full of mid-month days.   20
(CTS, P. 3504)   (TR. WILLIAM R. SCHULTZ)

A Song of Distant Waters

At the ninth month, our imperial soldiers ford distant waters,
Their horses treading the singing sands, startling geese aloft;
Piercing blasts in the thin air evoke longings for distant homes;
Border cold wounds the eyes like an arrow.
Frost encroaches upon chip fires along the ramparts;
Dry leaves ride the wind, heaven and earth wither.
Rhinoceros belts, squirrel jackets provide no warmth,
The moonlight, bright and cold, yellow gold the saddle.
Though barbarian dust enshrouded our encampment like a fog,
Year after year, the Flying General came to Lung-shou;   10
In Unicorn Hall unheralded, yet he has not returned;
Anxiously, a grieving wife waits in vain in her apartment.
(CTS, PP. 3503–4)   (TR. WILLIAM R. SCHULTZ)

A Crossing South of Li-chou

Tranquil, vacant is the river, girdled by the setting sun;
An island, vast, misshapen, merges with the flanking hills.
See, an oar is raised, a horse whickers across the waves;
By willow trees men rest, waiting the ferry's return.

From thick clumps of sand grass, seagulls flock, disperse,
While above endless fields along the river, a solitary egret rises.
But who will raise the sail in search of Fan li
Now oblivious to desire among the misty waters of Five Lakes.
(CTS, P. 3515)   (TR. WILLIAM R. SCHULTZ)

Early Autumn in the Mountains

Here, next the mountain, the cold comes early,
Crisp and clear, the air in the thatched hut.
Barren trees admit the sun to the window,
The cistern, brimming full, is still and silent.
Fallen nuts mark the monkeys' trail,
Dry leaves rustle to the passage of deer.
A plain zither—an untrammeled heart—
Hollowly accompanies the clear spring at night.
(CTS, P. 3526)   (TR. WILLIAM R. SCHULTZ)

An Early Walk on Shang Mountain

Departing at dawn, carriage bells ajingle—
The traveler grieves for his ancestral home.
A cock's crow, a thatched teahouse in the moonlight,
Human footprints on the frosted bridge planking,
Betel leaves fallen by the mountain road,
Orange blossoms bright on the station wall—
And so I dream a dream of Ch'ang-an,
Where ducks and geese settle, crowding the pond.
(CTS, P. 3527)   (TR. WILLIAM R. SCHULTZ)

A Spring Day in the Countryside

Astride a mount pawing misty sedge grass,
How can one be resentful of the vernal spring
Where butterfly wings dust the flowers at dawn
And the backs of crows glisten everywhere in the setting sun;
Where lush willows compete with the fragrant sash,
And melancholy hills tighten kingfisher eyebrows.

The feeling of separation, what is there to say
But that the heart is an endless river of stars.
(CTS, P. 3513)   (TR. WILLIAM R. SCHULTZ)

A Song of Wildfire

I rise to gaze upon southern hills,
A mountain fire burns mountain fields:
Specks of red, seeming long to be dead,
Shortly blaze anew, join together,
Raggedly move toward rocky cliffs,
Steadily traverse green slopes,
Follow closely, expire in eddying winds,
Gleams red on distant thatched eaves.

An aged neighbor, speaking the Ch'u dialect,
Leans on a shovel and, about to weep,   10
Remarks, "It is the custom in Ch'u and Yüeh
To burn the fields for dry cultivation.
Insects swarm among the sprouting beans,
Flowers in the hedge face the house.
Swine return late to rickety sheds,
Chickens pick at grain in spacious yards.
At the New Year, spring rains clear away;
Everywhere, the sounds of processions for the gods.
With cash, people consult the oracle,
Breaking tiles until the nearby woods resound;   20
A hexagram divined: climb the mountain,
Return under mulberry and buckthorn trees.
Fire blown upon white rushes,
Waist sickles glisten red as sugar cane.
Winds pursue the smoke of oak leaves
From oak trees which cover the mountain.
Driven sparks spread beyond sunset clouds,
Flying embers fall before the steps."
Raising his head, he sighs and sniffs,
Pretty maids curse the bountiful harvest,   30
For all know that kingfisher-blue silks
Will all go to official families for taxes.
(CTS, P. 3511)   (TR. WILLIAM R. SCHULTZ)

A Fishing Trapping Song

Fishing at dawn, trap them east of town;
Fishing at dusk, trap them west of town.
The oars make a distant, muffled sound
Among the lotus flowers, high and low.
Place the trap where the water is deep
For the golden scales as large as your palm;
Where tail fins scatter round ripples
And pearls that drip from the lotus on the Hsiang.
    Cool, cool is the breeze
      In the steadily falling rain.   10
    The water chestnut prickly
      Where mandarin ducks take wing.
Gleaming in the sunlight, water binds the woven wicker trap;
Drops of cold rain patter, patter on the boat's awning.
All aflower, the banks of Ch'u, its houses covered with bloom;
By golden ponds, glistening willows, is heard the Ballad of Ch'ien-chi.
Eternal, mysterious, unending the river flows onward,
A spectrum of color, clear and pure, its hue a teal blue.
(CTS, P. 3507)   (TR. WILLIAM R. SCHULTZ)

Tune: "Deva-like Barbarian" (*P'u-sa man*), Five Lyrics

[1]

Hills on paneled screen: sun-shadowed gold;
Hair-clouds drift over fragrant cheeks of snow.
Languidly, she gets up to paint her crescent eyebrows,
Then dallies and fusses with her makeup.

A mirror, front and back, frames a flower:
Twin beauties dazzle each other.
On her new robe of embroidered silk,
Pairs of golden partridges.
(CTS, P. 5125)   (TR. EUGENE EOYANG)

[2]

Within beaded, crystal curtains, a cool porcelain pillow
And warm incense waken a dream of mandarin duck brocade.
    Willows, smoke-like, bend by riverbanks;
    Wild geese wing across the waning moon.

    Lotus silks of pale, autumn hues
    And aigrette of cunning pattern she wears.
    Above each ear, flowers bright and fragrant,
    And a jade pin waving in her hair.
(CTS, P. 5125)   (TR. WILLIAM R. SCHULTZ)

[3]

A flower's borrowed gold brightly marks her forehead fair;
Gauze windows hide the night's disguise, an amorous glance.
    It was in the season of peonies they met,
    But too soon were they forced to part.

    Frozen in flight, two butterflies adorn
    A blue pin, golden-stemmed, in her hair.
    Who knows the inmost secrets of her heart?
    Only the bright moon and the flowering branches.
(CTS, P. 5125)   (TR. WILLIAM R. SCHULTZ)

[4]

A pair of mandarin ducks, mauve-feathered, flecked with gold,
Lightly ripple the blue waters of the springtime pond,
    Where, in bright reflection, stands a wild plum
    Incarnadine against the rain-washed sky.

    Brocade sleeves hide a dimpled cheek;
    Misted grasses cling to flying butterflies.
    Lacquered doors open on the fragrant scene,
    But not a word is heard from the Jade Pass.
(CTS, P. 5125)   (TR. WILLIAM R. SCHULTZ)

[5]

In the moonlit chamber, always she thinks of him.
Soft wisps of silken willows, languor in the air of spring.
    Verdant were the grasses beyond the gate;
    At their parting, she heard the horses neigh.

    Draperies patterned of gold kingfishers;
    Within, fragrant candle melts in tears.
    Falling petals, the morning plaint of the cuckoo,
    Green-gauze windows—fragments of an illusive dream.
(CTS, P. 5125)   (TR. WILLIAM R. SCHULTZ)

Tune: "Song of Water Clock at Night" (*Keng-lou tzu*), Three Lyrics

[1]

    The tendrils of willow are long
    And spring rains fine.
Beyond the flower bed, the clepsydra drip-drops.
    Wild geese start;
    City crows stir on the city wall—
On the painted screen, gold partridges.

    The fragrant mist is thin
    And seeps through the curtains.
Alas for the Hsieh family at their poolside pavilion!
    Behind the red taper   10
    Hangs a brocade screen
An old dream: you wouldn't know.
(CTS, P. 5126)   (TR. EUGENE EOYANG)

[2]

    A goldfinch in my hair,
    My cheeks brightly rouged,
For one brief moment we met among the flowers.
    You understood my heart,

And tender was your love.
Only Heaven knew the joys we shared.

The incense turns to ashes,
The candle dissolves in tears;
How like our innermost feelings for one another.
The peaked pillow is smeared,   10
The brocade covers cold,
When waking I find the water clock has stopped.
(CTS, P. 5126)   (TR. WILLIAM R. SCHULTZ)

[3]

Incense from a jade censer
And a tearful vermilion candle
Evoked autumnal moods within the painted chamber.
Penciled eyebrows worn,
Cloud-like locks in disarray;
Long is the night, the covers and pillow cold.

Upon the *wu-t'ung* trees
Falls a midnight rain,
Indifferent to the persistent pains of separation.
Leaf upon leaf,   10
Drop upon drop,
On empty stairs it drips until the dawn.
(CTS, P. 5126)   (TR. WILLIAM R. SCHULTZ)

Tune: "Pacifying the Western Barbarians" (*Ting Hsi-fan*),
Two Lyrics

[1]

Long years ago the envoy of Han departed.
Gather tender willows,
Pick chilled plum blossoms,
Climb the storied tower

Far away at Jade Pass swirl the snows of spring;
The migrant geese return, but not he.

A trill from the shepherd's pipe multiplies her grief;
    The moon pauses in its flight.

[2]

Poised in imminent flight, the petrel preens its wings.
    Green are the day-lily leaves,
    And pink the flowering apricot
    Beyond the trellised window.

Wearing aigrette of sunset hues and golden beads,
    Like a flower-decked branch in spring is she.
The full moon, a luminous disk above the pavilion,
    Enters the latticed room.
(CTS, P. 5124)   (TR. WILLIAM R. SCHULTZ)

Tune: "A Southern Song" (*Nan-ko tzu*)

In soft hanging coils, she embroiders her hair;
Eyebrows she traces like airy half-moons.
Remembered pledges haunt the long day through;
Because of him, harrowed by grief is she
    In this season of a hundred flowers.
(CTS, P. 5123)   (TR. WILLIAM R. SCHULTZ)

Tune: "Telling of Innermost Feelings" (*Su chung-ch'ing*)

Orioles warble
And flowers dance
At the midmorn of spring,
Midst the misting rain.
Gold is her ribboned pillow,
Royal the brocades
And phoenix tapestries.
Willows languish and butterflies glide by twos,
Averse to part.
Scarce a word is there from distant Liao-yang,   10
But in a dream he returns.
(CTS, P. 5124)   (TR. WILLIAM R. SCHULTZ)

Tune: "Dreaming of the South" (*Meng Chiang-nan*)[1]

Boundless, bitter is her sorrow,
Her painful longing for the wanderer at world's end.
The mountain moon ignores affairs that deeply touch the heart;
On wind and wave, in vain the transient bloom whirls and eddies.
Dark clouds scud across the sky.
(CTS, P. 5124)   (TR. WILLIAM R. SCHULTZ)

Tune: "River Messages" (*Ho ch'uan*)

From the riverbank
She hails a boat.
Bright is her morning dress
Amidst the fairy scene; alone she picks the lotus.
"Please, sir," the boatman urges, "don't go to the other shore!
Young sir,
Here are fresh flowers that fill the boat."

In the warm and gentle breeze, her red sleeves wave and flutter
On lissome wrists of jade;
Heartbroken, she faces the silken willows.   10
Has he gone to the southern
Or to the northern shore?
Unknowing, she
Waits as evening falls and all have gone.
(CTS, P. 5127)   (TR. WILLIAM R. SCHULTZ)

Tune: "Lotus-leaf Cup" (*Ho-yeh pei*), Three Lyrics

[1]

A single pearl of dew suspended clear and chill;
Shadowed riffles
Fill the courtyard pool.

---

[1] The tune-title given here follows the *Hua-chien chi*, not the CST, where it appears as *Yi Chiang-nan*. This tune also has a two-stanza version.

Green stems and radiant reds mixed in gay profusion;
My heart breaks,
The wind and waves are cold.

[2]

Mirrored on the lake at night floats an autumn moon,
White as snow,
At lotus-picking time.
A young girl, her cheeks rouged red, faces the cold waves,
Pained at heart,
Lost in sad reflection.

[3]

The girl of Ch'u dreams of returning to the southern cove;
The morning rains
Sprinkle the flowers with sorrow.
A small boat, pitching, tossing, approaches the flowered shore.
Waves spring up;
The west wind bars his way.

(CTS, P. 5123)   (TR. WILLIAM R. SCHULTZ)

Yü Wu-ling (9th century)

Offered to a Man Who Sells Pines

You come to market—seeking gain, to be sure—
Yet, sir, I am touched by the unique purity of your purpose.
You bring us trees hewn in chilly ravines—
To sell to the men in turquoise towers.

These meager leaves have undergone many passages of snow,
Their pale blossoms suited only for unripened spring.
But Ch'ang-an makes more of peach and plum
Merely to color the dust of its six boulevards.

(CTS, P. 3601)   (TR. EDWARD H. SCHAFER)

Lu Kuei-meng (?–c. 881)

Fisherman on a Southern Stream

I'm naturally lazy, carefree;
A secluded spot is what I like.
River flows north of the village;
Heart craves for aimless wanderings.
My rustic house far away from others,
Lonely and isolated, myself given to loftiness:
Going out, I first grip a bamboo staff;
Meeting people, I do not bother with a hat.[1]

On the southern stream is a fisherman
Who frequently takes children to visit me.   10
I asked him how he fished.
He answered truly in words of wisdom:
"From the start, I've speared fish and turtles,
Since I was a lad, right through to old age.
Their hideouts are second nature to me;
Thoroughly I know the secrets.
So I'd warn my people:
Heaven's gifts are not to be abused.
Reckon carefully: whether to spare or to kill the big or the small;
Wait for them to grow, multiply, and reap the reward.   20
All day I hunt fish for profit
And yet fish have never been exhausted."

We are housed together between sky and earth,
To abandon benevolence is to wrong heaven's bounties.
When I think of government officials,
I feel, this idea is hard for them to grasp.
People all die from extortion and fleecing,
None willing to show them pity or grief.
This year, rivers and marshes go dry;

---

1 Officials wore hats. Lu means that he is far from centers of bureaucratic activity.

Last season, mountain springs flooded.   30
Pleas and complaints fill the court:
Like the cawing of birds to my ears.
As (for instance) in the raising of chickens and ducks,
Surely you'll let them lay eggs and brood.
Mencius ridiculed the Man of Sung,[2]
Blaming him for hastiness in tugging rice sprouts.
I admire the fisherman's wise words,
In harmony with the teaching of the sages.
If I meet an official who collects poetry,
I'll dare to show him, in all sincerity, this little piece.   40
(CTS, P. 3724)   (TR. ROBIN D. S. YATES)

A Lone Wild Goose

I live between heaven and earth,
A wild goose, a lone visitor of the South.
Mournfully crying I long for my former companions;
And yet I can't avoid being late in drinking and eating.
Although I was praised in the *Hsiao Ya*,[1]
I can't escape the evils of fishing nets.
While indispensable in marriage rites,
I'm afraid of the hunter's attack with arrows.

The flashing hawks fight up and down through the sky,
Their spirit is bitterly insolent: 10
We often scare the fledgling mandarin ducks[2];
The likes of you are beneath our curse.
So I turn my head and speak to the flashing hawks:

"You're accustomed to eat putrid rats!
You're no different from a herd of jaded horses
That crave for mangers full of short beanstalks!
Surely you know not the banks of the Hsiao and Hsiang[3]

---

2 Mencius, a late fourth-century B.C. Confucian philosopher, tells a story about a
  man who pulled at his rice shoots because he was worried at their slow growth.
  He states that one should let all things take their natural course.
1 Alluding to one of the sections of the *Shih Ching*.
2 Mandarin ducks are symbols of marital harmony; the wild goose is one of
  separation.
3 The two scenic rivers that flow into Lake Tung-t'ing in Hunan.

Where bulrushes and duckweeds grow,
Where the stones assume strange shapes
And river coves have flowed cold from ages past.   20
Peacefully, you can watch the ways of stags and does
Who have no desire to be fed with hay and grain.

"What the world values are caps and gowns,[4]
So why should it object to a countryman's tufted hairstyle?
A *Sao* poet[5] praises orchids and iris;
The illustrations in the *Book of Change* use roots and vegetables.
In the essay 'Free and Easy,' the Master of the Lacquer Garden
Bases his philosophy on the quail.[6]
You are truly inferior in talent and nature,
No reproof can deter you from your lust.   30
Although your bodies love to soar high,
Dirt and dung are what you greedily look for.
I've heard that you commute with demons
And can quickly tell ghosts from goblins.
Though The Book on Robbing Nests[7] is still extant;
Your indulgence in black magic will not be tolerated!"
(CTS, PP. 3723–24)   (TR. ROBIN D. S. YATES)

Replying to Hsi-mei's [P'i Jih-hsiu's] "Thoughts in Early Autumn: Thirty Rhymes"

Idle, I enjoy only tranquillity:
Beyond the fence is wilderness.
The place being remote, I love all neighbors.
My courtyard filled with many nests, I weary of birds' chirping.
The banks resound as small boats lurch past;
By the light of the window I see long-legged spiders;
Only water birds swoop to the path;
Only country visitors knock on my door.

---

4 Metonymy for officials.
5 I.e., the poet Ch'ü Yüan, the author of *Li Sao.*
6 Chuang Tzu, the Taoist philosopher, once served as a minor official of Ch'i-yüan, or the Lacquer Garden. The first chapter of his work is entitled "Free and Easy Wandering."
7 *Author's note:* "In the *Rites of Chou,* in the chapter 'Autumn Officials, the Minister of Crime,' it is written: 'The nest robber is charged with seizing and overthrowing the nests of birds that have an evil cry.'"

A ridge of bamboos follows an ancient mound;   10
A pool lies in its original hollow:
Dawn lotus hold up their frosty stems;
Chilled blooms contract their purple tips.
Fishermen's thoughts follow the heavy nets;
Hunters' joy rises as their arrows whistle.

Happy dreams I recall after years have passed,
Rare prescriptions I copy from everywhere.
When my genius is careless, only I can mend it;
When my talent itches, who will scratch it but me?
The window is tranquil; curtain hangs constantly;
My whip idle, my scabbard remains untended;   20
My mountain clothes disdain to be elegant;
Quietly I strum heavenly music on string and gourd.

Orchids open, borne before the wind;
Peaches, sun-burnt, are sticky after rain.
Dried-up moss clings to stone steps at evening;
Damp smoke issues from the kitchen at dawn.
Shen Yüeh[1] described seals and books;
Yang Hsiung[2] valued wine and savories.
My eyes have peeped into unforgettable caves,
My ears aren't jolted by army bells.   30
I probe the months that slip by, looking beyond the calendar[3];
Using milfoil stalks, I record the trigrams in the *Change*.
No use for me, the silent stone forest;
Would you still tolerate wrangling in market places?
Why should pine and cassia hinder the tree grubs?
Turtles and dragons mock each other as they please.
If I can't make cinnabar into marrow,[4]
Who will help me turn purple into womb?
Don't suppose honor and disgrace are different:

---

[1] Shen Yüeh (441–512), a highly talented poet and philologist, was the first to
point out that the Chinese language is tonal.
[2] Yang Hsiung (53 B.C.–A.D. 18) was a poet, philosopher, and finally an official
under the usurper Wang Mang.
[3] Each year, the emperor promulgated the calendar on which was written in-
structions for farmers, dates of festivals, and other useful information.
[4] This was an alchemical experiment, the aim of which was to induce physical
immortality.

All things, large or small, live in peace. 40
Gibbons aren't nimble because of bows;
In wooden cages tigers forget how to roar.
An old friend remembers the Three Benefits[5];
The road home is flocked by the two Hsiao cliffs.[6]
My way grows antiquated, following my cartload of books.
My time is cast away with the casting line;
Desiring to be oblivious of schemes,
I aspire to become your bosom friend.
I see you busily dispatch the letters of remonstrance you drafted[7];
I pity myself lying among flattened reeds. 50
Although taking office has its dark secrets,
The fragrant and the fetid become confused.
Follow the prints of cranes on sandbanks,
While honey on the cliffs incites men to lean out too far.
White mushrooms fill withered trees resprouting;
Polygonatum is crammed into green baskets.
Being a transcendent means trusting to the recluse life;
Meditating is learning to still the urge for fame.
Do not say that rivers and lakes are eternal;
In the end you'll float away in a giant gourd.[8] 60
(CTS, PP. 3739–40)   (TR. ROBIN D. S. YATES)

P'i Jih-hsiu (c. 833–883)

Orthodox Music Bureau Ballads: Preface

Music Bureau ballads are those songs collected by the sage kings of antiquity, desiring through them to understand the strengths and weaknesses of the country, the joys and sorrows of the people. Once

---

5 "Three Benefits" (*san-i*) refers to the saying of Confucius that an ideal friend confers three kinds of benefits; namely, if he is straightforward, if he is forgiving, and if he is learned.

6 Mount Hsiao is situated in Honan province.

7 The last few lines of this poem urge P'i to return to the life of the recluse. Unfortunately, P'i did not take the advice: he was caught in 881 in Ch'ang-an by the rebel leader Huang Ch'ao and forced to become a Hanlin scholar. When Huang began to doubt P'i's loyalty to the rebel cause, he had him strangled.

8 Chuang Tzu had a friend called Hui Tzu. Hui Tzu was given a large gourd, but because it was so huge, he found no use for it and smashed it to pieces. Chuang Tzu told him he should have carved it into a boat and gone sailing over the lakes and rivers. Lu is suggesting P'i should not delay his return to the Taoist life.

obtained, they ordered the music officials to set them to music for porcelain instruments, to harmonize them with the bamboo instruments. The beauty of these songs was sufficient to exhort listeners to meritorious efforts. The satire of these songs was enough to admonish listeners with regard to governing. Therefore, the duty of the Grand Master[1] according to the *Rites of Chou*[2] was to direct the teaching of the six songs,[3] and the duty of the Lesser Master to direct the silent reading of the odes. In light of this, the way of the Music Bureau ballad is great! The so-called Music Bureau ballads today, however, are merely the lavish extravagance of the Wei and Tsin periods [A.D. 220–420], the ethereal beauty of the Ch'en and Liang eras [A.D. 502–88]. To call them Music Bureau songs is really not at all correct! Thus those things which should cause grief or fear I have at times made known in verse. In all there are ten pieces. Therefore, I have given them the name of "Orthodox Music Bureau Ballads."

Lament of a Woman Acorn-gatherer

Deep into autumn the acorns ripen,
Scattering as they fall into the scrub on the hill.
Hunched over, a hoary-haired crone
Gathers them, treading the morning frost.
After a long time she's got only a handful,
An entire day just fills her basket.
First she suns them, then steams them,
To use in making late winter provisions.

At the foot of the mountain she has ripening rice,
From its purple spikes a fragrance pervades.   10
Carefully she reaps, then hulls the grain,
Kernel after kernel like a jade earring.[1]
She takes the grain to offer as government tax,
In her own home there are no granary bins.
How could she know that well over a picul of rice

---

[1] This music master was always blind, cf. Arthur Waley, *The Analects of Confucius* (London: Allen & Unwin, [1956]), p. 100, n. 3.

[2] Cf. Burton Watson, *Early Chinese Literature* (New York, 1962), p. 139, for a short description of this work.

[3] Referring to the six modes of the *Shih Ching*: *feng* (persuasive), *ya* (liturgical), *sung* (paeanic), *fu* (descriptive), *pi* (metaphorical), and *hsing* (allusive).

[1] In a number of cases, where several characters are missing in the original edition, I have followed the emendations by modern editors of the text.

Is only five pecks in official measurement?
Those crafty clerks don't fear the law,
Their greedy masters won't shun a bribe.
In the growing season she goes into debt,
In the off season sends grain to government bin.   20
From winter even into spring,
With acorns she tricks her hungry innards.
I've heard that T'ien Ch'eng-tzu,
By feigning benevolence, made himself a king.[2]
Aah, meeting this old woman acorn-gatherer,
Tears come uncalled to moisten my robe.
(NO. 2 FROM A SERIES OF 10; CTS, PP. 3662–63)
                                        (TR. WILLIAM H. NIENHAUSER)

Song of a Farmer

A peasant oppressed by sorrow and misery
Described his feelings to me:

"It's hard for a single farming man
To provide for ten out on campaign.
Why are the grains of the South and East
Transported by boats to the ruler's domain?
In the Yellow River's lightning-like waters,
A half of the land overturns and sinks in vain.
If the adjuster or transport men profit in their service,
How dare we people criticize an official's gain?   10
Don't they farm along the Three Rivers' banks?
Don't they plow the Three Districts' plain?[1]
How is it they don't cart off theirs
To supply the imperial troops in grain?"

Beautiful! That peasant's speech,
But how are we to carry this message to the end of the king's road?
(No. 4; CTS, P. 3663)   (TR. WILLIAM H. NIENHAUSER)

---

2 T'ien Ch'eng-tzu (also known as Ch'en Heng) won the hearts of the people
  of the state of Ch'i by reducing the standard grain measure in collecting taxes
  and increasing the measure in redispensing the grain. He was only "faking
  benevolence," however, as he shortly thereafter assassinated his lord and
  usurped his rule.
1 Both "three rivers" and "three districts" refer to the region around the capital;
  the three rivers are the Wei, Lo, and Ching.

Lament for the People of Lung[1]

Lung Massif stands tens of thousands of feet;
Parakeets nest up on its peaks.
Pushed to lofty heights, then to further peril,
Even these mountains are not safe!
The simple folk of Lung
On hanging bridges they seem to mount the sky,
Spying a nest up in the void;
Many fall as they scramble in quest:
Out of one hundred, not one bird is caught,
Of ten, nine men die in the attempt.   10
By the Lung River there are border troops,
Border troops not idle either;
Under orders to carry the carved cages
Straight to the entrance of the Golden Hall.
Those feathers are no treasure of themselves,
That tongue doesn't learn to speak of its own.
Why make light of the lives of men,
To present these birds as objects of idle play.
I have heard that the ancient sage kings
Released all of their precious birds.   20
Now these people of Lung
Grieve unceasingly year after year.
(NO. 10; CTS, PP. 3663–64)   (TR. WILLIAM H. NIENHAUSER)

A Woodcutter's Ax

With a large ax handle tucked in at his waist,
Straight on and deep into the ravine he goes.
At the sound of a single blow in the empty grove,
Hidden birds call one another to flight.
Trees felled, tigers are driven off;
Nests overturned, forest goblins wail.

---

[1] Lung is the classical name of the area occupying the border between modern
Kansu and Shensi provinces.

I don't know of anyone who wields the big ax[1]
Who can do away with evils like this.
(CTS, P. 3679)   (TR. WILLIAM H. NIENHAUSER)

On a Crab

Before journeying to the vast sea, I already knew his name;
He has bones, but they grow on top of flesh.
Don't tell with no heart he fears thunder and lightning—
He even dares to amble sideways in the dragon king's watery domain.
(CTS, PP. 3704–5)   (TR. WILLIAM H. NIENHAUSER)

Mosquitoes

Buzzing darkly almost like thunder,
They bite one's flesh and know not surfeit.
As if high Heaven sensed something was amiss,
These little things are allowed to eat meat!
No crimson gauze curtain[1] for a poor scholar,
He bears his misery lying in a thatched hut;
Why do they search here for the sleek and fat,
In that belly there's nothing from the official granary!
(CTS, P. 3664)   (TR. WILLIAM H. NIENHAUSER)

Reading

What sort of thing is our family wealth?—
Piles of books arrayed up to the rafters.
In my lofty study at dawn I open a volume,
And alone share in the words of the sages.
Though men superior and wise have lived in every era,
We have all esteemed each other's minds.
But these bookworms I see on my desk
Still far surpass my ordinary companions.
(CTS, P. 3664)   (TR. WILLIAM H. NIENHAUSER)

---

1 I.e., law officials who administer the execution of evildoers.
1 The Han literatus Ma Jung (A.D. 79–166), known for his eccentricity, was said to have sat with his female musicians behind a crimson gauze curtain while teaching his students.

Thoughts in Early Autumn: Thirty Rhymes Sent to Lu-wang [Lu Kuei-meng]

Early autumn enters my rickety house,
Austere and bare like the level countryside;
Door and windows open into the depth of a grotto;
Books strewn about, littered like a bird's nest.
As I move my bed, I startle the crickets;
As I dust my boxes, I disturb the spiders.
On calm days, I draw spring water with cupped hands;
When idle, pick up the milkweed[1] to beat time with.
Junipers are nearly all short and scrubby,
Natural shallows form on the face of boulders.   10
Dwarf cassias sport leaves the size of fists;
New growth on pines, slender as fingertips.
The crying of cranes transmits the tones of the east,
Falcons swoop down with the twang of arrows.
Prescribed drugs I'm reluctant to take,
My writings done, I'm too lazy to copy them out.
My vexed heart is awake into the night;
My aching head I scratch in the cool breeze.

Elm leaves are pointed like arrows' barbs,
Fibers of creepers, tough like a whipcord.   20
Cracked fields hold purple taros,
Low-growing vines conceal green gourds.
Old cypresses all look scabby.
Moss in the shade suddenly feels like varnish.
One-eyed "king minnows"[2] fall into ruined moat,
Spiked "wolf-tails"[3] enter the empty kitchen.

---

[1] *Ju-kuan* (*laticiferous vessel*), a plant the stalks of which yield milky liquid when broken.

[2] The text reads *wang-yü,* literally "king's leftovers," the name of a fish said to resemble the pair-eyed fish (*pi-mu yü*), but with only half of its face showing. The name is believed to derive from a legend that when the king of Yüeh was dining on the delicacy of a fish, he threw the remainder into the water and it came to life; hence, it has only half of the face of the original. See Tso Ssu, *"Wu-tu fu"* ("Rhyme-prose on the Wu Capital") in *Wen-hsüan,* 5/8a.

[3] My conjectural reading of *hu* as "whiskered," or "spiked"; and of *meng* as "wolf's tail" (*lang-wei ts'ao*), a meaning found in the *Erh-ya.* Li Shih-chen's

All the long day I forget my cap and sash,
Only after some time do I remember food and drink.
Endowed with feeling, but no more than a wooden statue,[4]
Tongue-tied, like a bell without a clapper.[5]   30
When disposed, I wish to add to my knowedge of the Mysteries;
When restive, I want to revise the reading of the hexagram.

Only wise men are sparing of speech,
While the vulgar are disputatious.
Where is the strength to ward off disasters?
What face must I put on to dispel mockery?
I'd rather my bones were dissolved after I'm gone,
Still I must empty my bladder since sitting here.[6]
It should be hard to cling to vacillation,
But to be wary saves a fox from being trapped.   40
Off guard, one meets with venomous reptiles,
And easily comes upon the roar of beasts.
The world today teems with a thousand scorpions,
And the public road is blocked by the Mountains of Hsiao.[7]

My fame small, I'm content to be rejected by the world;
By nature stupid, I let the times cast me aside.
Broad daylight has become agreeable with me,
Blue clouds are fit to be my companions.

Pen-ts'ao kang-mu (*chüan* 23, p. 80) classifies *meng* as a type of grain. It is described as resembling the grain in every respect except that the ears have purplish yellow color. "It can be eaten as food in times of drought."

[4] Alluding to what is said of Liu Piao (144–208) in the *Hou-Han Shu* (*History of Later Han*) as a "wooden statue among men"; i.e., man of little worth or ability (*chuan* 74-*hsia;* Kai-ming ed., p. 866).

[5] *Jao,* "bell without a clapper," is smaller than the regular bell and is further differentiated from it by having a handle. According to the *Rites of Chou,* when it is held in the hand and sounded, it is so used to stop the beating of drums.

[6] For the meaning of *chuan pao,* see Hsi K'ang's letter to Shan T'ao (205–83), "Yu Shan Chü-yüan chüeh-chiao shu," *Wen-hsüan,* 43/2b.

[7] The two Hsiao Mountains, located in the border area between Honan and Shensi, were considered the most strategic defense of the ancient state of Ch'in. Here the poet alludes to the story about Chien Shu, an octogenarian officer of Ch'in, who warned his king against conducting a campaign against a distant state and foretold the death of his two sons in these mountains, where there were two imperial tombs. See *Tso Chuan* (*The Tso Commentary*), Third-second Year of Duke Hsi (Legge, J., *The Chinese Classics,* New York: Oxford University Press, 1961, Vol. V, pp. 220–21).

An official should emulate the Master of Five Willows[8];
Home, I'll never depart from the Mountain of Three Grass-spikes.[9] 50
The deer are left to roam the mountain torrent,
And the creepers grow freely, tangled in the mist.
The Warden of Monkeys, after the rumpus, plays a ruse,[10]
The Potion of Magic Mica,[11] when illness comes, is taken by the sick.

From now on I shall dwell in this ten-foot-square,
To cope with nitwits[12] is not my game.
When the Way is lost, it should be the demons' doing,
If my nature is stupid, it must be Heaven's will.
Endless affairs wherein I'm careless and lazy—
I'll count on you to cut loose this bitter gourd.[13]   60
(CTS, PP. 3685–86)   (TR. IRVING Y. LO)

Lo Yin (*833–909*)

The Book-burning Pit

Remnants and relics of a thousand years—here in a pit full of dust.
Even a plowman by the roadside is wounded in his soul.
As Grandfather Dragon[1] takes account of this affair, his abyss

---

[8] The sobriquet of the poet T'ao Ch'ien, who gave up his office rather than cringe before a superior.

[9] According to the *Biography of Immortals* (*Shen-hsien Chuan*), the Mountain of Three Grass-spikes (San-mao Shan) was said to be in the custody of three brothers who were respectively the Master of Fate, the Certifier of Records, and the Guardian of Fate.

[10] Referring to the story about Master Tsu, the monkey-keeper; cf. note 2 to Tu Fu's "Seven Songs."

[11] *Yün-mu*, literally the "mother (roots) of clouds," is the mica. Use of mica powder is associated with the story of the recluse Fan Hui during the time of the legendary emperor Yao. Yao conferred upon him a title and asked him to be in charge of refining mica (used in Taoist practices) with the promise that the mica dusts be given to cure sick people.

[12] *Tou-shao*, literally "peck-measures," referring to those in government who are of little ability and can only count or add; the expression comes from *The Analects* (13:20). Arthur Waley provides the note "mere thimblefuls" for the term "peck-measures" used in his translation, p. 176.

[13] *Pao* ("bitter gourd") alludes to what Confucius says about himself (*The Analects*, 17:7): "Am I indeed to be forever like the bitter gourd that is only fit to hang up [till it is dry to be used as a vessel], but not to eat?" (Waley's translation, p. 211). A "hanging gourd" comes to mean "a useless fellow."

[1] Old Dragon, in his deep watery domain, is thought to be the protector of the imperial race.

is discordant with shock—
Would he tell us: *Odes* and *Documents* must live to win men?
(CTS, P. 3931)   (TR. EDWARD H. SCHAFER)

Thinking of the Way Home: A Song

I don't plow my southern acre,
But care for the cassia by my eastern hall.

I am like the flowers of this tree:
We lose another year as they fall.

Relatives become estranged;
And good friends drift apart.

Daily I open wide those twelve gates[1]
But there's no way that takes me home.
(CTS, P. 3950)   (TR. GEOFFREY R. WATERS)

Sent to the Ch'an Master Wu-hsiang

People all talk about serving the King of Emptiness,[1]
And still their hearts are full of the cares of the market place;
Only this wanderer from the Horse Ridge Mountain
Has forgotten both the way of the living and the gate of death.
(CTS, P. 3954)   (TR. GEOFFREY R. WATERS)

Wei Chuang (836–910)

The Lament of the Lady of Ch'in

It was April in the year Kuei-mao
        of the Chung-ho reign,[1]
Flowers were like snow outside the walls of Lo-yang;

---

1 The twelve links in the chain of causation, as described in the first sermon Buddha delivered after his enlightenment at Bodhgaya. They are a common subject for contemplative exercises.
1 I.e., *Kung Wang*, an epithet for the Buddha.
1 I.e., A.D. 883.

East, west, north, south: all travel stopped:
Green willows muffled in silence, the fragrant dust had vanished.[2]
Suddenly I saw by the side of the road
 a girl like a flower
Resting alone under the shade of the green willows.
Her hairpins, shaped like phoenixes, were thrust in crooked,
 her sidelocks twisted awry;
Rouge was blotched, mascara streaked
 and her eyebrows wrinkled in pain:

"May I trouble to ask Your Ladyship
 where you come from?"

Contracting her eyebrows, about to speak,   10
 her voice at first choked;
Then she turned her head, gathered the sleeves of her robe
 and saluted her fellow traveler—

(Engulfed by destruction and chaotic revolution
 what would she say?)—
"Three years ago I was caught by the rebels
 and kept in the land of Ch'in.
Only vaguely can I remember what happened in Ch'in,
So now that you've unfastened for me your gold saddle,
I will halt my footsteps awhile for you.
On the eighth of January
 the year before last,
I had just closed the gold cage
 after teaching my parrot,
Had tipped open my phoenix mirror,
 was lazily combing my hair,
Leisurely leaning on the carved balustrade,   20
 relaxing in silence,
When, suddenly, I saw outside the gates
 red dust rising:
Now I was seeing in the streets

---

2 "Fragrant dust" is a Buddhist term for one of the six wordly environments,
smell. Here it is used as a metaphor for beautiful women, and, by extension,
the luxurious life led by the upper classes before the Huang Ch'ao rebellion.

men pounding gongs and drums.
Inhabitants rushed out of their houses
    half-crazed with panic;
Courtiers hurry to their offices
    still hoping it's all a mistake.
Now the government troops march in from the west
Preparing to hurry to the T'ung Pass[3]
    to meet the emergency.
All say that Po-yeh troops are holding the enemy,[4]
All shout that the rebels are coming
    but haven't yet arrived.
In moments my master
    gallops home in flight,
Dismounts and comes through the gate
    jabbering as though he were drunk:
'I happened to see the emperor's Purple Canopy
    hurtling into exile;
Already I had seen
    white banners[5]
    swarming in from all sides!'

"As they support their aged and lead their children
    people scream to each other for help,
Scramble over roofs and scrabble up walls
    with no thought for rank or order.
The south neighbors stampede
    to conceal themselves with neighbors in the north
And the east neighbors stampede
    to hide with neighbors in the west.
The north neighbors' women
    all surge together
While outside the rebels rage
    like stampeding beasts.

30

---

3 This pass, located in Shensi province, was the last barrier between the rebels and the capital.

4 This army was drawn from northwest China in modern Hopei province. On its retreat from the T'ung Pass, it encountered a force freshly levied in Ch'ang-an that was well armed and clothed. The Po-yeh troops were bitterly enraged, changed allegiance, and led the rebels into the capital, burning the West Market in vengeance.

5 These were the rebels' flags.

"Rumbling and tumbling, the sky and earth shudder
     with the clatter of chariots:
Thousands and thousands of horses   40
     cause thunder to crash from the ground.
Fire drives the Gold Star
     up into the nine heavens,[6]
The twelve broad streets of the city
     are choked with smoke from the roaring flames.
The wheel of the sun drops in the west,
     its cold light white:
The First Emperor gazes down dumbly,
     speaks not a word;
A misty moon is wound round with haze
     as though ringed behind many battlements;
The Eunuch stars slip away,
     seem to be smeared with blood;
The Purple Exhalation stealthily follows
     the shift of the Emperor's Throne;
Foul light secretly shoots to destroy
     the star Seats of the Ministers.[7]
In house after house blood flows
     like boiling fountains;
In place after place victims scream: 50
     their screams shake the earth.
Dancers and singing girls have
     all secretly disappeared,
Babies and young girls are abandoned alive.

"My neighbor in the east had a daughter,
     her eyebrow newly painted;
So pricelessly beautiful she seemed,
     capable of overthrowing a city or kingdom[8]:

---

6 According to tradition, the Chinese divided the sky into nine quarters. The
Gold Star is the dawn star, the planet Venus.

7 The Eunuch stars, the Purple Exhalation, the Emperor's Throne, and the Seats
of the Ministers are all heavenly constellations. The Chinese believed that
events in the sky were correlated with events on earth. So Wei Chuang is
using these lines not only as actual physical occurrences but also as metaphors
for the flight of the Emperor (the color purple was associated with the T'ang
royal family) and his eunuch entourage into exile and the destruction of the
government by the rebels (the foul light).

8 Alluding to Li Yen-nien's lines about a beautiful woman; cf. note to Li
Shang-yin's "Willow."

Long spears crowding round
    force her up into a war chariot;
Turning her head towards her perfumed chamber
    her tears stream down:
Soon she will draw out gold thread
    as she learns to stitch banners,
Then mounting a tattooed saddle
    she will be taught to gallop a horse;
And sometimes on horseback
    she sees her husband:
Not daring to gaze back   60
    her tears fall in vain.

"My neighbor in the west had a daughter,
    lovely as a goddess;
Her lustrous eyes flashed from side to side
    cutting the autumn waters
    like an inch of sword blade.
After she had finished with powder and rouge,
    all she did was to gaze at
    the reflection of spring in her mirror,
So young she knew not
    what was happening outside her doors.
Some thug leaps up her golden staircase
Rips the dress from her one bare shoulder,
    about to shame her,
But, clutching her clothes,
    she refuses to go through the vermilion gate,
So with rouge powder and perfumed cream on her face
    she's stabbed down till she's dead.

"My southern neighbor had a daughter
    (can't remember her name)
Only yesterday a go-between   70
    brought presents for betrothal;
Never heard to have stepped down
    her staircase of lapis lazuli,
Only her silhouette had been seen through the kingfisher blind.
Suddenly she hears, at the corner of the courtyard,
    sword blades clashing,
In seconds heads are chopped from bodies:

They look up to the skies, cover their faces
    and raise a single scream:
She and her sisters plunge together
    into the well.

"My northern neighbor's young wife
    is being urged to leave,
Soon she loosens her cloud-like tresses
    and wipes off the green from her eyebrows;
Now she hears men
    battering down the high gates,
Unwittingly she climbs up   80
    to the upper story;
In moments on all four sides
    leap up bright flames:
She wants to come down the stairs again;
    the stairs are already destroyed.
Deep in the smoke loud she shrieks
    still begging to be rescued;
Over the beams her corpse hangs,
    it's burnt to ashes.

"But, as luck would have it, I managed to keep myself
    safe from sword slashes
And I dared not look back long in hesitation.
Soon I combed out my hair that was shaped like cicada wings
    to follow the tramping army,
And I forced my moth eyebrows from frowning
    as I went out of the gates of my home.
From this time on, never was I able to return
    to my old street;
From this time on I had nowhere to look   90
    for any of my relations.

"Since I fell into the rebels' hands
    three years have passed;
Every day after day, all day,
    my heart and vitals shuddered in fear and dismay:
At night I rested encircled by thousand
    on thousand of lances and swords,

In the daytime I had one dish—
    minced human livers![9]
Though I lay behind mandarin duck curtains,
    how could I know pleasure?
Though I had many jewels, much finery,
    they were not what I longed for.
Their hair disheveled, faces filthy,
    even their eyebrows daubed with red:
Often I turned my eyes towards them
    and as often I couldn't stand the sight;
Their clothes untidy, slovenly,
    their speech barbaric,
Arrogance of success seemed tattooed on each face.   100
Almost all their Cypress Terrace officials are sly as foxes,
Nearly every courtier of their Orchid Office is a slimy rat![10]
They even try to stick ornate pins into their crew-cut hair!
But at night they wrap in embroidered quilts
    without stripping off their court robes;
They grip their ceremonial ivory tablets upside down
    when they act like Ministers of State;
They hang their Golden Fish wrong way up
    when they appear as High Officials![11]
I hear them in the morning
    entering the Imperial Hall to present their memorials,
I see them in the evening
    bellowing on their way to the wine shops.

"One morning, at around four o'clock,
    everyone scrambles up in panic,
Shouting and arguing   110
    as if in council of war:
Last night a mounted scout
    had entered the Imperial City

---

[9] That the rebels practiced cannibalism is well documented by the histories of the period; the royalist troops even sold civilians to them for food!

[10] Huang Ch'ao declared himself emperor when he captured Ch'ang-an and proceeded to organize his government along traditional lines. The Cypress Terrace and the Orchid Office were names of the Han dynasty censorate, the Yü-shih fu.

[11] These pendants were hung from the waists of high officials, a practice instituted at the beginning of the K'ai-yüan period (A.D. 713).

And reported that yesterday
    a royal army had occupied Russet River;
From Russet River to the City it is only thirty miles:
If they left in the morning,
    they could arrive by night!
Our savages sit in blank despair
    on their horses, quite, quite dumb,
But deep in the inner chambers the faces of us womenfolk
    light up in secret pleasure.
Every one of us says that now is the time
    when our wrongs will be wiped clean,
And each of us insists that today is the day
    when those fiends will perish.
Scurrying along on galloping horses
    messengers fan the flames of rumor,
And they say that the army is entering the city in full array.   120
P'eng Tsuan and Little P'eng gaze at each other in dismay[12];
Huang Ch'ao and Huang K'uei clutch their saddles as they snivel.
For several days matters drift, with no news:
We are certain that the rebels already
    hold jade tablets in their mouths in submission.[13]
However, flaunting their banners and brandishing their swords,
    they return triumphant,
And they say that the government army
    was completely smashed and annihilated.

"From this time on, starvation and misery
    redoubled on all sides:
A pint of grain costs ten pints of yellow gold;
In Shang Jang's kitchen, they eat the bark of trees,
Men's flesh is sliced on Huang Ch'ao's chopping board!   130
Communication with the southeast is cut:
    no way for grain supplies to be brought in.
Ditches and gullies gradually fill up level with the dead,
    as the population dwindles;

---

[12] Literally, Big P'eng and Little P'eng. Huang Ch'ao appointed P'eng Tsuan a Grand General of the Garrisons and Patrol Commander of the Four Fronts on his capture of Ch'ang-an. I have not been able to identify the other P'eng. Another commentator says Big P'eng and Little P'eng are two generals in Huang Ch'ao's army, who came originally from the city P'eng.

[13] According to the early historical work the *Tso Chuan,* Baron Hsü appeared before the King of Ch'u holding a jade tablet in his mouth as token of submission.

Stiff corpses lean against each other
    outside the Gates of the Six Armies,[14]
The Camp of the Seven Assembled Divisions[15] is stuffed full
    with victims of starvation.
Ch'ang-an is silent: what's there now?
In the abandoned markets and deserted streets
    wheat sprouts flourish.
To gather fuel wood, they chop down every flowering branch
    in the Apricot Gardens,
To construct barricades, they smash up
    the willows on the Imperial Canal;
The ornate carriages with their embroidered fine gauze curtains
    all have scattered and vanished,
Not one half of the noblemen's vermilion-gated mansions   140
    are left still standing;
Foxes and rabbits gambol up
    the Han Yüan Palace,
Thorn trees and brambles fill the entrance
    to the Flower Calyx Pavilion:
All the opulence of the old days is utterly
    obliterated and buried:
I raise my eyes with a shiver
    and see nothing familiar from the old days;
When the Inner Treasury was gutted,[16]
    it became just ashes of brocades and embroideries;
One trod along the Street of Heaven
    over pulverized bones of state officials.[17]

---

14 There were three imperial armies, the Yü-lin, the Lung-wu, and the Shen-ts'e. Each was divided into a left and right flank. The left armies were quartered outside the Gate of Eternal Peace, the right outside the Gate of the Nine Transcendents. These, presumably, are the gates to which the poet is referring.

15 The officers of the Seven Assembled Divisions is a phrase that occurs in the fragmentary late Chou work the "Biography of Emperor Mu." There is evidence that suggests "the Seven Assembled Divisions" was a designation in T'ang times for the Imperial armies stationed at the capital. This evidence, however, is not conclusive. An alternative rendition of the Chinese is "the Camp of the Seven Frames." While the location of a Pavilion of the Seven Frames in Ch'ang-an is known, there is no record of a camp of that name.

16 Two treasuries were located on either side of the Ch'eng-tien Gate, on the south-central side of the Palace City in Ch'ang-an.

17 These two lines were all that were left of the poem for a thousand years after it had been lost, and it was precisely to these lines that the high officials objected.

"It was dawn when we left the city[18]
    by a pathway leading east;
Outside the city, the landscape
    was like that on the northern frontier;
Sometimes by the side of the road
    we saw patrols of scouts roaming.
Beneath the slope, all was silence: 150
    no one there to greet or send off travelers;
Gazing eastward from Pa-ling
    not a single trace of smoke from a cooking fire;
On Mount Li, sealed off by trees,
    the gold and blue had vanished.
All main roads had become forests of brambles;
Travelers rest beneath the moonlight
    by crumbled walls.
Dawn, next morning, we reached
    the road to the Three Peaks:
Here, of a million households
    now not one survives;
Ruined fields and gardens
    grow only weeds;
Trampled-down trees and bamboo:
    none has an owner.
I try to question the Golden Heaven Spirit
    in his shrine by the roadside,
But the Golden Heaven Spirit doesn't speak: 160
    he's even more melancholy than mortals.
The ancient cypresses in front of his temple
    have been hacked down to stumps,
The golden incense burners in his hall
    exude somber dust:
'Ever since the mad Bandit[19] overwhelmed the Middle Kingdom,
Sky and earth have been darkened and dimmed
    with the black splash of wind and rain.
The sacred water in front of my altar
    has failed to be efficacious;

---

18 Time has passed. For the rest of the poem, the Lady of Ch'in recounts the
details of her flight from Ch'ang-an to Lo-yang.
19 The mad Bandit refers to Huang Ch'ao.

The Warriors of Hell, painted on my walls,[20]
    refused to obey me.
When days were leisurely,
    I merely accepted the libations and food offerings;
In times of danger,
    my spiritual power was of no assistance.
Now I am ashamed
    of being an ineffectual spirit:
I'd rather hide away   170
    deep in the mountains.
I haven't heard for some time
    pipes and flutes playing within my precinct;
Nowhere have I found on my bamboo mats
    sacrificial animals.
Soon I will make some demon of nightmares
    settle near the village
To kill and flay human beings alive
    so I could live on them day and night!'
When I'd heard his speech
    my sadness grew sadder:
Heaven sends down disasters
    which we cannot control.
If even a spirit can't escape calamities
    and wishes to flee into the mountains,
Why should we reprimand and rest our hope on
    the lords in the east?[21]

"Last year,
    I came out through the Yang-chen Pass;
When I raised my head   180
    I saw Mount Ching
    at the edge of of the clouds:
It was like leaving the grave
    and entering the land of the living,
For suddenly I realized that here

---

[20] The portraits of these two spirits were painted on either side of the entrance door. They were supposed to drive away evil influences.
[21] Those governors of provinces and generals who failed to suppress the rebels.

the seasons were clear
and the sky and the earth were at peace;
The governor general of Shen-chou[22]
was loyal and incorruptible,
He didn't raise shield and spear in rebellion,
but only defended his city;
The governor general of P'u-chin[23]
had been able to suppress all soldiery,
So for five hundred miles all was quiet,
no sound of lances clashing:
In the daytime, you could carry valuables
and no one would ask questions;
At night, you could just travel alone
with gold pins stuck in your hair.

"Next day, I passed Hsin-an,
traveling eastwards,
And met an old man   190
begging for rice-gruel;
His face was green,
green as moss,
His body concealed,
hidden in brambles and bracken.
I asked this old man:
'What village did you come from originally?
Why do you pass the night under bleak skies
in frost and dew?'

"The aged old man for a while stood upright
and was about to tell me his story
When he slumped back, rested his chin on his hands,

---

22 Shen-chou is the modern Shen prefecture in northwest Honan. The governor
general was probably Wang Ch'ung-ying, the elder brother of Wang Ch'ung-
jung, one of the T'ang generals successful in the later stages of the campaign
against the rebels.

23 P'u-chin was the name of a ford across the Yellow River east of Chao-yi
prefecture in Shensi. The name P'u-chin was probably used for the whole
region of P'u-chou, which in T'ang times was changed to Ho-chung fu.
Wang Ch'ung-jung (see note 22), who came from T'ai-yüan in Shansi prov-
ince, was Legate of Ho-chung in A.D. 881 and 882, and so it is probably he who
is mentioned. The modern scholar Chiang Ts'ung-p'ing, however, thinks it is
Cheng Ts'ung-tang who is meant.

looked up to the heavens and moaned:
'My farmhouse originally was in the Prefecture of Tung-chi;
Season after season I cultivated mulberries
    just near the Imperial Domain;
I sowed each season
    over five hundred thousand acres of arable fields;
Every year for household tax   200
    I paid thirty million cash;
My daughters were expert in weaving
    long gowns of serge and damask,
My daughters-in-law could prepare meals of red millet;
A thousand granaries!
    Ten thousand wagons!
After Huang Ch'ao had passed through
    still nearly half was left;
But ever since the troops encamped in and around Lo-yang,
Day and night patrols of foragers
    penetrated the walls of my village;
Like autumn waves, Green Snake
    swords were drawn from their scabbards;
A high wind blew
    on the White Tiger device in the flags.[24]
They entered my gates
    dismounted like whirlwinds
Pillaged the houses   210
    rifled the money bags
    as though they were sieving the very soil itself!
The wealth of my household was exhausted,
    my blood relatives snatched from me;
Today, in my failing years,
    I'm alone and utterly miserable.
Alone and utterly miserable,
    yet why should I groan?
There are a thousand, ten thousand families in the mountains:
Starved on mountain grass,
    they search every morning for brambleberries;

---

24 Green Snake was the name of a type of sword. The Green Snake was the
mythical beast that commanded the East, while the White Tiger controlled
the West. The rebels' flag was white, so the old man is saying that he was
plundered by both rebels and royalist troops.

At night they rest in the frost
    among reed flowers!'

"When I had heard this old man's heart-rending story,
All day my tears streamed down like rain.
Outside the gates, I hear only
    the ominous hoots of the owl;
I want to flee still farther east,   220
    but where am I going to?
I still hear that travel by boat or carriage
    on the Pien road is halted,
And they say too
    that they've been killing each other at P'eng-men.[25]
The somber hue of the plains only serves to chill
    a warrior's ghost:
Half of the rivers and streams are
    filled with the blood of innocent victims.
I happened to hear a stranger
    who had come from Chin-ling
Say that the scenery in Chiang-nan is different:
'Ever since the Great Bandit
    seized the Middle Plain,
War horses have not been bred on its four borders.[26]
The governor exterminates thieves
    as though he had spiritual power,
And showers affection on his people   230
    as if they were newborn infants.
His cities are secure
    as if protected by metal walls and moats of boiling water.[27]
His tax revenue, as abundant as clouds,
    provides for armies and ramparts.'

---

[25] It is not certain to what incident this line refers. There was a P'eng-men Mountain in Szechwan province to the southwest of Lo-yang, but any military action there would not have hindered the Lady of Ch'in from traveling eastward. Ch'en Yin-k'o has suggested that it may indicate an incident that took place in northwest Kiangsu: Ch'en Fan, a general under Shih P'u, murdered his superior officer Chih Hsiang at Ta P'eng Kuan. But the histories date this in late summer or fall 880, before Huang Ch'ao had captured Ch'ang-an, and the action mentioned in this line must have taken place in A.D. 882.

[26] A line drawn from the *Lao-tzu*.

[27] A metaphor taken from a poem by Wang Hung (A.D. 468–94).

"Why, when the four seas are completely in turbulence,
Is Chiang-nan as clear as water and smooth like a whetstone?
Fleeing from disaster, I have become
    a mere commoner beneath the capital gates,
In longing for peace, I envy
    even the ghosts in Chiang-nan.
I would like you, sir, to lift your oar
    and travel farther and farther east,
And sing this long song
    as an offering to His Excellency."[28]
(CFYCC, 1a–3b)   (TR. ROBIN D. S. YATES)

Spoken to Pines and Bamboos

Fragrant grass   in front of the courtyard
    greener than a green cloak
A poet   standing in the hall
    nearly gray-haired
Wracked by sickness   I cannot endure autumn's desolation
Pines in the rain   bamboos in the wind
    please do not sigh
(CTS, P. 4180)   (TR. ROBIN D. S. YATES)

Tune: "Sand of Silk-washing Stream" (*Huan ch'i sha*), Five Lyrics

[1]

A clear dawn adorns the day of the Cold Food Festival;
Among the curling willows, flowers bloom like filigree;
I roll up the curtain and step out of the painted hall.

I notice the peony buds are just beginning to blossom;
The sun is high, but still I lean against the red railing;
Frowning, I do not speak of my regret for the fading spring.

---

28 His Excellency is probably Chou Pao, the governor of Nanking, who entertained Wei when he visited that city after leaving Lo-yang in A.D. 883.

[2]

She wants to get on the swing, but she is too lazy;
She wants him to push the swing, but she is too timid;
The curtains in the painted hall shine in the moon and wind.

On this night who does not feel deep emotion?
The pear blossoms beyond the wall are again splendid;
Her jade-like face is sad as she lightly blushes.

[3]

I wake in sad reverie; the moon is slanting over the mountain;
A single lamp shines on the wall from behind the window curtain;
The beautiful one lives in a high apartment in the small tower.

I think of her lovely jade-like face—how shall I compare it?
A branch of cold plum blossoms in the spring snow.
The fragrant mist of her body is like the gathered clouds of dawn.

[4]

The green trees hide the crying orioles;
Slanting willow branches brush against the Pai-t'ung Dam[1];
On the Pearl-sporting River[2] the grass is luxuriant.

I return after drink; where else can I go?
Finely saddled and ready, the spotted horse neighs;
But I, covered with heavy perfume, am dead drunk!

---

[1] The Pai-t'ung Dam or *pai-t'ung t'i* is an allusion to songs written by Emperor
Wu of the Liang dynasty (reigned 502–50) and by the poet Shen Yüeh (441–
512) entitled "Pai-t'ung t'i" or "White Brass Hooves." Li Po (701–62) in his
"Song of Hsiang-yang" describes a scene of feasting and revelry during which
a song of this title is being sung. Wei Chuang uses *t'i*, "a dam" or "embank-
ment," as a pun on *t'i*, "hooves," and thus suggests this song and the idea of
carousal.

[2] The Pearl-sporting River is a reference to a folk song and to the story of Cheng
Chiao-fu of the Chou dynasty and his liaison with two goddesses at the foot
of Han-kao Mountain. The goddesses were wearing girdles trimmed with ex-
tremely large pearls. Cheng Chiao-fu asked for and received them as gifts, but
as he left, the pearls vanished and so did the women. Han-kao Mountain is
northwest of the district of Hsiang-yang.

[5]

Every night I think of you until the water clock fades;
Sadly, under the bright moon, I lean against the balcony;
I think you too feel the cold in your lonely quilt.

A short foot away, the painted hall is as deep as the sea;
In remembrance I have only your old letters to read;
When can we be together, hand in hand, in Ch'ang-an?
(CTS, P. 5130)   (TR. LOIS M. FUSEK)

Tune: "Deva-like Barbarian," Five Lyrics

[1]

The night of our parting in the red tower is enough for sorrow;
By the fragrant lamp, the tasseled screen is but half rolled up.
As I leave the moon is just fading;
She says goodby mixed with tears.

The guitar is ornamented with gold and kingfisher feathers;
From its strings come the caroling cries of orioles.
Urging me to return soon,
She is like a flower in the window!

[2]

Everyone says it is good to live south of the Yangtze;
The traveler can but stay there until he grows old.
The spring waters are more blue than the heavens;
On the painted boat drowsily I listen to the rain.

The girl who pours wine is like the moon;
Her wrists are as bright as frosted snow.
If you are not yet old, don't return home;
To return home is to be broken hearted!

[3]

Today I still remember my happiness south of the Yangtze;
Then I was young, and my spring robe was light.

On horseback I would draw near the slanting bridge;
From the towers red sleeves everywhere beckoned me.

Golden filigree and kingfisher feathers adorned the curved screen;
Drunkenly I entered that grove of flowers and stayed the night.
Now whenever I see a blossoming branch,
I vow not to return until my hair is white!

[4]

Host:

> I urge you to get very drunk tonight;
> Don't talk of tomorrow in front of the wine jar!

Guest:

> I greatly appreciate your sentiment;
> The wine is deep, but my feelings are even deeper!

Host:

> Only grieve that the spring night is so short;
> And don't complain that your cup is full!
> When there is wine we can laugh
> How long does human life last?

[5]

Spring is bright and splendid in the city of Lo-yang;
But the man of Lo-yang grows old in another land.
The willows darken on the Prince of Wei's embankment[1];
At this time I am confused and bewildered.

Alongside the blossoming peach, the spring waters run clear;
Mandarin ducks bathe in their freshness.
My regret gathers force in the setting sun;
I think of you, but you do not know it!
(CTS, P. 5130)   (TR. LOIS M. FUSEK)

---

[1] The Prince of Wei refers to Ts'ao Chih (192–232). The embankment was presumed to be on the bank of the River Lo; Po Chü-yi had described it as overgrown with willows.

Ssu-k'ung T'u (837–908)

Oxhead Temple

From my favorite place in the Chung-nan Mountains,
The chanting of the monks emerges into the dark sky.
Groves of trees stand out clearly in the somber solitude,
Thin mist floats in the desolate void.
(CTS, P. 3785)   (TR. HELLMUT WILHELM)

In the Country

From dusk to dawn I sit under the canopy of a pine,
Happily facing a calabash of wine.
The song of subtle rain fills my mind,
For no reason I dream of falling petals.
Trifling matters I while away playing chess,
Happy with a mirror that bears with my decrepit countenance.
The monk next to the brook, immersed in deep thought,
Has sent a letter inviting me to meet him again.
(CTS, P. 3781)   (TR. HELLMUT WILHELM)

In the Mountains

All birds love to babble where a man wants quiet;
Idle clouds seem jealous of the moon's full light.
In the world of men are a myriad problems—but none is my affair!
My only shame: autumn has come—and I have made no poems.
(CTS, P. 3788)   (TR. EDWARD H. SCHAFER)

In Heaven

Fallen flowers should still be mourned
       the same as falling leaves;
The songs of orioles will soon be followed
       by the cicadas' cries.

Flourishing and decay finish off all things,
    no more than so—
Only the idle people foolishly attach their feeling
    to these things.
(CTS, P. 3794)   (TR. IRVING Y. LO)

An Occasional Poem

A hall by the water where flowers grow dense,
A sunny day in spring just before noon—
A bird peeps at the mirror facing the rail,
A horse passes by—the crack of a whip beyond the wall.
(CTS, P. 3784)   (TR. IRVING Y. LO)

Exhorting Myself

My grandfather had the right-hand side of his seat inscribed
With wise counsel to bequeath to his grandsons.
Diligently following these sentences without tiring
Would make your reputation prevail day by day.
Conniving and display are the shame of scholars,
Compassion and frugality are revered by tradition.

Pines and cedars, do they not grow well?
And do peaches and plums not flower by themselves?
The mass of the people are all so sharp,
I alone am confused.[1]
I take my instructions from Master Lao,
And in a great dispute I choose to stammer.
(CTS, P. 3781)   (TR. HELLMUT WILHELM)

Yü Hsüan-chi (c. 843–868)

Composed on the Theme "Willows by the Riverside"

Kingfisher green lines the deserted shore,
the misty vision stretches to a distant tower.

---

[1] Quotation from *Tao-te-ching* 20.

Their shadows overspread the autumn-clear water
and catkins fall on the angler's head.
Old roots form hollows where fish hide;
limbs reach down to moor the traveler's boat.
Soughing, soughing in the wind and rain of night
they startle dreams and compound the gloom.
(CTS, P. 4665)   (TR. JAN W. WALLS)

Replying to a Poem by a New Graduate
Lamenting the Loss of His Wife

Immortals don't stay long in the world of men;
You've passed another fall, already ten.

Pairs of ducks on a curtain, beneath, her fragrance lingers;
In the parrot's cage her words are not yet stilled.

Morning dew pastes the flowers in a sad face;
Evening wind bends the willows like dropping eyebrows.

Colored clouds come once, then go away;
P'an Yüeh,[1] wistful, is going gray.
(CTS, P. 4667)   (TR. GEOFFREY R. WATERS)

To Tzu-an

A thousand goblets at the farewell feast
    can't dilute my sorrow,
my heart at separation is twisted
    in a hundred unyielding knots.
Tender orchids wilt and wither,
    return to the garden of spring;
willow trees, here and there,
    moor travelers' boats.
In meeting and parting I lament
    the unsettled clouds;
love and affection should learn from the river
    in flowing on and on.

---

1 A third-century poet who wrote three poems lamenting the loss of his wife.

I know we won't meet again
   in the season of blossoms,
and I won't sit by quietly
   drunk in my chamber.
(CTS, P. 4669)   (TR. JAN W. WALLS)

On the River

The Great River wraps an arm
   angling around Wu-ch'ang
Parrot Island faces the gates
   of ten thousand homes.
Spring sleep in a pleasure boat
   unfulfilled at dawn—
In dreams a butterfly
   still seeking blossoms.
(CTS, P. 4667)   (TR. JAN W. WALLS)

Tu Hsün-ho (846–904)

Climbing to a Mountain Monastery

Half into the mountains—a mountain monastery.
A man in the country now, I climb to it on an autumn day.
It is right in their midst, with lovely rocks askew—
Solitary on the summit on its very highest layer.

Where there is fruit, gibbons scramble up the trees;
When there is no fast, pigeons study the monks.
But my academic door never lacks for problems—
It's hardly possible that I shall come here again.
(CTS, P. 4136)   (TR. EDWARD H. SCHAFER)

Li Shan-fu (fl. 874)

My Detached Villa

On this ground I may look for rest;
Open the door—enough for bucolic feelings.
The window brightens—at least the rain is spent;
The sun goes down—again the wind is fresh.

Gray-green moss winds round the roots of felled trees.
Deep-blue haze quickens on the water's face.
Trifles and oddities—in these my heart finds its own joys.
Summer heat—the moon—listening to the cicadas call.
(CTS, P. 3848)   (TR. EDWARD H. SCHAFER)

The Temple of Hsiang Yü[1]

Captive or king, it's all a matter of chance.
Why ashamed to see Han boats on the river?
Contesting for the empire, the world wasn't big enough;
Would you now care for offerings of paper money from a traveler?
(CTS, P. 3846)   (TR. IRVING Y. LO)

T'ang Yen-ch'ien (fl. 880)

A Walk in the Country

Butterflies in love with evening flowers will not leave until
          the very end.
Gulls meeting spring waters find it sorely hard to fly away.
A man in the country, I keep no address at all under my heart;
A companion of butterflies, a follower of gulls, I will not go
          home either.
(CTS, P. 4007)   (TR. EDWARD H. SCHAFER)

---

[1] Hsiang Yü (232–202 B.C.), the defeated king of Ch'u. Cf. page 29.

Li Hsün (fl. 896)

Tune: "Song of the Southern Country" (*Nan-hsiang tzu*),
Five Lyrics

[1]

The way home is close—
She knocks on the gunwale and sings.
Where she was gathering pearls, water and wind were too much.
At a little bridge from the winding bank, hills and moon pass by.
Locked deep in the mist
Cardamom flowers droop: a thousand, ten thousand buds!

[2]

The fish market breaks up,
Ferrying boats are few—
The clouded trees of Vietnam visible afar in the middle murk.
A journeying stranger awaits the tide as the skies turn toward sunset:
Escorted to the river-reach in spring,
He listens sadly to a man-ape howling in the malarial rain.

[3]

She boards a painted skiff,
Sails over clear waves.
It is lotus-picking time—she sings a lotus-picking song;
Rhythmic sound of dragging oars—gauze sleeves pulled back.
Light on the pond wind-broken
Starts the gulls up from the sand—eight, nine flecks.

[4]

Her paired chignons fallen loose,
Small eyebrows arched—
She comes laughing down the spring mountain with her girl companions.
Jade-white, her delicate finger points far off to a spot deep in flowers.

We both look back
Where pair and pair of peafowl dance, welcoming the sun.

[5]

Pink cardamoms,
Purple thorn-roses[1]—
The house of the Zya woman adjoins the platform of the king of Viet;
One round of a village song, to rhythmic clapping of hands;
She is willing to wander and wonder—
To let wine flow free from whelk-shell cups, out on the flowing
water!
(CTS, P. 5152)   (TR. EDWARD H. SCHAFER)

Tune: "A Stretch of Cloud over Mount Wu"
(*Wu-shan yi-tuan yün*)

An old temple leans against the green hillside,
The Traveling Palace[1] nestles next to the emerald flow.
Sounds of waters, and the sheen of the mountain locked in the painted
tower.
Past memories send my thoughts far away.

Morning rain and clouds return at dusk,
Mist and flowers, in spring as in autumn.
Why should the screeching of the monkeys get so close to the solitary
boat?
The traveler has enough sorrows of his own.
(CTS, P. 5154)   (TR. HELLMUT WILHELM)

Han Wo (fl. 902)

Summer Night

Wild wind, chaotic lightning—black clouds are born.
Splashing, splashing in tall woods—the sound of dense rain.

---

1 Thorn-roses are the lovely *Rosa rugosa* of China.
1 An emperor's temporary residence while away from the capital.

Night wears on, rain lets up—wind, too, is settled.
Torn clouds—a floating moon once more slants down its light.
(CTS, P. 4079)   (TR. EDWARD H. SCHAFER)

Sent to a Ch'an Master

From non-being into being: the cloud peaks gather;
From being back to non-being: the lightning flash goes out.
To gather or to disperse is all illusory:
Only the meddlers keep up their useless jabbering.
(CTS, P. 4079)   (TR. IRVING Y. LO)

Anonymous

Lyrics from Tun-huang

Tune: "Willow Branches" (*Yang-liu-chih*)

Spring goes, spring comes, spring again will be spring;
    Cold and heat alternate constantly.
The moon waxes, the moon wanes, then again the new moon returns.
    Age urges people on.
What you see is the thousand-year-old moon before the hall,
    Eternally there, eternally present.
What you don't see are hundred-year-old people in the chamber:
    They have all turned to dust.
(JEN, PP. 81–82)   (TR. HELLMUT WILHELM)

Tune: "Deva-like Barbarian," Two Lyrics

[1]

Drizzle, drizzle, drop, drop, the rain at Winding Pond,
Two by twos, one by one, the mandarin ducks chatter.
    Sharp—the scent of wild flowers;
    Lush—the yellow of golden willows.

    Full of girls, the river shore:
    In pairs they dance next to the brook.

Bright, the sheen of their gauze dress,
Light as clouds, her powdered makeup.

[2]

In Tun-huang since old times we expect spirited generals,
Who will make all barbarians from afar submit to the throne.
Devoted and loyal, we look toward the Dragon Court,
And the Unicorn Terrace[1] of early fame.

I only regret that, separated by these tribes,
I can't make known our earnest emotions.
Sooner or later we'll wipe out these wolfish barbarians,
Then we will all bow before the Holy Countenance.
(JEN, PP. 33, 36)   (TR. HELLMUT WILHELM)

Tune: "Eternal Longing" (*Ch'ang hsiang-ssu*), Three Lyrics

[1]

A traveling merchant west of the river[1]
Displays wealth rare in this world,
All day long he stays in pleasure quarters
. . . dancing and singing.[2]

Incessantly drinking until drunk like mud,
Lightheartedly exchanging the golden goblets,
Pursuing pleasure, seeking happiness, until nightfall.
This is: not to return in wealth.

[2]

A sad merchant west of the river,
His loneliness he keeps to himself;
His whole face covered with dust,
Every day cheated by people.

---

1 *Ling-t'ai*, or the *Ch'i-ling* ("Unicorn") Pavilion, was the name of the imperial
secretariat during the reign of Emperor Wu of Han.
1 *Chiang-hsi* may also be taken as the name of a town, located west of present-
day Nanking, a center of commercial activities in T'ang time.
2 Two words are missing from the manuscript; a variant reading of the word
for "singing" is *ch'i*, or "chess-playing."

Mornings he stands in front of the western city gate,
The cold wind blowing tears from both his eyes;
He gazes toward home, many post stations away.
This is: not to return in poverty.

[3]

A merchant makes his home west of the river,
Lying sick in the Temple of the Earth-god.
People look in to ask for the latest news,
And to find out if there's a chance for departing.

The villagers just drag him off to the west of the road,
Mom and Dad know nothing about his fate.
On his body he carries his identification tag.
This is: not to return in death.

(JEN, P. 71)   (TR. HELLMUT WILHELM)

PART IV

Cross-pollination: The Predominance of the Tz'u, or Lyric Meters

(In the Five Dynasties and the Sung Eras, 10th–13th Century)

Ku Hsiung (fl. 928)

Tune: "Telling of Innermost Feelings"

In the endless night, having deserted me, where have you gone?
    No news of your coming!
    My perfumed chamber closed.
        My eyebrows knit—
    The moon is about to set.
How can you bear not to seek me?
    How lonely in my quilt!
Only if you bartered your heart for mine
    Would you know how much I miss you![1]
(CTS, P. 5142)   (TR. JAMES J. Y. LIU)

Feng Yen-ssu (903–960)

Tune: "Magpie on the Branch" (*Ch'üeh t'a chih*),[1] Two Lyrics

[1]

Who says that sadness can be cast away for long?
    Every year when spring arrives,
    Sorrow and remorse return as they were before.
Day after day by blossoms I am forever drunk with wine;
If only I could avoid the mirrors in which my once bright face grows
    thin.

By riverbanks the weeds are green, upon the dikes the willows;
    I wonder why this new sorrow,
    How such things remain, year after year:
Standing alone on a small bridge, wind billowing my sleeves,

---

[1] The last two lines remind one of Sir Philip Sidney's famous poem "My true love hath my heart, and I have his," but while Sidney's poem rests on a rhetorical conceit intellectually worked out, the present poem is a passionate cry, moving in its simplicity and naïveté. Cf. Wang Kuo-wei, *Jen-chien Tz'u-hua* (with notes by Hsü T'iao-fu, Peking, 1955), p. 47.

[1] After the time of Yen Shu (991–1055), this tune-pattern of *Ch'üeh t'a chih* with two stanzas was also known as *Tieh lien hua*.

And a new moon even with the woods when all have gone
    their ways.   10

[2]

In curve after curve the balustrade caresses jade-green trees,
    Willows in the light breeze
    Break out all their golden strands.
Someone takes up an inlaid lute, tuning it with pegs of jade;
A pair of swallows flies away in alarm through the screens.

As far as eyes can see, floating gossamer and falling willow-down;
    As the pink almond-flower clusters open,
    For a moment, a light Ch'ing-ming rain.
She awakens from deep slumber to orioles' flurried chatter,
Startled from the last of a happy dream that cannot be found again. 10
(CTS, P. 5172)   (TR. DANIEL BRYANT)

Sun Kuang-hsien (*?–968*)

Tune: "Paying Homage at the Golden Gate" (*Yeh Chin-men*)

    I cannot stay,
And if I could it would be senseless.
The spring shirt of light gauze had the color of snow
    The day I first left Yang-chou.

    I take the parting lightly,
And sweet it is to throw the past away.
The river was full of sails in the swift wind,
And I admired the bright-colored pairs of mandarin ducks, thirty-six of
    them.
    But then there was still the solitary swan.[1]
(CTS, P. 5164)   (TR. HELLMUT WILHELM)

---

[1] *Luan;* literally, a legendary bird which stopped singing when his mate died.

Tune: "Eight-beat Barbarian Tune" (*Pa-p'ai man*)

The peacock drags its tail with its long golden threads,
Frightened by people, it flies up into the clove tree.
Girls from Yüeh hurry to pick up from the sand those green feathers,
They call out to each other and return home,
> the slanting sun shining on their backs.

(CTS, P. 5164)   (TR. HELLMUT WILHELM)

Tune: "Song of a Dandy" (*Feng-liu tzu*)

With golden reins and jade bridle, a neighing horse
Tied to the green willow, standing in its shadow.
> The red gate is shut,
> The embroidered curtain let down.

Meandering through the courtyard water flows, and flowers fade.
> The welcome is over,
> Return now

Again through the nine thoroughfares in the depth of the night.

(CTS, P. 5163)   (TR. HELLMUT WILHELM)

Li Ching, Second Ruler of Southern T'ang (916–961)

Tune: "Echoing Heaven's Everlastingness" (*Ying t'ien-ch'ang*)

A single slender crescent brow before her dressing mirror,
Her cicada-wing hairdo and phoenix pins indolently left awry,
> Still, within many curtains,
> Remote, in her storied tower,

Sad and grieving over falling flowers the wind will not let rest.

On the willow banks there were paths in the fragrant grass,
But her dream was broken by the windlass of an ornate well.
Last night as the watches ended, she awoke from wine;
Her spring grief worse than any illness.

(NTECTHC, 1a)   (TR. DANIEL BRYANT)

Tune: "Sand of Silk-washing Stream," Two Lyrics

[1]

I myself have rolled the pearl screens up to their jade hooks,
And as before, spring regret locked in my storied tower.
Who is truly master of the falling blossoms borne by the wind?
  Long and brooding thoughts.

Black birds[1] bring me no news from beyond the clouds;
In vain the wisteria blossoms knot my sorrow in the rain.
I look back to the dusk over the green rapids of Ch'u,
  Flowing on to reach the sky.

[2]

The lotus flowers' fragrance fades, their blue-black leaves decay;
The sadness of the west wind rises over the green waves.
My features too are worried and worn like all these things,
  And I cannot bear to look upon them.

In the fine rain my dreams return from faraway Ch'i-sai[1];
Through a low tower blows the cold sound of jade pipes.
How many teardrops, and what end to my remorse,
  As I lean upon a balustrade?
(NTECTHC, 2a–2b)   (TR. DANIEL BRYANT)

Li Yü, Last Ruler of Southern T'ang (937–978)

Tune: "A Casket of Pearls" (*Yi-hu chu*)

Her morning adornment finished now,
She touches her lips with a few drops of sandalwood stain,
Showing off her tiny clove-like tongue:
  A single song in her clear voice
Breaks teasingly for a moment between her cherry lips.

---

1 The legendary goddess Hsi-wang-mu, "Queen Mother of the West," was said
to have sent messages to a Chinese emperor by way of these birds.
1 A small frontier outpost in the northwest.

Her gauze sleeves are moistened and soiled with deep red stains,
For her cup is deep, and again she blots away the fragrant unstrained
    wine;
She leans across the embroidered bed, so pampered and indolently
             Chewing bits of red basting
And spitting them, with a smile, at her Master Sandalwood.[1]   10
(NTECTHC, 6b)   (TR. DANIEL BRYANT)

Tune: "Song of Tzu-yeh" (*Tzu-yeh ko*)

How may one be spared the sorrow and regret of human life?
Why am I alone so overwhelmed, what end to my grief?
To my former kingdom I return in dreams again,
And awaken to find my tears already brimming.

With whom did I climb the high towers then?
How often I remember how we gazed into the clear autumn.
These things past are already drained and dead,
As though they were moments from within a single dream.
(NTECTHC, 7a–7b)   (TR. DANIEL BRYANT)

Tune: "Gazing at the South" (*Wang Chiang-nan*), Two Lyrics

[1]

    So much to regret:
    Last night my soul within a dream
Seemed again, as in former days, to wander into the imperial gardens,
Where carriages drifted like flowing water, the horses like dragons;
    And the breath of spring was just upon the moonlit flowers.

[2]

    So many tears:
    They stain your cheeks and run down along your chin,
Sorrows of the heart should not be told with tears,

---

1 "Master Sandalwood" is a reference to the poet P'an Yüeh (d. A.D. 300),
who was considered irresistibly handsome as a young man. In later poetry he
becomes a stock figure with some of the associations of Romeo or Valentino.

And neither should you play your phoenix flute as tears come on,
    For surely then your heart would tear still more.
(NTECTHC, 9a–9b)   (TR. DANIEL BRYANT)

Tune: "Pure Serene Music" (*Ch'ing-p'ing yüeh*)

Half the spring has gone by since our parting,
All before my eyes brings heart-rending sorrow.
The plum blossoms fall down below the steps like whirling snow,
No sooner brushed away than covering me over again.

The calls of the wild geese bring no word;
The road is so long, my dreams can't reach home.
The sorrow of separation is like the new grass of springtime:
However distantly you wander, you find it growing still.
(NTECTHC, 9b)   (TR. DANIEL BRYANT)

Tune: "Deva-like Barbarian," Two Lyrics

[1]

Bright flowers and dim moon, enmeshed in thin drifting mist;
Tonight is a perfect time to steal out to her lover's side.
    Stockinged feet tread the fragrant steps,
    As she holds in her hands her gold-sewn shoes.

They meet in a pathway south of the painted hall,
And she trembles for a moment in his nestling arms;
    "Because it is so hard for me to come out,
    I allow you now to fully indulge your love."

[2]

A sound of brass reeds crisp as the brittle clatter of cold bamboo,
As delicate jade fingers drift slowly through new music—
    Their secret amorous glances entice them on,
    And desire flows across their gaze in autumn waves.

In clouds and rain deep within the embroidered doors,
Never easy to express true feelings.
    The feast finished, a void returns again,
    In dreams bewildered within the spring rain.
(NTECTHC, 14b, 16a)   (TR. DANIEL BRYANT)

Tune: "Ripples Sifting Sand"

    The things of the past may only be lamented,
    They appear before me, hard to brush aside:
An autumn wind blows in the courtyards and moss invades the steps;
A row of unrolled beaded screens hangs idly down,
    For now no one comes for all the day.

    My golden sword now lies buried deep,
    And all my youth is turned to weeds.
In the cool of evening, when the heavens are still and the moon blossoms forth,
I think of all those towers of jade and marble palaces reflected,
    Shining emptily in the Ch'in-huai.[1]   10
(NTECTHC, 17a–17b)   (TR. DANIEL BRYANT)

Tune: "Spring in Jade Pavilion" (*Yü-lou ch'un*)

Their adornment for the evening finished now, their bright skin like snow,
The splendid Spring Palace maids form lines like swimming fish;
The blowing of phoenix-flutes breaks off and lingers among water and clouds,
As once again they play through the "Song of Rainbow Skirts."

From whom on the wind floats this fragrant scent?
Drunken, beating upon the railings, I taste the keen flavor of my heart.
As I return, leave no candle blossoms glowing red;
I wish to hear the clatter of my horse's hooves in the clear moonlight.
(NTECTHC, 18b–19a)   (TR. DANIEL BRYANT)

---

[1] Ch'in-huai is a minor stream which flowed through Chien-k'ang (Nanking), the Southern T'ang capital.

Tune: "Dance of the Cavalry" (*P'o-chen tzu*)

These forty years past, our house and our domain;
A thousand miles broad, the mountains and the rivers.
The Phoenix Pavilion and the Dragon Tower reached up to the stars at
     night.
Jade trees with jasper branches formed a cloud of vines;
     Never had we knowledge of the weapons of war.

One day, suddenly I surrendered and became a captive slave;
With Shen's thin waist[1] and P'an's streaked temples[2] I'm worn away.
Hardest of all was the day I took hurried leave of the ancestral shrine:
The Royal Academy of Music then performed the farewell songs,
     And I wept before my palace women.   10
(NTECTHC, 21a)   (TR. DANIEL BRYANT)

Tune: "Ripples Sifting Sand: A Song"

Outside the screen rain drips and splashes,
And the mood of spring is dead and gone.
My satin cover cannot ward off the chill of the last night-watch;
But within my dreams I do not know my present life in exile,
     And for a moment yearn for joy.

I should not lean alone upon this railing;
The endless streams and hills—
So easy it seemed to take my leave, how hard ever to meet again!
Flowing water, flowers falling, and spring gone all away:
     There is heaven; and there is the world of men.   10
(NTECTHC, 22a–22b)   (TR. DANIEL BRYANT)

---

[1] Shen Yüeh (441–513) was a famous poet and literary theorist. His biography
quotes a letter which he wrote to a friend while ill; in it, he complains that
he is constantly having to take in his belt.

[2] At the age of thirty-two, the poet P'an Yüeh (see note to the lyric "A Casket
of Pearls") found that his hair was beginning to turn gray. He wrote his
famous "*Fu* on the Height of Autumn" in which he bemoans his advancing
age.

Tune: "Crows Crying at Night" (*Wu yeh t'i*)

The spring scarlet of the forest blossoms fades and falls
  Too soon, too soon;
There is no escape from the cold rain of morning, the wind at dusk.

  The tears on your rouged cheeks
  Keep us drinking together,
  For when shall we meet again?—
Thus the eternal sorrows of human life, like great rivers
  flowing ever east.
(NTECTHC, 11b)   (TR. DANIEL BRYANT)

Tune: "Joy at Meeting" (*Hsiang-chien huan*)[1]

Silent, I go up alone to the Western Pavilion,
  The moon's like a hook,
Lonesome *wu-t'ung* trees lock clear autumn in the courtyard.
  Cut, it will not break;
  Ordered, yet still unruly:
  It's the sorrow of parting
Like the bittersweet taste in the heart.
(NTECTHC, 24b–25a)   (TR. EUGENE EOYANG)

Tune: "The Beautiful Lady Yü (*Yü Mei-jen*)

Spring blooms, autumn moon, when will they end?
How many yesterdays have passed?
Last night, at my little pavilion, the east wind again!
Oh, lost country, when moon is bright, I can't bear to
  look back.

Carved balustrades, marmorean stairs no doubt will stand;
Only the once bright faces have changed.

---

[1] The title of this tune-pattern, *Hsiang-chien huan,* is sometimes given as *Wu yeh t'i* ("Crows Crying at Night").

Ask the sum of grief there's to bear,
It's just a river in full spring flood flowing east to sea.
(NTECTHC, 4a–4b)   (TR. EUGENE EOYANG)

Wang Yü-ch'eng (954–1001)

Random Thoughts Written in Spring

Spring clouds look like beasts,
    sometimes like fowls;
Sunlit, wind-blown,
    one moment thin, the next thick:
Who says they are without designs
    and therefore carefree?
They are as devious and fathomless
    as a base, scheming mind.
(HCC 8/19b–20a)   (TR. IRVING Y. LO)

Journeying to the Village

My horse threads the mountain path as chrysanthemums begin to
    yellow;
Aimlessly, leisurely, I ride—my wandering mood unrestrained.
The noises from ten thousand ravines mingle with the sound of dusk;
Mountain peaks stand silent as I linger in the slanting sun.
Leaves of crab apple and pear trees drop their deep rouge color;
Field buckwheat flowering shed a snow-white fragrance.
How could I have, after humming this song, suddenly grown dispirited?
Hamlet and bridge, plain and trees—all look like my native village.
(HCC, 9/9a)   (TR. IRVING Y. LO)

Song of the Crow Pecking at My Scarred Donkey

Old crow of Shang Mountain, you are cruel!
Beak longer than a spike, sharper than an arrow.
Go gather bugs or peck at eggs—
Why must you harm this poor scarred beast of mine?
Since I was exiled to Shang-yu last year

There has only been this one lame donkey to move my things.
We climbed the Ch'in Mountains and the Ch'an to get here;
He carried a hundred volumes for me on his back.
The ropes cut his skin to the spine: the scar reached his belly;
Now with half a year's healing he's nearly well again.   10
But yesterday the crow suddenly swooped down
And pecked through his wound to get the living flesh.
The donkey brayed, my servant cried out and the crow flew away!
Perched on the roof he preened his feathers and scraped his beak.
There was nothing my donkey and my servant could do
Without a crossbow to shoot or nets to spread.
But Shang Mountain has many birds of prey;
I'll ask our neighbor to lend me his autumn hawk:
With claws of iron and hooked talons
He'll snap the crow's neck and feed on his brain!   20
And this won't serve only to fill his empty gut;
No! It's revenge for my donkey's pain.
(HCC, 12/10a–10b)   (TR. JONATHAN CHAVES)

P'an Lang (?–1009)

Written on Lake View Tower

Standing all day on Lake View Tower,
Too lazy to think of going home,
I listen to the river flow off toward the Milky Way
And watch the clouds pass an isolated peak.
A lonely boat is pulled up on the bank;
A bird stands facing me in perfect calm.
—I turn my head, the double gates are closed;
Bullfrogs are croaking in the sunset.
(HYC, 3a–3b)   (TR. JONATHAN CHAVES)

Tune: "Song of the Wine Spring," Two Lyrics

[1]

I always remember West Lake—
On the lake, when spring comes, there's an endless view:

The girls of Wu,[1] every single one a goddess,
Vying with one another in rowing their magnolia boats.

Clusters of pavilions and towers that look like the Magic Isle[2]—
There, and only there should a rustic grow old.
Since I left, it's been twenty years already.
 Gazing eastward; my eyes will soon wear out.

[2]

 I always remember West Lake—
All day long leaning on the balcony and gazing:
 Fishing boats in twos and threes,
 Islets in the clear autumn air,

The vague sound of a flute among flowering rushes,
A row of startled white birds, suddenly rising.
Since I left, I've repaired my fishing rod at leisure;
 My thoughts penetrate the cold water and clouds.
(CST, P. 5)   (TR. JAMES J. Y. LIU)

Lin Pu (967–1028)

An Autumn Day—
Leisurely Boating on West Lake

Water's breath mingles with reflected mountains;
Autumn has come to the vast sky.
I rejoice to see temples hidden deep in the forest,
Regret the broken silence when my boat moves from the shore.
Sparse reeds are snapping, though it isn't cold yet;
A rainbow's fragment arches in the setting sun.
Which way now to my little hut?
The fishermen's songs bring thoughts of home.
(HCSC, 1/1a)   (TR. JONATHAN CHAVES)

---

1 Name of ancient kingdom, famous for its beautiful girls.
2 P'eng-tao, paradise in Taoist legends.

A Trail Among the Pines

Seed pods of frost falling in autumn—
    a bamboo staff breaks open.
Hairpins of rain piled on the ground,
    pairs of wooden clogs level by treading.
There's no way to halt on command a traveler from Ch'ang-an[1]
Who loves to thread deep woods and walk among the chill lush green.
(HCSC, 4/2a)   (TR. IRVING Y. LO)

Yang Yi (974–1020)

Untitled

Blue mist rises from fragrant herbs in the bronze plate;
Incense sachets hang at the four corners of the round canopy.
Shen Yüeh, grieving, grows emaciated in vain;
Hsiang-ju's feelings are secret: who can convey them for him?
The rain has passed at the golden pond; it still seems a dream.
Kingfisher sleeves turned back in the wind: perhaps it was a fairy.
—Every day she climbs the Ch'in tower, but cannot send him poems:
He rides to the east in a screened carriage, surrounded by a thousand
    horsemen.
(HKCCC, 2/15a)   (TR. JONATHAN CHAVES)

Lang Mountain Monastery

Rolling mountains push toward the city;
A monastery stands on the highest peak.
Evening fog darkens the gold Buddhas;
A waterfall moistens winding stone steps.
Empty valleys echo the voice of the bell;
The pagoda's shadow mingles with scruffy clouds.

---

1 Alluding to the Han general Li Kuang (d. 119 B.C.). The story has it that a
    drunken officer, unwilling to recognize Li's former rank, refused to let him
    pass the guardpost at night.

A thousand horsemen sometimes visit here,
But I seek solitude, alone with my bramble cane.
(WYHC, 4/12a)   (TR. JONATHAN CHAVES)

The Prisons Are Full of Convicts

Iron chains and silver cangues: crowds of prisoners.
Distinguished laws and humble proposals are continuously issued.
No more is heard of memorials to empty the prisons;
How ashamed I must feel before the man of "half a word!"
The pure Ying, land of Mr. Huang, is near;
Shao-po of the sweet pear tree is our neighbor.
I long for those sages, but cannot follow their ways;
Are the people responsible for all these punishments?
(YSW, 1/1a–1b)   (TR. JONATHAN CHAVES)

Yen Shu (991–1055)

Tune: "Treading on Grass" (*T'a so hsing*)

Little path dotted with red,
Fragrant country covered with green.
By the lofty tower the trees spread their dark, dark shades.
The spring wind knows not how to forbid the willow catkins,
All fuzzy and fluffy, to dab a walker's face at random.

Emerald leaves hide the orioles,
Vermilion curtains bar the swallows.
The incense smoke quietly follows the gossamers drifting around.
At the moment of awakening from a sorrowful dream induced by wine,
The slanting sun is still shining on the deep, deep courtyard   10
(CST, P. 99)   (TR. JAMES J. Y. LIU)

Tune: "Spring in Jade Pavilion"

Green willows, fragrant grass, the many-stationed road—
Fickle youth finds leave-taking easy.
In my chamber a dream fades at the fifth-watch bell,
Beneath the flowers the sorrow of parting is April's rain.

Unloving never hurts as much as loving:
An inch can grow into a million skeins.
Heaven and earth have their end;
There's only longing that's interminable!
(CST, PP. 108–9) (TR. AN-YAN TANG)

Mei Yao-ch'en (1002–1060)

A Solitary Falcon Above the Buddha Hall
of the Monastery of Universal Purity

My newly rented home commands a view of the temple hall;
gold and jade-green glitter before my crumbling house.
I gaze at the temple, and watch the flocks of pigeons
bring food and drink to their nested young,
          unaware of the year's drawing to a close.
Bird droppings have dirtied all the carved eaves and painted walls,
and fallen on the heads and shoulders of clay-sculpted Buddhas.
The monastery monks would never dare to shoot the birds with cross-
    bows;
but suddenly there comes a dark falcon, baring his dangerous claws.
Crows caw, magpies screech, mynah birds cry out;
the falcon, excited, flies close in and catches the scent of flesh.   10
Determination in his heart, outnumbered but unafraid,
in a flash he has crushed the head of a bird and terrified the others.
The dead bird plunges in the void, has not yet reached the ground
when the falcon sweeps down with whirlwind wings and snatches him
          in midair.
Alone on the rooftop, he freely rips and tears,
pecks at the flesh, pulls at the liver, casts away the guts.
The scavengers with no skill of their own, crafty and cowardly,
circle above, waiting to descend, staring with their hungry eyes.
Soon the falcon has eaten his full and leisurely flies off;
who can distinguish kites from crows in the struggle for the
    leavings?   20
All the children point and gesture, the passers-by laugh,
while I thoughtfully intone my poem by the autumnal riverbank.
(WLC, 11/12b–13a) (TR. JONATHAN CHAVES)

Chiang Lin-chi Treats Me to Mudfish

Mudfish are the lowest of all fish—
one never serves them to honored guests.
And then they are so stubborn and slimy,
a terrible nuisance for the cook to prepare.
While frying they give off a wretched smell;
I've never been anxious to taste them!
Mr. Chiang has been south on official duty,
so his kitchen is expert at making this dish.
Yesterday he invited me to dine with him
and I found it more delicious than the finest fish.   10
Now I know that things of the humblest kind
depend on their spicing, bitter or sweet.
(WLC, 17/8b)   (TR. JONATHAN CHAVES)

The Boat-pullers

Wild goose, broken-legged on the sandbank:
he limps like a man, dragging spread wings.
The sun is setting—how can he bear the rains
and the chilly winds now starting to blow?
There are splashes of mud on his damp feathers;
head drawn in, he doesn't cackle.
—Boat-pullers, this is how you live,
and yet it's better than shouldering the tools of war.
(WLC, 34/10a)   (TR. JONATHAN CHAVES)

Elegy for a White Cock

White cock in my courtyard,
feathers white as white lard:
wild dogs were his daily fear;
malicious foxes never worried him.
Evenings, he'd roost in a nook in the eaves;
mornings, he'd peck by the foot of the stairs.
He crew before all the other birds,
even in wind and rain.

My granaries were running low
but I always gave him rice to eat.   10
Last night when the sky turned black,
a creature of darkness prowled and spied.
Stealthily it seized the cock—
I only heard the squawks of pain.
When I came to the rescue through the gate,
it was already past the eastern wall.
At the sound of my shouts, not daring to eat,
it dropped the cock and made its escape.
Throat covered with gushing blood,
the cock gasped for air on the brink of death.   20
Brilliant white breast stained deep vermilion,
frosty pinions broken and torn.
Compassionate, I wished him to live,
but his head was crushed and could not be healed.
I'll accept his fate and bury him;
who could bear to use cinnamon and ginger on him now?
Still I see his scattered feathers
floating, dancing with the breath of the wind.
I remember when he first came to this place,
how many favors he received: 30
he never had to fear the block,
and never passed his days in hunger.
Why did he meet this vicious beast?
Who ever thought he'd be destroyed!
Though this may be a trifling matter,
a deeper meaning may be discerned:
Mr. Teng[1] could coin a mountain of cash,
but starved to death in the end.
Such too, then, is the way of man—
I bow my head, full of sorrow.   40
(WLC, 1/3a–3b)   (TR. JONATHAN CHAVES)

---

[1] Alluding to the story of Teng T'ung (fl. second century B.C.), an official of
the Former Han dynasty and a favorite of Emperor Wen, who bestowed on
him a mountain rich in copper ore in Szechwan, from which he could coin
money. But Teng incurred the displeasure of the next emperor. His wealth
was confiscated and he died of starvation.

Swarming Mosquitoes

The sun has set, the moon is in darkness;
now the mosquitoes fly forth from cracked walls.
They swarm in the void with a thunderous hum,
dance in the courtyard like a veil of mist.
The spider's web is uselessly spread;
the mantis can't slash them with his ax.
The vicious scorpion helps them in their mischief
and freely stings with his belly's poison;
because he has no wings to use,
he patters and scratches up the darkened wall.   10
Noblemen reside in lordly mansions,
silken nets encircling their beds.
Would that in such homes as these
the mosquitoes flaunted their lance-like beaks!
Instead they frequent the poor and humble
with no compassion for their gauntness.
Suckers sharp, they race to the attack;
drinking blood, they seek self-increase.
The bat flits back and forth in vain;
he cannot kill or capture them.   20
The chirping cicada, sated with wind and dew,
shamelessly goes on sipping more.
—This hum and buzz can't last much longer:
The east will soon be bright.
(WLC, 3/7a–7b)   (TR. JONATHAN CHAVES)

On the Thirteenth Day of the Eleventh Month I Went to the Granary for the First Time Since My Illness

I am not a sparrow or a rat.
What am I doing here in this huge granary?
The warmth is gone from my tattered fox-fur robe,
mended with patches of yellow dogskin.
Frost crystals appear as the moon descends
weaving garlands on withered branches:

and I, a man of more than fifty,
lie gaunt with illness as ice forms on my skin.
(WLC, 16/7a–7b)   (TR. JONATHAN CHAVES)

Mourning for My Wife, Three Poems

[1]

We came of age, and were made man and wife.
Seventeen years have gone by since then.
I still have not tired of gazing at her face
but now she has left me forever.
My hair has nearly turned white,
Can this body hold out much longer?
When the end comes I'll join her in the grave;
until my death, the tears flow on and on.

[2]

Whenever I go out I seem to walk in a dream;
meeting people, often forcing myself to answer.
Then home again to the silent loneliness;
I want to talk, but there's no one I can talk to.
A single firefly flits through the chilly window;
a solitary wild goose flies in the endless night.
There is no greater pain for a man than this:
here my spirit is crushed, and dies.

[3]

There have always been long life and early death.
Who dares lay the blame on azure heaven?
I have seen many wives in this world of men,
yet none so beautiful and wise as she.
The foolish, it seems, are granted long life:
why was she not lent some of their years?
Can I bear to lose this jewel worth a string of cities
sunk and buried in the Ninefold Springs?
(WLC, 10/16a–16b)   (TR. JONATHAN CHAVES)

On the Night of the Fifteenth Day of the First Month
I Go Out and Return

Only depression if I stay at home:
out to the festival to ease my pain.
Every man, rich or poor, is together with his wife;
my heart is moved only to greater grief.
Pleasures cloy so easily as old age comes;
I would go walking but desire fades.
Home again, I see my boy and girl;
before a word is spoken my eyes smart bitterly.
Last year their mother took them out;
they smeared on rouge, trying to be just like her.   10
Now their mother has gone to the Springs below;
their faces are dirty, few of their clothes untorn.
When I reflect how young they both still are,
I can't bear to let them see my tears.
        Push the lamp aside
                lie facing the wall
a hundred sorrows clumped in me.
(WLC, 11/14a–14b)   (TR. JONATHAN CHAVES)

Second Marriage

I married a second time the other day,
happy about the present, still grieving for the past.
Once more there is someone to take care of the household;
my shadow is no longer alone in the moonlight.
Yet from force of habit I still call old wife's name—
my heart is just as troubled as before.
Luckily both women are kind and gentle
and I have married again the best of wives.
(WLC, 28/8b–9a)   (TR. JONATHAN CHAVES)

The Year Wu-tzu [1048], First Month, Night of the
Twenty-sixth: A Dream

Two years now since my second marriage;
in all that time, I've never dreamed of her.

Last night I saw her face again;
midnight was a painful hour.
The dark lamp glowed with a feeble light,
silently glimmering on the rafters.
And the unfeeling snow that beat against my window
was whirled to a frenzy by the wind.
(WLC, 31/9b)   (TR. JONATHAN CHAVES)

Poverty on the Bank

They can't plow and harvest.
They've no chickens or pigs.
Instead, they dry driftwood for roasting mussels
and strip bark from roots for making rain capes.
They build their houses with reeds,
twisting green creepers into makeshift gates.
The children gather lotus leaves
to wear as short pants.
(WLC, 33/12a)   (TR. JONATHAN CHAVES)

A Little Village

On the broad River Huai, dotted with islets, a village suddenly
    appears:
gateways here are bramble hedges, broken and full of gaps.
Scrawny chickens cluck at their mates as they peck for food;
old men with no robes to wear hold grandchildren in their arms.
Birds perch on the frayed hawsers of simple skiffs;
the river eats at withered mulberries, exposing the gnarled roots.
—That's how they live in this village.
How wrong to register the population in the emperor's tax books!
(WLC, 34/2a)   (TR. JONATHAN CHAVES)

Meeting the Herdsmen

Army horses, gangs and droves,
come to graze in the outer fields.
Larger herds of mingling hundreds;
smaller herds of galloping tens.
Some swarm together like warring ants;

Some scatter quickly like startled crows.
Wheat is trampled to the root.
Trees are gnawed—stripped of bark.
The soldier-herdsmen don't care,
but come to the market carrying their whips.   10
If they call for wine they get it;
if they want to eat, they're given food.
At sunset, drunk and full,
they lie at the road-bend, pillowed on their whips,
oblivious: this is not their land.
They don't worry about the taxes that have to be paid.
(WLC, 26/10a)   (TR. JONATHAN CHAVES)

On Hearing that Holders of the *Chin-shih* Degree
Are Dealing in Tea

The fourth and fifth months are when the tea is best in mountain
    groves;
then southern traders like wolves and jackals sell it secretly.
Foolish youths risk crossing the dangerous peaks
and work at night in teams, like soldiers with swords or spears.
The vagrant students also lust for profit,
their book bags are turned into smugglers' sacks!
Officers may apprehend them at the fords,
but the judges let them off, out of pity for their scholars' robes.
And then they come to the cities, where they prate of Confucius and
    Mencius,
not hesitating to criticize Yao and T'ang in their speeches.   10
If there are three days of summer rain, they rant about drowning in
    floods;
after five days of hot weather, they complain of a drought.
They make money in a hundred ways, dining on roast meat and wine,
while their hungry wives at home lack dry provisions.
—If you end up in a ditch, you're only getting your deserts:
the *chin-shih* degree of generals and ministers is not for the likes of
    you!
(WLC, 34/15a)   (TR. JONATHAN CHAVES)

Eating Shepherd's-purse

Men are ashamed to eat shepherd's-purse,
but I'm happy enough to eat it.
I just saw the gatherer of shepherd's-purse
walk out alone from the capital's south gate:
brittle iron knife eroded by the earth;
green bamboo basket mottled with frost.
He carried these to a frozen pond
where he plucked out the purse, roots and leaves.
His hands were chapped; he was hungry.
He'd have been thankful to eat even this plant!   10
Let others be greedy for such meats
as lamb and red-tail fish.
(WLC, 31/5b)   (TR. JONATHAN CHAVES)

On Seeing a Painting of Plants and Insects
by Chü-ning

When the ancients painted swans and tigers
they turned out looking like ducks and dogs.
But now I see these painted insects,
successful both in feeling and in form.
The walkers truly seem to move,
the fliers truly seem to soar,
the fighters seem to raise their limbs,
the chirpers seem to swell their chests,
the jumpers really move their legs,
the starers really fix their eyes!   10
And so I learn that the Creator's power
can't match the agility of the artist's brush.

There are many painters in P'i-ling,
drawing and scribbling, wasting scroll after scroll.
But Chü-ning is divinely endowed—
effortlessly he brings the others to their knees.
His roots and grasses are done with meticulous care;
his drunken ink is masterfully applied.

Men of influence and power cannot summon him at will;
for virtuous conduct he stands alone in his time.   20
(WLC, 10/13a)   (TR. JONATHAN CHAVES)

Borrowing Rice from Ju-hui

My family complains like cackling geese—
the chimney is cold, there's no fire for breakfast.
Penury must beg from poverty;
how can we help but laugh at each other?
Luckily, Mr. Yen's calligraphy[1] is preserved
and we have the poem of Mr. T'ao[2] as well.
They show that men of former times
also went begging for rice, begging for food.
(WLC, 38/4b)   (TR. JONATHAN CHAVES)

Liu Yung (fl. 1034)

Tune: "Midnight Music" (*Yeh-pan yüeh*)

Frozen clouds in the dark gloomy air—
                In a tiny leaf of a boat
        I left the river islet in high spirits.
Passing a myriad valleys and a thousand cliffs,
                I sailed where the Yüeh stream[1] ran deep.
        The angry waves gradually calmed,
        The forest wind suddenly rose.
Then I heard the traveling merchants calling to one another.
                Hoisting high my single sail,
                I drifted on in the "painted fish hawk"[2]
        Which fluttered past the southern shore.   10

---

1 Referring to the celebrated "Calligraphy on Begging for Rice" by the callig-
  rapher Yen Chen-ch'ing (709–84).
2 Referring to T'ao Ch'ien's poem "Begging for Food."
1 Identified by commentators with the Jo-yeh stream situated in the ancient
  kingdom of Yüeh (modern Chekiang). The famous beauty Hsi Shih (fifth
  century B.C.) is said to have washed silk gauze in this stream when she
  was a village girl. Later she was presented by the king of Yüeh to his
  old enemy, the king of Wu, and brought about the latter's downfall.
2 Boats were painted with the fish hawk on the prow as an auspicious sign,
  since this bird is strong in flight and not afraid of the wind. Consequently,
  "painted fish hawk" became a common literary substitute for a boat.

Now a gleaming tavern's sign comes into view,
  Then a cluster of misty villages,
  And several rows of frosty trees.
   In the fading sun,
Fishermen, knocking their boats[3] with poles, return home.
  Faded lotus leaves fall away,
  Withering willows shimmer faintly.
On the bank, in twos and threes,
  The girls washing their silk clothes
   Avoid the traveling stranger
While shyly laughing and talking among themselves. 20

  Coming here makes me think:
  "I've too easily deserted her chamber;
  Now the drifting duckweed can hardly stop!"
   I sigh over the date of our reunion,
Which she kept telling me to remember—Can it be counted on after
 all?
   My heart saddened by separation—
Useless to resent that it is late in the year and my return has been
 delayed.
   I fix my tearful eyes
  On the road that stretches far, far towards the capital.
A stray wild goose cries in the distance; the vast sky darkens. 30
(CTS, P. 37)   (TR. JAMES J. Y. LIU)

Tune: "Eight Beats of a Kan-chou Song" (*Pa-sheng Kan-chou*)

Facing me, the blustering evening rain besprinkles the sky over
 the river,
  Washing the cool autumn air once more.
  Gradually, the frosty wind rises chilly and hard,
   The landscape looks more forlorn,
   The fading sun falls on the balcony.
  Everywhere, the red withers and the green fades away:
   One by one, the glories of nature cease.
  Only the water of the Long River[1]
   Flows in silence to the east.

---

[3] It is said that fishermen knocked their boats with long poles to startle the
fish so that they would leap into the net.
[1] The Yangtze.

I cannot bear to climb high and look far,   10
    For to gaze at my native land in the dim distance
      Would release endless homeward thoughts.
I sigh over the past year's wanderings;
  Why should I desperately linger on?
      I imagine the fair one
    Is now gazing, head raised, from her chamber.
      How often has she
  Mistaken a returning boat on the horizon for mine?
      How would she know that I,
    Leaning here on the railings,   20
    Should be congealed with sorrow like this?
(CTS, P. 43)   (TR. JAMES J. Y. LIU)

Tune: "Chrysanthemums Fresh" (*Chü-hua hsin*)

Before lowering the perfumed curtain to express her love,
She knits her eyebrows, worried that the night is too short.
    She urges the young lover to go to bed
First, so as to warm up the mandarin-duck quilt.[1]

A moment later she puts down her unfinished needlework,
And removes her silk skirt, to indulge in passion without end.
    Let me keep the lamp before the curtain
That I may look at her lovely face from time to time!
(CST, P. 38)   (TR. JAMES J. Y. LIU)

Tune: "Jade Butterflies" (*Yü hu-tieh*)

where I gaze
the rain is ending and the clouds break up
as I lean at the rail in anxious silence
seeing off the last of autumn's glow
the evening scene is lonely
enough to chill Sung Yü to sadness
though touch of wind and rain is light
the duckweed gradually grows older

---

1 A brocade quilt with two holes for the necks.

in moon's frost cold
the *wu-t'ung* leaves whirl yellow   10
giving love is taking pain
where are you now?
the misty waters vast, and vague.

it's hard to forget
writing or drinking
how many nights alone beneath a clouded moon
again the changes, stars and frost
the seas are broad, the heavens far
and no way home.   20
the swallows pair
and I depend on letters
I point into the evening sky
to sight in vain the returning boat
at dusk we'll gaze toward one another
in the sound of the swan's cry
standing till the slanting sun is set.
(CST, P. 40)   (TR. JEROME P. SEATON)

Tune: "Wanderings of a Youth" (*Shao-nien yu*)

On the road to Ch'ang-an my horse goes slowly
in the tall willow confused cicadas cry
slanting sun beyond the isles
and winds of autumn on the plain
only where the heavens hang
the view cut off.

the clouds go back, but gone they
leave no track
where is the past?
unused to indulgence   10
wine becomes disconsolate
it's not
as it was
when I was young.
(CST, P. 32)   (TR. JEROME P. SEATON)

Tune: "Prelude to Allure Goddesses" (*Mi-shen yin*)

a leaf this boat, its light sail rolled
lies moored by the Ch'u's south bank
as dusk descends on the lonely wall, the post horn
draws mournful notes like those of a Tartar whistle
the waters vast
wild geese on flat sand
settle, startled, scatter
mist gathers in the cold woods
the painted screen is spread
horizon's far, the mountains small   10
like faintly traced eyebrows.

old joys cast off lightly
I'm here to seek an official post
but weary of this journeying
and the waning year
the manners and the sights of this strange place
are desolate and mournful
the eyes despair
the capital's far away
the towers of Ch'in cut off,   20
the soul of a traveler dismayed
the fragrant grass spreads in
empty vastness
and the evening glow spreads
no news of her,
a few broken clouds
far off.
(CST. P. 44)   (TR. JEROME P. SEATON)

Ou-yang Hsiu (1007–1072)

In Imitation of the "Jade Pavilion" Style,[1] Two Selections

[1]

A Song of "Hand-in-Hand"

The sun sets on the dike where I walk,
As I sing alone the song of "Hand-in-hand."
Then I remember the one whose hand I once held,
And everywhere I look, spring is radiant and green.

[2]

A Song of "Night After Night"

The drifting clouds disgorge a bright moon,
Its fleeting shadow darkens the jade staircase.
A thousand *li* away we share the same reflection,
But how can I let you know this heart night after night?
(OYWCC, 51/1a)   (TR. IRVING Y. LO)

A Song of Spring at West Lake,
Sent to Circuit Officer Hsieh [Po-ch'u][1]

The colors of spring have returned to West Lake,
The waters of springtime greener than the dye.
Full-blown flowers in bright hue
Drop their petals in the east wind, in disarray.

---

1 I.e., the style of *Yü-t'ai hsin-yung* ("New Songs of Jade Pavilion"), the sixth-century collection of love poetry.
1 Written on his way to Hsü-chou, in 1037, where the poet was remarried. The poem was addressed to his friend Hsieh in the Bureau of Justice at Hsü-chou, who had sent him a poem to comfort him during his exile at Yi-ling.

Tangled like clouds[2] are the spring sentiments of this magistrate—
A whitehead, versifying, grieves in bidding farewell to spring.

From far away at the lake, a goblet of wine, I imagine,
Can bring back the memory of someone at world's end.
Many thousand *li* away, I still can cherish the spring;
But suddenly confronting spring, a traveler's heart's startled.   10
Snow melting outside my door, a thousand hills turn green;
Flowers open on the riverbank, a sunny day in March.
As a young man, I drank wine to dally with spring's radiance;
Encountering spring today, I discover my hair's already white.

Everything in a strange land looks unfamiliar:
Only the east wind acts like my old acquaintance.
(OYWCC, 52/6b)   (TR. IRVING Y. LO)

Thoughts on the First Day of Autumn, Sent to Su Tzu-mei [Su Shun-ch'in]

The tree in the courtyard turns color suddenly,
As autumn wind stirs among the branches.
The nature of things isn't always like this,
But I'm already inclined to feel sad.
It's true I dread the flowers' fading,
Still the return of cool days makes me glad.
As I get up and pace, the moon is obscured by clouds;
As I look around, the stars and the Dipper shift positions.
The four seasons revolve with great regularity;
Who can arrange the appointment of myriad things?   10
My old friend is now a thousand miles away,
The months and years have caused me grief—
Distressed that great works come off too tardily,
I begrudge not merely the fading of rosy-cheeked youth.

---

[2] Author's note: Mr. Hsieh's poem contains the following two lines: "Sentimental, still young, yet already white-haired,/Rustic thoughts at springtime are like tangled clouds."

What is the great plan today for recovering the lost territory?[1]
The Tartar horses are daily growing more sleek.
(OYWCC, 53/6b)   (TR. IRVING Y. LO)

Inscribed on the Arbor of the Old Drunkard
(Tsui-weng-t'ing) at Ch'u-chou

At forty, a man's not yet old,
"Old Drunkard" is just the way I sign my name.[1]
A drunkard takes his leave of all things,
How could I then recall my age?

I love only the water below the arbor,
It comes somewhere from those jagged peaks.
It sounds as if falling from the sky,
Cascading down the eaves when it rains.
As it flows into the brook beneath the cliff,
Each drop adds to the hidden spring.   10
Its echoes never jar the ear like the voices of men,
Though its music is not that of pipes and strings.
Not that I don't find pleasure in strings and pipes,
But their notes at times are shrill and loud.

That's why I often bring my wine when I come,
And take long walks to get close to the waterfall.
Birds in the wilds peer at me as I lie drunk,
Clouds above the brook induce me to stay and take my rest.
Mountain flowers have no expression but a smile.
They do not know how to talk with me.
There's only the wind from the cliffs,
That blows upon me until I'm sober again.
(OYWCC, 53/9a)   (TR. IRVING Y. LO)

---

1 *Miao-mo,* literally "temple-plan," referring to the government plans in the early Northern Sung period to repossess the land in North China lost to the Khitans.
1 Literally, *t'i-pien,* i.e., to be inscribed at the end of a piece of his writing.

"Song of the Radiant Lady,"
Replying to a Poem by Wang Chieh-fu [Wang An-shih]

The Tartars make their home on saddle horses;
Shooting and hunting are their custom.
Where they find good grass or fresh spring, they camp;
To startle birds or put beasts to fright, they ride in pursuit.
Who'd let a daughter of Han marry a Tartar man?

Wind and sands had no feeling, though she was as lovely as jade;
Journeying on and on, she never met a single Chinese.
On horseback she sang "Longing for Home," the song she wrote,
From her strumming back and forth came the tunes of her lute,
All the Tartar men who heard marveled and sighed.   10

A face as fair as jade perished at the edge of the world,
But her lute was brought back to the families of Han.
As palace girls vied in composing new tunes,
Deep was her buried grief but the music sounded more bitter.

The delicate hands of a girl belong to the inner room;
Trained in the lute, she alone would never leave the hall.[1]
Not having seen the frontier road under dusty clouds,
How could she know the music that breaks one's heart?
(OYWCC, 8/5b)   (TR. IRVING Y. LO)

Tune: "Butterflies Lingering over Flowers" (*Tieh lien hua*)

Back in the painted pavilion, again in late spring,
　　Swallows fly by two and two,
　　Toward the soft willow, the pale peach tree.
A fine rain fills the sky; wind fills the yard:
Melancholy eye takes it all in, but no one sees.

---

[1] The last three words of this line, *pu-hsia-t'ang* ("never come down the hall"),
allude to the story of a lady named Po-cho, who died in a fire rather than
leave the hall at night when not accompanied by her tutor's wife (*Kung-
yang Chuan*, Thirtieth Year of Duke Hsiang; SPTK edition, 9/19a–19b).

Alone by the balustrade, my heart entangled;
    Lush grass, full foliage:
    I think of the banks south of the river.
Wind and moon heartless, people quietly change;
The memory of old friends like a dream afflicts my heart, to no
    purpose.   10
(CST, P. 128)   (TR. EUGENE EOYANG)

Tune: "Butterflies Lingering over Flowers"

ruffed blue-green garden, red blossoms
clear skies fill the eye.
above embroidered mats long drift
the orioles, flit up and down, together
on purpled paths and dust-gold wagon tracks
everywhere my horse's hooves tread spring land's green.

sudden's a spring dream crowded with my years
the past so far so far
enough, a hundred kinds of pondering
though the misting rain fills the tower   10
the line of mountains stands unbroken
idly a man tries everywhere
to find some crook of rail to lean on.
(CST, P. 128)   (TR. JEROME P. SEATON)

Tune: "Song of Picking Mulberry" (*Ts'ai-sang tzu*)—
Recollections of West Lake,[1] Six Lyrics

[1]

a little boat with stubby oars, and West Lake's good.
green water winds a vagrant wake
fragrant grasses stretch the dike
soft, the small song of the reed-pipe trails

windless the water's face is shimmering smooth
unnoticed the boats ply
the slightest motion, and the ripples flow
startled, sand birds thrash up the bank.

[2]

deep spring, rain past, yet West Lake's good.
the grasses vie in elegance
a butterfly confusion, clamor of the bees
clear day, the buds about to burst to flames of sun

---

[1] Originally consisting of thirteen lyrics, this series is given the title of *Hsi-hu nien-yü* (*Recollections of West Lake*) and a preface, written in "parallel prose" style. In a condensed form, the preface may be translated as follows: "Though the West Lake enjoys the reputation as the most scenic spot of eastern Ying-chou, it is the chance discovery of a fine day or a fine view that is more preferable to planned excursions and formal parties. What is to be treasured is the sudden inspiration or the excitement of a mood that leads to pleasurable activities, whether it is to listen to the croaking of frogs or to drink wine by a stream. When one is engrossed in enjoying himself, he becomes oblivious of even the people around him. Therefore, occasional visits are more pleasant than special trips and each visit is a new experience. Therefore, I look through my old verse compositions and find those that can be set to tunes of new melodies but merely as a pastime to make the joy on such occasions more complete."

Hsi-hu, here translated as West Lake, is located at Fu-yang in Ying prefecture (Ying-chou) in Anhwei province, where the River Ying confluences with the other streams. Ou-yang Hsiu was once the governor of Ying-chou and wrote these poems about West Lake, which is not to be confused with the more famous West Lake in Hangchow.

far off, magnolia oars, a painted barge sails on
or perhaps, a band of sprites reflected in the waves
tossed on broad waters, riding the wind high up
music, flute and strings.

[3]

painted skiff with a load of wine, and West Lake's good.
lively music from pipes and strings
wine cups quickly passed along
secure afloat on calming waves
slip off
to drunken stupor

the clouds float on beneath the moving boat
sky and the water, pure and fresh
look up, look down, stay, or go on
seems there's another heaven
in this Lake.

[4]

flocks of blossoms gone, yet West Lake's good.
shattered scattered residue of red
as willow down comes misting down
the willow hangs across the wind the whole day through

the pipe song wanders off, the traveler goes
and spring spring's emptied to my heart
I let the thin gauze curtain fall
fine rain, a mated pair of swallows, coming home.

[5]

when lotus opens, West Lake's good.
just come with wine
no need for pageantry
or serried ranks of carriages in train

the painted skiff slips deep among the flowers
fragrance drifts round the golden cup

misting rain misting
go back, drunk in a phrase from the reed pipe.

[6]

a whole life of saying, West Lake's good.
now I come, in my official carriage
wealth and honor
     floating clouds
look up, look down, the rushing years
twenty.

I come back, old white head, ancient crane
the people of the city and the suburbs
all strange, all new
who'd recognize the old coot, their master, on another day?
(CST, PP. 121–22)   (TR. JEROME P. SEATON)

Tune: "Treading on Grass"

 Withering plum blossoms by the wayside station,
 Sprouting willows at the bridge over the stream,
Fragrant grass, warm breeze, a traveler slowly riding away.
Parting grief multiplies, the farther one goes:
Endless, unbroken, like the floods of spring.

 Inches of aching heart,
 Lines of rouge tears;
In a high tower, don't lean against the rail:
Where the wild plain levels off, spring hills rise,
And the traveler is farther beyond the spring hills.   10
(CST, P. 123)   (TR. AN-YAN TANG)

Su Shun-ch'in (*1008–1048*)

Summertime

Behind secluded screens the hush of daytime scenes:
Breezes stir quietly at the bamboo weathercock,

In the lush green pond, fish lay golden roes,
In a shady yard a swallow guides her chicks.
Children squabble over dates fallen in the rain,
Under a clear sky my visitor helps me dry worm-eaten books:
Even this cozy nook is not free from dusty care;
To let things go, make do with a bowl of wine.
(SSCC, P. 80)   (TR. MICHAEL E. WORKMAN)

Commandeering the Wind

Long wind coming from beyond the horizon,
Ten stout sails spread out wide.
Raising my head, I watch the clouds join in flight;
My heart tangled among green bamboos finds release.
Idly viewing the water, I know the nature of things;
A tranquil mind, sweet inducer of sleep.
I know now the joy of sailing fast,
But shouldn't tired nags also deserve pitying?
(SSCC, P. 86)   (TR. IRVING Y. LO)

Wang An-shih (1021–1086)

Walking in the Countryside

Tender mulberry leaves picked so clean
    green shade is sparse;
On reed beds silkworms grow
    into corpulent cocoons.
Casually I ask the villagers
    of local ways,
And why after all their hard labor
    they still go hungry.
(LCC, 32/5a)   (TR. JAN W. WALLS)

On the Yangtze

River waters shiver in the west wind;
river blossoms shed their late red.

Separation's sorrow is blown by a flute
over the jumbled hills to the east.
(LCC, 26/5b)   (TR. JAN W. WALLS)

Hastily Composed on the Mo-ling Road

The harvest ripe, the farmers rejoice;
in the autumn wind the traveler alone grieves.
On and on winds this crooked road
and a homeward horse in the slanting sun.
(NO. 2 FROM A SERIES OF 2; LCC, 26/6a)   (TR. JAN W. WALLS)

At the Chiang-ning River Mouth

I lower sail at river mouth
    under a pale moon;
a lampless inn is there,
    about to close up.
A half-dead maple leans
    over the sandy bank;
tying the boat, I seem to see
    scars from former years.
(NO. 3 FROM A SERIES OF 3; LCC, 31/5b)   (TR. JAN W. WALLS)

A Sketch of Mount Chung

Noiselessly, the mountain stream
    circles the bamboo grove;
West of the bamboo, flowers and grasses
    sport with the tenderness of spring.
I sit under thatched eaves
    facing this all day;
Not a single bird sings,
    the silence of the hills deepens.
(LCC, 30/5a)   (TR. JAN W. WALLS)

In the Mountains

I follow the moon into the mountains,
I search for clouds to accompany me home.
A spring morning, dew on the flowers:
and the fragrance clings to my gown.
(LCC, 26/5a)   (TR. JAN W. WALLS)

Written on the Wall of Halfway Mountain Temple

Cold, we sit in the warmth,
hot, we walk in the cool:
everything is nothing but Buddha,
and Buddha is everything.
(NO. 2 FROM A SERIES OF 2; LCC, 3/2a)   (TR. JAN W. WALLS)

In the Style of Han Shan and Shih Te, Two Selections

[1]

Had I been an ox or horse
I would rejoice to see grass and beans;
If, on the other hand, I were a woman,
the sight of men would please me.
But if I were really me
I would always settle for what I be.
If liking and dislike keep you upset
surely you are being used:
Big man, with all your dignity,
don't mistake what you have for what you are.   10

[2]

The wind blew, a tile fell from the roof,
gave me a crack right on the head.
The tile too smashed itself to bits,
so mine was not the only blood let.
Yet I do not curse it, after all,
the tile didn't mean it.
Hatreds are the creation of creatures,

often drawn from a single accident,
but unaware that accidents happen
they must place blame somewhere.   10
And this alone is lamentable:
I beg you, cultivate the Truth.
Surely you can't deceive yourself
and swear enmity with that!
(NOS. 2, 4 FROM A SERIES OF 20; LCC, 3/3b)   (TR. JAN W. WALLS)

An Old Pine

Towering, thick, its straight trunk soars
    a hundred rods and more,
up into blue depths,
    no forest can claim him.
Winds born of a myriad valleys
    become its voice in the night;
the moon shining on a thousand hills
    hangs in its autumn shade.
This strength couldn't have come
    from tending with manure;
it is endowed with a mind
    in tune with creation.
The court that lacks men of talent
    would do well to take it;
but a world without a good carpenter
    had better leave it alone.
(LCC, 23/8a)   (TR. JAN W. WALLS)

By a Stream on Mount T'ien-t'ung

The stream ripples pure,
    trees hoary-gray,
I stroll through woods along the stream,
    treading the spring.
The stream grows deep, the wood thick,
    in an unfrequented spot,
only the fragrance of flowers unnoticed
    crosses the water.
(LCC, 34/8a)   (TR. JAN W. WALLS)

Plum Blossoms on Solitary Hill

What shall I compare them to—
    these plum blossoms on Solitary Hill?
Halfway between flowering and fading
    in the midst of thorns!
The fairest woman
    leaning against briers and trees;
A despondent statesman
    abiding in the weeds.
Stark straight, their lone loveliness
    carries the winter sun;
still, soundless, their fragrance from afar
    trails the wild wind.
Too late for transplanting,
    their roots grow old;
They glance back at the Imperial Park,
    their colors drained.
(LCC, 10/5b)   (TR. JAN W. WALLS)

Autumn Sun over the *T'ung* Tree

Autumn sun over the *t'ung* tree
spins its shadow like a speeding hub;
the garden, once so dark in its shade,
at next glance is bared to the light.
The cicada chirps no more in its heights,
a cold crow roosts on the tip of a branch.
A withered old man circles it a hundred times,
singing as he walks, waiting for spring to green.
(LCC, 8/5b)   (TR. JAN W. WALLS)

Composed on Horseback, Returning from Lakeview Pavilion at Hangchow, Presented to Yü-ju and Lo-tao

River's glint and mountain mist were floating in green;
At sunset we made to return, they stayed a little longer.

Hereafter this scene shall always enter into my dreams;
In dreams I can wander with my old friends.
(LCC, 33/6a)   (TR. JAN W. WALLS)

Written at Hsiang-kuo Temple on the Occasion of Watching Actors in the Hsing-hsiang Garden of the T'ung-t'ien-chieh Tao-ch'ang

Actors in the theatre,
One noble, the other low;
Knowing in their hearts they are truly the same,
They bear neither joy nor plaint.
(LCC, 10/3a–3b)   (TR. JAN W. WALLS)

"Song of the Radiant Lady"

When the Bright Consort first stepped out of Han palace,
Her tears damp in the spring wind, her temple locks hung limp.
Lowering her head, glancing at her shadow, her face paled;
And there was the emperor whose passion couldn't be held back.
Returning to court, he blamed the master painter
And asked if *his* eyes had ever laid on such a rare beauty.

But exquisiteness can never be captured in a painting,
That day a terrible wrong took the life of Mao Yen-shou!

Once gone, she knew in her heart she could never return;
How pitiable, she wore out one by one her palace-style gowns.   10
Secretly she longed to find out things south of the border,
But year after year, only the wild geese kept flying.
News from home were brought her from ten thousand miles away;
Luckily, in the town of felt tents, her memory often failed!

Have you not seen: within a foot of Long-gate Palace,
    Ah Chio[1] was locked in her room?

---

[1] Alluding to Empress Ch'en, whose nickname was Ah Chiao, a favorite consort of Han Wu-ti until her banishment to Ch'ang-men ("Long-gate") Palace for failure to give birth to an heir after over ten years of marriage.

To fall out of favor—
    no difference is there between north and south!
(NO. 1 FROM A SERIES OF 2; LCC, 4/7a–7b)   (TR. IRVING Y. LO)

Tune: "Sand of Silk-washing Stream"

The garden in the middle of a hundred acres is
        half-covered with moss.
The white water before the gate meanders on and on;
How many men would love peace so much as to come here?

In the corridors around the small courtyard spring is quiet:
Peaches on the hill, apricots by the stream, planted in twos
        and threes—
For whom do they blossom, for whom do they wither away?
(CST, P. 206)   (TR. JAMES J. Y. LIU)

Tune: "Mountain Hawthorns" (*Sheng Cha Tzu*)

Rain beats on trees south of the river;
In one night, innumerable flowers have blossomed.
    The green leaves gradually form a shade;
Below, there is a road on which the wanderer can go home.

Here, where you and I meet,
Not thinking that spring will soon end,
Let's lift our winecups and pray to the east wind:
"Don't go back in such a hurry!"
(CST, P. 208)   (TR. JAMES J. Y. LIU)

Yen Chi-tao (1030?–1106?)

Tune: "Partridge Sky" (*Che-ku t'ien*), Two Lyrics

[1]

Bright-colored sleeves attentively offered the jade cup,
Years ago, when I risked getting my face flushed with wine.

You danced till the moon over the center of the willow
               pavilion had set,
And sang till the wind by the peach-blossom fan died down.

          Ever since we parted,
            I've remembered our meeting—
How often has my dreaming soul been with you!
Tonight, let the light of the silver lamp shine on you fully,
For I'm still afraid that we are meeting in a dream.
(CST, P. 225)   (TR. JAMES J. Y. LIU)

[2]

Drunk with wine, I slap my spring robe
        and miss the old perfume:
Must heaven send the grief of parting
        to vex a carefree soul?
Year after year
        autumn grass grows over the fields;
Day after day
        setting sun comes to my pavilion.

          Clouds distant and dim,
            Waters vast and endless—
How many miles does the traveler still have to come home?
Lovesickness is but a fickle word,
These flowered scrolls[1] do not deserve your tears!
(CST, P. 226)   (TR. AN-YAN TANG)

Tune: "Mountain Hawthorns," Two Lyrics

[1]

A handsome youth with a golden whip
Left galloping on his piebald horse,
Entangling the lady in the jade pavilion,
Under embroidered quilts on a cold spring night.

---

1 *Hua-ch'ien;* i.e., letter paper with ornamentation.

Now news of him has come back;
Now it's April,[1] and pear blossoms fall.
Nowhere for her to express her lovesickness,
She turns her back on the garden swing.

[2]

From where is spring coming back?
Try to find out by the stream:
The willows on the bank display their delicate yellow,
The wheat in the fields regains green moisture.

A handsome youth full of feelings
Counts the time before the flowers will bloom.
Who will send him a twig of plum blossoms from the peak
To tell him news from the South?[2]
(CST, PP. 228, 229)   (TR. JAMES J. Y. LIU)

Tune: "Butterflies Lingering over Flowers"

Drunk, I left the western pavilion;
        sober, I can't recall.
Spring dreams, autumn clouds,
        easily they gather and disperse.
The slanting moon halfway up the window—
        still I lie awake,
Watching Mount Wu spread out its kingfisher green
        on the painted screen.

---

1 The original has *han-shih* or "Cold Food," a festival that occurs on the one
    hundred and fifth day after the winter solstice.
2 The last two lines allude to the anecdote about Lu K'ai (third century A.D.),
    who sent a twig of plum blossoms from the South to his friend Fan Yeh in
    the North, with a poem reading:
                    I pluck plum blossoms on meeting a courier,
                    To send them to the man by the fields.
                    What do we have here in the South?
                    Let me present you with a twig-ful of spring.
    Further, the peak refers to the Yü-ling, where, it is said, the plum blossoms
    on the southern branches are already faded when those on the northern
    branches bloom, the climate on both sides being so different.

Wine stains on my robe,
    words in my song—
Drop after drop, line after line
    tell of my desolate feeling,
The red candle pitying
    its own helplessness,
Weep for me in the cold night
    tears in vain.
(CST, P. 224)   (TR. AN-YAN TANG)

Su Shih (1037–1101)

In a Boat, Getting Up at Night

A gentle breeze rustles through reeds and rushes—
I open the hatch to watch the rain, as moonlight floods the lake.
Boatmen and waterfowls share alike the same dream;
Big fish, startled, speed away like scurrying foxes.
Late at night, men and objects do not feel for one another;
I alone am amused by things and their shadows.
Tides rising unseen from the bank, I mourn the wintry earthworms;
A setting moon caught by the willows, I watch a spider strung.
This fleeting life spent in sickness and worry—
The pure vision passes before my eyes just for a moment.   10
When cocks crow and bells sound, flocks of birds scatter—
Soon the drum beats at the prow and people call to one another.
(TPC, 10/10a)   (TR. IRVING Y. LO)

At the Heng-ts'ui[1] Pavilion of Fa-hui Monastery

Mornings I see the Wu Mountain[2] recumbent,
Evenings I see the Wu Mountain standing erect.

---

1 Heng-ts'ui (literally, "kingfisher recumbent"), a name given to this pavilion, refers to the mountains in front of it. This phrase is also a poetic epithet referring to women's eyebrows; the fashion at that time was to paint them green.
2 Wu Shan, actually a range of seven mountains southwest of Hangchow, one of which is also called Hsü Shan (named after the temple of Wu Tzu-hsü built on its top).

The Wu Mountain wears more than one face—
Tossing and turning to look its best for you.[3]

A recluse, I rise from my painted pavilion;
Holding everything empty, I see no object before me.
There's only this ridge a thousand paces high,
A barrier and screen from east to west.

Since spring I've had no date of return to my old country.
Who speaks of autumn's sadness? Spring is sadder still.   10
Having sailed on these placid waters, I long for the Brocade River[4];
Now, looking at these recumbent green hills, I'm reminded of Mount
  O-mei.[5]

When will the carved railings ever look their best?
Not just the man who leans against railings easily grows old.
A hundred years' flourishing and decay, far more lamentable,
Though I know pools and pavilions will turn to briers and brambles.

Wanderers who look for the place where once I've wandered
Need only to come to where the Wu Mountain lies recumbent.
(TPC, 4/6b)   (TR. IRVING Y. LO)

On Chao Ch'ang's Flower Paintings in
Wang Po-yang's Collection, Three Selections

[1]

Plum Blossoms

Southward I once traveled, crossing mountain passes,
To where the sand and water gleamed pure as silk.
On a traveler already afflicted with grief,
Sleet began to fall as the day dusked.

---

8 This line contains two allusions. First, the words "toss" (*chuan*) and "turn"
(*ts'e*) come from the first poem in the *Shih Ching*, generally interpreted
as an epithalamium ode. The comparison of the mountain to a woman
is reinforced by the second allusion: *wei chün jung*, the last three words
of the line (literally, "to wear makeup for you"), a common idiom de-
scribing a wife's duty.
4 Cho-chin ("wash-brocade") River in Ch'eng-tu, Szechwan, near the poet's
birthplace.
5 O-mei, the name of a famous mountain in Szechwan.

How graceful were these tiny plum blossoms,
The blurred vision of a lovely girl's[1] face.
Furtive fragrance lingered with me as I went away;
I looked back and was pelted by hundreds of petals.
Even today when I unroll this painting,
My old eyes grow dim and moist with tears.   10
Such secret longings cannot be sketched,
I'll go home and dream of your beauty.

[2]

Sunflower

Too fragile to endure the heat of a long summer day,
Yet pretty enough to cheer the cool morning—
Head stooped, a golden cup raised high,
Reflecting the splendor of the sun's first light.
A heart[2] of sandalwood color forms its own halo;
Its leaves of kingfisher sheen grow dense and prickly.
Of all who sketched from still life since ancient times,
Who could have excelled the art of Chao Ch'ang?[3]
Fresh morning makeup, or drunken stupor at noon:
Its true likeness holds the *yin* and the *yang*.   10
Just look within this flower and its stem,
There you'll find the fragrance of wind and dew.

[3]

Hibiscus

Pleasant winds brushing the forest grove,
Floodwater gathering slowly into pools.
Beside the creek a wild hibiscus grows—

---

1 The text reads: *Wu-chi,* literally "girl of Wu [modern Soochow]."
2 Punning on the word *hsin,* which means both "center" and "heart." Here it refers to the dark-brown color at the center of a sunflower.
3 Chao Ch'ang, or Chao Ch'ang-chih (998–1022), the painter of this series of four paintings, enjoyed a wide reputation for his paintings of flowers and fruits. One hundred and fifty-fours works by him were listed in the Sung imperial catalog, *Hsüan-ho* [1119–26] *hua-p'u.*

The water and the blossoms enhancing each other's beauty.
It sits there and watches the shriveled lotuses in the pond.
Alone it keeps company with withered chrysanthemums in the frost—
Ethereal beauty is but a moment's forced smile,
As old age presses on to crush and kill.
Sad and dismal, it is like a girl from a poor family,
Who's married late and startled by aging too soon.   10
Who can sketch the complexion of fair youth?
Only the Old Woodcutter of southern Szechwan.[4]
(TPC, 15/2b)   (TR. IRVING Y. LO)

Spring Day

Cooing pigeons, nursling swallows, all quiet without a sound;
Sunlight pierces western window, splashes my eyes sparkle.
Awakened from noontime torpor, I find nothing to do
Except in spring sleep to enjoy a sunny spring day.
(TPC, 15/3b)   (TR. IRVING Y. LO)

Two Poems on Insect Painting by Candidate Yin

[1]

On a Toad

Its savage eyes, at whom do they glare?
Its whitish belly swells in vain.
Just take care not to worry the centipede,
A hungry snake will never let you go free.

[2]

On a Snail

Its rancid saliva can't fill up a shell,
Barely enough to quench its own thirst;

---

4 Referring to the artist who signs the painting with his style-name of "Ch'iao-
jen Chien-nan lao."

Climbs high and never knows to turn back,
Ends up stuck on a wall—shriveled.
(NOS. 3, 7 FROM A SERIES OF 8; TPC, 14/8b)   (TR. IRVING Y. LO)

The Fisherman, Four Poems

[1]

The fisherman drinks,
Where does he go for wine?
All at once he disposes of his fish and crab.
Not too much wine, but he won't quit until drunk:
Neither he nor the others are particular about money.

[2]

The fisherman's drunk,
His straw cloak dances;
In his drunken state, he looks for his way home.
A light boat and a short oar, whichever way they slant—
When he wakes up, he doesn't know where he is heading.

[3]

The fisherman wakes
At noon on the spring river;
Fallen blossoms, flying catkins intrude into his dream.
Sobered up from wine and still drunk, drunk and yet sober—
He laughs at the human world, both past and present.

[4]

The fisherman, laughing,
Takes off like a light seagull,
Into a misty river of wind and rain.
On horseback, along the riverbank, is an official
Asking me for my little boat to ferry him southward.
(TPC, 15/1a–1b)   (TR. IRVING Y. LO)

Drinking at the Lake, First It's Sunny, Then It Rains

Shimmering water at its full—sunny day is best;
Blurred mountains in a haze—marvelous even in rain.
Compare West Lake to a beautiful girl,[1] she will look
Just as becoming—lightly made up or richly adorned.
(NO. 2 FROM A SERIES OF 2; TPC, 4/7a)   (TR. IRVING Y. LO)

Rain at Cold-Food Festival,[1] Two Poems

[1]

Since coming to Huang-chou,
Three Cold-Food Festivals have come and gone.
Each year I wish to linger with spring,
But spring's departure admits no delay.
This year we again suffered from rain,
Two months of autumn's dreary weather.
Lying in bed, I smell the crab-apple blossoms.
Mud splatters the rouge and the snow.
All in secrecy spring is stolen and wasted,
Wreaking vengeance in the middle of the night—   10
How does it differ from a sickly youth,
Up from his sickbed, his hair already white?

[2]

Spring flood is coming up to my door,
But the rain shows no sign of letting up.
My small house is like a fishing boat,

---

1 The text reads "Hsi-tzu," or "girl from the West Village." The name is some-
times given as Hsi Shih; she is considered the most beautiful girl in ancient
China, who rose from humble origins to become the consort of the king
of Wu kingdom.
1 Cold-Food (*han-shih*) Festival, the day before the Ch'ing-ming Festival,
marks the end of the three-day period when families refrain from starting
cooking-fires at home (in commemoration of the death of Yen Chih-t'ui).
It is also the season when Chinese families visited their ancestral burial
mounds. Hence, the reference in the second poem to paper money, which is
usually burned on such occasions.

Blurred in misty waters and clouds.
I boil winter vegetable in an empty kitchen,
And burn wet reeds in a cracked stove.
Who can tell it's the Cold-Food Festival
Except for scraps of paper on crows' beak?
The sovereign's gate is nine layers deep,
Grave mounds lie thousands of miles away.   10
I'd also lament my fate at the end of the road,[2]
But dead ashes can't be ignited by fanning.[3]
(TPC, 12/9b)   (TR. IRVING Y. LO)

Bathing the Infant[1]

Most people expect their sons to be clever,
My whole life was ruined by cleverness.
I only wish my son to be dull and stupid
And without suffering or hardship to reach the highest rank.
(TPHC, 2/23b)   (TR. CHIANG YEE)

Sent to Chief Abbot of Tung-lin Monastery

The brook speaks with an eloquent tongue,[1]
And the color of the mountain, isn't it the pure form?
Last night you read more than eighty thousand hymns,
How can you preach them to others then?
(TPC, 13/10b)   (TR. CHIANG YEE)

---

[2] Alluding to the poet Juan Chi, who was said to weep when he came to the end of a road.

[3] Alluding to the story of Han An-kuo (in the *Shih Chi*), who, while in prison, said to the jailer T'ien Chia who tried to shame him, "Couldn't the dead ashes be ignited again?" The jailer replied, "As soon as it is ignited, I shall smother it."

[1] The original title *"Hsi-erh"* refers to the ceremony of giving the infant its first bath on the third day after a child's birth.

[1] *Kuang-ch'ang she,* a Buddhist term referring to one of the thirty-two features of Buddha. According to the scriptures, a man who tells no lies can extend his tongue to the nostril, but when Buddha extends his, it touches the hairline.

A Monk of Auspicious Fortune (*Chih-hsiang*) Monastery
Asking Me to Name a Pavilion

Fleeting glory or decay—are wind and lightning;
How can they stay for long like the flowers in bloom?
The abbot meditates in the Hall of Perceiving-the-Illusion;
To perceive the sensory and then the Illusion—the senses
    and Illusion become one.
(TPC, 3/5b)   (TR. CHIANG YEE)

Tune: "Water Dragon's Chant" (*Shui-lung yin*)
After Chang Chi-fu's Lyric on the Willow Catkin,
Using the Same Rhyming Words[1]

It seems to be a flower, yet not a flower,
And no one shows it any pity: let it fall!
    Deserting home, it wanders by the road;
    When you come to think of it, it must
    Have thoughts, insentient as it may be.
    Its tender heart twisted by grief,
    Its delicate eyes heavy with sleep,
    About to open, yet closed again.
  In its dream it follows the wind for ten thousand miles,
    To find where its lover has gone,   10
But then it is aroused by the oriole's cry once more.

I do not grieve that the willow catkins have flown away,
    But that, in the Western Garden,[2]
    The fallen red cannot be gathered.
    When dawn comes and the rain is over,
    Where are the traces they have left?

---

[1] Chang Chih-fu is the courtesy-name of Chang Chieh, a friend and colleague of Su Shih's. It was a common practice to write a poem to "harmonize" (*ho*) with another one written by someone else, and if one used the same rhyming words as in the original poem, it was then called "following the rhymes" (*tz'u-yün*). This poem was written in 1087.

[2] Possibly a reference to an actual garden so named in Lo-yang, or used loosely for any fine garden.

A pond full of broken duckweeds![3]
Of all the colors of springtime,
Two-thirds have gone with the dust,
And one-third with the flowing water!   20
         When you look closely,
      These are not willow catkins,
   But, drop after drop, parted lovers' tears!
(CST, P. 277)   (TR. JAMES J. Y. LIU)

      Tune: "Prelude to Water Music" (*Shui-tiao ko-t'ou*)

The bright moon, when will she appear?
Wine cup in hand, I ask the blue sky.
I don't know inside the gates of heaven
What time of year it would be tonight.
I was just about to ride there on the wind,
But feared that heaven's crystalline palaces and towers
      So high, would be for me too cold.
Instead, I dance and cavort here with my shadow
      And know what it is to be among men.

         Circling the red-trimmed chamber,   10
         Peering down through doors of silk,
         She shines on the sleepless.
No cause for her to be spiteful—
Then, why, when we part, does she shine so round and full?
As man has both sorrow and joy, being apart and being together,
So too the moon has her waxing and her waning, increase and diminu-
      tion:
         This has always been less than perfect.
      So, let us both live to a ripe old age,
      And be together, though a thousand miles apart,
         To share her beauty.   20
(CST, P. 280)   (TR. EUGENE EOYANG)

---

3 Su Shih's own note reads, "It is said that when willow catkins fall into the
water, they turn into duckweeds. I have tested it and found it true."

Tune: "Song of Divination" (*Pu-suan tzu*)

Half-moon hangs on sparse *wu-t'ung* tree;
The water clock stops, people settle down.
Who sees the recluse passing by, all alone:
A haunting shadow of a fugitive swan.

Then, suddenly startled, it turns its head,
With a grief that no one can know.
Looking over each wintry bough, it settles on none:
The lonely sandbank's cold.
(CST, P. 295)   (TR. EUGENE EOYANG)

Tune: "Immortal at the River"

Wining at the Eastern Slope tonight,
        I sobered, then got drunk again.
About third watch as I got back home,
Snores thundered from my houseboy.
I rapped the gates, but no one answered.
Leaning on my cane, I listened to the river's sound.

I long regret I can't muster my own body,
Much less come to terms with worldly problems.
Night advances, quiet breeze quivers on ripples.
How I wish to sail away in my little skiff
And, high on the waters, live out the rest of my life!   10
(CST, P. 287)   (TR. MICHAEL E. WORKMAN)

Tune: "As in a Dream: A Song"

Make yourself pure before you purify others.
Myself, I perspire and I pant.
Let me say this to the bathers:
Why not play with your naked body?
        Splash!
        Splash!
Stoop yourself for the world's every living thing.
(CST, P. 311)   (TR. IRVING Y. LO)

Tune: "Joy of Eternal Union" (*Yung-yü lo*)—
Passing the Seven-league Shallows[1]

A leaf of a light boat,
A pair of oars startling the wild goose—
 Pure water and sky,
 Clear shadows, calm waves—
Fish gambol and play among the mirrored water grass,
And egrets dot the misty riverbank;
I pass by a sandy brook, fast-flowing,
 A frosted brook, cold,
 A moonlit brook, bright.

Layer after layer as in a painting,   10
Bend after bend like a screen—
 I recall those years:
When Yen Ling wasted his life till old age,
Ruler and minister shared the same dream.
Then as now, the vanity of fame!
Only the distant hills stretch on and on,
 And jagged clouds over the hills,
 Then dawn spreads the hills green.
(CST, P. 303)   (TR. IRVING Y. LO)

Huang T'ing-chien (1045–1105)

Buffalo Boy

Astride an ox, you pass the village far in the distance;
Low winds bring the notes of your flute across the paddies.
Ch'ang-an played host to many guests of fame and gain—
Their resources soon spent—not so with you, my cowherd!
(SKPC, I/3b)   (TR. MICHAEL E. WORKMAN)

---

1 The place where Yen Kuang, or Yen Tzu-ling, fished while living under
an assumed name because he wished to refuse the offer of a high post
from his former schoolmate, who became the first emperor of the Eastern
Han dynasty. Sometimes called Yen-ling Shallows, the place is located on
the banks of the Che River in modern T'ung-lu, Chekiang.

Following the Rhymes of Fellow Graduate P'ei Chung-mou[1]

Carriage tops flapping in spring wind by the waters of the Ju,
Inside, our beds faced each other as we slept on the monk's felt quilt.
The distance between Wu-yang and She an easy hundred leagues,
While you and I, sir, once were young men.
Our white hairs grow out like sprouting seeds;
We'd give anything for Green Mountain, but who has the cash?[2]
The tideland mists and bamboo groves south of the river,
We yield to the carefree cormorants falling asleep along her shores.
(SKWC, 1/11b)   (TR. MICHAEL E. WORKMAN)

Out in the Snow, Spending the Night at the New Stockade, Extremely Depressed[1]

Over my district north to south, when will my days in office end?
Once more at New Stockade, I untie the weary saddle.
Mountains swallow up the Sky Ladle—three stars have sunk[2];
Snow glistens in the moonlight in frozen land of a thousand leagues.
Minor officials must sometimes cringe before authorities[3];
Old friends often inquire why I haven't laid down this post.

---

1 Upon passing the 1067 imperial examination, Huang and P'ei served at their first official posts in North China. Huang became the sheriff of She-*hsien* in present Honan province. This poem was composed during Huang's middle period when the poet looked back over a lifetime of friendship with P'ei, which began twenty years earlier, in leisurely visits at the Buddhist monastery near the Ju River in Honan.
2 Alluding to the story of the Man of Tai-fu Mountain (Tai-fu Shan-jen), who sent a boy out with scrolls to beg for money to buy a mountain (*mai-shan ch'ien*).
1 New Stockade (*Hsin-chai*), a military outpost in present Honan province. Huang served as the sheriff of She-*hsien* from 1068 71. (An anecdote relates that the controversial political reformer Wang An-shih was so impressed with the sentiments in this poem that he promptly had Huang appointed instructor in the National University.)
2 Sky Ladle: the Big Dipper; three stars: Orion. The poet describes a winter sky in North China in the early morning hours.
3 Literally, "to buckle up the belt" of an official gown in the presence of a superior. T'ao Chi'en (365–427) refused to buckle up and he quit his post for early retirement to the "fields and garden" of his home in Kiangsi province. According to another version of this poem, the third couplet reads, "By now I know my meanness, too late to turn away;/This sick body hurts all over, too hard to bend the waist."

Everywhere south of the river tall bamboos touch the clouds—
Shall I head there in a spring breeze and snap off a fishing cane?
(SKWC, 2/3b)   (TR. MICHAEL E. WORKMAN)

Climbing K'uai Pavilion[1]

Idiot me has ended one more day's official grind!
At K'uai Pavilion, from east and west, I move in the clear evening air:
Trees shed leaves on a thousand peaks, the heavens far and wide;
The moon shines bright, a vast expanse of shimmering river.
For the fair one, bright zither strings once were slashed,[2]
Now only good wine could coax a smile from my eyes.[3]
Gliding endlessly homeward, the boatmen play their flutes—
Come what may, I'll pledge this heart to the white seagulls.
(SKWC, 11/6b–7a)   (TR. MICHAEL E. WORKMAN)

Upon Passing the Homestead[1]

Crickets' chirps become increasingly urgent
As a cold season idles the field pump.
Boyhood hands rooted those willows
Now rise to a darkened sky.
Our homestead neighbors simple folks,
Younger faces have replaced the oldtimers'.
Dark ancient woods rise above the graves,
Fields and orchards changed into ridged paths.

Clan elders inquire after my health;
Wife's kinsmen come to pay their respects.   10
Coming home, I feel like a stranger,
I look at myself and start to laugh.

---

1 Located in T'ai-ho *hsien* in present Kiangsi province, where Huang served as administrator from 1081–83.
2 Referring to the story of Po Ya and Chung Tzu-ch'i. Cf. Meng Hao-jan's "Parting from Wang Wei," note 1.
3 Leader of the "Seven Sages of the Bamboo Grove," Juan Chi (210–63) would irritably roll the whites of his eyes at an unwelcome visitor, but the pupils of his eyes sparkled on greeting a friend.
1 Huang's birthplace Shuang-ching, Fen-ning district, in present Kiangsi province, was famous for tea.

Life is duckweed floating on the river,
Its cares streak my temples with snow.
In deep night the wind stirs cascading frost,
The dry leaves whirl down in drifts.

Why does this candle sputter so gladly?
Probably for all the good news I've heard.
Mother's age causes both joy and worry[2];
My daughter is about to shed her baby teeth.   20
The boat will be moored a hundred leagues from home;
Dreams of return bring home an inch away.
(SKWC, 14/1b–2a)   (TR. MICHAEL E. WORKMAN)

Following the Rhymes of Chang Hsün, in My Study in Late Spring

Studying the ancient manuscript crumbly with age,
I cherish my friends across long rivers and lakes.
Visitors' horses and carriages are not missing here,
But the heart being distant, the scene is still tranquil.
I pick homegrown greens in the evening drizzle;
I draw icy well water to brew some fine tea.
Spring left me undiverted by the lush garden,
Though the yellow oriole would have welcomed me.
This court position of mine lacks prestige;
With luck, I'll next serve at a provincial post.   10
I'd like to paddle a dinghy on the choppy waves
Then scrub my hair dry on halcyon-crested peaks!
(SKNC, 3/5a)   (TR. MICHAEL E. WORKMAN)

Following the Rhymes of Wang An-shih's Poem
"Inscribed on the Wall of the Temple of Western Great Unity"[1]

In raging winds the crows' cries continue without end,
Ants battle just as fierce during the storm.

---

2 *Lün Yü* IV: 21, "The age of one's parents is always of great concern, giving rise to feelings of joy and trepidation." Huang's aged mother and young daughter were not able to accompany him on this official trip.
1 A Taoist temple in K'ai-feng, built in 1028. The Great Unity is the supreme deity of the Taoist religion.

Be it true, or be it false, who knows?
Men who head north wind up in the south.²
(SKNC, 3/10a)   (TR. MICHAEL E. WORKMAN)

Teasing Hsiao-te,¹ My Son

This young boy on my hands at middle age,
A prodigal offspring in the years of decline.
Learning to speak—he trills like a spring bird!
He smears the windows black—a bevy of dusky crows!
He's never been scolded for Grandma dotes on him;
Big sister glorifies his least show of wit.
Perhaps he'll compose someday Treatises by a Hermit²:
Don't let low family status³ stand in your path.
(SKNC, 10/2b)   (TR. MICHAEL E. WORKMAN)

Passing Hung-fu Monastery with Yüan-ming: Inscribed in Jest

In Hung-fu Monastery we brush off the dust from purple window
   gauze,¹
On dusty walls old poems cling like nestling crows;
Spring is about gone, already the season of wind and rain—
And still the visitors shake down the falling blossoms.
(SKNC, 11/3b)   (TR. MICHAEL E. WORKMAN)

---

2 Wang An-shih (1021–86) retired after a stormy career in 1076. His reform
   policies eventually were dismantled by the conservatives which included the
   poets Su Shih and Huang T'ing-chien.
1 Literally, "Minor Virtue," Huang's only son, born of a concubine in 1084.
   Huang's first wife had died at age twenty-five in 1070. A daughter was
   born to his second wife, but she, too, died at age twenty-six in 1079.
2 A set of political treatises compiled by Wang Fu (c. 76–157) of the
   Eastern Han dynasty. Scorned by his neighbors for his low birth as a
   concubine's son, he styled himself "a Man of Obscurity."
3 The text reads *wai-chia,* which means "mother's side of the family."
1 Monks usually washed off most inscriptions on temple walls or left them
   untended, but covered with gauze those done by famous calligraphers.

In My Study in the Monastery, Rising after a Nap, Two Poems

[1]

Short on brains, long on stupidity, the mantis seizes the cicada;
Grossness without limit, the one-legged K'uei pities the millepede.[1]
During the court recess, I'm back dreaming under the north window—
Moonlight stirs on the river, just right for fishing boats.

[2]

Peach and plum blossoms, speechless, keep swaying in the wind,
Yellow orioles see nothing beyond green rustlings.
Nine times out of ten, words of officials become regulations;
Should the river send a boat for me, I would head east.
(SKNC, 11/2a–2b)   (TR. MICHAEL E. WORKMAN)

Living in Exile at Ch'ien-nan[1]

Frost falls only to melt in the valley;
Wind strews the leaves over the hills.
By and by the bright year will dim
And all the wood mites hibernate.
(NO. 2 FROM A SERIES OF 10; SKNC, 12/8a–8b)

(TR. MICHAEL E. WORKMAN)

On a Painting of Ants and Butterflies

Butterflies paired in ecstatic flight
Unpredictably perish on spider webs;
Ants scramble for the broken wings—
Reward awaits upon return to the Southern Bough.
(SKNC, 16/5b)   (TR. MICHAEL E. WORKMAN)

---

[1] The poet draws on fables in the *Chuang-tzu* which point to the folly of inordinate desire that only succeeds in self-destruction.
[1] Traveling with his elder brother, Huang reached this exile-post in Szechwan in 1095.

Inscribed on a Scroll "Plum Blossoms by the Water" Done for Mr. Tseng by the Old Priest of Hua-kuang Temple

These plum buds move one's imagination,
Braving the cold, yield snow-like blossoms:
How pitiable: in the evening breeze upon the water,
Petal after petal, the flowers dot the rocky shoals.
(SKWC, 17/12b)   (TR. MICHAEL E. WORKMAN)

Tune: "Pure Serene Music"

Where has spring returned to?
Quiet, desolate, no path to follow.
If anyone knows where spring has gone,
Let him call her back to stay with me!

No trace of spring: who knows where?
Unless you go and ask the yellow oriole.
It sings a hundred tunes that no one understands,
And flies away past the roses, riding the wind.
(CST, P. 393)   (TR. JAMES J. Y. LIU)

Tune: "Partridge Sky"

The chill of dawn grows on the tips of yellow chrysanthemum twigs.
In this life, don't let the winecups be dry!
Before the wind, play the flute aslant in the rain;
When drunk, pin flowers on the hat and wear it upside down!

While my health remains,
Let me eat well,
And enjoy dancing skirts and singing castanets to the full!
Let the yellow flowers and my white hair entangle each other
To make a spectacle for the scornful eyes of my fellow men!
(CST, P. 394)   (TR. JAMES J. Y. LIU)

Tune: "Pleasure of Returning to the Fields: A Prelude"
(*Kuei-t'ien-lo yin*)

Fine view, but I'm still getting thinner.
How I've been toyed with by this man.
    I too have a heart!
    He misses me and calls me;
    When he sees me, he scolds me:
Heavens, how can one put up with this!

We were lucky to have been so thick;
Now, before the winecups, I knit my brows again.
    This man wonders why!
He wronged me and made me give way to him.   10
    So let it go! I don't care!
    This time it's really all over!
But when we meet, it's just the same as before.
(CST, P. 407)   (TR. JAMES J. Y. LIU)

Ch'in Kuan (1049–1100)

Returning from Kuang-ling

The day is chilly, birds each lean upon another,
Tens, hundreds, they flock to sport in the fading light.
Gone past, the travelers, and none arose,
But suddenly hearing ice break, they fly away together.
(NO. 4 FROM A SERIES OF 4; HHSC, 10/3b)   (TR. STEPHEN WEST)

Spring Rain

A night of gentle thunder fells a thousand catkins,
rays of clearing float on tiles of jagged blue.
Full of feeling, peonies hold spring tears,
sapped of strength, hedgeroses sleep along dawn branches.
(NO. 2 FROM A SERIES OF 5; HHSC, 10/2a–2b)   (TR. STEPHEN WEST)

Tune: "Happy Events Approaching" (*Hao-shih chin*)
Written in a Dream

By the road in spring, rain has added flowers,
And the flowers have stirred up a hillful of spring colors.
I walk to the deep-hidden source of a little stream,
    There are hundreds and thousands of yellow orioles.

The flying clouds opposite me turn into dragons and snakes,
    Soaring and twisting in the azure air.
Lying drunk under a shady ancient wisteria,
    I cannot tell south from north at all.
(CST, P. 469)   (TR. JAMES J. Y. LIU)

Tune: "Courtyard Full of Fragrance" (*Man-t'ing fang*)

Mountains rubbed by light clouds,
Sky adhering to the withered grass—
The painted horn's sound breaks at the watchtower.
Let me stop my traveling boat
And share a farewell cup with you for a while!
How many past events of Fairyland—
To look back is futile: only scattered mists remain.
Beyond the slanting sun:
A few dots of cold crows,
A river winding round a solitary village.   10

Soul-searing
Is this moment when
The perfume bag is secretly untied,
The silk girdle lightly torn apart.
All this has merely won me the name
Of a heartless lover in the Green Mansion!
Once gone, when shall I see you again?
In vain have I brought tear-stains to our lapels and sleeves!
Where my heart saddens,
The tall city wall stops my gaze;   20
The lights are up: it is already dusk.
(CST, P. 458)   (TR. JAMES J. Y. LIU)

Chou Pang-yen (1056–1121)

Tune: "Six Toughies" (*Liu-ch'ou*)
Written After the Roses Have Faded

Time for summer clothes and wine-tasting—
How I regret the wasted days and nights away from home!
  I wish spring would stay for a while,
  But spring goes back like passing wings,
    Once gone, no trace left.
  If you ask, Where are the flowers?
  Last night, amid wind and rain,
The beautiful ladies of the Ch'u Palace[1] were buried.
Where their filigreed ornaments fell, they left fragrance behind,
  As they dotted the peach-paths at random,   10
  And lightly fluttered above the willowy roads.
Who is there so loving as to pity their fall?
Only the matchmaker-bees and messenger-butterflies
  Knock on the window from time to time.

  The eastern garden lies quiet,
  Gradually overgrown with dark green.
A silent stroll beneath the precious clusters
    Turns into a sigh.
The long twigs purposely entangle the passer-by,
  As if pulling his clothes, about to speak,   20
    With endless parting sorrow.
  A tiny remaining bloom
I force myself to wear on the turban,
  But after all it's not like
One that softly wavers at the tip of a hairpin
  And leans towards you.
Ah, do not drift away by the morning or evening tide!
  For I fear that on the fallen red[2]

---

[1] The original for "beautiful ladies" is *ch'ing-kuo;* cf. note to Li Shang-yin's "Willow." The mention of Ch'u Palace alludes to the story about court ladies who starved themselves to death to keep slim; cf. note on Chao Fei-yen accompanying Wen T'ing-yün's "A Song of Chang Ching-yüan Picking Lotus Flowers."

[2] These lines allude to the story about Lu Wu, who saw a fallen red leaf drifting in the canal that led from the palace, with this poem written on it:

There may still be words of lovesickness—
How could anyone see them then?   30
(CST, P. 610)   (TR. JAMES J. Y. LIU)

Tune: "Prince of Lan-ling" (*Lan-ling Wang*)
On Willows

Willow's shadow straight up,
Hanging threads branch out, a mist of green.
    Along Emperor Sui's embankment
    how many times have I seen them
caress the water, let fall the catkins, while sending off a departing guest?
    I climb here, gazing toward home:
        Who could recognize
    a tired traveler in the capital—
    along a pavilion-dotted road,
    in years come and gone,   10
having broken off these soft branches by more than a thousand feet?

        Idly I search for familiar places:
    again, wine accompanies mournful music;
    again, a lamp shines upon farewell feast—
Pear blossoms and burned elm-leaves hasten the Cold-Food Festival.
    Grieved by the wind's coming like an arrow,
    and the waves warmed with a boatman's pole,
I look back from afar, and there are many post stations;
    The one I long for, in the farthest north of the world!

        Sad and forlorn!   20
    Sorrow on top of sorrow—
    now the banks of the river wind and turn,
    the ferry station silent and empty.
The setting sun lingers, spring never ends.
I remember how we held hands in a moonlit pavilion,
or listened to a flute on a dew-moistened bridge;
        Pondering on past affairs—

"How rapidly does the water flow!/Deep in the palace, nothing to do all day./
Diligently I ask the red leaf:/Go forth into the human world!"

everything is like a dream—
    I shed secret tears.
(CST, P. 611)   (TR. IRVING Y. LO)

Tune: "The Beautiful Lady Yü," Two Lyrics

[1]

About to leave, yet by the lamplight she lingers—
    Heartbroken, far from the vermilion door.
No need for the rouge-rain to cleanse fragrant cheeks:
    Wait till the roses have faded,
        he will come back.

In idle moments, limber up your waist and dance to the beats of songs,
    And let other people watch.
In the golden censer there should still be some dying embers:
    Just don't let love quickly turn
        into cold ashes.   10

[2]

Sparse fence, winding path, a small farmhouse—
    Clear dawn breaks above clouds and trees;
In the chilly air the mountain hue is here and nowhere.
The fields beyond send up the sound of a single bell,
        to send off a single boat.

I put on more clothes, gallop away, looking for a post station;
    Huddled with grief, only wine is best.
The ducks that doze among the reeds seem to own the pond:
    Though they may be surprised and scattered by the traveler,
        they'll pair up again.
(CST, P. 618)   (TR. IRVING Y. LO)

Tune: "Distant Red Window" (*Hung ch'uang chiung*)

    For days now,
    It's been a real binge.

I hardly noticed
heaped red petals outside my window
already half a finger deep.
Shadows of flowers shatter in the wind,
And, huddled in spring sleep, I suddenly wake up from wine.

Here's that lovely one,
Finely featured,
Comes to whisper in my ear,
And asks, "Haven't you sobered up yet today?"   10
Such tenderness,
softly and slowly,
Teases me drunk again.
(CST, P. 619)   (TR. IRVING Y. LO)

Chu Tun-ju (1081?–1159?)

Tune: "Happy Events Approaching"

Shaking my head, I left the world of red dust,[1]
No longer caring when to be sober, when drunk.
My livelihood—the green grass cloak and the straw hat;
I'm used to wearing frost and braving snow.

When night falls, the wind settles and the fishing line lies idle.
Above and below is the new moon.
For a thousand miles, water and sky are the same color.
Watch the single wild goose appear and disappear!
(CST, P. 854)   (TR. JAMES J. Y. LIU)

Tune: "Magnolia Blossoms, Abbreviated"
(*Chien-tzu mu-lan-hua*)

No one invited me—
I spread a rug under the pines and sit down by myself;
Sipping wine, composing verse,
Playing with the plum blossoms as my handmaids.

---

1 Conventional phrase for the world of hustle and bustle.

Being happy, I'm easily drunk,
And when the bright moon comes flying, I sleep under the flowers.
Who will see my drunken dance
But the flowers that fill my silk cap and the moon that fills my cup?
(CST, P. 858)   (TR. JAMES J. Y. LIU)

Tune: "The Charm of Nien-nu" (*Nien-nu chiao*)

What pleases me in my old age
Is that I've traveled every corner of the world,
    Known clearly what lies beyond things,
    See through all emptiness.
    Oceans of regret and mounds of grief,
    All will be quickly crumpled up.
      Lest I be lost among flowers,
      Or be stupefied with wine,
    Everywhere I shall keep an alert eye,
    Find a place to sleep when I'm full,   10
And waking up, play the actor's part to suit the occasion.

Don't speak of the past that's gone, or what's still to come;
    In the heart of this old man,
    There is no such concern.
I've neither prayed to the immortals nor fawned before Buddha,
    Nor have I aped the bustling Confucius;
    Too lazy to compete with the worthies,
    I'll allow them to have their laughs at me.
      Thus-so is just thus-so.
      When the play[1] is ended,   20
I'll take off my actor's gown and give it to the dummies.
(CST, P. 836)   (TR. IRVING Y. LO)

---

1 *Tsa-chü*, or "variety plays," were theatrical shows performed by professional actors. In the Sung capital of K'ai-feng, many playhouses were located in the so-called "tile district," offering a variety of entertainments which included puppet shows.

Li Ch'ing-chao (*1084?–c. 1151*)

Tune: "Pure Serene Music"

Year after year in the snow
we'd pick plum blossoms while we drank,
Pulling at all the petals to no good purpose,
drenching our clothes with pure white tears.

This year I'm at the end of the world,
strand by strand my hair turns gray.
Judging by the force of the evening wind
plum blossoms will be hard to come by.
(CST, P. 926)   (TR. EUGENE EOYANG)

Tune: "Spring at Wu-ling" (*Wu-ling ch'un*)

The wind subsides—a fragrance
        of petals freshly fallen;
it's late in the day—I'm too tired
        to comb my hair.
Things remain but he is gone
        and with him everything.
On the verge of words: tears flow.

I hear at Twin Creek spring it's still lovely;
how I long to float there on a small boat—
But I fear at Twin Creek my frail "grasshopper" boat
could not carry this load of grief.
(CST, P. 931)   (TR. EUGENE EOYANG)

Tune: "A Southern Song"

In the sky the Milky Way turns;
here on earth a curtain drops.
A chill collects on the pillow-mat, wet with tears.
I get up to untie my silk gown,
        wondering what hour of night it is.

The blue-tinted lotus pod is small
the gold-spotted lotus leaves are sparse.
Old-time weather, old-time clothes
only bring back memories
    but nothing like real old times.
(CST, P. 926)   (TR. EUGENE EOYANG)

Tune: "Tipsy in the Flower's Shade" (*Tsui hua-yin*)

Thin mists—thick clouds—sad all day long.
The gold animal spurts incense from its head.
Once more it's the Festival of Double Nine[1];
On the jade pillow—through mesh bed curtain—
the chill of midnight starts seeping through.

At the eastern hedge[2] I drink a cup after dusk;
furtive fragrances fill my sleeve.
Don't say one can't be overwhelmed:
when the west wind furls up the curtain,
I'm more fragile than the yellow chrysanthemum.   10
(CST, P. 929)   (TR. EUGENE EOYANG)

Tune: "Manifold Little Hills" (*Hsiao-ch'ung-shan*)

Spring has come to the gate—spring's grasses green;
some red blossoms on the plum tree burst open,
others have yet to bloom.
Azure clouds gather, grind out jade into dust.
Let's keep this morning's dream:
break open a jug of spring!

---

1 The Double Nine refers to the ninth day of the ninth month by the lunar
calendar (which corresponds to early October), which the Chinese call
Ch'ung Yang. On this day, the custom is to climb to high ground, take some
wine in which chrysanthemum petals have been dropped, and compose poetry.
The festival was especially important to Li Ch'ing-chao, because it was associ-
ated with T'ao Ch'ien, the poet whom she and her husband preferred to all
others and who was known for his poems on the chrysanthemum.
2 Referring to T'ao Ch'ien's famous lines "Picking chrysanthemums by the
eastern hedge/I catch sight of the distant southern hills."

Flower's shadows press at the gate;
translucent curtains thin out pale moonlight.
It's a lovely evening!
Over two years—three times—you've missed the spring.   10
Come back!
let's enjoy this one to the full!
(CST, P. 929)   (TR. EUGENE EOYANG)

Tune: "Magnolia Blossoms, Abbreviated"

From the pole of the flower vendor
I bought a sprig of spring about to bloom,
tear-speckled, lightly sprinkled,
still touched by a rose mist and dawn's early dew.

Should my beloved chance to ask,
if my face weren't fair as a flower's,
I'd put one aslant in my hair,
then ask him to look and compare.
(CST, P. 932)   (TR. EUGENE EOYANG)

Tune: "The Charm of Nien-nu"

Lonely courtyard,
once more slanting wind, misty rain,
the double-hinged door must be shut.
Graceful willow, delicate blossoms,
    Cold Food Day approaches,
and with it every kind of unsettling weather.
    I work out a few ingenious rhymes,
    clear my head of weak wine,
    exceptional, the taste of idleness.
Migrating wild geese wing out of sight
but they cannot convey my teeming thoughts.   10

In my pavilion, cold for days with spring chill,
    the curtains are drawn on all sides.
I am too weary to lean over the balustrade.
The incense sputters, the quilt feels cold,
    I am just awake from a dream.

No dallying in bed for one who grieves,
  when clear dew descends with the dawn,
  and the *wu-t'ung* tree is about to bud.
There are so many diversions in spring.
The sun is rising: the fog withdraws;
see: it will be a fine day after all.   20
(CST, P. 931)   (TR. EUGENE EOYANG)

Tune: "As in a Dream: A Song," Two Lyrics

[1]

How many evenings in the arbor by the river,
when flushed with wine we'd lose our way back.
The mood passed away, returning late by boat
we'd stray off into a spot thick with lotus,
       and thrashing through
                  and thrashing through
startle a shoreful of herons by the lake.

[2]

Last night, a bit of rain, gusty wind,
a deep sleep did not dispel the last of the wine.
I ask the maid rolling up the blinds—
but she replies: "The crab apple is just as it was."
       Doesn't she know?
                  doesn't she know?
The leaves should be lush and the petals frail.
(CST, P. 927)   (TR. EUGENE EOYANG)

Tune: "Sand of Silk-washing Stream," Two Lyrics

[1]

Mild and peaceful spring glow, Cold Food Day.
From a jade censer, incense curls out in wisps of smoke.
My dream returns me to the hills of my pillow, hiding my hairpins.

The sea swallows have not yet come,
　　idly we duel with blades of grass.
By the river the plum trees have bloomed,
　　catkins sprout from the willow,
and at dusk scattered showers
　　sprinkle the garden swing.

[2]

In the little courtyard, by the side window,
　　spring's colors deepen,
with the double blinds unfurled
　　the gloom thickens.
Upstairs, wordless,
　　the strumming of a jasper lute.

Far-off hills, jutting peaks,
　　hasten the thinning of dusk,
Gentle wind blowing rain
　　plays with light shade.
Pear blossoms are about to fall
　　but there's no helping that.
(CST, P. 928)   (TR. EUGENE EOYANG)

Tune: "Song of Picking Mulberry"[1]

In the evening gusts of wind and rain
　　washed away embers of daylight.
　　I stop playing on the pipe
and touch up my face in front of my mirror.

Through the thin red silk my cool flesh glistens
　　lustrous as snow fresh with fragrance.
　　With a smile I say to my beloved:
"Tonight, inside the mesh curtains, the pillow and mat are cool."
(LCCC, P. 43)   (TR. EUGENE EOYANG)

---

1 This lyric has also been attributed to anonymous authorship and appears
under the tune-title *Ch'ou nu-erh.*

Tune: "Telling of Innermost Feelings"

Night found me so flushed with wine;
    I was slow to undo my hair.
The plum petals still stuck onto a dying branch.
Waking up, the scent of wine stirred me from spring sleep;
    my dream once broken, there was no going back.

    Now it's quiet,
    the moon hovers above,
    the kingfisher blinds are drawn.
Still: I feel the fallen petals;
still: I touch their lingering scent;
still: I hold onto a moment of time.   10
(CST, P. 930)   (TR. EUGENE EOYANG)

Ch'en Yü-yi (1090–1138)

Journeying to Hsiang-yi[1]

Speeding flowers along the shores mirror my boat red;
A bank of elms for a hundred *li*, half a day's breeze
Lying, I watch the clouds motionless everywhere in the sky,
Not knowing that the clouds and I are both traveling east.
(CCSC, 4/1b)   (TR. IRVING Y. LO)

Sitting on a Rock by Mountain Stream

Green mountains on three sides, a bamboo fence all around—
But no road in the world is marked safe or unsafe.
Holding a thornwood staff, I sit on a craggy rock
While the mountain stream ceaselessly makes its mournful sound.
(CCSC, 17/5b)   (TR. IRVING Y. LO)

---

[1] In Honan province, near the Northern Sung capital Pien-ching (modern K'ai-feng).

Tune: "Immortal at the River"
Ascending a Little Tower at Night and Recalling Old
Friends in Lo-yang

I recall a drinking party on the bridge, the Meridian Bridge,[1]
Where most of the guests were outstanding men.
  In the long canal, the moon flowed away in silence.
  Amid scattered shadows of apricot blooms,
    We played our flutes till dawn.

More than twenty years have become a dream;
  Though I am still alive, I should be alarmed.
Leisurely I ascend the little tower to watch the newly cleared sky.
  Innumerable events ancient and modern—
  The fisherman's song rises at midnight!   10
(CST, P. 1070)   (TR. JAMES J. Y. LIU)

Yang Wan-li (*1124–1206*)

Replying to a Poem by Li T'ien-lin

Writing poetry needs a mind that's nimble and free;
Thus even casual lines may appear sublime.
No cassock-and-bowl can be handed down for a thousand ages,[1]
Whether a hill or a feather it demands equal care.[2]
Sometimes as natural as a pond with spring grass[3];
Other words suggest dust-clouded eyes.[4]
How delicious is the taste of a good poem?
—Like that of a frosty crab, slightly wine-cured.
(NO. 1 FROM A SERIES OF 2; YCCSC, 4/1b–2a)   (TR. SHERWIN S. S. FU)

---

1 Wu-ch'iao, a bridge to the south of Lo-yang.
1 According to the Buddhist tradition, the robe and the bowl were handed
  down generation after generation as insignia of the patriarch's authority.
2 I.e., an accomplished poet can handle everything with equal ease and felicity.
  To him a hill would seem just as light as a feather.
3 Alluding to Hsieh Ling-yün's celebrated line: "Spring grass grows by the
  pool," a verse much admired by critics for its freshness and spontaneity.
4 The image of dust-clouded eyes is derived from the *Chuang-tzu*, where the
  sages are described as having dust-clouded eyes when they gaze at and
  worry about the world.

Early Summer Waking from a Nap

Plums leave their tartness, weakening my teeth.
Banana fronds lend their green to my gauze window.
On a long day I rise listless from my nap;
Idly I watch children catch willow catkins.
(NO. 1 FROM A SERIES OF 2; YCCSC, 29/6b)   (TR. SHERWIN S. S. FU)

Fallen Blossoms

Petals red and purple turn to mud, and mud to dust.
The mad wind doesn't care for those who love flowers.
Though the blossoms have fallen from trees without saying goodby,
They've entrusted the orioles with a message for spring.
(YCCSC, 42/22b)   (TR. SHERWIN S. S. FU)

Stanza Written in Jest

Field daisies, wild lichens—each a mint coin;
Their bright yellow or patina green[1] rival in beauty.
Wages paid by Heaven to poor poets—
They buy only grief, and not land.
(NO. 1 FROM A SERIES OF 2, YCCSC, 14/11a–11b)
                                              (TR. SHERWIN S. S. FU)

Staying Overnight at the Temple of the Holy Vulture

I thought it rained last night yet it's sunny this morning;
It was only a mountain spring that roared all night long.
Meeting the stream ahead, it becomes mute and still;
But it made so much noise in the mountains!
(NO. 2 FROM A SERIES OF 2; YCCSC, 13/14a–14b)
                                              (TR. SHERWIN S. S. FU)

---

[1] The daisies' bright yellow refers to the color of gold coins; the lichens' dark green, to the color of copper coated with patina.

Taking the Ferry at Ta-kao at Dawn[1]

Fog veils the river and the mountains,
but sounds of dogs and chickens
                    show that a village lies ahead.
The wooden planks of the ferry deck are covered with frost—
my boot makes the first footprint.
(NO. 1 FROM A SERIES OF 2; YCCSC, 15/1a)   (TR. JONATHAN CHAVES)

Passing By Waterwheel Bay

Reading in my palanquin, I fall asleep and dream—
dream of a fishing boat, lapped by waves.
When I awake, the wind is riffling the pages of my book,
and I can't even find the right chapter.
(NO. 2 FROM A SERIES OF 2; YCCSC, 17/15b)   (TR. JONATHAN CHAVES)

Crossing Ts'en River

Skinny rocks—verdigris green;
putrid water—bile yellow.
Here, there are no hoofprints;
the twisting trail has run out.

Now the path starts again,
rougher than anything ever dreamed of.
Even with cold scraping our faces,
sweat pours down like sap.
(YCCSC, 17/6a)   (TR. JONATHAN CHAVES)

Master Liu Painted a Portrait of Me in My Old Age and Asked Me to Write a Poem About the Picture

Few hairs, made fewer by the comb;
short moustache, made shorter by the tweezers—

---

1 The complete title reads: "Taking the Ferry at Ta-kao in the Dawn of the
Fifth of the First Month in the Year Keng-tzu [February 2, 1180]."

scratching my hair, and twisting my moustache,
when will I ever stop looking for poems?
(YCCSC, 41/16a)   (TR. JONATHAN CHAVES)

Sitting at Night on the Moon-viewing Terrace

This autumn the days have been hot,
but each evening cool weather returns.
The last few nights I have sat outside
until the water clock struck the third watch.

Brisk wind, stars glittering and fading;
floating clouds, welcomed and seen off by the moon.
When I pursue happiness I can never find it;
now happiness has come of itself.
(NO. 1 FROM A SERIES OF 2; YCCSC, 32/1a)   (TR. JONATHAN CHAVES)

A Trip to Stone Man Peak[1]

Two friends took a trip together to Stone Man Peak.
They walked far through green bamboo and yellow brush.
The narrow path made walking difficult;
halfway up the mountain, the path ran out.
When the friends started, they could hear dogs barking from the
    villages,
but as they walked and as they talked, they got farther and farther
    away.
Soon, there were no footholds above and no ledges below,
no way to climb on, no way to retreat.
Green bamboo and yellow brush, deeper and deeper—
Suddenly, the notes of a flute sounded from the dark woods.   10
Below them in the grass was the skeleton of a cow
and a pool of blood moistening the ground.
The two men looked at each other, their faces drained of color
and ran around the mountain to a Buddhist temple.
When the monks heard their story, they cried out in fear,

---

1 The original title is: "Account of a Trip Made by Messrs. Yang and Lo to
Stone Man Peak of the Southern Ridge." A preface to the poem reads:
"My younger brother [Yang] T'ing-pi and Lo Hui-ch'ing visited Stone
Man Peak and were almost captured by tigers. They once talked to me about
this experience, so I wrote the poem to record the event."

kicking over meditation benches and falling against the walls.
"How could you have heard a flute on this desolate mountain?
It was the breath of a crouching tiger!"
The friends came home and told me their story—
they said it was a fantastic trip.   20
Yes, it must have been fantastic—
their lives were worth a handful of sand.
(YCCSC, 14/17b–18b)   (TR. JONATHAN CHAVES)

Songs of Depression, Two Selections

[1]

I don't feel like reading another book,
and I'm tired of poetry—that's not what I want to do.
But my mind is restless, unsettled—
I'll try counting raindrop stains
                    on the oilcloth window.

[2]

I finish chanting my new poems,
                    and fall asleep—
I am a butterfly, journeying to the eight corners
                    of the universe.
Outside the boat, waves crash like thunder,
but it is silent in the world of sleep.
(NOS. 5, 7 FROM A SERIES OF 12; YCCSC, 35/10b)
                                    (TR. JONATHAN CHAVES)

The Cold Lantern

Old and young, everyone's asleep,
                    but I am awake;
the cold lantern, flickering at midnight,
                    is my only companion.
The two flowers I've been looking at
                    become dragonfly eyes;
the single flame, a jade vase hanging in the air.
(YCCSC, 40/17a–17b)   (TR. JONATHAN CHAVES)

The Cold Fly

I see a fly
warming himself on the window sill,
rubbing his legs, enjoying the morning sun.
He seems to know when the light will shift:
a sudden buzz
and he's at another window.
(YCCSC, 11/5a–5b)   (TR. JONATHAN CHAVES)

Drying Clothes

At noon, I leave my clothes out to dry;
            at sunset, I fold them up
and carry them home in a willow-wood box.
The women laugh and ask each other—
"Who's that old man with bare feet?"
(YCCSC, 40/8a)   (TR. JONATHAN CHAVES)

Bubbles on the Water

The most precious treasure is never fully known.
The black dragon's pearl appears for an instant,
            then sinks again.
The jewel on the forehead of the Golden Buddha
is only half-visible to common men.
(NO. 2 FROM A SERIES OF 2; YCCSC, 32/10b)   (TR. JONATHAN CHAVES)

Lu Yu (1125–1210)

Blue Rapids

A hundred men shouting at once, helping to rattle the oars;
in the boat, face to face, we can't even hear ourselves talk.
All at once the men have scattered—silence, no more scuffle;
the only sound, two winches reeling out hundred-yard towlines:
whoo-whoo, whaa-whaa—how fast the winches unwind,
boatmen already standing there on the sandy shore!

Fog lifts from reedy villages, red in the setting sun;
rain ended, from fishermen's huts the damp smoke of cooking fires.
I turn my head, look toward home, now a thousand mountains away;
a trip up the gorges—we've just passed rapids number one.   10
When I was young I used to dream of the joys of official travel;
older now, I know just how hard the going can be.
(CNSK, 2/7b)   (TR. BURTON WATSON)

Third Month, Night of the Seventeenth, Written While Drunk

Years ago feasting on raw whale by the eastern sea,
white waves like mountains flinging me their beauty and awe;
last year shooting tigers, south mountain autumn,
coming home at night, thick snow plastered on my sable coat;
this year—so worn and broken it really makes you laugh;
hair flecked gray, ashen face—I'm ashamed to look at myself.
Who'd think, given some wine, I could still raise a fuss,
yanking off my cap, facing men, a big shout for every one?
Traitorous barbarians still not crushed, my heart never at peace;
the lone sword by my pillow sings out its clanging cry.   10
In a fallen-down posthouse I wake from dreams, the lamp about to
          die;
tapping at the window, wind and rain—third watch by now.
(CNSK, 3/17a–17b)   (TR. BURTON WATSON)

In a Boat on a Summer Evening, I Heard the Cry of a Water Bird. It Was Very Sad and Seemed to Be Saying, "Madam Is Cruel!" Moved, I Wrote This Poem.[1]

A girl grows up hidden in innermost rooms,
no glimpse of what may lie beyond her wall and hedge.
Then she climbs the carriage, moves to her new lord's home;
father and mother become strangers to her then.

---

[1] In this poem, written in 1183, Lu Yu employs a narrative framework—and the sound of the water bird's cry, *ku-wu* (which the poet transcribed by the two words meaning "Madam is cruel")—to recall a personal experience. Lu Yu married his first wife when he was about twenty and divorced her shortly thereafter, apparently because his mother found fault with the girl, whom he was very fond of; he wrote of her often in his poems.

"I was stupid, to be sure, yet I knew
that Madam, my mother-in-law, must be obeyed.
  Out of bed with the first cock's crowing,
  I combed and bound my hair, put on blouse and skirt.
  I did my work, tidied the hall, sprinkling and sweeping,
  in the kitchen fixed their plates of food.　　　　　　　　10
  Green green the mallows and goosefoot I gathered—
too bad I couldn't make them taste like bear's paws.[2]
  When the least displeasure showed in Madam's face,
  the sleeves of my robe were soon damp with tearstains.
  My wish was that I might bear a son,
  to see Madam dangle a grandson in her arms.
  But those hopes in the end failed and came to nothing;
ill-fated, they made me the butt of slander.
  Driven from the house, I didn't dare grumble,
  only grieved that I'd betrayed Madam's kindness."　　　20
On the old road that runs along the edge of the swamp,
when fox fire glimmers through drizzling rain,
can you hear the voice crying "Madam is cruel!"
Surely it's the soul of the wife sent home.
(CNSK, 14/18a)　　　　　　　　　　　(TR. BURTON WATSON)

It Has Snowed Repeatedly and We Can Count On a Good Crop of Wheat and Barley; in Joy I Made This Song

Bitter cold, but don't complain when Heaven sends down snow—
snow comes to bring us next year's grain!
Third month: emerald waves dancing in the east wind;
fourth month: clouds of yellow hiding paths in the southern fields.
How easy to see it—rows of houses raising shouts of joy,
already certain that officials will ease their load of taxes.
Sickle at waist, every young man in the village turns out;
gleaning kernels, each day little boys by the hundred and thousand.
Dust of white jade spills from the mill wheel, whirling up to the rafters;
noodles, silver threads into the pot, to be melted in boiling water.　10
Winter wine beginning to work, cakes of steamed malt bursting;

---

2 Bear's paws are the epitome of delicious food.

in oil pressed from fresh sesame, Cold Food dumplings smell sweet.[1]
The wife steps down from her loom, neglecting her morning weaving;
little sister helps in the kitchen, forgetful of evening makeup.
Old men, stuffed with food, laugh and thump their bellies,
under the trees, beating time on the ground, singing of the season of
        peace.
(CNSK, 19/18a)   (TR. BURTON WATSON)

The Rain Cleared and the Breeze and Sunshine
Are Superb as I Stroll Outside the Gate

Old man Chang, sick three years, finally up and died;
Grandpa Wu in one evening went where he couldn't hear us calling.
I alone, with this body strong as iron,
leaning by the gate, always looking at the green of evening hills.
(CNSK, 45/9a)   (TR. BURTON WATSON)

Autumn Thoughts

Sumac showing faint traces of red,
    chrysanthemums bit by bit unfolding;
a tall sky where winds keep company
    with the sadness of wild geese calling—
Should not a poet's mind be
    as keen as the blades of Ping[1]
to slice off a bit of autumn scene
    to bring it unto my page?
(NO. 1 FROM A SERIES OF 3; CNSK, 54/10b)   (TR. BURTON WATSON)

In a Dream I Traveled Among
Ten Thousand Acres of Lotuses

Shoreless breeze from heaven over an endless road—
Serving the moon, my master, I'll always be the custodian of wind
    and dew.

---

[1] The dumplings were prepared ahead of time for the Cold-Food Festival, when
all cooking fires were put out.
[1] Ping was a region famous for its swords.

I will take only a thousand goblets as my lunar[1] salary,
Because I dislike the smell of copper mixed with the flowers' scent.
(CNSK, 85/6b)   (TR. IRVING Y. LO)

Impressions

Crying unseen, birds awaken me from my sleep.
Thick layers of dewy leaves filter the morning light.
Looking into the pond, I wish only to dispel the lingering torpor,
But what can I do if those geese look as yellow as wine?
(NO. 8 FROM A SERIES OF 8; CNSK, 83/3a)   (TR. IRVING Y. LO)

Written at Random

Each day I grow poorer by the day,
        yet I can't arouse myself from poverty;
Each year I grow older by the year,
        yet old age comes as if prearranged.
The Yellow River will one day become pure,
But my white hair will never turn black again.
(NO. 4 FROM A SERIES OF 10; CNSK, 71/1b)   (TR. IRVING Y. LO)

Shown to My Son Yü

When I first learned how to write poetry,
I only tried to turn out elegant phrases.
In midyear I began to have some understanding;
Gradually I felt as if I had peeped into something great.
At times the marvelous and the spectacular also appeared,
Like mountain torrents dashing at rocks.
But before the hundred-foot wall of Li Po and Tu Fu,
I often regret, I stand dumbfounded.
Yüan and Po[1] just stay outside the door;
For Wen and Li[2] I really have no comment.   10

---

1 Punning on the word *yüeh,* which can mean both "moon" and "month."
1 Referring to Yüan Chen and Po Chü-yi, who are described by Lu Yu as "merely leaning against the door" of others; i.e., that their poetry relies on imitation or borrowing from others.
2 Referring to Wen T'ing-yün and Li Shang-yin, for whom Lu Yu reserves comment, implying that he does not think highly of their works.

Even though their pen may be mighty enough to lift a tripod,
The great essence has not yet been attained.
Poetry is one of six ancient arts[3];
It's more than a game of playing with words.
If you really want to master this art:
Excellence lies in something beyond poetry.
(CNSK, 78/11b)   (TR. IRVING Y. LO)

In a Dream[1]

The shadows of the *t'ung* tree, glistening and clear,
      having just passed,
Bells under the eaves tinkle in the wind,
      breaking off my daytime sleep.
In a dream I found myself in a painted hall with no one around,
And only a pair of swallows softly treading zither strings.
(CNSK, 12/10b)   (TR. IRVING Y. LO)

Inscribed on My Grass-script
Calligraphy Written While Drunk

In my breast are stored weapons of every description[1];
I want to try them out but there's no way, despite my lofty thoughts.

I seize upon wine as banners and drums,
            and make of my pen a long lance;
Heaven-born strength comes to men
            like the Silver River[2] rushing down.

---

[3] The Six Ancient Arts here refer to the *Book of Poetry*, the *Book of Documents*, the *Book of Changes*, the *Book of Rites*, the *Book of Music*, and the *Spring and Autumn Annal*; i.e., the Six Classics.

[1] The original title reads: "Taking a nap on a summer day I dreamed of visiting a courtyard all quiet without people, shadows of curtain all over the hall, and only swallows on the strings of a *cheng* [a thirteen-string zither] making a sound. Awakened, I heard iron bells tinkling in the wind and I suddenly realized that this might have been what I had dreamed of. Hence, this quatrain."

[1] *Wu-ping*, literally "five [kinds of] weapons" of ancient China, referring to lances, halberds, and others; a metonymy for weapons of war.

[2] I.e., the Milky Way.

On the inkstone hollow from Tuan Brook,[3] I grind my ink thick;
Under the flitting candlelight, my pen crisscrosses as if flying.
In a moment I roll up the scroll and take again my wine cup,
As though all across ten thousand *li* had been cleared of dust and
    smoke!

A man of valor leaves behind deeds of renown,
Rebellious foes will be conquered when their luck runs out.   10
When shall we steal a night's march out of Wu-yüan Pass[4]—
Hearing no voice of men, but only the sound of whips?
(CNSK, 7/6a)   (TR. IRVING Y. LO)

Sounds of Autumn

Everyone speaks of the sad autumn with a heavy heart,
But I delight in listening to its sounds from my pillow:
Fast-flying hawks loosened from leather thongs, strong in beak and
    claws;
Stalwart fellows stroking their sword, high in spirit.
Though feeble and sick, I, too, would like to be roused quickly,
And, spitting on my hand,[1] feel the urge to seize Tartar foes.
Bowstring taut, the wild geese fall, and my poem is done;
The force of my brush isn't any weaker than my bow is strong.
Let the grasses of Wu-yüan wither and the clovers wilt,
And the soughing wind of Koko Nor send briers swirling into the
    sky.   10
Once I've dispatched the report of victory, I shall remount my horse,
Then I'd follow the imperial carriage all the way to Liao-tung.[2]
(CNSK, 5/7a)   (TR. IRVING Y. LO)

---

[3] The inkstones from Tuan Brook, located at the foot of the western slope
of Lan-k'o Mountain in modern Kwangtung, were highly valued in T'ang
and Sung times for their coloration and quality.
[4] Also called the Elm-and-Willow Pass (Yü-liu Sai), located in modern
Sui-yüan province.
[1] Alluding to the words of Kung-sun Tsan (d. 199 B.C.) in the *Hou-Han Shu*,
"When the army was first raised in the empire, I called it a truly happy
event that could make one want to spit on the hand (*t'u-shou k'o-k'uai*)."
[2] In modern Liao-ning province, Manchuria.

An Occasional Poem

The ancients lie buried under barren hills,
Their bygone traces can be found in tattered pages.
Who knows the right and wrong concerning them?
Lifting my wine cup, I wish to ask the great void.
(NO. 6 FROM A SERIES OF 12; CNSK, 79/8b–9a)   (TR. CHIANG YEE)

Tune: "Phoenix Hairpin" (*Ch'a-t'ou-feng*)[1]

Pink creamy hands,
Yellow-labeled wine,[2]
Spring colors filling the city, willows by the palace walls.
East wind hateful,
Joys of love scarce,
One heart full of sad thoughts,
How many years of separation!
Wrong, wrong, wrong!

Spring the same as before,
She grows thin in vain;   10
Red are the stains of tears[3] that have soaked the mermaid-silk[4] scarf.
Peach blossoms fall,
Ponds and pavilions quiet;
Though mountainous vows[5] remain,

---

1 This lyric is said to have been written in 1155 under the following circumstances: The poet was happily married to his cousin T'ang Wan, but was forced by his mother to divorce her. After they had both remarried, they met by chance at Shen's Garden on a spring day. She asked her second husband to send the poet some food and wine, whereupon Lu Yu wrote the poem.

2 A kind of official brew. Yellow was the imperial color.

3 Red stains: One of the commentators explains this as a reference to the rouge on the lady's face, but it is also possible that the poet implies that she was shedding blood mingled with tears, a not uncommon conceit in Chinese poetry.

4 This alludes to the legend that mermaids can spin silk, and further alludes to the story about a mermaid who, on parting from her human host, shed tears that turned into pearls.

5 A conventional way of describing lovers' vows, which are as lasting as mountains. Sometimes the phrase is coupled with "sea-oaths" (which bears a resemblance to Dylan Thomas's "sea-faiths").

Letters of brocade[6] can't be sent.
No more, no more, no more!
(CST, P. 1585)   (TR. JAMES J. Y. LIU)

Tune: "Song of Divination"
On the Plum Tree[1]

By a broken bridge outside the courier station,
In silent solitude it blossoms without a master.
Already grieving by itself at nightfall,
How much more so when wind and rain come!

Not wishing to compete bitterly for spring
It allows the other flowers to be jealous.
When its blossoms are scattered in the mud and ground to dust,
Only their fragrance will remain as before.
(CST, P. 1586)   (TR. JAMES J. Y. LIU)

Tune: "Bean Leaves Yellow" (*Tou-yeh huang*)

All through spring, nothing but wind and rain;
When wind and rain give way to fair weather, spring is gone.
Who pities the innumerable dots of red[1] on the mud?
            Endless regret—
Just like my whole life, old man that I am!
(CST, P. 1594)   (TR. JAMES J. Y. LIU)

Tune: "Immortal at the Magpie Bridge"
(*Ch'üeh-ch'iao hsien*)

A rod full of wind and moon,
A cloak full of mist and rain,
I make my home to the west of the Fishing Terrace.[1]

---

6 This is possibly an allusion to the story about Su Hui, who sent her absent
  husband a palindromic poem woven in a piece of brocade to express her
  longing for him.
1 The poem is a symbolic self-portrait.
1 Fallen flowers.
1 On Mount Fu-ch'un in Chekiang, where Yen Kuang supposedly lived. A
  famous recluse, Yen was a friend of Emperor Kuang-wu's but refused to

Scared to death to get near the city gate when selling fish,
How would I ever go where the red dust is deep?

> When the tide rises, I get ready my oars;
> When the tide subsides, I tie up my cables;
> And when the tide recedes, I go home singing loudly.
> Others wrongly compare me to Yen Kuang—
> I am really just a nameless old fisherman!   10

(CST, P. 1595)   (TR. JAMES J. Y. LIU)

Tune: "Immortal at the Magpie Bridge"
On Hearing the Cuckoo at Night[1]

Under thatched eaves people are quiet,
By the straw window the lamp is dim,
While wind and rain spread over the river in late spring.
The orioles in the woods and the swallows in their nests are all silent,
Only the cuckoo cries often in the moonlit night;

> Urging limpid tears to fall,
> Startling me from lonely dreams,
> And then flying away to a chosen branch deep among many.
> Even among native hills I could not bear to hear it,
> Let alone after drifting around for half of my life!   10

(CST, P. 1595)   (TR. JAMES J. Y. LIU)

Tune: "Telling of Innermost Feelings"

Years ago, I traveled ten thousand miles in search of honor[1];
Riding alone, I guarded the Liang-chou frontier.[2]
Where are my broken dreams of mountain passes and rivers?
Dust has darkened my old sable coat.[3]

---

serve as an official. Also cf. note 1 to Li Po's "Thoughts While Studying at Hanlin Academy . . ."

[1] The cuckoo has strong associations with homesickness in Chinese poetry, and its cry is supposed to sound like the words for "Better go home."

[1] The original, *mi feng-hou*, literally means "in search of enfeoffment as a marquis."

[2] In modern Shensi province, where the poet served in a military capacity in his middle age.

[3] An allusion to Su Ch'in (third century B.C.), who wore out his sable coat while trying in vain to persuade the king of Ch'in to adopt his policies.

The Tartars have not been defeated,
My hair has turned gray first,
My tears flow in vain.
Who would have thought that in this life
My heart should be with the T'ien Mountains[4]
And my body grow old by the seashore![5]   10
(CST, P. 1596)   (TR. JAMES J. Y. LIU)

Fan Ch'eng-ta (1126–1193)

Four Songs in Imitation of Wang Chien[1]

[1]

Rejoicing the Spirits

A pig's leg fills the plate, wine overflowing the cups;
A clear wind soughing, the spirits are about to descend.
So the spirits' departure will be as auspicious as their coming,
The boys prostrate in greeting and the girls dance.

An old man, stirring the incense, says it with a smile:
"Farming families are better off this year than last.
Last year we pawned our clothes to pay land rent;
This year we have clothes to wear for the village sacrifice."

[2]

Reeling Silk

Autumn wheat turns green and lush as spring wheat yellows;
Above the plain the sun rises and the day is cool.
Womenfolk, calling to each other, are busy at work—
Behind the house the scent of boiling cocoons reaches the door in
    front.

---

4 See note 1 to Li Po's "Moon over Mountain Pass."
5 A phrase associated with the life of a recluse.
1 Wang Chien (768–833), a T'ang poet, some of whose poems are included in
    this volume.

The reeling wheel turns noisily like wind and rain,
As thick cocoons yield long, unbroken threads.
This year, there's no time to weave gauze for dress;
Tomorrow, we'll go to the west gate to sell our silk.

[3]

A Farming Family Invites the Guest to Stay Overnight

Traveler, don't ridicule this farming house as too small,
The doorway may be low, but it's easy to sprinkle and sweep clean.
My older boy will tie your donkey to the mulberry tree,
And the little one will brush a mat that's softer than felt rug.

In the wooden mortar is newly hulled grain, white as snowflakes;
Quickly, we can boil this fragrant rice to entertain our guest.
"When a good man enters the door, a hundred affairs prosper."
This year, we'll have no worry over late wheat and cocoons.

[4]

Pressing for Tax Payment

The farmer has got a receipt,[2] but the yamen still presses for tax
    payment—
In staggering steps a sheriff comes to knock at the door.
Tax receipt in hand, he mingles joy with resentment:
"I'm here just to ask for a drink before going home."

"The piggy bank by my bedside is the size of a fist;
Break it and you'll find there three hundred coins.
This money isn't enough for you to get drunk,
But it will reimburse you for wearing out your straw sandals."
(FSHC, PP. 30–31)   (TR. WU-CHI LIU)

---

[2] *Chao,* or *hu-chao,* as used in Sung times, refers to the official receipt given by the government to a farmer after he has paid his tax. Here the sheriff comes to collect the tax, not knowing that it has already been paid. While glad about the payment, he is resentful that he has made the trip in vain and so he demands a *pourboire.*

Written While Lying on My Pillow in the Morning on the Twelfth Day of the Eleventh Month

Bamboos rustle, the wind in battle array;
Windows brighten up in the blossoming snow.
By the thatched gates whines a shivering cur;
On paper tiles pecks a hungry crow.
Last night's wine strengthens me against coldness;
A new poem will sing the season's splendor.
The sun high, I'm still wrapped in a quilt,
Ashamed that the neighbors take their morning meal in bed.[1]
(FSHC, P. 43)   (TR. WU-CHI LIU)

Consoling the Yü Farmers

The author's preface: "The *yü* fields are those lands on the Gorge cultivated by cutting and burning. Early in spring, the mountains are slashed so that all the woods are cleared. When it is time for planting, they wait for signs of rain. Then the night before, they set fire to the land so as to use the ashes for fertilizer. The next day, it rains, and taking advantage of the warm soil, they sow seeds. The grains sprout and crops are doubled. Without rain, it will be the opposite. The mountains are barren and have a stony soil, its fertility so low that the land has to be slashed and burned several times before it can be tilled. In spring, they plant legume and wheat, from which to make cakes and dumplings to last for the summer season. By autumn, the grains will ripen. Government taxes are light. The people on the Witch Mountain average a crop of three hundred pecks and use only thirty to forty pecks for two installments of tax payment. Thus, all year long they have enough to eat on these three things [legume, wheat, and grain]. Even though they have not seen rice all their lives, they do not suffer from hunger. So I record the fact that in the Wu [Soochow] district, which is supposed to have an abundance of good rice, the taxes, both public and private, are so heavy that farmers

---

[1] I.e., they have breakfast before daybreak and will be ready for work early in the morning. The Western idea of "breakfast in bed" as a way of relaxation or self-indulgence would never occur to the Chinese farmers of the Sung period.

hardly have any grain left for themselves and are even worse off than those on the Gorge. To console the latter, I write this poem."

Farmers on the Gorge lead a hard life—
They slash and burn the big mountaintops.
Barren, soggy, the soil is worthless;
Three times they slash and only once they till.
With some of the cave dwellers' wisdom,
They divine rain before burning the plains.
When rain comes, they must hurry to plant,
Lest the growth won't be thick and plentiful:
Ears of wheat, luscious yellow;
Legume sprouts, vibrantly jade-green.   10
Cakes and dumplings they have all summer long,
Then wait for an abundant crop in autumn.
Tax on the acreage is less than a tithe;
The leftovers are enough for meals.
They know nothing about paddy rice,
But their bulging stomachs are always full.

I am familiar with farming in the Wu region,
So let me tell it to the farmers on the Gorge:
Wu fields have fertile black soil,
Each grain of Wu rice is lustrous as a gem.   20
"Long waists" are thin like melon seeds,[1]
"Even heads" round as pearls;
"Red lotus" is more delicious than the *ku* grain,[2]

---

[1] *Author's note:* "The 'long waist,' also known as the 'arrow,' is long and narrow; the white 'even head' is round and clean like a pearl; the 'red lotus' has a slightly reddish color; the 'scented rice,' also named 'nine *li* fragrance,' fills the table with fragrance if some half pint of it is cooked with a peck of other rice; the 'King Shun's rice,' its grain scorched and beardless, is popularly said to have been burned, while under cultivation, by Shun's father before given to Shun; the 'Chan-ch'eng' [south Annam] species comes from the South Seas; the 'pa-ya' and the 'hsien-ho' [respectively common rice of the late and early varieties] are the least expensive. These different kinds of rice are all produced in the Wu district."

[2] *Ku* is a rare variety of rice which grows in swamps.

Sweet rice more scented than autumn orchids.
Some came from species left by King Shun;
Others originated from regions in South Vietnam.
Common rice of early and late varieties
Fill to overflowing cooking pots and earthenwares.

They won't mind the toils of spring cultivation,
But fear only government tax in the fall.   30
Greedy officials are big rats and sparrows,
Yamen runners plunder like caterpillars and locusts.
With extra large measures they rob people of their reserve,
And take the surplus in strings of cash.
For eight pecks farmers have to pay the tax of ten,
And they are still sore from the wounds of tax levy.
Over and again, pressed by private debts,
They flee, leaving their kitchen fires untended.

Those rice grains gleam like tiny marbles,
Yet, what they taste like, the farmers will never know.   40
The idle rich are those who feed on them.
As for the tillers, their mouths must constantly drool.
They cannot fill their stomach like farmers on the Gorge,
Who feed on legume and wheat till the end of their life.
(FSHC, PP. 217–18)   (TR. WU-CHI LIU)

"Seasonal Poems on Fields and Gardens," Four Selections

Late Spring

Crow after crow darts into the woods; the passers-by are few.
From the far mountain, dark mists have reached my thicket gate.
A boy on a boat that's as small as a leaf
Alone rounds up rows of ducks to gather them home.

Summer

Myriad cicadas seethe and buzz in the setting sun;
Frogs and toads, tirelessly croaking, dote on long night.
Should I not face the world by being deaf and dumb,
How else could a restful dream come to my wicker cot?

Autumn

Behind a vermilion gate, on the eve of the Skills Festival,[1]
    come the seething sounds of merriment;
A farmhouse stands quietly in the evening,
    its thatched door shut:
When a boy is good at herding
    and a girl knows how to weave,
There's no need to invoke blessings
    from stars that cross the river.

Winter

Under the eaves, their back burned by the sun as hot as fire—
As if flushed with wine, they doze off half-asleep.
Galloping past their door, what titleholder is this man,
With his hat askew and whip tucked in his sleeves, battling the north
    wind?
(FSHC, PP. 374–76)   (TR. IRVING Y. LO)

Huang Shu (*1131–1191*)

Tune: "Song of River Goddess" (*Chiang-shen tzu*)
Mooring My Boat at Fen-shui[1] at Night

Autumn wind soughs and sighs, the setting sun is red;
                Twilight mist thickens,
                Evening clouds multiply.
        Ten thousand folds of blue mountains—
        Beyond them a returning wild goose cries.
Alone I mount the tower three hundred feet high,
                Leaning on the jade rail,
                Gazing at the tiered skies.

---

1 *Ch'i-ch'iao,* the Skills Festival, occurs on the seventh day of the seventh
lunar month; according to popular belief, only once a year on that day do
the stars, Herd Boy and Weaving Maid, meet across the Heavenly River
(the Milky Way).
1 There are several places so named; the one mentioned here is most likely the
Fen-shui Pass near Ch'ung-an, the poet's native district.

In the human world, days and months quickly pass by;
        Over the green *wu-t'ung* trees,   10
        Once more the west wind blows.
    Wandering north and south,
    How many heroes have worn themselves out?
Let me throw my jade goblet beyond the heavens!
        So many things
        Must remain unsaid!
(CST, P. 1677)   (TR. JAMES J. Y. LIU)

Hsin Ch'i-chi (1140–1207)

Tune: "Partridge Sky"
Written at the Po-shan Monastery

I did not take the road to the capital:
Instead, I made mountain monasteries tired of greeting me.
Finding flavor among the flavorless, there I sought my joy.
Showing talent in being untalented, I passed my life.

    I would rather be myself:
    Why pretend being someone else?
Having traveled everywhere, I've returned to farming.
    One pine, one bamboo, is a real friend;
    Mountain birds, mountain flowers are my brothers.
(CST, P. 1924)   (TR. IRVING Y. LO)

Tune: "An Immortal's Auspicious Crane" (*Jui-ho hsien*)
On Plum Blossoms

The cold of autumn's frost penetrates the curtain,
As light clouds shelter the moon;
    New ice still thin,
    The brook mirrors her makeup.
Think of dallying with scent and powder?
The seductive art is hard to learn.
    Her flesh, pale and thin;
    Fold upon fold
    Of colored silk, her foil.

Leaning in the east wind— 10
One pleasant smile from her,
In a wink, ten thousand blossoms fall in shame.

Forlorn!
What place can be called her home?
Garden after a snow?
Pavilion by the water's edge?
For a promised meeting by Jasper Pond,
Yet who can be sent
As her courier?
Butterflies know only 20
How to chase after peach trees and willows;
The southern boughs laden with flowers, they do not sense.
Still her heart would grieve
On some desolate evening
At the scattered sounds of the post horn.
(CST, P. 1955) (TR. IRVING Y. LO)

Tune: "Green Jade Cup"
Lantern Festival[1]

One night's east wind made a thousand trees burst into flower;
And breathe down still more
Showers of fallen stars.[2]
Splendid horses, carved carriages, fragrance filled the road.
Music resounded from paired flutes,
Light swirled on water-clock towers.
All night long, the fabled fish-dragons[3] danced.

---

[1] Yüan-hsi, or *yüan-hsiao,* is celebrated on the fifteenth day of the first month of the lunar year. In Sung times the lantern festival lasted three days, and later extended to five.

[2] A day-by-day account of the festivities of the three-day period in the capital of the Northern Sung is given in Meng Yüan-lao's (fl. 1126) *Tung-ching Meng-hua-lu* (*Recollections of the Splendor of the Eastern Capital*), published in 1147. Under the entry of the sixteenth day of the first month, it is recorded that from the numerous stages erected along the street, lanterns were hung from bamboo poles and "far and near, high and low, they appeared like flying stars."

[3] Referring to lantern dances in general. The term *yu-lung,* or "fish-dragon," is borrowed from Shih-ku's annotations of *Ch'ien-Han Shu* (*History of Former Han*), where it is identified as a dance imported from Central Asia

Gold-threaded jacket, moth- or willow-shaped hair ornaments[4]
Melted into the throng, giggling, a trail of scents.
In the crowd I looked for her a thousand and one times;   10
    And all at once, as I turned my head,
    I was startled to find her
Among the lanterns where candles were growing dim.
(CST, P. 1884)   (TR. IRVING Y. LO)

Tune: "Groping for Fish" (*Mo yü-erh*)
Written in the sixth year of Ch'un Hsi [1179], upon being
relieved of my duty as Assistant Fiscal Intendant of
Hupeh and sent to Hunan; at a farewell party given
by my colleague Wang Cheng-chih[1] at Hsiao-shan
(Small Hill) Pavilion[2]

    How much more
    Of wind and rain?
Too, too hastily, spring will leave again.
Cherishing spring, I've long dreaded flowers budding too soon,
    Still more, those fallen petals numberless!
    Spring, please stay!
    I've heard it said
Fragrant grasses at world's end obscure the way home.
    No word has been uttered against spring,
Except, I imagine, there must be those untiring   10
    Spiders at their web
    By painted eaves
All day long, chafing at blown catkins.

---

in which Han emperors took great delight. *Yu-lung* was said to be an exotic
animal from She-li, which first played in the courtyard, then jumped into
water to become a paired-eye fish, and finally emerged as a yellow dragon
eighty feet long. This custom continued to be observed on the fifteenth day
of the first month in the Later Han dynasty.

4 Hair ornaments in the shapes of a moth, bee, or willow were common
objects for sale at the booths during the Festival, as mentioned in
Meng, op. cit., and in *Tai-Sung Hsüan-ho Yi-shih* (*Recollections of Events
of the Hsüan-ho Period of Great Sung*), an anonymous work of the
Sung-Yüan period, under the entry for the sixth year of Hsüan-ho (1124),
the fourteenth day of the first month.

1 Wang Cheng-chi (d. 1192), whose courtesy-name was Cheng-chih, was an official
known for his high integrity, later made Lord of the Imperial Treasury (*t'ai-fu-
ch'ing*).

2 Located near the official residence in O-chou, Hupeh. *Yu-ti-chi-sheng* (*Record
of Famous Places in the Empire*), *chüan* 66, p. 5b.

Alas, the affair of Long-gate![3]
Likely, the hoped-for reunion again miscarried
When Delicate Beauty[4] has earned another's spite!
True, a thousand taels of gold could buy a reconciliation[5];
Yet, so full and deep, to whom could this longing be told?
        Please do not dance!
        Have you not seen   20
Jade Bracelet and Flying Swallow[6] all returned to dust?
    Bitterest sorrow is aimless grief.
    Do not lean against an overhanging rail,
    For where the sun has gone down,
Beyond the mist and willow, is where my heart breaks!
(CST, P. 1867)   (TR. IRVING Y. LO)

Tune: "Slow Song of Chu Ying-t'ai" (*Chu Ying-t'ai chin*)
Late Spring

    Since we halved the hairpin[1]
    At Peach-Leaves Ferry,[2]
Mist and willow have darkened the south bank.
I dread to climb the upper story:
Nine days in ten are filled with wind and rain.
Swirling petals, one by one, rend my heart:
    They fall unnoticed.
    And who's there to plead
    With orioles to still their song?

---

3 Allusion is to Ssu-ma Hsiang-ju (179–117 B.C.) to whom was attributed the "*Ch'ang-men Fu*" ("On the Long-gate Palace"), which treats as its central theme the grief of Empress Ch'en after she fell from favor. Cf. note to Wang An-shih's "Song of the Radiant Lady."

4 The text reads *o-mei*, or "moth-brow," a standard epithet for either a woman's beauty or the beauty of a man's moral character as used in *Li Sao* (line 45).

5 For "reconciliation," the text reads "Hsiang-ju's *fu*."

6 Referring to Yang Kuei-fei, whose nickname was Yü Hüan (Jade Bracelet), and to Chao Fei-yen (Flying Swallow)—respectively imperial concubines of Emperor Ming-huang of T'ang and Emperor Ch'eng-ti of Han.

1 Referring to the pledge of love exchanged between Yang Kuei-fei and T'ang Ming Huang, with each of them keeping half of a pair of ornamented hairpins.

2 "Peach-Leaves" (*T'ao-yeh*), was said to be the name of the concubine of the poet Wang Hsien-chih (344–397), who said goodby to her with a song at a ferry also named T'ao-yeh.

Peering at my temples,　　　　　　　　　10
I try to divine the date of your return with a flower.[3]
Once fastened to the hairpin, I take it down to count the petals again.
Lamplight flickers on the silk curtain;
Words choke in my mouth as I wake from dream:
"It must be spring that has brought sorrow back!
Then where does spring go when it leaves?
Yet I do not understand why
It does not take sorrow along when it goes away."
(CST, P. 1882)　　　　　　　　　　　　　(TR. IRVING Y. LO)

Tune: "Full River Red" (*Man-chiang hung*)

Parting sorrow shattered
Beyond the gauze window
Where the wind sweeps through bamboo.
　　Her lover gone,
The sound of the flute breaks off.
Alone she leans against the railing.
Her eyes cannot stand late April's dusk;
Her head overwhelmed by the green of a thousand hills.
　　She tries to read
One page of a letter from him,　　　　　10
Tries to read from the beginning.

Words of longing
Fill the page in vain;
Thoughts of longing
When would they suffice?
Upon her silken lapel tears fall, drop after drop;
Cascades of pearls brim her two hands.
Fragrant grass mustn't obscure a traveler's way home,
But hanging willow obstructs the eyes of someone left alone.
　　Bitterest sorrow is　　　　　　　　20

---

3 I.e., petals of flowers secured on hairpins worn by women as ornaments. The act of counting the numbers of petals to see if they agree with a random-selected number refers to a superstitious game played by people trying to guess at an answer to a difficult personal question, almost similar to what some people do in the West with daisy petals.

To stand and wait out the dusk moon
    Near a winding balustrade.
(CST, P. 1888)   (TR. IRVING Y. LO)

Tune: "Song of the Southern Country"
Presented to a Courtesan

What a fine hostess!
Says not a word but tipsies to bed,
Causing that man to put on airs.
    Hurry, hurry!
Fasten your skirt, make it secure.

    Shed no tears of parting:
Oaths by hills and sea are hard to redeem.
Remember to take your new love today,
    My child,
Ten years later you will feel just like her.   10
(CST, P. 1908)   (TR. IRVING Y. LO)

Tune: "Spring in [Princess] Ch'in's Garden"
(*Ch'in-yüan ch'un*)
Trying to cure myself of the habit of drinking, I wrote
this poem to admonish the wine cup and
ask it not to come near me

Wine cup, you come here.
    The old man today
    Resolves to mend his ways.
For many long years I have sustained the thirst;
My throat is parched like a scorched pan.
    And now I love to sleep;
    My snore is loud like thunder.
    You speak of Liu Ling,
    The wisest man in history, who said
"Once I'm drunk, bury me where I happen to die."[1]   10

---

[1] Liu Ling (?221–300), one of the Seven Worthies of the Bamboo Grove,
was said to be inordinately fond of drinking. Liu used to ride on a deer
cart which he would load with wine, accompanied by a servant with a
shovel, who was instructed that Liu should be buried wherever he hap-
pened to die.

If this is all true,
I should say with a sigh that you to your friend
   Have shown little gratitude.

You still rely on song and dance as your matchmakers,
   To scheme and conspire
   To men's deadly harm—
You know, too, that all grudges, large and small,
   Grow from what is loved.
Things are neither good nor bad;
Only excess makes calamities of them.   20
   Let this be our compact:
"Do not linger, but be quick to withdraw.
I am still strong enough to beat you down."
   Wine cup bows twice, and says,
   "Wave me away and I leave,
   Call me back and I come."
(CST, P. 1915)   (TR. IRVING Y. LO)

Tune: "Song of Divination"
Using Quotations from *Chuang-tzu*

"One of them takes himself to be an ox;
   Another takes himself to be a horse."[1]
When people give them names, they accept and won't refuse;
They're those who've learned well from Chuang Chou.

"Set an empty boat adrift in rivers and seas,"[2]

---

[1] The quotation, from the *"Ying Ti Wang"* chapter of the *Chuang-tzu*, describes a philosopher surnamed T'ai who "would sleep tranquilly and awake in contented simplicity. He would consider himself now (merely) as a horse, and now (merely) as an ox. His knowledge was real and untroubled by doubts . . ." (Translation by James Legge, *The Texts of Taoism*, pp. 307–8.)

[2] From the *"Shan-mu"* chapter: "If a man is crossing a river in a boat, and another empty vessel comes into collision with it, even though he be a man of choleric temper, he will not be angry with it. If there be a person, however, in that boat, he will bawl out to him . . . Formerly he was not angry, but now he is; formerly (he thought) the boat was empty, but now there is a person in it. If a man can empty himself of himself, during his time in the world, who can harm him?" (Ibid., p. 471.)

"Let wind and rain blow down loose tiles."[3]
"A drunken fellow falls from his cart and is not hurt."
All things are ordained by Heaven, for sure!
(CST, P. 1946)   (TR. IRVING Y. LO)

Ch'en Liang (1143–1194)

Tune: "The Beautiful Lady Yü"
Spring Sorrow

The east wind whirling, light clouds in strands,
The season sends whistling rain.
To the pavilion next to the pond the swallows have recently returned;
With a beakful of fragrant mud,
Its moisture containing faded flower, they fly.

Crab-apple blossoms scattered on the path spread out a brocade,
Time passing has changed into the old age of spring.
At dusk on the courtyard willows, crows chatter,
And I recall with whom I plucked pear blossoms in this same month.
(CST, P. 2109)   (TR. HELLMUT WILHELM)

Tune: "Water Dragon's Chant"
Loathsome Spring

Where the noisy flowers are deepest, a storied building,
The painted curtain half rolled up, a soft east wind.
Spring returns, kingfisher green, to the paths between the fields,
 Sedge sprouting delicately,
 Weeping willows in faded gold,
 Late in the season the flowers urging on.
 Thin clouds, the rain has just stopped,
 Light chill, then light warmth.

---

3 From the *"Ta-sheng"* chapter: "Take the case of a drunken man falling
from his carriage; though he may suffer injury, he will not die. His bones
and joints are not the same as those of other men . . . his spirit is entire.
He knew nothing about getting into the carriage, and knew nothing about
his falling from it . . . A man in the pursuit of vengeance would not
break the (sword) Mo-ye . . . nor . . . wreck his resentment on the fallen
brick." (lbid., pp. 453–54.)

How I loathe this scented world!
The wanderer remains unrewarded,   10
      Everything is committed
      To the orioles and swallows.

In my loneliness I climb high and think afar—
Toward the southern tower the honk of a returning wild goose.
      The meadow game played with golden hairpins,[1]
      The horse reined with black silk threads,[2]
      Drifting winds and scattered clouds.
      Tied with a gauze ribbon, distributed perfume,[3]
      Wrapped in a green kerchief, accumulated tears.
        What heaps of sorrow!   20
      Thus, then, the soul is overwhelmed.
      This mist and a faded moon,
      And the cuckoo's voice trailing off.
(CST, PP. 2108–9)   (TR. HELLMUT WILHELM)

Chiang K'uei (*1155?–1235?*)

Written at Lakeside Residence

The wind over the lake is mild, the moon fair;
I lie down and watch the clouds' shadow on the glass.
A light boat suddenly passes by the window,
Disturbing one or two green reeds.
(NO. 2 FROM A SERIES OF 14; PSTJSC, II/7a)   (TR. CHIANG YEE)

Tune: "The Charm of Nien-nu"

[*Preface*] Formerly I sojourned at Wu-ling, where the office of the judicial intendant of the Hupeh Circuit was located. By the ancient city wall were wild waters and tall trees that reached toward the sky. With

---

[1] The meadow game was played by children on the fifth day of the fifth moon. "Golden hairpins" is an expression for concubines. The meaning might also be that the silly children's game is played with a much too precious instrument.
[2] According to the *yüeh-fu* song "Mulberry by the Path," black thread was meant to dress up a horse's tail, and gold should be used as a bridle.
[3] Tied as a farewell present would be.

two or three friends I daily rowed a boat thereabout and drank when
we approached the lotus flowers. The atmosphere was secluded and
peaceful, unlike the human world. When the autumn water was almost
dried up, the lotus leaves stood about eight or ten feet above the
ground. Thereupon we sat in a row under them. When we looked up,
we could not see the sun; and when a cool wind came slowly, the green
clouds moved by themselves. Occasionally, from where the leaves were
sparse, we could peep at the pleasure seekers in their painted boats,
which also provided us with some enjoyment. Since I came to Wu-
hsing, several times I have been able to wander among the lotus
flowers. I have also sailed over the West Lake by night once and found
the view wonderful beyond compare. I therefore wrote these lines to
describe the lotus.

Stirring the red: a single boat—
I remember when I came,
Mandarin ducks were my companions.
Over the thirty-six pools where no one has reached,
Water-pendants and wind-skirts are numberless.
The emerald leaves breathing chill,
The jade-like faces wearing off the wine—
Then a sprinkling rain over the rushes and reeds.
Gracefully swaying,
The cold fragrance flies up my lines of verse.   10

At sunset
The green canopies stand erect.
Not having seen your lover,
How can you bear to leave, treading the ripples?
I only fear your dancing dress will easily fall in the cold;
And grieve to enter the west-wind-blown southern shore.
Tall willows casting shades,
Old fish puffing at the waves
Invite me to stay and dwell among the flowers.
How many spreading leaves?   20

How frequent the return journey by the sand?
(CST, P. 2177)   (TR. JAMES J. Y. LIU)

Tune: "Pale-golden Willows" (*Tan-huang liu*)

[*Preface*] While taking up my temporary residence in the southern part of Ho-fei City [in modern Anhwei], west of the Red Railing Bridge, I notice the streets and alleys have a desolate air, different from the scene south of the Yangtze. Only the color of the willows that line the road is lovely. I therefore compose this tune to comfort a traveler.

In the empty city a morning horn
Blows through the weeping willows.
On horseback, in a thin cloak, I shiver in the chilly air.
I've seen all the pale yellow and tender green,
They are all my old acquaintances south of the river.
It is so quiet and lonely,
Tomorrow will be the Cold-Food Festival again.
I force myself to bring wine
To a young lady's home.
I fear the falling of pear blossoms will complete the autumn scene. 10
When swallows come to ask where spring is,
Only pool and pond are decked in green.
(CST, P. 2181)   (TR. CHIANG YEE)

Tune: "Dim Fragrance" (*An-hsiang*)
Plum Blossoms

In the winter of the year Hsin-hai [1191], I went to visit Shih-hu [Fan Ch'eng-ta] in the snow. I stayed with him for a whole month; then he gave me papers and asked me to compose new *tz'u* patterns. I made these two tunes, which were much admired by Shih-hu. He made a talented singing girl learn to sing them, and the music was harmonious and charming. They were entitled *"An-hsiang"* ["Dim Fragrance"] and *"Su-ying"* ["Sparse Shadows"].[1]

The moonlight of a former time,
How often has it shone on me?—
I play on a flute by the plum tree,

---

[1] In naming this tune, Chiang K'uei uses as the title the first two words from two famous lines of Lin Pu's poem on plum blossoms: "Sparse shadows lie aslant across waters clear and shallow,/Dim fragrance gently floats beneath the moon at dusk."

Awakening the fair one,
　　To pluck a sprig, defying the chill!
But Ho Sun[2] has grown old,
And has forgotten how to sing of the spring breeze.
　　　　I wonder why
From the sparse blossoms beyond the bamboo,
Chill fragrance still seeps in to my mat of jade!   10

　　　　This land among the rivers—
　　　　So quiet and still!
I sigh for a friend far away,
The night's snow beginning to pile up.
Tears come easily before a kingfisher goblet.
Red blossoms, wordless, tell of my longing.
I'll always remember the place where we held hands:
A thousand trees in bloom press down on the cool green of West Lake;
　　Then one by one, the petals were blown away,
　　When can we see them again?   20
(CST, P. 2181)   (TR. AN-YAN TANG)

Tune: "Sparse Shadows" (*Su-ying*)
Plum Blossoms

On a branch covered with jade-green moss—
　　A pair of tiny birds of kingfisher blue
　　Roost side by side.
Myself a stranger, I encounter her
　　By the fence at dusk,
　　Leaning without a word on a tall bamboo.[1]
Chao-chün: unused to distant Tartar sands,[2]
Secretly longs for the land south and north of the river.
I think of her, pendants clinging, returning under the moon,
　　Turned into this blossom all alone.   10

---

2 Ho Sun (also Ho Hsün; d. c. 527), a widely acclaimed poet of his time, has also written a poem on plum blossoms.
1 Alluding to Tu Fu's poem "Ballad of a Virtuous Lady" (*"Chia Jen"*), which describes a woman leaning on a tall bamboo at dusk.
2 Referring to Wang Chao-chün's being married to a Tartar chieftain before the Han emperor discovered how beautiful she was. Cf. Tu Fu's poem "Thoughts on Historical Sites: Wang Chao-chün."

I still can recall the ancient palace affair:
    When the princess lay asleep,[3]
    A blossom flew near her dark, fine eyebrows.[4]
    Be not like the spring wind,
    Callous of beauty and charm,
    Hastily sending her away to a chamber of gold.[5]
Still another petal is allowed to drift with the waves;
Mournful is the song from the Jade Dragon flute.
    Time passes,
    Again I seek the furtive scent—   20
Only it has entered this small latticed window!
(CST, PP. 2181–82)   (TR. AN-YAN TANG)

Yen Yü (fl. 1200)

My Boat Moored on a River

At the edge of the world, a traveler long used to grief;
By the riverbank, the familiar post station.
The wind lowers the wild geese by the riverbank,
Snow dims the cabin lamp at night.
Poor and old, I sigh at life's stupidities;
Madly singing, I dread sobering after wine.
When can this body find a resting place?
A drifting duckweed on the river.
(TLYC, 2/7b–8a)   (TR. IRVING Y. LO)

Yüan Hao-wen (1190–1257)

A Quatrain

Above the creek dallies a bright moon;
Wind and dew issue their crisp command.

---

[3] Alluding to the story of Princess Shou-yang of the Liu-Sung dynasty. She once took a nap under the palace eave, and plum blossoms dropped petals on her forehead, leaving a delicate impression which started a fashion among the court ladies.
[4] Literally *o-lü* ("moth-green"), referring to well-shaped eyebrows painted green.
[5] Referring to the story of Emperor Wu of Han and Ah-chiao. See Wang An-shih's "Song of the Radiant Lady."

A heart that's empty, not a trace of dust;
Across a stand of bamboo sweeps autumn's shadow.
(NO. 1 FROM A SERIES OF 3; YYSSC, 11/1a)   (TR. IRVING Y. LO)

Autumn Sentiments

Chill leaves soughing
    scatter sounds of rain;
Swishing noises across an empty room
    disguise a light frost.
Yellow flowers must keep their tryst
    with the west wind;
White hair comes early
    to one far from home.
Humming verses like seasonal insects,
    I find autumn more bitter;
Dreaming of a winter magpie to echo my song,
    I start up in the night.
When will the road over the mountain pass,
    above Stone Cliff,
Offer me one glance of home to brighten
    my eyes for an instant?
(YYSSC, 8/1a)   (TR. IRVING Y. LO)

On Poetry, Three Quatrains

[1]

A croaking frog in a well sees the sky from end to end.
If only its eyes could sweep across rivers and hills of our world!
Damn well I know "spring grass by the pool"[1]
Was not conceived among charred timbers and chip fires.[2]

---

[1] A reference to a famous line, "spring grass grows by the pool," by Hsieh
Ling-yün (cf. "Climbing the Tower by the Pond"), often praised by Chinese
critics for its spontaneity. In explaining its origin, the poet attributed it to
a vision he had of his cousin-poet, Hsieh Hui-lien; cf. *Hsieh K'ang-lo chi-chu*,
p. 121; J. D. Frodsham, *The Murmuring Stream*, I, p. 36.

[2] Chip fires (*feng-huo*), or dried animal dung, were used as fuel by poor people
in China.

[2]

A poet's heart is wrenched and wrenched again until his head turns
    white;
From a paper crumbling to dust, the poet begs for inspiration in vain.
If you don't believe precious pearls aren't hard to find,
Just watch the golden-winged *gerudas* cleave the vast sea.

[3]

Fade the kingfisher blue, trim the red, blend the colors:
With each finger-touch bring out freshness anew.
The embroidery done, let the mallards be held up for viewing,
But do not assume the art of the gold needle can be taught.
(YYSSC, 14/10a)   (TR. IRVING Y. LO)

Crossing the Yellow River: June 12 [1233]

White bones scattered
like tangled hemp,
how soon before mulberry and catalpa[1]
turn to dragon-sands?[2]
I only know north of the river
there is no life:
crumbled houses, scattered chimney smoke
from a few homes.
(NO. 3 FROM A SERIES OF 3; YYSSC, 12/6b–7a)   (TR. STEPHEN WEST)

"Song of the Maidens"

Hungry crows sit and guard
corpses amid the grass,
blue cloth still there,
and old scarves.
South wind of the sixth month
that blows a myriad miles—
if mindful of these white bones,
should've turned them to dust.
(NO. 9 FROM 2ND SERIES OF 10; YYSSC, 6/12a)   (TR. STEPHEN WEST)

---

1 Standing for one's ancestral home.
2 I.e., desert.

Random Verses on Mountain Life, Two Selections

[1]

Clustered trees filled with the sounds of autumn,
In the deserted village the evening scene is calm.
The rainbow disappears, still the clear rain falls;
Clouds scatter, suddenly green mountains come to view.

[2]

A winding creek and scattered maple groves,
deep in the mountains, a stream fork hidden by bamboos.
Into the thin mist sink departing birds,
the setting sun follows homing cattle.

(NOS. 3–4 FROM A SERIES OF 6; YYSSC, 11/3a)   (TR. STEPHEN WEST)

PART V

The Rise of the San-ch'ü, *or Song-poems*

(In the Mongol-ruled Society, 1234–1368)

Kuan Han-ch'ing (*c. 1220–c. 1300*)

[Nan-lü] Tune: "Four Pieces of Jade" (*Ssu-K'uai yü*)
Idle Leisure

I

go where my mind will
sit when my heart's still
drink when I'm thirsty
eat when I'm hungry
and sing when I'm drunk
when hard times come
I find a pile of grass and sleep
the days and months are long
the world is vast
and idleness is happiness　　　　　　　　　10

II

toss off the vintage wine
use up the raw
laugh beside the earthen pot
ha, ha, ha,
hum harmonies together with this rude old mountain bonze
he has a pair of chickens
I've brought along a goose
and idleness is happiness

III

I've reined mind's horses
locked up my monkey-heart
leapt up from red dust and evil waves and wind
who woke me from my noonday nap beneath the locust's shade?
I've left the field of honor
and wormed into a nest of joys
where idleness is happiness

IV

he's plowed the southern field
and slept among the eastern hills
I've seen the way the world goes, often
vainly measured bygones in my mind
he's the saint
and I'm the fool
who'd argue that?
(CYSC, PP. 156–57)   (TR. JEROME P. SEATON)

[Shuang-tiao] Tune: "Intoxication in the East Wind"
(*Ch'en-tsui tung-feng*)
Two Songs

[1]

heaven in the South, earth Northward
pushed close together.
in an instant the moon wanes
and the blossoms fly.
my hand grasps
              the cup of this parting.
my eyes are screened with its tears.
I say take care, but the sound dies.
there is no way to bear this rush of sorrow.
may you fare well across ten thousand miles.

[2]

grief: I've grieved as a solitary phoenix grieves.
sadness: I've watched the moon wane, and the flowers fall.
why? only for you, my small foe.
ripped up: I've been before, but who'd get used to that?
sick: I've been sick, but never known till now.
have I despised? never, as I hate this cold quilt, this empty bed,
feared? never so much, that night would never come.
(CYSC, P. 163)   (TR. JEROME P. SEATON)

[Shuang-tiao] Tune: "Green Jade Flute" (*Pi-yü hsiao*),
Four Songs

[1]

fear, as I see the spring go
watch the silk of willow fly from bough.
quiet locks this perfumed chamber.
beyond the curtain the oriole cries the dawn.
I suffer, no word comes from earth's end.
last night I dreamed you here
beneath the blue-green coverlet.
weight of the gown loosened on my loins grown thin
it keeps getting dark, it goes on hurting.

[2]

wind sifts through the curtain
the empty stair is moonlight cold
the candle's gone out on its silver stand
the table's heaped in dying rings of perfumed smoke.
drunk, the spirit's hard to hold
the sparkle of things, fierce to endure.
why haven't you come?
you're somewhere mouthing "poetry."
Ha! I'll take another lover.

[3]

lightly she turns back her long red sleeves.
white fingers grasp the ropes.
the swing's hung high
and she comes falling, merry as a mountain spirit.
kingfisher hairpin fallen from her forelock
hair loose as willow leaves to one side, hanging.
beside the flowered path
she smiles, and fiddles with her spring gauze fan.
it chimes against the golden bracelet on her wrist.

[4]

this autumn scene is worthy of the brush.
red leaves fill up the mountain stream.

the path through the pines is set just so.
chrysanthemums glow gold around the eastern hedge.
I raise this very proper goblet, drain the dregs.
the commoner who offers you the cup's
fit for high post. but what's the use.
Get back!
I'll study T'ao Ch'ien, learn to be drunk
as he was.
(CYSC, PP. 164–65)　　　　　　　　　　　　(TR. JEROME P. SEATON)

[Shuang-tiao] Tune: "Song of Great Virtue" (*Ta-te ko*)
Spring

the cuckoo cries
go home, go home
but only spring returns
never my loved one.
how many more days of this languor?
willow fluff comes floating
fluttering, emptied, down.
all spring no word.
only a pair of swallows fly
mud in their beaks　　　　　　　　　　　　　　　　　　　10
to build a nest.
(CYSC, PP. 165–66)　　　　　　　　　　　　(TR. JEROME P. SEATON)

[Shuang-tiao] Tune: "Song of Great Virtue"
Winter, Two Songs

[1]

snow powder, flowery
dancing pear blossoms.
the misty hamlet's lost from view again.
thick falls fine rain: a picture.
evening crow caws in the distant grove.
yellow rushes screen the clear stream's glare.
there, in tangled halyards, a fishing boat.

[2]

toot once, strum once
give us a song
                to Great Virtue.
enjoy yourself, relax
stop setting snares.
how long can a man live, anyway?
be simple, plain
                and follow
where that leads you.
go find yourself a place to flop
and flop there.
(CYSC, PP. 167–68)   (TR. JEROME P. SEATON)

[Nan-lü] Tune: "A Sprig of Flowers" (*Yi-chih hua*)
Not Bowing to Old Age

[1]

I pluck the clustering flowers from the wall
snap off the greening roadside willow
the red unopened bud
the slimmest, the most supple green wand
I'm a dandy, and a rake I am
trusting this hand that plucks
the flower and the bough
that I can bear the willow's withering, the flower's fall
half a life I've picked as I pleased
half a life I've lain with flowers,   10
entwined in tender boughs

[2]

commander of the dandies' army
headman of the horde of rakes
when I'm red-faced old
I'll be the same
wasting my time with the flowers

losing my cares in wine
drinking and eating, carousing
punning and joking and playing with words
I'm smooth, I'm ripe
with the rhymes and the rules   10
there's no place in my heart
for mourning.
my companion's a girl with a silver guitar
she tunes it in front of a silver stand
and leans with a smile toward the silver screen;
my companion's an immortal of heavenly jade
I grasp her jade hand and shoulder
as we mount the tower of jade;
my companion's the "Gold Hairpin Guest"
she sings, "The Gold Lock of Hair"   20
offers the golden goblet up
fills the floating golden cup
you say I'm old, that I grow cold . . .

Don't think it.
I'm center stage, the boss
trimmer than ever
still slim and bold
I'm commander in chief of the brocade troupes
that throng this flowery encampment
and I travel the land   30
and wander the districts
for sport.

[3]

now your modern-day wastrel is nothing but that
a pile of straw, or a hole in the sand
a newborn bunny set loose for the hunt
I'm the hoary blue pheasant
always slipping the noose
and dodging the net
I've known the tramp of cavalry horses
and survived the cold arrows of ambush
I'll never fall behind
Don't tell me, "with middle age, the game is up"   10
I won't go gently to my dotage.

[4]

I'm a bronze bean with a pure bell tone
steam me: I won't get tender
boil me: I'll never be cooked
pound me: I'll never be bean paste
roast me: I'll never pop
who told you dandies you could come in here
where the harlot weaves her brocade net
a thousand layers
which can be hacked, but not hacked out
which can be chopped, but not chopped down   10
which can be loosened, yet never quite undone
even discarded, but never for long?
my play's beneath a storied garden's moon
my drink is fabled Kai-feng wine
my current love's a Lo-yang flower
I only pick the willows of Chang Terrace
I can play go
and I can play football
I'm a hunter and a wag
I can dance and sing   20
play the flute
I spread a rare table
and chant a fine poem
I'm great at chess.
you can knock out my teeth
and break my jaw
you can cripple my legs
and rip off my arms
let heaven lay all these curses on me
I still won't stop   30

except old Yama calls on me himself
and brings his fiends to fetch me
when my soul returns to earth
and my animal self falls straight to Hell
then, and only then
I'll quit this flowered path
I ramble on
(CYSC, PP. 172–73)   (TR. JEROME P. SEATON)

Lu Chih (*1246?–1309?*)

[Shang-tiao] Tune: "*Wu-t'ung* Leaves" (*Wu-yeh-erh*)
Written in Jest at a Banquet

Leisurely talk in low voices,
Pliantly sung melodies:
Distant rhymes even carry heavy feeling.
At the banquet
I marvel at her.
How is it,
Her gaze little by little fixes upon me?
(CYSC, P. 109)   (TR. HELLMUT WILHELM)

[Shuang-tiao] Tune: "Intoxication in the East Wind"
Autumn Scenery

From a precipitous cliff, a withered pine hangs upside down;
The last wisp of cloud and a wild duck fly together.
Endless mountains all around.
Boundless expanse of waters before my eyes,
Spread by the west wind, everywhere the feel of autumn.
Calm night, a low-silhouetted moon sailing beneath the clouds,
Carries me back to a painting of the Hsiao and the Hsiang rivers.[1]
(CYSC, P. 110)   (TR. SHERWIN S. S. FU)

[Shuang-tiao] Tune: "Song of the Lunar Palace"
(*Ch'an-kung ch'ü*)

Brother Number Three comes strolling along
Both legs black with mud
As he has been catching shrimps.
Old daddy, the head of the village,
In the shadow of the willows,
Beats open a watermelon.
Second brother, the little dirty one, his mouth watering,

---

1 Cf. note 4 to Tu Mu's poem "Early Geese."

Sits on a stone-roller, strumming a guitar.
See how the buckwheat blooms
And how the green beans sprout.   10
Beyond good and evil,
Happy this village life!
(CYSC, P. 115)   (TR. HELLMUT WILHELM)

[Shuang-tiao] Tune: "Pleasure in Front of the Hall"
(*Tien-ch'ien huan*), Two Songs

[1]

Be a loafer—
Wash off the dust of fame and gain in the vast waves,
Turn my head away from distant Ch'ang-an.
Content with my lot and my poverty.
If I do not wear a turban and socks,
Who will blame me?
Nothing disturbs my heart;
I keep company with mists and clouds
And have wind and moon for neighbors.
(CYSC, P. 134)   (TR. SHERWIN S. S. FU)

[2]

Wine in the cup is heavy.
A calabash of spring color inebriates this old man of the mountain,
A calabash of wine presses heavily on the flower stems.
Following me, boy,
Even when the calabash is dry, my merriment does not end.
But who is with me
To accompany me to the dark mountains?
It is Lieh Tzu who rode the wind.
Lieh Tzu rode the wind.
(CYSC, P. 134)   (TR. HELLMUT WILHELM)

Ma Chih-yüan (*1260?–1334?*)

[Nan-lü] Tune: "Four Pieces of Jade"
Retirement

Beside the green water,
Against the blue mountains,
With two hundred acres of good land and a house,
Enough for a leisure life beyond the pale of red dust.
Fat purple crabs—
Yellow chrysanthemum blooms.
It's time to return home.
(CYSC, P. 233)   (TR. SHERWIN S. S. FU)

[Yüeh-tiao] Tune: "Sky-clear Sand" (*T'ien-ching sha*)
Autumn Thoughts

Withered vines, old trees, crows at dusk;
A small bridge, flowing water, a few houses;
An ancient road, a lean horse in the west wind.
The evening sun sinking in the west—
A heartbroken traveler still at world's end.
(CYSC, P. 242)   (TR. SHERWIN S. S. FU)

[Shuang-tiao] Tune: "Song of Shou-yang [Palace]"
(*Shou-yang ch'ü*), Autumn Moon Above Lake Tung-t'ing,
Two Songs

[1]

Voices are still,
The moon's bright.
Outside the gauze window are reflected the slanting twigs of a plum
    tree.
Let the plum blossoms not flaunt their shadows to sneer at me—
You will be just as lonely when the moon falls.

[2]

Lovesickness—
What is the cure?
It needs only a lover for a doctor,
To hug, to embrace, while taking the pulse—
Then all will be well even without medicine.
(CYSC, PP. 248–49)   (TR. SHERWIN S. S. FU)

[Pan-she tiao] Tune: "Slow Chant" (*Shao-pien*)

I

Half a lifetime now, I've played my part on the stage,
Yet I almost fail to get ready for life's last act.
White hair advises me:
The West Village is best for a recluse,
Good just for old age—
A thatched hut, bamboo trails,
A well of medicinal water, a vegetable patch.
I'd then curb my aspiring thoughts;
If time should be as tasteless as chewing wax,
I'd just watch like a spectator the ways of the world,   10
Or quietly shut my wicker gate.
Though Chu-ke's Sleeping-dragon Knoll[1] is no more,
There's still a fisherman's jetty like Yen Ling.[2]
There's perfect joy in the southern garden,
With azure hills facing my couch
And green water flowing around my door.

II

Though I'm poor, I can sleep like a log—
I've no need of servants to till the field or maids to work the loom.
Two acres of fish pond dotted with lotus blossoms,

---

[1] Sleeping-dragon Knoll was the place where Chu-ko Liang (181–234) had lived as a hermit before he became Liu Pei's chief adviser.
[2] Yen Kuang, a close friend of the first emperor of the Eastern Han dynasty, preferred retirement to officialdom. The place where he used to go fishing is known as Yen Ling.

A clear stream receiving a hundred freshlets—
And the breeze and the moon for the old man to dally with,
But leave the meddlers to settle right and wrong.
Herein lies perfect happiness!
There'll be bamboo shoots and bracken roots for the monks,
Lute and chess for guests.

III

Lucky to own a melon patch by the Green Gate;
Who would envy the marquisate of a hundred square miles?[3]
Watered from the well-pump, leek shoots grow thick and broad.
How Fan Ch'ih[4] was elated to learn gardening!
Three cups of wine beneath the pear tree,
A mat in the shade of willows—
What unrestrained freedom!
My meal: a schoolteacher's meager porridge,
A poor fellow's yellow leek.

IV

I have a coat to keep me from freezing,
A mouthful of food to keep me from starving.
To be poor yet free from worry is to know the virtue of idleness.
For example: how could riding a boat in wind and storm
Compare with throwing away an official's robe to return home?
I've always disliked competing for fame and gain:
To protest against poverty only defiles my ears.
In the company of birds, I forget all wordly schemes.

V

I enjoy beckoning to the brightly coated pigeons on cloudy days,
And I love to whistle to thrushes among scented flowers;
Or, among dewy lotuses, in windy rushes, beyond misty willows,
To keep company with green-headed cackling ducks and chirping
    orioles.
(CYSC, P. 262)   (TR. SHERWIN S. S. FU)

---

3 Shao P'ing, a marquis during the Ch'in dynasty, was later reduced to
  poverty; he had to raise melons for a living and sell them at East Gate.
4 Fan Ch'ih was one of Confucius' disciples.

[Shuang-tiao] Tune: "Sailing at Night" (*Yeh hsing chu'an*)
A Song Sequence[1]

I

A hundred years are but a butterfly's dream.
Looking back, I sigh for things past.
Spring comes today;
Tomorrow flowers will fade.
So make haste with the penal cup[2]—
The night is dying, the lamp burning out.

II

Think of those palaces and pavilions of Ch'in and Han—
Now fields of withered grass for herding sheep and oxen.
Were it not like this, fishermen and woodcutters
        would have little to talk about.
Here and there, desolate tombs, broken monuments—
Hard to tell dragons from snakes.[3]

III

Thrown into fox trails and rabbit holes,
How numerous are the heroes!
The tripod's firm legs were broken in the middle.[4]
Was it Wei, or Tsin?

IV

Riches come from Heaven,
But do not overspend.
Days of fun and nights of pleasure won't last forever.
You sons of wealthy families, how in your steely hearts,
In the richly painted hall, you have wasted away the wind and the
        moon.

---

1 This translation differs from the complete text in CYSC by omitting the
    first three songs.
2 A cup of wine forced upon the loser of a game during a banquet.
3 They refer to inscriptions on the tombstones.
4 Like the three legs of a tripod, the Chinese empire was divided into Three
    Kingdoms during the third century. All three, including Wei, were eventually
    overthrown by the Tsin.

V

Before my eyes the red sun is again slanting westward,
Fast as a carriage going downhill,
Indifferent to my snow-white hair in the mirror.
When I go to bed, I part with my sandals.
Don't laugh at the clumsy wile of the pigeon,[5]
He only plays the fool, as I've done all the time.

VI

Profit and fame all gone,
Right and wrong cease to have meaning—
Red dust no longer lures me at my door.
Green foliage fittingly shelters a corner of my house;
Blue hills fill to perfection the gaps in the wall,
Then there are also the bamboo fence and a thatched cottage.

VII

Only after the insects have ceased to chirp can I sleep well,
When the cocks begin to crow, myriad affairs will have no rest.
When will all this come to an end?
Look at the ants thick as soldiers in battle formation,
Or bees sucking honey, buzzing here and there,
Or flies fighting over a drop of blood.
Lord P'ei's Hall of Green Wilds,[6]
Magistrate T'ao's White Lotus Society[7]—
What does one love to do in such places during autumn?
To pluck yellow flowers wet with dew,   10
To open purple-hued crabs covered with frost,
To warm wine by burning red leaves.
Think of the limited number of cups in one's lifetime!
How many Double Nine Festivals can one have?
Remember, my naughty page boy, if people ask where I am

---

[5] The pigeon was believed to be a foolish bird which seizes the sparrow's nest because it doesn't know how to build its own. A stupid person is therefore often likened to a pigeon.

[6] The village of P'ei Tu (765–839), a famous T'ang statesman.

[7] T'ao Ch'ien, who was not a member of the White Lotus Society, was on good terms with its members.

(Even if the governor of the North Sea[8] should come to see me),
Just tell them, "The Master of the Eastern Hedge is drunk."
(CYSC, PP. 268–70)   (TR. SHERWIN S. S. FU)

Chang K'o-chiu (1265?–1345?)

[Huang-chung] Tune: "Full Moon in the Human World"
(Jen yüeh yüan)
Spring Evening: Replying to a Song

Spreading fragrant grass, random spring clouds:
Sorrow in the setting sun.
Farewell wine at the five-mile station,
A painted boat on a calm lake,
A proud horse under hanging willows.

The sound of a bird crying,
A sudden rain at night,
A gust of east wind.
Peach blossoms all blown away.
Where is the beautiful one now?—   10
Only fallen red petals outside the gate.
(CYSC, PP. 756–57)   (TR. SHERWIN S. S. FU)

[Chung-lü] Tune: "Red Embroidered Slippers"
(Hung hsiu-hsieh)
Spring Night

When swallows come I'm sick with wine;
Where peonies bloom poetic feelings are rife.
In a courtyard at dusk the rain is over,
A heart as lucid as a mirror, the moon hangs quietly;
A hand plucking the zither fractures the frozen notes.
Before the wine goblet, spring night is long.
(CYSC, P. 797)   (TR. SHERWIN S. S. FU)

---

[8] K'ung Jung (153–208) of the Later Han dynasty was the Governor of Po-hai (North Sea).

[Shuang-tiao] Tune: "Celebration in the Eastern Plain"
(*Ch'ing tung-yüan*)
Replying to a Lyric Song by the Senior Poet Ma Chih-yüan

The mountain looks gaunt,
Leaves have withered.
Outside the west window everything to inspire a poet:
    Gray mist above treetops,
    A wisp of snow on willow twigs,
    The sun's red glow upon tips of flowers.
When successful, he laughs at the idle people;
When he stumbles, the idle people laugh at him.
(CYSC, P. 808)   (TR. SHERWIN S. S. FU)

[Chung-lü] Tune: "Sheep on Mountain Slope" (*Shan p'o yang*)
Boudoir Thoughts

Loose as clouds, the curled hair;
Fragrant and warm, the mandarin-duck quilt;
One feels: the bedroom conceals spring and sleep damages spring.
Willow catkins fly,
The handsome little maiden
Feels propitious under the snowflakes of her voice
And wakes up from her dream of lovers' reunion.
Who
Is in a bad mood?
Well,   10
Nobody but you!
(CYSC, P. 912)   (TR. HELLMUT WILHELM)

Chang Yang-hao (*1269–1329*)

[Shuang-tiao] Tune: "Tartar Tune of Eighteen Beats"
(*Hu shih-pa*)

While still young,
I didn't know I was aging.
To my mind the past

Seems only yesterday.
Good time passes relentlessly by, like flowing water.
Better get drunk
And sleep—
Let the sun stage the rise and fall of an empire;
I just pretend I know nothing about it.
(CYSC, P. 402)   (TR. SHERWIN S. S. FU)

[Shuang-tiao] Tune: "Wild Geese Have Come Down;
Song of Victory"
(*Yen-erh lo chien Te-sheng ling*)

In the past I brought trouble upon myself when I sought rank and
   honor;
Now facing hills and streams, I forget fame and gain.
In the past I attended court at the crowing of cocks;
Now I'm still sound asleep at noontime.
In the past, I stood on vermilion steps in the palace, holding an official
   tablet;
Now I pluck chrysanthemums by the eastern hedge.
In the past I fawned upon the powerful and the mighty,
Now I have leisure to visit old friends.
In the past, I was wild and foolish,
And narrowly occuped flogging and banishment;   10
Now I'm taking it easy:
Have learned to write songs on wind and flowers, snow and moon.
(CYSC, P. 407)   (TR. SHERWIN S. S. FU)

Teng Yü-pin (fl. late 13th century)

[Shuang-tiao] Tune: "Wild Geese Have Come Down—
Song of Victory"
(*Yen-erh lo kuo Te-sheng ling*)[1]
Idle Leisure

Heaven and earth a rotating ball,
Sun and moon a pair of flying arrows,

_____

1 This song has also been attributed to Teng Yü-pin Tzu, or the son of Teng
Yü-pin.

The floating life a dream act,
And the affairs on earth a thousandfold changing cloud.

Ten thousand miles away there is the Jade-gate Pass,
Within seven miles a fishing pond,
In the morning sun Ch'ang-an is near,
In the autumn wind the road to Shu is hard.
Why should one care?
Many a hero has been unjustly killed.
Just watch
Like stars the two spots on your temples.
(CYSC, P. 399)   (TR. HELLMUT WILHELM)

Tseng Jui (fl. 1300)

[Chung-lü] Tune: "Sheep on Mountain Slope"
Lamenting the Times, Two Songs

[1]

The cock's crow means profit
Only when daws flock, stop scheming.
Do we ever wake from this hazy dream?
We work the mind with plotting
And blind the soul with seeking.
Our labors call down a mountain of troubles
For riches . . . only a dream in spring.
Money
bubbles in water,
Men   10
damned souls in Hell.

[2]

Great success need not be proud
Nor does poverty merit scorn,
The cycle of worldly events turns all upside down.
A morning in spring
Soon is autumn night.
Flowers bloom and flowers fall, everyone knows;

This year early spring flowers come earlier still.
Flowers
pretty as ever,
Men   10
vainly cursing old age.
(CYSC, P. 493)   (TR. WAYNE SCHLEPP)

Sui Ching-ch'en (fl. 1300)

[Pan-she tiao] Tune: "Slow Chant"
[Han] Kao-tsu's[1] Homecoming

I

The village chief made the announcement from door to door:
"Whatever the assignment, there's no excuse to put it off."
This is no ordinary assignment—
On the one hand, we're ordered to provide fodder and food[2];
On the other, some of us are sent on errands.
Well, we have no choice but to comply.
Some say the royal chariot is coming;
All agree it's the imperial carriage—
Because the emperor is returning home today.
Wang, the village elder, holds an earthen plate;   10
Chao, the cowherd, grasps a wine gourd.
Wearing a newly brushed turban,
A silk gown just starched and ironed,
They jump at the chance to pose as village squires.

II

A bunch of fakers led by the blind musician Wang Liu
Rush in headlong on horseback, playing flutes and beating drums.
Then a large crowd of men and horses arrive at the village gate,
Several flags fluttering at the very front:

---

[1] A posthumous title given to the first emperor of Han after his death. For
humorous effect, it is translated literally as the "Great-Great-Grandfather" of
Han in the last line of the poem.

[2] The text reads *yeh kên*, which has no specific meaning and is often thought
to be padding words in a tune. But it has been suggested that *kên* may be
a variant of *liang,* meaning "food."

One featuring a frosty rabbit enclosed within a white circle,[3]
One decorated with a three-legged crow inside a red curve,[4]
One with a picture of hens learning how to dance,
One presenting a dog with two wings,
And another a gourd entwined by a snake.

III

Red-lacquered two-pronged pikes,
Silver-plated axes;
Some weapons like gilded sweet-melons and bitter-melons.
Shiny stirrups carried at the tip of spears;
Snow-white palace fans made of goose quill.
These fakers hold some implements never seen before;
They wear all kinds of bizarre clothes.

IV

Horses are hitched to the crossbars of the carriage,
Not a single donkey can be seen in harness.[5]
The handles of yellow-silk parasols are naturally curved.
In front of the carriage are eight officers, looking like judges in
    Heaven[6];
A lot of attendants follow the carriage.
There are also several lovely girls,[7]
Their dresses alike,
Their hairdos identical.

V

When that tall fellow[8] gets off the carriage,
Everyone salutes him,
But the tall fellow acts as if he didn't see them at all.
The village elders all bend their knees and lie prostrate before him,

---

[3] The white circle represents the moon, where the jade rabbit was supposed to dwell.

[4] Legend has it that there is a three-legged crow in the sun. Hence the expression "golden crow" (the sun).

[5] This is from the point of view of the villager who saw mules and donkeys more often than horses.

[6] Referring to mural paintings, sculptures, and the like seen in most temples.

[7] I.e., female musicians who served as attendants to an emperor or a commander in chief.

[8] According to his biography in the *Historical Records,* Liu Pang was a tall fellow.

But the tall fellow doesn't even bother to help them stand up.
All of a sudden I raise my head and look up;
By looking closely at him for some time I know who he is,
How my bosom almost bursts with anger!

VI

Your family name was originally Liu, wasn't it?
And your wife's was Lü.
I could trace the origin of your two families right from the beginning—
You used to be a village constable, fond of a few drinks[9];
Your father-in-law used to teach the kids of our village to read.
Once you lived to the east of our village,
Hired by me to feed cattle, cut grass,
Build dikes, and hoe the fields.

VII

In the spring you used to pick mulberry leaves;
In the winter you borrowed grain from me.
Bit by bit, you bought on credit a lot of rice and wheat.
By signing a new land contract, you made a profit of three steelyardfuls
    of hemp;
To repay wine debts, you once stole several bushels of beans.
These are not groundless accusations:
They are clearly recorded in ledgers and calendars;
I still have in my keeping all the documents.

VIII

The money you owe me you can pay me back with the bribes you
    collected,
The grain you owe me you can repay by reducing my taxes.[10]
Nobody would arrest you, Number Three Liu[11]—
Why did you bother to change your name to "Great-Great-Grand-
    father of Han"?

(CYSC, PP. 543–45)   (TR. SHERWIN S. S. FU)

---

9 The description of Liu Pang's humble origin and knavish personality is
based on historical facts.
10 The implication is clearly that there is no difference between the taxes
imposed by the emperor and the money he once stole.
11 Originally Liu Pang had no name and was known as Number Three Liu
because he was the third son of the family. After he became the emperor
he named himself *Pang*.

Hsü Tsai-ssu (*fl. 1300*)

[Chung-lü] Tune: "Joy All Under Heaven" (*P'u-t'ien lo*)
Sunset on the Western Hill

> Evening clouds dispersed,
> Setting sun hanging in the sky,
> A stream of maple leaves,
> And two banks of reed flowers,
> Where gulls and egrets perch,
> And oxen and sheep come down the road.
Ten thousand acres of gleaming water, as in a heavenly picture—
Crimson clouds are immersed in the chill of the depths.[1]
> Congealed mist, twilight scene,
> Flickering sunlight, ancient trees,   10
> And dark shadows of crows flying away.

(CYSC, P. 1040)   (TR. SHERWIN S. S. FU)

[Shuang-tiao] Tune: "Clear River, a Prelude" (*Ch'ing-chiang yin*)
Lovesickness

Lovesickness is like a creditor
Who daily presses his debtor.
He always carries a load of grief,
Yet can't even obtain three-percent interest,
And the capital is lost unless he can meet her again.
(CYSC, P. 1054)   (TR. SHERWIN S. S. FU)

---

[1] The text reads: *Shui-ching kung* (literally, "crystal palace"), the palace of the dragon king.

Chung Ssu-ch'eng (*1275?–1350?*)

[Nan-lü] Tune: "A Sprig of Flowers"
Written for My "Ugly Studio"[1]

I

Living between heaven and earth,
Endowed with the forces of *yin* and *yang*,
Because I am a man,
I should be versed in worldly ways;
Everything I do should be nice and fitting,
And to my heart's content.
But I've often run into trouble
With the critical remarks I wrote.
So even my friends, old or new,
Couldn't help laughing at me whenever they see me.   10

II

Just because my appearance is not presentable,
My talents have not won me any advantage,
And my writings never served me well half my life.
All in vain: my bosom full of marvelous thoughts,
My mouth spitting out flowery phrases.
But alas! my face is ashen-gray, my manners clumsy;
I'm gap-toothed, double-chinned,
Plus small eyes, thin eyebrows,
Short moustache and sparse sideburns.
Oh, where could I find Ch'en P'ing's elegant airs,[2]   10
Ho Yen's romantic appearance,
Or Pan An's handsome and charming looks?
I know all that.
I'm tired of looking at myself in the mirror,[3]

---

[1] The text reads *ch'ou chai*, meaning "ugly studio," which was also the poet's style-name (it was customary to name one's studio after one's style-name). Hence the poem is a description of the poet's appearance rather than of his studio.
[2] Ch'en P'ing, Ho Yen, and Pan An were among the most handsome men in ancient China.
[3] The text reads *ch'ing luan* ("green phoenix"), meaning "mirror."

Hating my dad and mom for doing so poorly!
Should one day an imperial decree recruit ugly men as candidates,
Surely I'd come out first on the list.

III

At times, with my hair tied up by a piece of soft black gauze
      into a "sky-piercing knot,"
My black boots sticking out of my wind-rustling gown,
I'd stand leisurely by the back door at dusk;
Then, all of a sudden, I'd burst into laughter.
What do I look like?—
Just like a latter-day Chung K'uei[4]
      who can scarcely scare the ghosts to death.

IV

If my cap is cocked my acquaintance will fault me;
But if my looks are not striking whom can I blame?
My bearing simply isn't imposing—majestic—awe-inspiring!
When I think about all this as I lie on my pillow,
Anger mounts in my breast.
In vain I've lived for thirty years;
In vain I've thought of it for nine thousand times!
I'm just like the gnarls on a tree trunk that can't be shaved off—
Like congenital diseases for which there's no cure.

V

In this world those that can walk can't fly,
Despite their talent in a thousand things,
Or their cleverness on a hundred occasions.
At my leisure I've come to understand this principle.
Privately I've explained it to myself:
I'm simply tired of roaming about because
If I come to a pond the fish would be startled and sink to its bottom;
If I pass the frontier the wild geese would fly away in fright;
And if I enter a garden even the common birds would avoid me.

---

4 A fabulous personage who was believed to be able to ward off ghosts. It was
a custom for people to post his image on the door because he looked so
extremely ugly that even evil spirits would be scared away at the sight of him.

While alive I am not a fit subject for a painting[5];   10
After my death no one will write my epitaph.

VI

A portrait painter should grasp the essence of painting:
"I'm afraid the skillful strokes of your brush
    can hardly communicate the secret of creation.
But you should be able to make, short of a draft,
    the copy resemble the original.
Just follow the pattern of a sheath in drawing a knife,
And if you draw a ghost, don't forget to add a mouth and a nose.
If your eyes are keen enough, you don't even need a model."

VII

For all your fog-lifting skill and sky-soaring plan,
Your dragon-killing devices and phoenix-catching contrivances,
You're subject to the way of the world
Which judges people in terms of high and low:
If you're loaded with money you're noble;
If you're broke you're mean.
They won't care whether you're a dashing, handsome youth:
Even if you look like the god of the River of Libations,[6]
Or your face surpasses that of an immortal;
Even though you were a Lü Tung-pin reborn into this world,   10
Or the reincarnation of Sung Yü[7]—
What if you hold only to the back of a coin,[8]
What if you don't have a cent in your name!—
Nobody will pay you the slightest attention.
It's useless for you to argue, to discuss this and that[9]
Or to discourse about right and wrong.

---

[5] This and the next line simply mean that he was so ugly no one would either paint his portrait or write a poem in praise of his appearance.

[6] I.e., the deity Erh-lang, nephew of the Jade Emperor, noted for his handsome countenance. He appears several times in the novel *Hsi-yu Chi* (*Journey to the West*).

[7] Lü Tung-pin was supposed to be a handsome immortal, while Sung Yü, also noted for his attractive appearance, was the disciple of Ch'ü Yüan and a famous *fu* writer.

[8] An approximate translation of an obscure line.

[9] Literally, "to talk about the yellow and to count the black"—a Yüan colloquial expression.

VIII

There was a dragon-killing scholar, a distinguished disciple of
    Confucius,[10]
Who had entered the inner chambers of learning—
None could compare with him past or present;
There was an archer (he hit the bull's-eye of a gold coin)
      who later became a prince's son-in-law[11]—
"Matchless in strategy."
"Profound in knowledge of military arts."
Sure, there are among the ugly and the handsome
Those who are praised and others who are wronged.
And here, this scholar and this warrior are good examples—
Both were wise in judgment,   10
Amiable and candid,
Never said anything they didn't mean, their conscience not the least
    tarnished.
If I should lie, God would know the truth.

IX

I often recall, with night rain tapping at my window and
    the lamp just beginning to grow dim,
And gusts of wind at my pillow before I woke up from a dream—
I saw a man
Invited me to visit him.
He said that I should have
A noble and prosperous career,
Become adept at both Confucianism
And the craft of government,
Become intelligent and clear-minded,
And also clever and cautious.   10
But due to a moment's oversight

---

10 The allusion is rather obscure, but it could refer to Tan-t'ai Tzu-yü, one
of Confucius' disciples, mentioned in *The Analects* (VI. 12). His appearance
was very ugly, yet it was with reference to him that Confucius said we
shouldn't judge a person by his appearance. In *The Annotated Classic of
The Rivers and Seas* (*Shui-ching Chu*) there is a story about his killing
two dragons.
11 Probably it alludes to Hsüan Tsan, one of the 108 heroes in the novel *Tale
of the Marshes* (*Shui-hu Chuan*). Despite his ugliness, he became the son-in-
law of a prince because the prince loved his strength and strategy.

He had made me in my present shape.
And in order to show his remorse,
He would offer me
An official's salary,
Numerous offspring,
A happy marriage,
Plenty of goods and money,
A granary filled to the top,
More and more honors and blessings,   20
And the fullest measure of a long life.
He said he had come here
Just to tell me about this.
As he bade me goodby,
He asked for my forgiveness.
He sighed several times,
Showed a moment's regret.
I woke up and remembered—
Remembered who he was—
He was none other than that evil spirit   30
Who kneaded me into such a shape when I was yet in the womb.
(CYSC, PP. 1371–72)   (TR. SHERWIN S. S. FU)

Ch'iao Chi (1280–1345)

[Cheng-kung] Tune: "Overtures" (*Lu-yao pien*)
On Myself

I was not chosen to head the dragon list,[1]
Nor was my name entered into the biography of worthies;
From time to time I'm a sage of wine,
Finding everywhere the Zen of poetry—
Highest graduate of the college of clouds and mists,
Drunken angel of rivers and lakes,
My talks and jokes are fit for the Imperial Academy of Compilation.[2]
Loitering,

---

1 I.e., a scholar who came out first in the Imperial Examination.
2 *Pien-hsiu Yüan*, an institute set up for the compilation of historical records; its members were appointed by the emperor.

I've been writing commentaries on the wind and the moon for forty
   years.
(CYSC, PP. 574–75)   (TR. SHERWIN S. S. FU)

[Chung-lü] Tune: "Sheep on Mountain Slope"
Expressing My Feelings on a Winter Day

Three chestnuts for morning, four at night[1];
What is right today is wrong tomorrow.
The fools understand neither failure nor success!
They amass family fortunes,
Cavort with loose women.
How boldly money excites mean minds;
Hundreds of ingots buy the ruling of a judge!
The body
come to this,
And the soul
not yet dead!
(CYSC, P. 584)   (TR. WAYNE SCHLEPP)

[Shuang-tiao] Tune: "Song of Plucking Cassia" (*Che-kuei ling*)
Composed for a Singer at a Banquet I Attended with
Mr. Po Tzu-shui and Others on an Autumn Day Among the
Lakes and Hills

The sound of autumn from a stretch of reed flowers,
The sinking sun shining on mountains and rivers,
And rustic houses bathed in a shower.
I long for the gaiety of songs and dances,
For a peaceful age,
And for a life spent in poetry and wine.
Wait till the willows come out on a sunny day, and I'll gallop my horse
                    in the spring breeze;
When cassia flowers look chilled by the night moon, I'll sail on a raft,
Listening to a song of the beautiful Wu girl,

---

1 Refers to a parable in the *Chuang-tzu;* see note 2 to Tu Fu's poem "Seven
   Songs Written While Living at T'ung-ku . . ."

I cannot but laugh at the Prefect of Chiang-chou,[1]   10
Whose tears stained the lute.
(CYSC, P. 604)   (TR. SHERWIN S. S. FU)

Liu Chih (*c. 1280–c. 1335*)

[Cheng-kung] Tune: "Decorous and Pretty" (*Tuan-cheng hao*)
Respectfully Offered to Circuit Inspector Kao

I

Disaster has struck the people
And a year of famine is upon them.
But thanks to your gracious efforts, all are free from suffering;
So I've composed this song for the people to sing.

II

Last year just when planting the new rice,
The weather went all wrong.
Where could one find rain when there should be!
The drought demon brought ruin to the whole countryside.
Rice wasn't fit for harvest;
Wheat didn't mature,
And the people lost hope.
Day by day prices went up;
They lost thirty percent when exchanging old currency for new,[1]
And a peck of grain smaller by almost half.[2]   10
What a wretched situation!

---

1 I.e., Po Chü-yi was the Assistant Prefect of Chiang-chou when he wrote
"The Song of the Lute."
1 In 1298 the government decreed that the old currency (*hun-ch'ao*) be re-
placed by new currency (*liao-ch'ao*). Earlier, in 1282, it set the regulation
that a three-percent commission or exchange charge be paid when cur-
rencies were exchanged, but by the end of the century inflation was so bad that
thirty percent was charged.
2 Literally, forty percent.

III

The local rich were underhanded, dishonest.
Granary managers deceptive, unjust.
Filled with elephantine greed and maliciously clever
They mixed husks with grain,
Slipped bran into the rice.
But how can they hope that their heirs would long survive!

IV

Dust gathered in cooking pots, the very old and the very young
    starved.
A grain of rice cost a pearl, so even those in their prime went hungry.
The rich had gold and silver but couldn't pawn them anywhere
And with bellies quite empty lay idly in the setting sun.
Peel elm bark to chew;
Pick wild greens to eat:
"Yellow-never-age" tastes better than bear's paws,
And bracken-root starch makes substitute of provisions.
"Goose guts," "bitter greens"—stew them with the roots;
"Reed-shoots," "rush lettuce"—eat them leaves and all,   10
But leave alone the trunks of the willow and the camphor![3]

V

Some pounded hemp-stalk pith to concoct a thick soybean milk;
Others boiled wheat bran to make a watery gluten.
Even so they didn't hesitate to raise clasped hands reverently
    and thank azure Heaven.
One after another more yellow than yellow scripture paper,
Each thinner than a jackal,
They lay about in the alleys and the lanes.

VI

Secretly they slaughter wide-horned buffalo or
Sneak out and cut down large-leafed mulberry trees,[4]

---

3 The wood of these is needed to make coffins.
4 Since the water buffalo was essential to agriculture and the mulberry essential
to sericulture, the state forbade their destruction.

But if an epidemic comes along, they'll be buried alive without a coffin.
Sell off, at tremendous loss, family assets and property,
Also, sons and daughters,
As if unrelated, never seen before[5]—
So what if it's painful to part!
No one ever wants suckling babes and they are cast in the great river,
Yes, where can one find food to spare in the kitchen, wine in the cup?
When I saw infants drowning in the river and mothers standing on the
    bank,   10
How could I but choke over such misery and pain!

VII

The grain broker's smuggling boat lies hidden in the creek beyond the
    bay
After slipping across the river in the middle of the moonlit night.
Now the double-dealing grain merchants make their play—
Still they'll have to pay a double brokerage fee.
But the flour seller will want it both ways too, and
The broker, with his old currency, will be done out
       of four taels before he knows it!

VIII

In our river district there's a public granary.
Year after year it's been under the control of the revenue officer.
The accounts of outlay and income were juggled to appear in perfect
    order—
Everything had been grabbed up, the government blocked from doing
    its duty.
Recently an official recommendation to release public grain
       has come down to the district:
Distribute a month's ration to each family according to its size.
But the rich had used their wealth and bought themselves off,[6]
And in the end this phony kindness meant nothing at all.
Try to satisfy your hunger with a painted picture of a rice cake—what
    a joke!
That one can rely on official seals and pronouncements is all a lie—   10
They just make the village headmen and section heads happy.

---

5 Shen and Shang (Orion and Lucifer), which never see each other.
6 The rich had bribed the tax men to let them get away with not paying their
grain tax into the granary and to falsify the books to cover up for them.

IX

Even brave, strong men were crushed and dispirited,
And idle vagabonds sent off to the grave.
Clutching baby to bosom, leading a boy by the hand and
    leaning on a bamboo staff—
Frail, weak, hunched over like a prawn,
He's utterly out of breath, stricken by the side of the road,
Stifling sobs, eyes filled with tears.

X

I saw the living dead line up on the streets—
They came out begging, blocking doors, fighting over what they had
    got.
Even the wealthy merchants, hugging gold to their breasts,
    stood anxiously there, waiting for death.
But now we can give our heartfelt thanks for the good offices
    of the circuit inspector,
Who opened up the granaries like Chi An.[7]
Aflame with enthusiasm by day and night,
He gave order to have the grains released and personally went
    around distributing them.
Having seen the orphans, the widows, and the sick—
    who had no one to turn to for help—
He sent doctors, had gruel prepared and portioned out
    throughout the outlying lanes.
He was superb in making proper and multiple use of stolen money 10
    confiscated and grain stockpiled.
All the starving multitude give him their utmost respect.
They're like a winter-brittle tree meeting spring,
Like new shoots getting another chance to grow.

XI

The rich, buying up grain and acquiring properties, became
    all the more rapacious.

---

[7] Chi An was a provincial governor during the reign of Emperor Wu of Han
(140–87 B.C.). When famine resulted due to floods, he opened the public
granaries on his own personal authority.

The poor, lacking the means to live, flesh and blood separated,
    became all the more hopeless.
The rich took concubines and purchased servants—they had
    more than their share of prosperity.
The poor starved to death and their corpses filled the ditches—
    what a disaster it was!
How bitter is the lot of the common folk!
How bitter is the lot of the common folk!
Even in autumn harvest time, they sold their wives and children,
    and lost all they possessed.

XII

This official loves the people, worries for the state,
    is unbiased and impartial.
He exercises benevolence in his conduct of government—
    he's an ardent, zealous man.
He pities the old, has compassion for the poor,
And looks upon the people as his own children.
He restores the dead to life;
Helps the weak, curbs the strong.
The great mass of people give heartfelt thanks for his wise virtue.
It is carved on their bones, engraved upon their hearts.
How they wish they could "dampen the grass" or "let the
    reins hang down."[8]
They were as underneath an overturned tub,   10
But now can all enjoy the brilliance of the sun.

XIII

He is endowed with the attributes of a great minister,
His talent fitting to be the very beams and rafters of the court.
In deliberations he is broad and profound,
At heart benevolent and forgiving.

---

[8] This involves two stories, both probably apocryphal. Li Hsin-ch'un (third century A.D.) was taking a nap in the fields near a river when the local governor, out on a hunt, had a fire started to drive the game. Li's faithful dog then kept running back and forth from the river to Li, circling him with a band of wet grass—thus saving his life.
    Fu Chien, founder of the Former Ch'in dynasty (351–94), was once being pursued by bandits, and he fell into a river and was about to drown when his faithful horse let his reins hang down—saving his life as well.

His conduct of government—fair and just,
Attendance to official duties—merciful and charitable.
He can compare favorably with Hsiao and Ts'ao,[9]
May stand shoulder to shoulder with Yi and Fu,[10]
And form ranks with Chou and Chao.[11]
Someday a document with purple seal will proclaim the
    Imperial Edict,   10
And in brocaded blouse he'll urge on his fleet horse's hooves.[12]

XIV

We pray that he'll soon be ranked with the most illustrious at court,
And anxiously look to the day when the fragrance of his name
    lies hidden under the golden goblet.[13]
He shall enter court at the Imperial Capital,
Cling to the dragon, cleave to the phoenix,[14]
His food in the bronze tripod flavored and his soup well seasoned;
He will discourse on the way of government, and make the state
    prosper.
How noble in his sable cicada-shaped cap!
How distinguished in robes of the highest rank!
With jeweled girdle-pendants tinkling as he walks.
When the myriad folk of the whole empire again delight in their
    labors,   10
They'll know it's all due to this circuit inspector who once did his duty.

XV

A prime minister's family produces prime ministers—
    this to the honor of one's forebears;

---

9 Hsiao Ho and Ts'ao Shen served in turn as prime minister during the reign of Emperor Kao of the Han (reigned 206–195 B.C.).

10 Yi Yin and Fu Yüeh were great officers of the Shang dynasty (1765–1122 B.C.).

11 Duke of Chou, the son of King Wen of Chou, and duke of Chao, a son of King Wen by a concubine—both were great state officers who assisted King Wu (reigned 1121–1116 B.C.) to establish the Chou dynasty.

12 The implication is that Circuit Inspector Kao will someday be summoned to court to become prime minister.

13 When Emperor Hsüan of the T'ang (reigned 712–55) decided to appoint a new prime minister, he wrote the name down on a sheet of paper and left it on his desk. When the crown prince, the heir apparent, came in, he covered the name by turning a golden goblet over on top of it.

14 I.e., as the emperor's closest confidant and principal assistant.

To win promotion upon promotion—this to the glory of one's
    descendants.
The people will never forget his mercy as he gave life back to them!
How could they ever repay his virtue when he saved them from
    starvation!
The elderly and small children carefully weigh his merits,
Old wood gatherers and fishermen meet and talk about them.
They say that at East Lake beside the willow banks
Where serenity and peace uplift the heart,
And to Su Yün-ch'ing's vegetable garden,[15]
He, together with Hsü Ju-tzu,[16] will bask in the fragrance of   10
    their reputations.
There people will build a sacrificial temple to make offerings,
And erect a monumental stone with an inscription in several lines,
Giving an account of the particulars of his virtuous government,
So that for countless generations to come, when officials and
    commoners see it, they'll remember and revere.

(CYSC, PP. 669–71)   (TR. RICHARD JOHN LYNN)

Kuan Yün-shih (1286–1324)

[Chung-lü] Tune: "Rapt with Wine, Loudly Singing—
Joy in Spring's Coming"
(*Tsui kao-ko kuo Hsi ch'un lai*)
My Love

Natural demeanor warm and soft
Winsome face demure.
When we chance to meet, her sidelong glances encourage me,
Kindling the pangs of my lovesickness.

Matchmaker bees and go-between butterflies fail to coax her:
Swallows or orioles can't do as they please.

---

[15] During the Shao-hsing era of Southern Sung (1131–62) a commoner, Su
Yün-ch'ing moved to the shore of East Lake (Tung-hu), built a small hut,
lived alone, and started up a vegetable garden. He was generous to the
common folk in the neighborhood and often helped them when times were
bad.
[16] Hsü Ju-tzu (97–168), or Hsü Chih, a famous recluse of the Later Han
period.

Just like a sprig of red almond blossoms peeping over a wall
She lies beyond the reach of plucking hand.
How I feel, in vain, that for those blossoms' sake the wind
   and rain bear shame!
(CYSC, P. 365)   (TR. RICHARD JOHN LYNN)

[Shuang-tiao] Tune: "Song of the Lunar Palace"
Sending Off Spring

Ask the Lord of the East,[1] "Where lie the ends of the earth?"
Setting sun and singing cuckoos,
Flowing water and peach blossoms,
Dim, dim distant mountains,
Lush, lush fragrant grasses,
Dark, dark red sunset clouds.
Pursue willow catkins and where would the wind transport you?
Chase floating spider silk and to whose house would you be enticed?
Languidly tuning a balloon lute
She leans on the swing,   10
The window gauze reflecting moonlight.
(CYSC, P. 367)   (TR. RICHARD JOHN LYNN)

[Shuang-tiao] Tune: "Song of Shou-yang [Palace]"

Porpoises spout amid the waves;
Wild geese settle on the sands.
Leaning on Mount Wu,[1] a kingfisher-blue screen hung up high,
I see the tidal bore,[2] its drum the sound of ten thousand drummers.
A girl fair as jade, rolling up the pearl blinds,
   is pretty as a picture.
(CYSC, P. 372)   (TR. RICHARD JOHN LYNN)

---

1 The god of spring.
1 Actually a spur of mountains to the southeast of Hangchow which stretch
 from the West Lake to the Ch'ien-t'ang River.
2 The Ch'ien-t'ang tidal bore—a spectacular sight, especially in autumn.

[Nan-pei ho-t'ao]¹ "Medley of Southern and Northern Tunes"
Scenic Tour of West Lake

Tune: "Butterflies" [Northern Melody] (*Fen-tieh-erh*)

I

Unportrayable on the light silk of a small fan
You're more lovely than P'eng-lai fairy mountain
(Though you haven't mountains and streams where twenty
        thousand can stand off a million).²
Over there, inlaid gem-like in the lake, embankments link green
        lowlands—there must be a hundred lofty villas.
I think to myself: Tung-p'o and
The Immortal Pu, who's there now to echo your poems?³

Tune: "Happy Events Approaching" [Southern Melody]
(*Hao-shih chin*)

II

Don't say: How can Phoenix Hill
Rival the glories of the Left Bank!⁴
Throughout the endless stretch of time
There's been, of course, an infinite number of picturesque places,
But when mists envelop and vapors enclose—
Winding your way across the six bridges, peaks of kingfisher
        hue seem to spire up like conch shells,
Blue tinged mountains caress azure skies and
Golden waves float on water as green as pure green jade.

---

1 While the northern tunes were those of Ta-tu (modern Peking), the southern
  tunes were sung in Hangchow. The mode for this sequence is *Chung-lü*.
2 Said of the strategic location of the ancient state of Ch'in (modern Shensi).
3 I.e., the poets Su Shih and Lin Pu, both known for the poems they wrote
  about the West Lake.
4 "Phoenix Hill" (*Feng-huang-p'o*), a famous scenic area near West Lake;
  "the Left Bank" (*Chiang-tso*) refers to Chin-ling or Chien-k'ang (Nanking),
  the capital of several dynasties during the third–sixth centuries.

Tune: "Pomegranate Blossoms" [Northern Melody]
(*Shih-liu hua*)

III

Now I see lotus-pickers singing the lotus-pickers' song.
Truly, this picturesque place surpasses all others!
Then there's that inverted image of the distant mountains
        plunged beneath clear waves—
Bright mists embrace kingfisher hues,
Strange rocks thrusting precipitously.
Now I see sand gulls marring the lake surface's gleam here and there.
Yi-yi ya-ya,
The breeze brings across the sound of oars.
Now I see this charming beauty sitting and leaning still on
        the carved railing,
Just like Ch'ang-o[5] facing her jeweled mirror.

Tune: "Chilly East Wind" [Southern Melody]
(*Liao-ch'iao tung-feng*)

IV

How is it that
There's so much pleasure and enjoyment?
Singing with my poet friends and drinking companions,
Flowers are thick, the wine rich.
We rid ourselves of all troubles, but never overdo it.
In carefree delight while away time or
Peacefully sit and face the pure breeze and bright moon.
Whether spring, summer, autumn, winter—
All four seasons can be your inspiration.

---

5 Ch'ang-o (or Heng-o): goddess of the moon.

Tune: "Squabbling Quails" [Northern Melody] (*Tou an-ch'un*)

V

Excited woodwinds, staccato strings in noisy clamor,
Magnolia boats, painted barges in tidy array.
With powder and mascara the girls follow one upon the other,
Their cloud coiffures in verdant tints a myriad blossoms quivering.
Truly, scour the past and grind the present—there's no
          exquisite nest like this!
If you don't believe me, try it and see.
A thousand green wispy willows,
Ten thousand red ambrosial lotus flowers.

Tune: "Moth Fluttering Against Lamp" [Southern Melody]
(*P'u-teng o*)

VI

Fresh breezes waft across marsh orchid fragrance as
The moon bursts through mountain clouds.
Jade-green mist floats upon pure deep water.
Dang-dang, dawn bells ring out in the temples.
Wu-yeh-yeh, apes cry out on the ancient ridges.
See the pairs and pairs of mandarin ducks playing in the clear waves!
Far, far off there seem to be fishing boats and skiffs,
In the jade-green mist bamboo rain hats and cloaks crowding each
    one.

Tune: "Going Up Small Pavilion" [Northern Melody]
(*Shang hsiao-lou*)

VII

How crowded and bustling it is over there.
How spaced out and peaceful these few nests are.
Here looking out on a clear day,
I lean on blue mountains and
Steep myself in clear waves.

A fine rain's just finished.
The thin mist's just dispersed,
A gentle wind's just stopped.
But really! Don't quote again: "Whether unadorned or all made up."[6]

Tune: "Moth Fluttering Against Lamp"

VIII

Tier upon tier of storied buildings, decorated pavilions.
Cluster upon cluster of extraordinary flowers, exotic fruits.
In the distance, green sedges and bottom grasses,
Lush, lush slopes of fragrant shrubs.
Geh-deng geh-deng, the clatter of hoofbeats—
In dim darkness the Long Bridge[7] seems to straddle the waves,
Slender wispy willows like spun gold.
Far, far off there seem to be fishing boats and skiffs,
In the jade-green mist bamboo rain hats and cloaks
            crowding each one.

Tune: "Coda" (*Wei-sheng*)

IX

Here you can find joy in cloudy weather or bright, day or night.
From ancient times till now many have sung of your charms—
Snow, moon, and wind-blown flowers, anything can happen!
(CYSC, PP. 378–79)   (TR. RICHARD JOHN LYNN)

---

6 From a famous poem by Su Shih, "Drinking at the Lake . . ." (included in
  this volume), in which the lake was compared to a peerless beauty of the
  fifth century B.C.
7 Ch'ang-ch'iao ("Long Bridge") is at the southeast side of West Lake below
  Nan-p'ing Mountain.

Yün-k'an Tzu (*date unknown*)

[Chung-lü] Tune: "Greeting the Immortal Guest"
(*Ying hsien-k'e*), Eight Songs

[1]

No tricks
      nothing doing
the sun and moon endure *their* rush
and don't grow old

sail backwards?
paddle against the flow?
to hell with that
you'd better be known
as being
      quiet.

[2]

Light wind in bamboo
deep flower shadows, drinking
a cup of strong brew, striking
a couple of lute chords
reveal world's dark contrivance
hoard marvels I may use

dream an empire of ants
wake to know the world is vapor
is a dream.

[3]

My home's in the flowering mountain
my joy is purest idleness
in a rush hut by a blue grotto
at the end of a crazy winding path
at noon I take a simple meal

and when I'm full
I take my staff
and wander to the mountaintop
and gaze.

[4]

Who envies you
oh high and mighty
all done up in purple
trailing your robe of rank
my heart's at peace
I'm satisfied with me
there aren't many in the world today
to match this
               crafty rascal.

[5]

Done with the world
and pure
         as darkness
nothing to hold me
nothing restrain
the old guy here
within the grove
before blue cliffs
               the wind, the moon's companion
madly singing   10
drunk and dancing
smashed, polluted with the wine
of endless life

[6]

When I'm drunk I sleep
and even when I'm not
I loll my head and
stagger east and west completely
shameless
there is no spring
there is no fall

toot-toot, woo-woo
this music keeps me young.

[7]

Gathering simples, going home
white clouds flying
mist seals green mountains

and this wandering mystic's straight astray

black apes call and green birds cry
a magic crane goes before me, dancing
leads me to my cave.

[8]

The flour's gone sour
the grain in the bag has gone stale
my ladle's busted, and even
my old wooden bowl's got a harelip
no salt, just a couple of onions
contentment is my portion: it's sweeter
than the dainties of the world.
(CYSC, PP. 1883–88)   (TR. JEROME P. SEATON)

Anonymous

[Chung-lü] Tune: "Joy in Spring's Coming" (*Hsi ch'un lai*), Seven Songs[1]

[1]

The first time I saw her between her embroidered curtains
she looked at me with eyes of love.

---

[1] These seven *ch'ü* songs, to the tune of "Joy in Spring's Coming," were written presumably by a young scholar undergoing the various stages of a love affair with a courtesan. The freshness of language and the tendency to ignore classical rules of prosody for the sake of immediate thought and melody as it then was sung are reminiscent of song-lyric writings of our own day.

I cannot say all that swells in my heart.
Heaven, O Heaven!
Let me meet her sometime.

[2]

I'm so sick that food and drink aren't food and drink,
so miserable, living or dying's neither living nor dying.
When does such heartsickness heal itself?
This misery is like the sea!
Oh let my torment be quickly over.

[3]

Her plum-apple face charms the sweet rain,
her willow-slender figure shames the wind,
her small cherry lips are barely red-tinted.
Lovely thing!
How have you come to such a place?

[4]

We heard "The Gold Thread" sung through,
and never noticed when the silver flask was empty,
nor when the moon went down outside our music chamber.
I was drunk,
and can't remember what time my darling left.

[5]

Her dreams pass and she wakes. The first watch is over.
The moon circles the south wall and another watch begins.
Gently she rouses her lover:
"Don't sleep!
There's so little left of the night."

[6]

For a while words can feign feeling but not the heart;
it is too soon to forget our love.
To friends you insist you never think of me.
But you lie.
Deep down I know it. I cannot be fooled.

[7]

Her eyes full, in two clear waves overflowing,
the brows drawn in winter peaks of sadness . . .
And when I leave, who comes to your room?
Always too soon
the trees are startled by autumn.
(YJHLC, PP. 96–99)   (TR. WAYNE SCHLEPP)

PART VI

In the Long Tradition: Accommodation and Challenge

(Ming, 1368–1644; Ch'ing, 1644–1911;
The Republic, 1912–   )

Kao Ch'i (1336–1374)

"Lament of a Soldier's Wife"

My husband never desired the official seal of a marquis,
But a tiger's tally[1] sent him to join the ranks in a foreign land.
For many nights I was visited in my bedroom by bad dreams,
Now I hear from the general's headquarters of the army's defeat.
His body perished, yet his faded soldier's cloak remains;
His old comrade-in-arms has brought it home for me.
A woman, I'd never find the road to the border—
How could I get to far Wu-wei[2] to find his unburied bones?
I can only cut out paper pennants to summon back his soul;
And turn them toward that place where we once parted.   10
(chcsc, 1/20b)   (TR. IRVING Y. LO)

"Ballad of a Ferocious Tiger"

Dark wind blows in the forest, crows and magpies mourn:
People sense a ferocious tiger's coming before it appears.
Eyes burning bright, it crouches in the middle of the road;
Once espied by the general, arrows fly off the bow.
Homes plant thorny stakes as high as their door;
Hogs and suckling pigs are corralled before sundown.
How fierce indeed a tiger, yet all still rejoice
If only it keeps to its swaggering far off in the mountains' depths.
(chcsc, 1/25b–26a)   (TR. IRVING Y. LO)

Picking Tea: A Ballad

Thunder roars past creeks and mountains,
        dark clouds bringing warm days;
From shady clusters, sprouts begin to rear their spear-like heads.
Wearing silver hairpins, girls respond to each other in songs—

---

[1] I.e., wartime dispatch. The term is derived from the ancient custom of employing messengers to carry important messages carved on tallies of bamboo or metal.
[2] Wu-wei, also known as Liang-chou, is a district in modern Kansu province.

Whose basket shows that she has picked the most?
As they come home, the fragrance still clings to their hands;
Their choicest crop is offered first to the magistrate.
The freshly roasted leaves aren't theirs to taste by bamboo stove;
Hamper after hamper they are sold to merchants south of the lake.
Mountain families don't know about raising rice and wheat;
Each year's food and clothing depend on these spring rains.[1]   10
(chcsc, 2/11a)   (TR. IRVING Y. LO)

Sunflower[1]

Its radiance bursts forth in summer's bright light,
In clusters nestling along the dense green shade.
Evenings, it droops like the common hibiscus,
But blazes at noon with the pomegranate flowers.
A subtle scent spreads across our mat,
A fresh splendor shines upon our feast.
When all the other flowers have bid us farewell,
This last survivor now rouses our pity.
(chcsc, 6/10b)   (TR. IRVING Y. LO)

Cold Spring[1]

Far away the spring comes down among clustered peaks;
Evenly it flows above a flat boulder.
The moon shines to transfigure it into a pool;
The wind blows on it without causing a ripple.
Its noise blends with the fall of frosty leaves,
Its sheen reflected on autumn's overspreading moss.
A rustic traveler peers in it at his gaunt face—
He has come here, leaning on his bamboo staff.
(chcsc, 5/11a)   (TR. IRVING Y. LO)

---

[1] The stormy days of spring, mentioned in the first and last lines, were felt to be the best time to pick the choice crop of new tea leaves.
[1] From a series entitled "Three Songs Written by the Pond of Western Studio."
[1] Han-ch'üan is located in Mount Chih-hsing [Mount Whetstone], distinguished by a flat rock over which a broad stream flows (author's note). The place, where the monk-poet Chih-tun (314–66) once lived, lies southwest of Soochow.

On a Painting by Hsia Kuei[1] Entitled
"Returning in Wind and Snow to a Village Home"

Clouds hover over the river's waves, the evening's in a haze;
The green hills suddenly disappear as might a fugitive.

A universe glitters, pure as crystals of ice;
Spring sentiments all dispersed into a grove of trees dry and sere.
Rustic bridge, ancient ferry, no travelers in sight;
Echoes are heard loud and clear and withered reeds sing.
Beneath the river sky, an old man ten thousand *li* from home—
In a short rush rain cloak, he looks like a hedgehog; his boat like a
    waterfowl;
Fish, burrowing deep in winter mud, evade his fishing nets.
Coming home, he recognizes from afar the isolated fishing village,   10
Knocks at a bramble gate in the night and hears dogs bark.
Bamboos along the trail bend and break, none to prop them up;
A country wife is steaming the rice, a child sent to fetch wine.

I cast no envious eyes on meats roasted around a glowing fire;
I sigh that my career has often ruined my plan—
A bagful of poems[2] accompanying my donkey, and my whiskered
    servant on foot.
Where in Ch'ang-an will I find drinking companions?
Their heads pelted by falling flowers so their caps no longer black?[3]
Lying awake in an inn, I once again am a wanderer;
Ashamed of myself, I face this painting of "Returning
    in Wind and Snow to a Village Home."[4]   20
(chcsc, 10/2a–2b)   (TR. IRVING Y. LO)

---

1 Hsia Kuei (fl. 1190–1225), a leading Sung landscape painter, especially noted
    for his snow sceneries.
2 Alluding to the story about the T'ang poet Li Ho, who went out each morn-
    ing riding on a nag, followed by a servant carrying a silk bag, in which he
    would deposit lines of poetry as he composed them; then he would complete
    these poems each evening when he got home.
3 Black caps were what the commoners wore. The highly evocative line, as
    Professor F. W. Mote points out, has many layers of implied meaning; an
    alternative English translation of this line could be "Hair graying, official
    caps no longer on their heads."
4 "Much of Kao Ch'i's poetry written away from home is devoted to the theme
    of regret and grief of one who cannot return home. The theme of this paint-
    ing is a reminder of that desire to return—fom Nanking to his home in
    Soochow." (F. W. Mote.)

On a Painting of the Radiant Emperor's Night Revels by Candlelight[1]

Behind Calyx Hall's towers the sun has just set,
Purple-robed eunuchs hurry to lock up the palace gates.
His Majesty feasts tonight in the West Garden,
Flames leap from silver plates, a hundred torches burning.

The blossoming trees wish to shut their eyes and sleep, but can't[2];
Her red dress stands out more dazzling bright in the glare.
Purple flames filling the courtyard turn into a spring mist;
Unnoticed, the moon glides by across the sky.

New scores for the Rainbow Skirt Dance having been tried,
Attendants shout for fresh candles to be brought;   10
Palace girls' brass rattles announce the time of night,
But singers and dancers mustn't hurry, the night's only halfway
    through.

Together they say that the night is to be spent in revels,
And officials are excused from court attendance next day—
Their only care, the wind and dew may bring a hint of chill;
The royal consort, thinly clad, feigning coy restraint.

Lute sounds soon give way to drumbeats close behind;
Daylight pleasures aren't enough to rejoice an emperor's heart.
What hope then the radiance would "turn into something bright,
To cast its gleam in the lowly huts of poor, wandering folk?"[3]   20

---

[1] Ming Huang ("Radiant Emperor," sometimes translated as "Bright Emperor")
or T'ang Hsüan-tsung, whose infatuation for Yang Kuei-fei was popularly
linked to the An Lu-shan rebellion, has inspired a number of poems and
plays in Chinese literature. The title of the painting here includes a saying:
"Hold candles aloft and enjoy the night."

[2] Alluding to the story that Ming Huang once remarked to his royal consort
when she appeared with flushed cheeks, "Haven't the blossoms of the red
flowering crab apple had enough spring sleep?"

[3] Alluding to a folk song by Nieh Yi-chung which reads: "I wish the heart of a
ruler/ Could be turned into something bright/ Instead of shining on feasts
and silken mats/ To shine into a fugitive folk's home."

On the lofty terrace above Soochow, the long night's singing;
In palaces at Chiang-tu, the swarms of fireflies[4]—
Those who pursue only pleasure never know when to stop,
And helpless they become when beacon fires are suddenly lit.

Pity the travelers who have returned along that Szechwan road,[5]
The palace attendants all white-headed now in their lonely inner
    chambers!
The light of his lonely lamps never falls on the returning spirit;
Night rain beats on the *wu-t'ung* tree through the sad, dreary autumn.
(chcsc, 8/15a–15b)   (TR. IRVING Y. LO)

Lin Hung (c. *1383*)

Drinking Wine

Confucian scholars love strange antiquity,
No sooner open their mouth than gab about Yao and Shun.
If they were born before the time of Fu-hsi,[1]
What'd have been the topic of their discourse?
Now the ancients have all passed away,
And their ways are found in what they left behind.
But since not a single word in them can be made good,
Ten thousand volumes are all useless things.
So I wish only to drink my wine,
And not to know the rest.   10
Look, the people in the Land of the Happy-drunk
Lived long before Heaven and earth began.
(WANG, SER. 2; 3.II/3a)   (TR. IRVING Y. LO)

---

4 Here the poet refers to the story about the revels of Emperor Yang of the
Sui dynasty, who is said to have collected thousands of fireflies and then
released them in the imperial park in Chiang-tu (modern Yang-chou).

5 Upon the outbreak of the An Lu-shan rebellion, Ming Huang took refuge
in Szechwan; after the emperor's return to Ch'ang-an (following the sac-
rifice of Yang Kuei-fei at Ma-wei), he is said to have employed Taoist
mediums in a vain attempt to summon back her soul.

1 The earliest of the three mythical emperors in Chinese culture, to whom was
attributed the invention of the hexagram.

Saying Farewell to Magistrate Ch'en Ta-yu

Old friends sigh at long separation;
Once met, we have to part again.
The road of parting follows autumn rain;
Returning carriage enters the evening clouds.
In the maple grove a thousand leaves have fallen,
The river's flow divides into many streams.
When I see the moon over an empty bridge,
Full of longing, it'll remind me of you.
(WANG, SER. 2; 3.II/8a)   (TR. IRVING Y. LO)

Sailing at Night on Flowing-sand River[1]

The sun is about to set when I board the boat;
As it comes out of the cove, the clouds are calm.
The moon darkens where I cross the river,
In the north wind I hear the marsh reeds whistle.
(WANG, SER. 2; 3.II/11b)   (TR. IRVING Y. LO)

Inscribed on the Painting "Pleasures of the Lute by the River"

The Uncarved Block[1] professes no activity,
Greatest hearing is attuned to the slightest sound.
But how about Po Ya the master musician
Who still longed for hills and stream?
I have a tune of hoary antiquity
Which yearns for the accompaniment of a lute.
The world is now given over to solitude,
Let's not startle the dragons from the depth.
(LYWSH, 20a)   (TR. IRVING Y. LO)

---

1 Liu-sha River, located south of Ch'ang-p'ing *hsien*, Shensi.
1 *Ta-p'o,* a Taoist metaphor from the *Tao-te-ching* which symbolizes the original state of complete simplicity, the highest ideal.

Yü Ch'ien (1394–1457)

A Poem on Coal

Split open the massive chaos to obtain black gold;
Genial warmth stored in its veins, there's the mystery.
When kindled into flame, it brings back the bright spring;
Cast in a huge burner, its light shatters the long night's gloom.
On it depends the tripods' and wine vessels' life-giving strength;
In iron and stone there still remains a deathless heart!
Its only wish, enough food and warmth for the people—
And so, enduring much hardship, it forsakes the mountain grove.
(CKLTSH, P. 910)   (TR. WU-CHI LIU)

Shen Chou (1427–1509)

Inscribed on a Painting

White clouds, like a belt, wind around the waist of the mountains;
A path narrow and long soars into the void, off a stony ledge.
Alone, I lean on a thornwood staff and gaze peacefully into the
  distance;
Wishing to respond with my flute playing to the singing of the
  mountain stream.
(PAINTING IN NELSON GALLERY, KANSAS CITY, MO.)

                                        (TR. DANIEL BRYANT)

Returning Home at Dusk from Town, on the Fifteenth of the Seventh Month

Why should I have raced my boat home from town at dusk?
For fear my fisherman's cloak of rush would be soiled
  by the dust of the market place.
Only when I reached home did I realize
  I had fought with wind and rain;
On my two banana trees were many broken leaves.
(STC, PP. 687–88)   (TR. IRVING Y. LO)

Inscribed on the Fan of a Wealthy Old Man

Deep in a kingfisher hall, someone is heavy with wine,
The wind-blown curtain flaps against a silver hook.
In front of the gate, he's startled to see spring helter-skelter,
Then he begrudges the blown petals scattered to the neighborhood.
(STC, P. 690)   (TR. IRVING Y. LO)

Wine Cup and Bright Moon

The moon is coming up the blue sky,
It falls into my wine cup.
When wine is gone, the moon suddenly disappears,
But in Heaven, eternally, it lives on.
(STC, P. 679)   (TR. IRVING Y. LO)

Inscribed on a Painting

Looking at the clouds,
    one might say the green mountain moves;
Who would imagine
    the clouds so busy, the mountain so serene?
How laughable he is:
    this man of the mountain—he won't keep still—
All morning long,
    washing his inkstone, sketching the mountain and the clouds.
(STC, P. 760)   (TR. IRVING Y. LO)

T'ang Yin (1470–1523)

Inscribed on a Painting of a Cock

The red comb on its head needs no adorning,
It struts, its body covered in snow-white feathers.
All its life it dares make few utterances,
But when it crows, ten thousand doors burst open.
(LJC, 3/1a)   (TR. CHIANG YEE)

Inscribed on a Painting

Light mist girdles the mountain,
Cool winds gather round the treetops.
Listening to the brook, he practices quietness,
Standing upright, his face level with the bridge.
(LJC, 3/31b–32a) (TR. CHIANG YEE)

Hsü Wei (1521–1593)

Inscribed on a Painting of Windy Bamboo, to Be Presented to Tzu-kan

A gift for you should not be vulgar,
I paint for you bamboo in the wind.
Just listen to the sound of the topmost branches,
Is it the wind or someone weeping?
If only one could paint the windy bamboo as if weeping:
The old saying is "in painting a tiger,
    it's difficult to paint the bones."
(HWCSC, P. 457) (TR. CHIANG YEE)

Abandoning the Plan of Visiting West Lake

Don't say there are only hills and slopes at West Lake,
It has always been a prince's preserve of wild geese and ducks.
When autumn water overflows the embankment, level as a glass,
Seagulls fly off in a row to peck at fishes.
(HWC3C, P. 820) (TR. IRVING Y. LO)

Untitled

Colossal:
    like towers and pavilions from the flat plain;
Infinitesimal:
    like particles of dust on a clear day at sunrise—

Taken together, these two things just can't stand comparison:
Clearly, the rolling waves of the sea in endless chase.
(HWCSC, P. 803)   (TR. IRVING Y. LO)

Lotus

When the flower droops and the leaf wilts,
    the lotus can barely hold up the dew;
Lowering their heads, the wild geese fly by in silent grief.
Slowly the light of the lake spreads, level as one's palm—
When autumn comes, there's no place for a dragonfly to perch.
(HWCSC, P. 888)   (TR. IRVING Y. LO)

Ch'ien Ch'ien-yi (1582–1664)

On the Road to Western Hill

How lovely the Imperial Mound, but when can I visit it?
In my dreams the Western Hill has often eased my longing.
Rocks in the stream, parched for rain, show only their skeleton;
Orioles among flowers, when spring is aging, are quite without charm.
Homing crows, above the night watchman's beat, sound sad and
    urgent;
A lean horse in the slanting sun is relaxed and slow of gait.
Coming and going, the phoenix birds[1] fly in measured formation;
Only those tired wings alone are flapping ineffectually.
(NO. 1 FROM A SERIES OF 2; MCCHC, 2/4b)   (TR. IRVING Y. LO)

Poems Written in Prison, Three Selections

[1]

Nightly the watchman's rattle startles my sleep,
    awaking me from my everyday dream;
Broad daylight appears darker than the night,
    the night as long as a year—

---

[1] *Wan-hung,* identified as birds of the phoenix family, are sometimes mentioned in poetry with the connotation of "officials."

All in an interminable day, to wear out a long imprisonment,
My soul in solitude, my only companion on a solitary bed.
Where the cell ground is painted, there's still earth under my feet[1];
An inverted basin[2] above my head, there's but a tiny patch of sky.
In this midst before I understand the principles of roaming the
    universe,
I've studied in vain the first chapter of the Nan-hua scripture.[3]

[2]

Spluttering burnt-out lamp blazes in the dusk,
Winter's blast, rasping and shrill, beats upon the matted door.
I seize a pretext for sorrow to sustain myself through the long night;
And count on bad dreams to call back my fettered soul.
Fame and renown vanishing before my eyes, only a caged lamp is
    here;
Lying on my pillow, I recount wordly affairs from the start.
Rising from my sleep, with blurred eyes, I prop up my white head;
It's easy to tell that the web of law is the imperial favor.

[3]

A fishing cove and long lines of fishermen's huts,
Winter plum blossoms on thousands of trees, and a painted boat—
Soft green leaves burgeon from under the eaves in the ample heat of
    the sun;
Unsuspecting red flowers emerge from water, leaning on the breeze.
An ornamented carriage always chary of the flower-strewn ground.
A screened balcony most pleasant on a drizzling day—
My dream trails off to fine spring scenes south of the river;
From my prison pit, I talk to you about the fairyland.
(NOS. 1, 19, 20 FROM A SERIES OF 30; MCCHC, 12/2b, 7a)

(TR. IRVING Y. LO)

---

1 Referring to the practice of marking a circle on the floor of a prison cell,
where a prisoner's feet are allowed no freedom of movement for a period
of time.
2 Referring to the expression "It's difficult to see light under an inverted basin";
the meaning here is that it is not easy to right an injustice.
3 The first chapter of Chuang Tzu, also known as *Nan-hua Ching*, is entitled
"Roaming the Universe."

A Rebuttal of [Su] Tung-p'o's Poem on "Bathing the Infant," Written on the Ninth Day of the Ninth Month in the Year *I-ssu* [1629]

Master Tung-p'o, in raising children, was afraid of their being clever;
All my life I was ruined because I was dull and dumb.
I still wish my son to be born cagey and cunning,
So he could drill through heaven and earth to attain the highest rank.
(MCCHC, 9/2a)　　　　　　　　　　　　　　　　(TR. IRVING Y. LO)

Drinking Wine

The world is full of those who love to be officials,
Never again can they savor the sweet taste of wine.
There are also those who love wine,
They have no time to ponder how good it is to be an official.
Love of wine makes people wild,
Love of official life turns them base.
Even when his insides rot, a drinker won't quit drinking;
In the wee hours of the night, an official won't stop working.
To be fond of wine or to crave for titles,
Each in its own way can cause death.　　　　　　　　　　10

I have always loved being an official,
A junior secretary[1] wasn't too lowly for me.
But I'm also among those who love wine,
My cellar is always full.
This year my luck runs afoul—
Dismissed from office, I didn't do well with wine either.
With a long sigh, I say goodby to the capital:
I know it's time to pack up and leave!
(NO. 5 FROM A SERIES OF 7; MCCHC, 7/3b)　　　　(TR. IRVING Y. LO)

---

1 *Shih-lang,* "junior secretary," is the title Ch'ien held in the Board of Ceremonies during the early 1620s.

"Willow Branch Songs," Two Selections

[1]

Must I lament the time that's gone because I've been cast aside?
I've had my days when flowers bloom and flowers fall.
The green bank by the river is said to be like fragrant grass:
It'll ever follow the wanderer to the end of the world.

[2]

A crescent moon hangs on the tip of the willows,
New leaves are like eyebrows, the moon's like a hook.
Wait till the moon is round and reflected in a mirror
To lift from my eyebrows ten thousand layers of grief.
(NOS. 7, 9 FROM A SERIES OF 10; MCCHC 11/12b–13a)

(TR. IRVING Y. LO)

T'an Yüan-ch'un (1586–1631)

Heard on a Boat

Willows cannot hide a bright moon's sorrow,
Cast upon the river's gleam and a small boat.
If distant bells crossing the water should seem moist,
It's because, when they reach my ears, autumn is here already.
(TYHHC, P. 374)

(TR. IRVING Y. LO)

Ch'en Tzu-lung (1608–1647)

A Ballad of the Little Cart

Rattling little cart and patches of yellow dust at dusk—
Husband pushed,
Wife pulled.
Leaving home, hapless, where could they go?

"Green are the elm leaves, they can cure our hunger.
Oh, would there be a happy land where to eat our gruels together!"

The wind blew on the yellowing weeds.
They gazed toward the walls of a house,
Hoping the host inside would feed them.

Knocks on the door, no one answers;   10
    inside, not even a cooking pot.
Aimlessly pacing the empty lane, they shed tears like rain.
(WANG, SER. 1; 7.1/7a–7b)   (TR. WU-CHI LIU)

A Parable

East of the river there's a foul bird
Which calls itself the bald pelican.[1]
It feeds on fish, barely cramming its throat;
Its feathers are simply a disgrace.
That's why from the bank where it stands,
Gulls and egrets always fly far away.

Whence comes this grayish hawk,
With iron plumage and pupils flashing gold?
Though not at all elegant or refined,
Still it plots to swoop and strike.   10
It chooses not to soar high to the heavens,
But comes down, hovering over the cold river stream.
Sidewise, it edges to the pelican and eats its fill;
Then, spreading both wings, it flies off to roam the skies.

How could a lower stream become habitable?
Noble or base: each seeks what he will.
That's why the mind of an aged crane
Remains aloof and disdains the high autumn.
(WANG, SER. 1; 7.1/8a–8b)   (TR. IRVING Y. LO)

-----

[1] *T'u-ch'iu*, a type of water bird, or bald crane, larger than a crane and of dark gray color. It has a bald, red top, yellow beak, and a pouch like a pelican's; it loves to feed on refuse, fishes, and snakes.

Tune: "Telling of Innermost Feelings"
Wandering in Spring

Beneath the small peach branches,
She tried on her silken dress:
A butterfly's powdered wings struggling with the lingering scent.
The carriage's jade wheels ground fine the blossoms;
On her half-hidden face, annoyance showed in her rouge makeup.

Wind suddenly was warm,
As the sun began to climb.
In the curled willow branches,
A pair of dancing swallows,
Ten thousand swirling flowers,   10
And the ground flooded by the setting sun.
(CKLTTH, P. 354)   (TR. BRUCE CARPENTER)

Wu Wei-yeh (1609–1671)

View of the Countryside

The Yangtze rushes past the capital
Where can the traveler's thoughts find a resting place?
White bones lie buried beneath new mounds of earth;
Green mountains surround the city in several ranges.
Past the lofty tower drive sheets of rain;
Above the solitary pagoda marshal armies of returning clouds.
At dusk, sad notes sound from a reed-leaf whistle;
Wintry crows fly silently across a tractless sky.
(WSCL, 8.11/13a)   (TR. CHANG YIN-NAN AND LEWIS C. WALMSLEY)

Sailing at Dusk from T'u-sung[1]

The lonely moon loiters above the village;
Shivering waves scutter back and forth.

---
[1] A city about 10 miles north of T'ai-ch'ang in Kiangsu province.

Voices come from beneath the bamboo matting on the boats;
Heavy ropes sink in the water by the tree at the bridge.
I shall risk sailing my light boat in the frost;
As I put on my clothes, I hear cocks crow in the early dawn.
The bamboo weir sounds like roaring rapids,[2]
Rushes in the islet rustle like summer rain.
Fishermen chatter as they enter the estuary;
Farmers, frightened, call their families from the gate.   10
Some lights from the lamps can still be seen;
Voices of old men and women merge with the market clatter.
The river changes its course, and shops have moved away;
Until now I have met only one sailboat.
For a livelihood, there're sedges and wild rushes[3] to be gathered;
This marshland becomes isolated from the world.
I should now say goodby to friends and relatives,
Pole my boat in and settle here the rest of my life.
(WSCL, 1.I/3a–3b)   (TR. CHANG YIN-NAN AND LEWIS C. WALMSLEY)

On the Twenty-fourth of the Third Month, in the Year Ting-wei [1667] I Sailed Across Lake T'ai from Behind the Mountain and Stayed Overnight at the Fountain-of-Good-Fortune Monastery

Twilight has already descended upon a thousand trees,
But a solitary peak is still aglow in the setting sun.
With each flight of steps I climb, my body seems to grow taller;
The woodland path is soon lost in the distance.
Looking back through the gap of the mountain pass,
From above the treetops, I see the lake's shimmering light.
Pine cones drop in front of me,
As the priest opens the door of his stone lodge.
The rent from an orange grove allows him to cultivate his mind;
Sufficient unto himself, this man with silver eyebrows and white
    hair.   10
Sporadic sounds of musical stones tinkle clearly,
Flowing water meanders through the bamboo thicket.
How fortunate I am to be able

---

2 When run over by the moving boat.
3 Implying that the people make their living by cultivating a kind of inferior rice (*ku*) and making mats, bags, etc. from a kind of rush (*p'u*) plant.

To rest for a while in Master Chih's[1] bed!
When the traveler's dream enters the blue-green mountains,
The affairs of the world can indeed be put aside.
(WSCL, 3.II/1a)   (TR. CHANG YIN-NAN AND LEWIS C. WALMSLEY)

Visiting the Garden at Monk Wen Ko's Home

Shadows of the sails pass across his window;
The toll of a monastery bell floats above the treetops.
Ripe fruits hang under the eaves of his house;
Reclining pine trees lean upon one another beyond the terrace.
Pods on the legumes ripen early this spring;
Tea leaves sprout late after the rain.
While visiting this quiet study, leisurely, alone,
I expect to meet there this saintly man.
(WSCL, 8.I/2a)   (TR. CHANG YIN-NAN AND LEWIS C. WALMSLEY)

Tune: "Sand of Silk-washing Stream"

A faint flush spreads all over her cheeks, still sleepy-eyed,
Softly, swiftly, she walks down the steps.
Plucking flowers from a tall branch, she shows off her lissome body.

Gently stirring incense in the burner —
    fragrance spreads all around;
Gingerly writing a line of verse on paper—
    the ink runs aslant.
Used to guessing trivial things,
    she thinks of herself as clever.
(WSCL, 19.I/6b)   (TR. IRVING Y. LO)

Tune: "Song of River City" (*Chiang-ch'eng tzu*)
On a Kite

Willow floss in the swift wind races against the Spring Festival.
    Hoisted by children,

---

1 Chih-tun, a Buddhist monk who devoted his life to studying and interpreting
Buddhism in a monastery on Chih-hsing Mountain in Kiangsu province; cf.
note to Kao Ch'i's poem "Cold Spring."

Running everywhere,
A sheet of paper, wind-driven, it desires to ascend to the heavens;
And the wandering thread, ten thousand feet long, cannot hold its
    course.
            But when it hits the ground,
            Suddenly it grows still.

Upon whose manipulation shall it depend to fly again and whistle?[1]
            To ride with ease on the wind,
            To startle a few people?   10
In March, south of the river, one can hear hawks cry:
The zither of Chao and the lute of Ch'in sound from beyond the
    heavens;
            Melodies inexhaustible,
            "East of the Blue Sea."[2]
(WSCL, 19.II/4b)   (TR. IRVING Y. LO)

Chu Yi-tsun (*1629–1709*)

Majestic Valley

Birds become frightened when the mountain moon sets;
Trees stand still when the valley wind dies.
When the monastery drum rolls through the deep forest,
The hermit monks have already prepared their meal.
(PSTC, 6/3a)   (TR. CHANG YIN-NAN AND LEWIS C. WALMSLEY)

---

1 *Feng-yüan*, or a Chinese kite, makes a whistling sound in the wind; hence,
  it is also called *feng-cheng;* the second character in the compound is also the
  name of a musical instrument (line 12), here translated as "lute."
2 This line is believed to allude to two lines of poetry: "The Song of Liang-chou
  in new melodies,/Played the story of the Heavenly Geese fleeing from the
  Blue Sea." The term *"hai-tung-ch'ing,"* literally, "sea-east-blue," is actually
  the name of a species of hawk from Liao-tung (eastern Manchuria). Its
  blue feathers are valuable for use in making fur coats. Chin Jung-fan, the
  editor of the 1775 edition of *Wu-shih chi-lan,* offers the interpretation
  that this is an allegorical poem, describing the political career of Wu's
  former enemy Juan Ta-ch'eng, whose courtesy-name was "Yüan-hai," or
  "Round Sea."

West Cliff

Early in the morning I hear monkeys call from the mouth of the
    gorge;
In the evening I sleep with the moon on a rocky cliff.
Through the long night winds blow from the heavens;
On the west precipice cassias burst into bloom.
(PSTC, 5/11b)   (TR. CHANG YIN-NAN AND LEWIS C. WALMSLEY)

Deepening-Green Pavilion

A single pavilion looms dark against cloud and forest;
The mountain ravine echoes the monkeys' plaintive cry.
As the heavy mist dampens my clothing,
The setting sun suddenly pours down on me.
(PSTC, 5/12a)   (TR. CHANG YIN-NAN AND LEWIS C. WALMSLEY)

Inscribed on the Painting of "Garden for Retirement": Pavilion of Sincerity, on Rocky Mountain

From distant grove I hear the occasional knell of a monastery bell;
Rays of the setting sun climb up the tallest trees.
Facing each other, I suddenly forget words,
My heart's delight lies in quiet solitude.
(PSTC, 6/16b)   (TR. CHANG YIN-NAN AND LEWIS C. WALMSLEY)

Listening-to-the-Rain Studio

The wind sways the blossoms of the rock orchids;
Tender reeds grow quickly in the rain.
Vivid dreams carry me back to deserted mountains:
A mass of fallen petals, and the babbling of a crimson creek.
(PSTC, 6/17a)   (TR. CHANG YIN-NAN AND LEWIS C. WALMSLEY)

Written at Mauve Garden: Pine Wind Terrace

The mountain moon shines on a cloudless sky.
Deep in the night the wind rises among the pines.

I wish to weave my thoughts into a song for my jade lute,
But the pine wind never ceases blowing.
(PSTC, 11/5a)   (TR. CHANG YIN-NAN AND LEWIS C. WALMSLEY)

Tune: "Song of Divination"

Fading dream lingers by the hills on the screen,
Incense smoke dissolves into tiny ancient scripts.[1]
All day the curtain at the window hangs limp,
Swallows chatter, but human voice is still.

On courtyard grass, the mist has already gathered;
From willows by the gate, catkins are ready to float down.
I've heard enough of last night's wind on the pear blossoms,
And tonight there's rain at dusk.
(PSTC, 27/1b)   (TR. IRVING Y. LO)

Tune: "Song of the Southern Country"

Tomorrow we part,
     Don't linger over tonight's moon bright as silver.
I wish only the wind and rain at daybreak
          Will last till dusk,
And the cuckoo wearies of crying, "Rush me, I won't go."[1]
(PSTC, 27/5a)   (TR. IRVING Y. LO)

Tune: "Song of the Southern Country"
Spring Thoughts at Pearl River[1]

Soft colored clouds obscured by the sun; [Wang Wei]
Red upon red, green upon green, flowers in the park: [Wang Chien]
How can I enhance this fine poetic feeling? [Ssu-k'ung T'u]

---

[1] I.e., the seal script (*chüan-shu*) a style characterized by angular strokes.
[1] A variation of the onomatopoeic transcription of the cry of the cuckoo from *pu-ju kuei* ("Better go home") to *ts'ui pu-ch'ü;* cf. note to Lu Yu's poem "On Hearing the Cuckoo at Night."
[1] This is an example of the "collected lines" (*chi-chü*) verse. The names appearing in brackets following each line are the original authors. Also see Huang T'ing-chien's "Living in Exile at Ch'ien-nan" where the four lines were all taken from the works of Po Chü-yi.

  Listen to the spring birds: [Ku K'uang]
After they've flown, the flowering branches still dance gracefully.
  [Wei Ying-wu]
(PSTC, 30/2a)   (TR. IRVING Y. LO)

Wang Shih-chen (1634–1711)

What Strikes My Eye

Desolate, this rainy autumn evening;
Gray and vast, the Yangtze dusk in Ch'u.
At times I see a boat gliding
Dim and indistinct beyond the river's clouds.
(YYCHL, 5.1/18a)   (TR. RICHARD JOHN LYNN)

Dawn at Chiao Mountain, Seeing Off K'un-lun on His Way Back to Ching-k'ou

In the mountain temple they beat the Dharma Drum,[1]
As the river moon hangs suspended over wintry trees.
Far away I see off this man from the South;
A cock crows as the tall, narrow sail departs.
(YYCHL, 5.1/21a)   (TR. RICHARD JOHN LYNN)

Written Beneath Hui Mountain, When Tsou Liu-yi Comes by for a Visit

After rain a bright moon appears;
Its gleam lights the view down the mountain path.
Across the mist-shrouded stream, someone is talking:
"Can you tell me where I can moor my boat?"
(YYCHL, 5.1/28a)   (TR. RICHARD JOHN LYNN)

---

[1] The Dharma Drum, or Drum of the Law (*fa-ku*), is sounded in temples to summon the monks to the dawn service.

On the Way to Huang-ch'ang River[1]

Cloud reflections float on flooded paddies;
The clear spring still crookedly courses down.
This river country suits the evening glow—
As water plants enter into cool autumn.
On the sands birds fly about then rest,
Caltrop tendrils scatter and again pause.
Slowly I look down over Kua-pu's banks:
Beyond the flowers lie several fishing boats.
(NO. 2 FROM A SERIES OF 2; YYCHL, 6.I/11a) (TR. RICHARD JOHN LYNN)

Occasional Poem: Upon Seeing Lotuses Bloom in a Vase

On that day when I brought wine to Red Bridge,
I sailed in a small boat east of the lotus pads.
Quietly resting on the sand, the birds were white;
Scattered about the islet, the flowers were red.
The bright mirror created a lucid glow;
The clear stream was placid in the gentle breeze.
Since we've parted it's been a thousand days,
And now again I meet you in this pear-shaped vase.
(NO. 1 FROM A SERIES OF 2; YYCHL, 6.I/22b) (TR. RICHARD JOHN LYNN)

Moonlit Night at Fragrant Mountain Temple[1]

The bright moon appears from the east ridge,
And the summits become still all at once.
Melting snow still covers the ground,
Lying in shadow before the western lodge.
The hue of bamboos makes the solitude complete,
As pine shadows bewitch the shimmering ripples.
All this brilliance shines forth at once—
A myriad of images all pure and fresh.

---

[1] A small river that flows into the Yangtze in the vicinity of Kua-pu Mountain.
[1] Fragrant Mountain Temple on Fragrant Mountain (Hsiang-shan), a summit of West Mountain, is in Yüan-p'ing—then a suburb northwest of Peking.

Now there's someone rapt in meditation;
It's midnight and he still hasn't gone to sleep.   10
(YYCHL, 2.II/9b)   (TR. RICHARD JOHN LYNN)

Arriving After Rain at the Temple of Heavenly Peace

Having gone out through the west city wall in the chilly dawn,
I arrived at the Buddhist temple just after a fresh rain.
As the sun came up there was no one to meet,
But the whole courtyard was filled with the chatter of wind bells.
(YYCHL, 9.I/18b)   (TR. RICHARD JOHN LYNN)

Lieh Mountain

The red walls of the old temple emerge from the blur of
   the blue-green mountain;
Water from the lichen- and moss-covered precipice
   spatters our clothes.
A formation of white herons takes off and rushes at our boat,
And then flies to the top of a pine tree halfway up the cliff.
(YYCHL, 10.I/10b–11a)   (TR. RICHARD JOHN LYNN)

Sailing Along the Tai Stream from Stone Bridge
to the Foot of Mo-ho Peak

As the sun sets, the mountain air becomes cool;
The clear stream winds back and forth on its course.
Searching for its source, I forget my weariness;
Gradually I become unaware of how far I've traveled.
Dark rocks thrust themselves upward into sharp precipices,
While tall trees stand graceful, beautiful.
The path before me is hard to make out;
The trail behind changes its shape many times.
Out of the silence strange sounds echo from the elephantine range;
In the desolate air, how pleasant is the evening breeze.   10
From a hidden path, a woodcutter emerges at dusk;
And above stiff cliffs, birds winging homeward appear.
Quickly as the evening mists fade,
Twilight floods the mountains all around.

Then a new moon rises, clear, enchanting,
While rosy clouds spread out and roll up in billows.
I feel my linen gown a little too thin,
But my bamboo staff makes me feel agile and strong.
A "man of mountain and valleys"[1] all my life—
I hope I shall be able to carry out this promise.   20

(YYCHL, 1.1/6b–7a)   (TR. CHANG YIN-NAN AND LEWIS C. WALMSLEY)

Na-lan Hsing-te (1655–1685)

Tune: Remembering the Prince" (*Yi Wang-sun*)

All night the west wind cuts the banana leaves;
through the autumn, wearied eyes have endured the loneliness.
Grudgingly, I give myself up to the unstrained wine.
While reading the *Li Sao*,
my sorrow resembles,
day after day, night after night,
the Hsiang River tides.

(NLT, 1/1a)   (TR. WILLIAM GOLIGHTLY)

Tune: "Partridge Sky"
Parting Sorrows

Back to him,
        exquisite, graceful, coy
        she stands there
        pretending.

Plum pistils roll between her palms,
        the petals tap her shoulder.

She has meant to tell her lover how much she detests partings;
        and yet, here he is, and she—.
                Grief strangely quiets.

---

1 The poet had in mind to visit all the famous mountains of China.

The clouds are untroubled,
    the waters, edgeless;

a sound of flute locks emptiness to the room.

When can these two drift as one
    with the spring moon
    in flood—

A leaf of a boat
    between steep banks
    of drooping willows?
(NLT [ADDENDA], 1a)   (TR. WILLIAM GOLIGHTLY)

Tune: "Remembering the Lady of Ch'in (*Yi Ch'in-o*)
    At the Mouth of Dragon Pool

Mountain after mountain
            fold by fold
Each overhanging cliff
    like a thread splits the sky;
        Like a thread splits the sky;
And on the broken headstones
Old mosses gnaw at inscribed words.

Thunderous winds
    clang like metal;
Dark, forbidding, at the bottom of the pool,
    the cave of the landslide dragon;
        The cave of the landslide dragon;
    we watch prosperity,
    we watch decline,   10
the rise and the fall of dynastic houses,
        under an old moon.
(NLT, 2/4b–5a)   (TR. LENORE MAYHEW AND WILLIAM MCNAUGHTON)

Tune: "A Big String of Words" (*Yi-lo-suo*)
The Great Wall

The moorland fires are gathered up
      into the green clouds.
The west wind howls in the night.
Over the dark fields the wings of wild geese
      pattern the autumn sky
Like mountaintops sketched on a screen.

Through how many panels of mountains and seas
Do the high parapets of the long wall
      wind and wind?
Our eyes follow, slope after slope,
      and we understand
How it ate up the dragon hearts of our grandfathers.
And in the end they built it for whom?
      For the benefit of what clan?   10
(NLT, 2/3a)   (TR. LENORE MAYHEW AND WILLIAM MCNAUGHTON)

Tune: "Butterflies Lingering over Flowers"
Leaving the Border

Today as in the past, who is the master of these rivers and
    mountains?
In the sound of the Tartar bugle,
Herds of horses have often come and gone.
With desolation everywhere before my eyes, what's there to say?
The west wind blowing ages the red maple trees.

To whom can I tell my hidden grief?
Golden lances, armored horses,
Green mounds, the twilight road.
Deep are my feelings, but how deep?
Setting sun deep in the mountain, late autumn rain!   10
(NLT, 3/8b–9a)   (TR. AN-YAN TANG)

Tune: "Song of a Dandy"
Hunting in Autumn

Withered grass on the plain.
After the Festival of Double Nines
From trees yellow leaves begin to flutter down.
I recall the jade bridle, my hair all black, the season of fallen
    blossoms,
And people gathering kingfisher feathers;
Suddenly I remember the notes of a flute.
But now there are only parched traces of the green that is gone,
Everywhere, shadows of frost on faded swirls of red;
Autumn waters reflecting the sky,
Chilling mist like a brocade,   10
Where the vultures fly,
The sky is somber, the clouds are high.

A man must take his pleasure,
Don't you know,
Easily the temples turn gray?
Since I've parted from the east wind,
I've suddenly grown crestfallen.
Why should I care for fame?
All my life,
I have worn a short cloak and shot at tigers,   20
Bought wine in the western suburb;
But I'll turn toward the sun's setting rays
And, leaning on my horse, put on a hero's air.
(NLT, 4/6b)   (TR. BRUCE CARPENTER)

Tune: "Autumn Waters" (*Ch'iu-shui*)
Listening to Rain

Who claims one needs wine to dispel grief?
Upon sobering up, my heart becomes intoxicated.[1]
Just then the fragrance dissolves from the kingfisher quilt.
Across the screen, I'm startled to listen:

---

[1] In the sense that "a grieved heart is like drunk."

Drop after drop, threads of rain, mixed with tears.
I recall the time I snuffed out the candles by a dark window,
A light nap, and a dream of loveliness just formed,
Then awakened again and again—
A pair of eyes brimming with tears.

The same as in the old days, amid the buzzing of crickets—   10
A low lamp glows, then dims;
How can I sleep?
Pondering on my life's footprints several years past
The storm waves higher than my head—
All that I needed was a glance from her beneath blossoms;
To press close to her tall dressed hair before the lamp;
I asked when we could again share together
The taste of night rain on vacant stairs.

(NLT, 4/3b–4a)   (TR. BRUCE CARPENTER)

Tune: "Immortal at the River"
Winter Willow

Flying catkins, flying floss, where have they gone?
Layers of ice, banks of snow, have hastened their withering.
One tree with sparse twigs stands in the dawn's chill.
I love that nice bright moon there,
But it might be that I'm wearied and worn.

Most surely, when the thick silken strands have fallen off,
The memory of green hills will come back again.
A dream of skirt-splashing[1] once broken, it'll be hard to renew.
With so much remorse in the west wind,
Still it cannot smooth out my knitted brows.

(NLT, 3/7b)   (TR. IRVING Y. LO)

---

[1] Alluding to the meeting with a girl, as in the preface to Li Shang-yin's poem about his meeting with a girl named Willow Branch. Cf. James J. Y. Liu, *The Poetry of Li Shang-yin*, p. 139, and notes. The splashing of a woman's skirt in the river refers to a springtime ritual a kind of purification rite. It may also contain a hidden reference to an illicit love affair.

Cheng Hsieh (1693–1765)

For Contemporary Artist Pien Wei-ch'i[1]

You paint the wild geese as if I could see them crying,
And on this double-threaded silk, the rustling sound of river reeds.
On the tip of your brush, how infinitely chill is the autumn wind;
Everywhere on the mountain pass is the sorrow of parting.
(CPCC, P. 89)   (TR. IRVING Y. LO)

Inscribed on a Painting

Green hills on both banks—mounds of rice kernels[1];
The Long River, narrow and straight—a bolt of cloth on the shuttle;
In a thousand years, those who have gone to battle
All are gathered up in the torn net of a fisherman.
(CPCC, P. 49)   (TR. IRVING Y. LO)

The Small Garden

Moonlight, harsh and clear, floods the high pavilion.
The night still young, the wicket gate is half-open.
A lantern moving among trees announces the guest's arrival;
Smoke rises from the bamboos in answer to my call for tea.
The dog barks now and then at the falling of autumn stars;
Gusts of wind disperse the sad sounds of a distant flute.
Rapt in talk, we sit till the dawn slowly comes up,
As brightly colored clouds and cool dew overspread the green moss.
(CPCC, P. 109)   (TR. WU-CHI LIU)

---

[1] *Author's note:* "Pien Wei-ch'i, whose courtesy-name is Yi-kung, also called
Shou-ming, is a *hsiu-ts'ai* from Shang-yang [in modern Honan] and is
especially skilled in painting the wild geese."
[1] Referring to one technique of Chinese painting, the application of tiny dots,
similar to Western pointillism.

Tune: "Full River Red"
A Four-season Song on the Hardships and Joys of Farming Life

I [Spring]

Fine rain, gentle thunder,
 After Startling-of-the Insects,[1] warm breeze stirs the earth—
It's the season for the elders to send farmhands early to work,
 On the eastern acres or southern field.
Hoe on shoulders under an evening moon—the village dogs bark;
Calves mooing beneath dawn stars—the hills shrouded in mist.
Rising at fifth watch, when startled by cocks crowing out of turn,
 Such are the hardships of farming life.

Beyond a distant fence
Peach trees abloom;   10
Above the banks of the pond
Tender willow branches—
 Slowly the sun warms the thatched eaves;
 Young girls put on thin dress.
Everywhere in the garden spring leeks ready for cutting;
 New Year wine, half a jug, to share with friends.
It's a delight to see white-heads get drunk, leaning on white-heads.
 Such are the joys of farming life.

II [Summer]

Ripples of wheat toss in the wind,
 It's again the early sprouting of grain seedlings, now halfway out.
Just watch those whirring spars above the dikes,
 Splattering silver streams, splashing milk!
Take off your straw hat, let the rain comb smooth the hair on your
head;
While weeding, let your sweat fall on the root of the growing grain.
And busy at raising silkworms, women rush about, gathering mulberry
leaves.
 Such are the hardships of farming life.

---

1 *Ching-chih* ("Startling-of-the-insects") refers to a period in the lunar calendar,
corresponding to March 5–20.

Flustering wind
Shakes the broad bamboo leaves; 10
Amid the rustling sound
Float down new bamboo-skins.
Just the season of green river-reeds on the surface of the water,
And red pomegranate by the corner of the house.
Boys giggle in the field picking melons,
Wash their feet in the pond in the slanting sun.
In the evening breeze, everyone talks of nonsense.
Such are the joys of farming life.

III [Autumn]

Light clouds, swift wind,
Send off one mournful sound of the wild goose.
The farmers' chief worry is the weather for drying the grain:
Should the day be cloudy, or should it rain?
But before you store up the frosted stalks to last the whole year,
District officers are searching everywhere for tax-dodging households,
And ferocious agents as a rule more demanding than the magistrate!
Such are the hardships of farming life.

When the purple crabs mature,
Reddish caltrops are peeled, 10
The coir nuts[2] give out a ringing sound,
And village ditties are heard;
Listen to the shattering sounds of festival drums
Fill up the mountain and shake the city walls.
Clasping his zither, the divine shaman spreads words of auspicious omen;
Leaning on their canes, old people raise their wine cups,
To invoke blessings for abundant harvest each year.
Such are the joys of farming life.

IV [Winter]

When the branches of old trees are trimmed,
Winter's angry howl shakes loose the four walls of the house;
Ox urine, all over the ground, can't be cleaned out,
And cow dung's right by the gate.
As the sun slants above the thatched house, clouds gather, snow comes;

---

2 *Kuang-chieh,* or *Arenga saccharifera.*

The road along the embankment blocked, the wind blows down rain.
All night long, villagers hulling the rice, keep fire lit till dawn.
>   Such are the hardships of farming life.

>   Bundles of hay for a bed,
>   Dry rushes for roof,   10
>   Pottery for frying pan,
>   And gourd for a ladle.
>   Cut down some snow-laden pine branches
>   To cook mallow and boil beans;
Bring out the fermented millet wine to rejoice with neighbors.
After you've paid your taxes at the yamen, you leave the city;
Then laugh at your country wife for powdering her face for the New
  Year.
>   Such are the joys of farming life.
(CPCC, PP. 143–44)   (TR. IRVING Y. LO)

Chao Yi (1727–1814)

Rising Early in the Morning

I hate to hear those crazy cocks crowing around a thatched inn;
I get up, half awake, half asleep.
What a clear picture of a traveler's life:
My horse chews the scrap heaps of fodder while a mouse stares at
  the lamp.
(CSPCTP, II, 37)   (TR. CHANG YIN-NAN AND LEWIS C. WALMSLEY)

Strolling in the Countryside

A fierce wind urges me to change into my quilted cotton gown.
Staff in hand, I start strolling across the nearby lonely countryside.
The autumn wind is particularly fond of meddling in other people's
  affairs—
It reddens those maple leaves and whitens man's hair.
(MCSH, P. 95)   (TR. CHANG YIN-NAN AND LEWIS C. WALMSLEY)

In Search of Solitude

I never tire in my search of solitude;
I wander aimlessly along out-of-the-way trails
Where I have never been before,
The more I change my direction, the wilder the road becomes.
Suddenly I come to the bank of a raging river;
The path breaks off, all trails vanish.
No one is there for me to ask directions:
Only a lone egret beside the tall grass, glistening white.
(MCSH, P. 91)   (TR. CHANG YIN-NAN AND LEWIS C. WALMSLEY)

Writing Poetry in the Back Garden

For years I've suffered from extreme poverty,
And this year is even more difficult.
One day my wife came out and told me
That we had nothing for breakfast the next morning.
With a smile I thanked her and turned her away:
"Please do not come here to disturb me:
I'm trying to compose a short poem,
One word still does not sound right.
Wait till my poem has been finished,
Then we can settle our mustard, our salt and our leeks.   10
Woman, look at all those officials on the Ch'ang-an road,
Has a single one of them ever starved to death?"
(MCSH, P. 91)   (TR. CHANG YIN-NAN AND LEWIS C. WALMSLEY)

Huang Ching-jen (1749–1783)

Spring Sentiments

There is good news that spring's in the air,
But how about the rain and the wind?
Sorrowing for me, two candles shed tears;
After conversing with me, a wild goose wings homeward.
The Imperial Palace is as remote as the heavens,
My homeland is unreachable except in dream.

How nasty can the god of spring become—
He won't let the little peach tree burst into red blossoms.
(MCSH, P. 106)   (TR. CHANG YIN-NAN AND LEWIS C. WALMSLEY)

Mixed Emotions

Abstruse Buddhahood and Taoist immortality are both unattainable,
I know only to complain on lonely nights, of my unjust fate.
Like tumbleweeds, my sad songs have all but vanished into the air;
Like willow catkins, my shallow reputation has sunk into mud.
Nine people in ten deserve only the whites of my eyes,[1]
And one hundred percent useless is a scholar!
Should I grieve because my poems have caused me sadness?
Spring birds and autumn insects know how to voice their feelings.
(MCSH, P. 107)   (TR. CHANG YIN-NAN AND LEWIS C. WALMSLEY)

Sentiments on New Year's Eve in the Year Kuei-ssu [1773]

Laughter pours from a thousand homes, as the water clock drips and
    drips—
One learns grief and anxieties in secret, from matters beyond oneself.
Silent and alone, I stand on the market bridge unknown to anyone;
A single star bright as the moon, I watch for a long, long time.
(CSH, P. 59)   (TR. CHANG YIN-NAN AND LEWIS C. WALMSLEY)

Traveling at Break of Day

Having traveled ten *li* from the high city walls,
I can still hear the sound of the night watchman's rattle.
My horse's neigh awakens the birds from their dreams;
My own voice heralds the cocks for their crowing.
Trees huddle together, darkening a thousand hillocks;
Sands drift, brightening the single road.
Anxiously I watch the waning moon,
How sad I am traveling so early in the morning!
(MCSH, P. 106)   (TR. CHANG YIN-NAN AND LEWIS C. WALMSLEY)

---

1 Alluding to the poet Juan Chi, who used to look at people whom he disliked
with only "the whites of his eyes."

Questing-for-Spring Arbor

This idiotic me is left alone to enjoy this solitude,
While boatmen call one another through the mist.
My boat adrift, on which bank of the river shall I sleep tonight?
I can only paddle towards more fragrant waters.
(CSH, P. 59)   (TR. CHANG YIN-NAN AND LEWIS C. WALMSLEY)

Kung Tzu-chen (1792–1841)

The Lute Song

There is a fair one,
Her joy surpasses all joys,
Her sorrow surpasses all sorrows.

The moon shines in the hall:
No, it's not the light of the moon,
It's the light of her eyes.

The fair one is melancholy,
Mountains and rivers fill her heart;
The setting moon has faded;
How can she stop her yearning?

The fair one is melancholy,
Mountains and rivers fill her heart;
Alas, separated across darkness,
She has no one to yearn for!
(KTCCC, P. 446)   (TR. AN-YAN TANG)

Miscellanies of the Year Chi-hai [1839], Seven Selections

[1]

Deep and vast is parting sorrow as the sun slants;
Eastward, a poet's riding whip points to the edge of the world.

Fallen blossoms aren't by nature without feeling:
Changed into mud in spring, they still nurture flower's growth.
(NO. 5 FROM A SERIES OF 315; KTCCC, P. 509)   (TR. IRVING Y. LO)

[2]

Ghosts wailed at night when the ancients invented words;
A hundred anxieties beset men of later ages who know how to read.
I dread neither ghosts nor anxieties:
Night after night I work on ancient texts as autumn lamp turns green.[1]
(NO. 62; KTCCC, P. 515)   (TR. WU-CHI LIU)

[3]

Just to tow one tracking rope takes ten boatmen or more;
I carefully count to a thousand boats that crossed this river.
I have once wasted the grains in the imperial granary[2];
Hearing their harrowing cries, I shed my tears like rain.
(NO. 83; KTCCC, P. 517)   (TR. WU-CHI LIU)

[4]

When young I fenced with sword and played the flute;
The sword's strength and the flute's soul are now both spent.
Who is to share my desolation as my boat comes home?
Countless joy and grief gather on this day.
(NO. 96; KTCCC, P. 518)   (TR. IRVING Y. LO)

[5]

Her message of grace comes down from lofty clouds;
Numerous kalpa will turn to dust before my feelings can be quenched.

---

[1] The title for this quatrain reads: "I always regretted that Hsü Shen [the compiler of *Shuo-wen*, the first Chinese dictionary, in A.D. 100] saw but little of the ancient texts. So based upon a study of the inscriptions on the sacrificial bronze vessels, I added to Hsü's *Shou-wen* 147 words with a description of their forms and meanings. The work was completed in the fourth month of the Year *Wu-hsü* [1838]."

[2] I.e., the salaries of a government official. The title of this quatrain reads: "Written on the twelfth day of the fifth month after I have arrived at Huai-p'u."

A *Ch'an* initiate[3] is naturally timorous at the shadows of flowers—
Awakened from dream, I offer my *gatha* to thank Ling-hsiao.[4]
(NO. 98; KTCCC, P. 518) (TR. IRVING Y. LO)

[6]

A nation's vitality comes from wind and thunder—
How pitiable, the myriad horses have all become dumb!
I urge the Lord of Heaven to reassert himself,
And send down to earth talented men of every description.[5]
(NO. 125; KTCCC, P. 521) (TR. WU-CHI LIU)

[7]

Alone by candlelight in a hall in autumn,
    I listen to the beatings of my heart;
Beyond the screen, who has brought the news of heavy rain?
Tomorrow the scenery along the creek won't be the same:
The bridge there is already sunk under water a foot deep.
(NO. 225; KTCCC, P. 530) (TR. IRVING Y. LO)

My Neighbor's Child Cries in the Middle of the Night

My neighbor's child cries in the middle of the night;
Some say he is thinking of his previous existence.
What does he remember of life before his birth?
He might have wished to be born without literary fame.

I have a portfolio of manuscripts;
Often I worked on them but never completed any.
As I have scribbled away for more than a decade,
Sweet and bitter feelings mingle a thousandfold.

---

3 *Ch'u-ch'an,* in Hinayana Buddhism, refers to the first of the four degrees in the achievement of *dyana* (*ch'an*); in Ch'an Buddhism it also means the "first (*ch'u*) awakening."

4 Name of a woman not identified by the poet.

5 The title of this quatrain reads: "When I passed by Chen-chiang I witnessed temple sacrifices to the Jade Emperor, god of wind, god of thunder, etc. Prayers were said in the thousands. I wrote this at the request of the Taoist priest."

With half the night spent in endless worrying,
I feel the urge to get up and work.   10
I trim the candle and tumble out of bed,
My maid laughs at me and my wife scolds.

When I think I might die the next morning,
My tears crisscrossing my cheeks, fall to the ground.
(KTCCC, P. 441)   (TR. WU-CHI LIU)

Tune: "Decorous and Pretty" (*Tuan-cheng hao*)

Recalling the past years, my heart is often bewildered.
No more can I remember to whom I owe favors or spite.
From a gold incense-burner smoke rises in the gloom of daylight,
       Puff upon puff, to form
       Clouds of idle grief.

A bright moon, flowers in full bloom, and every wish fulfilled by
    Heaven—
But there will still be a time when wine is gone and the lamp blown
    out.
Much better for the quilt to be cold and the fragrant smoke to
    dissolve . . .
       When all alone,
       I ponder upon it a thousand times!   10
(KTCCC, P. 543)   (TR. AN-YAN TANG)

Tune: "Green Jade Cup"

I don't complain that time passes too soon,
    My only regret:
    I've wasted my youth.
My gaze stretches afar toward a floating gossamer—a thread of my love;
A broken bridge and flowing river,
    Sunset and drifting catkins—
       Is that the spring's journey home?

On the pavilion, all day I stood and gazed.
I wish to tell of my grief, but to whom?

On the orchid banks flowers scatter as the day dusks.   10
    Awake I feel as if drunk,
        Drunk, I seem to be dreaming;
           Yet did I really dream?
(KTCCC, P. 547)   (TR. AN-YAN TANG)

Tune: "Butterflies Lingering over Flowers"

Wine presses hard upon spring grief,
    as spring whirls up willow catkins—
When swallows return,
    they bitterly tell of springtime missed.
For a moment, recalling the loved one,
    I stand and wait, scratching my head;
Plums fall in a gusty wind,
    in the lonely courtyard at dusk.

Of my sad and doting thoughts,
    what's the use of telling?
Wreath upon wreath of fading fragrance
    curls up until it leaves no trace;
When I have stilled my passion for flowers,
    I shall thank last night's wind and rain.
(KTCCC, P. 559)   (TR. IRVING Y. LO)

Ku-t'ai-ch'ing (*1799–?*)

Tune: "Partridge Sky"
Puppet Theater

Puppets on stage let people do what they will;
Bogus tales are meant to delude doltish children.
No shreds of evidence in stories about the royal houses,[1]
Still they charm with marvels wrought by evil genius.

---

[1] The text reads: "Li T'ang and Chao Sung," referring to the royal houses of Li and Chao, respective founders of the T'ang and Sung dynasties.

Mounted on dark-red leopards,[2]
Escorted by striped civets,
In fresh gowns and bright caps they fake dignity.
After the show, they are strung up high and useless;
But carved wood and pulled strings belong to another time.
(THCK, I:2 [1933], P. 152–53)   (TR. IRVING Y. LO)

Tune: "Phoenix Hairpin"
Crab Apple

Dew clear and bright
Drips drop after drop.
Red and tender, each dot finely traces a flower's heart.
Blossoms like teardrops,
Leaves kingfisher-green,
The same tart flavor. Remember? remember? remember?

Told in the sounds of insects,
Envied by the west wind—
At autumn's coming, in whom can I confide?
Idle grief gathers,   10
I cannot sleep.
Half of a waning moon,
And the embroidered quilt feels cold. Sleep, sleep, sleep!
(THCK, I:2 [1933], 159)   (TR. IRVING Y. LO)

---

2 Alluding to line 5 of "The Mountain Goddess" (*Shan-kuei*) in the *Nine Songs* (*Chiu-ko*); cf. David Hawkes's *The Songs of the South*, p. 43.

Tune: "Ripples Sifting Sand"
Accompanying My Husband[1] on a Spring Outing to Stone
Pavilion, Passing by Mercy Brook and Sighting a Flock of
Mandarin Ducks[2]

Where the flowers and trees grow dense,
  Spring is best.
In a clear stream floats the water grass row after row.
A small bird, shy at people, unsettled in its perch,
  Flies up to a willow branch.

Returning horses tread on scented path,
  Hill's shadow sinks west.
Mandarin ducks break through the gray mist in flight:
  Thirty-six pairs in a lovely pattern,
   Together they bathe in the clear brook.   10
(THCK, I:2 [1933], 153)   (TR. IRVING Y. LO)

Chiang Ch'un-lin (1818–1868)

Tune: "Magnolia Blossoms, Slow" (*Mu-lan-hua man*)
Traveling on the Yangtze, Passing the Pei-ku Mountain at Dusk

Anchored on the Chin-huai River, the rain has vanished;
A lamp's glow sees off a boat going home.
Trees are caressed by twilight clouds;
Stars fall upon the wide wilderness.
The colors of dusk pervade the sky,
By the rushes, evening tide suddenly bolts.

---

1 *Fu-tzu* in the text, an honorific referring to her husband, the Manchu imperial clansman I-hui (1799–1838), who inherited his father's title as Prince Jung in 1815. Taken as a concubine by the prince, she shared with him many years of happy life, devoted to poetry and the collection of art objects.
2 *Yüan-yang*, male and female drake, symbols of conjugal happiness. This reference reinforces the allusion to the "water grass" (*hsing*) in line 3, which occurs in the first poem in the *Shih Ching*, a poem traditionally accepted as an epithalamium.

In the heart of vaporous waves, flickering light becomes a full moon.
From a dream I wake, and ask who chanted the Song of Ch'u—
The ripple of chords, strings made taut by frost?

The lovely moon   10
Is speechless as it looks upon the sad one asleep;
What is gone is hard to cast from the heart.
I look at the lush Nan-hsü,
And the majestic Pei-ku Mountain,
Such scenes!
Gone are the linked iron chains to block the river,[1]
And tall-masted boats are left free to turn around.
Silent, the fish-dragon sleeps in the water's depth,
My wounded heart entrusted to the autumn mist.
(CKLTTH, PP. 445–46)   (TR. BRUCE CARPENTER)

Huang Tsun-hsien (1848–1905)

Folk Songs (*Shan-ko*), Two Selections

Author's Preface: It is the custom of the local people [of Kwang-
tung] to be fond of singing. These are refrains sung by boys or girls,
preserving some of the characteristics of the Tzu-yeh songs. I have
selected only those that can be written down, resulting in the following
verses. [Manuscript copy of these poems, totaling fifteen, indicate 1891
as their date of composition.]

[1]

I cook the lotus soup, slice fine lotus roots;
I await my husband's return to relieve his hunger.
If he should covet pairs of chopsticks[1] elsewhere,
Just so he forgets not the key[2] in his heart.

---

1 Alluding to the naval expedition of Wang Chün against the Wu kingdom,
  when the Wu forces attempted to block the Yangtze with linked iron chains;
  see Liu Yü-hsi's poem "Sorrowing for the Past at Western Pass Mountain."
1 *Chu* ("chopsticks") is probably a pun for *shu*, also read *ch'u*, meaning "a
  pretty girl."
2 *Ch'ih*, which may be pronounced as *shih*, means both "door key" and "spoon";
  it is homophonous with another character which means "vow."

[2]

When you buy pears, don't buy those core-nibbled by bees;
If only the heart rots nobody will know.
Because we once shared a pear,[3] we formed our close bond—
Who could have known that close bond has now turned to separation?
(NOS. 1, 3; JCLST, PP. 19–20)   (TR. IRVING Y. LO)

Miscellanies of the Year Chi-hai [1899], Eight Selections

[1]

I'm a man of east and west, south and north,[1]
All my life I style myself a "citizen of wind and waves"[2];
I've visited four continents[3] in half a century,
That still leaves fifty more springs for my garden at home.

[2]

My back against the slanting sun,
    I stood at the bridge for a long time;
Once or twice people passed me by,
    once or twice I nodded at them.
We talked of the clearing that followed the rain,
    then each left and went his way.
I've met with none of my acquaintances,
    nor could I recall who they were.

[3]

Elements of water and fire within the clouds
    contend for mastery;
Rubbing against each other when they meet,
    they cause a roaring sound.

---

3 The phrase translated as "shared a pear" is *fen-li* (literally, "to divide or
  halve a pear"); it is homophonous with *fen-li*, meaning "separation" in the
  line below. ("Close bond" is a translation of *ch'in-ch'ieh;* literally, "affection,"
  "intimacy," or "love.")
1 Actually a quotation from *Li Chi* (*Book of Rites*), first said by Confucius about
  himself.
2 A quotation ("*feng-p'o min*") from the *Tien-hsia* chapter of the *Chuang-tzu.*
3 Referring to Asia, America, Europe, and Africa.

What is only ordinary force
    that comes from drive and resistance—
Is in the human world rashly taken
    as frightful thunderbolt.[4]

[4]

Returned from dream, I rested for a while
    and wept profuse tears:
The fleeting time that I have misspent,
    already fifty years.
There's only the past and what's to come,
    the present nowhere to be found.
For the eternal cycle of birth and extinction,
    come and watch the incense smoke.

[5]

Beams of sunlight, particles of dust
    breathe on one another;
When the night air is still,
    ten thousand noises die down.
If you have truly arrived
    at the state of no sight and no sound,
Swarms of insects will still be hovering
    around the tip of your nose.

[6]

I threw away my book and dozed off at noon;
    and when I woke up
I came to hear the blind old man's song
    sung to the beat of his drum.
Do not tell me of right or wrong, or
    of life's errors after death:

---

4 *Author's note:* "Buddhist scriptures explain thunder as caused by friction when clouds bring the wind and the earth into contact with each other, or when the wind and the water come in contact, or when the wind and the fire come in contact. For example, fire is produced when two branches of wood rub against each other; when two electric currents meet, there is lightning. This explanation is similar to the Western theory that it is friction in the dry air that produces electricity—proving that physical sciences concerning force and air have all been encompassed in Buddhist scriptures."

Human affairs played on stage
    are but a children's game.

[7]

Transplant the peach tree, graft the plum,
    and everywhere it's spring;
Fruits are more plump, flowers more lush,
    the newer the tree.
No wonder in the Western Hemisphere,
    in the newly settled land,
The white men have supplanted
    the red Indians of former times.

[8]

At year's end, I dream all of a sudden
    of the time of Great Commonwealth[5];
Sobered up from wine, I feel the quilt's cold
    and lament my feeble old age.
Who has shown me the greatest cordiality
    and is thus dearest to me?
I bolt my gate, and return to read
    my own poetry.
(NOS. 1, 4, 5, 8, 9, 10, 23, 86; JCLST, PP. 286–303)   (TR. IRVING Y. LO)

Recuperating in Chang Villa

Hidden in my trousers, winter lice have all been wiped out;
Buzzing around my temple-hairs, the mosquitoes won't cease humming.
As I lie high on my pillow, my heart is free from every care—
After one sleepless night, how could another day have dawned?
(NO. 8 FROM A SERIES OF 17; JCLST, P. 228)   (TR. IRVING Y. LO)

---

5 *Ta-t'ung,* the Confucian vision of universal brotherhood and peace, which
  gained popularity from the advocacy by K'ang Yu-wei (1858–1927), a leader of
  the 1898 Reform Movement.

Sent in Lieu of a Letter to Shih-wu, Lan-ku, and Other Friends

From among ten thousand trees autumn wind rises—
My heart alone it cannot blow home.
In my sleeve I still carry a lonely visiting card;
My books form an enclosure like a hundred city walls.
The vast ocean is a home for the seagulls,
While in soaring clouds birds fly high.
But wine stains and tear marks
Still disfigure my commoner's robe.
(NO. 2 FROM A SERIES OF 2; JCLST, P. 47)   (TR. AN-YAN TANG)

Spending the Night in an Inn at Swatow[1] and Writing About My Feelings, Sent to Liang Shih-wu

Flap, flap, the sounds of autumn
    among seared branches and leaves;
A hundred skeins of rustling sorrow
    enter deep into my heart.
Wild wind stops the ferry,
    bells anxious to talk;
An ancient moon hangs in the sky—
    a mirror that I watch alone.
Not yet middle-aged,
    I've known both sadness and joy;
When few true friends are left,
    I find parting difficult.
Under the eaves, in my room,
    a thousand times I've paced.
Now I face the lone lamp,
    now I lean on the railings.
(JCLST, PP. 26–27)   (TR. AN-YAN TANG)

---

1 Swatow, in Kwangtung province, became a treaty port in 1858.

To Send Away Melancholy

Flowers bloom, flowers fall,
  I bolt my gate and sleep.
Wasting fine spring days?
  How could I help it?
Affairs of this world
  seldom turn out as we wish;
People before my eyes
  die off more and more each day.
The patterings of evening rain
  a rustling tune[1]
Of flowing, fleeting time
  an immortal treads and sings.[2]
This day, this hour,
  and there's this "I";
Tea mists, a meditation couch,
  and a sick Vimalakīrti.
(JCLST, PP. 157–58)   (TR. AN-YAN TANG)

Wang Kuo-wei (1877–1927)

To Try to Find

To try to find my heart, it's hard enough;
How could I hold it in tranquillity?
Illness impedes poetry, and all I feel is useless;
Sorrow comes from birth, not without cause.
I rise to watch, in the moonlight, frost on ten thousand roof tiles;
I lie down hearing, in the wind, a thousand spears of bamboo.

---

[1] *Hsiao-hsiao ch'ü,* alluding to a line from Po Chü-yi's "Song of Wu Erh-niang," which reads: "Evening rain rustling, but the lover has not returned."
[2] *T'a-t'a ko,* alluding to the song of Lan Ts'ai-ho, one of the Eight Immortals, which reads in part: "Tread and sing/Lan Ts'ai-ho!/How long will one world last?/Ruddy cheeks, a tree in springtime/Of time gone by, a shuttle in a loom . . ."

North of Ts'ang-lang Pavilion, a huge date tree[1]—
Ceaseless, the cawing of crows in the evening cold.
(WKTCC, P. 1783)   (TR. IRVING Y. LO)

Tune: "Song of Picking Mulberry"

The drum sounds from the high city wall as the lampwick burns out.
     Asleep, yet awake;
     Drunk, yet sober—
Suddenly I hear the two or three notes of a wild goose's lone cry.

Life is no more than willow catkins in the wind:
     Joy in fragments,
     Grief in fragments—
All turn to patches of duckweed spreading on the river.
(WKTCC, PP. 1512–13)   (TR. CHING-I TU)

Tune: "Immortal at the River"

I heard my love was gone on garrison at Chin-wei Mountain.[1]
     Last night my dream took me there,
     Not knowing that he had gone already to Liao-hsi,[2]
Where the sky darkens over a thousand camps on the sand
     And ten thousand horses neigh beneath the moon.

My love is like a plum blossom and I am the leaf,
     But all I can caress is a barren branch.
I mourn that flowers go and leaves bud at different times;
     Don't say that flowers fall before their time:
     It's only the leaves that grow too late.   10
(WKTCC, P. 1523)   (TR. CHING-I TU)

---

[1] *Chün-ch'ien shu, Diospyros Lotus,* is a variety of date tree, the fruits of which
are sometimes used to make varnish.
[1] In present Mongolia.
[2] Referring to the area from the present Hopei province to the Liaotung penin-
sula.

Tune: "Butterflies Lingering over Flowers," Two Lyrics

[1]

How much regret in my dream last night?
    I on horseback and you in a carriage,
    The two of us drawing closer to each other.
Face to face, you seemed sorry for my haggard look;
Under many eyes, you drew up the curtain to ask for my health.

Then down the road the rumble of your carriage gently died away.
    In my dream I find I cannot follow;
    Where, on waking, can I have news of you?
By my window, candle's tears have gathered an inch;
Longing, in this human world, is our common lot.   10

[2]

I have tasted the bitterness of parting at world's end.
    Little was I aware, before my return,
    How the flowers would be scattered.
When we look at each other without a word beneath the flowers,
Spring, by the green window, fades with the passing day.

I would like to tell of my feelings by the lamp light:
    One skein of new joy,
    A thousand skeins of old regret.
Things hardest to keep in this human world—
Rosy cheeks which fade in the mirror and flowers that fall   10
    from trees.
(WKTCC, PP. 1201, 1516)   (TR. CHING-I TU)

Tune: "Echoing Heaven's Everlastingness"

A horse with a chestnut mane reflected in the green waves
    of the spring river;
Upon the waves, rowing a boat, a girl pretty as jade.
    She seems to know him,

Yet too shy to follow—
For a moment she lowers her head and sends him a side glance.

Her cloud-like hair aslant,
Her painted eyebrows knitted—
Does she regret this brief meeting,
Or feel annoyed by the uncertainty of a moment?
Rowing with a pair of oars, she speeds away.   10
(WKTCC, P. 1531)   (TR. CHING-I TU)

Tune: "Sand of Silk-washing Stream"

A mountain temple dim and far away, its back against the
        setting sun—
No birds can reach that height far in the shade.
From above, at the single note of its chime, clouds pause in their
        passing.

When I try to climb the peak, to peer at the bright moon,
By chance I obtain the Eye of Heaven[1] to look at the mundane
        world—
And I find in its revelation, alas, I am but a man.
(WKTCC, P. 1517)   (TR. CHING-I TU)

Lu Hsün (*1881–1936*)

In Remembrance of the Forgotten[1]

Used to long nights, springtime is past;
Leading wife, clutching child, my temples are thin.
In visions vague, indistinct, a loving mother's tears[2];

---

1 *"T'ien-yen"* is a Sanskrit term (*divyacaksus*) meaning "divine sight or unlimited vision."

1 This poem was originally untitled and included in an essay named "Remembrance of the Forgotten." Lu Hsün later referred to the poem as "A Lament for Jou Shih" in a letter to a friend. Jou Shih (1901–31), the pen name of Chao P'ing-fu, a young writer, was arrested and later executed along with twenty-two other young people by the police.

2 Referring to the poet's mother, worrying over Lu Hsün's safety.

Atop city walls, changes again of royal standards.[3]
Compelled to watch companions turned newly into ghosts,[4]
Angered, I turned to a forest of swords to seek words that rhyme.
Finished, I lower my eyes; but this is no place to write.
Moonlight, bright as water, glistens on my black robe.
(LHCC, IV, p. 374) (TR. WILLIAM R. SCHULTZ)

Sending Off O.E. Who Brought an Orchid Home to Japan[1]

The pepper in ashes, cassia branches broken, the good man grows old,
Dependent solely on secret crags to reveal his pure heart.
How begrudge a fragrant blossom, a gift for a distant one,
My homeland in a drunken stupor, ridden with thorns![2]
(LHCC, VII, P. 143) (TR. WILLIAM R. SCHULTZ)

Self-mockery[1]

Fortunes locked in the Hua-kai[2] stars, why seek anything,
For before I turn about, I've cracked my head.
Tattered hat shielding my face, I cross the noisy market
To a leaky skiff, wine in hand, to drift down the river.

With knitted brows, frozen glances, the officials I accuse;
With bowed head, willingly I'll be the children's ox.[3]

---

3 A reference to the constantly shifting political climate.

4 Cf. the line by Tu Fu, "After battle cry many new ghosts."

1 I.e., a Japanese acquaintance named Ohara Eijiro, a friend of Mr. Uchiyama Kanzo.

2 The pepper, cassia, and orchid are classical symbols of honesty and purity of spirit; on the other hand, thorns represent dishonest, corrupt men.

1 According to an entry in the author's personal diary, this poem was originally written for Liu Ya-tzu (1887–1958) at a dinner hosted by the novelist Yü Ta-fu (1896–1940).

2 According to the "Astronomy Monograph" in the *Tsin Shu*, the nine stars associated with the Celestial Emperor were called Hua-kai. Literally "flower-canopy," the term is used in fortunetelling and means "a year of bad luck"; but Lu Hsün characteristically chose it as the title of one of his collections, the *Hua-kai chi*. Cf. the postscript he wrote to the volume.

3 This couplet was quoted by Mao Tse-tung in his celebrated talk on literature and art at the Yenan Forum in 1942. "To play the child's ox" is an allusion to *Tso Chuan* (Legge, *The Chinese Classics*, New York: Oxford University Press, 1961, VI, pp. 809–910), referring to the story about Duke Ching of Ch'i, who once held a rope in his mouth, pretending to be an ox, and asked his son T'u

Stealthily I enter a small tower to design a "Grand Unity,"
Heeding neither winter, summer, spring, nor fall.
(LHCC, VII, P. 151)   (TR. WILLIAM R. SCHULTZ)

Hesitation[1]

Lonely, desolate, the new literary scene;
Peaceful, tranquil, the old battlefields.
'Tween earth and sky remains a single warrior
Shouldering a lance, wandering aimlessly, alone.
(LHCC, VII, P. 158)   (TR. WILLIAM R. SCHULTZ)

Call to Arms[1]

Take up the pen: fall into the net of law;
Resist the times: offend popular sentiments.
Accumulated abuse can dissolve the bones,
And so, one gives voice to the empty page.
(LHCC, VII, P. 158)   (TR. WILLIAM R. SCHULTZ)

Lamenting Yang Ch'uan[1]

How can there be heroic feelings, as in bygone days?
Flowers bloom, flowers fall: one thing follows another.
How could I know tears would fall like southern rain,
Or the common man would weep again for a champion?
(LHCC, VII, P. 159)   (TR. WILLIAM R. SCHULTZ)

---

to pull it. A later minister, Pao Mu, was reported to have said, "Have you forgotten now when our [late] ruler was playing ox [to T'u], the child [fell down and] broke his teeth?"

[1] Lu Hsün's second collection of short stories was compiled in 1925 and published under the title *P'ang-huang* (*Hesitation,* literally "wandering aimlessly"), to which this poem is inscribed.

[1] Sometimes translated as "The Outcry," this is the title of Lu Hsün's first collection of short stories, 1923, which included his most famous work, "The True Story of Ah Q."

[1] Yang Ch'uan (1893–1933) was prominent in scientific and political circles, and, in addition to numerous public responsibilities, he founded the Science Society of China, served as secretary-general of Academia Sinica, and held a key post in the China League for Civil Rights. He was assassinated on June 18, 1933.

Su Man-shu (1884–1918)

Written During My Stay at White Clouds Monastery on West Lake

Dense white clouds embrace Thunder Peak;
Wintry plum blossoms blush in the snow.
After a vegetable meal I sink slowly into deep meditation,
As scattered bell sounds fall on shadows in the monastery pool.
(MSCC, P. 43)   (TR. WU-CHI LIU)

Passing by Kamata

Deep under the willows' shade the horse treads proudly.
A vast expanse of silvery sand pursues the ebbing tide.
The ice-flag atop a thatched store signals a nearby market;
Red leaves all over the hill, the girls gather them for fuel.
(MSCC, P. 44)   (TR. WU-CHI LIU)

Chanting These Verses on My Way to Yodoe

From this lone village rises dimly a wisp of smoke;
Everywhere is heard the rice-sprout song as farmers toil in the field.
A lean horse need not worry about the long road ahead—
The peach blossoms, lovely and red, leap onto my singing whip.
(MSCC, P. 47)   (TR. WU-CHI LIU)

Addressed to a Koto-player

[1]

A Zen mind is unperturbed by the envy of moth-browed beauties;
In Buddha's precept anger is the same as affection.
I shall return home in a rain hat and bamboo cloak
With neither love nor hatred for mankind.

[2]

I loathe flowers blooming and willows shrouded in mist—
For twenty years I've been a lone wanderer on the Eastern Sea.
All ties of affection severed, indifferent to looks and appearance,
I shall sleep on the shore of Lake Biwa[1] with a sutra as my pillow.

[3]

Having stolen the dew from the lips of the heavenly maid,
Many times I have wiped away tears as I stand in the wind.
Thinking of you day after day has aged me.
On the lonely window—how unbearable—twilight descends.
(MSCC, P. 50)   (TR. WU-CHI LIU)

Inscribed on Byron's Poetic Works[1]

An autumn wind blows across the sea in the deepening twilight—
Alone, I bewail Byron's fate as I read his poems.
Poets, you and I, are like fluttering reeds in a storm.
Could I summon your soul from a strange land?
(MSCC, P. 53)   (TR. WU-CHI LIU)

Poems Written During My Sojourn in Japan, Three Selections

[1]

She puts on a silken blouse and comes down from the western chamber
With the warm fragrance of a tender bloom[1]; she talks endlessly.

---

1 A scenic spot near Kyoto.
1 *Author's Preface:* "Hsüeh-hung, a poetess from Spain, came to visit me on my
sickbed and personally presei ed me with a lovely portrait of hers, a volume
of Byron's poetic works, and a bunch of camellia flowers and sensitive plants.
Very solicitously she urged me to make plans for a trip homeward. Alas! Early
in my youth I shaved my head to learn the Buddhist law but failed to accom-
plish anything. Whenever I think of my life, I have no words to express my
pain. So, ill as I am, I write down these twenty-eight words on the front leaf
of Byron's book. This sentiment will be appreciated only by Hsüeh-hung."
    The poet met the young Spanish lady to whom he gave this Chinese name
("Snowy Swan") on a boat from Shanghai to Singapore, where the poem was
written.
1 *T'ou-k'ou*, literally, nutmeg and its flowers.

But when asked about her age, she turns bashful
And disappears behind a crystal screen to practice the lute.

[2]

Shouldn't I pilfer wantonly this famed fragrance of a foreign land?
Her smile behind the window screen casts a gloom over my thoughts.
A lustrous pearl I would like to present her, but I despair and falter,
For fear it will kindle sorrows anew when next year the twin stars
    meet.[2]

[3]

On the bank of Lake Rouge a chestnut steed treads proudly.
The flowing stream and perched crows reveal a small bridge,
Where, seeking tidings of him from the leaves of the banana palm,
The tears she sheds every morning have swelled into a red tide.
(NOS. 3, 5, 15 FROM A SERIES OF 19; MSCC, PP. 61–63)

(TR. WU-CHI LIU)

Liu Ya-tzu (1887–1958)

On the Second Day of the Fifth Month [1908], Written After Drink.
At That Time the News Has Spread of the Defeat of the Revolutionary Army in Yunnan

[1]

Some affairs are hard to relate and painful to hear.
Into a goblet of wine my tears flow like silken thread.
We enjoy here these carefree days of elegant feast,
But, out yonder, the tall city walls are splashed with blood.

[2]

For twenty years I've erred in learning the skills of "insect-carving."[1]
This skull of mine in the mirror has betrayed its owner's trust.

---

2 He feels sad because even the two separated star-lovers in the Milky Way, the
   Cowherd and the Weaving Maid, could meet once a year.
1 To carve insects on stone is considered a small artistic skill; here it refers to
   poetry writing.

Were I to build a hill of wine dregs and drink myself to death,
I would only have earned an unheroic name.
(LYTSTH, P. 18)   (TR. WU-CHI LIU)

Strange Tears

What would I do with these strange tears in a cold night?
Youthful years on swift horses have gone by as in a dream.
I have not yet cultivated a good name upon the approach of old age;
Before the mirror of history, my face easily flushes with shame.
In my young days I drafted the summons of war on Mount Yen-jan,[1]
Now I am too timid to listen to the song at Kai-hsia.[2]
When I think of my aged mother and ailing wife,
How could I forsake the warmth of home[3] for a soldier's life?[4]
(LYTSTH, P. 46)   (TR. WU-CHI LIU)

Filled with Emotions on the Moon-ferrying Bridge at Arashiyama

A dragon never rears its head before sending down torrential rain.
Spring water flows noiselessly in the mountains.
Why should this stream alongside Moon-ferrying Bridge
Complain forever to the humans of its murmuring grievances?
(LYTSTH, P. 56)   (TR. WU-CHI LIU)

---

[1] The Han general Tou Hsien, after having defeated the Hsiung-nu and pursued them into their desert home in Inner Mongolia, had an inscription (compiled by Pan Ku, the historian) carved on the rock surface of Mount Yen-jan to celebrate his victory. Many well-known writers of the past were entrusted with the task of drafting war proclamations against the enemy. The most famous instance is the summons to war against Empress Wu of the T'ang dynasty written by the poet Lo Pin-wang. In this line, Liu Ya-tzu has merged the two historical references.
[2] For a translation of this song, see Hsiang Chi's "Song of Kai-hsia."
[3] Literally, "to cut off the lapel of a warm robe"; the equivalent of the English expression "to forsake the warmth of the hearth."
[4] Literally, "to carry a spear."

Miscellaneous Poems on Lake Biwa, Three Selections

[1]

Beyond the stream at Seta stretches an endless view.
On a silk kerchief, warm and fragrant, a pair of tiny hands ply the
    needle.
I can't help feeling nostalgic about my native country:
In the embroidered picture, a T'ang-style bridge![1]

[2]

By Flower-and-Moon Pavilion, I stay my carriage
To stroll under thatched eaves that overlook the lake.
The master painter, dotting with his brush, habitually forgets
        his hunger;
He feeds himself on the colors of the mountain and the river's gleam.

[3]

Cataracts flying down a thousand fathoms roll up a raging billow.
Bright lamps, flares numberless, cast their shadows into the distance.
All my life, my excursion boots have never taken me to such a place
Where my soul dissolves at the sight of White-wave Bridge.
(NOS. 4, 5, 11 FROM A SERIES OF 12; LYTSTH, PP. 56–57)

(TR. WU-CHI LIU)

To a Friend, Using the Same Rhymes of a Poem He Sent Me

Four decades, I've aroused the southeast with flute and sword;
For three years now, I've found myself buried alive within those
        four walls![1]
Who would expect that dead ashes have blazed anew like
        torches?
And I still wish to conjure up huge waves and sport with the long
        wind.

---

1 According to the author, some of the silk handkerchiefs on sale in the gift shop
  are embroidered with pictures of a T'ang bridge (Chinese-style bridge) at
  Seta, one of the eight scenic views of Lake Biwa.
1 The poet lived in enemy-occupied Shanghai during the first three years of the
  Sino-Japanese War.

Swearing to tame fierce tigers and slay ferocious crocodiles,
I disdain to imitate the cold cicada that mourns the lone swan.
On this ancient earth, under a hoary sky, to whom could I tell
     my thoughts?
This new poem I shall "broadcast" tonight through the mail.
(LYTSTH, PP. 92–93)   (TR. WU-CHI LIU)

Dragons and Snakes[1]

Dragons and snakes tangle in my dream; they can hardly recoil.
Beacon fires everywhere, our ailing country is sad without spring.
The Allies' victory consoles us but a little[2];
History is replete with lessons of the "overturned cart."[3]
I raise my voice to call for the people's democracy.
No more can we bow our head to serve the lords.
Cinnabar caves and a hermit's dodder robe[4]—these things are
       full of contradictions;
Thinking of the suffering masses, I'm ashamed to plot a living
       for myself.
(LYTSTH, P. 137)   (TR. WU-CHI LIU)

Overjoyed at Soviet Russia's Entry into the War

Blind clouds, poisonous vapors hang over this mountain city,
But today, one war dispatch suddenly brightens many eyes.
As the Red Army moves east to aid its friends,
All black-haired people can celebrate victory in the west.
The tyrant's dying flames will be quenched;
Democracy and prosperity will be ours forever.

---

1 "The hibernation of dragons and snakes is to preserve the self": a quotation from the Appendix in the *Classic of Changes*.

2 A reference to Russia's victory over Germany at the end of World War II.

3 The Chinese proverb goes: "One should learn a lesson from an overturned cart." Here it means no one heeds the repeated warning of the mistakes the country has made in the last thirty years since the founding of the Republic.

4 *T'u-ch'iu*, here translated as "dodder robe," is the name of a place in Shantung, where one of the feudal princes in ancient times retired. *Tan-hsüeh*, or "cinnabar caves," is also the name of a place in Shantung, where the mountain veins yielded rich cinnabar deposits, which enriched their owners. The feelings of wealth and retirement, of course, are contradictory.

How I wish the war horses would be sent straight down
To forge a link of ten thousand miles between Ulan Bator and
      Yenan, our capital!
(LYTSTH, PP. 141–42)   (TR. WU-CHI LIU)

On Hearing the News of the Japanese Surrender[1]

Fireworks explode like thunderclaps all over Chungking,
Bringing to the long night the brightness of dawn.
Peasants and workers, exhausted, still deplore their heavy burden,
While shameless scoundrels appropriate Heaven's merit as their own.
Dark currents continue to flood the country, my fears multiply,
But in this righteous war fought to a finish, the nation can take pride.
Raising their head southward, to await fresh reports of victory,
The people of the Huai and the Yangtze look to the recovery of
      their capital.[2]
(LYTSTH, P. 142)   (TR. WU-CHI LIU)

For Guests After Their Visit[1]

Rotten wood is unfit for carving,[2] so I slept at noon.
Hurriedly I came out to greet you, my cap and gown in disarray.
How could I, a man of Nan-yang,[3] trouble you to visit me three times?

---

1 The full title of the poem: "On the night of August 10 [1945], the wireless carried the news of the Japanese surrender; written afterwards on the twelfth."
2 A reference to the New Fourth Route Army (Communist) operating in the Huai and Yangtze regions in southeast China; the capital referred to here is Nanking.
1 Original title: "On that day [May 1, 1949] I was soundly asleep in my noonday nap when it was announced suddenly that Chairman Mao was coming to visit us with his wife Chiang Ch'ing and their young daughter. I immediately got up to receive them. I showed Chairman Mao all my recent writings and asked him for comments. Then we went out for a walk. We rambled together along the 'long corridor' and sailed across Lake Kunming on a painted boat before we returned. It was already twilight when the guests left. I wrote this poem to record the event." Liu Ya-tzu was then living in the guest quarters of the former Summer Palace (noted for its long corridor and lake) in the western outskirts of Peking.
2 Confucius remarked of his pupil Tsai Yü, who napped while the master was teaching, "Rotten wood cannot be carved."
3 When Chu-ko Liang, the famous third-century scholar-general, was retiring in his hut in Nan-yang, Liu Pei, who later founded the Shu Han kingdom, visited him three times to ask him to help in Liu's campaigns against his rivals, Wei and Wu. See note 1 to Ma Chih-yüan's "Slow Chant."

In this northern land, I can still compose a hundred songs.
You came with your lovely wife and daughter;
We shared a boat, strolled and talked together.
If I could stay long as your guest in this famous garden,
I'd feel happier here than in the gold-powdered pavilions across
       the Yangtze.[4]
(LYTSTH, P. 208)   (TR. WU-CHI LIU)

Mao Tse-tung (1893–1976)

Tune: "Spring in [Princess] Ch'in's Garden"
Snow

    Northern landscape,
Thousand miles around covered by ice,
Ten thousand miles under snowdrifts.
      On both sides of the Great Wall,
      I see vast wastes;
      Up and down the Great River
      Suddenly the torrents are still;
Mountains wind around like silver serpents,
High headlands ramble about like waxen elephants,
On the verge of challenging heaven.   10
      A sunny day is best
      For watching the red against the white:
      Extraordinary enchantment.

The rivers and mountains have this special charm
That inspires countless heroes to great deeds.
Pity the First Sovereign and the Martial Emperor
      Had small talent for literature,
And the founding fathers of T'ang and Sung
      Lacked both grace and charm.
In his own generation—favored by heaven—   20
      Genghis Khan
Knew only how to bend the bow, bringing down the great vulture.
      All these are gone now,

---

[4] Said of the gay and extravagant palaces in Nanking in the Six Dynasties period.
Nanking is situated south of the Yangtze.

To single out the men of high character,
We must look to now, the present.
(MCHST, II, P. 130)   (TR. EUGENE EOYANG)

Tune: "Song of Divination"
On the Plum Tree, After a Poem by Lu Yu

Wind and rain see spring off;
    Fluttering snow greets her coming.
Already, on the high precipice, a hundred yards of ice,
Yet there's still the beauty of blossoms on the branch.

    That beauty doesn't rival spring,
    But only heralds spring's approach.
Wait till the mountain flowers blaze out and bloom:
There, amid the brush, she will be smiling.
(MCHST, IV, PP. 126–27)   (TR. EUGENE EOYANG)

Tune: "Full River Red"
A Reply to Kuo Mo-jo

    On this tiny planet,
    There are flies that fly against a wall,
    With a buzzing sound,
    Sometimes screeching,
    Sometimes weeping.
Ants climbing the locust boast of a large domain;
But for beetles to bring down a tree is no easy matter.

It was just when the west wind and falling leaves
        descended on Ch'ang-an—
    That arrows whistled by.

    So many things,
Since the beginning, need to be done.
Heaven and earth revolve,
    While time presses on.
    Ten thousand years is too long:
    It's the moment that counts.

The four oceans in turmoil, clouds and rivers are in a fury;
The five continents rumble, wind and thunder rage.
We must rid ourselves of all those pests who prey on man
　　　　And stand completely unopposed.
(MCHST, IV, P. 186)   (TR. EUGENE EOYANG)

Tune: "Spring in [Princess] Ch'in's Garden"
Ch'ang-sha

Alone I stand in autumn cold,
As Hsiang River goes north, past Orange Island.
I see a thousand mountains red-tinted,
Forest after forest dyed deep red,
　　Wide river blue right through,
　　A hundred boats fight the current;
　　Eagles strike out in the lofty sky,
　　Fish eddy in the shallows,
A host of creatures vies for freedom in the frost-nipped air.
　　Bewildered by this immensity,
　　I ask: "This vast expanse, this great earth,
　　Who is master of it all?"

I have led a hundred companions here:
I think back to those many months and years, those lofty plans;
　　We were schoolboys, and still young,
　　With an air of strength and of life,
　　The spirit of scholars,
Quick to censure, upright in manner.
We pointed to this river, that mountain,
　　Stirring ourselves with words: 20
　　To us, the marquisates of old are dung.
　　　　Do you remember,
How, in the middle of the river, striking against the waves,
　　We almost toppled our fleet little boat?
(MCHST, I, P. 1)   (TR. EUGENE EOYANG)

Tune: "Song of Picking Mulberry"
Double-Ninth Festival

How quickly we age. Not so the heavens.
　　Year after year, the Double Nine;

Now, once again, the Double Nine,
And on the battlefield, the yellow flowers smell sweet.

Once a year, the autumn wind rages,
    So unlike spring's brightness
    Yet better than spring's brightness,
With skies vast, waters full, and frost miles around.
(MCHST, I, PP. 78–79)   (TR. EUGENE EOYANG)

Tune: "Deva-like Barbarian"
Ta-po-ti[1]

Red, orange, yellow, green, turquoise, blue, violet:
Who's waving this rainbow flag against the sky?
    After the rain, sunlight slants down again,
    And the mountain passes, range after range, turn green.

That year a bloody battle raged;
Bullet holes dotted the wall of the village just passed.
    The scars on the mountain pass
    Make it lovelier today.
(MCHST, II, P. 1)   (TR. EUGENE EOYANG)

Tune: "Remembering the Lady of Ch'in"
Loushan Pass

Fierce west wind,
Geese call in the open air, there's frost under the morning moon,
                        frost under the morning moon
    Shattering sounds of horses' hooves
    And of the bugles' wail.

Do not say the mountain pass is like steel,
For today we have marched right up to the summit,
                    right up to the summit,
    Atop green hills like the sea,
    Under a dying sun like blood.   10
(MCHST, II, PP. 33–35)   (TR. EUGENE EOYANG)

---

1 A town in Kiangsi province, the base of the Red Army in 1933.

Tune: "The Charm of Nien-nu"
Kunlun Mountains

Into the atmosphere, out of this world,
Unruly Kun-lun,[1] witness to the buoyancy of every spring on earth.
You fly up, three million white dragons of jade,
Stirring the heavens with your snowcapped scales;
  Then, melting on a summer day,
  Flooding rivers and creeks,
  Turning men into fish and turtles.
In a thousand autumns of works good and bad,
Who could tally up your score?

  And yet, Kun-lun, I say to you now   10
No need for such height, nor for all that snow.
If I could only, leaning against the sky, draw the sacred sword,
  I'd slice you into three parts:
  One part I'd leave for Europe,
  Another bequeath to America,
  And the third will remain here in the East.
So that the whole world would be at peace,
And we would all share your coolness, and your warmth.
(MCHST, II, PP. 78–79)   (TR. EUGENE EOYANG)

---

[1] The highest mountain in China, with a height of twenty thousand feet, along the border of Tibet and Sinkiang, which separates into three main ranges cutting across north, central, and southwest China.

Bibliography

I. Bibliography

Davidson, Martha, ed. *A List of Published Translations from Chinese into English, French, and German,* Part II. New Haven: Yale University, Far Eastern Publications, 1957.

Hightower, James Robert. *Topics in Chinese Literature: Outlines and Bibliographies.* Cambridge: Harvard University Press, 1962. Revised Edition. Harvard-Yenching Institute Studies, Volume III.

Yuan, Tung-li. *China in Western Literature: A Continuation of Cordier's Bibliotheca Sinica.* New Haven: Yale University, Far Eastern Publications, 1958.

II. Translations, or Renditions of Chinese Poetry (Excluding Individual Poets and General Anthologies), Arranged by Date of Publication

1898   Giles, Herbert. *Chinese Poetry in English Verse.* London: Bernard Quaritch, 1898. Reissued as *Gems of Chinese Literature,* Volume II, Shanghai: Kelly and Walsh, 1923; New York: Paragon Reprint, 1965.

1909   Cranmer-Byng, L. A. *A Lute of Jade* (Wisdom of the East Series). London: Murray, 1909.

1915   Pound, Ezra. *Cathay.* London: Elkin Mathews, 1915.

1916   Cranmer-Byng, L. A. *A Feast of Lanterns* (Wisdom of the East Series). New York: Dutton, 1916.

1918   Fletcher, W. J. B. *Gems of Chinese Poetry.* Shanghai: Commercial Press, 1918. Together with *More Gems of Chinese Poetry* (Shanghai, 1933) reissued in one volume by Paragon, 1966.

1918   Waley Arthur. *170 Chinese Poems.* London: Constable, 1918; New York: Knopf, 1919.

1921   Ayscough, Florence and Amy Lowell. *Fir-Flower Tablets.* Boston: Houghton Mifflin, 1921.

1923   Waley, Arthur. *The Temple and Other Poems.* New York: Knopf, 1923.

1929   Bynner, Witter and Kiang Kang-hu. *The Jade Mountain.* New York: Knopf, 1929. New York: Doubleday reprint, 1964, Vintage reprint, 1972, another Taiwan reprint with parallel text.

1932   Ts'ai, Ting-kan. *Chinese Poems in English Rhymes.* Chicago: University of Chicago Press, 1932.

1933   Candlin, Clara. *The Herald Wind* (Wisdom of the East Series). London: Murray, 1933.

1933   Hart, Henry. *A Hundred Names*. Berkeley: University of California Press, 1933.

1937   Ch'u Ta-koa. *Chinese Lyrics*. Cambridge: Cambridge University Press, 1937.

1937   Waley, Arthur. *More Translations from the Chinese*. New York: Knopf, 1937.

1938   Hart, Henry. *A Garden of Peonies*. Stanford: Stanford University Press, 1938.

1940   Jenyns, Soame. *Selections from the 300 Poems of the T'ang Dynasty* (Wisdom of the East Series). London: Murray, 1940.

1944   ———. *A Further Selection from the 300 Poems of the T'ang Dynasty* (Wisdom of the East Series). London: Murray, 1944.

1946   Waley, Arthur. *Chinese Poems*. London: Allen & Unwin, 1946.

1947   Payne, Robert. *The White Pony*. New York: John Day, 1947.

1949   Ives, Mabel L. *Chinese Love Songs*. Upper Montclair, New Jersey: B. L. Hutchinson, 1949.

1950   Wong, Man. *Poems from the Chinese*. Hong Kong: Creation Books, 1950.

1958   Alley, Rewi. *The People Sing*. Peking: Foreign Languages Press, 1958.

1959   Rexroth, Kenneth. *One Hundred Poems from the Chinese*. New York: New Directions, 1959.

1960   Ch'en, C. J. and Michael Bullock. *Poems of Solitude*. London: Abelard-Schuman, 1960.

[1962] Demiéville, Paul. *Anthologie de la Poésie Chinoise Classique*. Paris: Gallimard, 1962.

1962   Davis, A. R. (ed.). *The Penguin Book of Chinese Verse*. Translations by Robert Kotewall and Norman L. Smith. Baltimore: Penguin, 1962.

1965   Graham, A. C. *Poems of the Late T'ang*. Baltimore: Penguin, 1965.

1965   Ayling, Alan and Duncan Mackintosh. *A Collection of Chinese Lyrics*. London: Routledge & Kegan Paul, 1965.

1967   Liu, Shih Shun. *One Hundred and One Chinese Poems*. Hong Kong: Cathay, 1967.

1967   Sackheim, Eric. *The Silent Zero, in Search of Sound: An Anthology of Chinese Poems from the Beginning Through the Sixth Century*. New York: Grossman Publishers, 1967.

1967   Frodsham, J. D. and Ch'eng Hsi. *An Anthology of Chinese Verse: Han Wei Chin and the Northern and Southern Dynasties*. Oxford: Clarendon Press, 1967.

1967 Yang, Richard F. S. and Charles R. Metzger. *Fifty Songs from the Yüan: Poetry of Thirteenth Century China.* London: Allen & Unwin, 1967.

1968 Wells, Henry W. *Ancient Poetry from China, Japan and India Rendered into English Verse.* Columbia, South Carolina: University of South Carolina Press, 1968.

1969 Ayling, Alan and Duncan Mackintosh. *A Further Collection of Chinese Lyrics.* London: Routledge & Kegan Paul, 1969.

1970 Morris, Ivan (ed.). *Madly Singing in the Mountains, An Appreciation of Arthur Waley.* New York: Walker & Co., 1970.

1972 Rexroth, Kenneth and Chung Ling. *The Orchid Boat: Women Poets of China.* New York: McGraw-Hill, 1972.

1972 Scott, John. *Love and Protest: Chinese Poems from the Sixth Century B.C. to the Seventh Century A.D.* New York: Harper Colophon Books, 1972.

1972 Mayhew, Lenore and William McNaughton. *A Gold Orchid: The Love Poems of Tzu Yeh.* Rutland, Vermont: Charles Tuttle, 1972.

III. Background and Genre Studies (Most Containing Translations)

A. Books

Demiéville, Paul. *Airs de Touen-Houang.* Paris: Centre National de la Recherche Scientifique, 1971.

Liu, James J. Y. *The Art of Chinese Poetry.* Chicago: University of Chicago Press, 1962.

———. *Major Lyricists of the Northern Sung.* Princeton, New Jersey: Princeton University Press, 1974.

Luh, C. W. *On Chinese Poetry.* Peiping, 1935.

Pulleyblank, E. G. *The Background of the Rebellion of An Lu-shan.* London: Oxford University Press, 1955.

Schafer, Edward H. *The Golden Peaches of Samarkand: A Study of T'ang Exotica.* Berkeley: University of California Press, 1963.

———. *The Vermilion Bird.* Berkeley: University of California Press, 1967.

Schlepp, Wayne. *San-ch'ü, Its Technique and Imagery.* Madison: University of Wisconsin Press, 1970.

Teele, Roy E. *Through a Glass Darkly* (A Study of English Translations of Chinese Poetry). Ann Arbor, Michigan: University of Michigan Press, 1949.

Watson, Burton. *Chinese Lyricism: Shih Poetry from the Second to the Twelfth Century.* New York: Columbia University Press, 1971.

Wu, John C. H. *The Four Seasons of T'ang Poetry.* Rutland, Vermont: Tuttle, 1972.

Yip, Wai-lim. *Ezra Pound's Cathay.* Princeton: Princeton University Press, 1969.

Yoshikawa, Kojiro. *An Introduction to Sung Poetry.* Translated by Burton Watson. Cambridge: Harvard University Press, 1967.

B. Articles

Baxter, G. W. "Metrical Origin of the Tz'u," *Harvard Journal of Asiatic Studies,* 16 (1953), 108–45.

Bishop, John L. "Prosodic Elements in T'ang Poetry," in *Papers of Indiana University Conference on Oriental-Western Literary Relations,* pp. 48–60, Horst Frenz (ed.). Chapel Hill: University of North Carolina Press, 1955.

Boodberg, Peter A. "Cedules from a Berkeley Workshop in Asiatic Philology," *Tsing Hua Journal of Chinese Studies,* New Series VII (August 1969), 1–39.

Chen, Shih-chuan. "The Rise of the Tz'u, Reconsidered," *Journal of the American Oriental Society,* 90:2 (1970), 232–42.

Downer, C. B. and A. C. Graham, "Tone Patterns in Chinese Poetry," *Bulletin of the School of Oriental and African Studies,* 24:1 (1963), 145–48.

Eoyang, Eugene. "The Solitary Boat: Image of Self in Chinese Nature Poetry," *Journal of Asian Studies,* 32:4 (1973), 593–621.

Fang, Achilles. "Some Reflections on the Difficulty of Translations," in *On Translations,* pp. 111–33, Reuben A. Brower (ed.). Cambridge: Harvard University Press, 1959.

Frankel, Hans. "The 'I' in Chinese Lyric Poetry," *Oriens,* 10 (1957), 128–30.

———. "The Chinese Ballad 'Southeast Fly the Peacocks,'" *Harvard Journal of Asiatic Studies,* 34 (1974), 248–71.

———. "The Contemplation of the Past in T'ang Poetry," in *Perspectives on the T'ang,* pp. 345–65, Arthur F. Wright and Denis Twitchett (eds.). New Haven: Yale University Press, 1973.

Frodsham, J. D. "The Origin of Chinese Nature Poetry," *Asia Major,* 83:1 (1960), 68–103.

Hawkes, David. "Chinese Poetry and the English Reader," in *The Legacy of China,* pp. 90–115, Raymond Dawson (ed.). London: Oxford University Press, 1964.

Kao, Yu-kung and Mei Tsu-lin, "Syntax, Diction, and Imagery in T'ang Poetry," *Harvard Journal of Asiatic Studies,* 31 (1971), 49–133.

Lattimore, David. "Allusion and T'ang Poetry," in *Perspectives on the T'ang,* pp. 405–39. Arthur F. Wright and Denis Twitchett (eds.). New Haven: Yale University Press, 1973.

Lee, Joseph J. "An Explanation of the 'Universe' in Chinese Poetry," *Literature East & West,* 10:3 (1966), 211–20.

Li, Chi. "The Changing Concept of the Recluse in Chinese Literature," *Harvard Journal of Asiatic Studies,* 24 (1962–63), 234–47.

Lo, Irving Y. C. "Style and Vision in Chinese Poetry: An Inquiry into Its Apollonian and Dionysian Dimensions," *Tsing Hua Journal of Chinese Studies,* New Series 7:1 (1968), 99–113.

Miao, Ronald C. "The 'Ch'i Ai Shih' of the late Han and Chin Periods (I)," *Harvard Journal of Asiatic Studies,* 23 (1973), 183–223.

Miller, James W. "English Romanticism and Chinese Nature Poetry," *Comparative Literature,* 24 (1972), 216–36.

Schafer, Edward H. "The Idea of Created Nature in T'ang Literature," *Philosophy East & West,* 15 (1965), 153–60.

IV. Studies and Translations of Individual Poets

A. *Shih Ching*

TRANSLATIONS

Allen, C. F. R. *The Shih Ching or Classic of Poetry.* London: Kegan Paul, 1891.

Cranmer-Byng, L. *Book of Odes, Shih-king.* London: Murray, 1906.

Jennings, William. *The Shi King, the Old "Poetry Classic" of the Chinese.* London: Routledge, 1891.

Karlgren, Bernhard. *The Book of Odes.* Stockholm: Museum of Far Eastern Antiquities, 1950.

Legge, James. *The Chinese Classics.* 5 Vols. (Hong Kong, 1861–72). New York: Oxford University Press, 1961.

———. *The She King, or the Book of Ancient Poetry* (Translated into English Verse). London: Trubner, 1871. Reprint: *The Book of Poetry.* New York: Paragon Book Gallery, 1967.

Pound, Ezra. *The Classic Anthology as Defined by Confucius.* Cambridge: Harvard University Press, 1954.

Waddell, Helen. *Lyrics from the Chinese.* London: Constable, 6th Printing, 1934.

Waley, Arthur. *The Book of Songs.* London: Allen & Unwin, 1937.

STUDIES

Chow, Tse-tsung. "The Early History of the Chinese Word *Shih* (Poetry)," in *Wen-lin: Studies in the Chinese Humanities,* pp. 151–209, Chow Tse-tsung (ed.). Madison: University of Wisconsin Press, 1968.

Couvreur, S. *Cheu King, Texte Chinois avec une Double Traduction en Français et en Latin* (Peking, 1896). Taichung: Kuangchi Press, 1967.

Dembo, L. S. *The Confucian Odes of Ezra Pound, A Critical Appraisal.* Berkeley: University of California Press, 1963.

Dobson, W. A. C. H. *The Language of the Book Songs*. [Toronto]: University of Toronto Press, 1968.

Granet, Marcel. *Festivals and Songs of Ancient China*. Translated by E. D. Edwards. London: Routledge, 1932.

Hightower, James R. *Han Shih Wai Chuan (Han Ying's Illustrations of the Didactic Application of the Classics of Songs)*. Cambridge: Harvard University Press, 1952.

McNaughton, William. *The Book of Songs*. New York: Twayne Publishers, 1971.

Wang, C. H. *The Bell and the Drum: Shih Ching As Formulaic Poetry in an Oral Tradition*. Berkeley, California: University of California Press, 1974.

B. Poets Before T'ang

Ch'ü Yüan (343?–278 B.C.)

Hawkes, David (tr.). *Ch'u Tz'u, The Songs of the South*. London: Oxford University Press, 1959.

Lim, Boon Keng. *The Li Sao, An Elegy on Encountering Sorrows*. Shanghai, 1929.

Waley, Arthur. *The Nine Songs: A Study of Shamanism in Ancient China*. London: Allen & Unwin, 1955.

Yang, Hsien-yi and Gladys Yang (tr.). *Li Sao and Other Poems of Chu Yuan*. Peking: Foreign Languages Press, 1953.

Hsi K'ang (A.D. 223–62)

Gulik, R. H. van (tr.) *Hsi K'ang and His Poetical Essay on the Lute*. Tokyo: Sophia University, 1941.

Hsieh Ling-yün (385–433)

Frodsham, J. D. (tr.). *The Murmuring Stream: the Life and Works of Hsieh Ling-yün*. 2 Vols. Kuala Lumpur: University of Malaya Press, 1967.

Mather, Richard. "The Landscape Buddhism of the Fifth-Century Poet Hsieh Ling-yün," *Journal of Asian Studies*, 18 (1958), 67–78.

Liu Hsieh (465–522)

Shih, Vincent Y. C. (tr.). *The Literary Mind and the Carving of Dragons (Wen-hsin tiao-lung)*. New York: Columbia University Press, 1959.

Lu Chi (261–303)

Ch'en, S. H. *Lu Chi: Essay on Literature*. Portland, Maine: Anthoensen Press, 1953.

Hughes, E. R. (tr.). *The Art of Letters*. New York: Pantheon, 1951.

T'ao Ch'ien (365–427)

Acker, William (tr.). *T'ao the Hermit: Sixty Poems by T'ao Ch'ien*. London: Thames & Hudson, 1952.

Chang, Lily Pao-hu and Marjorie Sinclair (tr.). *The Poems of T'ao Ch'ien*. Honolulu: University of Hawaii Press, 1953.

Hightower, James Robert (tr.). *The Poetry of T'ao Ch'ien*. Oxford: Oxford University Press, 1970.

———. "T'ao Ch'ien's 'Drinking Wine' Poems," in *Wen-lin: Studies in the Chinese Humanities*. pp. 3–44, Chow Tse-tsung (ed.). Madison, Wisconsin: University of Wisconsin Press, 1968.

———. "Allusion in the Poetry of T'ao Ch'ien," *Harvard Journal of Asiatic Studies*, 31 (1971), 5–27.

Ts'ao Chih (192–232)

Kent, George W. (tr.). *Worlds of Dust and Jade: 47 Poems and Ballads of the Third Century Chinese Poet Ts'ao Chih*. New York: Philosophical Library, 1969.

Whitaker, E. P. K. "Tsaur Jyr's 'Luchshern Fuh,' " *Asia Major*, New Series, 4 (1954), 36–56.

C. T'ang Poets

Han Shan (early 8th century?)

Snyder, Gary. "The Cold Mountain Poems of Han-shan," *Evergreen Review*, 2:6 (1958), 69–80. Also in *Evergreen Review Reader 1957–1967*. New York: Grove Press, pp. 211–15.

Waley, Arthur. "27 Poems by Han-shan," *Encounter*, 3:3 (1954), 3–8.

Watson, Burton. *Cold Mountain: 100 Poems by the T'ang Poet Han-shan*. New York: Columbia University Press, 1962, 1970.

Wu, Chi-yu. "A Study of Han-shan," *T'oung Pao*, 45:4–5 (1957), 392–450.

Han Yü (768–824)

Von Zach, Erwin. *Han Yü's Poetische Werke*. Cambridge: Harvard University Press, 1962.

Li Ho (791–817)

Frodsham, J. D. *The Poems of Li Ho*. Oxford: Clarendon Press, 1970.

South, Margaret Tudor. *Li Ho: A Scholar-official of the Yüan-ho Period, 806–821*. Adelaide, Australia, 1967.

Li Po (701–762)

Cooper, Arthur (tr.). *Li Po and Tu Fu*. Baltimore: Penguin, 1973.

Eide, Elling O. "On Li Po," in *Perspectives on the T'ang*, pp. 367–403, Arthur F. Wright and Denis Twitchett (eds.). New Haven: Yale University Press, 1973.

Obata, Shigeyoshi (tr.). *The Works of Li Po*. New York: Dutton, 1922.

Waley, Arthur. *The Poetry and Career of Li Po*. London: Allen & Unwin, 1950.

Li Shang-yin (813–858)

Liu, James J. Y. *The Poetry of Li Shang-yin: Ninth-Century Baroque Chinese Poet*. Chicago: University of Chicago Press, 1969.

————. "Ambiguities in Li Shang-yin's Poetry," in *Wen-lin: Studies in the Chinese Humanities,* Chow Tse-tsung (ed.). Madison, Wisconsin: University of Wisconsin Press, 1968.

Liu Tsung-yüan (773–819)

Nienhauser, William H. *et al. Liu Tsung-yüan* (Twayne World Authors Series). New York: Twayne Publishers, 1973.

Meng Hao-jan (689–740)

Frankel, Hans (tr.). *Biographies of Meng Hao-jan* (Chinese Dynastic Histories Translations, No. 1). Berkeley: University of California Press, 1952, 1961.

Po Chü-yi (772–846)

Feifel, Eugene. *Po Chü-i as a Censor.* Mouton, 1961.

Levy, Howard S. *Translations from Po Chü-i's Collected Works.* 2 Vols. New York: Paragon, 1971.

Waley, Arthur. *The Life and Times of Po Chü-i.* London: Allen & Unwin, 1949.

Tu Fu (719–770)

Alley, Rewi (tr.). *Tu Fu: Selected Poems.* Peking: Foreign Language Press, 1962.

Ayscough, Florence. *Tu Fu: The Autobiography of a Chinese Poet,* Volume I, A.D. 712–759. Boston: Houghton Mifflin, 1929.

————. *Travels of a Chinese Poet: Tu Fu, Guest of Rivers and Lake,* Volume II, A.D. 759–770. Boston: Houghton Mifflin, 1934.

Davis, A. R. *Tu Fu.* New York: Twayne Publishers, 1971.

Hawkes, David. *A Little Primer of Tu Fu.* Oxford: Clarendon Press, 1967.

Hung, William. *Tu Fu: China's Greatest Poet.* Cambridge, Massachusetts: Harvard University Press, 1952.

Lee, Joseph J. "Tu Fu's Art Criticism and Han Kan's Horse Painting," *Journal of the American Oriental Society,* 90:3 (1970), 449–61.

Mei, Tsu-lin and Kao Yu-kung. "Tu Fu's 'Autumn Meditations,' An Exercise in Linguistic Criticism," *Harvard Journal of Asiatic Studies,* 38 (1968), 44–80.

Stimson, Hugh M. "The Rimes of 'Northward Journey' by Duh-Fuu, 712–770," *Journal of the American Oriental Society,* 93:2 (1973), 129–35.

Von Zach, Erwin. *Tu Fu's Gedichte* (Harvard-Yenching Institute Studies, VIII). 2 Vols. Cambridge: Harvard University Press, 1952.

Yoshikawa, Kojiro. "Tu Fu's Poetics and Poetry," *Acta Asiatica,* 16–17 (1969), 1–26.

Wang Wei (701–761)

Chang, Yin-nan and Lewis C. Walmsley (tr.). *Poems by Wang Wei.* Rutland, Vermont: Tuttle, 1958.

Ch'en Yi-hsin. "Wang Wei, the Nature Poet," *Chinese Literature,* 7 (1962), 12–22.

Robinson, G. W. (tr.). *Poems of Wang Wei.* Harmondworth: Penguin, 1973.

Walmsley, Lewis C. and Dorothy B. Walmsley. *Wang Wei, the Painter-Poet.* Rutland, Vermont: Tuttle, 1968.

Yip, Wai-lim (tr.). *Hiding the Universe, Poems by Wang Wei.* New York: Grossman Publishers, 1972.

Yüan Chen (779–831)

Hightower, James R. *"Yüan Chen and 'The Story of Ying-ying,'"* *Harvard Journal of Asiatic Studies,* 23 (1973), 90–123.

D. Poets Since T'ang

Fan Ch'eng-ta (1126–1193)

Bullett, Gerald. *The Golden Year of Fan Ch'eng-ta.* Cambridge: Cambridge University Press, 1946.

Hsin Ch'i-chi (1140–1207)

Lo, Irving Yucheng. *Hsin Ch'i-chi.* New York: Twayne Publishers, 1971.

Kao Ch'i (1336–1374)

Mote, F. W. *The Poet Kao Ch'i, 1336–1374.* Princeton: Princeton University Press, 1962.

Li Ch'ing-chao (1084?–c. 1151)

Hsu, K'ai-yu. "The Poems of Li Ch'ing-chao (1084–1141)," *Publication of the Modern Language Association,* 77 (1962), 521–28.

Hu, P'in-ch'ing. *Li Ch'ing-chao.* New York: Twayne Publishers, 1966.

Li Yü (937–978)

Liu, Yih-ling and Shahid Suhrawardy (tr.). *Poems of Lee Hou-chu.* Bombay: Orient Longmans, 1948.

Lu Yu (1125–1210)

Candlin, Clara M. (tr.). *The Rapier of Lu.* London: Murray, 1946.

Watson, Burton. *The Old Man Who Does as He Pleases.* New York: Columbia University Press, 1973.

Mao Tse-tung (1893–)

Barnstone, Willis (tr.). *The Poems of Mao Tse-tung.* New York: Harper & Row, 1972.

Boyd, Andrew (tr.). *Nineteen Poems by Mao Tse-tung.* Peking: Foreign Languages Press, 1958.

Ch'en, Jerome and Michael Bullock (tr.). "Thirty-seven Poems by Mao Tse-tung," in Jerome Ch'en, *Mao and the Chinese Revolution,* pp. 315–60. New York: Oxford University Press, 1965.

Engle, Hua-ling Nieh and Paul Engle (tr.). *Poems of Mao Tse-tung.* New York: Dell Publishing Co., 1972.

Ng, Yong-sang. *"The Poetry of Mao tse-tung,"* in *Chinese Communist Literature,* Cyril Birch (ed.). New York: Frederick A. Praeger, 1963.

Tay, C. N. "From Snow to Plum Blossom," *Journal of Asian Studies,* 25 (February 1966), 287–303.

Wong, Man (tr.). *Poems by Mao Tse-tung.* Hong Kong: Eastern Horizon Press, 1966.

Su Man-shu (1884–1918)

Liu, Wu-chi. *Su Man-shu.* New York: Twayne Publishers, 1972.

Su Shih (1037–1101)

Le Gros Clark, Cyril D. (tr.). *The Prose-Poetry of Su Tung-p'o.* London: Kegan Paul, 1935. Reprint: New York: Paragon, 1964.

Lin, Yutang. *The Gay Genius.* New York: John Day, 1947.

Watson, Burton (tr.). *Su Tung-p'o: Selections from a Sung Dynasty Poet.* New York: Columbia University Press, 1965.

Yüan Mei (1716–1797)

Waley, Arthur. *Yüan Mei: Eighteenth Century Chinese Poet.* London: Allen & Unwin, 1956. Reprint: New York: Grove Press, n.d.

Background on
Poets and Poems

PART I

Shih Ching (Book of Poetry)

Literary historians and critics have from time to time tried to point out that the Chinese had an imaginative literature dated before even the oldest songs in the *Shih Ching*. While this may be true, they must, nevertheless, agree that the poetry in the *Shih Ching* is the fountainhead of Chinese literature. In the shaping of a basically lyrical tradition, no single book in the Chinese language is more powerful and significant than this Confucian classic. The *shih* form, from which is derived the generic name of poetry (*shih*), originated from the *Shih Ching*. Furthermore, its contents embody some of the most trenchant and surging themes that are to recur in varying forms throughout the Chinese poetic tradition.

We are not sure whether Confucius was responsible for the compilation of the book. We only know that by his time the book had already taken a definite shape, and the "three hundred poems" were said to furnish one of the main textbooks in the Confucian education, in which poetry played an important role. The *Analects* and the *Mencius*, for instance, abound in quotations from the *Shih Ching* on ethical and philosophical mattters. Along with the other classics, the book was banned in the third century B.C., but was restored in four versions in the early Han dynasty. Of the four, the so-called Mao version has survived almost intact through the next two millennia. It is to this particular version, now containing 305 poems, that we refer when we talk about the *Shih Ching*.

Traditional scholarship assigns most of the 305 poems to a period from the twelfth century B.C. to the seventh century B.C. in the Chou dynasty. Based upon both external and internal evidences, we believe that the *Shih Ching* did not take its final shape until the seventh century B.C. and that the period from the twelfth to the seventh century B.C. was a formative period for almost all the 305 poems, including the so-called Shang hymns (Nos. 301–5), which were composed in the state of Sung after the fall of the Shang dynasty. Moreover, many of these poems were constantly modified and altered in form and language throughout the centuries until the time of Confucius, when they assumed their final shape. The poetry of the *Shih*

Ching exemplifies the plenitude of Chinese literature in an oral tradition and the humanistic essence of Confucius' teaching.

The corpus of the *Shih Ching* is traditionally divided into four sections: the *feng* ("ballads of the states"), the *hsiao ya* ("festive songs on lesser occasions"), the *ta ya* ("festive songs on greater occasions"), and the *sung* ("hymns and eulogies"). The *feng* section (Nos. 1–160) is comprised of poems from fifteen states, mainly folk ballads ranging from love songs to political complaints; the *hsiao ya* section (Nos. 161–234), primarily of festivity chants and very refined poems of praise and protest; the *ta ya* section (Nos. 235–65), mostly of verse compositions in sophisticated structure about dynastic histories and vicissitudes; and the *sung* section (Nos. 266–305), basically liturgic hymns sung in ancestral temples of three noble houses: the Chou, the Lu, and the Shang. There are, of course, thematic overlappings and exceptions in this classification.

(C. H. WANG)

Ch'ü Yüan (343?–278 B.C.)

The poems of Ch'ü Yüan, China's first major poet, are found in the *Ch'u Tz'u (Verses of Ch'u)*, the second important anthology of ancient Chinese poetry, which also includes poems by Ch'ü Yüan's followers and imitators from the third century B.C. to the first century A.D. A southern state, Ch'u occupied the vast Yangtze region which developed a flourishing culture in Ch'ü Yüan's time and was fertile in myth and religious beliefs.

Besides being a poet, Ch'ü Yüan was known as a virtuous statesman loyal to the king and patriotic to his country. A descendant of the noble family of Ch'u, he attained in his youth a high position at court and was entrusted with the compilation of government edicts and regulations. But his youthful brilliance and integrity of character soon aroused the jealousy of other courtiers, who slandered him before the king. Subsequently, Ch'ü Yüan was banished from court, to which he never returned, the only other official business he undertook being a diplomatic mission to a neighboring state. During this period Ch'u contended for the hegemony of the Chinese world with Ch'in, a powerful state in the northwest. This rivalry led to more diplomatic activities, military expeditions, and political intrigues. Against Ch'ü Yüan's advice, the king of Ch'u set out for a meeting with the king of Ch'in, but was detained and died in captivity in Ch'in. Ch'ü Yüan thus became further alienated from the new king who came to the throne, and throughout his long life Ch'ü Yüan was so overwhelmed with grief and disappointment that shortly after the capture of the Ch'u capital (Ying) by the Ch'in forces, he drowned himself in the River Mi-lo.

Ch'ü Yüan's poetic works consist of some twenty-five titles, including the *Li Sao, Chiu Ko (The Nine Songs), Chiu Chang (The Nine Declarations), T'ien Wen (Heaven Questioned)*, and *Chao Hun (Summoning the Soul)*. Although his authorship of these works has been questioned by modern critics, there is little evidence to prove that Ch'ü Yüan could not have written them. In fact, everything in Ch'ü Yüan's background—his career, temperament, and knowledge of Chinese history—convinces the reader that he was the most likely author of these poems.

The Nine Songs (actually eleven in number, the last two being added later to the sequence) are shamanistic hymns to the various deities and spirits in the land of Ch'u. Sometimes, the songs can be erotic in tone, as in "Lord of the River Hsiang," while at other times a more serious and reflective mood pervades poems such as "The Great Arbiter of Fate." In *The Nine Declarations* are poems written during different periods in the poet's life. Except for "Hymn to the Orange," apparently a work of his youth, the poems in this group reveal a poet's agonizing soul beset by grief and sufferings in life. These sentiments reach their climax in "A Lament for Ying," where the poet's personal sorrow for the loss of the king's favor merges with his broad sympathy for the sad plight of the Ch'u people at the fall of their capital.

The title of the poem *Li Sao*, of which two selections are given here, has been variously rendered as "The Lament," "Encountering Sorrow," and "An Ode on the Sorrows of Departure." A long autobiographical poem, it begins with an account of the poet's parentage and birth, his cultivation of moral qualities, his subsequent fall from the king's favor, and his resolve to continue in the righteous path. The laments are interwoven with sections which recount the poet's adventures and journeys, and the counsels he receives from men and spirits, including a visit with a shaman wizard. The most lyrical part of the poem is a description of an imaginary journey to Heaven and the quest for beauties in mountains and streams as well as in the realm of legendary history. When all these efforts prove futile, the poet finally but reluctantly decides to leave his country and the world.

It has been suggested, somewhat unconvincingly, that the author of the *Li Sao* could have been a magician and its theme mythmaking. Whatever the merit of this speculation, the *Li Sao* poet has created in the poem, through an abundance of similes and allegories, a supremely beautiful world of fantasy. It exemplifies, moreover, the poetry of moral persuasion at its best. In sheer artistry and poetic power, the *Li Sao* has never been equaled and, together with the *Shih Ching,* remained a source of inspiration for countless poets of later generations.

(WU-CHI LIU)

PART II

Hsiang Chi (232–202 B.C.)

Hsiang Chi, better known by his courtesy-name of Hsiang Yü, was the unsuccessful contender with Liu Pang for the Chinese empire toward the end of the Ch'in empire. A native of Hsia-hsiang in the state of Ch'u, he led an uprising against Ch'in in 209 B.C. and had himself declared the "Hegemon

King of Ch'u" (*Ch'u pa-wang*). His valor and strategy won him many bat-
tles until he emerged as Liu Pang's strongest rival. The "Song of Kai-hsia"
was sung on the night of his last battle. In later centuries, his heroic life was
often romanticized in Chinese dramatic and operatic literature.

Liu Pang, Emperor Kao-tsu of Han (*256–195* B.C.)

Liu Pang (*Liu Chi,* whose posthumous title Kao-tsu means "Exalted An-
cestor") was the founder of the Han dynasty. A man of humble birth, he
led a band of rebels against the Ch'in empire and became the first among
many rebel groups to enter the Ch'in capital of Hsien-yang in 207 B.C. and
thus, by prior agreement, was declared the ruler of the land of Ch'in. Liu
Pang is not known either for his learning or for his respect for scholars;
the "Song of the Great Wind" is the only poem attributed to him.

Liu Ch'e, Emperor Wu of Han (*156–87* B.C.)

Liu Ch'e was a great patron of literature whose long reign of over half a
century (140–87 B.C.) was probably the most flourishing period of Han
China. Trade and expansion carried Chinese power and influence to Central
Asia, Korea, and the modern Vietnam. At home, he fostered the study of
Confucianism by establishing in 136 B.C. the degree of the Doctor of
Classics and created China's first imperial university twelve years later, for
the training of officials and prospective degree candidates. Although in the
later years he engaged in Taoist pursuit of the elixir of immortality and
other occult activities, it was his efforts which produced the entrenchment
of the classics and the syncretization of Confucianism with other popular
beliefs of the time.

Being particularly fond of music and poetry himself, Liu Ch'e greatly
expanded the staff and activities of the institution known as *Yüeh-fu* (the
Music Bureau) for the supervision of musical compositions and the col-
lection of folk songs; the name itself became an important subgenre of
Chinese verse. He was said to be especially partial to the *sao* meter and to
the "rhyme-prose" (*fu*), which remained the favorite of the literati of Han
times.

Nineteen Poems in Ancient Style

No one knows for certain who invented the pentasyllabic form of Chinese
poetry (*Wu-yen shih*), or exactly when this became established as an ac-
cepted poetic medium. What we know as classical Chinese poetry (excluding
the *Shih Ching* and *Li Sao*) grows out of this oldest and the basic meter—
with five words, or characters, per line and usually divided by a caesura be-

tween the second and the third. It should be pointed out that the first four songs in Part II of this anthology were still composed in the *sao* meter, which made use of an extra caesural particle (*hsi* in modern pronunciation) to break up an otherwise unwieldy line of nine or more syllables.

The "Nineteen Poems in Ancient Style" (*ku-shih shih-chiu shou*) by anonymous writers hold a pre-eminent position in Chinese poetry, for tradition considers them the earliest preserved poetry written in the pentasyllabic meter, which became the dominant form of the next thousand years. Later Chinese poets cultivated and imitated the pensive melancholy of these poems. Readers and commentators seized on their ambiguity to give the poems political interpretations—the virtuous minister alienated from his sovereign—a theme common in the *Shih Ching* and *Ch'u Tz'u*. In short, the "Nineteen Poems in Ancient Style" were produced at that happy juncture in poetic evolution when old traditional themes are summarized and first expressed in a new revitalized language. As Diény says in his excellent study of the series (Jean-Pierre Diény, *Les dix-neuf poèmes anciens*, Paris: Presses Universitaires de France, 1963), "gathering the heritage of the past, they announced the future."

(CHARLES HARTMAN)

Ts'ai Yen (c. A.D. 200)

Authorship, style, and content mark "The Lamentation" (*Pei-fen Shih*) by Ts'ai Yen as a special poem. Consisting of 108 lines, with alternate lines rhyming (with just a few exceptions), this is the earliest and the longest composition in the five-word *shih* category. Ts'ai Yen's authorship of this poem is well authenticated, despite the skepticism expressed by critics.[1] This poem is sometimes known as the First Part of "The Lamentation" since there exists a second poem with the same content but written in the *sao* meter (also believed to have been written by Ts'ai Yen). Attesting to the popularity of this work, there exists still another version, known as *"Hu-chia shih-pa p'o"* ("Eighteen Beats of the Tartar Whistle"), a definitely later work.[2]

---

[1] Among those who questioned Ts'ai Yen's authorship is the Sung poet Su Shih, who argued on the grounds of internal evidence (denunciatory opening lines against Tung Cho) and stylistic sophistication of the poem, which Su considered as too similar to "The Ballad of Mulan." Among contemporary scholars, Yü Kuan-ying has put forth the most convincing argument for Ts'ai Yen's authorship. For more information, see quotations in the *Wei-Tsin Nan-pei-ch'ao wen-hsüeh ts'an-k'ao tzu-liao* (*Research Materials for Literary Works of the Wei, Tsin, and Northern and Southern Dynasties, 220–588*), Peking, 1962, Vol. 1, pp. 172–73. For historical background of this poem, see Yi-t'ung Wang, "The Lamentation of Ts'ai Yen (c. A.D. 200)," *Delta* (Jan.–Mar. 1960), 11–14, from which this translation has been taken and revised by the author.

[2] A contrary argument, that this song was also Ts'ai Yen's, has been presented by Kuo Mo-jo, cf. *Hu-chia shih-pa p'o t'ao-lun chi* (*Essays on "Hu-chia shih-pa p'o"*), Peking, 1959.

Ts'ai Yen (*Wen-chi*) was the daughter and the only child of Ts'ai Yung (133–92), a prominent official of the Later Han dynasty, known for his erudition and his large private collection of books. He lived through one of the darkest periods in Chinese history which included the misrule of the eunuchs (generally hostile to intellectuals), an unsuccessful palace coup (against the eunuchs), and finally the rebellion of Tung Cho (d. 192), a frontier general who seized power in the central government. Ts'ai Yung, one of Tung Cho's close associates, was imprisoned at the time of Tung Cho's downfall and shortly afterward died in prison. The turmoil of this period came to an end in 208 when Ts'ao Ts'ao, a statesman and man of letters, declared himself the prime minister. (His son became the founder of the Wei kingdom following the demise of the Later Han dynasty.)

When the civil war broke out, Ts'ai Yen had returned to live with the family as a young widow (from a former and childless marriage). Later, during the Tartar invasion, she was captured, carried north as a prisoner, and married to a Tartar chieftain. Two children were born to her during the twelve years of her captivity. When Ts'ao Ts'ao, who was a friend of her father's, came to prominence, he provided enough gold and treasure to ransom her from the Tartars so that the Ts'ai family line would not become extinct. Upon her return to China, she married for a third time.

"The Lamentation" tells about this bizarre and bitter life of the author. It not only describes in vivid detail the hardship and suffering of a war prisoner and hostage[3] but also reveals her resentment, joy, and resoluteness in the face of extreme adversity. The poem may be viewed both as a political and social document of the time and as an early record of the heroic and tragic elements in Chinese literature.

(YI-T'UNG WANG)

Hsü Kan (*171–214*)

A native of Po-hai in what is now a part of Shantung province, Hsü Kan's contemporary literary fame rested upon his prose tract *"Chung lun"* ("Disquisition on the Middle Way"). Only a handful of his verses have survived, of which the elegant series titled *"Shih ssu"* or "Boudoir Thoughts" is the most complete and representative. Hsü Kan's last years were spent in the service of the statesman and military leader Ts'ao Ts'ao and he became a member of the famous Pleiad, the *Chien-an ch'i tzu* (The Seven Literary Masters of the Chien-an Reign-period [196–220]).

(RONALD C. MIAO)

---

3 See Yi-t'ung Wang, "Slaves and Other Comparable Social Groups During the Northern Dynasties (386–618)," *Harvard Journal of Asiatic Studies,* II (1953), 301–7.

Wang Ts'an (177–217)

Wang Ts'an (*Chung-hsün*), another member of the Chien-an Pleiad, was a scion of a distinguished family of statesmen. Known for his prodigious memory and literary gift, he was appreciated as a boy genius by the Han scholar Ts'ai Yung. Sometime after A.D. 193, he fled the capital, Ch'ang-an, for Ching-chou, a vast territory in the south of China governed by Liu Piao, a friend of the Wang clan's. He sought Liu Piao's patronage; and it was at this time he wrote his "Seven Poems of Lament," describing life in the war-torn territories. Later his political allegiance shifted to Ts'ao Ts'ao, who appointed him to high office. He wrote a total of five poems entitled *"Ts'ung chün shih,"* or "Songs on Joining the Army," probably around A.D. 216, when he followed Ts'ao Ts'ao's military campaign against the rival state of Wu. One selection given here is a good example of Chinese eulogistic verse, expressive of a martial spirit combined with a loyal subject's protestation of duty and honor. His "Occasional Verses," though they celebrate royal hunts and excursions or other important events, suggest something of the animation and high spirit on such occasions.

(RONALD C. MIAO)

Ts'ao P'i, Emperor Wen of Wei (187–226)

Ts'ao P'i (*Tzu-huan*) was the second son of Ts'ao Ts'ao, upon whose death he succeeded to the prime ministership. In A.D. 220 he brought about the abdication of the last Han emperor and established himself as the first emperor of the Wei kingdom, with the capital in Lo-yang.

Ts'ao P'i was also known as a great patron of literature and as a poet and critic. A coterie of writers who gathered around him became known as the Chien-an Pleiad. In addition to his poems, he left an "Essay on Literature," which may be regarded as the earliest work of Chinese literary criticism. "The Lotus Pond" is an example of the poetry written on formal occasions, the Western Gardens being a favorite excursion spot of the Chien-an poets. The "Song of Yen" is regarded as the oldest and most complete example of *shih* in the seven-word form. Again, it employs a *yüeh-fu* title to treat a then popular theme, the separation and longing between husband and wife.

(RONALD C. MIAO)

Ts'ao Chih (192–232)

As one studies the biography of Ts'ao Chih, one is faced with three different personalities: first, the historical Ts'ao Chih; second, the literary image which he presents of himself in his writings in prose and verse; and third, the legendary figure of an enormously talented and singularly unhappy prince, a mixture of fact and fiction, developed over the centuries from historical, literary, and anecdotical sources.

Ts'ao Chih (*Tzu-chien*) was born as the third son of the mighty warlord Ts'ao Ts'ao (155–220). At that time the Han empire was breaking up, and Ts'ao Ts'ao was gaining control of North China, which was still the heartland of China. It was becoming clear that sooner or later the Ts'ao family would abolish the Han dynasty in name as well as in fact, and establish a dynasty of its own. This did happen in 220, when Ts'ao Ts'ao died and his eldest son Ts'ao P'i accepted the abdication of the last Han emperor and became the first emperor of a new dynasty, Wei, which was to rule North China for forty-six years. This event was a bitter disappointment for Ts'ao Chih, who had himself long had ambitions for the throne. But he lost in the rivalry with his elder brother. The contest between the two brothers Ts'ao P'i and Ts'ao Chih, each supported by a coterie of friends at Ts'ao Ts'ao's court, lasted from 211 to 217. In the latter year, Ts'ao Ts'ao made his final decision to appoint Ts'ao P'i as his heir apparent.

In his early years, Ts'ao Chih seems to have led a gay and extravagant life. He was addicted to luxury and worldly pleasures. Contemporary records as well as his own poetry and prose writings reveal him to have been fond of eating and drinking at sumptuous banquets, of horseback riding, hunting, and swordplay, of watching cockfights, of outings and gay parties with music, dancing, and beautiful women, and of poetry improvisations. But the Ts'ao family placed severe restrictions on all of its princes, limiting their freedom of movement and frequently changing their enfeoffments, so that they often had to move from one enforced residence to another. Ts'ao Chih was enfeoffed no less than ten times, in eight different locations. The legendary picture of Ts'ao Chih presents him as having been persecuted by his brother the emperor, but in fact the policy was not directed against Ts'ao Chih personally but applied equally to all the Ts'ao princes, so as to keep them from plotting against the leaders of the clan.

Having been an unsuccessful contender for the throne, Ts'ao Chih was naturally an object of suspicion at the newly established Wei court, and relations were cool between him and his brother Ts'ao P'i (known to history as Wei Wen-ti, reigned 220–26). Ts'ao Chih's frustration in this respect continued when Ts'ao P'i died in 226 and was succeeded by his son Ts'ao Jui (Wei Ming-ti, reigned 226–39); the new emperor kept his uncle under the same restrictions. Throughout his life (he died in 232 at the age of forty) Ts'ao Chih never held an important government post.

Ts'ao Chih came from a family of literary men. His father Ts'ao Ts'ao and his brother Ts'ao P'i were both distinguished poets and prose writers, but Ts'ao Chih was the most gifted of the family. His poetry marks an important stage in the development of Chinese lyric poetry. In his time, men of letters were struggling to establish literature as an authentic art form, independent of other forms of writing, but their attempts at self-expression were usually clumsy and crude. Ts'ao skillfully combined this incipient lyricism of the literati with the well-established folk art of the anonymous *yüeh-fu* ballads that had been flourishing for three or four centuries. He used different meters but preferred the five-syllable line, which had become prominent in the second century A.D. Among his favorite poetic themes are the glitter and luxury of court life, the restless wanderer, the deserted wife, the Taoist immortal ascending to Heaven, and other highly imaginative fantasies. His diction and imagery are characterized by contrasting extremes and rapid changes. Among recurring images there are tall objects, lofty and remote places, soaring birds, roads, rivers, roaming animals, and drifting plants. His influence on other poets, in his own time and in all succeeding ages, has been great.

(HANS H. FRANKEL)

Juan Chi (210–263)

Juan Chi (*Ssu-tsung;* also known by his sobriquet of "Pu-ping," from his service as Chief of Infantry [Commissary]), native of Ch'en-liu, Honan, was a musician and an iconoclastic poet whose works, though not extensive, had a wide appeal among some of the early T'ang poets. Son of Juan Yü, a prominent poet of the Chien an era, he was known in his lifetime for his erudition, his familiarity with the Taoist canon, and his adroit defiance of authorities. Witnessing the rapid decline of the Wei dynasty and at the same time unwilling to lend his support to the rising political fortune of the Ssu-ma family (who founded the Tsin dynasty), Juan Chi shared with many other intellectuals a violent disdain for politics and sought safety by espousing the trend known as the "Pure Conversation" (*ch'ing-t'an*), or "Philosophical Discourses." These were usually held in a bamboo grove outside the capital of Lo-yang, accompanied by much drinking; hence, the seven leaders, including Juan Chi, were known as the "Seven Sages of the Bamboo Grove"! Juan himself was known to have kept himself in a state of inebriation for months on end, just to head off a quasi-political discussion with an agent of the Ssu-ma family. His series of eighty-two *Yung-huai* poems, like those untitled poems of Ts'ao Chih, continued to employ the allegorical framework, but contained more explicit and personal references. All written in five-syllabic lines, these lyrical verses nonetheless marked a departure from the works of Juan Chi's predecessors by a strict avoidance of *yüeh-fu* topics.

T'ao Ch'ien (365–427)

T'ao Ch'ien, popularly known as T'ao Yüan-ming, was born the son of an official family in a district near modern Kiukiang in Kiangsi. During his youth the family fortune declined and, after several frustrating attempts to secure an appointment, he gave up all worldly ambitions and retired to his home and gardens while he was still in his early forties.

T'ao spent the remaining years of his life as a gentleman farmer, whose activities he sang in his poems. He was able to lead a simple, leisurely, and contented life, devoted to books, poetry, and music, but he also knew extreme poverty (cf. "Begging for Food"). Quiet pleasures (drinking with neighbors) or stark tragedies (when his house was burned down)—these events he recorded in his poems with great candidness, thus setting an example for the kind of intimate, personal poetry which later became popular with Chinese poets.

An essential quality of T'ao Ch'ien's poetry is his serene philosophical attitude toward life in the midst of adversities. In spite of the political turbulences of his time, which culminated in the usurpation of the Eastern Tsin throne by Liu Yü, founder of the [Liu] Sung dynasty in 420, and his personal misfortunes, T'ao Ch'ien remained constant in the pursuit of a good, meaningful life marked by happy family relationship, friendly contact with neighbors, and a contemplative peace of mind in harmony with nature.

Like Hsieh Ling-yün, a younger contemporary, T'ao Ch'ien was a lover of nature, preceding by several centuries the T'ang nature poets such as Wang Wei and Meng Hao-jan. But whereas Hsieh wrote landscape poems on the mountains and streams, T'ao described in his verses the more homely aspects of nature in the fields and gardens, especially the delights of a rural community in which he found himself. He was well known for his poems on the chrysanthemums, with which he is inevitably linked by later poets. But in addition to a sheer delight in the beauty of nature, he often gives a philosophical and allegorical interpretation of his nature poems far beyond their original meaning.

Though resigning himself to the life of a commoner, T'ao Ch'ien was not totally unconcerned with current political events and situations in the country, and in spite of his Taoist and Buddhist leanings—he made friends with Buddhist monks of the White Lotus Society, which later was to develop into Ch'an Buddhism—he upheld Confucian views on moral virtues and uprightness as symbolized by the chrysanthemums and pines. His vision of a utopian community was described in his famous essay, the "Peach Blossom Spring"—an account of indescribably beautiful scenery, as well as a record of ancient costumes, mores, and virtues, which became a favorite theme of many poets of later centuries.

Another important topic of T'ao Ch'ien's poetry is drinking, which appears more frequently in his poems than in any of his predecessors'. He is the first known Chinese poet who made it a habit to sing of wine and its pleasures, setting up a recurrent tradition in the works of later poets, notably Li Po. It should be noted, however, that in the Chinese tradition, drinking is not to be equated with alcoholism; among its redeeming virtues, the most important is the inspiration it gives the poet. Wine did inspire T'ao

Ch'ien to write some of his best poems in the series entitled "Drinking Wine," four of which are included in this volume.

In Chinese poetry T'ao Ch'ien occupies an eminent position as the foremost writer of the five-word verses in the ancient style. At a time when Chinese poetry and prose suffered from overelaborateness and artificiality, T'ao Ch'ien stood staunchly for the simplicity of style and content. His language is direct, precise, and devoid of the ornateness and affectation that was the hallmark of the works of his contemporaries. By running against the current, he was rated by a later critic (Chung Yung, 469–518, in his *Shih-p'in*) as a poet of the second rank. But his warm appreciation of life, his moral rectitude, his philosophical insights, as well as the truthfulness of his sentiments and the freshness of his nature images, have won him recognition since the T'ang dynasty, and his fame has grown with time. Today he is generally regarded as one of China's major poets.

(WU-CHI LIU)

Hsieh Ling-yün (385–433)

Hsieh Ling-yün, the duke of K'ang-lo, belonged to one of the most wealthy and influential families of his day. He enjoyed great popularity as a poet during his lifetime; he was also a noted calligrapher, painter, lay Buddhist, and author of rhyme-prose (*fu*). His "Rhyme-prose on Dwelling in the Mountains" (*Shan-chü fu*) is one of the finest examples of its genre.

The best of Hsieh's poetry (in all close to one hundred poems have survived) dates from the decade beginning with the year 422. Prior to that time Hsieh had held several official posts, and with his talents and family connections could have expected a brilliant career at court. However, in the summer of 422 he unsuccessfully supported his friend Liu I-chen (the prince of Lu-ling) for the throne. In the ensuing power play the prince was exiled and murdered, while Hsieh was demoted to the position of magistrate of Yung-chia, where he remained about a year before retiring to his family estate in Shih-ning (near Shao-hsing, Chekiang). Some of Hsieh's best-known poems (including the first five in our selection) were written during this year. Clearly Hsieh underwent a fierce spiritual struggle to recover from the sudden ruin of his political career. The Yung-chia poems abound with barbs against the government, and at the same time reveal growing aesthetic interest in mountain landscapes together with a Taoist affirmation of living in harmony with nature, cleansed of worldly ambitions.

Hsieh intermittently held other official positions, and came increasingly into disfavor for his neglect of duty, riotous parties, and arrogant behavior toward men who could make their influence felt at court. In 431 he was once more assigned an "exile" post in the south (the disillusioned last poem of this selection probably dates from this period), and barely escaped execution when he resisted arrest and staged a small uprising. Exiled again to the region of modern Canton, in 433 he finally suffered public execution on trumped-up charges of rebellion.

The poems written after 423 confirm Hsieh's reputation as China's first great "nature poet." Many of these describe the poet's wanderings about the hills surrounding his Shih-ning estate. In his "nature" poetry Hsieh seeks, and sometimes achieves, a mystical vision of nature; often the landscape will suddenly be transformed at the moment the poet becomes so immersed in it that he loses all sense of normal distinctions, including that of self. It has been suggested that this manner of revealing a landscape is related to the Buddhist concept of "instantaneous enlightenment," which Hsieh himself strongly supported. The transcendental visions generally are not sustained throughout the poem, but perhaps we should not consider them any less valid even if discordant subjective concerns, usually expressed as longing for absent friends, do impinge.

(FRANCIS WESTBROOK)

Pao Chao (?–466)

Pao Chao (*Ming-yüan*), native of Tung-hai in Kiangsu, was the major poet of the middle decades of the fifth century. Though he came to maturity only shortly after the death of T'ao Ch'ien and Hsieh Ling-yün, his style of poetry is very different from that of the earlier poets. In particular, he was the first great master of the *yüeh-fu* ballad. In these poems, often using the persona of the aging and embittered ex-military man, Pao expresses the disappointments of his own life. Born into an obscure family, he never succeeded, in spite of his literary genius, in breaking into the ruling elite.

Pao himself was killed by mutinous soldiers during the confusion which followed the unsuccessful attempt at rebellion by his patron, the prince of Lin-hai. Some two hundred of his poems, about one third of them in the ballad style, have survived, to win the admiration of both Li Po and Tu Fu, and to pave the way for the "heroic" or "frontier" poetry of Kao Shih and Ts'en Shen. His best-known poems are eighteen ballads of "The Weary Road," in which the ordinary incidents of life are charged with intense lyricism.

(DANIEL BRYANT)

Liu Chün, Emperor Hsiao-wu of [Liu]-Sung (430–464)

Liu Chün (*Hsiu-lung*), native of P'eng-ch'eng in Kiangsu, was a grandson of Liu Yü, the founder of the Sung kingdom. When his father, Emperor Wen (reigned 424–53), was murdered by the heir apparent, he led a punitive campaign against his brother and succeeded in having himself proclaimed emperor. He was known posthumously as Emperor Hsiao-wu (reigned 454–64) of Sung.

Shen Yüeh (441–512)

Shen Yüeh (*Hsiu-wen*) sprang from a military family of relatively low status in the area of what is now Chekiang province in southeastern China. His great-grandfather, Shen Mu-fu, had been executed for his implication in the peasant rebellion led by the Taoist-magician Sun En in 399, and his grandfather, Shen Lin-tzu (377–422), in a heroic effort to restore the family honor, had distinguished himself in military service to the Liu-Sung court (420–79). Yüeh's father, Shen P'u (416–53), unjustly accused of disloyalty by a rival, was put to death when Yüeh was only twelve, but through the intervention of family friends Yüeh himself escaped with his life. These experiences of his forebears made him extremely circumspect throughout his life and help to explain how he managed to hold positions of trust through three dynasties: the Sung, Ch'i (479–502), and Liang (502–57)—though at his death he was plagued by feelings of guilt at having betrayed the last ruler of Ch'i.

Precisely because of his powers of survival in a particularly bloody period of the Southern Dynasties, some critics faulted him for a fundamental lack of integrity. Others caviled at his literary innovations, claiming his rules for tonal euphony did violence to the spontaneous outpouring of simple feeling which lyric poetry should be. Some even complained that his love poems were "heterogeneous and lascivious." There were murmurings, too, that a man whose family for generations had been devotees of the Taoist sect of the Heavenly Master (*T'ien-shih Tao*) should have been such an ardent lay supporter of Buddhism that no fewer than twenty-four essays signed with his name appear in the "Expanded Collection of Apologues on the Propagation of the Light" (*Kuang hung-ming-chi*) in the Chinese Buddhist canon. Still others castigated his major historiographic work, his monumental *History of the Sung Dynasty* (*Sung-shu*), as a bilious tract shot through with narrow prejudice.

Viewed from the perspective of fourteen centuries, however, Shen Yüeh clearly emerges as a major poet. Certainly no one of minor talents could have stirred his contemporaries to such violent reactions. His reputation today stands largely on his contribution toward making the inherent music of the tonal language of medieval China sing for the poet, and on his self-conscious manipulation of the initial and final sounds occurring within a couplet (the so-called "four tones and eight defects" which formed the basis of later rules for versification in the T'ang period). But he also deserves recognition for his sensitivity in capturing the tender feelings of lovers in such pieces as "Hand in Hand" and "Four Recollections," and for his light-hearted enjoyment of nature and sympathy for other living things, coupled with keen observation, as seen in poems like "The Fishing Rod" and "Wild

Geese on the Lake." One of his mature pieces, "Spending the Night in the Eastern Park," written when he was sixty-six, is an almost perfect exemplar of his own rules of euphony—a facet, alas, which is totally lost in translation—yet at the same time it conveys the somber weight of his years and sense of approaching death, giving us a hint of the truly broad reach of his humanity.

(RICHARD B. MATHER)

Hsieh T'iao (464–499)

Hsieh T'iao (*Hsüan-hui*), native of Yang-hsia in Ch'en-chün, Honan, was considered, along with Shen Yüeh, one of the most elegant court poets and exponent of the Yung-ming (reign period 483–93) style. A descendant of the same prominent Hsieh family as the poet Hsieh Ling-yün, he held high positions in court under the Ch'i dynasty and also served as magistrate of Hsüan-ch'en, Anhwei (hence his sobriquet Hsieh Hsüan-ch'eng). Later he antagonized a powerful prince and died in prison. Some one hundred fifty of his poems are extant, mostly lyrical in character, which won critical appreciation of many T'ang poets, especially Li Po.

Hsiao Yen, Emperor Wu of Liang (464–549)

Hsiao Yen (*Shu-ta*), native of Nan-ling (Wu-chin), Kiangsu, was a commoner who rose to a position of power under the Ch'i dynasty and eventually reigned as Emperor Wu of Liang. Known for his erudition and devotion to Buddhism, he enjoyed nearly half a century of benevolent rule (reigned 502–49). He and his two sons were accomplished poets and great patrons of literature.

Anonymous
"The Ballad of Mulan"

"The Ballad of Mulan" is an anonymous work of the Northern Dynasties, written (c. fifth–sixth century A.D.) toward the end of a very ancient tradition of compiling and collecting folk ballads by the court or the literati. By the time of its composition, poets had already begun to use the ballad form to compose their own original works. This ballad exhibits in many ways the transition that had begun. It is not merely a recording of an oral work, but lies somewhere between, linking works like "Barbara Allan," "Sir Patrick Spens" to literary ballads such as "Judas" or "St. Steven and King Herod."

The extent of literary refinement in this poem—although in some cases one might suspect an oppposite effect created by a recorder who did not totally understand the aesthetics of the oral mode—is difficult to determine. Some obviously oral elements remain. The first line, for example, when read or sung could represent either the sounds of a girl sighing or the hum of a loom. Other devices, such as the repeating of the same syllable thrice in succession (lines 11–12), are not as effective and may possibly have resulted from the combination of several texts or traditions of the story. Some of the images are also aural. As the listeners waited, the ballad singer told of how the sounds of the Yellow River and then the noises of the enemy cavalry muffled the cries of Mulan's parents (lines 21–28). The four-directional description (lines 17–20), the sunrise and sunset accounts (lines 21–22 and 25–26), the successive portrayal of each member of the family as Mulan arrives home (lines 43–48), and the first eight lines of the poem (cf. note 3 to the translation) are formulaic. Lines 29–32, an interpolation generally regarded as the most blatant incursion of the literary tradition, add little to the overall effect of the poem.

The poem itself consists of sixty-two primarily five-character lines divided into several scenes tracing Mulan's resolve to fight in place of her father (lines 1–6), the campaign (lines 17–32), an imperial audience and reward (lines 33–42), her return home (lines 43–58), and an epilogue (lines 59–62). The campaign is generally considered to have involved the Hsien-pi people (to which Mulan belonged) of North China defending their holdings in one of their endless wars against the nomadic Jou-jan. Though the narrative often focuses on detail, the description and characterization remain so general as to afford us, who have neither an appreciation of oral poetry nor the advantages of hearing this work performed, less difficulty than one might expect in appreciating the poem in translation.

(WILLIAM H. NIENHAUSER)

PART III

Wang Fan-chih (590?–660?)

The poetry of Wang Fan-chih enjoyed an immense popularity in the T'ang dynasty, was relatively familiar in the Sung eras, but has been virtually forgotten since. That he was known as late as the tenth century (some three hundred years after his lifetime) is attested by the scroll fragments found in Tun-huang datable from this period. The Sung encyclopedia, *T'ai-p'ing kuang-chi* (978–81), mentions him in a brief, no doubt apocryphal, biography. According to this account, he was said to have come from the town of Li-yang in Wei-chou, Honan. He was purportedly found in a tumescence of the trunk of a crab apple tree at birth by Wang Te-tsu, who raised the child and gave him his name. The story is more revealing for its anecdotal than for its biographical value, as it indicates that Wang Fan-chih's fame was such as to inspire legends about his life.

But Wang's poetry is of interest not just to students of oral literature. He left his mark on a number of important poets, including Han Shan, Huang T'ing-chien, and Fan Ch'eng-ta, among whose verses echoes of some of Wang's famous lines may be found. In these poems, we can see a ready wit, bold and idiomatic diction, a manner that is endearing and totally natural. These translations aim at capturing the spontaneity of the original in recognizable idioms. Whenever possible, vernacular expressions are used in preference to literary locutions because Wang Fan-chih's poetry is not so much to be read as to be heard. He was anything but a formal or "correct" academy poet.

(EUGENE EOYANG)

Wang Chi (590?–644)

Wang Chi (*Wu-kung;* TUNG-KAO TZU), a native of Lung-men in Chiang-chou (Shansi), was acclaimed for his literary genius in Ch'ang-an while he was in his teens. Later, unhappy at court, he led an unconventional life and was known for his capacity for wine. Like T'ao Ch'ien, whom he admired, he wrote his own obituary; besides his poetry, he was the author of several prose works including the *Classic of Wine* (*Chiu Ching*) and an imaginary account of the *Land of the Happy-Drunk* (*Tsui-ḥsiang chi*).

Wang Chi's poetry breaks away from the formalistic, decorative "palace style," the vogue of the early T'ang. His anti-Confucian stand (cf. "Sent to Recluse Ch'eng") and his espousal of Taoist sentiments represent a departure in content as well as in style. While his eight-line poems do not have all the features of the "regulated verse" poem (*lu-shih*), they may be regarded as the precursors of this type of poetry; they anticipate the works of Wang Wei and Meng Hao-jan, both in form and in spirit.

Lu Chao-lin (c. 641–680)

Lu Chao-lin (*Sheng-chih*), a native of Fan-yang, in Yu-chou (Hopei), was known as one of the "Four Talents" (*ssu-chieh*) of the early T'ang (the other three being Wang Po, Yang Chiung, and Lo Pin-wang). After securing government preferment, he was appointed military officer of Hsin-tu, west of Ch'eng-tu, in Szechwan. Forced to resign because of ill health, he retired to Mount T'ai-po to study Taoism. While there, he was said to have collected and eaten large quantities of magic herbs and, perhaps as a result, contracted a disease which crippled his hands and feet. He moved to Chü-tz'u Mountain in Honan, where the climate was more salutary, and spent the rest of his life at his retreat near the River Ying. The last ten years of his life were made unhappy by his sickness and by the political climate of

he time under Empress Wu. Finally, he drowned himself in the Ying about
80. In his works he shows a preference for the "ancient style," and gener-
ally avoids the ornate diction of the "palace style." His poems show an un-
usual clarity of imagery and a sensitivity to suffering.

(ROBIN D. S. YATES)

Ch'en Tzu-ang (661–702)

Ch'en Tzu-ang (*Po-yü*) was born in Tzu-chou, Szechwan. After an unsettled
youth, he began his studies comparatively late, earning his *chin-shih* degree
at the age of twenty-nine. Appreciated by Empress Wu for his literary tal-
ent, he was summoned to court and awarded with high ranks. Under the
new dynasty of Chou, following Empress Wu's usurpation, he rose to high
position in court. Later he was accused of involvement in an intrigue and
died in prison.

The poetry of Ch'en Tzu-ang exercises a strong, healthy influence on other
T'ang poets. Tu Fu and Li Po, among others, claim allegiance to him. Best
admired by his contemporaries were his thirty-eight poems entitled "Impres-
sions of Things Encountered" (*Kan-yü*), which, in theme and style, are
reminiscent of another series of poems by Juan Chi entitled "Expressing My
Thoughts" (*Yung-huai*). Ch'en's style is distinguished by a strict avoidance
of the euphuistically beautiful diction of the late Six Dynasties poetry and a
return to the simpler, more robust, and more personal style of an earlier
period.

(WILLIAM NIENHAUSER)

Han Shan (date uncertain)

Han Shan means "Cold Mountain." It is the name of a place, but also the
name of a person. Little is known for certain about the man who made that
mountain his place of refuge, the symbol of his spiritual aspirations, and his
own pseudonym. Possibly he lived in the early T'ang period. Probably he
was a farmer who left his family from time to time to embark on obscure
pilgrimages to Buddhist shrines or into the wilderness. In his poems he
sometimes rants about the vanity of power, glory, wealth, and female beauty
—all mere filth to him. But he could also write tenderly of misty peaks and
bird song, and the spiritual satisfactions of quiet and isolation. Centuries
after his death he became a Ch'an myth, especially in Japan. In these later
times he was frequently represented in art as a freak in tattered garments,
grinning imbecilely, a happy social reject. It is hard to relate this popular
image to the contents of the poems attributed to him.

(EDWARD H. SCHAFER)

Shih Te *(date uncertain)*

Shih Te is a pseudonym for a T'ang Buddhist poet who was said to be a younger contemporary of Han Shan and another monk, Feng Kan, with both of whom he was friendly. Strictly speaking, little is known about the life of Shih Te. Only legends have been associated with his life. The majority of his poems are either vehement denunciations of the evils of mortal men, or Buddhist sermons calling upon the unenlightened to mend their evil ways and awaken to the Buddha. His best poems are those which combine description of landscapes with delineation of the poet's mental and spiritual states of mind. All his poems are untitled and are written in the ancient-style form, usually of eight lines with rhymes occurring on the even-numbered lines.

(JAMES M. HARGETT)

Meng Hao-jan *(689–740)*

Meng Hao-jan, a native of Hsiang-yang, Hupeh, was the most successful poet in the early years of the High T'ang, preceding by a decade Wang Wei and Li Po, both of whom were his friends and admirers. Meng Hao-jan was best known as a recluse poet though it cannot be said that he did not have ambitions of passing the examinations and, as he himself said in a poem, offering his talents to serve an illustrious ruler. He waited, however, until he was forty before he went to the capital to take the *chin-shih* examination, and his failure in achieving his goal was a great disappointment in his life. Before returning to the Dear Gate (Lu-meng) Mountain of his native Hsiang-yang to live as a recluse, he took an extensive trip down the eastern and central Yangtze regions. His travels and his secluded life in the mountains form the main themes of his more than two hundred extant poems.

In the poems of Meng Hao-jan are combined the two mainstreams of Chinese nature poetry: the calmer and homelier aspects of nature as described by T'ao Ch'ien, and the more awesome sceneries of Hsieh Ling-yün. Like T'ao Ch'ien, Meng was a philosophical poet; he also excelled in more realistic descriptions and showed greater originality in the use of poetic imageries. He wrote mostly in the five-word meter of the modern school, revealing a greater depth and range of personal emotions than some of the nature poets who wrote in Wang Wei's style.

Wang Wei *(701–761)*

Wang Wei (*Mo-chieh*, after the popular Buddhist saint Vimalakīrti, known in Chinese as Wei-mo-chieh) was a native of T'ai-yüan prefecture in modern

Shansi. Admired by his contemporaries as poet, musician, and painter, his poetic genius saw fruition during the reign of Emperor Hsüan-tsung (reigned 713–55); his career, on the other hand, remained miraculously unscathed by the upheavals during the An Lu-shan rebellion.

Wang Wei's life, on the surface, is not much different from that of many T'ang poets. He was considered a prodigy in his teens (when he wrote several of the long narrative poems, including the "Ballad of the Peach-Blossom Spring"), and he earned his *chin-shih* degree at twenty-one. Then followed government service, which led him, after several minor setbacks, to the appointment as Minister to the Right and, later, as Censor; travels to various parts of the empire; banishment from the capital, sometimes to remote outposts. When Ch'ang-an fell to An Lu-shan in 756, Wang Wei was said to have refused service under the rebel government by feigning illness. But, unable to resist the pressure, he finally had to compromise his stand. Upon the suppression of the revolt and the return of Emperor Su-tsung (reigned 756–62) to the capital, a charge of sedition was made against him but later dropped.

Unlike many other T'ang poets, Wang Wei's life, even during its most active periods, was often combined with deliberate seclusion, or withdrawal from society. Before he was thirty, following his first period of banishment, he lived for a brief time as a recluse on Mount Sung, near the Eastern Capital, Lo-yang. Later, while holding office in the capital, he led the life of a semi-recluse at a scenic villa at Wang-ch'uan in the Chung-nan Mountains near Ch'ang-an. At the villa he spent many quiet years studying Buddhist scripture with his poet-friend P'ei Ti, to whom he addressed the series of quatrains of Wang-ch'uan, which became the subject of many of his poems und at least one horizontal handscroll painted by him. He remained a devout Buddhist to the end of his life.

Traceable to the twin influences of Buddhism and landscape painting, Wang Wei's poems are distinguished by a visual immediacy on the one hand, and by meditative insight on the other. An often quoted dictum in praise of Wang Wei, attributed to the Sung poet Su Shih, is that "in his poetry there is painting and in his painting there is poetry." Whether describing the simple rustic life on a farm, or writing about the joy and peace he found in nature, Wang Wei has an eye for details. In his poetry he often blends the most concrete vocabulary with the abstract (like "empty," "being," "non-being," etc.) to create a special atmosphere.

Wang Wei is widely regarded by Chinese critics as a worthy successor to T'ao Ch'ien in the tradition of *t'ien-yüan* ("fields and garden") poetry, which also commanded a large following among Wang Wei's contemporaries. Preeminently among them was Meng Hao-jan, as well as a host of others, such as Ch'u Kuang-hsi, Tsu Yung, and Wei Ying-wu. Technically, however, Wang Wei's poetry represents a great advance over T'ao Ch'ien's in that he has turned the five-syllabic meter (he seldom employed the seven-word line) into a more supple tool of self-expression through many devices such as parallelism, inversion, the careful placing of pivotal words, and variations in the placing of the caesura in each line (some of these qualities, we hope, may be evident even in translation).

For many Western readers, perhaps the most appealing quality of Wang Wei's poetry lies in the poet's ability to explore the world of nature and men, to communicate directly with the reader, and to express what is seldom expressible in any language, namely, the profound insight of a poet to "see into the life of things."

(IRVING Y. LO)

Ch'u Kuang-hsi (*fl. 742*)

Ch'u Kuang-hsi, a native of Yen-chou, Shantung, was considered a major poet by his contemporaries, but he never has enjoyed wide popularity, and only a small fragment remains of his works. Although generally grouped as a member of Wang Wei's school, he is more a pastoral poet than a nature poet. He writes convincingly of farm routines, the change of seasons, and the life of peasants.

Although Shantung might have been Ch'u's ancestral home, he actually came from Kiangsu. After failing the examination in Ch'ang-an, he traveled widely and might have settled as a farmer in southwestern Honan (cf. "The Cowherd: A Song"). Sometime after 726, he passed the *chin-shih* examination and became a local official. Despite his reputation as scholar and promising statesman, he remained a political unknown until 753, when he gained the attention of General Ko-shu Han. When the An Lu-shan rebellion broke out in 755, he escaped to the South, where he might have cast his lot with one of the imperial princes (possibly the same Prince Yung with whom Li Po had the misfortune to associate). After the rebellion, Ch'u was banished and died in Kwangtung.

(JOSEPH J. LEE)

Wang Ch'ang-lin (*?–756*)

Although Wang Ch'ang-lin was regarded by his contemporaries as "the supreme poet of the empire," there exists extremely meager biographical information about his life. Not even his birthplace has been established. We only know that he passed his *chin-shih* examination in 727, never rose to high position, and was twice exiled. Also, he died at the outbreak of the An Lu-shan rebellion.

During his lifetime, Wang's reputation as a poet outranked that of Li Po and Tu Fu. In a T'ang anthology of twenty-four poets, compiled in 752, by Yin Fan—entitled *Ho-yo ying-ling chi* (*Anthology of Geniuses of the Land*) —Wang was placed next to Wang Wei and above Ch'u Kuang-hsi. And it is on him that Yin Fan lavished the highest praise. His poetry was considered the embodiment of vigor and power. Especially admired were his quatrains and his seven-word ancient-style poems. He also wrote a treatise on poetic criticism called *Shih-ko* (*Delineation of Poetry*), now lost. According to the famous Japanese monk-scholar Kukai, this work was much consulted by his contemporaries, and fragments of it can still be found in Kukai's *Bunkyō Hifu Ron*.

(JOSEPH J. LEE)

Ch'ang Chien (fl. 749)

A native of Ch'ang-an, Ch'ang Chien passed the *chin-shih* examination in the same year as Wang Ch'ang-lin. Soon dissatisfied with a minor position in local government, he gave up officialdom for the life of a Taoist recluse. Little else is known about his life. He was much admired as master of eremitic poetry even in his own time; Yin Fan in his anthology considered him the equal of Liu Chen, Tso Ssu (fl. 300), and Pao Chao (d. 466)—men of genius who seldom rose to enjoy wealth and power.

(JOSEPH J. LEE)

Li Po (701–762)

Against a rich body of legends of Li Po's ancestry and birth, it is generally agreed that, whether he was born in Kansu, Central Asia, or some other region, Li Po grew up and spent his boyhood in Szechwan. His writings indicate that in 725 he left home for central and east China, partly to travel, partly to gain recognition for his talent. But fame did not come his way until many years later. In the meantime he married and made his home first in Hupeh, then in Shantung, then in the lower Yangtze. Finally he went to Ch'ang-an, where he was presented to Emperor Hsüan-tsung and given a position in the Hanlin Academy, in either 742 or 743. Li Po, however, was not destined to enjoy the imperial favor for long. In 744 he fell victim to court intrigues and was allowed to leave Ch'ang-an to "return to the hills."

Li Po was in Honan when the An Lu-shan rebellion broke out in 755. The war compelled him to leave for the South, where he eventually entered Prince Yung's service. When the prince was found guilty of treason, Li Po was also implicated and sent into exile—this time to Yeh-lang, far in the southwestern corner of the T'ang empire. But before he got there, amnesty came and he was able to resume his wanderings along the Yangtze; he was then fifty-nine. Three years later he died while visiting his kinsman, the famous calligrapher Li Yang-pin.

Much has been written about Li Po's drinking bouts, his restlessness, his Taoist inclination, or his seeming casualness toward wealth and fame. The point to be kept in mind is that Li Po's life-style is actually a reflection of High T'ang cultural milieu and is shared by many of his contemporaries such as Wang Ch'ang-lin, Kao Shih, and others. We need to look at the poet also as a common mortal: a friend, a husband, a father, an aspiring literatus, or a despairing soul.

The translations are arranged in a roughly chronological order. This arrangement, though by no means strictly followed, may serve to highlight the various periods of Li Po's creative life. The placement of other yet undated pieces is arbitrary. Chan Ying's *Li Po shih-wen hsi-nien* is among the best chronologies of Li Po's poetic and prose writings. Kuo Mo-jo's *Li Po yü Tu Fu* (*Li Po and Tu Fu*) adds much new insight.

With the possible exception of "Climbing Phoenix Terrace . . . ," practically all the poems represented here are either *yüeh-fu* songs, *ku-shih* (ancient verse), or *chüeh-chü* (quatrain). This is characteristic of the entire corpus of Li Po's poetic work. Unlike the *lü-shih* (regulated verse), with its strict requirement of tonal arrangements and grammatical parallelism, the ancient verse forms afford exceptional freedom of expression; they give wing to Li Po's imagination.

Traditional Chinese criticism never fails to note the river-like quality of Li Po's poetic power: its gushing energy, its tumbling fall, or its majestic flow. In Chinese critical terminology this flow or rhythm is called *ch'i* (breath). Li Po was fully aware of his own art and in his "*ku-feng*" (ancient airs) poem he identified his art with the tradition of the Chien-an masters—a tradition particularly notable for its directness of expression, the easy flow of its lines, and its social concern. In terms of High T'ang's own division of contemporary poets into the school of *feng-ku* (wind-bone) and that of *sheng-lü* (sound-pattern), Li Po would most probably have regarded himself as among the former.

(JOSEPH J. LEE)

Kao Shih (702?–765)

Kao Shih (*Ta-fu*, CHUNG-WU), a native of Po-hai in Tsang-chou, Hopei, followed a career which began in obscurity and ended in his enfeoffment as a marquis. Probably with some exaggeration, his biographers claimed that he started writing poetry only in his fiftieth year and went on to achieve instant fame. Little is known of his early life except that he traveled widely and settled down to farming in southeastern Honan, after disappointments in Ch'ang-an, while he was in his twenties. In 735 he failed a second time in his examination and returned to Honan, where in the autumn of 744 he met both Li Po and Tu Fu. With the latter poet, he developed a lifelong and warm friendship, despite the two men's vastly different political fortune.

In 749 Kao passed a special examination in Ch'ang-an and was appointed to a minor post as district police commissioner in Feng-ch'iu, near K'ai-feng;

soon he was disgusted with the routine business of administration, such as the flogging of culprits, and left for the northwest. His political fortune soared after he gained the attention of Governor General Ko-shu Han, whom he aided in the Battle of T'ung-kuan during the An Lu-shan rebellion. Subsequently, he was said to have warned the emperor against the rebellion of Prince Yung and, unlike Li Po, to have attempted to block it. In 756 he was appointed a censor. A year later he earned the enmity of a court minister and was sent to Szechwan. He became prefect of P'eng-chou and then of Shu-chou when he renewed his friendship with Tu Fu. As governor general of Ch'eng-tu in 763, he tried unsuccessfully to repel the attacks of the Tibetans; he died in Ch'ang-an as advisory chancellor (*shih-lang*) in the Ministry of Punishment.

The poetry of Kao Shih is generally considered along with that of Ts'en Shen as exemplifying the "heroic" mode. His songs about military campaigns, which dominate his works, are largely devoid of anti-war sentiments and mirror the ambitions of adventurous young men. Most of his poems are somber and melancholy. Stylistically, Kao is heavily indebted to the *yüeh-fu* poetry of the earlier era, infusing it with contemporary setting and idiom, and thus assuring it a new lease of life.

(IRVING Y. LO)

Liu Ch'ang-ch'ing (709–780?)

Liu Ch'ang-ch'ing (*Wen-fang*), born in Ho-chien, Hopei, earned his *chin-shih* degree in 733. He served as Censor and held other provincial posts under Emperors Hsüan-tsung and Su-tsung; later involved in a legal suit, he was banished as Marshal of Mu-chou, in Chekiang, and then as Censor of Sui-chou, in Hupeh. Hence, he was also known as Liu Sui-chou.

Although sometimes considered a Mid-T'ang poet, Liu had actually enjoyed wide reputation during the K'ai-yüan (713–41) and T'ien-pao (742–56) reigns. Among his contemporaries, he was especially admired for his five-word poems; one of his fellow poets referred to him as the "Great Wall of the Pentasyllabic Verse" (*wu-yen ch'ang-ch'eng*). Both his quatrains and his "regulated verse" poems are often simple sketches of nature and of quiet pastoral life—understated and yet charged with feeling—in the tradition of Wang Wei.

Tu Fu (712–770)

Tu Fu (*Tzu-mei*) has dominated Chinese literature for almost ten centuries as a master poet. His position is not likely to be seriously challenged despite mild rumblings of dissent from post-Cultural Revolution critics such as Kuo Mo-jo in his study of Li Po and Tu Fu (*Li Po yü Tu Fu*, Peking, 1971). Certainly, no Chinese writer has mirrored in his work more completely the world he lives in than Tu Fu. Nor has anyone revealed himself with greater passion and candor, or displayed a greater dedication to his craft, or achieved such consummate mastery of his art.

Paradoxically, however, the man remembered by posterity as the "poet-sage" or the "poet-historian" was very much neglected by his contemporaries. Of the ten extant anthologies of poetry compiled before the end of the tenth century, only one of them—*Yu-hsüan chi* (*Second Anthology of Choicest Verses*) by the poet Wei Chuang (d. 910)—included Tu Fu's poems (seven). Tu Fu's literary fame did not come to him in his lifetime.

Nor could Tu Fu's political career be regarded in any way as a success—and this despite the advantages of his birth and education and the patronage of friends. He was born in Kung-hsien, in modern Honan (though he often spoke of himself as a native of Tu-ling, Capital Prefecture, the original home of the Tu clan), into a distinguished literary family. His grandfather, Tu Shen-yen (d. 708), was a leading poet at the beginning of the T'ang era; a still more illustrious ancestor, Tu Yü (222–84), wrote an important commentary on one of the Confucian classics and was ennobled as a marquis after a successful military career. This Confucian heritage bred in him a strong sense of duty, which colors much of Tu Fu's works; never in his life did he abandon his goal of serving the empire and promoting the well-being of his sovereign.

Yet twice in his career, in 735 in Lo-yang and in 747 in Ch'ang-an, Tu Fu took and failed in the imperial examinations (his second failure was due chiefly to political reasons). For several years both before the first examination and immediately subsequent to it, he traveled extensively in south-central China, visiting centers of ancient civilization. His poems of this period reflect a wide range of interests which included painting, music, riding, and hunting, and even a mild curiosity about the occult practices of Taoism. In other poems of this period are found the records of his first meeting with the poets Li Po and Kao Shih, which led to lifelong friendships, and sketches of both the affluence ("The Elegant Women") and the uglier aspects of T'ang society at the height of Hsüan-tsung's reign ("Song of the War Chariot" etc.).

In 752 Tu Fu took a special examination in Ch'ang-an and again failed. During the next three hard years in the capital, the poet was unsuccessful either in securing the patronage of some powerful military governors, such as Ko-shu Han (as did other poets like Kao Shih and Ts'en Shen) or in obtaining an appointment by demonstrating his literary ability through the special presentation of rhymed-prose compositions to the emperor. In the meantime, he found it necessary to move his family away from the capital, and his homesickness made his life even unhappier. Finally, in 755, his long years of waiting resulted in an appointment as District Police Commissioner of Ho-hsi (in Shensi). Upon declining it, he was given a post only slightly more palatable, as an adjutant in the office of the Right-Commandant attached to the Crown Prince's Palace, a position fifth from the bottom in the official ladder.

In the winter of 755, the An Lu-shan rebellion broke out and the emperor Hsüan-tsung sought refuge in Shu (Szechwan), while the heir apparent was installed as the new emperor (Su-tsung) at Lin-wu in Kansu. Swept by these events, the poet was again separated from his family, left at the Ch'iang Village, and made a politically tactful move to join the exile court of the new emperor, which had moved to Feng-hsiang in Shensi. He arrived there in 757 and was later reunited with his family. "Journey North," the longest of his five-word ancient-style poems, describes both his physical suffering and his spiritual agony during this most trying period of the poet's life.

Tu Fu's loyalty was rewarded with an appointment, in 757, as Commissioner to the Left (*tso shih-yi*) in the chancellery, the highest rank he ever attained. He continued in the same position upon the return of the court to Ch'ang-an that winter. Shortly thereafter, because of his persistent outspoken defense of a general who had lost a battle, he incurred the emperor's displeasure and was exiled to a minor position in Hua-chou, in Shensi. Scenes of deprivation and sorrow which he witnessed on the road become the subject matter of such poems as "Recruiting Officer of Shih-hao" and the three "Farewell" poems; in all of these poems (and there are many others) he employs the *yüeh-fu* ballad conventions for reportage of current events.

In 759, for unknown reasons, Tu Fu left his post in Hua-chou for Ch'in-chou (T'ien-shui, Kansu) and then went south from there through T'ung-ku (Ch'eng-hsien, Kansu) to Ch'eng-tu in Szechwan. Although several local rebellions beset this province, 761–62, it was in Ch'eng-tu that the poet began the most tranquil and also the most productive period of his life. More than half of his extant 1,450 poems were written during this last decade of his life. In 762 the appointment of Yen Wu, his former friend at the chancellery, as governor general of Ch'eng-tu was welcome news to the poet, and he served briefly on Yen Wu's staff. Shortly before the death of Yen Wu in 765, Tu Fu decided on a river journey, down the Yangtze, which might take him home to Honan; en route he became ill and was detained at K'uei-chou for two years. At the ancient site of the White Emperor City nearby, overlooking the famous gorges, on the border of Szechwan and Hupeh, Tu Fu wrote some of his most mature "regulated poems," including the series of "Autumn Thoughts." In 768 he continued his travel through Hupeh and Hunan, and he wrote his last poem while lying sick in a boat on Lake Tung-t'ing, in which vicinity he died in 770.

Tu Fu's achievement as a poet is apparent in the plenitude of his themes and in his inimitable style. His works include poems written in every one of the known verse forms: poems in the ancient style (416), regulated poems (772, of which 621 are in the five-word meter and 151 in the seven-word meter), and quatrains (138). And in all these different genres he is able to make them accommodate not only new themes and ideas but also a new language. For example, his "Song of the War Chariot," which owes its structure to "The Ballad of Mulan," employs a set of entirely contemporary idiom to tell about the plight of the people of his own day. In his regulated poems, he takes pride in what he calls "meticulousness" (*hsi*), with both meaning and structure, which is a record of his innovative uses of the language. In his quatrains, nearly all written during the last decade of his life, he again turns to the diction and the speech pattern of the folk songs, which he employs not in the service of timeworn motifs and themes, but in the description of his immediate personal situation.

It is hard to sum up Tu Fu's poetic style in a paragraph or two. "Objectivity," "realism," "candor," or "verisimilitude"—any of these words describes only one aspect of his poetry, and all can be amply illustrated in poem after poem. Whether in simple language ("Only the old man was there to see me off," from "Recruiting Officer of Shih-hao") or through symbols ("broken ripples and waves/from an old embroidery," from "Journey North"), the poet touches on every human emotion: joy, grief, anger, or indignation. Sometimes the rich texture of Tu Fu's poetry is woven out of historical allusions (as is the case of the "Autumn Thoughts" series), but it can also be appreciated on the verbal level. Regrettably, a translation cannot reproduce all the various kinds of purely linguistic features, such as assonance and alliteration, or his innovations in the skillful discrimination of end rhymes or in the modulation of the cadence in each line. But attempts have been made in the translations to preserve as much as possible all the semantic ambiguities and subtleties of Tu Fu, and not to leave out anything from the original. For it is our conviction that Tu Fu's verses often overwhelm the readers with a wealth of details, and his meticulous art is the degree of precision and control he exercises over them. It is the accumulation of such little-noticed details in life, blending thought and feeling, which makes Tu Fu's poetry uniquely impressive and which accounts for the universality of his appeal.

(IRVING Y. LO)

Ts'en Shen (715–770)

Ts'en Shen (sometimes pronounced Ts'en Ts'an), native of Nan-yang in modern Honan, was born into a poor family. After passing his *chin-shih* examination in 744, Ts'en served in a number of official positions in the capital, but in 749, feeling that his ambitions were not being realized quickly enough, he took service as a subordinate to General Kao Hsien-chih, then engaged in a series of military campaigns to extend T'ang rule into Central Asia. Ts'en spent much of the next ten years under the command of Kao and later Feng Ch'ang-ch'ing. His duties seem to have been literary rather than military, and he probably missed the historic Battle of Talas (751) in which the newly emergent Arabs blocked further Chinese expansion into what is now Soviet Turkestan. After his return to metropolitan China, Ts'en spent most of his time in provincial posts in Szechwan, where he died.

Ts'en Shen was one of the leading "heroic" poets of the High T'ang period. Although he wrote many fine poems on subjects common to his contemporaries, he is best known for his long *yüeh-fu* ballads written during his years in the far west. These rugged poems, with their descriptions of the harsh climate, unearthly topography, and barely civilized natives of the Central Asian deserts, stand in marked contrast to the nature poems of such poets as Wang Wei and Meng Hao-jan.

(DANIEL BRYANT)

Yüan Chieh (719–772)

Yüan Chieh (*Tz'u-shan;* CHUI-SHOU), a native of Honan, matured in the era of corruption which dominated the Chinese court in the 740s and lived through the rebellion-swept decade as an upright official and then as a recluse. Besides his poetry, he was known as an editor of one of the earliest extant anthologies of T'ang verse (760). This volume, containing twenty-four poems by seven of his contemporaries, is appropriately entitled *Ch'ieh-chung chi* (*A Portfolio Anthology*).

Yüan Chieh's writings reflect his dissonance with contemporary society. He is known as a promoter of the classical in style and tone. His poetry, often didactic, paves the way for the "New Music Bureau Ballads," and he is thus considered a precursor of the Mid-T'ang period (765–835). Many of his works which show Buddhist influence are not, however, untypical of his time.

(WILLIAM NIENHAUSER)

Ku K'uang (725?–c. 814)

Ku K'uang (*Pu-weng*), a native of Hai-yen, Chekiang, was both a painter and a poet. He passed his *chin-shih* examination in 757, but did not hold any high government post. Instead, he traveled extensively in South China, became a recluse, and lived to his ninetieth year. He was known for his sense of humor, and his works include some "limerick" verses. He experimented with unconventional meters, juxtaposing lines of unequal lengths, and deliberately introduced dialectal words into classical Chinese poetry. Thus, in both form and content, he anticipated Po Chü-yi's "New Music Bureau Ballads" as well as the lyric meter (*tz'u*) of the ninth century.

Tai Shu-lun (732–789)

Tai Shu-lun (*Yu-kung*) was a native of Chin-t'an, Jun-chou, Kiangsu. His education included tutelage under the scholar Hsiao Ying-shih (717–68); his career reached prominence when he served under the T'ang financial genius Liu Yen (715–80?), during the reign of Emperor Tai-tsung (reigned 763–79). Although the poet was banished after Tai-tsung's death and spent the next decade primarily in the provinces, the new emperor often sought his criticism of poems written at court. He was summoned to return to court in 789 and died en route. His works include many *yüeh-fu* titles in which realistic depiction of contemporary society was the primary concern.

(WILLIAM NIENHAUSER)

Wei Ying-wu (737–?)

Wei Ying-wu, native of Ch'ang-an, once served as an imperial guardsman under Emperor Hsüan-tsung; he quit his job to begin his formal education. After passing his *chin-shih* examination, he served at various provincial posts as Censor of Chiang-chou, Kiangsi, and then as Censor of Soochow. Hence, his sobriquet as "Wei Chiang-chou" or "Wei Su-chou."

Wei's poetry exhibits a markedly different style from that of his contemporary Ku K'uang. Shunning realistic themes, he (along with Liu Ch'ang-ch'ing) carried on the tradition of nature poetry in the style of T'ao Ch'ien and Wang Wei. Distinguished by their gentle reflectiveness and quiet serenity, his poems were highly esteemed by later poets and critics, especially in the Sung eras.

Wang Chi-yu (fl. 766)

Wang Chi-yu, a native of Honan, was one of the few neglected T'ang poets. Without holding any office all his life, he was known to be erudite and to cultivate the writing of "the strange and the unexpected." His poetry, however, was esteemed by his contemporary poet-friends, including Tu Fu (who immortalized him in a poem entitled *K'o-t'an*, "The Lamentable"), and was included in two T'ang anthologies, the *Ho-yo Ying-lin chi* and Yüan Chieh's *Ch'ieh-chung chi*. Only a dozen of his poems are extant.

(JOSEPH J. LEE)

Chang Chih-ho (c. 742–c. 782)

Chang Chih-ho, or Chang Kuei-ling (*Tzu-t'ung*), was a native of Chin-hua in Wu-chou, Chekiang. He passed his Classical (*ming-ching*) Examination at the age of sixteen and was appointed to the Hanlin Academy by Emperor Su-tsung. Later, after a demotion, he decided upon retirement and adopted the style-name of "Fisherman of Mist and Waves" (*Yen-po tiao-t'u*). His "Fisherman's Songs" was considered as one of the earliest *tz'u* tunes.

Lu Lun (*fl. 770*)

Lu Lun (*Yun-yen*), native of Ho-chung, Shansi, was one of the ten "Talented Poets of the Ta-li Era" (766–79) under Emperor Tai-tsung, along with Ssu-k'ung Shu and others. He held many high government posts, including the censorate, but was later maligned and demoted. Admired for his deft use of parallelism, his verses are often distinguished by the presence of realistically sketched scenery.

Li Yi (*c. 749–c. 829*)

Li Yi (*Chün-yü*), native of Lung-hsi, was, along with Li Ho, a leading poet during the reign of Emperor Hsien-tsung (reigned, 806–20). Known also for his testiness, he was unhappy at court and served on military posts in various parts of the empire. Later reinstated and returned to the capital, he continued to hold high positions and to enjoy a wide reputation. He was recognized especially as a master of the quatrains.

Meng Chiao (*751–814*)

Meng Chiao (*Tung-yeh*) was the oldest of an entire constellation of important poets who dominated the last decade of the eighth century and first decades of the ninth century. After he met Han Yü in Ch'ang-an in 791, Meng Chiao joined the ranks of the young intellectuals who sought to create an ancient-style prose with enough aesthetic appeal to compete with the then dominant rhymed parallel prose. Han Yü and others saw in Meng Chiao's work a poetic counterpart to their efforts in prose. However, when Han Yü passed the examination in the famous class of 792, Meng Chiao failed. After several attempts, Meng finally did pass the examination in the 790s but received only a minor post, which he soon lost due to incompetence. He spent the rest of his life living off friends and powerful patrons. His long life was a history of failure, poverty, and the bitterness which went along with them. While this provided the impetus and theme for much great poetry, it is certain that Meng would have preferred moderate political success:

> I don't know what good literature is—
> You meet your death in fruitless wandering.

Since the T'ang Confucian sentiment which Meng Chiao supported gener-
ally identified political and artistic genius, Meng and his friends came to
emphasize less popular Confucian ideas, the virtues of suffering and poverty,
to account for their political failure. In an extreme case, the poet's suffering
comes to be understood as the internalization of a cosmic and political
disorder. Meng Chiao writes of an earlier moral exemplar, Yüan Lu-shan[1]:

> The good man is not naturally crippled,
> Thus there was cause for Lu-shan's crippling:
> If within him lay the universe's finest seed,
> Then his body was of the universe,
> And since the universe was greatly crippled,
> Lu-shan's way was tortuous.

This sense of resonance between the poet and the external world may help
to explain the peculiar way Meng perceives his relation to autumn and the
apricot tree in his poems. The apricot tree which has lost its blossoms is
more than simply a metaphor for the loss of his sons: it is a parallel identity
and, in a poem of the sequence not translated here, Meng Chiao eventually
becomes the tree:

> I stand alone like a bundle of twigs.

But if the poet's suffering can be explained by his resonance with a disturbed
universe, at times it seems Meng Chiao turns angrily to blame the universe
for what it has done to him:

> I eat hermit's greens, my belly aches,
> I force a song, but there's no joy in it,
> I go out the door and there's a stumbling block—
> Who claims that Heaven and Earth are broad?

Meng Chiao's intense bitterness, his bizarre imagination, and his violent
imagery ultimately cost him the popularity which his works enjoyed in the
ninth and tenth centuries. As Chinese poetry turned to understatement and
self-conscious simplicity in the late twelfth and thirteenth centuries, Meng
Chiao's position in the canon of T'ang poetry was questioned, on the
grounds that, as the thirteeenth-century critic Yen Yü put it, "he makes one
unhappy."

(STEPHEN OWEN)

---

[1] Yüan Te-hsiu (696–754), scholar who served as the Magistrate of Lu-shan, af-
ter passing the *chin-shih* examination, and gave away his entire income for a
year to feed the orphans and the destitute. Then he left the office to become a
recluse, and won the praise of his contemporaries.

Wang Ya (*c. 764–835*)

Wang Ya (*Kuang-chin*), native of T'ai-yüan, Shansi, passed his *chin-shih* examination in 792 and later the rhetoric (*po-hsüeh hung-tz'u*) examination. He held important posts under six emperors; when his attempt to join a counterplot against some powerful eunuchs failed, he was executed. Many of his poems are in the *yüeh-fu* style.

Han Yü (*768–824*)

Han Yü (*T'ui-chih*) was born into a literary family of landed gentry in Honan. His father died in 770, and the young boy, age two, was raised in the family of Han Hui, a man of some reputation in literary circles. From 774 until 777 the family lived in Ch'ang-an, where Han Hui was employed in the coterie of the powerful minister Yüan Tsai. When Yüan Tsai fell from power, Han Hui and his family were banished to the South. After Han Hui's death in 781, the family suffered greatly, returning north during the 783–85 rebellion.

In 786 Han Yü came to the capital to study for the *chin-shih* examinations, which he passed in 792. However, he failed three consecutive times to pass the Rhetoric Examinations (*po-hsüeh hung-tz'u*) and in 796 took service under Tung Chin (724–99), the Military Governor of Pien-chou. After Tung Chin's death, Han accepted a similar post under Chang Chien-feng (735–800), Military Governor of Hsü-chou. In 802, Han Yü finally obtained his first post in the central government—an instructorship at the Imperial University. He was exiled in 803 for opposing the Wang Shu-wen reform clique, but recalled in 806 after the demise of this group and promoted to a professorship at the university.

From 806 until 819 Han Yü resided at either Ch'ang-an or Lo-yang. He rose through the bureaucratic ranks with uneven success, always returning to the Imperial University. His fame as a scholar, writer, and teacher grew steadily during this period. In 819 he wrote an inflammatory memorial protesting the Emperor's attachment to Buddhism and was again exiled to the South, but wrote an abject apology, was recalled in 820, and made Rector of the University. After serving in several high posts in the government—Vice-president of the Ministry of War, Vice-president of the Ministry of Personnel, and Metropolitan Governor—he died in Ch'ang-an in 824 at age fifty-six.

As a literary figure, Han Yü meets each of the three tests that T. S. Eliot proposed as requisites of a major poet: abundance, variety, and complete competence. His fame as a prose writer had unjustly overshadowed the high quality of his poetry. He was a daring innovator in both forms. His reform of Chinese prose style, the so-called *ku-wen* (ancient-style prose) movement, was totally accepted in the Sung, but debate continues to this day over the success of his innovations in poetry.

Han Yü, perhaps more than any other Chinese author, had a heightened awareness of the need for vitality in literary language. He avoided the clichés, the overworked metaphors, the dead wood that floats throughout much of even good Chinese literature. His works aim at the ideals of purity and vividness that, as a scholar of the Han and pre-Ch'in classics, these texts exhibited to him. He knew that the perennial appeal of the classics lay in the simple directness of their language, and so based his reforms on a return to the rhythm and syntax, if not always the vocabulary, of common speech.

The scope of Han Yü's poetry is vast; his major poems are long, which makes him a difficult poet to anthologize. That he is virtually excluded from the popular Chinese anthologies partially explains the failure of modern Chinese literary critics to acknowledge his poetic achievements. Our selections attempt to illustrate Han Yü as a philosophical and speculative poet ("Sentiments at Autumn," "Occasional Poem"), a satirist ("The Girl from Flower Mountain"), a humorist ("On Losing One's Teeth"), a surprisingly good writer of regulated verse ("Demoted I Arrive . . ."), and a writer of dialect and colloquial poetry ("The Officer at the Rapid"). The "Southern Mountains" can be read on several levels. For example, it could be interpreted as a personal allegory of the author's political career.

When Emperor Ch'ien-lung (1710–99) ordered the compilation of an anthology of the best of Chinese poetry—in a volume known as *T'ang-Sung shih-ch'un* (*The Essence of the Poetry of the T'ang and the Sung*) published in 1750—only four poets of the T'ang were chosen to be included: Tu Fu, Li Po, Po Chü-yi, and Han Yü. (The two Sung poets included were Su Shih and Lu Yu.) This belated tribute came at a time when Ch'ing poets were rediscovering the subtleties of style among late T'ang poets. Chao Yi (1727–1814), for example, recognized Han Yü as "a true pioneer" (*pi-shan k'ai-tao*) and "founder of a new school" (*tzu-ch'eng yi-chia*). Chao Yi summed up Han Yü's achievement this way: "What Tu Fu achieved so effortlessly through talent (*ts'ai*) and thought (*ssu*), these Ch'ang-li [Han Yü] made it his special effort to excel in" (*Ou-pei shih-hua*). It is hoped that these translations will vindicate for the reader this basically sound assessment of an eighteenth-century poet-critic.

(CHARLES HARTMAN)

Hsüeh T'ao (768–831)

Hsüeh T'ao, though a minor figure, is the most famous woman poet of the T'ang dynasty, with the possible exception of Yü Hsüan-chi. Very few facts are known of her life, and the problems are multitudinous. An important biographical notice written during the T'ang era by Li Yü, and contained in the *History of Women of the Green Window* (*Lü-ch'uang nü shih*), fails to record her dates. A number of references published during the Ming dynasty suggest that she lived into her middle or late seventies. Wen Yi-to, in his *Anthology of T'ang Poetry* (*T'ang-shih ta-hsi*), gives her dates as 768 to 831, now widely accepted, and earlier a Japanese scholar named Kondō Moku arrived at much the same conclusion, indicating that she lived to her early sixties. It is almost certain that she was born about the year 768.

She was the daughter of "a good Ch'ang-an family." Her father, a government official, was transferred to Ch'eng-tu in Shu (modern Szechwan)—the date is lost to history—where he died while Hsüeh T'ao was still quite young. By one account, the only other dating from the T'ang era, it was the widow, in straitened circumstances, who turned her daughter into a singing girl. Evidently Hsüeh T'ao's poetic talents were widely known even while she was still in her teens (if our dating is correct), and there are the usual stories of her composing poetry well in advance of age ten. In 785, Wei Kao arrived in Shu as Regional Commander, the post he was to hold until his death in 805. Unlike his predecessor, who exhibited no interest in the approved avocations of his class, Wei Kao summoned Hsüeh T'ao, bade her serve him wine and compose poetry. Li Yü says that it was Wei Kao who turned her into a singing girl. Within a year Wei Kao had the audacity to recommend her for the honored post of Collator at the Imperial Court, and there was, of course, overwhelming opposition. Yet in one leap Hsüeh T'ao became famous within government circles. In fact, the term "collator" (*chiao-shu*), as a result, acquired the additional meaning of "singing girl," a usage found even as late as Republican China.

During her lifetime Hsüeh T'ao served eleven regional commanders of Shu that we know of, several of whom were very talented in poetry, like Wu Yüan-heng. It is from one of his poems, one which alludes to the great sadness Hsüeh T'ao felt on Wei Kao's death, that we learn she had great beauty, undoubtedly an asset she made good use of. Only ninety of her poems have come down to us. The *Chin River Collection* (*Chin-chiang chi*), which purportedly contained five hundred of her poems, was already lost by the beginning of the Ming dynasty.

(ERIC W. JOHNSON)

Wang Chien (768–833)

Wang Chien (*Chung-ch'u*), a native of Ying-ch'uan, Honan, was official, soldier, courtier, and recluse during his long career. He had a wide circle of poet-friends, including Han Yü and Chang Chi (c. 765–830). He was especially well known for his "Palace Poems," totaling one hundred, said to be written and based upon true happenings in Emperor Te-tsung's (reigned 806–20) harem, told to him by a kinsman who served as a eunuch. Wang

Chien's works include many *yüeh-fu* titles with realistic themes, which typify the social concern of Mid-T'ang poetry.

(WILLIAM NIENHAUSER)

Liu Yü-hsi (772–842)

Liu Yü-hsi (*Meng-te*), often said to be a native of P'eng-ch'eng, Kiangsu, was actually born in Wu-chi in Chung-shan, Hopei. He passed his *chin-shih* examination at the age of twenty and, together with Liu Tsung-yüan, rose to prominence in the service of Wang Shu-wen. When Wang fell from favor, he was among the eight people banished to the provinces, with the title of marshal (*ssu-ma*) of Lang-chou in Hunan. Nine years later, when recalled to the capital, his satiric and humorous verses written at revisiting the Hsüan-tu Monastery so offended the authorities that he was again exiled, first to Lien-chou in Kwangtung, then to K'uei-chou in Szechwan, and finally to Ho-chou in Anhwei. He ended his career as a high court official in the Board of Rites.

As a poet, Liu Yü-hsi was deeply imbued with a sense of history (cf. "Sorrowing for the Past at Western Pass Mountain") and he constantly experimented with folk idioms and the prosodic arrangements of popular songs (cf. "Bamboo Branch Song" and "Willow Branch Song"). He enjoyed a wide reputation in his own lifetime, and his name was often linked to that of Po Chü-yi, after the death of Yüan Chen, as two of the leading Mid-T'ang poets.

Po Chü-yi (772–846)

Po Chü-yi (*Lo-t'ien;* HSIANG-SHAN) could probably be regarded as China's earliest popular poet and also the first serious poet who took great pride in his poetical activities. This twin distinction—popular success and semi-professionalism—makes him unique in Chinese literary history.

Like Li Po and many others, Po Chü-yi achieved fame in his lifetime, but while the other poets were chiefly admired by a small circle of literary men, Po was widely acclaimed by the common people. Po himself recorded that, in his travels, he had seen his poems copied on the walls of inns and monasteries and that singing girls who knew his songs would demand a higher price. His fame also reached far beyond the borders of China—to Korea and Japan. It was said that foreigners in Ch'ang-an would pay large sums of money for copies of his poems and that Emperor Saga (768–842) of Japan had the works of this Chinese poet stored in the Imperial Secretariat. (In Japan, Po is known by his courtesy-name Po Lo-t'ien and continues to enjoy immense popularity. Even today he is honored, together with Japan's mythical and historical heroes, in Kyoto during the Gion Festival held in July each year. Included in the traditional parade is a shrine dedicated to

Po, which depicts him in a pose of being engaged in a debate with a Buddhist priest.)

As a man of letters, Po's attitudes and activities also mark a departure from the normal Chinese pattern and bear a striking similarity to those of professional writers today. Tu Fu and Li Po, for instance, wrote far more poetry than what was preserved and handed down to posterity. But Po was not only a poet and critic; he was also his own editor. Nearly all that he ever wrote, over two thousand eight hundred poems, was collected and arranged in seventy-five *chüan,* according to his own system of classification; and as many as five copies were made and stored in separate places. This extraordinary act underscores Po's basic belief in the redeeming power of poetry in troubled times.

The period covering the reigns of eight T'ang emperors spanned by the poet's long life was marked by intense political instability and profound economic change. Factional strifes and eunuch intrigues in the court, border invasions, and the rebellions of local commanderies (including another sack of Ch'ang-an in 783) severely crippled the empire. The introduction of a new system of biannual land tax, along with other abuses and inequities— notably the royal commissary system (cf. "An Old Charcoal Seller")— brought much suffering to the people. From the chaotic conditions of the time and the poet's own experience grew Po Chü-yi's staunch belief in the function of poetry as a means of social criticism, for which he became the chief apostle.

Po Chü-yi was born into an old family of T'ai-yüan, Shansi (his actual birthplace was Hsin-cheng *hsien* in Honan province), although his father had occupied only a minor post in a prefectural government. Though recognized as a literary prodigy since childhood (cf. "Grass on Ancient Plain," written as an exercise when he was fifteen), he did not pass the *chin-shih* examination until he was twenty-nine. In A.D. 802, he was given a lowly appointment as Collator of Texts (*chiao-shu-lang*). Then, because of his extraordinary gift as a writer, he was appointed (in 807) a member of the Hanlin Academy and given the title of Commissioner to the Left (*tso shih-yi*). As might be expected, he took his assignment seriously and soon made many enemies. He frequently criticized government policies and loyally defended many of his friends, including the poet Yüan Chen, who had incurred the court's disfavor. As a result, he was sent several times to provincial posts, once as Marshal (*ssu-ma*) to Chiang-chou (815) in Kiangsi and twice as governor, to Hangchow (822) and Soochow (825). Midway in his career, he developed a serious interest in Buddhism and studied the doctrines of the Southern Ch'an school. He included among his friends many learned monks and later adopted the style-name of "Lay Buddhist of the Fragrant Mountain" (*Hsiang-shan chü-shih*). He held important posts in the later years of his long life and retired from government service for the last time in 842, four years before his death.

The poet's long experience in the various parts of the empire, coupled with his keen observation of the lives of the people and his broad sympathy with their plight, have produced some of the most poignant, realistic poems in Chinese literature. His early interest in the tradition of narrative poetry was expressed in the "Song of Everlasting Sorrow" (a long poem many times translated and anthologized) in 806, followed by "Watching the Wheat-reapers" a year later. In 809, Po created what he termed the "New Music Bureau Ballads" (*Hsin yüeh-fu*), a series of fifty poems on contemporary events. These "satirical and didactic" (*feng-yü*) pieces, which formed the first category of his collected works, were those by which the poet wished to be best remembered. In a famous letter of 815, written to Yüan Chen, with whom he discussed his literary principles, Po called this group of poems "compositions written for the purpose of saving the world."

Another division in his collected works consists of poems which he had "written to perfect his own character, and to express his feelings of release and pleasure while away from his duties"; they are mostly meditative pieces, appropriately titled "Idle Leisure" (*hsien-shih*). The third category, under the heading of "Being Moved to Mourn" (*kan-shang*), contains elegiac pieces such as "Painting Bamboo: A Song." To the fourth and largest group of poems, Po assigned the title of "Miscellaneous Poems Written According to Prosody" (*tsa-lü*), containing poems he valued the least. The determination of categories is not always strict, and the arrangement of the poems has been changed by later editors; nevertheless, the method employed by the poet is classification by content (categories 1–3) and style (the last category). That his works also include lyrics written to such popular tune-patterns as "Ripples Sifting Sand" etc., which began to proliferate only after the poet's time, also reflects his sensitivity to a new artistic milieu.

Modern readers will probably find some of Po Chü-yi's poems lacking in subtleties and overcharged with didacticism. But there is a certain freshness and spontaneity and sincerity of emotion in his poems. And in the best of his "regulated verse" poems—"On a Moonlit Night, Sent to My Brothers and Sisters," for example—he shows a mastery of form equal to the best of T'ang poets. It is said that he would often rewrite his lines to make his poems intelligible to unlettered women. If this story can be believed, it points up an almost Wordsworthian concern that the principal object of poetry is to relate or describe "incidents and situations from common life" and "in a selection of language really used by men." In the *Preface to Lyrical Ballads* (1800), Wordsworth has also written, "The poet binds together by passion and knowledge the vast empire of human society"—with this ideal, we believe, Po Chü-yi could not have agreed more completely.

(IRVING Y. LO)

Liu Tsung-yüan (773–819)

Liu Tsung-yüan (*Tzu-hou*) is traditionally recognized as a master essayist of the *ku-wen* movement and one of the more eclectic minds of his era. He has endeared himself to Chinese readers for centuries through his descriptions of scenic landscapes he discovered during two periods of exile in south-central China.

Liu Tsung-yüan was born and raised in the capital, Ch'ang-an. After a meteoric rise in the civil government under the aegis of Wang Shu-wen and his faction, he fell from imperial favor and was sent to a rural district in Yung-chou, Hunan, and given a minor provincial post in A.D. 805; ten years later he was reassigned as prefect in the aboriginal region of Liu-chou, Kwangsi. Virtually all of his extant poems were written during the fifteen years of his service in the South.

Liu Tsung-yüan's poetry is a record of his struggle with himself during this exile. Although he took an interest in Buddhism, especially in the Ch'an school, which was then popular in South China, he was a servant of the state at heart. Early in his years away from court he adopted the poetic garb of the neglected or misunderstood official with all its motifs, allusions, and symbols. In his descriptions of the people and scenes about him, his sense of isolation can be seen to diminish gradually. His later poetry is simpler, appealing directly to the emotions. The selections included in this anthology mirror the world of early ninth-century provincial China seen through the eyes of a cosmopolitan northerner who gradually came to feel at home in the towns of southern China.

(WILLIAM NIENHAUSER)

Yüan Chen (779–831)

Yüan Chen (*Wei-chih*) enjoyed wide popularity in his time and was probably the most colorful poet of the Mid-T'ang period. A native of Lo-yang, Honan, Yüan Chen was a descendant of the royal house of the Northern Wei dynasty that ruled over northern China in the fifth and sixth centuries. His father died when he was seven years old, and the family was left in difficult circumstances. It was his mother, a highly cultured woman, who supervised Yüan's early education. A precocious child, Yüan Chen passed the Classical Examination (*ming-ching*) by the time he was fourteen. In 806 he finished first in a more competitive degree examination in Ch'ang-an. It was then that he met Po Chü-yi, with whom he formed a lifelong and deep friendship. Many of the letters and lyrical poems Yüan Chen wrote after their separation, especially during his banishments, were addressed to Po-Chü-yi.

Yüan Chen shared with his friend the philosophy that literature should reflect social concerns, and during the Yüan-ho period (806–20) they also advocated a poetic form known as the *Hsin yüeh-fu* ("New Music Bureau Ballads"). One of the most important poems by Yüan Chen written in this style is "On Lien-ch'ang Palace." According to historical records, Emperor Mu-tsung, who came to the throne in 821, was so impressed by this new ballad with political overtones that he soon had Yüan Chen promoted as a member of the imperial secretariat.

Yüan Chen's political career suffered from many setbacks and repeated banishments. His life as an exile, however, may have brought him closer to the common people and made him sympathize with their sufferings (e.g., "Song of the Weaving Woman"). In private life, he also had his share of personal tragedy—the loss of his only son, and the death of his wife. The works that show his true feelings are those elegies and poems of parting and separation from Po Chü-yi. The impression that the poet was a heartless man incapable of intense emotions lacks substantiating evidence, but may have stemmed from a supposedly autobiographical prose romance Yüan Chen wrote—*Ying-ying chuan* (*The Story of Ying-ying*).[1] It is generally assumed that in this popular tale of romantic love (which was later adapted by Yüan dramatists and became known as the *Romance of the Western Chamber*, or *Hsi-hsiang chi*) the hero, Scholar Chang, who deserted his first love for the sake of political advancement, was in effect Yüan Chen himself.

Most Chinese critics who have relatively low regard of Yüan Chen's poetry share the bias of Su Shih, who once said that Po Chü-yi's poetry was "common" (*su*) and that Yüan Chen's poetry was "frivolous" or "light" (*ch'ing*). It is true that Yüan Chen's shorter poetry sometimes deals with frivolous subjects, such as ladies' fashions, or that these verses are merely impromptu compositions, more characterized by spontaneity than by conscious effort. But his longer poems can be complex and show genuine attempts at creating fresh imagery. In the *Hsin yüeh-fu* pieces, the poet's quick intellect is often coupled with his ability to grasp many tangled issues at once and direct his satirical thrust in many directions. His *oeuvre* (*Yüan-shih Ch'ang-ch'ing chi*), in one hundred *chüan*, consists of poems and prose of various genres, and this variety of subject matter and style could perhaps best explain his immense popularity and the sobriquet by which he was generally known, "Yüan the Genius" (*Yüan Ts'ai-tzu*). His artistic creed, a belief in simplicity, clarity, and sincerity, set the style and tone of Yüan-ho (806–20) poetry.

(ANGELA JUNG PALANDRI)

Chia Tao (779–849)

Chia Tao (*Ch'ang-chiang*) was originally from far northeast China, a region from which relatively few poets came. He began his adult life as a monk, with the religious name Wu-pen, but in 810 went to Ch'ang-an in order to meet Han Yü, Meng Chiao, and Chang Chi. His early poetry affected the bizarre exaggeration of the age, even more so than most, so that his poetic daring became something of a joke. Han Yü wrote of him:

His body is large, but not so large as his gall.

---

[1] See James R. Hightower, "Yuan Chen and 'The Story of Ying-ying,'" *Harvard Journal of Asiatic Studies*, 30 (1973), 90–123.

Meng Chiao spoke of him cryptically as a "lean monk lying in ice," and wrote jokingly:

> Too bad Li Po and Tu Fu are dead
> Not to see such madness as this.

Shortly thereafter Chia Tao became a layman and took up residence in the capital.

Chia Tao had a relatively undistinguished political career. Most of the rest of his life was spent in the capital in the company of the poets of the day. As the literary fashion shifted away from the hyperbolic style of the early ninth century toward a characteristically Late T'ang aestheticism, Chia Tao became one of the principal figures in the creation of the new style along with Chang Chi and others. He spent the last years of his life in several provincial posts.

(STEPHEN OWEN)

Chang Yu (*fl. 810*)

Chang Yu, or Chan Hu (*Ch'eng-chi*), born either in Ch'ing-ho, Hopei, or Nan-yang, Honan, was known primarily for his *yüeh-fu* verses, many of which contain pointed references to contemporary or near-contemporary events and personalities. The poets Yüan Chen and Po Chü-yi had a low opinion of his works, which, however, won the praise of Tu Mu.

Li Ho (*791–817*)

Li Ho (*Ch'ang-chi;* CH'ANG-KU), a native of Ch'eng-chi in Lung-hsi, Kansu, came of age with every reason to believe that he would be a success in the government. He had the opportunity of meeting and winning the patronage of the essayist and poet Han Yü prior to his taking the Prefectural Examination in 809 in Honan, where the family estate was located. At the start of 810 he was in the capital, Ch'ang-an, for the literary examination; but he was barred from taking it on the basis that if he became a *chin-shih* he would violate the taboo of using his deceased father's given name, which was Li Chin-su. (The *chin* of the degree and the Chin of his father's name, while sounding alike, are two different characters, yet the custom was to observe the taboo even with homonyms.) Thereafter, Li Ho occasionally referred to his failing health as well as to his deep disappointment. Because of hereditary privilege, he still managed to obtain a lowly position as Supervisor of Ritual at the Court of Imperial Sacrifices. He kept this position for three years, 811 to 814, and then, after a brief stay at his home, he joined the staff of one of the generals fighting a rebellious military governor. In 817 his illness caused him to return home, and he died shortly thereafter.

The talented literati found, during Li Ho's time, that their ability was largely ignored in favor of those who possessed financial and military influence. It was precisely through his rich, allusion-laden poetry that Li Ho responded to his era. Because he was fond of using mythological themes and the shamanistic imagery of the *Ch'u Tz'u* in the same way that more traditional poets used nature and history as the source of their allusions, Li Ho has long been considered a mystic whose poems are obscure and even depressing. But this is not the case. Li Ho found in Taoist and shamanist sources congenial imagery which allowed him to comment on the social and political evils of his day. His most "mystical" poems include the criticism of his own society, as do some of his less controversial poems.

(MICHAEL FISH)

Chu Ch'ing-yü (*fl. 826*)

Chu Ch'ing-yü, also known as Chu K'o-chiu, was a southerner from either Chekiang or Fukien. He passed his *chin-shih* examination in 826 and became a friend of the poet Chang Chi. His works consist mostly of quatrains and "regulated verse" poems.

Tu Mu (*803–852*)

Tu Mu (*Mu-chih*), poet and essayist, who was often referred to as "the Lesser Tu" as distinguished from Tu Fu, "the Greater Tu," was born in Wan-nien in the Capital District (Sian, Shensi), the scion of a distinguished family. When he was three years old, his grandfather Tu Yu (735–812) was ennobled as the Duke of Ch'i; a prominent statesman and scholar, Tu Yu was the compiler of the huge encyclopedia known as *T'ung-tien,* which contains the source material for the political and social history of China from the earliest time. A deep sense of the past pervades much of Tu Mu's own poetry.

Tu Mu obtained his *chin-shih* degree in 828 and received appointments in the provinces. In the faction-ridden court of Emperor Wen-tsung, he served at one time as secretary to Niu Seng-ju (779–848), but he was never happy with either the Niu clique or that of Li Te-yü (787–850), Niu's chief rival. Thwarted in his political ambition to strengthen the royal house and restore it to the past glory, Tu Mu chose to pursue a life of pleasure in Lo-yang, Yang-chou, and other metropolitan centers, and was known to be a connoisseur of beautiful women. In his poetry he prized himself for having shunned both the "ornate and the strange" on the one hand and "the commonplace and the vulgar" on the other. His own voice speaks most eloquently in his "regulated verse" poems and his quatrains; they are admired especially for their visual immediacy and delicacy of feeling.

Li Shang-yin (813?–858)

Li Shang-yin (*Yi-shan;* yü-hsi-sheng, or "Scholar of the Jade Stream") was born in Huo-chia, Honan, in 812 or 813, the son of a junior official. Orphaned young, he showed early literary brilliance but had an unsuccessful official career, serving under various military governors in different parts of China, including modern Shantung, Shensi, Kansu, Kwangsi, and Szechwan. He died in Cheng-chou in 858.

Li's extant poems, numbering about six hundred, may be divided into three groups. The first consists of ambiguous poems, often untitled or titled after the first line or ostensibly written to describe certain objects (*yung-wu*), which may involve several levels of meaning. Many of these deal with clandestine love, but have also been interpreted as political allegory. The second group is those poems addressed to friends and relatives or for his own amusement. Though they contain definite references to circumstances in the poet's life, their significance transcends the actual occasions that prompted their writing. The third group consists of poems dealing with contemporary sociopolitical situations, either directly or obliquely through historical allusions. As a whole, his poetry explores many different worlds, in a variety of styles ranging from the archaic to the colloquial, but at his most typical his worlds are rich and complex, and so is his language, in imagery and structure. He exerted great influence on some later poets and is generally considered a major poet in spite of the "obscurity" of many of his poems. (For a detailed study see James J. Y. Liu, *The Poetry of Li Shang-yin.*)

(JAMES J. Y. LIU)

Wen T'ing-yün (813?–870)

Wen T'ing-yün (*Fei-ch'ing*), native of T'ai-yüan, Shansi, was well-known in his own times as an accomplished musician and man of letters. Although his name was linked publicly with Li Shang-yin and other prominent literary figures such as Tuan Ch'eng-shih (?–863), very little is known with certainty about Wen T'ing-yün's family background, public career, or personal character. The historical records reflect a man of independent outlook and romantic temperament. Caring little for Confucian standards of public morality and bureaucratic behavior, he performed badly in the civil service examinations, despite the name he enjoyed as an accomplished writer of the examination *fu* poetic style. His official career was therefore uneven and lacking in distinction. A habitué of the cabarets and bordellos which flourished in the large metropolitan centers, he developed a reputation for irresponsible and unmannered behavior; however, that environment, with its popular music and song, also contributed to his development as a poet.

Until his day, the *tz'u,* or lyric poetry, was little cultivated by the literati class, though popular among professional entertainers and singers. As a skilled performer on the flute and the zither, Wen contributed to *tz'u* poetry by adapting that flexible medium to the requirements of polite literature and by creating a number of new *tz'u* patterns. Traditionally regarded as the first major poet to make extensive use of this new form, his example exerted a powerful influence on the early phase of development of the genre of lyric poetry.

Among the seventy *tz'u* poems in his *oeuvre*—the largest representation by one poet in the *Hua-chien chi* (the earliest *tz'u* anthology, preface dated 940)—two main styles predominate: a richly embellished depiction of the emotional and psychological pains experienced by the abandoned woman (either wife, lover, or professional entertainer), and a simple narration in the popular folk song manner of the joys and sorrows of young love. His verses in the "Deva-like Barbarian" and "Song of Water Clock at Night" tune-patterns best exemplify the former style, which shows the influence of "palace-style" verse (*kung-t'i shih*) of preceding periods. The movement seen in these poems is typically from exterior to interior scene, often lavishly appointed; and the emotional state of the neglected woman, which ranges widely from ennui to pensive longing to despair, is amplified by or is contrasted with her surroundings. Allusive, richly textured in language and metaphor, and compressed in form, these lyrics convey a feeling of both profound sensitivity and decadent affluence.

The latter style is represented best by verses set to the "Dreaming of the South" and "A Southern Song" patterns, where, in contrast to the ornate rhetoric of the former style, the diction is simple and direct. Thematically, the former style is concerned with a single individual, a woman, in isolation; and the latter with the interplay between young men and women, as in the folk songs (*yüeh-fu*) of the Southern dynasties. In both styles, however, the point of view is objective, detached, thus lending an air of realism to the individual poem.

Wen T'ing-yün is most often thought of as a *tz'u* poet because of his important contributions to the early development of that form. His *shih* poetry, which is also richly varied in theme, manner, and diction, is however no less interesting. Among the two hundred-odd *shih* poems which have been preserved, he shows a strong preference for the seven-syllabic line and the *ko-hsing,* or ballad, forms, which better suited his descriptive manner. In his use of theme and metaphor, a sense of vanished glory, of past heroic ages, is invoked, most frequently the luxuriant, self-indulgent world of the fifth and early sixth centuries, when his own ancestors were highly placed in society. The "Wildfire" poem, on the other hand, strikes an entirely different note, revealing both a fine descriptive sense and a larger sensibility than he is often credited with. In general, the densely textured qualities and the ornate diction found in his lyrics are also characteristic features of his *shih* poetry written in the more traditional forms.

(WILLIAM R. SCHULTZ)

Yü Wu-ling (9th century)

Almost nothing is known of this poet of the mid-ninth century. The small corpus of his extant poems reveals a preoccupation with the sorrows of separation from friends and nostalgia for an unrecoverable past, tempered by a deep involvement with wild nature.

(EDWARD H. SCHAFER)

Lu Kuei-meng (?–c. 881)

Lu Kuei-meng (*Lu-wang;* PU-LI HSIEN-SHENG) was born into a poor family in Ch'ang-chou (Wu-hsing) near Soochow, Kiangsu. Having failed many times in his attempts to pass the imperial examinations, Lu lived as a recluse in his native province. Lu seems to have found happiness only in boating through the beautiful Lake T'ai district, visiting temples and monasteries and practicing alchemy. An authority on tea, he was partially responsible for making that beverage an integral part of Chinese social life. His friends included P'i Jih-hsiu, to whom he dedicated most of his poems, Lo Yin, and other recluse poets. His nature poetry abounds in allusions to the texts of philosophical Taoism, and he is also known for his satirical prose in which he expresses his intense dislike of the vulgar people and harsh officials.

(ROBIN D. S. YATES)

P'i Jih-hsiu (c. 833–883)

P'i Jih-hsiu (*Hsi-mei,*), native of Hsiang-yang, Hupeh, was a recluse before he became an official in the chaotic years of the late ninth century. He earned his *chin-shih* degree in 867 and served on the staff of Ts'ui P'u, Censor of Soochow, when he became a friend of Lu Kuei-meng's. Ten years later, he was appointed Doctor of Letters in the Imperial University in Ch'ang-an. When the Huang Ch'ao rebellion broke out, he was captured, made to serve in the Hanlin Academy of the rebel government, and eventually killed. P'i Jih-hsiu's poetry, on the one hand, shows vast erudition (cf. "Thoughts in Early Autumn"), and on the other, incorporates realistic themes and everyday language (cf. "Orthodox Music Bureau Ballads"). In their simplicity, irony, and attention to detail, his verses foreshadow the development of Sung poetry.

(WILLIAM H. NIENHAUSER)

Lo Yin (833–909)

Lo Yin (Chao-chien), native of Ch'ien-t'ang (Hangchow), led an indifferent career in the Late T'ang government, his progress impeded by his liking for barbed, satirical language when alluding to government officials and other magnates. Still, he enjoyed a widespread reputation as a poet. He was an ugly man; the story is told that the daughter of an influential friend fell in love with him through his poetry, but when Lo Yin came to visit her father and she saw his face, she gave up his writings altogether. Late in the ninth century Lo Yin was attracted to the court of Ch'ien Liu, founder of the semi-independent state of Wü-Yüeh in Chekiang, where he died in high office. He was particularly famous for his poems on historical themes, a fact that may explain the indignation expressed in the poems translated here.

(EDWARD H. SCHAFER)

Wei Chuang (836–910)

Wei Chuang (Tuan-ssu) was born into an impoverished old family of Tu-ling, the Capital District (Sian, Shensi); struggled through poverty to become a poet; lived to witness the most turbulent period of the T'ang dynasty; and eventually became an accomplished writer of both shih and tz'u in an age of transition.

On January 8, 881, when the poet was in his mid-forties, Huang Ch'ao led an army of sixty thousand peasant rebels into the T'ang capital. The emperor, Hsi-tsung, fled south to Ch'eng-tu in Szechwan; Huang Ch'ao proclaimed himself emperor and appointed his lieutenant Shang Jang "the Grand Exterminator of T'ang." It was no idle boast. Hundreds of government officials were murdered and so were eighty thousand of Ch'ang-an's inhabitants. By the time Li K'o-yung recaptured the city in 883, the population was worse than decimated and only four government buildings out of hundreds had survived the conflagrations. Although Huang Ch'ao was finally defeated, the T'ang dynasty never recovered, finally falling in 907.

Wei Chuang was in the capital when Huang Ch'ao made his triumphal entry, and endured great privations until he made his escape in the spring of 882. A year later, while resident in Lo-yang, he wrote one of the longest and probably most dramatic political poems in Chinese literature, "The Lament of the Lady of Ch'in," a realistic account of the sack of Ch'ang-an. It was said that after Wei Chuang had become a high government official in the independent state of Shu, he regretted the harsh realism of the following two lines: "When the Inner Treasury was gutted, it became just ashes of brocades and embroideries;/ One trod along the Street of Heaven over pulverized bones of officials" and forbade the perpetuation of this poem by his descendants. The poem survived only by title until handwritten copies of this poem were found among the Tun-huang (Kansu) manuscripts, discovered a thousand years later.

Wei Chuang achieved immediate literary fame with the writing of this poem. He traveled through south-central China, visiting many provinces, and did not return to Ch'ang-an until 893. Three years later he was assigned a government post in Shu (Szechwan), where his admiration for Tu Fu was such that he found and purchased the poet's dilapidated house in Ch'eng-tu and renovated it for his own use. His poems, from 881 on, convey in austere language his intense concern for the social and political conditions of the time. When Wang Chien set up an independent kingdom in Shu on the demise of the T'ang dynasty, Wei Chuang served as his chief minister. He also became a leader among the *tz'u* poets of the kingdom; fifty of his lyric compositions were included in the *Hua-chien chi,* and his style greatly influenced later lyric poets. He was also known as a compiler of one of the T'ang *shih* anthologies called *Yu-hsüan chi.*

(ROBIN D. S. YATES)

Ssu-k'ung T'u (837–908)

Ssu-k'ung T'u (*Piao-sheng*), native of Ho-chung, Shansi, divided his time between the rigors of exalted government office and the peace and quiet in his old home. During the final agony of the dynasty, he lived as a recluse in a remote valley in Shansi, where he enjoyed the company of learned monks and other scholars, writing beautiful poems about the mountain landscape. When the last scion of T'ang was murdered by Chu Ch'üan-chung, the founder of the Liang dynasty, he starved himself to death. His works include a long poem in twenty-four stanzas, known as the "Categorization of Poetry" (*Shih-p'in*), an attempt at describing and ranking the essential qualities manifested in verse (for a partial translation of this poem, see pp. 179–88 of Herbert A. Giles's *A History of Chinese Literature*, New York: D. Appleton, 1923).

(EDWARD H. SCHAFER)

Yü Hsüan-chi (c. 843–868)

The poet Yü Hsüan-chi was a courtesan, a concubine, and a Taoist nun, all in the twenty-five years of her short life. As a courtesan in the city of Ch'ang-an, teeming capital of the T'ang empire, she met Li Yi, whom she addresses in her poems by his sobriquet, Tzu-an. This man apparently purchased her freedom from the brothel and took her as his concubine. Later he abandoned the poetess in the south, where she languished in the mountains for a time, returning eventually to the business of pleasure. At length she was able to travel back to the metropolis of Ch'ang-an, but she found herself living in serious poverty without a regular patron. It was probably this series of misfortunes that turned her thoughts toward the Taoist religion, for we soon find her leading the life of a nun. Following a period of asceticism, Yü began again to accept visitors, and she spent the rest of her life as a courtesan-nun. Popular tradition has it that she was executed after being found guilty of beating a maid to death, but recently more sympathetic critics have suggested that she could have been framed on trumped-up charges.

Yü Hsüan-chi's poems require little explanation, for none of them contains the kind of historical or mythical allusion that makes so much of Chinese poetry incomprehensible without the aid of cumbersome notes. Rather, the poetess relies more heavily upon symbolism: willow trees and blossoms usually represent the courtesan; the butterfly, the rake; the pine tree, fidelity; silken gowns, the worldly life. The concerns of society, the musings of philosophers, the rise and fall of dynasties, all find little place in her fifty extant poems. She was a woman in a man's world, and though she resented it she was helplessly dependent upon men. Her poems are an intensely personal but real reflection of her life and feelings, and as such they will be found worth reading.

(JAN W. WALLS)

Tu Hsün-ho (846–904)

Tu Hsün-ho (*Yen-chih*), native of Ch'ih-chou, Anhwei, was the illegitimate son by a concubine of the poet Tu Mu. He enjoyed the patronage of Chu Ch'üan-chung, who overthrew the T'ang dynasty. Despite the eminent position he obtained at court, the younger Tu's barbed comments made enemies among influential magnates, some of whom even plotted his assassination. He died of natural causes before the fruition of these plans.

(EDWARD H. SCHAFER)

Li Shan-fu (fl. 874)

Bitterly disappointed by his failure to achieve a position in the official hierarchy late in the ninth century, Li Shan-fu gave himself to melancholic drinking and periods of wild singing. He drifted about the disturbed world of the declining T'ang, from war lord's government to Taoist monastery, leaving many unfinished poems. A mad genius.

(EDWARD H. SCHAFER)

T'ang Yen-ch'ien (fl. 880)

T'ang Yen-ch'ien (*Mao-yeh;* LU-MEN HSIEN-SHENG) was a native of Chinyang in Ping-chou, Shansi. A learned man, he passed his *chin-shih* examination in 873 and held important provincial posts, both civil and military, during the troubled years at the end of the T'ang era. He was an accomplished painter, calligrapher, and musician as well as a writer.

(EDWARD H. SCHAFER)

Li Hsün (fl. 896)

Li Hsün (*Te-jung*) was a luminary at the court of the independent state of Shu in tenth-century Szechwan. His ancestors were Persian. The fact that his younger brother was a dealer in drugs and aromatics adds color to the probability that the poet was identical with the Li Hsün who is known to have written a pharmacopoeia on exotic drugs. He was one of the eighteen poets represented in the *Hua-chien chi;* many songs he wrote in the new popular form are colored with banana groves, palm leaves, elephants, hibiscus blossoms, and earringed native courtesans. They suggest an intimate acquaintance with the tropical South.

(EDWARD H. SCHAFER)

Han Wo (fl. 902)

Han Wo (*Chih-yao*) was a native of Wan-nien (Sian), Shensi. He passed his *chin-shih* examination in 889 and had a distinguished career in the court of Emperor Chao-tsung. Later he incurred the enmity of Chu Ch'üan-chung, the subverter of the dynasty, and early in the tenth century he was forced to flee to the safety of a secessionist military court in Fukien. His poems are richly colored: one of them has the curious distinction of containing the first reference to the binding of women's feet.

(EDWARD H. SCHAFER)

Lyrics from Tun-huang

Among fresco paintings, banners, embroideries, and other articles unearthed in one of the cave-chapels in a Buddhist monastery in Tun-huang, Kansu, there were found over ten thousand items of hand-copied manuscripts that had been sealed and preserved there for almost a thousand years. Over a half of the Tun-huang findings, brought to Europe by the Hungarian adventurer Mark Aurel Stein (later Sir Aurel Stein), who was in the service of the British government, and the French Sinologist Paul Pelliot, have become the permanent collections respectively of the British Museum and the Bibliothèque Nationale. These materials include popular literature of various kinds in T'ang China, of anonymous authorship, often involving works of oral transmission, copied by unskilled hands onto the cramped spaces in a single sheet of paper or in a scroll.

This extraordinary find contains over eighty pieces of a type of composition known as *pien-wen* (tales and ballads written mostly in alternating passages of prose and poetry, which deal with stories in the lives of Buddhist saints or Chinese folk heroes and historical figures), as well as *shih* compositions by neglected T'ang poets, such as Wang Fan-chih, and the only surviving text of Wei Chuang's "Lament of the Lady of Ch'in." What testifies to the immense popularity of *tz'u* in tenth-century China, or even earlier, are the 500 or so verses known as *ch'ü-tzu* or *tz'u* (318 "fixed-pattern sequential verse" and 227 isolated lyrics[1])—all by anonymous authors with the exception of a few known compositions by three or four popular T'ang poets. (For many of these lyrics, interestingly enough, the names of the singers were given.) As many as sixty-nine different tune-titles occur in the Tun-huang lyric collection, and forty-five of these titles are identifiable as *chiao-fang* (Imperial Music Training School) tunes played by musicians in the T'ang capital of Ch'ang-an. Somewhat cruder in style than those written by the literati, these anonymous songs depict the life of ordinary people in a remote mercantile and garrison town, on the crossroad from China to Central Asia and thence India.

(IRVING Y. LO)

PART IV

Ku Hsiung (fl. 928)

Nothing else is known of Ku Hsiung except that he was one of the court poets of the Shu kingdom during the Five Dynasties period and a man of flippant humor. Fifty-five of his lyrics were included in the *Hua-chien chi*.

Feng Yen-ssu (903–960)

Feng Yen-ssu (*Cheng-chung*), a native of Kuang-ling (modern Yang-chou, Kiangsu), held various high positions in the court of Li Ching, the second Ruler of Southern T'ang. His nearly one hundred extant *tz'u* poems were a major influence on later poets for over a century, although they are now often overshadowed by the works of Li Yü. Many of his poems show both the subtle refinement of a courtier and sometimes cynical pessimism.

(DANIEL BRYANT)

---

[1] These figures are taken from Jen Erh-pei [Jen Na], *Tun-huang ch'ü ch'u-t'an* (*Songs of Tun-huang Explored for the First Time*), Shanghai, 1954. For a study of the *pien-wen* literature, see Arthur Waley, *Ballads and Stories from Tun-huang* (New York: Macmillan, 1960), and Eugene Eoyang, *Word of Mouth: Oral Storytelling in the Pien-wen* (unpublished dissertation, Indiana University, 1971).

Sun Kuang-hsien (*?–968*)

Sun Kuang-hsien (*Meng-wen*), native of Kuei-p'ing, Szechwan, was a high official in the Nan-p'ing kingdom (907–63), ruling over Hupeh and eastern Szechwan, the smallest and weakest of the ten kingdoms. He was responsible for arranging the surrender of Nan-p'ing to Sung and was rewarded by Sung T'ai-tsu with a post as Censor in Huang-chou but he died before assuming office. He left a collection of essays and eighty-two *tz'u,* sixty of which were in the *Hua-chien chi.*

Li Ching, Second Ruler of Southern T'ang (*916–961*)

Li Ching (*Po-yü*), native of Hsü-chou, Kiangsu, was the son of a man of obscure origins who succeeded in becoming the dominant political figure in the state of Wu and eventually ursuped the throne in 937. In 943, Li Ching succeeded his father as Second Ruler of the new state of Southern T'ang (its territory roughly equivalent to the modern provinces of Kiangsu, Anhwei, and Kiangsi) and attempted a vigorous expansion of his domain. His military campaigns resulted in costly defeats in Fukien and Hunan, and they so weakened his state that he was unable to fend off an invasion from the north. With his enemies in control of the shore opposite his capital, Chien-k'ang (modern Nanking), he left his son Li Yü behind to administer the old capital and moved his court to Hung-chou (modern Nan-ch'ang, Kiangsi), where he died soon after.

In contrast to his military failures, Li Ching's court was one of the leading cultural centers of the age. The poet Feng Yen-ssu and the landscape painter Tung Yüan were only two of the many brilliant men who gathered under his protection in Chien-k'ang.

There is no record of Li Ching's collected works having survived the fall of Southern T'ang in 976, and we have today only four *tz'u,* two *shih,* and a few fragments and prose pieces left.

(DANIEL BRYANT)

Li Yü, Last Ruler of Southern T'ang (*937–978*)

Li Yü (*Ch'ung-kuang*), also known as Li Hou-chu, the last Ruler of Southern T'ang, was pre-eminently noted for his painting and calligraphy as well as for his lyrics. Born only months before the coup in which his grandfather founded the state, he succeeded in 961 to a throne for which he was suited by neither temperament nor training. He seems to have been extravagant and impulsive as a ruler, but he avoided war and encouraged Buddhism. He took refuge from the cares of state and later from personal tragedy—the death of his beautiful and accomplished wife and their young son—in poetry and art. Southern T'ang was doomed even before Li Yü ascended the throne, but it was not until 974 that the Sung court dispatched its armies against him. His capital fell in the winter of 975 and he was taken as a captive north to the Sung capital of Pien-ching (modern K'ai-feng, Honan). He wrote many of his best lyrics during this period of his captivity. On his forty-first birthday, the Sung emperor sent him a gift of poisoned wine and he died after drinking it.

Li Yü's court equaled that of his father's in literary and artistic splendor, and included some of the men who would later figure importantly in the cultural life of the early Sung. The *tz'u*, which had hitherto been limited almost exclusively to themes derived from the palace-style poetry began in his hands to acquire a more personal style and to establish a new identity. Especially the lyrics of his last period were acclaimed by later critics for the delicacy and poignancy with which he expressed not just his personal grief, but a sense of waste in all human endeavors. The modern poet-critic Wang Kuo-wei (1877–1927) ranked Li Yü above both Wen T'ing-yün and Wei Chuang and considered him to epitomize Nietzsche's concept that all literature must be written in blood.

(DANIEL BRYANT)

Wang Yü-ch'eng (954–1001)

Wang Yü-ch'eng (*Yüan-chih*), native of Chü-yeh in Ch'i-chou, Shantung, served as a high official under the emperors T'ai-tsung (reigned 976–92) and Chen-tsung (reigned 993–1022). He was three times banished to the provinces because of his outspoken criticism of court policy. Urbane and erudite, he was entrusted with the drafting of government documents and the writing of the *shih-lu* (veritable records) of T'ai-tsung's reign. As a writer, Wang advocated a rejection of the literary style of the Five Dynasties and a return to that of T'ang. He was one of the earliest Sung poets to praise the poetry of Tu Fu. His own poetry shows the influence of both Tu Fu and Po Chü-yi, the former in the matter of diction and syntax and the latter in the choice of theme and general attitude toward poetry.

P'an Lang (?–1009)

P'an Lang (*Hsiao-yao*) was a native of Ta-ming, Hopei (another account has it that he was of Ch'ien-t'ang, or modern Hangchow, Chekiang, near the famous West Lake mentioned in his works), who lived in the period between the Five Dynasties and the Sung. In 955 he received the *chin-shih* degree and was appointed an acting assistant professor in the Imperial

Academy, but was soon deprived of his post. After years of wandering as a herbalist, he was given another minor post in the Sung period. Only ten of his lyrics have survived.

Lin Pu (967–1028)

Lin Pu (*Chün-fu*), native of Ch'ien-t'ang (modern Hangchow), Chekiang, was a recluse poet. He lived alone for twenty years on the Orphan Hill (Ku Shan) in the famed West Lake region of his native district. Never married, he was known to prefer plum blossoms to a wife, and cranes as companions rather than children.

Yang Yi (974–1020)

Yang Yi (*Ta-nien*), native of P'u-ch'eng in Fukien, and an official during the reign of the third Sung emperor, Chen-tsung, is best known as the chief poet of the Hsi-k'un school. This school was named after an anthology of poems entitled *Hsi-k'un ch'ou-ch'ang-chi,* which was issued in 1004 and attained considerable popularity in its day. Most of the poems in this collection were modeled on the verse of Li Shang-yin, but in the hands of Yang and the other Hsi-k'un poets, the elegant richness of Li's style degenerated into artificiality.

Later reactions to the Hsi-k'un school were often quite violent. The critic Shih Chieh (1005–45), for example, said of Yang Yi that he was "excessive in his artfulness, extravagant in his loveliness, and superficially beautiful." Shih even attacked Yang for "corrupting the Way of the Sage," the "Sage" being Confucius!

On the other hand, the great poet and thinker Ou-yang Hsiu admired Yang, describing him as "a great literary hero of his time." Ou-yang must have noticed that a number of Yang's poems did not fit the usual stereotype of the Hsi-k'un style. He would certainly have approved of two of the poems translated here, which come from Yang's personal collection, rather than from the Hsi-k'un anthology. "Lang Mountain Monastery" is a finely balanced nature poem, free of the obscure bookishness which mars Hsi-k'un poetry. "The Prisons Are Full of Convicts" does contain three literary and historical allusions, but they are woven into the fabric of a social protest poem, a type not ordinarily associated with the name of Yang Yi.

(JONATHAN CHAVES)

Yen Shu (991–1055)

Yen Shu (*T'ung-shu*), native of Lin-ch'uan in Wu-chou, Kiangsi, was one of the many prominent statesmen-poets of the early Sung, and one of the few

southerners attaining the highest rank in court. Recognized as a child prod-
igy, he was awarded the associate *chin-shih* degree at fourteen and granted
the privilege of using the Imperial Library. A stylist in the drafting of docu-
ments, he served in many important posts, including that of the Executive
Censor. He advocated the establishing of private schools, and his own home
became the literary salon of his time. Skilled especially in the *hsiao-ling*
(short lyrics), his elegant poems continued the tradition of Feng Yen-ssu
and other Southern T'ang poets.

Mei Yao-ch'en (1002–1060)

Mei Yao-ch'en (*Sheng-yü*) is a major figure in the early development of
Sung poetry. The poet and critic Liu K'e-chuang (1187–1269), using a
technical term for the founder of a Buddhist sect, described him as "the
Mountain-Opening Patriarch of the poetry of this dynasty."

Mei's life was that of a scholar-bureaucrat, and he counted among his
friends some of the greatest statesmen of the day, most notably Ou-yang
Hsiu, with whom he maintained a deep, lifelong relationship. Nevertheless,
Mei never rose above the relatively unimportant position of Auxiliary Secre-
tary of the Ministry of Justice.

In addition to the frustrations of official life, Mei suffered the early loss of
his first wife, who died in 1044 at the age of thirty-six, of a baby son who
died less than a month later, and of a baby daughter by his second wife less
than four years afterward. In a preface to Mei's collected works, Ou-yang
Hsiu wrote that "a man must undergo hardship before he can become an ac-
complished poet." The tragic deaths of Mei's wife and children moved him
to write some of the finest poems of personal emotion in Chinese literature.

Through his association with Ou-yang Hsiu and other figures in Ou-yang's
circle of friends, Mei was involved in a major revival of Confucianism. Dur-
ing the T'ang dynasty, Buddhism had become the dominant school of
thought in China. Only the poet and thinker Han Yü had the courage to at-
tack what he regarded as a foreign intrusion into Chinese life, and to call
for a return to native ways of thought. Ou-yang and Mei admired Han Yü,
both for his defense of Confucianism and for his accomplishment as a poet.
For Mei in particular, the revivification of the humanistic Confucian tradi-
tion was associated with the creation of a more realistic poetic style which
could encompass descriptions of everyday life and protest against social
injustice.

Mei lived at a time when the Tangut Hsi Hsia state was threatening
Chinese sovereignty in the North. The Hsi Hsia invasions reached their
height in 1040, when Mei was an official in Honan province, where floods
and a great windstorm added to the misfortunes of the people. The war gave
rise to the forced conscription of militiamen, causing enormous hardship.

Mei responded to these and later events with a number of powerful protest poems, of which "Meeting the Herdsmen" is an example.

In his few pronouncements on poetry, Mei called for originality and for skill in the depiction of "scenes that are difficult to describe, in such a way that they seem to appear right before the reader's eyes." He also advocated relatively simple diction, which would nevertheless express a "meaning beyond the words themselves." The term he used for this poetics of understatement was *p'ing-tan,* literally, "even and bland." Han Yü too had called for simpler diction in literature, and like Han, Mei was reacting to earlier styles in which complex language concealed an inner emptiness.

Mei was a poet of the real, whether he was writing about his personal life or the social and political realities of his time. His personality impressed all who met him, including such men as Wang An-shih and Su Shih, who were to become major Sung poets. Ou-yang Hsiu described Mei in this way: "As a person, Mei Yao-ch'en was humane, generous, good-natured, and casygoing. He was never intractable in his relations with others. When he desired to satirize or mock because of the angry feelings to which his poverty and sorrow gave rise, he did so in poetry. But this was for his own pleasure, and not out of resentment or hatred. Thus he can be considered a Superior Man."

(JONATHAN CHAVES)

Liu Yung (fl. 1034)

Liu Yung (original name San-pien; *Ch'i-ch'ing*), native of Ch'ung-an, Fukien, was a popular lyric poet skilled in music. He was a contemporary of Yen Shu and Ou-yang Hsiu, but neither his birthdate nor the year of his death is known for certain. He earned his *chin-shih* degree in 1034, but disdained an official career. He remained a junior secretary all his life in a local administration in Chekiang, supervising agricultural work (known as *t'un-t'ien*), for which he earned the nickname of Liu T'un-t'ien. The majority of his two hundred lyrics belong to the subgenre called *man-tz'u,* or "slow tunes," some of which have three stanzas (cf. Tune: "Midnight Music"). Many of his lyrics reflect the gaiety of urban life as found in such prosperous cities as Hangchow, Soochow, or the Sung capital K'ai-feng. He was especially noted for songs depicting the sorrow of farewell and separation, endowing them with thought and emotion. As a *tz'u* expert, he succeeded so well in blending colloquial idiom with the requirements of music that his verses were sung at every village, but the popularity of his poetry notwithstanding, he died in extreme poverty. It was said that at his death many of the women of the demimonde whom he had befriended raised money to give him a proper burial.

Ou-yang Hsiu (1007–1072)

Ou-yang Hsiu (*Yung-shu*) was born in Mien-chou, Szechwan, though he claimed his paternal lineage from Lu-ling, Kiangsi, as his place of origin. He became one of the first few southerners to rise early to national prominence in the court of Northern Sung. Statesman, historian, philosopher, archaeologist, he was best known as an essayist (for his leadership role in the prose reform movement) and as a poet.

Ou-yang earned his *chin-shih* degree in 1030 and served on a minor administrative post in Lo-yang, where he became a good friend of the poet Mei Yao-ch'en. Upon the recommendation of the senior statesman Fan Chung-yen (989–1052), he was soon brought to the capital, K'ai-feng, and appointed to the Imperial Academy. Political factionalism shortly caused his banishment to Yi-ling, in modern Hupeh, where he spent his time writing his private history of the Five Dynasties. A political conservative, he enjoyed power for only eight years (1060–68) in the central censorate; he was exiled for the second time when he opposed the new economic measures advocated by Wang An-shih—this time as magistrate of Ch'u-chou, Anhwei. There he adopted the style-name (*hao*) of the "Old Drunkard" (*tsui-weng*), and built the famous pavilion which he immortalized in both prose and poetry. Unsympathetic to Wang An-shih's fiscal policy all his life, Ou-yang had a high regard for the reformist prime minister's literary ability and remained Wang's steadfast friend.

Ou-yang's own contribution to literature rested on his reform of the current prose style and on his many innovations in poetry. Early in his life he developed a great admiration for the works of the T'ang writer Han Yü, which led to his advocacy of the ancient-style prose (*ku-wen*) movement, stressing vigor and simplicity in opposition to the florid style of the Six Dynasties prose.

Ou-yang's eclectic genius found expression in a wide variety of literary genres, which included *shih* and *tz'u* as well as the rhyme-prose composition (*fu*). (His descriptive account of an outing at the "Old Drunkard's Pavilion" is considered a masterpiece in prose literature.) As a writer of *shih* poetry, he was adept in all verse forms and considered by some of his contemporary poets as the equal of Li Po. Also known for his knowledge of music and for his unconventionality in personal life (for which he was heavily censured, especially by later Neo-Confucianist critics), Ou-yang turned his artistic sensitivity to good account by becoming a dominant writer of *tz'u*, then popular in the opulent life of the Northern Sung society. No less than Liu Yung, he enlarged the themes and the language of love poetry, but he was more successful as a writer of short songs (*hsiao-ling*). Often by incorporating into his lyrics many popular, colloquial expressions, he brought new verve and a greater depth of feeling to a tradition that began with the

Hua-chien poets nearly a century earlier. He embellished upon this tradition and, with his more refined sensibilities, created for it a new audience.

Also known as a *bon vivant,* Ou-yang gave himself the other style-name of Liu-yi, which literally means "six (in) one," referring to his desire to see himself, as one of the sixes, constantly in the presence of five other things; namely, his archaeological collection of a thousand *chüan,* his library of ten thousand *chüan,* his zither (*ch'in*), his chess set, and his wine. Possibly also a good raconteur, his comments on poetry and poets, included in a volume entitled *Liu-yi shih-hua* (*Liu-yi's Talks on Poetry*), became the first *shih-hua* treatise ever written; and it established a tradition of impressionistic criticism of poetry, which was continued in China until the time of Wang Kuo-wei in the twentieth century.

(IRVING Y. LO)

Su Shun-ch'in (*1008–1048*)

Su Shun-ch'in (*Tzu-mei*), native of T'ung-shan in Tzu-chou, Szechwan, later moved to K'ai-feng, Honan. Along with Mei Yao-ch'en, he was one of the two early Northern Sung poets who were critical of the Hsi-k'un style of poetry and advocated a return to greater realism and simpler diction. He passed the *chin-shih* examination in 1034 and was appointed a Registrar in the Court of the Imperial Banquets; he showed great concern for the welfare of the people in memorials he submitted, explaining the causes of natural disasters. In 1044, as a member of the General Memorial Acceptance Bureau, he was implicated in a political scandal leveled at Fan Chung-yen and others, and was demoted to a post in Soochow, where he lived in retirement in his Ts'ang-lang villa. His poems often contain stark imagery, sometimes reminiscent of the T'ang poet Meng Chiao, and even his poems about nature are likely to express some bitter thoughts and to give the appearance of being roughhewed.

Wang An-shih (*1021–1086*)

Wang An-shih (*Chieh-fu;* PAN-SHAN) was a native of Lin-ch'uan, Kiangsi. After winning his *chin-shih* degree, Wang An-shih began his official career serving mostly in provincial posts away from the capital. Surprisingly this was at his own request, and despite repeated efforts of influential men like Ou-yang Hsiu to bring him into higher circles of the central government. He claimed that on his small salary he could support his family better in the outlying districts than in the capital, where the cost of living was much higher. There are indications, however, that even then he saw himself as one destined for greatness, waiting only for an enlightened sovereign to authorize the radical reforms he had in mind (cf. "An Old Pine").

His chance came during the reign of Emperor Shen-Tsung (reigned 1067–85), when Wang was given the highest post in the government. He immediately began to impose sweeping political, economic, and military reform measures, which aroused great opposition among the conservative forces of the empire. Nine years later, when the success of his program appeared to be certain, he turned over his position of leadership to a trusted associate and retired to his home in present-day Nanking, where in the decade that followed, he wrote some of his finest poetry. In 1085 Shen-Tsung died, and Wang's party fell from power to be replaced by a conservative group, which immediately set about canceling the controversial reforms one after another. Wang died the following year, a disappointed man.

Known as one of the Eight Prose Masters of the T'ang and Sung periods, Wang An-shih was also one of the great *shih* poets of his time. There are thirty-eight *chüan* of poetry in his complete works; they contain approximately four hundred ancient-style poems, and one thousand in the regulated form, including *chüeh-chü*. He composed only a few verses in the *tz'u* form, which flourished in the hands of other Sung masters. Thematically, his poems may be divided into such categories as political and historical concerns, personal relationships, idleness, and Buddhistic matters. The historical and political poems mostly reflect the strong views of Wang's youth, while poems of idleness and Buddhistic thought stem largely and naturally from his later years in retirement; poems to friends and relatives span his whole life.

His verses often contain an allegorical comment, as in "An Old Pine." In others, especially those on political subjects and composed in his younger years, he makes no attempt to conceal his dissatisfaction with the system that feeds silkworms fatter than peasants ("Walking in the Countryside"). His Buddhistic poems, mostly composed in his later years of retirement, are often strongly didactic, as for instance the Han Shan and Shih Te series. By far his best poems, and those upon which his reputation as an adept of regulated verse rests, are his shorter verses written in idleness, wherein a single mood or observation is crystallized by skillful juxtapositon with images that echo and reinforce a primary feeling (cf. "By a Stream on Mount T'ien-t'ung").

Wang was among the first Sung poets to recognize and acclaim the surpassing achievement of Tu Fu; his fondness for the style of this all-time master of the regulated verse form is apparent in the most successful of his own works.

(JAN W. WALLS)

Yen Chi-tao (*1030?–1106?*)

Yen Chi-tao (*Shu-yüan;* HSIAO-SHAN) was the youngest son of Yen Shu. Leading a free, unconventional life, he held only local administrative posts in Honan and was at one time implicated in a political case and imprisoned. In 1105 he was appointed a prefectural judge in K'ai-feng. Written primarily for his own enjoyment, his lyrics are characterized by natural diction and fresh imagery and represent a complete break from the *Hua-chien* tradition. He and his father are known as the Two Yens of lyric poetry.

Su Shih (1037–1101)

Su Shih (*Tzu-chan;* TUNG-P'O), regarded by some as "the greatest of Sung poets" (Burton Watson, *Su Tung-p'o,* p. 4), achieved pre-eminence in many fields which included *shih, tz'u,* belletristic prose, as well as calligraphy and painting. Born in Mei-shan, Szechwan, into a family of modest means (his father, Su Hsün, 1009–66, a self-taught man, did not win recognition as a scholar until the last decade of his life), Su Shih passed his *chin-shih* examination, with Ou-yang Hsiu as his examiner, in 1057, along with his younger brother, Su Ch'e (*Tzu-yu,* 1039–1112). The father and the two sons all became outstanding prose writers and poets of their age and were known as the Three Sus.

Su Shih's checkered political career was marred by a series of defeats and banishments, primarily due to his opposition to Wang An-shih and also due to the acerbity of his writing, which at one time brought about his imprisonment. He was exiled to the provinces no fewer than twelve times in places like Mi-chou in Shantung; Hu-chou in Chekiang; Hangchow, twice; Huang-chou in Hupeh; Ting-chou in Hopei; Hui-chou in Kwangtung; and as far as Ch'iung-chou on Hainan Island. As a provincial administrator, he had the reputation of introducing benevolent policies and establishing a wonderful rapport with the people, especially in the area of public construction and relief work. From his experience in these various posts, he derived an immense knowledge of the lives of the common people, which was revealed in much of his poetry.

Su Shih's philosophical orientation also came from diverse sources. Trained in the writings of Taoist philosophers since early adolescence, his mind was attuned to the teachings of Lao Tzu and Chuang Tzu. He included among his friends several of the eminent Buddhist monks of the time, and he acquired a profound knowledge of Ch'an Buddhism. A spirit of real detachment, akin to what can be loosely called a sense of humor, informs some of his best verses.

Su Shih's works include over two thousand poems (*shih*) and over three hundred compositions in the lyric meter (*tz'u*). In either genre, he writes not only with great gusto but also with sufficient attention to the minutest details. Some critics prefer to describe his style as exuberant, spontaneous, or unrestrained; but, together with this display of powerful sentiments, there is always an astonishing degree of verisimilitude. Subjects as large as the tidal bore of the Ch'ien-t'ang River or as small as a snail or a toad, as somber and serious as the plight of the farmers, or as lighthearted as a day in a fisherman's life, are accorded the same kind of meditative scrutiny. His poetry usually combines description with narration and these two with philosophical affirmation. His achievement as a *tz'u*-writer is considered extraordinary in that he has accommodated lyric poetry to all kinds of themes and broadened its scope. His harsher critics claim that, in so doing, he was oblivious of the demands of music; but whatever might have been lost in the finer points of tonality (we lack detailed information about Sung music to confirm or refute this charge) has been amply made up for by the sweep and power of his poetry.

(IRVING Y. LO)

Huang T'ing-chien (1045–1105)

Huang T'ing-chien (*Lu-chih;* FU-WENG, SHAN-KU), native of Fen-ning, Hung-chou, in Kiangsi, poet and calligrapher, was known as the founder of the Kiangsi school of poetry. He passed his *chin-shih* examination in 1067 and served as a magistrate of She-hsien, in modern Honan, for a while before he was appointed professor in the National University and later one of the compilers of the Veritable Records of Shen-tsung's reign. As a scholar-official, he had an extremely checkered career: a victim of political dissensions, he was exiled many times to the provinces; and he died at his exile post in Yi-chou, Kwangsi, in 1105.

A study of Huang's some two thousand extant *shih* poems and over a hundred *tz'u* compositions reveals that he is a poet's poet. Though he never sought to establish a coterie, his style of poetry exerted great influence on his contemporaries and on later poets. Huang's fastidious taste for unique states of feeling can be bizarre; it once led a critic to warn that his poems must be chewed like olives. His best work meditates on the vicissitudes of human life, and often strikes at the knowledge of death. Huang believed in detaching emotions from the artistic process and in organizing a method of composition that would allow the creative transmutation of ancient literature into contemporary poetry. He advocated the techniques of "changing the bones" (*huan-ku*, borrowing certain images and phrases from past writers but altering the meaning) and "snatching the embryo" (*tuo-t'ai*, expressing the idea of another writer but altering its wording). Thus, he maintained, a poet could forge the unwieldy "ironlike" matter culled from extensive reading into golden new wholes (*tien-t'ieh ch'eng-chin*). Later on, this aspect of Huang's poetic theory became a subject of derision by intuitionist critics, such as Yen Yü (fl. 1180–1235) of the Southern Sung and by Wang Jo-hsü (1177–1246) of the Chin dynasty (1115–1234), who condemned Huang as a resourceful plagiarist. Yet Huang's speculation on the reciprocity of tradition and individual talent is strongly modern.

Huang enjoyed a reputation as a connoisseur of paintings by scholars, executing colophons and poems on scroll and fan paintings by artist friends. He took delight in the company of scholarly recluses like the monk Chung-jen, a specialist in ink plum blossoms. He is one of the four great calligraphers of the Sung dynasty.

(MICHAEL E. WORKMAN)

Ch'in Kuan (1049–1100)

Ch'in Kuan (*Shao-yu; T'ai-hsü;* HUAI-HAI CHÜ-SHIH), native of Kao-yu, Yang-chou, Kiangsu, was one of the followers of Su Shih. He obtained the *chin-shih* degree in 1085 and was appointed Correcting Editor of the Imperial Library and Officer of the Bureau of Compilation. When Su Shih fell from power in 1095, Ch'in Kuan was demoted as collector of wine revenue in Ch'u-chou in Chekiang. Later he was exiled to Ch'en-chou in Hunan, and to Lei-chou in Kwangtung. Upon the ascension of Hui-tsung in 1100, he was allowed to return to the capital but died en route. He left less than a hundred lyrics, all of excellent quality. Restricted in the type of subject matter, his verses, nonetheless, present successfully the moods of sorrow in a wide range of nuances.

Chou Pang-yen (1056–1121)

Chou Pang-yen (*Mei-ch'eng*), native of Ch'ien-t'ang (modern Hangchow), Chekiang, was a court musician and poet. As a young man, he was a student at the Imperial University, to which he was later appointed its Administrative Assistant. He was said to lead an unconventional life; and, according to one story, he was once the rival with Emperor Hui-tsung himself for the love of a famous singing girl. He held teaching and administrative posts in the provinces before he was appointed Intendant of the Bureau of Great Splendor (*Ta-ch'eng Fu*), an institution set up since 1075 to engage in the writing and the preservation of musical scores. Skilled especially in the composition of the "slow tunes," i.e., the longer lyrics, Chou created a number of new patterns, including the famous "Six Toughies" (*Liu-ch'ou*). When the term, literally "Six Uglinesses," was first introduced, it puzzled the Emperor. Asked to explain what the title meant, Chou replied that the number refers to the intricate parts of the music he had composed, and the Emperor was satisfied. Chou's verses offer the familiar themes from the *Hua-chien* poetry in a new guise and in a style characterized by a greater use of realistic details. He frequently employs color words to enhance the emotional appeal, and also concrete imagery by coining new noun-compounds such as "plum-blossom-waves" (*mei-lang*) or "dancer's-waist, song-tablets" (*wu-yao ko-pang*), which present difficulties in translation. Innovative only in this regard, he is primarily an embellisher of the *tz'u* tradition.

(IRVING Y. LO)

Chu Tun-ju (1081?–1159?)

Chu Tun-ju (*Hsi-chen;* YEN-HO), native of Lo-yang, expressed in his poetry the nostalgia and disillusionment of the early Southern Sung period. When the Jurched people overran North China, he moved to Kwangtung. In 1135 he obtained the *chin-shih* degree, but refused many appointments. Later he held the post of Judicial Intendant in modern Chekiang and also served as junior master of ceremonies at court. As a displaced northerner, he constantly wrote of his longing to be free and of the pleasure he found in being close to nature. His lyrics are a happy mixture of lofty sentiments and a free and easy style, with effective use of colloquial idioms.

Li Ch'ing-chao (1084?–c. 1151)

Li Ch'ing-chao (YI-AN CHÜ-SHIH), native of Li-ch'eng (modern Tsi-nan), Shantung, who lived in the intervening period between Northern Sung and Southern Sung, may be said to be one of the foremost lyric poets. She is both the successor to Su Tung-p'o and the precursor of Hsin Ch'i-chi. She was the daughter of a distinguished man of letters, daughter-in-law of a minister, wife of an educated minor official who was antiquarian, book collector, and epigrapher. Her reputation as a poet was established early with her contemporaries. Unfortunately, due to the loss of her home at the time of the Jurched invasion, the early death of her husband, and the tragedy of her later life, only a portion of her total poetic output is now extant, some fifty lyrics out of some six volumes. Yet, of the poems that remain, there is sufficient evidence to show that she was a remarkable poet, resolutely personal yet far from self-indulgent or tawdry. Her happy marriage figures in most of her poems, either actively celebrated or nostalgically recollected. At one time, husband and wife collaborated on the *Chin Shih Lu,* a monumental catalogue of stone and bronze *objets d'art,* of considerable archaeological interest, to which she added a postscript after his death.

The poetry of Li Ch'ing-chao reveals a mastery of language, a disarming directness of diction, a ruthless honesty of tone. Her attitudes are those of a woman, but her femininity is never servile or shrill. As a poet, she could be both bold and delicate, languid and boisterous. In short, though we have but a sampling of her work, there is world enough in what we have to hear the many voices of a true poet. Her attempt was to establish life in words: poetry was for her a stay against time, a surety to blot out oblivion. She tried to recapture the past, to preserve the present: in her own words, what she wanted to do was "still . . . hold onto a moment of time."

(EUGENE EOYANG)

Ch'en Yü-yi (1090–1138)

Ch'en Yü-yi (*Ch'ü-fei;* CHIEN-CHAI) originally from Mei-chou, Szechwan, later moved to She-*hsien* in Honan. He became *chin-shih* in 1113 under the last Northern Sung emperor; later, after North China was occupied by the Jurcheds, he moved south and rose to high rank under the first Southern Sung emperor. He is known mainly for his *shih* poems but his few extant *tz'u* lyrics are also remarkable.

Yang Wan-li (1124–1206)[1]

Yang Wan-li (*T'ing-hsiu;* CH'ENG-CHAI YEH-K'E, or "Rustic Man from the Studio of Sincerity") was one of the so-called Four Masters of Southern Sung Poetry, the others being Lu Yu, Fan Ch'eng-ta, and the little-known Yu Mao (1127–93), whose works have largely disappeared. All these men wrote primarily in the traditional *shih* form, although they also wrote a small number of *tz'u*.

Yang's life was relatively uneventful. A native of Chi-shui, Chi-chou, in Kiangsi, he earned his *chin-shih* degree in 1154, and embarked upon a fairly typical career in the government bureaucracy. The highest office he held was Director of the Imperial Library, to which he was appointed in 1189. Yang's most significant political act was the submission in 1167 of a famous memorial, *Ch'ien lü ts'e* (*A Thousand Concerns*), in which he advocated maintaining a strong defense against the Jurched Chin dynasty, which had occupied northern China as far as the Huai River. After retiring from official life at the age of sixty-five, he showed considerable courage by refusing to write an essay about a garden being constructed by the notorious Han T'o-chou, the most powerful official of the time. When Lu Yu, Yang's friend, agreed to write an essay for Han, Yang criticized Lu in a poem.

But Yang's main concern was literature. As he himself wrote, "In my life I have loved nothing else—I have only loved literature, as other men love beautiful women and I have especially loved poetry." Yang was extremely prolific; his collected writings include some four thousand two hundred poems, and this number does not include over a thousand early poems which he burned in 1162, when he seemed to have undergone an artistic crisis. Yang wrote nine collections of poetry, "a book of poems for each office he held," as a later critic put it.

In the preface to the second of these books, Yang describes his development as a poet. He began by studying the poets of the Kiangsi school (Huang T'ing-chien and his followers), and Ch'en Shih-tao, and then went on to the works of Wang An-shih and the Late T'ang poets. But in 1178,

---

[1] According to modern research, the probable dates are 1127–1206.

he experienced "enlightenment," and no longer felt a need to emulate earlier poets. Now "the ten thousand images of nature presented themselves" to him, and "it was no longer difficult to write poetry." From this time on, Yang advocated individuality in poetic style:

> I'd be ashamed to continue a school
> or carry on a sect—
> each writer must form his own style,
> with a beauty of its own.

The enlightenment of which Yang speaks reflects his interest in Ch'an Buddhism. The practice of Ch'an meditation may have helped Yang to develop his remarkable ability to concentrate on the details of the physical world; thus he could devote an entire poem to a description of the movements of a fly ("The Cold Fly"). Ch'an consciousness also informs this statement by Yang on the nature of poetry:

> "Now, what is poetry? If you say it is simply a matter of words, I will say, 'A good poet gets rid of words.' If you say it is simply a matter of meaning, I will say, 'A good poet gets rid of meaning.' But, you say, if words and meaning are gotten rid of, where is the poetry? To this I reply, 'Get rid of words and meaning, and there is still poetry.'"

Yang is often referred to as "the colloquial poet" (*pai-hua shih-jen*), because of his extensive use of colloquialisms, a feature which gives his diction an unusual flexibility and expressiveness. Later writers often criticized Yang as being "vulgar," but he has never been without his admirers. The Ch'ing poet Yüan Mei (1716–98), told that his poetry was like that of Yang Wan-li, replied: "Yang was one of the master poets of the Southern Sung. Later critics often made light of his poetry, but they didn't realize that he was a man of natural genius, like Li Po. It is true that he didn't polish certain flaws in his work, but this was the result of his honesty. I feel unworthy to be considered an imitator of his."

(JONATHAN CHAVES)

Lu Yu (1125–1210)

Lu Yu (*Wu-kuan;* FANG-WENG) was born into a scholar-official's family in Shan-yin (Shao-hsing), Chekiang, two years before the Jurched conquest of northern China and the establishment of Southern Sung with its capital in Lin-an (Hangchow). Early in his youth, he was taught to write poetry by his father, who also instilled in him a strong patriotic fervor; and he kept up a productive life as a poet for the next seven decades.

Lu Yu's personal life was marred by a tragic love affair when he, as a young man, was forced to divorce his beloved wife at his mother's behest. His political career was also beset with frustrations. Though successful in the examinations (1153, 1154), he incurred the displeasure of Ch'in K'uei, then prime minister, who blocked him from receiving any political appointments. In 1160, after Ch'in K'uei's death, he was recalled to the capital and was later appointed Assistant Commissioner in the Grand Court of Appeal and Compiler in the Privy Council, where he was a colleague of Fan Ch'eng-ta's. Because of his forthright views on government administration and war policy, he was dismissed from office in 1166. Four years later, he was sent as a prefectural administrator to K'uei-chou, Szechwan, where he spent a number of years in various posts which gave him the opportunity of visiting army garrisons in frontier regions. In 1178, Lu Yu's poetic fame had attracted the attention of the emperor, who summoned him to Lin-an; but, instead of being rewarded with a court appointment, he was sent out once again to provincial posts, serving successively in Fukien, Kiangsi, and Chekiang. He finally retired to his home in Shan-yin, in 1190. Thereafter he returned to the capital only twice: once (1202–3) to participate in the compilation of the Veritable Records of the two reigns of Hsiao-tsung and Kuang-tsung, and another time, in 1204, for an audience with the emperor (Ning-tsung, reigned 1195–1224). On his deathbed, he wrote his last patriotic poem, exhorting his sons not to fail to report to his spirit at family sacrifices the news of the eventual recovery of the Central Plains, a wish never fulfilled.

Lu Yu's works (mostly *shih*) consist of over ten thousand poems, which can be divided into three periods: 1) poems written while he was a young man, laboring under the influence of the Kiangsi school of poetry and striving for artistry and elegance; 2) those he wrote in his middle age as he evolved a new style marked by expansiveness and vigor; and 3) poems from his period of retirement which are mostly tranquil in tone. Lu Yu is not an innovator of forms and techniques; his poetry rises above narrow concerns and reveals an independent mind. In his later age he gave himself the style-name of Fang-weng, or "Emancipated Old Man." But while he felt himself emancipated from worldly concerns and the trammels of the spirit, he remained steadfast to the end of his life in his love of his country and in his vision of seeing China reunited. Patriotic sentiments permeate a significant part of his poetry.

(WU-CHI LIU)

Fan Ch'eng-ta (1126–1193)

Fan Ch'eng-ta (*Chih-neng;* SHIH-HU CHÜ-SHIH), a native of Wu-*hsien* (Soochow), Kiangsu, combined in his career active government service and the contemplation of nature and the countryside, for which his poetry was best known. He received his *chin-shih* degree in 1154, and became a high official in the court of the Southern Sung. In 1170 he carried out a diplomatic mission as a special envoy to the court of the Jurched (Chin) emperor in Yen (near Peking). On various other occasions he served as Pacification Commissioner and military or civil governor in Szechwan, Chekiang, Kwangsi, and Kiangsu. He also held high positions in the capital, as Grand Secretary and Acting President of the Board of Civil Service. During his retirement, and his old age, he lived in his scenic villa at Shih-hu (Stone Lake) in the outskirts of Soochow. It was there that he wrote (1186) the series of sixty poems on rural life in the four seasons. His love of nature is also reflected in the botanical treatises he wrote on the chrysanthemum and the winter plum.

Fan Ch'eng-ta continued the tradition of the "garden and field" poetry of T'ao Ch'ien and Wang Wei. But he differed from them in that he depicted not only the scenes and sceneries in the rural surrounding but also, in a realistic and intimate manner, the life and activities of the farmers. Moreover, he was seriously concerned with their social and economic plight, the hardships due to natural calamities or government oppressions, such as conscription and heavy taxation. His official duties took him to the remote regions of the empire, where he observed and recorded in poetry the folkways and living conditions of the primitive mountainous and coastal people. On his trip to the Jurched court, he was inspired and encouraged by the yearnings of the northern Chinese for the return of the Sung imperial army. Such patriotic sentiments are typical of Fan as well as other poets of the same period.

As a scholar-official, Fan Ch'eng-ta was guided by Confucian virtues and political ideals, especially by his love of country and people, but occasionally his verses echoed the Buddhist sentiments of resignation. As a poet, while he early came under the influence of the Kiangsi school, his best poems are simple and contain refreshing use of realistic details; sometimes they are satirical in the tradition of the New Music Bureau poems of Po Chü-yi and Wang Chien. Although Fan Ch'eng-ta was not as prolific a writer as his friend Lu Yu, the two of them could be considered as the most successful *shih* poets of the Southern Sung.

(WU-CHI LIU)

Huang Shu (1131–1191)

Huang Shu (*Tzu-hou*) was a native of Ch'ung-an in modern Fukien. He studied under Liu Tzu-hui, who also taught the great Neo-Confucian philosopher Chu Hsi (1130–1200). Huang did not enter official service but lived as a recluse. Of his works only three lyrics have survived, but they are of high quality.

Hsin Ch'i-chi (1140–1207)

Hsin Ch'i-chi (*Yu-an;* CHIA-HSÜAN), native of Li-ch'eng (modern Tsinan), Shantung, was a major poet of the Southern Sung dynasty. His collected works, then consisting of four *chüan*, were printed in an elegant block-print edition in 1188–1203. As a young man, Hsin distinguished himself in a personal exploit by capturing the leader of a minor rebellion, which gained him an audience with the emperor (Kao-tsung) at Chien-k'ang (modern Nanking). Later, he sporadically held government posts in the provinces, both civil and military, but he never succeeded in advocating a program of military preparedness and revitalization, or in opposing the peace policy toward the Jurched rulers of North China. For more than two decades in the last years of his life, he lived in retirement in his villa named Chia-hsüan, near the Fukien-Kiangsi border, surrounded by mountains and lakes, which he loved. There he gathered around himself a wide circle of friends (including the Neo-Confucianist philosopher Chu Hsi) and admirers.

Hsin Ch'i-chi was known by his contemporaries as an erudite poet and a patriotic poet par excellence. This reputation rests on his allusive style and on the heroic sentiments expressed in some of his verses. Especially adept in the composition of the longer tune-patterns, he frequently larded them with events and borrowings, sometimes direct quotations, not only from ancient poetry but also from prose classics such as history and philosophy. His efforts in this direction succeeded in broadening the scope of lyric poetry and contributing to the eventual separation between *tz'u* and music. Thus, he and Su Shih are frequently mentioned as the two great masters of lyric poetry and the exponents of the grand style hitherto unknown in lyric-meter compositions.

In other moments, however, Hsin also wrote bucolic poetry and love songs with wit and humor. His descriptions of nature are sometimes direct and simple but, more often, rich with nuances and ambiguities on both the verbal and metaphysical level. The most copious *tz'u* writer, he wrote over six hundred lyrics which reflect a wide range of styles, though he was rather undistinguished as a poet in the traditional *shih* form.

(IRVING Y. LO)

Ch'en Liang (1143–1194)

Ch'en Liang (*T'ung-fu*), native of Yung-k'ang, Chekiang, was known primarily as a philosopher and one of the leaders of the pragmatist school of Neo-Confucianism. His extant lyrics, though fewer than seventy, established him as a worthy successor to Hsin Ch'i-chi, his great friend and mentor. As a young man, he was fond of studying and discussing military stratagems; in 1163, as a private citizen, he presented to the throne a series of five essays entitled "Discourses on Revitalization of the Nation" (*Chung-hsing lun*). Rejected by the court, he began a more vigorous course of study of the classics and, in 1181, succeeded in impressing the emperor (Hsiao-tsung) with a new memorial but declined official posts offered him. As man of principle, he became the target of malignment and was imprisoned on more than one occasion. He took first place in the *chin-shih* examination under Emperor Kuang-tsung in 1193, a year before his death.

As a *tz'u* writer, Ch'en showed considerable prosodic sophistication, occasionally inventing new tune-patterns and refining upon existing ones. Written solely for his friends, these lyric songs reveal a high density of poetic feeling though deliberately couched in an admixture of colloquialism and allusions to the classics.

(HELLMUT WILHELM)

Chiang K'uei (1155?–1235?)

Chiang K'uei (*Yao-chang;* PAI-SHIH TAO-JEN), native of Po-yang, Kiangsi, was the first musician among the lyric poets of Southern Sung. He never held any official post but was highly esteemed by his contemporaries for his poetic gift and his connoisseurship of music, and be became a friend of all the leading poets of his time, including Fan Ch'eng-ta, Hsin Ch'i-chi, Yang Wan-li, and many others. As a composer of lyrical scores, he invented no fewer than seventeen tune-patterns, under the general rubric of "Songs Composed by Myself," the scores for which (along with scores he wrote to some earlier tunes) are still extant, though not all decipherable to the general reader.[1] In the writing of lyric songs, Chiang paid meticulous attention to diction and especially to the tonal quality. Disturbed by the general neglect of music by poets and the court alike, he had once, in 1199, submitted to the emperor an essay urging the reform of court music, but it failed to gain him attention. He led a rather unconventional life and visited many places of scenic beauty and large commercial cities. As a lyric poet, his style in akin to that of Chou Pang-yen, another craftsman-poet and musician of an earlier era. His finely chiseled verses have both admirers and detractors, and quite a few imitators among the less talented poets toward the end of the dynasty.

(IRVING Y. LO)

---

[1] Cf. Rulan Chao Pian, *Sonq [Sung] Dynasty Musical Sources and Their Interpretations* (Cambridge: Harvard University Press), 1967.

Yen Yü (fl. 1200)

Yen Yü (*Yi-ch'ing; Tan-ch'iu;* TS'ANG-LANG PU-K'E), about whom little else was known except that he was a native of Shao-wu, Fukien, was best remembered as the author of the most influential book of poetic criticism in the Sung dynasty, entitled *Poetry Talks from Ts'ang-lang* (*Ts'ang-lang shih-hua*), in which the poet-critic launched a systematic campaign to reinstate the all-mysterious quality of *shen* or "spirit" in poetry in opposition to what was advocated by the Kiangsi school (cf. Huang T'ing-chien) then popular among poets. Influenced by Ch'an Buddhism and its doctrine of "sudden illumination," Yen Yü maintains that the ideal poetry should be like "echoes in the air, reflection of the moon in water, or an image in the mirror" (translation by James J. Y. Liu; cf. his discussion of Yen Yü's contribution as a critic in *The Art of Chinese Poetry*, Chicago: University of Chicago Press, 1962, pp. 81–83). And he points to the poetry of the High T'ang period, especially that of Tu Fu, as embodiment of the best in poetry. Yen was critical of both the allusive and the discursive styles of poetry as exemplified in the works of Shu Shih and Huang T'ing-chien, which had been widely imitated. Yen's own poetic works, though limited in quantity, occasionally succeeded in expressing the ideal he upheld.

(IRVING Y. LO)

Yüan Hao-wen (1190–1257)

Yüan Hao-wen (*Yü-chih;* YI-SHAN), native of T'ai-yüan, Shansi, was the most eminent poet of the Chin (Jurched) dynasty in North China. He obtained his *chin-shih* degree in 1219 and became a high official in the Chin government. When the dynasty fell in 1234, he refused to serve under the Mongols and devoted his time to historical research and literary pursuits. Aside from traditional verses and lyrics, he also wrote critical studies of Tu Fu and Su Shih and compiled an anthology of the works by 240 Chin poets entitled *Collection of the Central Plains* (*Chung-chou chi*). His works include several titles of poetic criticism done in verse (cf. "On Poetry, Three Quatrains"), in which he revealed his partiality for the tradition established in the North, particularly by the Chien-an poets of the Wei dynasty, reserving his harshest criticism for the Six Dynasties poets and for the Kiangsi school of poetry.

PART V

Kuan Han-ch'ing (c. 1220–c. 1300)

Kuan Han-ch'ing (*Yi-chai-sou*), better known by his courtesy-name (Han-ch'ing) than his personal name of Yi-chai, was a native of Yen-ching (Peking), Hopei. It was the site of the Yüan capital, Ta-tu, where Kuan lived throughout his long life. Only once did he travel south to visit Lin-an (Hangchow), the Southern Sung capital, after its fall to the Mongols in 1276. It is unlikely that Kuan ever served as an imperial physician or in any other official capacity. A member of the theatrical profession, he performed on stage and earned his living by writing plays for the acting companies. He was the creator of the Yüan drama (*tsa-chü*) and certainly its most prolific writer, with some sixty plays to his credit, of which eighteen have survived and been attributed to him.

Kuan Han-ch'ing was not only the "leader of the Pear Garden" (i.e., the actors) and the "master teacher of the compilers of drama," but also a man of the world, "a leader of all the dandies under heaven" (cf. the song sequence "Not Bowing to Old Age"), who preferred the company of the sing-song girls, many of whom were also actresses. It could be that he indulged in these gay dissipations as a protest against the oppressive rule of his time, instances of which can be found in his plays. There is, however, little reference to political or social events in the more than fifty short song-poems (*san-ch'ü*) and thirteen song sequences (*t'ao-shu*) that he wrote.

These are mostly romantic poems on the beauty of nature, the change of seasons, the sorrows of parting, and the sentiments of love. As a poet and playwright, Kuan was expert in the use of the *ch'ü* form, which he successfully wielded as a fitting medium for the conveyance of his feelings and thoughts. His *ch'ü* songs are characterized by the ease and spontaneity of language, particularly his skillful use of vulgar, colloquial expressions; his peculiar brand of wit and humor; and his remarkable dramatic instinct, which enlivens all his works, dramatic as well as non-dramatic.

(WU-CHI LIU)

Lu Chih (1246?–1309?)

Lu Chih (*Ch'u-tao;* SU-CHAI), a native of Cho-chün, Hopei, was well known in his time as a scholar and poet. He passed the *chin-shih* degree in 1268, and though he followed a Confucian course as a high government official, he also expressed in his poems a desire to live in seclusion. The ideal life envisioned by him bears witness to the influence of Taoist escapism. Thus, despite his successful career, there is a note of pessimism in his writings.

In his extant one hundred and twenty song-poems, he made frequent reference to the historical past. Lives of the tragic figures, historical or legendary, or visits made to historical sites, would provide occasions for the poet's comments on the mutability of human affairs. He felt a spiritual kinship with the people and events he wrote about. In general, Lu Chih's poetry is graceful, but lacks intensity.

(SHERWIN S. S. FU)

Ma Chih-yüan (1260?–1334?)

Ma Chih-yüan (*Tung-li*) was born in Ta-tu (Peking), Hopei. Often considered the most outstanding *san-ch'ü* poet of the Yüan period, he was also one of its leading playwrights. Little is known about his life, except that he once served in the provincial government of the Kiangsu and Chekiang district. He seemed to have shown some interest in seeking an official career, and his lack of success was reflected in many of the songs he wrote.

Of the extant one hundred and fifteen songs and six song sequences, the dominant motif is that only an unencumbered life brings happiness. The poet appears to value the integrity of character far above fame and fortune. There is more jocularity than bitterness in his admonition that one had "Better get drunk, and once sober,/ Get drunk again." His well-known line— "Blue hills fill to perfection the gaps in the wall"—reveals that he is able to find peace in the natural world.

Ma Chih-yüan's position in the *ch'ü* genre has often been compared to Su Shih's in the *tz'u* and Li Po's or Tu Fu's in the *shih;* it was mainly through his contribution that the *ch'ü* emerged as a major form of Chinese poetry in the Yüan era. He succeeded in widening the range of its subject matter and in multiplying its levels of expression. He masters many styles, including the colloquial and the humorous, and shows particular skill in the description of nature.

(SHERWIN S. S. FU.)

Chang K'o-chiu (1265?–1345?)

Chang K'o-chiu (*Hsiao-shan*), a native of Ch'ing-yüan, Chekiang, was a minor official who had never risen above the lowest ranks in the Yüan bureaucratic system. It seems that he was a great traveler and a friend of many noted scholar-officials and poets.

A prolific writer of more than eight hundred extant *ch'ü* poems and nine song sequences, Chang K'o-chiu devoted his life to the writing and perfection of the *ch'ü* as a poetic form. His poems show a wide range of topics: love and friendship, knowledge of history combined with personal reflections, Ch'an Buddhism and Taoism, seasons and festivals, and appreciation of nature. Significant among his works is the song sequence on the West Lake in Hangchow, where he lived for a long time.

As a poet, the urbane sophistication of Chang K'o-chiu's technically perfect lines more than makes up for his relative lack of vigor and originality. The strength of his poems lies in their restraint, elegance, and lucidity, characteristics of the best *ch'ü* poets. Often he is able to incorporate famous verses and phrases from early writers. He also makes free use of clichés, puns, and epigrams by giving them new connotations. Thus, by cultivating an artistry that conceals art, his verses are often impregnated with meanings not easily comprehended by a careless reader. Mainly through these devices, he succeeded in elevating the *ch'ü* form to a high artistic level, and he enjoyed a wide reputation during his lifetime and later among Ming and Ch'ing critics.

(SHERWIN S. S. FU)

Chang Yang-hao (1269–1329)

Like Lu Chih, Chang Yang-hao (*Hsi-meng;* YÜN-CHUANG), native of Tsinan, Shantung, occupied important official positions. They both wrote about the vanity of human life and desires, but in Chang Yang-hao's poems the moralist always gets the upper hand of the esthete, and a number of his one hundred and sixty-three song-poems (including two song sequences) are no more than rhymed sermonizing, with special emphasis placed on predestination and retribution. But when the style is natural and lucid, this type of poetry creates its own charm. The tone is colloquial without being vulgar, straightforward without being superficial.

An eminent official, Chang Yang-hao showed in his poems some social concern and humanitarian compassion. In view of his public life, his comments and reflections on history take on a deep meaning. But most of his song-poems were composed during the years of his retirement. They describe the meaninglessness of officialdom and at the same time his happiness in returning to nature.

(SHERWIN S. S. FU)

Teng Yü-pin (fl. late 13th century)

Little is known of Teng Yü-pin, the author of four short *ch'ü* lyrics and four song sequences. He was listed in the *Lu Kuei-pu* (see Chung Ssu-ch'eng) as a subprefect and a poet of musical compositions (*yüeh-chang*).

Tseng Jui (*fl. 1300*)

Tseng Jui (*Jui-ch'ing;* HO-FU), a native of Ta-hsing (near Peking), Hopei, was one of those northern writers who moved south to settle in Hangchow toward the middle of the Yüan dynasty. He did not seek an official career but led the carefree life of a recluse. He did not disdain, however, to mix with the people in the market place and often receive gifts from his wealthy admirers. His extant work consists of one play, some one hundred *ch'ü* songs, as well as seventeen song sequences. He was also noted as a painter and a writer of riddles. His poems reflect his nonchalant and playful attitude toward life, his humor often accentuated by ridicule and satire.

Sui Ching-ch'en (*fl. 1300*)

Sui Ching-ch'en (*Ching-hsien*), the author of three plays (all lost) and a number of *san-ch'ü* poems, lived in the Hangchow region in the early years of the fourteenth century. He was noted for his poetic and musical talents and probably never attained any official position.

The song sequence "Kao-tsu's Homecoming" is an admirably original treatment of a historical event. Its protagonist, Number Three Liu (i.e., Liu Pang), had been a vagabond in his native district before he became the first emperor of Han. With a view to showing off, he made a spectacular public display of his homecoming. The poet availed himself of such an occasion to poke fun at the emperor and, more importantly, to castigate the traditional political system. So, instead of presenting Liu Pang as a hero, the poet stressed the suspicious, antagonistic attitude of the villagers; at the same time he attacked governmental policies. Most effective is his use of humor and irony in the description of the event, presented in detail and in logical order. First, through the eyes of an ignorant yet somewhat reluctant villager, the reader witnesses a theatrical presentation of the emperor, his carriage and retinue. Then the seemingly naïve description gives way to a tirade against the absurdity of politics. The last songs move with a compelling power to the unexpected yet inevitable conclusion, which is also the climax. The dynastic title in the last line, "the great-great-grandfather of Han" (the founder of the Han dynasty), was an honorific given to Liu Pang after his death. To use such a title here is a deliberate anachronism to bring about a surprising ending—an ironical contrast, on which hinges the humor of the poem.

(SHERWIN S. S. FU)

Hsü Tsai-ssu (fl. 1300)

Hsü Tsai-ssu (*Te-k'o;* T'IEN-CHAI), a native of Chia-hsing, Chekiang, was a lyricist who never tried his hand at drama; nor is there any song sequence in the extant collection of his poetry. He wrote nothing but short lyrics, in which he seems to have succeeded surprisingly well. But he is not as perfect an artist as Chang K'o-chiu and occasionally his verses sound too affected, his style too finical.

The two major categories of his lyrics are scenery and love. While his love poems are more or less conventional, he is sometimes capable of a realistic and colloquial style in presenting the lovers' psychology or in defining lovesickness. The immediacy of his lines adds much to Hsü Tsai-ssu's reputation as a love poet.

(SHERWIN S. S. FU)

Chung Ssu-ch'eng (1275?–1350?)

Chung Ssu-ch'eng (*Chi-hsien;* CH'OU-CHAI), the author of seven plays (now lost) and a number of *san-ch'ü* poems, was best known for his book *A Register of Ghosts* (*Lu kuei-pu*), first compiled around 1330 but continually revised until after 1345. The work provides lists of some 150 Yüan *ch'ü* writers, both dramatists and lyric poets. Much of our knowledge of the *san-ch'ü* writers is derived from Chung's book. Unfortunately, this material is rather meager, and equally sketchy is the biographical information on Chung himself.

A native of K'ai-feng, Honan, he lived most of his life in Hangchow, where he made the acquaintance of many writers, including Sui Ching-ch'en, whom he met in Hangchow in 1303 and whose death he mourned in a *ch'ü* poem in the *Register of Ghosts,* as he did many other authors in the same book. Chung Ssu-ch'eng failed repeatedly in the examinations, which had been restored in the later years of the Yüan dynasty. Humorously, he attributed the cause of his failure to his ungainly appearance. Previously, Kuan Yün-shih had called himself "The Sour Studio" (*Suan-chai*), and Hsü Tsai-ssu "The Sweet Studio" (*T'ien-chai*) because of his fondness for sweetmeats; so Chung Ssu-ch'eng now styled himself "The Ugly Studio" (*Ch'ou-chai*), referring to his ugly appearance, to which our selected song sequence bears ample witness.

Marred somewhat by digressions and antithetical verses, the poem has a loose structure and a tautological imagery. Nevertheless, it remains a highly delightful self-portrait in which humor is mixed with indignation not so much at the poet's own unhappy fate as at the snobbishness of society. More sophisticated than most writings of its kind, the poem shows its author as a wise, detached person who is able to look at himself frankly and dispassionately. Whatever amount of sentimentality he may have shown, he more than redeems it by his self-mocking irony. Indeed he never fails to keep an aesthetic distance from reality so as to make his self-analysis objective and interesting to the reader. Behind his analysis one can always perceive a sensitive soul full of comic imagination and originality.

(SHERWIN S. S. FU)

Ch'iao Chi (1280–1345)

Ch'iao Chi (*Meng-fu;* SHENG-HO-WENG), native of T'ai-yüan, Shansi, occupies an important position only next to Chang K'o-chiu in the later development of the *san-ch'ü.* The second most voluminous writer, with two hundred nine lyric songs and eleven song sequences, he is noted for his remark on the structure of an ideal *san-ch'ü*—"the head of a phoenix, the belly of a pig, and the tail of a leopard." Like Chang K'o-chiu, Ch'iao Chi covers a broad range of styles and subjects in his poems. He is sometimes refined and elegant, at other times facile and colloquial, but never vulgar. He writes on love and friendship, seclusion and the fisherman's life, the seasons and beautiful scenery, historical reflections, and humorous episodes. The best-known of his works are those that give an autobiographical account of himself and those that portray feminine beauty and amorous relationship with women. In addition to *san-ch'ü,* Ch'iao Chi is also the author of a number of well-known plays.

(SHERWIN S. S. FU)

Liu Chih (c. 1280–c. 1335)

Liu Chih (*Shih-chung;* PU-CHAI) is recorded as a native of Ning-hsiang in Shih-chou, Shansi, but was actually born in Kiangsi, where his father held an official post at the time. As a young boy he grew up in Ch'ang-sha and Wu-ch'ang. Later he became a disciple of the famous Confucian scholar Yao Sui (1239–1314). After having served in the provincial government of Kiangsi and later of Honan, he was called to the capital to be Grand Master of Imperial Sacrifices in the Bureau of Protocol (*T'ai-ch'ang li-yi-yüan po-shih*). In 1332 he became Imperial Adviser in the Hanlin Academy, but was soon afterward demoted to Chief Supervising Secretary in the Office of Scrutiny (Censorate) of Chiang-che province. He stayed in Hangchow and died there about 1335. He seems to have acquired a strong sense of Confucian justice from his teacher Yao Sui—something readily apparent in the song sequence included in this anthology.

Little of Liu Chih's prose and *shih* poetry has been preserved, but his *san-ch'ü* constitute one of the larger *oeuvres* preserved from the Yüan period —about seventy short songs and four song sequences.

In his *san-ch'ü* Liu Chih strives for a clean, direct style which is impressive in its studied simplicity. He uses allusions only sparingly, and these tend to be straightforward and easily recognizable. The piece translated here, "Respectfully Offered to Circuit Inspector Kao," is a long song sequence in fifteen stanzas, which describes the sufferings brought on by famine in Kiangsi and praises Circuit Inspector Kao for his efforts in bringing relief to the region.

(RICHARD JOHN LYNN)

Kuan Yün-shih (1286–1324)

Kuan Yün-shih (SUAN-CHAI) was a Sinicized Uighur whose original name was Hsiao-yün-shih-hai-ya (Sävinc Qaya). As a teen-ager he excelled in the military arts, horsemanship, and hunting, and when he inherited his father's (Kuan Chih-ko) office of garrison commander of the Liang-huai region, he quickly won the respect of the whole Mongol military establishment. However, he soon afterward underwent a drastic and complete reversal of his view of life, for he yielded his office to his younger brother, gave up the military for good, and became an earnest student of the leading Confucian scholar of the day, Yao Sui (1239–1314). Kuan seems to have studied with Yao until 1308. It was about then that he completed his *Exegesis in the Vernacular on the Classic of Filial Piety* (*Hsiao-ching chih-chieh*) and became tutor to the heir apparent (later Ying-tsung, reigned 1321–23). In 1313 Kuan was appointed to the Hanlin Academy and became an official state historiographer. Two years later he retired from all official duties and went into semi-seclusion at the West Lake in Hangchow, where he spent the remainder of his life. Kuan's official career seems to have been one of frustration and disappointment. At the West Lake he led a Bohemian existence, immersed himself in Ch'an, and indulged in alchemy, wine, poetry, and all the other distractions that the region had to offer. It is said that he even disguised himself and wandered about selling Taoist magic health pills which he had concocted himself.

Kuan's *shih* poetry (preserved in the *Yüan-shih-hsüan*) emulates the Late T'ang style, especially Li Ho's, and reveals an exotic, emotionally extravagant personality, with strong interests in shamanistic culture (allusions to the *Ch'u Tz'u* abound in his writings). Kuan's *san-ch'ü* is one of the larger *oeuvres* preserved from the Yüan period, about eighty *hsiao-ling* (short songs) and eight or nine song sequences—depending on the different attributions. The great majority of the *san-ch'ü* come from his days at the West Lake. They reveal an uncompromising zest for life, a free spirit, and a strong undercurrent of sensuality. His songs have been aptly termed *haofang* ("vigorous and unrestrained") by the traditional critics.

(RICHARD JOHN LYNN)

Yün-k'an Tzu (*date unknown*)

Yün-k'an Tzu is the religious pseudonym of an otherwise anonymous Taoist recluse who lived in the first half of the fourteenth century. His work of twenty-seven short poems, written in the *ch'ü* form, is in many ways similar in content to the *shih* poetry of the famous T'ang Buddhist poet Han Shan.

(JEROME P. SEATON)

PART VI

Kao Ch'i (*1336–1374*)

Kao Ch'i (*Chi-ti;* CH'A-HSÜAN, CH'ING-CH'IU), native of Ch'ang-chou (near Soochow), Kiangsu, is generally regarded as the best poet in the early period of the Ming dynasty. As a young man, he traveled extensively in south-central China, gaining an intimate knowlege of the living conditions of the people at a time when the Mongol empire was tottering and near collapse. Returning to his native city in 1360, he was recognized for his poetic genius, and emerged as the leader of a group of Ten Young Poets. Showing a penchant for the study of military stratagems, he was often seen in the company of Chang Shih-ch'eng, the rebellious leader who ruled Soochow until 1367 when the overwhelming army of Chu Yüan-chang (Ming T'ai-tsu), the new founder of the Ming dynasty, forced his surrender. The chaos of these times produced in Kao a greater disillusionment which sharpened his satirical wit and gave rise to a fascination with allegory.

In 1369, Kao received the honor of being summoned to the Ming capital in Nanking, along with fifteen other scholars, to engage in the compilation of Yüan history, under the auspices of a hastily convened historical bureau. At the completion of the project a year later, he declined court appointments and returned to Soochow. But just a few years afterward, the lengthening shadow of political autocracy caught up with him: accused of sedition because of an innocuous literary composition he wrote for his friend Wei Kuan, then governor of Soochow, on the occasion of the restoration of the prefectural hall, he was publicly executed.

Though writing in an age that fostered literary imitations, Kao showed a mastery of all traditional verse forms unmatched by his contemporaries. His works include many fine *yüeh-fu* poems in which realistic descriptions are combined with interpretation. Themes from nature or from history, all serve his purpose in sketching the precariousness of the human condition.

(IRVING Y. LO)

Lin Hung (c. 1383)

Lin Hung (*Tsu-yü*), a native of Fu-ch'ing, Fukien, was the most prominent member of a group of Ten Talents of Fukien. During the early years of the Hung-wu reign (1368–98), he was summoned to the capital and given examination in poetry by the emperor. After serving as a magistrate of Chiang-lo (modern Yen-p'ing in Fukien) for seven years, he was appointed Assistant Chief (*yüan-wai-lang*) in the Board of Ceremonies. But before the age of forty, he asked for permission to retire to his native place. As a poet, Lin advocated a return to the style of the great T'ang masters. Among his best works are some of the poems written in the five-syllabic meter, in a style that invites comparison with the T'ang poet Wei Ying-wu.

Yü Ch'ien (1394–1457)

Yü Ch'ien (*T'ing-yi*), a native of Ch'ien-t'ang, modern Hangchow, was a high government official who also left many literary works. He obtained his *chin-shih* degree in 1421 and rose rapidly to become Executive Secretary in the Board of War. As a military administrator in the northern provinces, he achieved wide reputation. For his success in defending the capital (Peking) against the invading Mongols, he was awarded the position of *shao-pao* (Junior Guardian of the Heir Apparent). However, he was later maligned by enemies at court and executed. A prolific writer, much of his poetry is derivative in style, but occasionally contains good lines.

Shen Chou (1427–1509)

Shen Chou (*Ch'i-nan;* SHIH-T'IEN, or "Field of Stone"), a native of Ch'ang-chou, Kiangsu, and the most outstanding painter of the Ming, was known to his contemporaries as "a man of three excellences" (*san-chüeh*). Besides painting, the other two fields in which he had achieved supreme mastery were calligraphy and poetry. Recognized as a literary genius in his teens, he nonetheless shunned the taking of imperial examinations and entering into an official career. Instead, he lived at home all his life, caring for his mother (who lived to almost a hundred years), and enjoyed wide fame as an artist and teacher. Many famous Ming painters, like T'ang Yin, were among his pupils. As a painter, he excelled in landscape, usually done on smaller scrolls or albums (he attempted large scrolls only in his later years), showing both men and nature in a state of blissful communion. His poetry is inspired by the works of Po Chü-yi and Su Shih and often reflects humor, spontaneity, and a sense of detachment.

T'ang Yin (1470–1523)

T'ang Yin (*Po-hu, Tzu-wei;* LIU-JU), a native of Soochow, was one of the most eminent calligraphers and painters of the Ming dynasty. Along with Wen Chen-ming (1470–1559), Chu Yun-ming (1460–1526), and the poet Hsü Chen-ch'ing (1479–1511), he was known as one of the Four Talents of Soochow. As a young man, he was given to drinking and led an unconventional life. He passed the *hsiu-ts'ai* ("Budding Talent") examination in 1498, but was quickly implicated in a lawsuit arising out of irregularities of the examination and was jailed. An uninhibited genius, his paintings and calligraphies have been much prized by collectors. Among his group of Soochow poets, he was considered a leading writer of *ch'ü* songs in the southern tune.

Hsü Wei (1521–1593)

Hsü Wei (*Wen-ch'ang;* CH'ING-T'ENG SHAN-JEN), of Shan-yin (Shao-hsing), Chekiang, was primarily known as a painter and calligrapher, but he also enjoyed a wide reputation in his own time as poet, prose writer, and the author of a series of four plays under the general title of *The Four Cries of a Gibbon* (*Ssu-sheng yüan*). He led a rather extraordinary and tragic life: he was imprisoned, once attempted to commit suicide, and spent the last years of his life in sickness and poverty. As a poet, he opposed both the rhetorical and the imitative, advocating the need for self-expression; his poetic style is sometimes reminiscent of that of the T'ang poet Li Ho.

Ch'ien Ch'ien-yi (1582–1664)

Ch'ien Ch'ien-yi (*Shou-chih;* MU-CHAI), of Ch'ang-shu, Kiangsu, was a scholar-official with a checkered career; he was an eminent poet, essayist, compiler, historian, and bibliographer. He obtained his *chin-shih* degree in 1610, followed by appointments to high positions including the vice-presidency of the Board of Ceremonies. In 1625 he was accused of being a member of the Tung-lin party and dismissed from office. He returned to literary pursuits in his native place, where he met and took as a concubine a famous singing girl and poetess. A fellow townsman's accusation of Ch'ien's neglect of official duties resulted in his imprisonment, 1637–38. When the Ming dynasty collapsed, he was among the first scholar-officials to declare his allegiance to the new Manchu regime. Two years later he was appointed to the same position in the Manchu government. Not long afterward, he was accused of plotting against the emperor and again imprisoned. Permitted

to return to Ch'ang-shu, he began an uninterrupted career of scholarship
compiling a large anthology of Ming poetry, Ming history, and a catalogue
of his own library; he then turned to Buddhist studies in his later years. A
hundred years after his death, he became a chief target of the infamous lit
erary inquisition of Ch'ien-lung (reign period, 1736–95). For ten year
(1769–79) the. emperor issued repeated edicts accusing Ch'ien of having
shown disloyalty by serving two masters and having written slanderou
remarks against the Manchus. The destruction and burning of all his book:
throughout the empire, however, failed to check the tide of his rising popu
larity. His poetic works alone are printed in one hundred and sixty *chüan*
yet, despite his extraordinary poetic gifts, he never succeeded in founding a
school of poetry as did Wang Shih-chen (1634–1711) a few decade:
later.

T'an Yüan-ch'un (*1586–1631*)

T'an Yüan-ch'un (*Yu-hsia*), a native of Ching-ling, Hupeh, was one of the
two leaders (the other was Chung Hsing, 1574–1624) toward the end o.
the Ming dynasty who violently opposed the revivalists of the ancient style
that had dominated the literary scene for a hundred years. Known as the
Ching-ling school, T'an and his group took their cue from the Kung-ar
(also in Hupeh) school, notably Yüan Hung-tao (1568–1610) and hi
two brothers, who were demanding similar reforms in prose. (The Yüan.
were great prose writers, although they also wrote some poetry, stressing
social concern and the need for self-expression.) T'an emphasized the im
portance of *hsing-ling*, or "native sensibility" (translation by James J. Y
Liu, *The Art of Chinese Poetry*, p. ·74), and they wrote a kind of in
troverted poetry,·always striving for originality of expression.

Ch'en Tzu-lung (*1608–1647*)

Ch'en Tzu-lung (*Wo-tzu;* TA-TSUN), a native of Hua-t'ing (near Sung
chiang), Kiangsu, was poet, essayist, and patriot. He obtained his *chin-shih*
degree in 1637 and served on district administrative posts in Chekiang jus
before the end of the Ming dynasty. When Peking fell to the Manchus, he
went south to join the forces of Prince Fu, who tried to establish an in
dependent kingdom at Nanking. When his native city fell a year later, Ch'en
fled to the mountains and became a monk. Then he joined another group o
rebels in defiance of the Manchus; and when this rebellion collapsed, he flec
in a boat and then committed suicide by drowning. Recognized as a skillfu
writer of the parallel-style prose, he was also noted for both his *shih* anc
tz'u. He was the compiler of a critical anthology of Ming poetry anc

another large volume of essays and memorials presented to the throne during the Ming dynasty.

Wu Wei-yeh (1609–1671)

Wu Wei-yeh (*Chün-kung;* MEI-TS'UN, "Plum Hamlet"), a native of T'ai-ts'ang, Kiangsu, was one of the leading poets of the early Ch'ing dynasty. He passed the *chin-shih* examination in 1631 and served briefly under the Ming emperor as a Hanlin compiler and tutor in the Imperial Academy. Disputes with other high officials led to his resignation, and he returned to his native place to devote himself to the writing of history. When the Ming dynasty was overthrown, he was said to have seriously considered taking his own life, but yielded to the plea of his family and friend to declare allegiance to the new government. Though he later became a libationer of the Imperial Academy, he expressed in much of his poetry a deep regret for the political action he had grudgingly taken. Later he was implicated in a lawsuit and dismissed from office. A prolific writer, he is noted especially for descriptive (and sometimes satiric) and narrative poems, many of which deal with contemporary events, very much in the manner of the T'ang poet Po Chü-yi.

Chu Yi-tsun (1629–1709)

Chu Yi-tsun (*Hsi-ch'ang;* CHU-CH'A, "Bamboo Knoll"), a native of Hsiu-shui (Chia-hsing), Chekiang, was a scholar, poet, and bibliophile. Though his great-grandfather had been a Grand Secretary in the Ming dynasty, he grew up in straitened circumstances and started his career in the early years of the Manchu regime by serving as secretary to many prominent men of letters. In 1678 when a special examination was decreed, he took and passed the *po-hsüeh hung-tz'u* ("Wide Learning and Grand Rhetoric") examination, followed by appointment as a Hanlin academician and an editor of the official history of the Ming. His writings include bibliographies of the Confucian classics and of philology as well as a critical anthology of Ming poets and another anthology of *tz'u* poets from T'ang to Yüan. As a poet, he exerted great influence and, along with Wang Shih-chen, was known as "Wang of the North and Chu of the South." A prolific *tz'u* writer, his poems are traditional, frequently allegorical, and sometimes obscure—reminiscent of the lyrics of the technician-poets of the Southern Sung period. Among his works, love lyrics make up one separate volume, the "descriptive of things" poetry written in the *tz'u* meter another, and still another titled *Fan-chin chi* (*Collection of Mixed Brocades*) contains only poems made up of lines collected from other poets' works.

Wang Shih-chen (1634–1711)

Wang Shih-chen (*Yi-shang;* YÜ-YANG SHAN-JEN, or "Man of Yü-yang Moun-
tain") was a native of Hsin-ch'eng, Shantung. He had a long and promi-
nent career in the state bureaucracy, where he rose to the highest offices as
President of the Censorate and President of the Board of Punishments. But,
despite his successful career, he made no substantial impact upon the society
and politics of his day and is now remembered almost entirely as a literary
figure—poet, essayist, critic, and anthologist.

As a poet, Wang was especially attracted to the "serene and placid" land-
scape poetry of the Wang Wei tradition, but he also wrote in other styles as
well; he was something of a "pluralist" who believed that there was a certain
kind of poetry most appropriate for each human experience—serene con-
templation, extreme emotion, homesickness, travel, narrative.

In general, in whatever style Wang wrote, he tried to realize in concrete
poetic examples his own particular theory of poetry—the essential features
of which he termed *shen-yün.* Basically, *shen,* which means "spirit" or
"spiritual," refers to both perfect, spontaneous, intuitive (spiritual) control
over the poetic medium and perfect, intuitive, enlightened (spiritual) ap-
prehension of reality. *Yün,* which means personal tone, mood, or atmosphere
—that particular feeling with which the poem is charged—refers to the
inner psychological and spiritual realities which characterize each individual
poet. The poem is then a fusion (or amalgam) of the poet's view of objec-
tive reality (scene) colored or charged with his expression of the mood
he feels at the time of composition.

Generally speaking, Wang was not interested in the direct expression of
strongly felt emotion or highly individualized personality. Poetry for him
was more an exercise in self-cultivation and an attempt to bring his own
personal feelings into harmony with nature. He used landscape poetry as a
vehicle for the indirect expression of his own sensibilities and moods and
regarded poetry as a bridge between the subjective self and the objective re-
ality with which he tried to come to terms.

(RICHARD JOHN LYNN)

Na-lan Hsing-te (1655–1685)

Na-lan Hsing-te (*Jung-jo;* LENG-CHIA SAN-JEN), his name sometimes spelled
Nara Singde, was a Sinicized Manchu noble descended from the Yehe Nara
clan, and the eldest son of Mingju (1635–1708), a powerful court official.
Trained by Chinese tutors, he was noted for his literary brilliance as a boy.
He passed the metropolitan examination at eighteen, but was prevented by
illness from taking the palace examination until 1676, followed by ap-

pointment to the imperial bodyguard. At that time his *tz'u* compositions were widely admired by the leading poets in Peking, and two collections were printed by 1678. He accompanied Emperor K'ang-hsi (reigned 1661–1722) on many tours to Inner Asia, to the Amur region, or to the coastal provinces of the Yangtze area. He was known to have befriended many Chinese men of letters and subsidized their literary activities. A major *tz'u* poet of the Ch'ing period, he excelled in lyrics modeled after those of the earliest period, and shunned the use of artificiality and ornamentation in poetry. He has often been compared to Li Yü, the Last Ruler of Southern T'ang, whom he greatly admired.

Cheng Hsieh (1693–1765)

Cheng Hsieh (*K'e-jou;* PAN-CH'IAO, or "Plank Bridge"), a native of Hsing-hua, Kiangsu, best known today for his paintings and calligraphy, was an artist-turned-official and an original poet. As a young man, he excelled in painting and calligraphy and led a Bohemian life. The death of his father forced him to seek employment, and he eked out a living by selling his paintings. Many years of hardship made him a changed person; devoting himself to study, he passed the *chin-shih* examination in 1736. His later life was known for his benevolent administration as a magistrate in Shantung and for his wide circle of friends which included Buddhist monks and Manchu nobles. He cultivated in his poetry a forceful, simple style, which became known as *tao-ch'ing* ("mere expression of feeling"); sometimes, this type of poetry has been set to music and popularly taught in schools. His poetic works include, in addition to *shih* and *tz'u,* a separate volume of poems written as colophons on paintings, which type of verse is generally known as *t'i-hua shih.*

Chao Yi (1727–1814)

Chao Yi (*Yün-sung;* OU-PEI), a native of Yang-hu, Kiangsu, was a historian and poet. His family was poor, and like his father, he made his living by private tutoring before he won the *chin-shih* degree in 1761. He held administrative posts in the provinces and later became the head of a private school in Kiangsu. His writings include critical notes on the twenty-two dynastic histories, noted on military campaigns in Burma and Taiwan (in both of which he had participated), a chronology of the poet Lu Yu, and remarks on poetry (*Ou-pei shih-hua*). As a critic, he was opposed to the school of *shen-yün* (intuition and tone) as advocated by Wang Shih-chen; rather, he would call attention to the importance of *hsing-ling,* or native sensibility. Less concerned with rhetorical effects, his verses are sometimes humorous and sometimes discursive in the tradition of Sung poetry.

Huang Ching-jen (1749–1783)

Huang Ching-jen (*Chung-tse*), of Wu-chin (Ch'ang-chou), Kiangsu, was a fourteenth-generation descendant of the Sung poet Huang T'ing-chien. His family was poor, and he repeatedly failed the higher examinations after he won the *hsiu-ts'ai* degree in 1765. Though his poetic talents were recognized early by many leading scholars of his day, he remained depressed and impoverished all his life. At his death his friends raised money for his burial; the tragic circumstances of his life spread his poetic fame even further. In 1793 he was among the sixteen contemporary poets included in an anthology compiled by Pi Yüan (1737–97), the famous epigrapher and historian, and before 1799 there had been two editions of his collected works in print. A great admirer of Li Po, he excelled in both *shih* and *tz'u*, and was also known for his painting and calligraphy.

Kung Tzu-chen (1792–1841)

Kung Tzu-chen (*Se-jen;* TING-AN), of Hangchow, was a patriot, poet, and scholar whose interests embraced many diverse fields: political reform, foreign trade, geography, archaeology, Confucian classics, and Buddhism. Born into a family of scholars—his maternal grandfather and tutor was the eminent Ch'ing philologist Tuan Yü-ts'ai (1735–1815)—Kung wrote some of his extant poems at the age of fifteen. Though he did not pass his *chin-shih* examination until 1829, after repeated failures, he had by then already published several political articles urging reform of the Manchu government and restraints in trading with Western nations. He experienced many frustrations in his personal and political life. Because of his poor calligraphy, he was barred from appointment to the Hanlin Academy after passing the *chin-shih* examination; his proffered service to Commissioner Lin Tse-hsü (1785–1850), of Opium War fame, in 1838, was rejected. According to an account of his near contemporaries, he was the lover of the poetess Ku-t'ai-ch'ing, who was the concubine of the Manchu prince Yi-hui (1799–1838). For some inexplicable reason, Kung left Peking hurriedly in 1839, and he died in Hangchow two years later.

Kung was a prolific writer, but only a small body of his prose and poetry is now extant. As a poet, he showed the mastery of many verse forms, including the four-word poetry ("The Lute Song"), a rare form since T'ao Ch'ien, for whom Kung had great admiration. But in his yearning for freedom and in the spontaneity of expression, he was probably more akin to Li Po, while his strong sense of moral outrage and indignation directed at a decadent society, coupled with his preference for an allegorical style, could justify a comparison with Ch'ü Yüan. Similarly, these moral and social views, as well as his patriotic stand and romantic tendencies, influenced such Southern Society (Nan-she) poets in the beginning of the twentieth century as Liu Ya-tzu and Su Man-shu.

Ku-t'ai-ch'ing (1799–?)

Ku-t'ai-ch'ing (*Tzu-ch'un;* YÜN-CH'A WAI-SHI, "Unofficial Historian on a Raft from the Clouds"), also known as Tai-ch'ing ch'un, or Hsi-lin ch'un, was a poet of either Chinese or (Manchu) Bannerman origin. As a concubine to Prince Yi-hui, who was himself a lyric poet and calligrapher, she shared with him a life devoted to poetry and the collection of art objects. Upon the prince's death in 1838, his son by an earlier marriage, who inherited Yi-hui's title as Prince Jung, expelled her from the family mansion. Little else is known of her subsequent life except that she became blind in 1875 and was still living a year later. Her collected works, consisting of both *shih* and *tz'u,* existed in manuscript and were partially printed in two volumes in 1910 and 1914. Additional poems appeared in the August 1933 issue of the *Quarterly Journal on the Study of Tz'u* (*Tzu-hsüeh chi-k'an*).

Chiang Ch'un lin (1818–1868)

Chiang Ch'un-lin (*Lu-t'an*), a native of Chiang-yin, Kiangsu, enjoyed early fame as a writer of *shih* and later became a leading lyric poet. During the 1850s he served as a salt administrator in the Huai River district. After leaving office, he led an unconventional life; he turned to the printing of books on lyric poetry to eke out a living, was involved in a lovers' quarrel with a young woman whom he had married, and died by taking poison.

Huang Tsun-hsien (1848–1905)

Huang Tsun-hsien (*Kung-tu*), of Chia-ying-chou (Mei-hsien), Kwangtung, was a diplomat, political reformer, and poet who sought to establish a new school of poetry within the tradition of classical verse. After passing the provincial examinations in 1876, he was appointed Counselor to the Chinese Legation in Tokyo. During the two years he spent in Japan, 1877–79, he wrote a series of descriptive verse entitled *Miscellaneous Poems About Japan* (published by the Tsung-li Yamen, i.e., the Foreign Office, 1879), which enjoyed a wide circulation; he also began his larger work, a history of Japan, which he completed in 1887 and which was printed in 1890. He served as Consul General in San Francisco, 1882–85, Counselor to the Chinese Legation in London in 1890, and Consul General in Singapore, 1891–94. He was named Minister to Germany in 1896, but the appointment was canceled because of Germany's alleged opposition. During the next few years, as salt administrator in Hunan, he sponsored reform movement among the gentry in the provinces and founded the School for Contemporary Affairs (Shih-wu hsüeh-t'ang), which became a center of political reform. He was named Minister to Japan in 1898, but was prevented by illness from taking his post. In the same year, he was granted an audience with Emperor Te-tsung (Kuang-hsü, reigned 1875–1908), the last hope of the reformists. Upon the failure of the reform movement, he returned to his native place and devoted himself to teaching and writing and to the study of Buddhism.

As a political theorist, Huang exerted great influence on such reform leaders as T'an Ssu-t'ung (1865–98), K'ang Yu-wei (1858–1927), and Liang Ch'i-ch'ao (1873–1929), although his ideal of a constitutional monarchy proved too quixotic for his time. An eclectic and original thinker, he expressed the same concern for the fate of classical poetry and advocated the need to discard all distinctions with respect to modes and other formalistic considerations. He titled his collected verses *Jen-ching lu shih-ts'ao* (*Draft Poems Written in the Hut of the Human World*), with the implied notion that poetry is simply the "world" (*ching*) experienced by men (*jen*). (*Ching* is a word derived from Buddhist terminology which was later discussed by Wang Kuo-wei in terms of "emotion" and "scene"; cf. James J. Y. Liu, *The Art of Chinese Poetry,* p. 84, pp. 96–98.) He found no useful purpose in classifying his poems as *chüeh-chü* or *lü-shih;* instead, he used the term *ku-chin-t'i shih* (poems in old-and-new style) to designate what he wrote. He evolved his style from all sources, including the Confucian classics, historical writings, the philosophers, as well as the colloquial speech. His keen interest in folk poetry led to his collection of scores of folk songs from his native district, Kwangtung. He wrote a great number of poems on contemporary events, including the presidential election in the United States; and, like Po Chü-yi, more than a millennium earlier, sought the revitalization of classical verse by creating a new language.

(IRVING Y. LO)

Wang Kuo-wei (1877–1927)

Wang Kuo-wei (*Ching-an;* KUAN-T'ANG [after the name of his studio, Yung-kuan T'ang]), a native of Hai-ning, Chekiang, was a poet, critic, and philosopher, whose contributions to literature included his pioneer studies of Chinese drama and the Oracle Bone scripts. Disdaining the imperial examination system, he enrolled in a modern private school in Shanghai in 1895, and began his study of Japanese and Western languages. In 1902 he went to Japan to continue his education, but was forced to return after only a few months because of poor health. He taught schools in Shanghai and Soochow for a few years. In 1906 he published his first collection of lyrics, which won immediate praise of his peers as the most outstanding lyric poetry to appear since Sung times. Four years later, he published his famous *Jen-chien tz'u-hua* (*Poetry Talks of the Human World*), in which he defined the essence of poetry as the fusion of internal emotion and external scene, for which he used the term *ching-chieh,* or the "world." This was also the first work of Chinese literary criticism in which Western sources were cited.

Since his student days, Wang was fascinated with the philosophies of Kant, Schopenhauer, and Nietzsche, and he translated some of their writings into Chinese. He also applied his knowledge of Western philosophy to his criticism of the *Hung-lou meng* (*The Dream of the Red Chamber*), producing the first important modern critical study of the Chinese novel.

When the Revolution of 1911 broke out, Wang moved his family to Japan, where he stayed until 1915. Upon his return, he continued a productive career of research and teaching, and served on the faculty of National Peking University and, later, of the Institute of Chinese Studies at Tsing Hua University (in Peking). In the summer of 1927, he took his own life by drowning himself in the K'un-ming Lake of the Summer Palace in the western suburb of Peking.

The collection of Wang's lyric poetry, *T'iao-hua tz'u,* consists of one hundred and fifteen poems, the majority of them written between 1905 and 1909, when he was disappointed with philosophy and began to seek consolation in literature. Nevertheless, philosophical ideas, particularly German voluntarism, seem to dominate his verse, though expressed by means of conventional themes. A pessimistic outlook on life and a desire for emancipation are its recurring motifs. In his avoidance of artificiality and of the use of remote allusions, and in his ability to express complex human emotions in a fresh manner, his lyrics reveal a close affinity with the works of the early *tz'u* masters, of the Five Dynasties and the Sung eras.

(CHING-I TU)

Lu Hsün (*1881–1936*)

Lu Hsün, the pen name of Chou Shu-jen, was born in Shao-hsing, Chekiang, of once prosperous gentry parents. He received a classical education before entering a modern technical school. After a period of study in Japan, he returned to China to enter governmental service. His early efforts as a writer went virtually unnoticed until the appearance of a short story "A Madman's Diary" in 1918, which, with the publication of later stories in a similar satirical vein, established him as one of the foremost literary figures of his time.

The major portion of his imaginative writings, namely, the two dozen short stories collected in *Na-han* (*Call to Arms*) and *P'ang-huang* (*Hesitation*) and a similar number of poetic essays included in *Yeh-ts'ao* (*Wild*

Grass), were all written before he left Peking in 1926. Thereafter, he devoted his energies largely to the short topical essay, which, vested with the same sardonic wit and mordant humor characteristic of his fiction, he used to lay bare the foibles of his age.

In addition to the short stories, the impressionistic prose-poems, the polemical essays, and various scholarly works and translations from Western literature and critical theory upon which his reputation as a writer is based, Lu Hsün turned occasionally late in life to classical verse forms as a medium of private expression. Among the sixty-odd verses which have been preserved, over forty were written between 1931 and 1935, and a large proportion of these were addressed to friends and acquaintances, many of whom were Japanese. Written for the most part in the septisyllabic regulated verse pattern, these poems are nevertheless contemporary in meaning, richly allusive, characteristically warmly humorous and bitingly satirical in manner, and, above all, profoundly moving in spirit and humane in temperament. The late critic T. A. Hsia aptly likened Lu Hsün's classical verse to "the strange beauty of 'frozen flowers.' "

(WILLIAM R. SCHULTZ)

Su Man-shu (1884–1918)

Su Man-shu (original name, *Hsüan-ying;* TZU-KU), a native of Hsiang-shan, Kwangtung, was born in Yokohama, Japan, of a Cantonese merchant and a Japanese woman. He had an unusual and romantic life. After returning to China to spend his childhood in his native Hsiang-shan, he went back to Yokohama, where he was educated in a Chinese community school. Later, he went to Tokyo and became a fledgling revolutionary in the Chinese student movement opposed to the Manchu government. Following his comrades, he returned to China and engaged in journalistic activities. After staying with friends in Shanghai and Hong Kong, he left unexpectedly, shaved his head, and became a Buddhist monk, retiring briefly to a small temple in southern Kwangtung, and adopting the Buddhist name Man-shu (Manju). In the latter part of his short life, although he did not take his vow seriously and often feasted and drank in the company of singing girls, he remained celibate and never knew the warmth of a connubial life.

Su Man-shu was an elusive and immature genius who charmed his contemporaries with poetry and fiction in the intervening period between the end of the Manchu dynasty and the first years of the Chinese Republic. He was associated with the leading literary men of his time, including writers of the Southern Society, of which he was a member. He traveled widely, once teaching school for two years in Surabaya, Java, and often plied the China Sea between Shanghai and Tokyo, where he visited his Japanese mother. By that time, his revolutionary ardor gradually gave place to Buddhist resignation and romantic melancholy as he brooded over his uncertain, rootless existence. He was beset by poverty and illness until his death. The deep sorrows he felt and expressed so poignantly in his short lyrics are never morbidly self-indulgent. The exotic experiences in his life, combined with his poetic sensibilities and his understanding of Buddhism and of Western literatures, endow his verses with fresh power and beauty.

(WU-CHI LIU)

Liu Ya-tzu (1887–1958)

Liu Ya-tzu (*An-ju;* YA-LU), a native of Wu-chiang (near Soochow), Kiangsu, was influenced in his youth by the revolutionary movement led by Sun Yat-sen in the early twentieth century. A veteran member of the Nationalist Party (Kuomintang) founded by Sun, he was active in provincial party affairs in 1924–27, but his leftist, pro-Communist stand prevented him from taking positions in the newly organized Nationalist government (1928–49). For five years (1932–37) he was Director of the Shanghai Gazetteer Bureau. During the Japanese occupation of the city, he retired from public life to engage in research on the historical materials of the Southern Ming (a historical term referring to the period in the mid-seventeenth century during which the princes of the Ming imperial house rallied their supporters in southern China to resist the invading Manchus). He joined the Communist government when it was founded in Peking in 1949, but he soon became inactive because of old age and ill-health.

Intellectuality and emotion characterize Liu Ya-tzu's new type of revolutionary verse, cast in traditional meters, just before the decline of classical poetry in the first decades of the twentieth century. As a young radical, he used poetry as a vehicle to express his ardent beliefs in revolutionary causes. Early in his career, he advocated the overthrow of the Manchu government and later, in the republican period, resistance to the war-lord regime. These were also the aims of the Southern Society, a large literary organization with a membership of several hundred, which Liu founded with his friends in 1909 and which he led for more than ten years. Many members of the society were revolutionaries who became prominent in the Nationalist government. Liu also made friends with many Communist leaders just as he had earlier with the Nationalists. He was responsible for launching Mao Tse-tung as a poet by publishing Mao's first poem in 1945 in Chungking.

Loyal to the memory of his poetic friends, Liu published the posthumous literary works of several of them, including Su Man-shu. He led the movement for a return to T'ang poetry but was also an admirer of the Sung patriotic poet Hsin Ch'i-chi, and adopted Hsin's name, Ch'i-chi, as his own personal name, which he later gave up in favor of Ya-tzu. Like Su Man-shu, he was greatly influenced by Kung Tzu-chen. Liu's poems, spanning a half century and totaling several thousand, express a poet's lofty imagination and visionary dreams, as he chronicled the fast-moving events of his time. He was at his best in this kind of historical and heroic poetry, which he endowed with his personal emotions, but he also wrote numerous occasional poems, especially those to his friends, and excursion poems, several of which are also included in this volume.

(WU-CHI LIU)

Mao Tse-tung (1893–1976)

Mao Tse-tung (*Jun-chih*) was born into a well-to-do peasant family at Shaoshan in Hsiang-t'an, Hunan. Alternating between work at his father's farm and attending schools, he finally left home for Peking and Shanghai in his mid-twenties, where he was exposed to Western ideas introduced into China following the May Fourth (1919) movement. He was soon drawn into the maelstrom of student movements and political agitations of the Chinese Communist Party, of which he was a founding member. He participated in the peasant uprisings (1927) in his native Hunan and spent the next few years with other Communist guerrilla groups in their strongholds in Kiangsi and other border areas. When pressed by the Nationalist armies, the Communists started the Long March (1934) that was to end next year in Yenan, Shensi, where Mao rose to power as the unchallenged leader of his party. After a short truce with the Nationalists during the Sino-Japanese War (1937–45), Mao led the Communists to victory, and in 1949 he became the Chairman of the Central People's Government in the People's Republic. For the next twenty-five years, he consolidated his power by eliminating his rivals and enemies, and wielded supreme authority over a nation of some eight hundred million people.

As a revolutionist, Mao is both a man of action and a theorist, whose written words and sayings have a tremendous impact both at home and abroad. In addition to his political writings and polemics, he is also the author of some forty poems (most of the *tz'u* form) in the classical meter. These have been eulogized by his followers and widely translated into foreign languages. The poems receive attention because of the unusual status of their author but they also have certain pronounced features. First, true to the saying that poetry expresses a man's sentiments and beliefs, Mao's writings reflect the aspirations and ambitions of a political leader during the different periods of his career. Secondly, there is originality in his verses characterized by a boldness in technical innovations or violations, as well as in his approach and outlook toward life. Lastly, it must be admitted that while he is not a poet of flawless skill, his peculiar genius illuminates most of his best lines with imagination and sensitivity.

Mao Tse-tung shared with his friend in poetry, Liu Ya-tzu, their common love of classical verse and the awareness that this accomplishment demanded long apprenticeship, incommensurate with the needs of modern

China. Accordingly, he warned the young readers not to emulate him in the writing of poems in the classical style. Perhaps, this three-thousand-year-old tradition of Chinese poetry that started with the Mao (Mao Heng and Mao Ch'ang of the early Han dynasty) version of the *Shih Ching* will aptly conclude with the works of another Mao, the Marxian revolutionist poet.

Appendix I:
Tune-titles and Translations

Lyric Meters (*tz'u*)

An-hsiang	"Dim Fragrance"
Ch'a-t'ou-feng	"Phoenix Hairpin"
Ch'ang hsiang-ssu	"Eternal Longing"
Che-ku t'ien	"Partridge Sky"
Chiang-ch'eng tzu	"Song of River City"
Chiang-shen tzu	"Song of River Goddess"
Chien-tzu mu-lan-hua	"Magnolia Blossoms, Abbreviated"
Ch'in-yüan ch'un	"Spring in [Princess] Ch'in's Garden"
Ch'ing-p'ing yüeh	"Pure Serene Music"
Ch'ing-yü-an	"Green Jade Cup"
Chiu-ch'üan tzu	"Song of Wine Spring"
Ch'iu-shui	"Autumn Waters"
Chü-hua hsin	"Chrysanthemums Fresh"
Chu Ying-t'ai chin	"Slow Song of Chu Ying-t'ai"
Ch'üeh-ch'iao hsien	"Immortal at the Magpie Bridge"
Ch'üeh t'a chih	"Magpie on the Branch"
Feng-liu tzu	"Song of a Dandy"
Huo-shih chin	"Happy Events Approaching"
Hsiang-chien huan	"Joy at Meeting"
Hsiao-ch'ung-shan	"Manifold Little Hills"
Ho ch'uan	"River Messages"
Ho hsin-lang	"Congratulating the Bridegroom"
Ho-yeh pei	"Lotus-leaf Cup"
Hua fei hua	"Flower Unlike Flower"
Huan ch'i sha	"Sand of Silk-washing Stream"
Hung ch'uang chiung	"Distant Red Window"
Ju meng ling	"As in a Dream: A Song"
Jui-ho hsien	"An Immortal's Auspicious Crane"
Keng-lou tzu	"Song of Water Clock at Night"
Kuei-t'ien-lo yin	"Pleasure of Returning to the Fields: A Prelude"
Lan-ling Wang	"Prince of Lan-ling"

Lang t'ao sha	"Ripples Sifting Sand"
Lin-chiang hsien	"Immortal at the River"
Liu-ch'ou	"Six Toughies"
Man-chiang hung	"Full River Red"
Man-t'ing fang	"Courtyard Full of Fragrance"
Meng Chiang-nan	"Dreaming of the South"
Mi-shen yin	"Prelude to Allure Goddesses"
Mo yü-erh	"Groping for Fish"
Mu-lan-hua man	"Magnolia Blossoms, Slow"
Nan-hsiang tzu	"Song of the Southern Country"
Nan-ko tzu	"A Southern Song"
Nien-nu chiao	"The Charm of Nien-nu"
Pa-p'ai man	"Eight-beat Barbarian Tune"
Pa-sheng Kan-chou	"Eight Beats of a Kan-chou Song"
P'o-chen tzu	"Dance of the Cavalry"
Pu-suan tzu	"Song of Divination"
P'u-sa man	"Deva-like Barbarian"
Shao-nien yu	"Wanderings of a Youth"
Shen-cha-tzu	"Mountain Hawthorns"
Shui-lung yin	"Water Dragon's Chant"
Shui-tiao ko-t'ou	"Prelude to Water Music"
Su chung-ch'ing	"Telling of Innermost Feelings"
Su-ying	"Sparse Shadows"
T'a so hsing	"Treading on Grass"
Tan-huang liu	"Pale-golden Willows"
T'iao-hsiao ling	"Song of Flirtatious Laughter"
Tieh lien hua	"Butterflies Lingering over Flowers"
Ting Hsi-fan	"Pacifying the Western Barbarians"
Tou-yeh huang	"Bean Leaves Yellow"
Ts'ai-sang tzu	"Song of Picking Mulberry"
Tsui hua-yin	"Tipsy in the Flower's Shade"
Tsui lo-p'o	"Tipsy and Dissolute"
Tuan-cheng hao	"Decorous and Pretty"
Tung-hsien ko	"Song of Grotto Fairy"
Tzu-yeh ko	"Song of Tzu-yeh"
Wang Chiang-nan	"Gazing at the South"
Wang hai-ch'ao	"Watching Tidal Bores"
Wu-ling ch'un	"Spring at Wu-ling"
Wu-shan yi-tuan yün	"A Stretch of Cloud over Mount Wu"
Wu yeh t'i	"Crows Crying at Night"

Yang-liu chih	"Willow Branches"
Yeh Chin-men	"Paying Homage at the Golden Gate"
Yeh-pan yüeh	"Midnight Music"
Yi Ch'in-o	"Remembering the Lady of Ch'in"
Yi-hu-chu	"A Casket of Pearls"
Yi-lo-suo	"A Big String of Words"
Yi wang-sun	"Remembering the Prince"
Ying t'ien-ch'ang	"Echoing Heaven's Everlastingness"
Yü hu-tieh	"Jade Butterflies"
Yü-lou ch'un	"Spring in Jade Pavilion"
Yü Mei-jen	"The Beautiful Lady Yü"
Yung-yü lo	"Joy of Eternal Union"

Song-poems (*ch'ü*)

Ch'an-kung ch'ü	"Song of the Lunar Palace"
Che-kuei ling	"Song of Plucking Cassia"
Ch'en-tsui tung-feng	"Intoxication in the East Wind"
Ch'ing-chiang yin	"Clear River, A Prelude"
Ch'ing tung-yüan	"Celebration in the Eastern Plain"
Fen-tieh-erh	"Butterflies"
Hao-shih chin	"Happy Events Approaching"
Hsi ch'un lai	"Joy in Spring's Coming"
Hu shih-pa	"Tartar Tune of Eighteen Beats"
Hung hsiu-hsieh	"Red Embroidered Slippers"
Jen yüeh yüan	"Full Moon in the Human World"
Liao-ch'iao tung-feng	"Chilly East Wind"
Lu-yao pien	"Overtures"
Man-t'ing fang	"Courtyard Full of Fragrance"
Nan-pei ho-t'ao	"Medley of Southern and Northern Tunes"
Pi-yü hsiao	"Green Jade Flute"
Po pu tuan	"Pluck, Not Break"
P'u-teng o	"Moth Fluttering Against Lamp"
P'u-t'ien lo	"Joy All Under Heaven"
Shan-p'o yang	"Sheep on Mountain Slope"
Shang hsiao-lou	"Going up Small Pavilion"

Shao-pien	"Slow Chant"
Shih-liu hua	"Pomegranate Blossoms"
Shou-yang ch'ü	"Song of Shou-yang [Palace]"
Shui-hsien tzu	"Song of Water Nymph"
Ssu-k'uai yü	"Four Pieces of Jade"
Ta-te ko	"Song of Great Virtue"
Tien-ch'ien huan	"Pleasure in Front of the Hall"
T'ien-ching sha	"Sky-clear Sand"
Tou an-ch'un	"Squabbling Quails"
Tsui kao-ko kuo Hsi ch'un lai	"Rapt with Wine, Loudly Singing— Joy in Spring's Coming"
Tuan-cheng hao	"Decorous and Pretty"
Wei-sheng	"Coda"
Wu-yeh-erh	"*Wu-t'ung* Leaves"
Yeh hsing ch'uan	"Sailing at Night"
Yen-erh lo chien Te-sheng ling	"Wild Geese Have Come Down; Song of Victory"
Yen-erh lo kuo Te-sheng ling	"Wild Geese Have Come Down— Song of Victory"
Yi-chih hua	"A Sprig of Flowers"
Ying hsien-k'e	"Greeting the Immortal Guest"

Appendix II:
Chinese Dynasties and Historical Periods, A Chronological Table

Hsia	21st–18th centuries B.C.
Shang (Yin)	1765–1122 B.C.
Western Chou	1122 or 1027–771 B.C.
Eastern Chou	770–403 B.C.
Spring and Autumn Period	722–481 B.C.
Warring States Period	403–221 B.C.
Ch'in	221–207 B.C.
Han	206 B.C.–A.D. 220
Former Han	206 B.C.–A.D. 24
Later Han	A.D. 25–220
Three Kingdoms Period	220–280
Wei	220–265
Shu-Han	221–263
Wu	222–280
Tsin (Chin)	265–420
Western Tsin	265–316
Eastern Tsin	317–420
Northern and Southern Dynasties	420–589
Sung (Liu-Sung)	420–479
Ch'i (Southern Ch'i)	479–502
Liang	502–557
Ch'en	557–589
Northern Wei	386–534
Eastern Wei	534–550
Northern Ch'i	550–577
Northern Chou	557–581
Sui	581–618
T'ang	618–907
Five Dynasties Period	907–960
Southern T'ang	937–975

Sung	960–1279
Northern Sung	960–1127
Southern Sung	1127–1279
Liao (Khitan)	916–1125
Hsi-Hsia (Tangut)	1038–1227
Chin (Jurched)	1115–1234
Yüan (Mongol)	1234–1368
Ming	1368–1644
Ch'ing (Manchu)	1644–1911
Republic	1912–
People's Republic	1949–

Index of Authors

Supplemental Bibliography
More Translations of Chinese Poetry
and Books on Poetics and Lives of Chinese Poets

Birrell, Anne (tr.). *New Songs from a Jade Terrace: An Anthology of Early Chinese Poetry*. London: Allen & Unwin, 1982.

———. *Popular Songs and Ballads of Han China*. London: Unwin Hyman, 1988.

Bryant, Daniel (tr.). *Lyric Poets of the Southern T'ang: Li Yu and Feng Yen-ssu*. Vancouver: University of British Columbia Press, 1982.

Chan, Marie. *Kao Shih*. Boston: Twayne, 1978.

———. *Cen Shen [Ts'en Shen]*. Boston: Twayne, 1983.

Chang, Kang-i Sun. *The Evolution of Chinese Tz'u Poetry: From Late T'ang to Northern Sung*. Princeton: Princeton University Press, 1980.

———. *Six Dynasties Poetry*. Princeton: Princeton University Press, 1986.

Chaves, Jonathan (tr.). *Heaven My Blanket, Earth My Pillow: Poems by Yang Wan-li*. New York: Weatherhill, 1975.

———. *Mei Yao-ch'en and the Development of Early Sung Poetry*. New York: Columbia University Press, 1976.

———. *Pilgrim of the Clouds: Poems and Essays by Yuan Hung-tao and His Brothers*. New York: Weatherhill, 1978.

——— (tr. and ed.) *The Columbia Book of Later Chinese Poetry: Yuan, Ming, and Ch'ing Dynasties (1279–1911)*. New York: Columbia University Press, 1986.

Ch'en, David Y. *Lu Hsun: Complete Poems*. Tempe, Arizona: Center for Asian Studies, Arizona State University, 1988.

Crump, J. I. (tr.). *Songs from Xanadu: Studies in Mongol-Dynasty Song Poetry (San-ch'u)*. Ann Arbor, Michigan: Center for Chinese Studies, 1983.

Cutter, Robert Joe. *The Brush and the Spur: Chinese Culture and the Cockfight*. Hong Kong: Chinese University Press, 1990.

Davis, A. R. *T'ao Yuan-ming: His Works and Their Meaning*. 2 Vols. Cambridge: Cambridge University Press, 1984.

Debon, Gunther. *Chinesische Dichtung, Geschichte, Struktur, Theorie*. Leiden: E. J. Brill, 1989.

Duke, Michael S. *Lu You*. Boston: Twayne, 1977.

Egan, Ronald C. *The Literary Works of Ou-yang Hsiu (1007-72)*. Cambridge: Cambridge University Press, 1984.

Eide, Elling O. (tr.). *Poems by Li Po*. 2 Vols. Lexington, Kentucky: Anvil Press, 1984.

Fong, Grace S. *Wu Wenying and the Art of Southern Song [Sung] Ci [Tz'u] Poetry*. Princeton: Princeton University Press, 1987.

Frankel, Hans H. *The Flowering Plum and the Palace Lady: Interpretations of Chinese Poetry*. New Haven: Yale University Press, 1976.

Frodsham, J. D. (tr.). *Goddesses, Ghosts, and Demons: The Collected Poems of Li He (790–816)*. London: Anvil Press Poetry Ltd., 1983.

Fusek, Lois (tr.). *Among the Flowers: The Hua-chien Chi*. New York: Columbia University Press, 1982.

Hargett, James M. *On the Road in Twelfth Century China: The Travel Diaries of Fan Chengda*. Stuttgart: Franz Steiner Verlag, 1989.

Hartman, Charles. *Han Yu and the T'ang Search for Unity*. Princeton: Princeton University Press, 1986.

Hendricks, Robert. *The Poetry of Han Shan (Cold Mountain): A Complete Annotated Edition*. Albany: State University of New York Press, 1990.

Holzman, Donald (tr.). *Poetry and Politics: The Life and Works of Juan Chi, A.D. 210–263*. Cambridge: Cambridge University Press, 1976.

Johnson, Dale R. *Yuarn [Yuan] Music Dramas: Studies in Prosody and Structure and a Complete Catalogue of Northern Arias in the Dramatic Style*. Ann Arbor, Michigan: Center for Chinese Studies, University of Michigan, 1980.

Knechtges, David R. *The Han Prosody: A Study of the Fu of Yang Hsiung, 50 B.C.–A.D. 18*. Cambridge: Cambridge University Press, 1976.

———. *Wen Xuan or Selections of Refined Literature*. Vols. 1 and 2. Princeton: Princeton University Press, 1982 and 1987.

Kroll, Paul W. *Meng Hao-jan*. Boston: Twayne, 1981.

Larsen, Jeanne (tr.). *Brocade River Poems: Selected Works of the Tang Dynasty Courtesan Xue Tao [Hsueh T'ao]*. Princeton: Princeton University Press, 1987.

Lee, Joseph J. *Wang Ch'ang-ling*. Boston: Twayne, 1982.

Levy, Dore Jesse. *Chinese Narrative Poetry: The Late Han through T'ang Dynasties*. Durham, North Carolina: Duke University Press, 1988.

Levy, Howard Seymour (tr.). *Translations from Po Chu-i's Collected Works*. Vols. 3 (Regulated and Patterned Poems, 822–832) and 4 (The Later Years, 833–846). San Francisco: Chinese Materials Center, 1976–78.

Lin, Shuen-fu. *The Transformation of the Chinese Lyrical Tradition: Chiang K'uei and Southern Sung Tz'u*. Princeton: Princeton University Press, 1978.

Lin, Shuen-fu and Stephen Owen (eds.). *The Vitality of the Lyric Voice: Shih Poetry from Late Han to the T'ang*. Princeton: Princeton University Press, 1987.

Liu, James J. Y. *Major Lyricists of the Northern Sung*. Princeton: Princeton University Press, 1974.

――――. *The Interlingual Critic: Interpreting Chinese Poetry*. Bloomington, Indiana: Indiana University Press, 1982.

――――. *Language, Paradox, Poetics: A Chinese Perspective*, Richard John Lynn (ed.). Princeton: Princeton University Press, 1988.

Lo, Irving Yucheng and William Schultz (eds.). *Waiting for the Unicorn: Poems and Lyrics of China's Last Dynasty, 1644–1911*. Bloomington, Indiana: Indiana University Press, 1986.

――――. *Tai Lin Chi: Chinese Character Text of Waiting for the Unicorn*. Bloomington, Indiana: Indiana University Press, 1986.

Lynn, Richard John. *Kuan Yun-shih*. Boston: Twayne, 1980.

Mair, Victor H. (comp. and tr.). *Four Introspective Poets: A Concordance to Selected Poems by Roan Jyi [Juan Chi], Chern Tzyy-arng [Ch'en Tzu-ang], Jang Jeouling [Chang Chiu-ling], and Lii Bor [Li Po]*. Tempe, Arizona: Center for Asian Studies, Arizona State University, 1987.

――――. *Mei Cherng's [Mei Sheng's] "Seven Stimuli" and Wang Bor's [Wang Po's] "Pavilion of King Terng [Teng]"*. Lewiston, New York: Edwin Mellen Press, 1987.

Marney, John. *Liang Chien-wen Ti*. Boston: Twayne, 1976.

――――. *Chiang Yen*. Boston: Twayne, 1981.

Mather, Richard B. *The Poet Shen Yueh (441–513), the Reticent Marquis*. Princeton: Princeton University Press, 1988.

Miao, Ronald. *Early Medieval Chinese Poetry: The Life and Verse of Wang Ts'an (A.D. 177–217)*. Wiesbaden: Franz Steiner Verlag, 1982.

Nienhauser, Wiliam H., Jr. *P'i Jih-hsiu*. Boston: Twayne, 1979.

―――― (ed. and comp.). *The Indiana Companion to Traditional Chinese Literature*. Bloomington, Indiana: Indiana University Press, 1986.

Owen, Stephen. *The Poetry of Meng Chiao and Han Yu*. New Haven: Yale University Press, 1975.

――――. *The Poetry of the Early T'ang*. New Haven: Yale University Press, 1977.

――――. *The Great Age of Chinese Poetry*. New Haven: Yale University Press, 1981.

――――. *Traditional Chinese Poetry and Poetics: Omen of the World*. Madison, Wisconsin: University of Wisconsin Press, 1985.

――――. *Remembrances: The Experience of the Past in Classical Chinese Literature*. Cambridge: Harvard University Press, 1986.

――――. *Mi-lou: Poetry and the Labyrinth of Desire*. Cambridge: Harvard University Press, 1989.

Palandri, Angela C. Y. Jung. *Yuan Chen*. Boston: Twayne, 1977.

Red Pine. *The Collected Songs of Cold Mountain*. Port Townsend, Washington: Copper Canyon Press, 1983.

Rickett, Adele Austin R. (ed.). *Chinese Approaches to Literature from Confucius to Liang Ch'i-ch'ao*. Princeton: Princeton University Press, 1978.

Schafer, Edward H. *Mirages on the Sea of Time: The Taoist Poetry of Ts'ao T'ang*. Berkeley: University of California Press, 1985.

Schmidt, J. D. *Yang Wan-li*. Boston: G. K. Hall, 1976.

Seaton, Jerome P. and Donald A. Riggs (tr.). *Chinese Poetic Writing* by François Cheng (with an anthology of T'ang poetry). Bloomington, Indiana: Indiana University Press, 1982.

Seaton, J. P. and James Cryer (tr.). *Bright Moon, Perching Bird: Poems [by Li Po and Tu Fu]*. Middletown, Connecticut: Wesleyan University Press, 1987.

Soong, Stephen C. (ed.). *Song without Music: Chinese Tz'u Poetry*. Hong Kong: Chinese University Press, 1980.

Tu, Kuo-ch'ing. *Li Ho*. Boston: Twayne, 1979.

Wagner, Marsha L. *Wang Wei*. Boston: Twayne, 1981.

————. *The Lotus Boat: The Origins of Chinese Tz'u Poetry in T'ang Popular Culture*. New York: Columbia University Press, 1984.

Watson, Burton (tr. and ed.). *The Columbia Book of Chinese Poetry: From Early Times to the Thirteenth Century*. New York: Columbia University Press, 1984.

Wixted, John Timothy. *The Song-Poetry of Wei Chuang (836–910)*. Tempe, Arizona: Center for Asian Studies, Arizona State University, 1979.

————. *Poems on Poetry: Literary Criticism by Yuan Hao-wen (1190–1257)*. Wiesbaden: Franz Steiner Verlag, 1982.

———— (tr.). *Five Hundred Years of Chinese Poetry, 1150–1650: The Chin, Yuan and Ming Dynasties* by Yoshikawa Kojiro. Princeton: Princeton University Press, 1989.

Wong, Shirleen S. *Kung Tzu-chen*. Boston: Twayne, 1975.

Yates, Robin D. S. *Washing Silk: The Life and Selected Poetry of Wei Chuang (834?–910)*. Cambridge: Harvard University Press, 1988.

Yip, Wai-lim (ed. and tr.). *Chinese Poetry: Major Modes and Genres*. Berkeley: University of California Press, 1976.

Yu, Pauline. *The Poetry of Wang Wei: New Translation and Commentary*. Bloomington, Indiana: Indiana University Press, 1980.

————. *The Reading of Imagery in the Chinese Poetic Tradition*. Princeton: Princeton University Press, 1987.

WU-CHI LIU, now retired, was Professor of East Asian Languages and Literatures at Indiana University when this volume first appeared.

IRVING YUCHENG LO has had a distinguished career at Indiana University as a Professor of Chinese Literature and Culture. He is also co-editor (with William Schultz) of *Waiting for the Unicorn: Poems and Lyrics of China's Last Dynasty, 1644–1911* (Indiana University Press).